MODELLING ACCELERATED PROFICIENCY IN ORGANISATIONS

DOCTORATE THESIS

MODELLING ACCELERATED PROFICIENCY IN ORGANISATIONS

PRACTICES AND STRATEGIES TO SHORTEN TIME-TO-PROFICIENCY OF THE WORKFORCE

Dr RAMAN K ATTRI

Copyrights © 2022 Raman K Attri

All rights reserved. No part of this publication may be reproduced, distributed, or transmitted in any form or by any means, including photocopying, recording, or other electronic or mechanical methods, without the prior written permission of the author and publisher, except in the case of brief quotations embodied in critical reviews, research papers and certain other noncommercial uses permitted by copyright law.

Printed in the United States of America /Australia

ISBN: 978-981-18-4290-0 (e-book)
ISBN: 978-981-18-4288-7 (paperback)
ISBN: 978-981-18-4289-4 (hardcover)

Republished by Speed To Proficiency: S2Pro© for Dr Raman K Attri with permission from Southern Cross University, Australia

Originally published electronically by Southern Cross University, Australia 2018 as DBA thesis

Original copyrights held by Dr Raman K Attri, 2018

https://www.speedtoproficiency.com
info@speedtoproficiency.com

National Library Board, Singapore Cataloguing in Publication Data

Name(s): Attri, Raman K., 1973-
Title: Modelling accelerated proficiency in organisations : practices and strategies to shorten time-to-proficiency of the workforce / Dr Raman K. Attri.
Description: Singapore : Speed To Proficiency Research, [2022]
Identifier(s): ISBN 978-981-18-4288-7 (paperback) | 978-981-18-4289-4 (hardback) | 978-981-18-4290-0 (Epub)
Subject(s): LCSH: Employees--Training of--Methodology. | Learning ability. | Performance.
Classification: DDC 658.312404--dc23

DOCTORATE THESIS
Dr RAMAN K ATTRI

Modelling Accelerated Proficiency in Organisations:
Practices and Strategies to Shorten Time-to-Proficiency of the Workforce

Raman K. Attri

May 2018

Submitted in fulfilment of the requirements for the degree of

Doctor of Business Administration

School of Business and Tourism

Southern Cross Drive, Bilinga

QLD, 4225, Australia

Declaration and Statement of Authorship

I certify that the work presented in this thesis is, to the best of my knowledge and belief, original, except as acknowledged in the text, and that the material has not been submitted, either in whole or in part, for a degree at this or any other university.

I acknowledge that I have read and understood the University's rules, requirements, procedures and policy relating to my higher degree research award and to my thesis.

I certify that I have complied with the rules, requirements, procedures and policy of the University (as they may be from time to time).

Raman K. Attri

Date: 29-May-2018

Acknowledgements

Though my name appears on the title page, there is more than one person who contributed to the success of this study. Without their help, completion of my doctoral degree would have been utterly impossible. First and foremost, my sincere appreciation to all the 85 participants of my study who took their precious time out of their busy schedules and extended all their support to me during data collection, in-depth interviews and review of the findings. Ultimately, this thesis is a reflection of their collective wisdom, made available to the rest of the world to utilise. Without their thoughtful sharing of their practical experience, this study would not have been possible.

My gratitude goes to my first supervisor, Dr Wing S. Wu, who has been instrumental in providing insightful directions, support and encouragement, in what has been a tedious journey of doctoral study. His practical experience of industry and academic expertise were instrumental to the directions I chose in this research study. I am also grateful to my second supervisor, Dr Scott Niblock, Southern Cross University (SCU), Australia for providing great support and guidance.

I am highly indebted to the distinguished thought-leaders and practitioners who critically reviewed the findings of this study and provided useful feedback. Without their guidance, I would not have been able to make this study practice-relevant and contemporary. Specifically, I am thankful to Glenn Hughes, a highly regarded facilitator and speaker and senior director of learning and development at KLA-Tencor Corp USA, for reviewing the study's findings and discussing and sharing insights with me throughout my journey. Further, I would like to express my gratitude to Sriman Venkatesan, senior manager of learning and development at Xilinx Asia Singapore, for critically reading the thesis as a potential corporate user. I am grateful to Dr Charles Jennings, co-founder of 70:20:10 Institute UK, for critically evaluating findings of this research and providing extremely useful suggestions from a practitioner standpoint. I would also like to extend my thanks to Charles Fred, a proponent of the concept of *speed to proficiency* and founder of The Reignite Group USA, for reviewing the model of accelerated proficiency developed in this research.

I am beholden to Dr Robert Hoffman, an eminent researcher on *accelerated proficiency* and Senior Scientist at the Institute for Human and Machine Cognition Florida, USA. I am also indebted to Dr Jorean (J.J.J. G.) van Merriënboer, a well-known researcher on *complex learning* and distinguished Professor at Maastricht University, Netherlands. Both spent their valuable time reviewing the scholarly relevance of my thesis and providing detailed feedback, despite their busy schedules. Further, I would like to express my gratitude to Dr David L. Morgan, Professor at Portland State University in Oregon USA, for his insightful answers and clarifications to my queries through the ResearchGate forum that positively influenced my methodological choices.

This thesis would not have taken its current shape and level of professionalism without thorough editing and proofreading during the final stages of the study by Dr Linda Riggs Mayfield, a highly detail-oriented proofreader and editing consultant based in Illinois USA. She ultimately provided valuable inputs to transform my research into an academic thesis. I am also thankful to Efren Lopez, Senior Director of Learning and Knowledge services at KLA-Tencor Corp USA, for graciously sponsoring a substantial portion of the cost of this doctoral study. I am also thankful to several of my team members at KLA-Tencor Learning and Knowledge group who tried and tested many of the methods generated from my findings, which gave me confidence that "this works".

Lastly, I would not have been able to complete this study without the support of my loving wife, Anh Chi, who gave me the good news of her pregnancy the day I started this study. She single handily managed all the hardships that come with pregnancy, raised our child, made financial compromises allowing me to invest in this study, and patiently waited for me to complete my study without complaint. More than my own time, I missed four beautiful years of the lovely childhood of my son, Rayan, who turned four years old the day I submitted this thesis.

Thanks to all of these individuals who directly or indirectly supported this research study.

List of Academic Publications

Attri, RK & Wu, W 2018, 'Model of accelerated proficiency at workplace: six core concepts to shorten time-to-proficiency of employees', *Asia Pacific Journal of Advanced Business and Social Studies,* vol. 4, no. 1, pp. 1-11, http://dx.doi.org/ 10.25275/apjabssv4i1bus1.

Attri, RK (in press), 'Accelerating speed-to-proficiency of project managers in fast-paced business world: practices that work', in O Manuel & P Andres (eds.), *Human Capital and Competence in Project Management*, ISBN 978-953-51-5544-7, INTECH, Rijeka, Croatia. [Peer reviewed]

Attri, RK & Wu, W 2017, 'Model of accelerated proficiency at workplace: six core concepts to shorten time-to-proficiency of employees', in L Holmes (ed.), *Proceedings of 1st Australia-New Zealand Conference of Advanced Research (ANZCAR-2017)*, Melbourne, 17-18 June, Asia Pacific Institute of Advanced Research (APIAR), Gordon, pp. 1-10, viewed 31 July 2017, <http://apiar.org.au/wp-content/uploads/2017/07/1_ANZCAR_2017_BRR713_Bus-1-10.pdf>. [Peer reviewed]

Attri, RK & Wu, W 2016a, 'Classroom-based instructional strategies to accelerate proficiency of employees in complex job skills', paper presented to the Asian American Conference for Education, Singapore, 12-15 January, viewed 10 April 2017, <https://www.researchgate.net/publication/303803099> [Presentation]

Attri, RK & Wu, W 2016b, 'E-learning strategies at workplace that support speed to proficiency in complex skills', in R Idrus and N Zainuddin (eds.), *Proceedings of the 11th International Conference on e-Learning: ICEl2016*, ISBN: 9781910810910, Kuala Lampur, 2-3 June, Academic Conference and Publishing, Reading, UK, pp. 176–184, viewed 10 April 2017, <https://www.researchgate.net/publication/303802961>. [Double blind peer reviewed]

Attri, RK & Wu, W 2015a, 'Conceptual model of workplace training and learning strategies to shorten time-to-proficiency in complex skills: preliminary findings', *Proceedings of 9th International Conference on Researching in Work and Learning (RWL)*, [Paper No. 100], Singapore, 12-15 December, Institute for Adult Learning, Singapore, viewed 10 April 2017, <http://www.rwl2015.com/papers/Paper100.pdf>. [Double blind peer reviewed]

Attri, RK & Wu, W 2015b, 'Accelerating speed-to-proficiency in complex jobs: conceptual model of e-learning strategies that works', [Abstract], *Proceedings of the 6th International Conference on Teaching,*

Education and Learning (ICTEL), ISSN 2454-5899, Singapore, 15-16 November, GRDS, pp. 87, viewed 10 April 2017, <http://www.grdsweb.com/files/documents/41.pdf>.

Attri, RK & Wu, WS 2015c, 'E-Learning strategies to accelerate time-to-proficiency in acquiring complex skills: preliminary findings', paper presented to the eLearning Forum Asia (eLFA) Conference, Singapore, 17-19 May, viewed 10 April 2017, <https://www.researchgate.net/publication/282647943>.

Attri, RK 2014, 'Rethinking professional skill development in competitive corporate world: accelerating time-to-expertise of employees at workplace', in J Latzo (ed.), *Proceedings of Conference on Education and Human Development in Asia (COHDA 2014)*, ISSN 2188-3432, Hiroshima, 2-4 March, The PRESDA Foundation, Kitanagova, Japan, pp. 1–11, viewed 10 April 2017, <https://www.researchgate.net/publication/282648062>. [Peer reviewed]

Abstract

This study aimed to explore practices and strategies that have successfully reduced time-to-proficiency of the workforce in large multinational organisations and develop a model based on them. The central research question of this study was: How can organisations accelerate time-to-proficiency of employees in the workplace? The study addressed three aspects: the meaning of accelerated proficiency, as seen by business leaders; the business factors driving the need for shorter time-to-proficiency and benefits accrued from it; and practices and strategies to shorten time-to-proficiency of the workforce. 85 participants (*n=85*) from 7 countries who represented 10 economic sectors, 20 business sectors and 28 industry groups contributed 66 successful bounded project cases. A qualitative research approach was used. Data were collected through in-depth interviews with project leaders and by collecting additional project case documents. Data were analysed using *thematic analysis* to identify the themes in the data. *Matrix analysis* was then used to perform within-case and cross-case analysis to compare the project cases.

11 overarching themes were developed from the data analysis, out of which two overarching themes explained the characteristics of job-role proficiency and accelerated proficiency, while three overarching themes described the magnituide and scale of time-to-proficiency business problem, business drivers for accelerating proficiency and business benefits of reduced time-to-proficiency. Six overarching themes revealed the business practices employed by organisations to reduce time-to-proficiency: (1) Defining business-driven proficiency measures in terms of expected business outcomes from a job role; (2) Developing a proficiency reference map of all the inputs, conditions and roadblocks that determine or influence how required business outcomes are being produced in a job role; (3) Sequencing an efficient proficiency path of activities and experiences ordered to produce the desired business outcomes in the shortest possible time; (4) Manufacturing accelerated contextual experiences by leveraging on-the-job opportunities or training interventions in a compressed time-frame; (5) Promoting an active emotional immersion through engagements, consequences, stakes, feedback and proficiency assessments; and (6) Setting up a proficiency eco-system, providing timely support to performers while doing the job such as enabling job environment, highly involved manager, structured mentoring from experts, purposeful social connectivity with peers, leveraging subject matter experts and on-demand performance support systems.

Organisations orchestrated these six business practices as an input-output-feedback system to reduce time-to-proficiency of the workforce. A conceptual model (*Accelerated Proficiency Model*) was developed representing interactions among six business-level practices/processes as a closed-loop system to explain the concept and process of accelerated proficiency in the workplace. These practices were implemented through a set of twenty-four strategies proven successful in various contexts. The strategies employed were much beyond the boundaries of conventional training interventions. The job itself acted as the primary mechanism to accelerate proficiency. A two-level hierarchical framework (*6/24 framework of strategies*) was also constructed in the form of a checklist consisting of six practices and twenty-four strategies for practitioners. Overall, the findings of this research study contribute significantly to the body of knowledge on accelerated proficiency. In particular, the conceptual model and the framework developed in this study can be implemented across a range of contexts, business sectors, job types and settings to reduce time-to-proficiency of the workforce.

Table of Contents

Declaration and Statement of Authorship	I
Acknowledgements	II
List of Academic Publications	IV
Abstract	VI
Table of Contents	VIII
List of Tables	XII
List of Figures	XIII
List of Boxes	XIV
List of Appendices	XV
List of Abbreviations	XVI
Chapter 1 INTRODUCTION	**1**
1.1 INTRODUCTION	1
1.2 BACKGROUND	1
1.2.1 Job performance	2
1.2.2 Proficiency	3
1.2.3 Acquisition of skilled performance	3
1.2.4 Proficiency progression	4
1.2.5 Accelerated proficiency	6
1.2.6 Business perspective of accelerating proficiency	7
1.2.7 Strategies and methods of accelerating proficiency	8
1.3 RESEARCH PROBLEM AND QUESTIONS	10
1.4 CONTRIBUTIONS OF THE STUDY	11
1.4.1 Contribution to knowledge	12
1.4.2 Contribution to business research methodology	12
1.4.3 Contribution to practice and education	12
1.5 JUSTIFICATION OF THE STUDY	13
1.5.1 Faster workforce readiness	13
1.5.2 Time-to-market competitiveness	14
1.5.3 Cost of training and non-proficiency	14
1.6 RESEARCH METHODOLOGY	15
1.6.1 Research design	15
1.6.2 Data collection	15
1.6.3 Data analysis	16
1.6.4 Validation and reliability	17
1.7 DELIMITATIONS AND ASSUMPTIONS	17
1.7.1 Scope	17
1.7.2 Delimitations	18
1.7.3 Assumptions	18
1.8 OUTLINE OF THE THESIS	19
1.9 CHAPTER SUMMARY	20
Chapter 2 LITERATURE REVIEW	**22**
2.1 INTRODUCTION	22
2.2 PERFORMANCE	24
2.2.1 Human resource development and performance improvement	24
2.2.2 Dimensions of job performance	29

2.2.3	Learning and performance	36
2.2.4	Acquisition of skilled performance	38
2.3	**PROFICIENCY**	43
2.3.1	Novice-to-expert transition	43
2.3.2	Stages of proficiency	45
2.3.3	Proficiency scaling	48
2.3.4	Proficiency	51
2.3.5	Expertise	53
2.3.6	Expert performance	55
2.4	**ACCELERATED PROFICIENCY**	58
2.4.1	Accelerating proficiency	58
2.4.2	Theoretical issues	63
2.4.3	Challenges to accelerate proficiency	66
2.5	**METHODS OF ACCELERATING PROFICIENCY**	69
2.5.1	HRD methods of employee development in the workplace	70
2.5.2	Cognitive task analysis (CTA) methods	74
2.5.3	Time-compressed simulations-based methods	78
2.5.4	Case-based and scenario-based methods	83
2.5.5	Representative part-task approach	87
2.5.6	Knowledge capture methods	88
2.5.7	Technology-based methods	89
2.5.8	Accelerated learning methods	90
2.5.9	Workplace training/learning methods	91
2.6	**CONCLUSION ON RESEARCH ISSUES**	95
Chapter 3	**RESEARCH METHODOLOGY**	**99**
3.1	**INTRODUCTION**	99
3.2	**RESEARCH DESIGN**	100
3.2.1	Inquiry framework and research process	100
3.2.2	Justification for pragmatic paradigm	104
3.2.3	Justification of qualitative research approach	107
3.3	**SAMPLING AND PARTICIPANT SELECTION**	108
3.3.1	Purposive sampling	108
3.3.2	Search for ideal participants	109
3.3.3	Connection with potential participants	110
3.3.4	Selection and invitation of target participants	111
3.3.5	Participation rate	111
3.3.6	Distribution profile of participants	112
3.3.7	Sampling unit/unit of analysis: Bounded project cases	114
3.4	**DATA COLLECTION**	114
3.4.1	Phase-1 interviews for general understanding	116
3.4.2	Phase-2 interviews for collection of bounded project cases	116
3.4.3	Phase-3 expert focus group for review of findings	118
3.4.4	In-depth interviews	119
3.4.5	Interview protocol	121
3.5	**DATA PROCESSING AND MANAGEMENT**	122
3.5.1	Data processing	123
3.5.2	Data management	123
3.5.3	Classification of project cases	124
3.5.4	Criterion sampling of bounded project cases	127
3.6	**DISTRIBUTION PROFILE OF SELECTED PROJECT CASES**	128

3.7	DATA ANALYSIS PROCESS AND METHODS	131
3.7.1	Thematic analysis	131
3.7.2	Miles and Huberman matrix analysis approach	132
3.7.3	Concept maps to identify themes	135
3.7.4	Project case summary and analytic memos to identify themes	138
3.7.5	A priori coding using Template Analysis (TA)	139
3.7.6	First cycle coding	140
3.7.7	Thematic network to analyse themes for relationships	141
3.7.8	Organising sub-themes, themes and overarching themes	142
3.7.9	Constructing matrices	144
3.7.10	Within-case analysis	148
3.7.11	Cross-case analysis	148
3.7.12	Validation of themes, relationships and conclusions	149
3.8	VALIDITY AND RELIABILITY METHODS	149
3.8.1	Framework for assessing trustworthiness	149
3.8.2	Sampling adequacy	151
3.8.3	Data triangulation	152
3.8.4	Data analysis triangulation	152
3.8.5	Prevalence Analysis	153
3.8.6	Audit trail and decision trails	153
3.8.7	Member (participant) checking	154
3.8.8	Peer reviews	155
3.8.9	Expert focus group	155
3.8.10	Thick and rich description	156
3.8.11	Reflexivity for credibility and controlling researcher's bias	157
3.9	ETHICAL CONSIDERATIONS	157
3.9.1	Informed consent	157
3.9.2	Confidentiality	158
3.10	CHAPTER SUMMARY	158
Chapter 4	**RESEARCH FINDINGS**	**160**
4.1	INTRODUCTION	160
4.2	THEMATIC STRUCTURE OF EMERGENT THEMES IN DATA ANALYSIS	161
PART-1: OVERARCHING THEMES		164
4.3	RESEARCH QUESTION #1: MEANING OF ACCELERATED PROFICIENCY	165
4.3.1	Overarching theme C1: Proficiency	165
4.3.2	Overarching theme C2: Accelerated proficiency	166
4.3.3	Conclusion of research question #1	167
4.4	RESEARCH QUESTION #2: DRIVING FACTORS AND BENEFITS OF REDUCED TIME-TO-PROFICIENCY	170
4.4.1	Overarching theme D1: Magnitude and scale of time-to-proficiency business problem	170
4.4.2	Overarching theme D2: Business drivers for accelerating time-to-proficiency	171
4.4.3	Overarching theme D3: Business benefits of reduced time-to-proficiency	172
4.4.4	Conclusion of research question #2	173
4.5	RESEARCH QUESTION #3: PRACTICES AND STRATEGIES TO ACCELERATE PROFICIENCY	173
4.5.1	Overarching theme (practice) P1: Defining business-driven proficiency measures	182
4.5.2	Overarching theme (practice) P2: Developing a proficiency reference map	183
4.5.3	Overarching theme (practice) P3: Sequencing an efficient proficiency path	184
4.5.4	Overarching theme (practice) P4: Manufacturing accelerated contextual experiences	186
4.5.5	Overarching theme (practice) P5: Promoting an active emotional immersion	188
4.5.6	Overarching theme (practice) P6: Setting up a proficiency eco-system	189
4.5.7	Conclusion of research question #3	190

PART-2: EMERGENT THEMES — 193

4.6 RESEARCH QUESTION #1: MEANING OF ACCELERATED PROFICIENCY — 194
- 4.6.1 Emergent themes grouped under C1: Proficiency — 194
- 4.6.2 Emergent themes grouped under C2: Accelerated proficiency — 198

4.7 RESEARCH QUESTION #2: DRIVING FACTORS AND BENEFITS OF REDUCED TIME-TO-PROFICIENCY — 203
- 4.7.1 Emergent themes grouped under D1: Magnitude and scale of time-to-proficiency business problem — 203
- 4.7.2 Emergent themes grouped under D2: Business drivers for accelerating time-to-proficiency — 205
- 4.7.3 Emergent theme grouped under D3: Business benefits of reduced time-to-proficiency — 206

4.8 RESEARCH QUESTION #3: PRACTICES AND STRATEGIES TO ACCELERATE PROFICIENCY — 208
- 4.8.1 Emergent themes (strategies) grouped under P1: Defining business-driven proficiency measures — 208
- 4.8.2 Emergent themes (strategies) grouped under P2: Developing a proficiency reference map — 209
- 4.8.3 Emergent themes (strategies) grouped under P3: Sequencing an efficient proficiency path — 213
- 4.8.4 Emergent themes (strategies) grouped under P4: Manufacturing accelerated contextual experiences — 217
- 4.8.5 Emergent themes (strategies) grouped under P5: Promoting an active emotional immersion — 222
- 4.8.6 Emergent themes (strategies) grouped under P6: Setting up a proficiency eco-system — 225

PART-3: ANALYSIS OF TIME-TO-PROFICIENCY RESULTS OF PROJECT CASES — 231

4.9 ANALYSIS OF RESULTS OF TIME-TO-PROFICIENCY REDUCTION IN PROJECT CASES — 232
- 4.9.1 Indicators of reduction in time-to-proficiency — 232
- 4.9.2 Effectiveness of practices/strategies in reducing time-to-proficiency — 233

4.10 CHAPTER SUMMARY — 234

Chapter 5 CONCLUSIONS & IMPLICATIONS — 236

5.1 INTRODUCTION — 236
5.2 SUMMARY OF EMERGENT THEMES — 237
5.3 DISCUSSION OF RESEARCH QUESTION #1 — 238
- 5.3.1 Overarching theme C1: Proficiency — 239
- 5.3.2 Overarching theme C2: Accelerated proficiency — 243
- 5.3.3 Propositions from research question #1: Meaning of accelerated proficiency — 247

5.4 DISCUSSION OF RESEARCH QUESTION #2 — 248
- 5.4.1 Overarching theme D1: Magnitude and scale of time-to-proficiency business problem — 249
- 5.4.2 Overarching theme D2: Business drivers for accelerating proficiency — 250
- 5.4.3 Overarching theme D3: Business benefits of a shorter time-to-proficiency — 250
- 5.4.4 Propositions from research question #2: Driving factors and benefits — 251

5.5 DISCUSSION OF RESEARCH QUESTION #3 — 251
- 5.5.1 Practice P1: Defining business-driven proficiency measures — 253
- 5.5.2 Practice P2: Developing a proficiency reference map — 255
- 5.5.3 Practice P3: Sequencing an efficient proficiency path — 260
- 5.5.4 Practice P4: Manufacturing accelerated contextual experiences — 264
- 5.5.5 Practice P5: Promoting an active emotional immersion — 271
- 5.5.6 Practice P6: Setting up a proficiency eco-system — 274
- 5.5.7 Propositions from research question #3: Practices and strategies to accelerate proficiency — 280

5.6 CONCEPTUAL MODEL AND FRAMEWORK — 281
- 5.6.1 Conceptual model of practices to accelerate proficiency — 282
- 5.6.2 Framework of strategies to shorten time-to-proficiency — 287

5.7 CONCLUSION ON RESEARCH FINDINGS — 287
- 5.7.1 Research question #1: meaning and nature of accelerated proficiency — 287
- 5.7.2 Research question #2: driving factors and benefits of accelerated proficiency — 288
- 5.7.3 Research question #3: practices and strategies to accelerate proficiency — 289

5.8 CONTRIBUTIONS OF THE STUDY — 291
5.9 CONTRIBUTIONS TO METHODOLOGY — 294
- 5.9.1 Using social media to recruit participants — 294

5.9.2	Internet-mediated in-depth interviews	295
5.9.3	Bounded project cases as sampling unit and unit of analysis	295
5.9.4	Goal-oriented pragmatic approach to research study	295
5.10	RECOMMENDATIONS TO PRACTITIONERS	296
5.11	LIMITATIONS OF THE STUDY	301
5.12	DIRECTIONS FOR FUTURE RESEARCH	302
5.12.1	Building theory of accelerated proficiency	303
5.12.2	Testing and expanding accelerated proficiency model	303
5.12.3	Analysing factors affecting accelerated proficiency	304
5.12.4	Generating context-specific guidelines for practitioners	305
5.12.5	Conducting case study of implementation	306
5.13	CHAPTER SUMMARY	306
REFERENCES		**307**
APPENDIX		**351**

List of Tables

Table 1-1: Summary of research questions and research objective 21
Table 2-1: Proficiency scaling proposed by Hoffman (1998) 49
Table 2-2: Summary of research questions and research objective 98
Table 3-1: Summary of research questions and research objective 99
Table 3-2: Response rate and participation rate in the study 112
Table 3-3: Distribution profile of research participants 113
Table 3-4: Participant distribution and outcomes of three-phase data collection process 116
Table 3-5: Profile of participants in expert focus group 119
Table 3-6: Participation rate in various data collection methods and modes 120
Table 3-7: Project cases by economic sector, business sector and industry group 125
Table 3-8: Project cases by nature of job role 127
Table 3-9: Project cases by critical-to-success (CTS) skill 127
Table 3-10: Project cases by complexity levels 127
Table 3-11: Distribution of project cases by contextual variables 130
Table 3-12: A priori thematic codes developed for the study 139
Table 3-13: Summary of major matrices constructed in this study 146
Table 4-1: Summary of research questions and research objective 160
Table 4-2: Thematic structure of emergent themes noted in data analysis 162
Table 4-3: Thematic structure of overarching themes noted in research question #1 165
Table 4-4: Thematic structure of overarching themes noted in research question #2 170
Table 4-5: Thematic structure of overarching themes in research question #3 175
Table 4-6: Thematic structure of overarching theme (practice) P1: defining business-driven proficiency measures 182
Table 4-7: Thematic structure of overarching theme (practice) P2: developing proficiency reference map 183
Table 4-8: Thematic structure of overarching theme (practice) P3: sequencing an efficient proficiency path 185
Table 4-9: Thematic structure of overarching theme (practice) P4: manufacturing accelerated contextual experiences .. 187
Table 4-10: Thematic structure of overarching theme (practice) P5: promoting an active emotional immersion 188
Table 4-11: Thematic structure of overarching theme (practice) P6: setting up a proficiency eco-system 190
Table 4-12: Prevalence of six overarching themes (practices) across project cases 191
Table 4-13: Three categories of indicators of proficiency measures reported in project cases ... 197
Table 4-14: Magnitude of time-to-proficiency across primary job nature 203
Table 4-15: Magnitude of time-to-proficiency across economic sectors 204
Table 4-16: Distribution of success indicators 233
Table 5-1: Summary of research questions and objective 236
Table 5-2: Comparison of emergent themes with the literature 238
Table 5-3: Emergent themes from research question #1 239
Table 5-4: Construct of job-role proficiency 243
Table 5-5: Emergent themes from research question #2 249
Table 5-6: Emergent themes from research question #3 252
Table 5-7: Contributions of this study 292

List of Figures

Figure 1-1: Simplified concept of accelerated proficiency 10
Figure 2-1: Map of literature review 22
Figure 2-2: Accelerated proficiency growth curve and time-to-proficiency 61
Figure 3-1: Inquiry framework used for present research study 101
Figure 3-2: The process of three-phase data collection 115
Figure 3-3: Five stages of a typical improvement or problem-solving project 117
Figure 3-4: Project case data classification framework 125
Figure 3-5: Data analysis process adopted in this study 134
Figure 3-6: Concept map #1 of an interview showing themes related to manager's involvement 136
Figure 3-7: Concept map #2 of another interview showing themes related to manager's involvement 137
Figure 3-8: Patterns captured in project case summary memos 138
Figure 3-9: Example demonstrating process of first cycle coding 140
Figure 3-10: Example of a thematic map of the theme 'purposeful social interconnectivity' 142
Figure 3-11: Clustering of first cycle codes to form themes, sub-themes and overarching themes 144
Figure 4-1: Concept map of overarching themes C1 and C2 (meaning of proficiency and accelerated proficiency) 168
Figure 4-2: Conceptual map of overarching theme D1, D2 and D3 (drivers for accelerating proficiency and benefits of reduced time-proficiency) 169
Figure 4-3: Concept map of overarching theme (practice) P1: Defining business-driven proficiency measures 176
Figure 4-4: Conceptual map of overarching theme (practice) P2: Developing a proficiency reference map 177
Figure 4-5: Concept map of overarching theme (practice) P3: Creating an efficient proficiency path............................. 178
Figure 4-6: Conceptual map of overarching theme (practice) P4: Manufacturing accelerated contextual experiences..... 179
Figure 4-7: Concept map of overarching theme (practice) P5: Promoting an active emotional immersion 180
Figure 4-8: Conceptual map of overarching theme (practice) P6: Setting up a proficiency eco-system 181
Figure 4-9: Concept map of interactions among overarching themes (practices) 192
Figure 5-1: Conceptual model of accelerated proficiency.. 285

List of Boxes

Box 5-1: Propositions from research question #1 248
Box 5-2: Proposition from research question #2 251
Box 5-3: Propositions from research question #3 280

List of Appendices

Appendix 1	Participants' profiles	352
Appendix 2	Detailed project case profiles with contextual variables	356
Appendix 3	Interview guide & questions	359
Appendix 4	Questionnaire interview template	362
Appendix 5	Excerpt from questionnaire interview	364
Appendix 6	Sample invitation letter to participate in research	365
Appendix 7	Research information sheet	366
Appendix 8	Web-based informed consent form at surveymonkey.com	369
Appendix 9	Web-based informed consent form at qualtrics.com	370
Appendix 10	Pre-interview expectation setting e-mail	371
Appendix 11	Concept map captured during interview (example)	372
Appendix 12	Concept map updated and refined (example)	373
Appendix 13	Interview summary (example)	374
Appendix 14	Analytic memo of an interview (example)	376
Appendix 15	Master tracker and checklist for the research study (excerpt)	377
Appendix 16	Job classification map	378
Appendix 17	Complexity levels (excerpt)	380
Appendix 18	The 3-digit DOT job complexity code	381
Appendix 19	Project cases excluded using criteria-based sampling	382
Appendix 20	Analytic memo for organising themes (example)	383
Appendix 21	Thematic map of strategies (excerpt)	385
Appendix 22	Matrix of analytic memo for project case summary	386
Appendix 23	Example of case-ordered context matrix (excerpt)	388
Appendix 24	Example of case-ordered themes (excerpt)	390
Appendix 25	Example of variable-ordered themes (excerpt)	391
Appendix 26	Checklist matrix for time-to-proficiency results reported in project cases	392
Appendix 27	Matrix of time-to-proficiency results reported in project cases	394
Appendix 28	Matrix of business benefits reported in project cases	397
Appendix 29	Proficiency measures matrix (excerpt)	399
Appendix 30	Code matrix (excerpt)	400
Appendix 31	Descriptive meta-matrix for themes and sub-themes arranged by complexity (example)	401
Appendix 32	Example of case-ordered conceptually clustered matrix (except only)	403
Appendix 33	Member (participant) checking questionnaire	405
Appendix 34	Example of data triangulation of interview codes with document codes	406
Appendix 35	Thematic prevalence of six practices arranged by contextual variables	407
Appendix 36	Feedback from expert focus group	409
Appendix 37	Explaining a project case using 6/24 framework of strategies	411
Appendix 38	Reflexivity journals (examples)	417
Appendix 39	Thematic structure of overarching themes and emergent themes in three research questions	419
Appendix 40	Summary of research propositions	421
Appendix 41	6/24 framework of strategies to reduce time-to-proficiency (research output #1)	423
Appendix 42	Accelerated Proficiency Model(APM) (research output #2)	424
Appendix 43	Research questions mapped to interview questions	425

List of Abbreviations

4C/ID	Four components instructional design
6D	Six-disciplines of breakthrough training
ACM	Adaptive course model
AFL	Acceleration of future learning
AP	Accelerated proficiency
APM	Accelerated proficiency model
ART	Above-real-time training
ASTD	American Society for Training and Development
BEM	Behavioural engineering model
CDM	Critical decision method
CFT	Cognitive flexibility theory
CLT	Cognitive load theory
CSAT	Customer satisfaction
CTA	Cognitive task analysis
CTS	Critical-to-success
CTT	Cognitive transformation theory
CWA	Cognitive work analysis
DOT	Dictionary of Titles
EPSS	Electronic performance support systems
GICS	Global Industry Classification System
GOMS	Goals, operators, methods, selections
HPL	How people learn framework
HPT	Human performance technology
HRD	Human resource development
HRM	Human resource management
HTA	Hierarchical task analysis
ILT	Instructor-led training
ISCO	International Standard Classification of Occupations
ITAM	Integrated task analysis model
JIT	Just-in-time
KADS	Knowledge analysis and documentation system
KPI	Key performance indicators
KSA	Knowledge, skills and attitudes (or behaviours)
OJT	On-the-job training
PSS	Performance support systems
RPD	Recognition primed decision
SBL	Scenario-based learning
SBT	Scenario-based training
SME	Subject matter expert(s)
SOC	Standard Occupational Classification
TLAC	Think like a commander
TNA	Training need analysis
TRBC	Thomson-Reuters Business Classification
TTP	Time-to-Proficiency
WDA	Work domain analysis
XBT	Expertise-based training

Chapter 1 INTRODUCTION

1.1 INTRODUCTION

This chapter introduces the study on accelerating proficiency in the workplace, its meaning, drivers and benefits and strategies to shorten time-to-proficiency of employees. This chapter is organised as follows: Section 1.2 provides the background of the research study by defining the basic terms such as *performance, proficiency* and *accelerated proficiency* used in the context of this study. This section also builds the rationale for the study by presenting the summary of the literature review and outlining the gaps briefly. Section 1.3 outlines the research problem and questions briefly. Section 1.4 provides a brief synopsis of contributions made by this research study to the theory and practice. Section 1.5 of this chapter justifies conducting this study based on its business value. Then Section 1.6 discusses a brief overview of the methodology used in the study. Section 1.7 explains the delimitations and assumptions used in this study. Section 1.7 gives the outline of the rest of the thesis.

1.2 BACKGROUND

This research study addresses a critical challenge in modern organisations: the workforce generally takes a significant amount of time to reach full proficiency in several job roles, which in turn puts market and financial pressures on organisations. This study aims to explore how organisations view the concept and process of accelerating proficiency, and the practices and strategies organisations have used successfully to decrease the time-to-proficiency of the workforce. The concepts of performance, proficiency, accelerated proficiency and time-to-proficiency are defined and discussed in the following sections. This section intends to summarise only the major inferences from the literature review and highlight the gaps that are the basis for this study. The detailed literature review is conducted in chapter 2.

This study takes forward the conceptualisation of *accelerated proficiency* and *accelerated expertise* proposed in experimental research studies conducted by Hoffman (Hoffman et al. 2008, 2009, 2014; Hoffman, Andrews & Feltovich 2012; Hoffman & Andrews 2012; Hoffman, Andrews, et al. 2010; Hoffman, Feltovich, et al. 2010) and Fadde (Fadde & Klein 2010, 2012; Fadde 2007, 2009a, 2009b, 2009c, 2012, 2013, 2016) during the last decade in training and work settings. In their studies, they have identified several theoretical issues and gaps.

In particular, the gaps such as lack of good understanding of the concept and process of accelerated proficiency, needs for accelerating proficiency and methods to accelerate the proficiency served to propose research questions in this research study towards accelerating proficiency in the organisational and workplace domain.

1.2.1 Job performance

Effective performance from employees in any job is a key business expectation that fuels business operations, profit and competitive advantage (Sonnentag & Frese 2002). The poor performance of an individual at the job may have far-reaching effects on the team performance, as well as an organisation's performance. There are two primary views about individual performance. One is the behavioural view, and the other is the outcome view. Emphasising the behavioural view, Campbell and Wiernik (2015, p. 48) maintained that 'individual job performance should be defined as things that people actually do, actions they take, that contribute to the organisation's goals'. The second view suggests that outcomes and results of the behaviours are equally important indicators of work performance. Supporters of the outcome view have positioned a contradictory view that business organisations value performance in terms of accomplishments (Gilbert 2013). Accomplishment can be the work outputs or things (such as decisions made, strategies identified) or end results (such as sales improvement). Binder (2017, p. 20) stated 'the value delivered by human performance is in the *accomplishments* it produces and that the behavior needed for producing those accomplishments is costly, not valuable for its own sake'. Reconciling these views, Viswesvaran and Ones (2000) suggested a middle ground based on their analysis of over four hundred different dimensions they found in last several decades' studies on work performance. They defined work performance as a combination of actions, behaviour and outcomes, which are linked to organisational goals.

Historically, literature has suggested several different perspectives to explain performance: task vs. contextual performance (Borman & Motowidlo 1993); behavioural vs. outcome performance (Campbell et al. 1993); task vs. job performance (Kanfer & Kantrowitz 2002); individual vs. team performance (Sonnentag & Frese 2002), and job vs. organisational performance (Griffin, Neal & Parker 2007; Sudnickas 2016). Recently, in a meta-analysis of 107 studies published until 2010 in four major databases, Koopmans et al. (2011) noticed a prominent trend toward measuring individual job performance as task performance or task proficiency. However, task performance is just one dimension of the overall job performance: 'There is not one outcome, one factor, or one anything that can be pointed to and labelled as job performance. Job performance really is multidimensional' (Campbell, McHenry & Wise 1990, p. 314).

Irrespective of how performance is measured, an individual's job performance is a critical determinant of an organisation's performance and competitiveness. In this thesis, the term *performance* refers to job performance an individual must demonstrate to meet organisational goals.

1.2.2 Proficiency

Performance measurement deals with how well someone meets the standards set for tasks, actions, behaviours, results or accomplishments to meet organisational goals. If performance is defined in terms of actions and behaviours, managers need to know how proficiently an individual is demonstrating those actions or behaviours. Thus, the concept of performance has an important dimension of proficiency (Griffin, Neal & Parker 2007; Koopmans et al. 2011). Campbell and Wiernik (2015, p. 48) highlighted the importance of proficiency: 'For those [actions and behaviours] that are relevant, the level of proficiency with which the individual performs them must be scaled'. Most commonly, an individual's proficiency indicates a level of performance. In business, for a given job, desired or target proficiency may be expressed in terms of the predefined level of performance expected from a given job such as customer satisfaction scores, revenue generated, number of transactions conducted or defect rates (Rosenbaum & Williams 2004, p. 14). A performer is said to be proficient when s/he meets these standards. 'Proficiency is when a new employee achieves a predetermined level of performance on a consistent basis' (Rosenbaum & Williams 2004, p. 14). *Business Dictionary* defines proficiency: 'Mastery of a specific behavior or skill demonstrated by consistently superior performance, measured against established or popular standards' [http://www.businessdictionary.com/definition/proficiency.html]. To do a job to satisfaction, one needs to have this minimal level of proficiency referred to as *desired or target proficiency* in this thesis.

Depending on how desired or target proficiency measures are defined, an individual may or may not have reached the desired or target proficiency in a given job. The definition of desired or target proficiency varies from organisation to organisation and from job to job. Enos, Kehrhahn and Bell (2003, p. 371) position proficiency as 'the primary objective of both formal and informal learning undertakings in organisations'. Nevertheless, workforce proficiency appears to be an important determinant of how successfully organisations handle business challenges on a daily basis (Hoffman, Feltovich et al. 2010). Having employees with high proficiency level is crucial to organisations:

> Domain practitioners who achieve high levels of proficiency provide technical judgment to speed decision-making in time-critical events. They provide resilience to operations by resolving tough problems, anticipating future demands and re-planning, and acting prudently by judgment rather than by rule. (Hoffman et al. 2014, p. 2)

1.2.3 Acquisition of skilled performance

An individual's knowledge and skills are an inseparable part of job performance. Campbell (1990) explained that job performance could be predicted with the help of three direct determinants—declarative knowledge (i.e., knowledge of facts, principles and procedures); procedural knowledge and skills (i.e., knowing what to do and actually doing the task), and motivation (i.e., wilfully exerting effort, extent and length). 'An underlying mechanism of cognitive ability' helps an individual acquire job knowledge and skills, which positively influences the job performance (Sonnentag & Frese 2002, p. 10). Thus, learning plays a central role in skill acquisition. To deliver a performance to certain standards, one needs to acquire skills to a certain level of mastery. In general, the goal of acquiring skills is to perform the task to desired standards or produce outcomes as per desired organisational goals.

Most of the skill acquisition studies are either approached from a learning standpoint or expertise development standpoint. Since the 1980s an immense amount of research has been conducted to understand the nature of expertise (cf. Cambridge Handbook of Expertise and Expert Performance by Ericsson et al. 2006). The classic scholarly works have suggested that experts are highly skilled individuals who think remarkably in a different way than novices (Anderson 1981). From that perspective, expertise can be defined as 'the possession of a large body of knowledge and procedural skills' (Chi, Glaser & Rees 1982). Ericsson et al. (1993) explained that the mechanism of attaining expertise in certain closed domains such as sports, chess, music was to engage in highly intense and focused practice on domain-specific activities under a coach, termed as deliberate practice. Chi (2006, p. 23) made an argument that expertise is acquired and is an outcome of skill acquisition as 'presumably the more skilled person became expert-like from having acquired knowledge about a domain, that is, from learning and studying and from deliberate practice'. Charness and Tuffiash (2008) viewed expertise as a superior performance, which is achieved through a combination of high-level skills and domain-specific knowledge and skilled memory.

Most of the methods in the literature for development of proficiency and expertise (*high proficiency,* as Hoffman et al. called it) were informed by expertise studies (Fadde 2016). However, the limitation of those methods is noted as being mostly focused on developing the expertise of individuals on specific representative tasks and often time within laboratory settings (Hambrick, Oswald et al. 2014). The notion of expertise specifies deliberate practice in a specific set of non-changing tasks. However, in the workplace, professionals hardly ever get to work on the same set of tasks that long. For those reasons, Fadde and Klein (2010) contended that deliberate practice, and hence, achievement of expert performance, is not an even realisable goal in any job for any organisation.

1.2.4 Proficiency progression

Several researchers have maintained that expertise is not an end state, rather it is a journey that is characterised by progressively increasing skills, experience and intuition (Benner 2001; Dreyfus & Dreyfus 2005, 2004; Hoffman 1998). Staged view of expertise has been used to conceptualise how a novice progresses or develops towards expertise. This view reports a level-like shift in qualitative characteristics of the individual, thus giving the notion of stages one passes through towards higher level of skill mastery or higher performance.

Accordingly, the journey towards expertise involves a progression through several stages of proficiency acquisition. For instance, Dreyfus and Dreyfus (2005; 2004) suggested a progression in terms of how a performer handles a situation. They suggested that an individual acquires intuitive grasp on situations and problems while passing through five stages—novice, advanced beginner, competent, proficient and expert. This staged model could explain the progression towards expertise reasonably well in nursing and medicine professions (Benner 2004). A similar but characteristically grounded on different criteria, Hoffman, Feltovich et al. (2010) proposed the continuum view of progression in terms of proficiency: 'We are considering a concept of expertise referred to as "high proficiency."' (p. 28). They viewed proficiency as an indicator of one's level of experience or expertise in the skills, and thus there was a need for some sort of mechanism to scale proficiency. They further stated, 'The analysis of proficiency and proficiency scaling can usefully commence by distinguishing experts (high and very high proficiency) from novices (very low proficiency)' (id. 32). On this continuum, one progresses towards higher proficiency through stages like naïve, novice, initiate, apprentice, journeyman, expert and master (Hoffman 1998). In this thesis, the research is aligned with the Hoffman et al.'s (2014) concept of proficiency as a continuum of mastery in a skill or function or job. In this view, a novice is someone who has low or very low proficiency, while an expert is someone with very high proficiency in that particular aspect (skill, task, function or job).

While most of the staged model gave a theoretical framework on progression towards expertise, the staged view did not explain the actual mechanisms or methods of developing an individual to the next level of performance (Dall'Alba & Sandberg 2006; Peña 2010). The issue is that the actual mechanism of acquiring proficiency is not elaborated upon in the current expertise literature the way it could be applied or used in organisations. Moon, Kim and You (2013, p. 226) stated the limitation in expertise literature: 'Most studies can't explain how the expertise reaches to a specific level or stage by multiple mechanisms. Accordingly we have to develop specific and realistic model for how expertise develops'. Therefore, the basic issue that arises is the lack of understanding of the concept and process of proficiency in organisations.

An increasing trend in the literature revealed that several researchers thought employees should be prepared to proficient level or journeyman level as a minimum in organisations (Hoffman et al. 2014; Jung, Kim & Reigeluth 2016; Moon, Kim & You 2013). For instance, Hoffman et al. (2014) believed that skills of most employees needed to be developed at least at the journeyman level, that is, one who can do his/her job productively and independently. However, there is no easy answer on how to map any proficiency scale to the performance measures used in the workplace. Even among researchers, there is less agreement on performance measures in regards to whether to measure job performance in terms of tasks or behaviours or outcomes (Koopmans et al. 2011). Thus, the literature does not provide much guidance on nature of proficiency at each stage on any of the staged models. Further, the literature lacks guidance on how proficiency can be quantified from one stage to another in measurable terms. This issue raises several interrelated questions: What proficiency means to organisations? How do organisations measure proficiency? How do the stages of proficiency play a role in performance assessment at work?

1.2.5 Accelerated proficiency

Business leaders consider that it is very important to identify the point when an individual demonstrates performance that signifies his/her being operating at or above desired or target proficiency (Fred 2002). Every job role requires a certain amount of time to develop performance to the desired proficiency level. This time is referred to as *time-to-proficiency* (TTP). Bachlechner et al. (2010, p. 378) defined time-to-proficiency as 'the amount of time an individual spends in a new job environment before it [sic] is able to fulfil most tasks without help from colleagues or supervisors'. Time-to-proficiency is usually measured from the date of hiring or when someone takes up a new role or the first day of the training s/he attends. However, measurement of the starting point and end state may vary significantly based on the context and definition of desired proficiency. Time-to-proficiency is not measurement of one activity, rather it involves time required for several activities such as onboarding, formal as well as informal training required to understand the basics of the job, on-the-job training and on-the-job learning to understand specifics of job tasks, and other activities to gain experience on specific tasks or skills required to do the job (Attri & Wu 2015).

The overall time-to-proficiency could be in months or years depending on the jobs. Ericsson et al. (1993) estimated that at least ten years of deliberate practice was required to acquire expertise (time-to-expertise). Though developing every employee as an expert may not be a feasible goal for organisations, there is a general consensus that time-to-proficiency could also be long. For example, time-to-proficiency of new bankers in a study was estimated to be between eleven and fourteen months (Thompson 2017, p. 173). According to an estimate, a pilot takes a minimum of 1500 hours (the equivalent of two years flying two hours every day) to be certified to fly a commercial plane (Government Publishing Office 2013). Thus, time-to-proficiency is usually very long—much longer than any training program one attends to get initial operating readiness.

Organisations do not have that much time (Fadde & Klein 2010). Therefore, researchers appealed to hasten the process of acquiring expertise or at least acquiring a certain level of mastery in the skills (Fadde & Klein 2010, 2012; Fadde 2007, 2009a, 2009b, 2009c, 2012, 2013, 2016; Hoffman et al. 2008, 2009, 2014; Hoffman, Andrews & Feltovich 2012; Hoffman & Andrews 2012; Hoffman, Andrews, et al. 2010; Hoffman, Feltovich, et al. 2010). Hoffman, Andrews and Feltovich (2012, p. 9) pointed out that the fact that it takes a long time to achieve proficiency, is the basis of accelerating the same. Hoffman, Feltovich, et al. (2010, p. 9) called this concept *accelerated proficiency* and defined it as 'phenomenon of achieving higher levels of proficiency in less time'. Hoffman et al. (2014, p. 13) further qualified accelerated proficiency as 'getting individuals to achieve high levels of proficiency at a rate faster than ordinary'. They expressed accelerated proficiency in terms of time-to-proficiency (id. 169). Thus accelerated proficiency is the deliberate and conscious effort of shortening time-to-proficiency. Acceleration of proficiency is measured in terms of reduction in the time someone takes to reach the desired proficiency. In the business and academic literature, this deliberate effort is expressed with several synonyms or variations like *accelerating skill acquisition, accelerating proficiency acquisition, accelerating performance, accelerating time-to-proficiency, shortening time-to-proficiency* and *speed-to-proficiency* (Bruck 2015; Fadde & Klein 2010; Fred 2002; Hoffman et al. 2014; Rosenbaum & Williams 2004).

However, limited research has been carried out on this concept. Hoffman and Andrews (2012) raised the point that understanding of the concept of accelerated proficiency remains to be crystallised. Extending it to theoretical underpinning of the concept and process of accelerated proficiency, Hoffman et al. (2014) recently contended that there was no unified theory yet that could explain the nature of accelerated proficiency phenomenon. They implied that potentially two theories—cognitive flexibility theory (Spiro & Jehng 1990) and cognitive transformation theory (Klein & Baxter 2009), could be merged to form a new theory for accelerated proficiency: 'Both tap into same general empirical base about the phenomenon of proficiency, expertise, and high-end learning' (Hoffman et al. 2014, p. 136). While research and synthesis by Hoffman et al. (2014) advanced the understanding of the nature of accelerated proficiency, a unified theory remains elusive, more so in natural settings of organisations. The absence of a unified theory or model makes it even more important to understand this phenomenon, more specifically in organisations. Nevertheless, some questions have not been adequately addressed by the literature. For instance, how do business professionals view the concept of accelerated proficiency in an organisational context?

1.2.6 Business perspective of accelerating proficiency

Organisations have witnessed tremendous turmoil and growth between 2000 and 2016, which has led executives to be concerned about the success of their business in the new world (Deloitte 2017). The foremost organisational concern is increased competition. With globalisation, most organisations now have access to the same markets, similar technologies and similar capabilities (Kraiger, Passmore & Rebelo 2014; Kraiger 2014). The relative success of organisations may ultimately depend upon time-to-market of their products, services or solutions they develop or offer. Capabilities, competencies and skills of the workforce are the most critical determinants of time-to-market and hence the competitive distinction among organisations (Wright & McMahan 2011). Changing business landscapes and market dynamics bring different expectations on workforce competencies. A decade ago, the *Implications for 21st Century Work* report forecasted:

> One expected consequence of the technological advances is a continued growth in the demand for a high-skilled workforce capable of undertaking the basic R&D to develop new technologies, developing the applications and

production processes that exploit the technological advances, and bringing the resulting products to the commercial marketplace. (Karoly 2007, p. 3).

Researchers keep expressing similar views that the ability and readiness of the workforce to meet new business needs is a topic of constant concern to modern business managers (Salas et al. 2012). Thus, one of the critical business expectations is to bring the workforce up to speed to new job roles, new expectations, new standards or new business needs in as short a time as possible.

Several market forces collectively drive the need for shorter time-to-proficiency in the workplace, such as time-to-market competitiveness (Lynn, Akgün & Keskin 2003); constant obsolescence of skills (Korotov 2007); increasing complexity of jobs and skills (Hoffman, Feltovich, et al. 2010); attrition of senior or ageing workforce constantly getting replaced (Hoffman et al. 2014). The efforts to accelerate time-to-proficiency, thus lead to the faster readiness of workforce, cost savings and increased competitiveness in the market. Corporations and business leaders have emphasised the need for speed to proficiency and made recurring appeals to tackle this new business metric in several white papers, blogs, business case studies, commercial conferences and business books (Bruck 2007, 2015; Cross 2013; Harward 2017; Rosenbaum & Pollock 2015; Rosenbaum & Williams 2004). Leading workplace learning expert, Jay Cross stated that 'the faster a worker becomes proficient, the more profitable the firm' (Cross 2013). Similarly, leading business consultants, Rosenbaum and Williams (2004) stressed the importance of identifying the point at which desired performance is delivered: 'You need to know the *level of performance* required to do the job and *how long* it takes to get there.... when you can get employees up-to speed in far less time, productivity rises at far less expense'.

As a result of these appeals by business leaders, organisations now realise that the faster employees learn the skills required to do the job up to set performance standards, the faster they are able to handle new customer needs, meet new market needs, perform to new expectations, and deliver new technologies or adopt new changes (Attri 2014; Attri & Wu 2015). These appeals have indicated that time-to-proficiency is becoming one of the most important business metrics for fast-paced technological organisations. Accordingly, organisations worldwide are striving to figure out interventions, systems and strategies to shorten time-to-proficiency of employees (Fred 2002). However, the body of knowledge appears to be lacking even in the business domain. Notably, only three business books on this subject area were found: *Learning paths: increase profits by reducing the time it takes employees to get up-to speed* (Rosenbaum & Steve 2004); *Breakaway: deliver value to your customers—fast!* (Fred 2002); and *Speed to proficiency: creating a sustainable competitive advantage* (Bruck 2015). All of these books were based on practitioner experiences and not grounded in research-based evidence. However, the authors of these books recognised that shortening time-to-proficiency was a crucial business challenge that needs to be solved.

1.2.7 Strategies and methods of accelerating proficiency

The review of literature presented in chapter 2 reviews currently available methods for accelerating proficiency. The literature review indicated that some studies developed some promising methods with evidence to accelerate proficiency. These include cognitive task analysis (CTA) methods, time-compressed simulations-based methods, case-based and scenario-based methods, representative part-task approach, knowledge capture methods, technology-based methods, and accelerated learning methods. However, most of these methods are training methods for either classroom settings or simulation settings, and not all are transferable to workplace settings. Most are methods or techniques for addressing certain skill acquisition issues in specific contexts. These methods do not offer a comprehensive theory or model to guide acceleration of proficiency in the workplace. Hoffman, Feltovich, et al. (2010, p. 180) reiterated prevailing literature gaps on accelerated proficiency and appealed for researchers to address research questions such as:

> 1) How to quicken the training process while maintaining its effectiveness (*Rapidised Training*), ... 3) How to train and train quickly to higher levels of proficiency (*Accelerated Proficiency*). [emphasis in original]

To answer these questions, they recently synthesised a range of methods from the existing literature in their latest publication *Accelerated Expertise* (Hoffman et al. 2014, pp. 169–170). Despite the body of knowledge, they challenged that more research needs to be conducted, particularly to accelerate the stages of proficiency which are of interest to organisations by '(1) Facilitating the achievement of high proficiency, especially accelerating across the apprentice to senior journeyman levels of proficiency ... (3) Producing applications' (Hoffman et al. 2014, p. 173). This appeal was the trigger for this research study, positioning it in the organisational setting. Until recently, in scholarly research, as well as the practitioner literature alike, no systematic attempt has been put forward to develop a model for accelerated proficiency in the workplace.

While there is a lack of empirical studies in the mainstream academic literature regarding how to accelerate proficiency, the practitioner literature (such as magazines, intuitional reports, consulting blogs, industry awards and corporate white papers) continue to report several success stories and successful methods to reduce time-to-proficiency in business settings (Emily & Krob 2014; PetroSkills 2009; PTC 2005; Rosenbaum 2014; WalkMe 2013). Thus, it is understood that several organisations have pioneered certain methods and strategies to shorten time-to-proficiency, which unfortunately has not seen its way into mainstream scholarly publications. This gap fundamentally motivates this research study. Based on this gap, some questions arise in the organisational context: What are the methods or strategies used in organisations to accelerate proficiency? How successful are these methods?

This research study contributes to addressing the questions highlighted in the previous sub-sections, and in particular, explores the concept of accelerated proficiency in organisational settings, business factors that drive the need for accelerated proficiency, business benefits of doing so and strategies deployed by various organisations to successfully reduce time-to-proficiency of the workforce.

1.3 RESEARCH PROBLEM AND QUESTIONS

The business challenge this study intends to address is that organisations struggle with long time-to-proficiency of their workforce and that puts market and financial pressure on them. The intent is conceptually portrayed in *Figure 1-1*. Proficiency levels are plotted on the vertical axis and time is plotted on the horizontal axis. Proficiency paths are shown as a straight line for simplicity. The dotted horizontal line indicates desired or target proficiency. Assuming an employee starts a job role at time T_0, s/he reaches target proficiency following a traditional proficiency path at time T_1. Conceptually, if some strategies or mechanisms exist which could accelerate the rate of proficiency acquisition to follow the accelerated proficiency path; it could have allowed the individuals serving the same job role at time T_2. The difference, T_2-T_1, is a net reduction in time-to-proficiency. The result of shorter time-to-proficiency leads to substantial financial and operational benefits to the organisation and higher value to customers (Fred 2002).

Figure 1-1: Simplified concept of accelerated proficiency

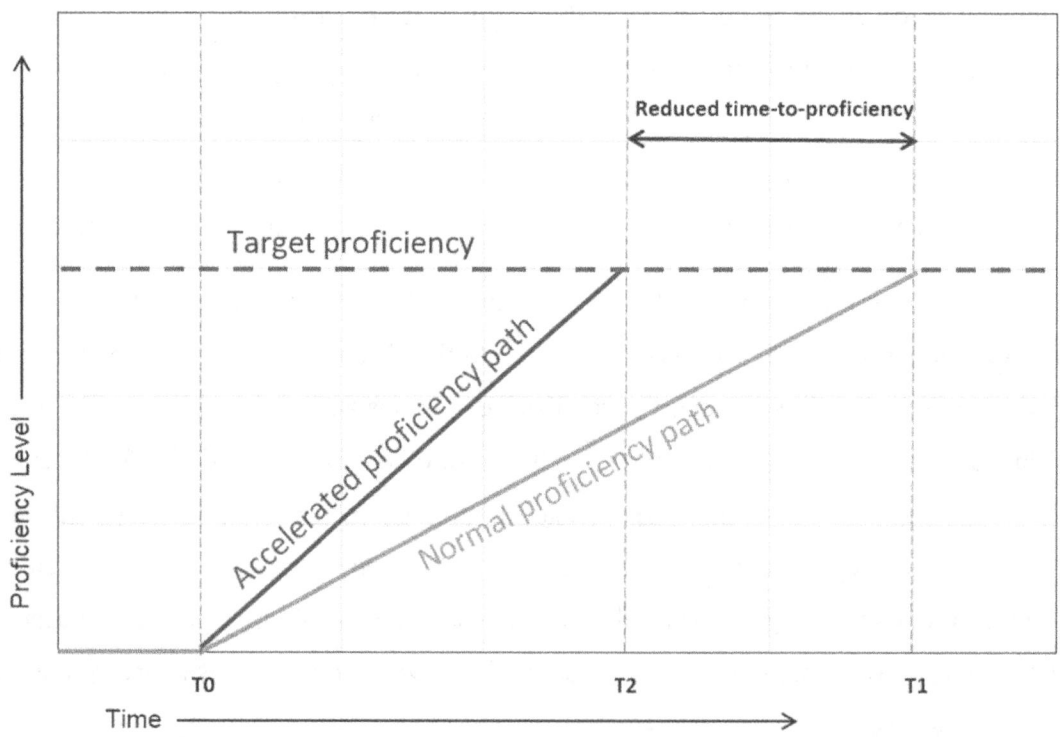

Source: modified from Rosenbaum and Williams (2004) and Hoffman et al. (2014)

Essentially, one of the aims of this research study is to examine the concept of accelerated proficiency and explore the strategies that have been used successfully in various organisations to shorten time-to-proficiency of employees. The central research question this study attempted to answer is:

How can organisations accelerate time-to-proficiency of employees in the workplace?

Three interrelated research questions were investigated to address the central research question:

1. *What does the concept of accelerating proficiency or accelerating time-to-proficiency mean to organisations?*

2. *What business factors drive the need for reducing time-to-proficiency of the workforce and how do organisations benefit from achieving it?*

3. *What core practices and strategies business leaders and practitioners adopt to achieve shorter time-to-proficiency of the workforce in a given job?*

Current studies have not investigated accelerated proficiency in business settings as practised or viewed by practitioners. The first research question was designed to analyse and understand the meaning practitioners place on the concept of accelerated proficiency in different contexts and to understand how they view this concept. The current scholarly literature does not specify the impact of this problem on an organisation's business, extent to which business leaders are concerned about this problem and the value of reducing time-to-proficiency. Thus, the second research question intended to understand the drivers, business reasons and pressures that influence organisations to pursue accelerated proficiency projects and the benefits of shortening time-to-proficiency. The third research question was designed to identify practices, strategies, methods and processes used by various organisations to reduce time-to-proficiency successfully. Currently, no guiding framework was found for accelerating proficiency in the workplace. To address this gap, the end objective of this research was to develop a conceptual model and framework out of these proven practices or strategies, which practitioners can use to reduce time-to-proficiency of the workforce in various settings.

This study's findings address gaps in the literature and offer guidance in solving the crucial business challenge of long time-to-proficiency. The thesis argues that practices and strategies to shorten time-to-proficiency are beyond training and learning interventions and require orchestration of several other processes, systems and strategies in the workplace. A conceptual model and framework of strategies is proposed which organisations can use to shorten time-to-proficiency. An agenda for future research is also presented to guide academic researchers and practitioners to explore other aspects of the accelerated proficiency phenomenon.

1.4 CONTRIBUTIONS OF THE STUDY

This section summarises three major contributions made by this study: (1) contribution to knowledge; (2) contribution to methodology; and (3) contribution to practice. A detailed description of the contributions is provided in chapter 5.

1.4.1 Contribution to knowledge

This study fills a gap in the literature in regards to limited research available on accelerating proficiency in organisations. The findings of the study contribute towards understanding theoretical and practical underpinning about how organisations currently accelerate proficiency in business settings. A major output of this research study is the identification of main practices and strategies that drive a reduction in time-to-proficiency in the workplace. A detailed framework of six practices and 24 strategies was developed. A conceptual model was developed to explain the dynamics and mechanism of how proficiency of workforce is accelerated in organisations. Further, this study established the magnitude and scale of the business problem of time-to-proficiency and clearly outlines the business benefits of shortening time-to-proficiency across a number of different contexts. This contribution to the body of knowledge lays the groundwork for further business research in this niche area. This research study also offers a list of topics and methods for future research to investigate various aspects of the accelerate proficiency phenomenon. Section 5.12 of Chapter 5 outlines these directions in detail.

1.4.2 Contribution to business research methodology

This study contributed to business research methodology in four areas. Details of this contribution are described in section 5.9 of chapter 5. Firstly, this research study demonstrates how professional social media sites like LinkedIn and other social media outreach tools like SlideShare, blogs, Google and others can be used be to establish credibility and reach out to difficult-to-reach business experts, particularly in niche areas (Robinson, Sinar & Winter 2013). Second, this study provides strong evidence that Internet-based interview methods are in fact powerful vehicles to get good reach, good quality data and good quality participation (Sturges & Hanrahan 2004). Thirdly, this research study demonstrates the use of bounded project cases as sampling units and units of analysis in today's organisations where most improvement initiatives in the organisations are conducted using temporary project teams (Turner & Müller 2003). Finally, this study demonstrates that the core business goal of 'what works' can be used in scholarly fashion to produce useful research outcomes (Fendt, Kaminska-Labbé & Sachs 2008; Gray 2014). This study demonstrates that managers in organisations can use goal-oriented methodologies they already may be using at their workplace on a daily basis to design their research and to collect/analyse data.

1.4.3 Contribution to practice and education

This study offers a practical framework for practitioners, which is grounded in successful real-world business practices. This framework consists of six practices and 24 strategies and is developed in the form of a hierarchical checklist with rich recommendations. Practitioners can use this framework in their context easily to plan and lead projects to shorten time-to-proficiency. A side outcome of the data collection in this research study is sixty success stories structured as bounded project cases which may find its use in a case-based method in a range of management, training and instructional design disciplines (e.g., Harvard case-based teaching - Roberts 2001).

1.5 JUSTIFICATION OF THE STUDY

In this section, the study is justified from the perspective of the benefits that organisations can realise from its outputs. In particular, the findings of this study helps to address three business needs in organisations and practice: (1) the need for faster readiness of the workforce to support business needs; (2) need to stay competitive in the market; and (3) need for cost benefits.

1.5.1 Faster workforce readiness

Organisations are increasingly becoming aware of the importance of bringing people up to speed faster. In a survey of over 10,000 business leaders, Deloitte recently reported that skills are becoming obsolete at an accelerated rate and indicated that software engineers must now redevelop skills every twelve to eighteen months and speculated similar trends in other professions (Deloitte 2017). New studies indicate that the half-life of job skills have gone down to five years, while the average tenure in a job is merely four and half years indicating that every new job in one's career potentially requires mastery of altogether new skills (Gratton & Scott 2016). Time-to-proficiency, thus, becomes very important where knowledge and skills become obsolete so soon.

Further to that, employees are required to solve increasingly complex business problems characterised by multiple goals, many possible actions, several different and uncertain consequences, and dynamically changing environments (Fischer, Greiff & Funke 2011). Complexity is also evident in the eco-system within which employees are required to operate in terms of processes, people and systems (Andersson et al. 2014; Marks et al. 2012; Schmid et al. 2011). To cope up with such complexity, employees now need to learn much higher-ordered skills (Karoly 2007; Levy 2010). However, in some jobs employees will simply leave the job due to the frustration of not being able to handle such complex assignments, not being able to produce and gain confidence quickly enough.

Recently, a *Workplace Learning Report* reported that the 'cost of replacing an employee is 50% to 250% of their annual salary benefits' (LinkedIn 2017, p. 32). It is very important for organisations to make their new employees productive as fast as they can. In a recent case study, a large insurance company in the US faced a very low retention rate of staff due to eighteen weeks long time-to-proficiency. When the time-to-proficiency was reduced to twelve weeks, the retention rate went up by 50% (Pollock, Wick & Jefferson 2015, p. 285). The effect of an organisation's inability to cope with above market forces could be far-reaching. Fadde and Klein (2010, p. 5) indicated such effect: 'The failure to get people up to speed can ripple through a team.... These kinds of pressures put a premium on methods to build expertise at all levels of an organisation rapidly'. Thus, the speed of skill obsolescence and pace of increasing complexity necessitate that organisations figure out methods and strategies to accelerate time-to-proficiency of their employees. The faster the workforce readiness, in turn, enables an organisation's competitiveness in the market.

1.5.2 Time-to-market competitiveness

Competition and the rapid rate of technological change have made the need for a shorter time-to-market as a critical business requirement for organisations. The competitiveness to distinguish one company's competitiveness from the other in producing new products comes from the capabilities, skills and competencies possessed by the workforce (Huselid & Becker 2011; Wright & McMahan 2011). Thus, organisations worldwide are spending a significant amount of money on training and development interventions to develop their workforce because they believe 'a skilled workforce represents a competitive advantage' (Salas et al. 2012, p. 74). However, not just the capabilities but the efficiency with which companies do so [update worker's skills] can thus be critical in helping them maintain a competitive edge' (Koller 2005, p. 3). In a recent survey, Deloitte observed the importance of speed: 'Instead of mere efficiency, successful organisations must be designed for speed, agility, and adaptability to enable them to compete and win in today's global business environment' (Deloitte 2017, p. 20).

There is a consensus among a large community of researchers that a team's time-to-proficiency in supporting a new product, service or technology does determine the "sweet spot" for the launch of the product or service (Langerak, Hultink & Griffin 2008). Shortening time-to-proficiency of the workforce is likely to lead to a certain advantage in time-to-market competitiveness for organisations (Fred 2002). This is one of the key motivations of this research study. Such financial implications of solving business problem of long time-to-proficiency justify undertaking this research study.

1.5.3 Cost of training and non-proficiency

Organisations depend on training and learning interventions as the first line of defence to prepare employees for initial operating proficiency (to start doing the job). Some figures suggest that every year organisations spend millions of dollars on training and learning programs to bring employees to the proficiency level to address their business needs. A recent *Training Industry Report* stated that the average annual training budget for large companies (those with over 10,000 employees) was $14.3 million, while total training expenditures in the US alone were $70.6 billion (Training Magazine 2016, p. 29).

There is also an opportunity cost or productivity loss while employees are away from their job undergoing training, no matter how long. Those times otherwise could have been utilised in producing revenues or handling critical jobs for the customers. In a case study, eighteen weeks of time-to-proficiency of financial services advisors at the US's largest insurance company caused hundreds of thousands of dollars of lost revenue opportunity for insurance agencies; which were subsequently reduced by 68% by decreasing time-to-proficiency to twelve weeks (Pollock, Wick & Jefferson 2015, p. 285). Further, in a case study involving fourteen new bankers, net income increased by 13% (approx. $250,000) in first twelve months of employment due to a 25% decrease in time-to-proficiency (Thompson 2017).

The consequential costs associated with a non-proficiency of an employee cannot be ignored either. Non-proficient employees performing below desired expectations may lead to errors or defects, customer dissatisfaction, financial losses for the business or even life-threatening situations. Thus, it is argued that bringing people up to proficiency faster leads to significant cost benefits.

1.6 RESEARCH METHODOLOGY

This section summarises the research design and methodology employed to conduct this study.

1.6.1 Research design

A qualitative exploratory approach was used in this study to explore the new under-investigated concept and process of accelerated proficiency in the workplace. The business problem of accelerating proficiency is relatively new and needs to be understood in its natural settings. Therefore, such a study warranted an exploratory qualitative research approach to understand the phenomenon (Mason 2002). The pragmatism paradigm was chosen for this study. The pragmatic stand informed the goal-oriented qualitative data collection and data analysis methods in this study (Johnson & Onwuegbuzie 2004). The study design involved purposive sampling and criteria-driven sampling for selection of participants using professional databases. The three-stage data collection process was used with in-depth interviews. Sampling units of bounded project cases were used to gather success stories across various contexts. Thematic and matrix analysis was employed to analyse the data and a focus group was used to validate the research findings.

1.6.2 Data collection

The goal of the data collection was to gather and understand successful project cases, which could provide insights into the need for shortening time-to-proficiency and strategies employed by business leaders to do so and results attained out of deploying such strategies. A systematic and criteria-driven selection was used in this study to recruit and select participants. A combination of purposive sampling and criterion-driven sampling was utilised (Mason 2002; Morse 1991; Patton 1990, 2014). Research participants consisted of selected worldwide training experts and business professionals with proven project experience in shortening time-to-proficiency of employees. The study employed several participant outreach strategies while employing social media platforms to secure participation from experts. These strategies are described in detail in section 3.3 of chapter 3. In total, 85 business and project leaders from 7 countries participated in this study.

The data collection was conducted in three phases using in-depth interviewing as the primary mode of data collection. Phase 1 involved in-depth interviews with industry experts and thought leaders to arrive at a general understanding of the concept of accelerated proficiency. That phase guided the understanding of key issues and approaches in this area and guided the interview questions for phase 2 data collection. 28 interviews were conducted at this stage. Phase 2 data collection involved in-depth interviews with project leaders who possessed specific experience in leading, designing or driving a project to reduce time-to-proficiency. The bounded project case was used as sampling unit, as well as a unit of analysis. In-depth interviews in phase 2 focused on understanding a complete project case, business challenge, previous models and new strategies used to reduce time-to-proficiency and project results. During this phase, 66 successful project cases, along with 50 associated project case documents were collected. These project cases spanned across 10 economic sectors, 20 business sectors, and 27 industry groups, covering 14 different types of jobs and 5 levels of complexity. Phase 3 involved an expert focus group with selected business leaders to review the findings and model developed in this study. The feedback was collected and analysed to understand how well the study's findings resonated with the expert group.

1.6.3 Data analysis

Data analysis in this study used two frameworks. Using thematic analysis techniques specified by Boyatzis (1998) and Braun and Clarke (2006, 2013), new themes and patterns were identified during this comparison, and emergent data-driven coding was used to code these themes and patterns. Coded data were displayed using several techniques such as matrices and thematic networks (Attride-Stirling 2001). At various stages in the data analysis, concept map techniques were also used for intuitive data analysis (Daley 2004; Wheeldon & Faubert 2009). The themes were analysed for the association, relationship and hierarchy among themes. The themes, sub-themes and overarching themes emerged during thematic analysis.

The themes were arranged in the form of matrices using the matrix analysis framework specified by Miles, Huberman and Saldana (2014). The matrix analysis reduced each project case into a number of matrices across several variables. These matrices were used to compare the themes across several variables across all the project cases (Stake 2006; Yin 2014). Project cases were compared for similarity, patterns and contrast, and relationship of those patterns across different contextual variables such as business sectors, industry groups, nature of jobs, nature of skills involved and complexity ratings. The bounded project case structure allowed efficient cross-case analysis for a large amount of data. Recursive processes of completing data reduction, creating data display and drawing conclusions led to the development of a conceptual model of accelerated proficiency and identification of six major practices and twenty-four strategies prevailing across all project cases.

1.6.4 Validation and reliability

Framework and techniques specified by Lincoln and Guba (1985) and Miles, Huberman and Saldana (2014) were used to ensure objectivity, dependability and credibility of the study data, data analysis and findings. Checking for usefulness and generalizability of the research findings and framework was a very important aspect of this research's objective to produce a framework that can be used readily in practice. The data collection across several contexts allowed assessment of the degree of generalisation of the concept of accelerated proficiency revealed in the study. Therefore, several techniques including prevalence scoring, member (participants) checks, and an expert focus group were used to implement guidelines suggested by Miles, Huberman and Saldana (2014) to check for external validity/transferability/fittingness and utilisation/applicability/action-orientation of the study's findings. It was concluded from the findings that the model is generalizable across several contexts.

1.7 DELIMITATIONS AND ASSUMPTIONS

This section describes the scope of this study, along with delimitations and assumptions made.

1.7.1 Scope

The topic of the research was accelerating proficiency in the workplace and shortening time-to-proficiency of the workforce from a business standpoint. Thus, this study approached the business problem of longer time-to-proficiency from the overall business standpoint, and hence, has been addressed within the business discipline.

The study has been conducted with practice orientation. Though there may be some overlap, this research study did not explore strategies for general performance improvement, training effectiveness or accelerating learning. The focus of the study has been exploring business strategies.

Based on preliminary research while locating the participants, it was understood that the organisations actively engaged in reducing time-to-proficiency were scattered thinly across various business sectors, contexts and different organisation types. Therefore, this research study is not positioned in any specific business sector, organisation type, job type or demographic location. Accelerated proficiency is relatively a new phenomenon/concept. Positioning the research in one specific setting would have led to non-representative samples not enough to build inferences for larger practice. Therefore, attempts have been made to approach the findings from a practical application standpoint, focus on the generalizability of findings and to provide a practical output as much as possible. Thus, this study investigates practices and strategies across various contexts to develop a generalizable model. The major phase of this research was conducted with data collected from project leaders and practitioners who have specifically worked on or led projects to shorten time-to-proficiency. Almost all of them were project leaders. Thus, the study represents the viewpoint of project leaders or project owners primarily, and not the views of the full project team and other stakeholders.

1.7.2 Delimitations

The topic of accelerated proficiency (or accelerated expertise) has been studied in the literature, primarily in the training, education, and psychology or cognitive domains. This study acknowledges that these topics generate considerable interest in training leaders, learning designers and educational researchers. However, no other study was found that was explicitly positioned in the business domain due to the nature of the problem it aimed to solve. No attempt was made to limit the study to any specific sub-discipline such as performance management or training management. This study was exploratory in nature, which required keeping it within the major discipline of business to build a holistic understanding of this phenomena. As such, this study was not designed to explore the general methods of improving training effectiveness, performance improvement or accelerating learning or similarly related topics, unless specifically linked to gains in shortening time-to-proficiency.

Historically, the topic of accelerated proficiency has been linked to human learning. However, the literature on general human learning, training and cognitive domains is immensely vast. One of the aims of this research is to explore the methods and strategies to shorten time-to-proficiency and to develop a conceptual model or framework. Therefore, instead of reviewing all main and allied areas of training, learning and cognitive sciences, the literature review in this study is guided by the goals of the research and has focused on finding evidence of accelerated proficiency in existing methods, models or theories.

Developing a theory on accelerated proficiency was not an objective of this study. Sampled population in this study were mainly the project leaders and practitioners. Their experience was best suited to provide insights into practical and useful frameworks that worked in the organisations. This study offers process view of accelerated proficiency in organisations. Other studies may be better positioned to motivate investigations to develop a theory on accelerated proficiency with a different population. This study offers directions in section 5.12 for extending the findings of this research towards building a theory of accelerated proficiency.

1.7.3 Assumptions

The participants in this study were selected from various business organisations. It was assumed that participants were free to express their views, provide details of their projects and sought appropriate permissions from their parent or client organisation to share the details of such projects. Therefore, it was assumed that the accounts provided by the participants were honest, truthful and evidence-based. It was also assumed that the sample size of 85 participants and 66 project cases was representative enough to reveal important aspects of the business problem of time-to-proficiency in various contexts.

The relevant literature on the topic of accelerated proficiency and time-to-proficiency is very limited in the mainstream scholarly research, which mainly informed the business challenge selected for this study. However, most of the literature is available on elite expertise development rather than workplace proficiency in business settings. The significance of the research and business challenges addressed in this study has been suggested by the practitioner literature such as commercial conferences, blogs, business books by practitioners, corporate case studies, and business analysis reports, among others. It was assumed that business challenges represented in the practitioner literature were worthwhile topics for research and a perceived gap in the mainstream literature.

1.8 OUTLINE OF THE THESIS

This research thesis is organised into six chapters:

Chapter 1: Introduction: The first chapter laid out and focused on introducing the research topic. The chapter also laid the foundation for remaining chapters by summarising the literature review, research problem and justification to conduct this study.

Chapter 2: Literature Review: This chapter reviews the existing literature and identifies the gaps in the literature regarding the focus area of study. This chapter reviews different theories, and models found relevant to accelerating proficiency. Gaps from existing theories and models are noted to establish a research context and problem for this study.

Chapter 3: Research Methodology: This chapter presents the research design and selection of the data collection methodologies and qualitative research methodology. It offers a justification for choosing the pragmatic paradigm and describes how data were collected and processed. Data analysis methodology is also explained. The methods employed for ensuring validation and reliability of the research study and its findings are described as well.

Chapter 4: Research Findings: This chapter discusses the details of data analysis performed on the collected data and presents the findings from the data analysis. Results are presented for each of the research questions in two parts. The first part of the chapter describes the summary of overarching themes that were formed during data analysis based on the emergent themes. The second part of the chapter describes the details of emergent themes noted under each research question. The part three of the chapter provides analysis of results of time-to-proficiency reduction seen in project cases analysed in this study.

Chapter 5: Conclusion and Implications: The final chapter discusses the results, explains the major interpretations and relates the findings to the existing literature. This chapter outlines an important section on a conceptual model of accelerated proficiency that is derived from the findings and discussions. This chapter also outlines the major contributions made by this study to the body of knowledge. The limitations are explained and a detailed agenda for future research for extending this study.

1.9   CHAPTER SUMMARY

The concept and process of accelerating proficiency and business need for shortening time-to-proficiency is critical in organisations. Solving such a business problem would have a significant impact and business value. Thus, this is a research problem of significance, impact and contribution to the literature. Leading literature on expertise and business informs the lack of understanding of mechanisms and strategies to shorten time-to-proficiency, and it also suggests a lack of any framework or conceptual model to guide practice. This research study strives to fill this literature gap. The central research question this study addressed is how organisations can accelerate time-to-proficiency of the workforce. Three research questions were explored to understand the meaning of accelerated proficiency for the organisations, significance and importance of shortening time-to-proficiency and strategies to shorten time-to-proficiency. A qualitative exploratory research approach was taken in this study. 66 project cases gathered from 85 participants were analysed using thematic analysis and a conceptual model was developed from the findings. This study contributes to knowledge, practice, methodology, teaching and society. The research questions and objectives are presented in a summary table, as shown in *Table 1-1*, to build an appropriate connection.

Table 1-1: Summary of research questions and research objective

Business problem		
The business challenge this study aimed to solve is that organisations are struggling with long time-to-proficiency of their workforce in certain job roles.		
Intents/aims		
To explore and understand the meaning practitioners place on the concept of accelerated proficiency in the workplace. To understand what makes the need for accelerating proficiency critical for organisations and what benefits they receive from reducing time-to-proficiency. To identify practices, strategies, methods and processes that have been proven to reduce time-to-proficiency successfully in different contexts.		
Central research question		
How can organisations accelerate time-to-proficiency of employees in the workplace?		
Research questions		
Research question #1	Meaning of accelerated proficiency	What does the concept of accelerating proficiency or accelerating time-to-proficiency mean to organisations?
Research question #2	Driving factors and benefits of reduced time-to-proficiency	What business factors drive the need for reducing time-to-proficiency of the workforce and how do organisations benefit from achieving it?
Research question #3	Practices and strategies to accelerate proficiency	What core practices and strategies do business leaders and practitioners adopt to achieve shorter time-to-proficiency of the workforce in a given job?
Research objective		
The objective of this research is to develop a conceptual model and/or framework of proven practices or strategies that practitioners can use to reduce time-to-proficiency of the workforce in various settings.		

Chapter 2 LITERATURE REVIEW

2.1 INTRODUCTION

This chapter identifies the research issues, highlights the gaps noted and proposes research questions based on those gaps towards accelerating proficiency in organisational and workplace domains. The topic of this research study is broadly linked to two parent topics: job performance and proficiency development. The conceptual relationships of broad topics which are the focus of this literature review are shown in *Figure 2-1*. The concept map of the literature review is based on the general premise that knowledge and skills play key parts in delivering desired performance at the job. As people gain more proficiency and expertise in the job, their performance level increases. Accelerating the pace with which people acquire proficiency thus sits at intersections of job performance, skill acquisition and proficiency development. Therefore, the literature review was conducted mainly on these three parent areas to draw the research questions which this study was designed to investigate.

Figure 2-1: Map of literature review

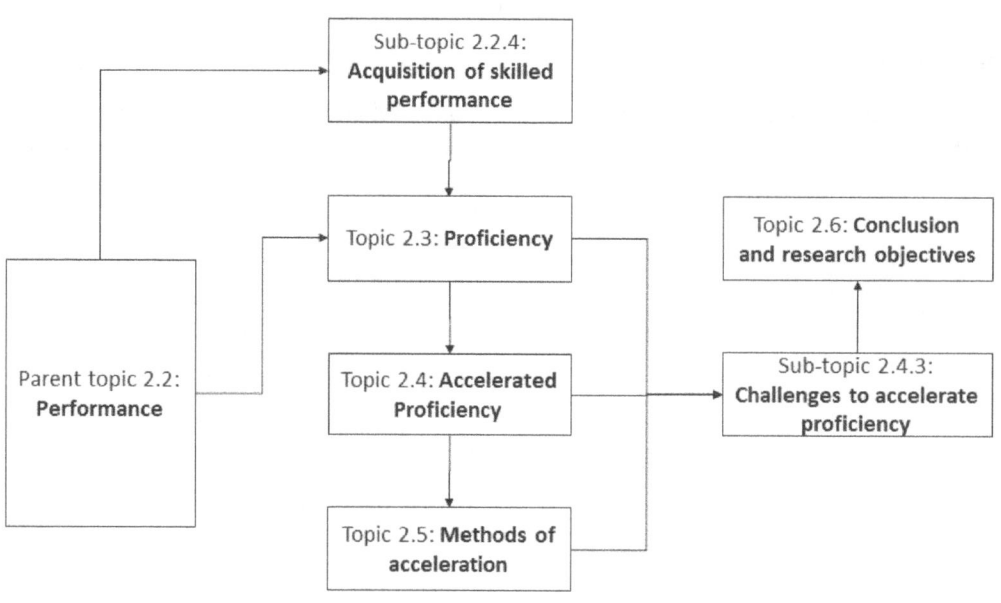

Source: developed for this research study

This chapter is organised as follows: Section 2.2 reviews the literature on the parent topic of job performance broadly and reviews the studies and major themes of performance from historical and classic studies relevant to the research problem. Sub-section 2.2.1 introduces the broader perspectives from studies and advances in human resource development (HRD) and performance improvement. Sub-section 2.2.2 explores the studies that characterised dimensions of job performance. Section 2.2.3 explores the studies on debate of linkage between learning and performance. Sub-section 2.2.4 reviews major themes on the sub-topic of acquisition of skilled performance. The classic and seminal work and historical work of significance such as theories of stages of skill acquisition are reviewed. Section 2.3 reviews the definition and nature of proficiency. In this section, the literature on proficiency is reviewed as it relates to the literature on parent topics of performance, knowledge/skill acquisition and expertise acquisition. Key studies on novice-to-expert transition and concept of proficiency scaling are reviewed. Section 2.4 then reviews the imperatives in the literature that assert the need for accelerated proficiency and the existing work on accelerated proficiency is reviewed. Theoretical issues, as well as challenges to accelerate proficiency, as noted in various studies, are highlighted. Section 2.5 reviews studies on various methods proposed by researchers for accelerating proficiency. The methods are reviewed for their implications and evidence towards acceleration of proficiency. Section 2.6 enumerates the gaps that lead to the development of the research questions for the study. The research problem and central research question are then explained based on the directions informed by the literature gaps.

The main goal of this study is to the explore the field of accelerated proficiency, which is a relatively new research topic. This study takes forward the conceptualisation of accelerated proficiency proposed in experimental research conducted by Hoffman (Hoffman et al. 2008, 2009, 2014; Hoffman, Andrews & Feltovich 2012; Hoffman & Andrews 2012; Hoffman, Andrews, et al. 2010; Hoffman, Feltovich, et al. 2010) and Fadde (Fadde & Klein 2010, 2012; Fadde 2007, 2009a, 2009b, 2009c, 2012, 2013, 2016). Their work reflects recent advances on the topic of accelerating proficiency of people in training and work settings. However, the general theories underlying the concept of accelerated proficiency are grounded in seminal and classic works conducted between the 1960s and 2000s by leading theorists such as Murphy (1989), Campbell (Campbell 1990; Campbell, McHenry & Wise 1990; Campbell et al. 1993), Borman and Motowidlo (Borman & Motowidlo 1993; Motowidlo, Borman & Schmit 1997; Motowidlo & Van Scotter 1994), Dreyfus and Dreyfus (Dreyfus & Dreyfus 1986, 2004, 2005), Fitt (Fitt 1964; Fitt & Posner 1967), Anderson (1981, 1982, 2000), Ackerman (1988, 1992), Chi (Chi 1982; Chi 2006; Chi, Glaser & Rees 1982; Chi, Glaser & Farr 1988; Chi, Glaser & Rees 1981; Glaser & Chi 1988), Ericsson (Ericsson 2000, 2002, 2003, 2004, 2006a, 2007, 2008, 2009a, 2009b, 2009c; Ericsson et al. 1993; Ericsson & Charness 1994; Ericsson, Prietula & Cokely 2007; Ericsson & Towne 2010; Ericsson & Ward 2007), Spiro (Spiro & Jehng 1990; Spiro et al. 1987; Spiro et al. 1990; Spiro et al. 2003) and Klein (Klein 1993, 1997, 1998, 2003; Klein & Baxter 2009; Klien & Borders 2016; Klien, Hintze & Saab 2013; Klein et al. 1997), among others. The work of these theorists is thoroughly reviewed, alongside recent developments in the literature. The literature review approaches the topics of performance, knowledge and skill acquisition, expertise and proficiency from a historical perspective first before reviewing the emergence of accelerated proficiency and methods to accelerate proficiency.

2.2 PERFORMANCE

In this section, the literature about the parent discipline of performance (more specifically job performance) is reviewed. Most of the work on modelling of performance is grounded in seminal and classic work, while modern researchers have extended this work further.

2.2.1 Human resource development and performance improvement

Human resource development

The business success of an organisation depends on skills, capabilities, potential and expertise of its people primarily among other resources (Jacobs 2003). The discipline of human resource development (HRD) has long been investigated for a range of issues related to human performance in organisational contexts. Most commonly, HRD is defined as 'a process for developing and unleashing human expertise through organisation development and personnel training and development for the purpose of improving performance' (Swanson & Holton 2001, p. 4). Traditionally, HRD has been associated with training and development (T&D) interventions. Training and development include workplace interventions to enhance the learning of employees towards developing their capabilities and expertise. However, over the last two decades, researchers such as Swanson and Holton (2001) have proposed that HRD processes focus on organisational development (OD), as well as T&D. Organisation development includes the processes to enhance the effectiveness of the organisation, as well as care for employees (Werner & DeSimone 2009). According to Swanson and Holton (2001), OD is the 'process of systematically unleashing human expertise to implement organisational change for the purpose of improving performance'. Thus, OD activities are central to any organisations towards preparing employees for changes and are indeed affected by HRD activities (Cummings & Worley 2001; Rothwell & Sullivan 2005). Nevertheless, the purpose of HRD processes and interventions is probably unquestionable towards improving performance and developing the expertise of employees and organisations as a whole. For instance, 'HRD should exist for the purpose of improving performance; it must be performance focused, considering the relationship of HRD to the organisational system it serves' (Swanson & Arnold 1996, p. 17).

Various studies have attempted to explore different aspects of HRD, emphasizing the key goals of HRD such as training and development (McLagan 1989a, 1989b), facilitating organisational change through learning (Chalofsky & Lincoln 1983), increasing human potential (Nadler, Wiggs & Smith 1988), delivering organisational performance (Jacobs 1989), improving work-related learning capacity (Watkins 1989), performance improvement (Gilley, England & Wesley 1989), performance and productivity improvement (Smith 1990), and unleashing human expertise through organisational development (Swanson 1995). HRD exhibits considerable overlaps in theory and practice with other domains such as career development, organisational and process effectiveness, performance improvement, strategic organisational planning, human resource management and human resources (Swanson & Holton 2001). Researchers most commonly divide studies on HRD into two separate paradigms: the learning paradigm and the performance paradigm (Swanson & Holton 2001).

Learning paradigm of HRD

The learning paradigm of HRD is dominated by three perspectives on learning: 1) individual learning which considers individual's learning as the outcome of various instructional and training interventions (Gagne & Briggs 1974); 2) performance-based learning that focuses on individual performance resulting from learning (Holton, Bates & Ruona 2000); and 3) whole systems learning which encompasses enhancing team and organisational performance through learning in addition to individual performance (Watkins & Marsick 1993). According to this paradigm, developing expertise of employees resides at the heart of any HRD intervention. In an organisational context, 'expertise almost always refers to the ability to use knowledge and skills to achieve outcomes that have value to someone else' (Jacobs 2003, p. 5). Further, Jones (1981, p. 188) asserted HRD as a 'systematic expansion of people's work-related abilities' (as cited in Swanson & Holton 2001, p. 5).

Training and development have been considered a critical part of HRD processes in this paradigm. Classic research studies on HRD are almost all focussed on the training and development function from the angle of workplace learning and employee education. Swanson and Arnold (1996, p. 17) highlighted the intersection of HRD and adult education in the workplace: 'First, the context is organisations. Second, the dependent variable, or desired outcome, is performance, which will directly affect the goals of the organisations. Third, the intersection includes education and training interventions'. Swanson (2007) proposed that employees need skills not only to maintain the system but also to change the system, later being significantly different from the former. Early studies on training and development focused on competence development of employees. Employee competence was defined as the use of a specific set of knowledge or skills (Jacobs 1997). However, early studies have argued that competence or employee abilities have a direct relationship with performance (Morf 1986), which in turn can be measured at the organisation, process or individual level (Swanson 1999). Some studies have shown that '[t]he primary outcome of HRD is not just learning but also performance' (Swanson & Holton 2001, p. 139). This aspect is reviewed in the following discussion of performance paradigm.

Performance paradigm of HRD

The second paradigm of HRD is performance paradigm, which focuses on enhancing individual performance through nonlinear, as well as learning interventions. In an organisational context, researchers have argued that competence is a limited construct (focusing on acquiring skills and knowledge only) which does not convey the true goals of HRD interventions (Swanson & Holton 2001). In a study conducted by Evers et al. (2011), the authors noted several organisational and tasks factors that influenced the professional development of teachers, and in turn, occupational expertise. While performance has been linked to the human lens which involves a focus on knowledge, skills and abilities of the individual (Clark 2008), improving performance in the workplace requires focusing on more than just human competencies. This school of thought represents the second paradigm of HRD, performance paradigm, which is dominated by two perspectives on performance: 1) individual performance improvement focuses on individual level performance systems; and 2) whole system performance improvement is a broader focus on performance improvement at multiple levels. The former approaches include human performance technology (HPT) (Gilbert 1978; Stolovitch & Keeps 1992), while the latter approaches include performance improvement or performance consulting (Holton 1999; Robinson & Robinson 1995; Rummler & Brache 1995)

A comprehensive review of the literature has indicated that there are over 50 different performance improvement models falling under individual, organisational and societal categories (Gok & Law 2017; Schaffer 2000). The studies on performance improvement are based on the premise of improving performance with or without a human lens (Swanson 1999). Given that performance of an individual in the organisation is not a singular function, researchers have suggested taking a system view to HRD that encompasses looking at different parts of the HRD as system elements which interact with each other through various processes (Jacobs 1989, 2014; Swanson 2001; Yawson 2013). A general system theory describes any performance improvement process that uses a simple thinking model of inputs, processes, outputs and a feedback loop (Swanson 1999). System theory also emphasises improving performance based on measurements: 'Performance improvement can only be manifest through outputs and change in outputs can only be assessed through some form of measurement' (Swanson 1999, p. 7).

An important implication of this line of thought was to investigate the role and impact of organisational development on how human expertise/performance was developed/improved in the workplace. Using a multidisciplinary approach based on their consulting engagements, Rummler and Brache (1995) proposed that there were three performance levels: organisation performance being the first level, process performance as the second level and individual performance as the third level. Their model fundamentally changed the way performance improvement was viewed in organisations. Extending Rummler and Brache's (1995) work further, Swanson (1994, 2007) proposed a performance diagnosis matrix that specified that performance should be measured at three levels, namely organisation, process, and individual, with all three of them being impacted by performance variables such as mission/goal, system design, capacity, motivation and expertise. Also, the integrated taxonomy of performance domains proposed by Holton (1999) suggested four domains of performance: mission, process, social sub-system and individual.

Among seminal studies that investigated performance paradigm in HRD, Gilbert (1978) coined the term 'worthy performance' to communicate the return on investment on performance. He proposed a behaviour-engineering model (BEM) which distinguished between a person's behaviours and the environment support that encourages or impedes performance. This model suggested that there was more than an individual's capability to produce a worthy performance (Gilbert 1978). Gilbert indicated that two sets of factors influenced performance: (1) environmental factors, which included information, resources and incentives; and (2) individual factors, which included knowledge, capacity and motives. While the environmental factors support or impede performance, the individual factors contribute towards performance at the individual level (Gilbert 2013).

Extending this work, Chevalier (2003) elaborated that the information element in the BEM model was about the role and performance clarity, relevant and frequent feedback about performance, description of expectations of performance and clear guides for performance. Resources element included tools, material, processes, procedures, and overall physical and psychological work environment and work conditions required to perform the job. The incentives element included adequate financial and non-financial incentives given to performers, enriched job designs, and positive work environment allowing further career opportunities. In contrast, knowledge represented the skills, knowledge, behaviours and experience to match the requirement of performance. Motives represented people's motivations and desire to work. Lastly, capacity represented the adaptation, flexibility and capacity to learn, which is free from emotional limitation. Chevalier (2003) postulated that final performance depended on push-pull forces exerted by environmental factors and individual factors. The major application of Gilbert's model is seen in identifying the barriers to expected performance (King Jr & Cennamo 2016). Some studies specifically used Gilbert's BEM model to evaluate performance improvement (Wooderson, Cuskelly & Meyer 2017), design safety interventions to improve performance (Crossman, Crossman & Lovely 2009), and justify the investment in human performance interventions (Humphress & Berge 2006).

There have been several implications of the studies using Gilbert's BEM model, one of them being that performance improvement requires several environment support systems in place, apart from skills, knowledge and behaviours possessed by an individual (Chevalier 2003). The second implication is that performance can be improved with or without training, with the latter being more prevalent (Dean 2016). The third is that accomplishments and outcomes should be the way to measure performance instead of behaviours, as they are just the means to achieve accomplishments (Binder 2017). While the influence of environment and organisational factors on performance cannot be denied, it was seen that organisations suffer more from performance issues related to organisational factors. For instance, in a meta-analysis of 327 performance improvement projects completed between 1986 and 2012, Hartt, Quiram and Marken (2016) noted that 65% to 74% performance issues targeted organisational or environmental factors, whereas 26% to 35% of the performance issues focused on individual performance factors only. This study indicated that causes related to an individual's performance issues could be a small percentage of overall performance causes at the organisational level. Research has contended that, when there are performance issues, the diagnosis needs to be carried out at the organisation, process, team and individual levels (Swanson 2007). Such a performance analysis of organisational and environmental factors is the foundation of Human performance technology (HPT), a framework developed from BEM to address the performance problems of organisations systematically (Pershing 2006; Van Tiem, Moseley & Dessinger 2004, 2012). HPT was defined as:

> A systemic and systematic set of processes for assessing and analysing performance gaps and opportunities; planning improvements in performance; designing and developing efficient, effective, and ethically justifiable interventions to close performance gaps or capitalize on opportunities; implementing the interventions; and evaluating all levels of results. (Guerra-Lopez 2016, p. 3)

Pershing (2006, p. 6) defined HPT as 'the study and ethical practice of improving productivity in organisations by designing and developing effective interventions that are results-oriented, comprehensive, and systemic'. Conceptually, HPT is similar to organisational development because it is an applied behavioural science and based on systems theory (Cho & Yoon 2010; Jacobs 1989; Pershing 2006). Both OD and HPT are concerned with improving organisational performance (Stolovitch 2007). The core of the HPT philosophy is a combination of three processes – performance analysis, cause analysis and intervention selection (Van Tiem, Moseley & Dessinger 2012). The HPT model emphasises heavily on analysis of possible performance issues and causes across different levels surrounding the worker. This includes analysis of mission, vision and goals of the organisation (organisational analysis); analysis of environment surrounding the job (environment analysis); analysis of difference between desired performance and actual performance (gap analysis); and analysis of causes of the gap between actual and desired performance (cause analysis) (Van Tiem, Moseley & Dessinger 2012). Similarly, Rothwell et al. (2000) presented a human performance improvement (HPI) model developed for the American Society for Training and Development (ASTD) based on key processes of performance analysis, cause analysis and intervention selection. This model was represented as a change management system in which performance is continuously measured and evaluated. Deterline and Rosenberg (1992) revealed the mission, strategy, and goal analysis, as well as analysis of work, organisation and competitive environment, as part of the organisational analysis. They argued that one should to assess several causes that may be leading to the performance gap. The cause analysis may include looking at consequences, incentives and rewards; data and information; resources, tools and environmental support; individual capacity; motives and expectations; and skills and knowledge.

Researchers have positioned the scholarly appeal and theory-driven practice value of HPT and attempted the development of theory from implications of HPT (Cho & Yoon 2010; Pershing, Abaci & Symonette 2016; Pershing, Lee & Cheng 2008). Implications of studies on HPT is its particular focus on more holistic understanding of processes, procedures and models used specifically towards improving workplace performance. A characteristics premise of HPT is that training is not the only solution to improve performance (Stolovitch & Keeps 1999). Deterline and Rosenberg (1992) indicated that interventions may include but are not limited to coaching, compensation, cultural change, documentation, environmental engineering, health/wellness, job aids, job/work design, leadership/supervision, performance management, performance support, staffing, team building and training/education. In recent studies, it was found that HPT practices described performance improvement processes followed by the practitioners to a reasonable degree (Kang 2017; Pershing, Lee & Cheng 2008). Nevertheless, the topic of performance and performance improvement is so widespread that it has expanded into several sub-disciplines. Performance is an important concept in HRD, which encompasses both learning and organisational performance: 'HRD will only be perceived as having strategic value to the organisation if it has the capability to connect the unique value of employee expertise with the strategic goals of the organisation' (Swanson & Holton 2001, p. 147). Performance of employees at the job that is job performance is an important aspect connected with developing employee skills, proficiency and expertise. The studies revealing this relationship are reviewed in the following sub-sections.

2.2.2 Dimensions of job performance

In the literature, business performance of an organisation is believed to be the result of collective forces of resources, strategies, technology and people: 'Organisations perform well and create value when they implement strategies that respond to market opportunities by exploiting their internal resources and capabilities' (Afiouni 2007, pp. 127–128). Researchers recognised skilled people in an organisation as one of the key contributors to business performance and organisational competitiveness (Afiouni 2007; Huselid

& Becker 2011). The critical value of individual performance of people in organisations was widely recognised: 'Organisations need highly performing individuals in order to meet their goals, to deliver the products and services they specialised in, and finally to achieve competitive advantage' (Sonnentag & Frese 2002, p. 4).

Despite its importance, the term *performance* does not seem to have one universal definition because there are several perspectives through which performance is viewed, defined and measured. Though numerous studies have been conducted in the field of individual performance, various disciplines have focused on different aspects of performance. The *Oxford English Dictionary* defines performance as 'the action or process of performing a task or a function' (https://en.oxforddictionaries.com/definition/performance). More generally, when an individual exhibits skill to desired standards to get the job done, this is what determines performance.

For a long period, task performance and job performance have been differentiated in the literature. While task performance indicates whether something was done to the desired specification or not, job performance indicates whether the job achieved the stated business outcomes. Job performance is viewed as the result of several cognitive, psychomotor tasks or abilities working together. Murphy (1989, p. 185) explained the distinction as:

> Job performance is certainly a function of the individual's performance on the specific tasks that comprise standard job descriptions but is also affected by variables such as success in maintaining good interpersonal relations, absenteeism and withdrawal behaviors, substance abuse, and other behaviors that increase hazards in the workplace ...

Thus, to produce overall job performance, several other things are required, such as teamwork, self-development, and personal attributes like perseverance, interpersonal and communication skills. Seconding Murphy's (1989) assertion, other studies also maintained similar view: 'Total [job] performance is much more than specific task or technical proficiency' (Campbell, McHenry & Wise 1990, p. 214). Viswesvaran and Ones (2000, p. 218) observed that several classic studies in the 1980s and 1990s had recognised that 'job performance entails more than just task performance'.

During the last several decades, the literature has generated a range of dimensions that characterised job performance. In the review of performance-related studies spanning last few decades, Viswesvaran (1993) and Viswesvaran and Ones (2000) observed 486 different performance dimensions across various occupations which were reported in literature prior to 2000. They classified these dimensions into ten groups: (1) overall job performance; (2) job performance or productivity; (3) effort; (4) job knowledge; (5) interpersonal competence; (6) administrative competence; (7) quality; (8) communication competence; (9) leadership; and (10) compliance with rules (Viswesvaran & Ones 2000). However, they found that there was not one dimension that could fully explain the dynamics of job performance and that each dimension was complexely interrelated:

> The existing research in this area [individual job performance] appears to be that each performance dimension is complexly determined (jointly by ability and personality) and that it is impossible to specify a sole cause or antecedent of a particular dimension of job performance. (Viswesvaran & Ones 2000, p. 224)

More recently, Koopmans et al. (2011) conducted a comprehensive meta-analysis across 58 studies related to individual performance framework. They found that performance had several different dimensions, which may be similar across several jobs and each of those dimensions could be measured with some indicators, varying from job to job. They reasoned that it was difficult to say if these measures captured the complexity of performance at work. Alongside the dimensions of job performance, the measures of job performance also showed the similar diversity that there was not one single measurement prevailing across occupations.

The complexity of job performance was discussed in the literature with reference to factors that impact performance as well. In a meta-analysis, Sonnentag and Frese (2002) found that there were two kinds of studies on the effects of situated work factors of on-the-job performance. They noticed that one set of studies indicated job characteristics such as job design interventions (e.g., meaningful tasks), control at work and group-work enhanced the job performance, while another set of studies showed factors such as role ambiguity, role conflict, and work environment stressors inhibit performance. This showed that job environment, as well as job design, impact job performance. Among others, team performance plays an important role for successful attainment of organisational goals within the team (or group). The interplay of such factors makes job performance a complex phenomenon.

In a study conducted by Campbell, McHenry and Wise (1990, p. 314), the authors elaborated on the complex nature of job performance as: 'There is not one outcome, one factor, or one anything that can be pointed to and labeled as job performance. Job performance really is multidimensional'. Swanson (1999) maintained the same view.

Collectively, various studies in the literature suggest a range of dimensions. Major dimensions include behaviour performance, task performance, outcome performance, contextual performance, individual and team performance. These dimensions are reviewed below.

Behavioural vs outcome performance

Sonnentag and Frese (2002) stated that performance has two different aspects that represent extremes - behavioural or action aspect (what an individual does) and an outcome aspect (what the consequence or result of the action is). Behavioural performance was one of the key dimensions found in the classic studies of Campbell (1990) and Murphy (1989). Murphy (1989) pioneered the work performance theory in which he emphasised behaviour as performance. Apart from task-related skills and behaviours, the contribution of other skills and attitudes affected overall task performance. Murphy (1989) believed that task performance is about the accomplishment of duties and tasks written in job descriptions. He theorised that work performance has four dimensions: (1) task behaviours; (2) interpersonal behaviours; (3) downtime behaviours (related to work avoidance); and (4) destructive/hazardous behaviours (related to noncompliance, violence, etc.).

Building on the work of Murphy (1989), Campbell (1990) considered not only task-related behaviours but also performance behaviours not directly related to the task. He acknowledged that performance is not just about job-specific task proficiency. Rather, an individual's proficiency in several non-job specific tasks as well, such as perseverance and discipline that is required to obtain reasonable performance. Campbell (1990) included eight dimensions to the work performance: (1) job-specific task proficiency; (2) non-job-specific task proficiency; (3) written and oral communications; (4) demonstrating effort; (5) maintaining personal discipline; (6) facilitating peer and team performance; (7) supervision; and (8) management and administration.

Studies by Campbell (1990), Campbell, McHenry and Wise (1990) and Campbell et al. (1993) led to an important demarcation and characterisation of job performance, in particular, the conceptual differences between behavioural performance versus outcome performance. Campbell (1990) and Campbell, McHenry and Wise (1990) maintained that only actions which are measured and those which lead to organisational goals count towards individual performance. Campbell et al. (1993) defined performance as behaviours or actions that are relevant to the goals of the organisation. This view implied that the outcome of the work such as the number of parts made, the number of sales made, among other metrics, was a result of individual behaviour. However, this view maintained that measuring an individual's performance in terms of job outcomes was problematic. Motowidlo, Borman and Schmit (1997) strongly made the argument that a performance model should not include results but should focus on behaviours only. They reasoned that results are a function of not only an individual's performance but also several other factors. Unless these factors are isolated, results do not represent an individual's contribution to the organisation's goals (Motowidlo, Borman & Schmit 1997, p. 73).

In contrast, supporters of the outcome view have positioned an argument that business organisations value performance in terms of accomplishments (Gilbert 1978, 2013). Accomplishments can be work outputs or things such as decisions made, strategies identified or end results (such as sales improvement). The supporters of this view reasoned that value of human performance is in the accomplishments it produces. This view also considered behaviours to produce those accomplishments were costly and not valuable in itself. Besides, there are challenges in defining performance only in behavioural terms too because not every action or behaviour is measurable. Unless someone focuses on results, it is difficult to identify the behaviours that are strongly correlated to produce the desired outcomes or results.

To reconcile these two aspects, researchers like Viswesvaran and Ones (2000) defined work performance as 'scalable actions, behavior and outcomes that employees engage in or bring about that are linked with and contribute to organisational goals'. This view combined behavioural aspects, as well as outcome aspects of job performance. Supporting this combined view, Moon, Kim and You (2013, p. 227) insisted on considering performance as an 'outcome and product in addition to behaviour or process in human resource development'. Several studies compared the strategies of behaviour-based versus outcome-based performance management systems (Oliver & Anderson 1994; Piercy, Cravens & Morgan 1998, 1999). However, studies exploring empirical relationships between the individual's behaviour aspects and outcome aspects are scarce. Yet, the implications of how performance is measured (at the behaviour level or outcome level) have a bearing on how one views the process of acquiring performance. For example, Farrington-Darby and Wilson (2006, p. 27) believed that '[d]isciplines that favour studying expertise [or performance] from an output perspective will look to the decision rather than the decision-making, the solution more than the process of problem solving ...'

Nevertheless, whichever way performance is defined or measured, individual performance is still shown to be one of the most critical workforce metrics in organisations. Moreover, studies have indicated that individual performance was an important component of work and organisational success (Sonnentag & Frese 2002). Maximising individual performance, therefore, is critical to the health of the organisation.

Task vs contextual performance

Campbell's (1990) model of eight dimensions of work performance, like Murphy's (1989), included task-related proficiency as one of the key dimensions that determine work performance. Borman and Motowidlo (1993, p. 73) proposed that task performance was 'the proficiency with which incumbents perform activities that are formally recognised as part of their jobs; activities that contribute to the organisation's technical core'. Other researchers defined task performance using terms like *job-specific task proficiency, technical proficiency* or *in-role performance*. For example, job-specific task proficiency was defined as the 'degree to which the individual can perform the core substantive or technical tasks that are central to a job and distinguish one job from another' (Viswesvaran & Ones 2000, p. 32). Early research suggested that task proficiency of an individual was the major source of variation in task performance (Borman & Motowidlo 1993). Thus, task proficiency represented one key element of task performance. However, task performance was shown to encompass many other aspects as well. Campbell (1990) and Murphy (1989) acknowledged that performance was not just about job-specific task proficiency, but organisations looked for an individual's proficiency in several non-job specific tasks, such as perseverance and discipline to achieve reasonable performance.

Borman and Motowidlo (1993) suggested dividing these aspects into two distinct categories of performance behaviors related to tasks, such as (1) job-specific task proficiency, which contributes to organisational effectiveness; and (2) performance behaviors such as non-job-specific task proficiency, written and oral communication, demonstrating effort, maintaining personal discipline, facilitating team and peer performance, supervision and leadership, and management and administration, which lead to organisational effectiveness in other ways. Based on that distinction, they developed the construct of task performance and non-task performance and called the latter as *contextual performance*. Contextual performance comprised of those activities which contributed indirectly and 'maintain the broader organisational, social, and psychological environment in which technical core must function' (Motowidlo, Borman & Schmit 1997, p. 75). Most of the contextual performance was believed to be behavioural-related competencies, social behaviour and personality traits. Borman and Motowidlo (1993) identified five categories of contextual performance: (1) volunteering to carry out tasks activities that are not formally part of the job; (2) persistence to complete a task successfully; (3) helping others; (4) following organisational compliance norms; and (5) supporting and defending organisational objectives.

Also, contextual performance was not considered mandatory but 'discretionary' (Motowidlo & Van Scotter 1994, p. 476). For instance, Motowidlo and Van Scotter (1994) postulated that knowledge, skills, abilities and experience are more correlated to task performance than contextual performance. However, personality traits such as interpersonal skills and motivations affected contextual performance. They also noted that task performance and contextual performance each contributed in its own way and independently to overall job performance. Further, Motowidlo, Borman and Schmit (1997) asserted that because performance was assessed through supervisory ratings, motivation was associated with both task performance and contextual performance.

Recent research suggests that performance could not be fully explained using this distinction of task vs. contextual performance. For instance, Bott et al. (2003) conducted a personality survey on 356 employees in a manufacturing organisation across a wide range of jobs and suggested that task performance and contextual performance demonstrated weak to moderate correlation. Similarly, at an Australian public sector agency, Bish and Kabanoff (2014) found by surveying 100 mid-level managers that managerial competencies of star performers, while most were categorised as task performance and contextual performance, there were several competencies like self-direction and willingness to lead that could not be contained in this model. This evidence indicated that there is more to the job performance of an individual beyond task and contextual performance.

Individual vs team performance

The literature suggests that while on one side, task performance alone did not define success in the job, at the same time, individual performance alone was not the sole contributor towards business outcomes. Individual performance and group performance intertwined together due to changes in work arrangements in modern organisations because people are working with others to meet stated business goals (Lynn, Skov & Abel 1999). Some studies proposed that the term performance should have an aspect of collective business results (Parker & Turner 2002). However, task-related skills at the individual level vs at the group level are not same. Sonnentag and Frese (2002, p. 7) maintained from their analysis that 'task-related skills and knowledge are not sufficient when accomplishing tasks in a team-work setting'. Further, since the work is performed in teams, the social aspect is also an important determinant of job performance. To lessen this divide, Griffin, Neal and Parker (2007) modelled work performance to be measured at three levels. That is, organisation level, group level and individual level.

Though there are several factors, known and unknown to the literature, the social aspect, team interactions and conflicts are some of the variables which make job performance in the organisational settings a highly complex phenomenon. How teams are structured, organised and interact with each other has a determining effect on individual's job performance. In a study involving 525 individuals in 54 teams, Tims et al. (2013) noticed that structuring the job for the team has a direct impact on an individual's job performance. Lynn and Kalay (2015) also found that if a team has strong clarity on its vision, it would positively influence the team's ability to succeed. Furthermore, in an analysis of 28 studies, Schmutz and Manser (2013) found that team behaviours, such as teamwork or coordination, affect overall business outcomes. These studies showed that social aspect of an individual's job performance could not be ignored.

At a team and organisational level, job performance is also impacted by employee engagement with management, their peers and overall organisational goals. Anitha (2014) conducted 383 questionnaires with employees from middle and lower management levels from small-scale organisations. The author noted that employee engagement had a significant impact on employee performance. Working environment and team and co-worker relationships were determining factors on employee engagement. Similarly, based on 110 questionnaires from front-line hotel staff in Romania, Karatepe (2013) established that employee engagement fully mediated the job performance of the employee, as well their extra efforts towards customer service. Employee engagement as a key factor to job performance, as well as a key determinant of organisational competitiveness, has been identified in recent studies (Albrecht et al. 2015; Bedarkar & Pandita 2014).

The above review of the literature on performance indicates that while organisational business performance is a much larger domain, job performance is more than just an individual's task-related performance. Both behaviour and outcomes are important for producing the performance for the job, among several other aspects. Contemporary research studies have recognised that developing individuals in the workplace to produce such overall encompassing performance is a challenge and been addressed by contemporary research studies (Campbell & Wiernik 2015; Dumas & Hanchane 2010; Houger 2006; Kanfer & Kantrowitz 2002; Khan, Khan & Khan 2011; Quartey 2012; Wallace 2006).

2.2.3 Learning and performance

Task performance and job performance are direct functions of abilities or skills acquired by an individual. In a seminal study based on 3,000 cases, Hunter (1986) reported that abilities influenced job knowledge and work samples, which in turn affected the supervisory rating of performance. He noted that abilities of the individual did not directly affect the supervisory ratings, but job knowledge and work samples produced by an individual correlated well with the supervisory ratings. His model supports that knowledge and skills are mediating variables when determining an individual's performance. Subsequently, other classic studies established that the knowledge, skills and abilities one acquires as a result of job experience or training are the primary determinants of performance of any job (McDaniel, Schmidt & Hunter 1988; Qui'nones, Ford & Teachout 1995).

Motowidlo, Borman and Schmit (1997) theorised that intervening variables to performance are knowledge, skills and work habits that are basically learned through experience. They postulated that task knowledge (procedures, judgement, heuristics, rules, and decisions), task skills (using technical information, solving problems, and making judgements) and task work habits (pattern of behaviours, tendencies, choices one makes in a situation, motivational aspects, persistence, and planning) affect task performance. Similarly, other sets of contextual knowledge (knowledge about effective actions in situations that call for volunteering, helping, supporting, persisting, and defending), contextual skills (carrying out actions deemed effective in a situation) and contextual work habits (ways of handling conflicts, tendencies, and interpersonal styles) also affect contextual performance. These skills and knowledge possessed by an individual manifest themselves in the form of differences in the job performance among workers performing the same job.

The literature indicated that the nature of knowledge and skills possessed by an individual also determined performance. Campbell (1990) explained that job performance could be predicted from one person to another with the help of three direct determinants: declarative knowledge (i.e., knowledge of facts, principles, and procedures), procedural knowledge and skill (i.e., knowing what to do and actually doing the task), and motivation (i.e., choice to exert effort, how much and how long). The level of training, education, experience, the range of skills and amount of practice, etc. determined the level of declarative and procedural knowledge or skills someone exhibited. This model supported the linkage of knowledge, skills, abilities and experience towards individual performance. Recent studies have suggested a strong linkage between providing appropriate knowledge and skills to employees through training and job performance (Dumas & Hanchane 2010; Khan, Khan & Khan 2011; Niazi 2011, 2011; Quartey 2012). Thus, the review indicates that performance is considered as a function of knowledge, skills and abilities of an individual, though performance is not solely attributable to these characteristics alone.

Several studies have proposed that learning has a central role in the performance concept and is a central underlying mechanism to acquire knowledge and skills (Campbell 1990; Hesketh & Neal 1999; London & Mone 1999). Learning has been viewed as a long-term behavioural change, which should positively affect performance. Historically, some classic work has shown that individual performance improved with learning in terms of time spent on the job (Avolio, Waldman & McDaniel 1990; McDaniel, Schmidt & Hunter 1988; Qui'nones, Ford & Teachout 1995). An employee's willingness and cognitive ability to learn task requirements were shown to be an important determinant of job performance. Sonnentag and Frese (2002) scanned 146 meta-analyses published in 20 years in twelve major journals of the workplace and organisational psychology, and discovered that most researchers believed that there was 'an underlying mechanism of cognitive ability' that helped an individual acquire job knowledge and skills to impact job performance positively. No two individuals may have the same cognitive ability. Thus variation in learning and job performance are inherent. Based on the analysis of several studies, Kanfer and Kantrowitz (2002, p. 32) observed that 'individual differences in general cognitive ability may account for more variance in performance when performance is defined in terms of skill acquisition or job proficiency'.

Learning a task or skill leads to eventual performance, whether it is behavioural, a task, an outcome or job performance. Thus, learning is considered to be a major dimension of performance. Though the role of learning in improving performance is well understood, the nature of the relationship has been debated extensively. The relationship between performance and learning is reversed during training versus after the training. During any training intervention, learning is contended as more important than in-training performance, while after the training, at the job performance is contended to be more important than learning. In a study, Bjork (2009, p. 313) expressed that performance during a training event may not be the right indicator:

> Performance during training is often an unreliable guide to whether the desired learning has actually happened. Considerable learning can happen across periods when performance is not improving and, conversely, little or no learning can happen across periods when performance is improving markedly.

From this perspective, learning becomes more important than performance during training. Soderstrom and Bjork (2015, p. 193) termed learning as 'the relatively permanent changes in behavior or knowledge that support long-term retention and transfer' while they termed performance during training as 'the temporary fluctuations in behavior or knowledge that are observed and measured during training or instruction or immediately thereafter'. Furthermore, the performance within a training intervention may not be the desired performance required at the job. However, what matters is the job performance of an individual after training. Bjork (2009, p. 319) highlights a challenge as: 'The problem for a training organisation is to maximise performance when it matters, that is, *after* training and, specially, when individuals are deployed'. The corollary to this assertion is that accelerating performance within training may have very short-term effects as 'expediting acquisition performance today does not necessarily translate into the type of learning that will be evident tomorrow' (Soderstrom & Bjork 2015, p. 193). However, at the job, the performance (i.e., outcomes and behaviours) matters more than learning. Sonnentag and Frese (2002, p. 6) suggested that as:

> One might argue that what ultimately counts for an organisation is the individuals' performance and not their learning—although learning might help to perform well. This line of reasoning stresses that learning is a highly relevant predictor of performance but is not performance itself.

In general, the review of the literature indicates that learning is one of the key determinants of performance. Knowledge and skill acquisition appear to be inseparable parts of job performance. In their study about pilots tackling direct problems, Dreyfus and Dreyfus (2005) noted that as an individual acquired experience, he passed through five stages: novice, advanced beginner, competent, proficient and expert. Such representation assumed that performance or skill proficiency was a continuum in which the novice was on the one end of the continuum, while the expert was on the other end. As such, the overall goal of knowledge and skill acquisition is to develop a higher level of competence, proficiency or expertise of an individual, which is then translated into performance through behaviours/actions or results.

2.2.4 Acquisition of skilled performance

In the literature, skill acquisition has been explained from different viewpoints. Knowledge and skill acquisition have been grounded in well-regarded classic and seminal work conducted in the 1960s, 1970s and 1980ssuch as Fitt and Posner (1967), Anderson (1981, 1982), Ackerman (1988) and Shiffrin and Schneider (1977). Some researchers in more recent times, such as Langan-Fox et al. (2002), have extended these theories further. For several decades, one of the most common trends was describing skill acquisition in terms of stages in which performance or the proficiency of skills was improved as individuals gained more practice and experience.

Some of the earliest explanations of how an individual progressed towards skilled performance were the notions of practice and automaticity. For several decades, the practice has been accepted as the most fundamental mechanism of skill acquisition towards mastery of skills. Fitt (1964) and Fitt and Posner (1967) suggested that perceptual-motor skill acquisition occurs in three stages: *cognitive stage, associative stage,* and *autonomous stage,* which support progression from conscious to a less conscious form of practice. Anderson (1981, 1982, 2000) proposed a general theory of cognition called Adaptive Control of Thought-Rational (ACT-R), which described learning progression in three stages: *declarative knowledge stage; knowledge compilation stage; and procedural knowledge stage.* Ackerman (1988) supported that skill acquisition followed similar stages, as indicated by the above theories.

In Fitt and Posner's (1967) version, the first stage was termed as a *cognitive stage*. In this stage, learners are still trying to get accustomed to the task, understanding the instructions and trying to develop strategies to perform the task. A performer at this stage tends to develop 'basic factual understandings, the broad outline, the essential nature of each of the steps and the order in which these must be performed' (Cornford & Athanasou (1995, p. 12). This stage is characterised by the learner's attempt to understand the demands of the task and then 'distinguish between important and unimportant aspects of the task' (Schneider 1993, p. 316). The goal of this stage is to acquire declarative knowledge about the task.

Then the learner progresses to next stage called a*ssociative (practice fixation stage).* At this stage, repetition of skill and involvement with reality increases the depth of understanding, and the steps and sequence of skill performance are imprinted in permanent memory. Performance strategies are also refined at this stage. Prior learning is leveraged to develop strategies in new situations. Associations are developed by the learners between clues and responses for 'making the cognitive processes more efficient to allow rapid retrieval, thus transforming declarative knowledge into procedural forms' (Schneider 1993, p. 316).

Finally, with practice, an individual reaches a stage called *autonomous stage*. At this stage, skills can be subconsciously executed, and the action becomes very automatic. The nature of skills at this stage is sometimes called *automaticity*. The learner is becoming skilled on the task to a level where s/he does not need many resources. More cognitive resources are available to process other activities. Problem-solving is usually done with the conscious mind. At this stage, accuracy, as well as speed, are improved. However, the rate of improvement will hit a plateau after a certain amount of practice.

The major implication of Fitt and Posner's (1967) learning model towards proficiency/expertise development was to lay out the instructional activities in stages. This model described the sequence of events proposed for the development of a skill and provides the mechanism and guidance for instructional events by which the automaticity is achieved (Clavarelli, Platte & Powers 2009). While Fitt and Posner's (1967) learning model appeared to explain the mechanism of psychomotor skills, it did not explain how the learning actually took place. To explain the learning mechanism, Anderson (1981, 1982, 2000) proposed a three-stage learning model, Adaptive Control of Thought-Rational (ACT-R). This model described learning progression in the form of three stages. First stage is declarative knowledge stage. Declarative knowledge stored in declarative memory refers to facts, processes, principles, concepts, and information, etc. The learner receives information, background, generation instructions, etc. about the topic of skill. For performing any skill, the knowledge relevant to or required to do so is learned in declarative form. Declarative memory mainly links the propositions, images, and sequences by associations. In the next stage of knowledge compilation, the knowledge about a skill is converted gradually from declarative to new procedures, which can be applied without much attention. Inferences are drawn from pre-existing factual knowledge in the declarative memory, and this leads to learning of procedural knowledge, which is third stage. Procedural memory, also called long-term memory, stores information in the form of representations in what Anderson (1981, 1982) called *productions*. ACT-R theory described three types of learning processes: (1) generalisation, which refers to productions becoming broader in application; (2) discrimination, which refers to productions becoming narrow in application; and (3) strengthening, which refers to the more frequent use of certain productions. New productions are formed by associating, disassociating or in terms of combining or un-combining existing productions. This stage involved domain-specific *proceduralization* and *composition*. The *proceduralization* involves creating domain-specific productions during interpretation of declarative knowledge. The *composition* is combining several steps or adjacent procedures into one. The number of steps is reduced on each iteration of the procedure. The reduction in steps, thus leads to improved learning in initial phases of practice. However, as one's speed increases with practice, learning does not appear to improve at the same rate that was in the initial phases of the practice. In the last stage, *procedural knowledge* is developed. This refers to a representation of what needs to be done in a given situation. Practice refines appropriate procedures. Responses become more generalised and automatic. With continuous use over time, the productions become automatic and part of the unconscious mind. Practice is essential for developing learned procedures into automaticity of expertise in any field (Ge & Hardré 2010). ACT-R theory indicated that both declarative and procedural knowledge resides in separate long-term memory systems. A major implication of ACT-R theory was that cognitive processes were involved in developing automaticity. The ACT-R theory incorporated several learning mechanisms which have been translated into instructional strategies (Oyewole et al. 2011). To implement ACT-R theory in skill acquisition training, Clark (2010) suggested instructional techniques like goal and reasons, overview, connection to prior knowledge, new knowledge, demonstrated procedure, practice, and feedback.

One limitation of Fitt and Posner's (1967) three-stage learning theory and ACT-R theory is that they do not explain the influence of task characteristics and task instructions on skill acquisition. To address this deficiency, Ackerman (1988) presented an integrated theory that was based on an analysis of measures of ability, nature of the information processing and nature of skill acquisition. On the skill portion, he supported that skill acquisition follows similar phases, as proposed by Fitt and Posner (1967), Anderson (1982) and Shiffrin and Schneider (1977). He stated that abilities are structured based on three components: complexity processing, the content of information (figural, verbal, numerical content) and speediness of processing. He described how one develops ability structures as s/he passes through stages of skill acquisition. He reasoned that ability-performance relations are a function of three task characteristics: consistency of information processing demands, task complexity and degree of task practice. He proposed that in tasks characterised by consistent information processing components, general ability and broad content ability determines the performance during the cognitive phase. However, for inconsistent tasks, general and content ability determined the performance across all three phases. At the cognitive stage, demand is the most attentional resource based on the task characteristics because the learner is trying to understand the task instructions, goals and 'formulating the strategies for task accomplishment' (Ackerman 1992, p. 599). In the associative phase, performance is determined by perceptual speed abilities, while psychomotor abilities determine performance in autonomous phases. Ackerman (1988) reasoned that to go beyond this stage to the autonomous stage, a learner needed first to develop consistent information processing characteristics. Similar to the account given by Fitt and Posner (1967) and Anderson (1982), Ackerman (1992, p. 599) explained the nature of performance at this stage: 'Performance at this phase of skill acquisition is typically highly speeded and highly accurate'. At this stage, the learner needs little or no attentional effort.

From the expertise building perspective, a major implication of this model was the proposition that more cognitive resources are required in the first two stages, which slows down the speed of performance. This happens more prominently on novel, complex and inconsistent tasks. Therefore, based on this model, it was inferred that the sequence of tasks based on task characteristics might be an important determinant of expertise development. Subsequent research studies identified few flaws in this model. Langan-Fox et al. (2002, pp. 104–105) mentioned that Ackerman's theories 'largely ignore the experiences and internal processes of a person (e.g., how they feel, what strategies they are using, the role of the external environment)'.

The popular three-staged models of Ackerman (1988), Fitt and Posner (1967), Shiffrin and Schneider (1977) and Anderson (1982) explain the mechanism of skill acquisition but do not provide any way to know where one may be in the process of skill acquisition. As one practice, not only cognitive ability varies, but also the task characteristics change over time and environment in which one performs the job also changes. Langan-Fox et al. (2002) contended that skill acquisition should be considered as a process that assumes influence of other variables, internal to human, as well as external on to performance. They proposed an integrated process model for skilled performance based on learning in general during skill acquisition. They considered two sets of factors that influenced skilled performance: internal influences and external influences. Among internal influences, Langan-Fox et al. (2002) believed several factors like changing levels of consciousness, automaticity, motivation, emotion, metacognition and memory influenced skill acquisition. Changing level of consciousness was based on Rasmussen, Pejtersen and Goodstein's (1994) observations that a performer may be conscious about when to choose between three types of behaviours: skill-based, rule-based and knowledge-based, depending on the task characteristics. The amount of practice determined how soon the individual would achieve the automaticity or automatic processing (Shiffrin & Schneider 1977). However, inconsistent tasks demand a higher level of practice than consistent tasks (Ackerman 1988). Langan-Fox et al. (2002) believed that motivation in the form of difficult goals, as suggested by Ackerman (1988), influenced acquiring complex skills. Self-regulatory processes and metacognition were assumed to impact skill acquisition in terms of how people perceived their skills in relation to the task difficulty. This observation indicated that performers were always able to monitor their state and change their cognitive strategies during skill acquisition. Langan-Fox et al. (2002) also postulated that emotions have a great impact on skilled performance, a factor previously missing from the skill acquisition theories but 'most central and pervasive aspects of human experience' (id. 109). Emotions may also have a positive or disruptive effect on performance depending on the affective state of the performer.

Memory is another component that influences skill acquisition profoundly, as explained by Anderson (1982). Langan-Fox et al. (2002, p. 111) contended that in stage one of skill acquisition, in which demand for attentional resources is high, working memory is most predictive of task performance. In stage two of skill acquisition, the associative memory is likely to be more predictive than in stage one, and procedural memory could predict higher performance in stage three of skill acquisition. Lastly, retention factors have a strong influence on skill acquisition because retention leads to 'improved capacity to draw an association between new and established information' (id. 112). All of these factors, to varying degrees, influence how someone progressed through skill acquisition and demonstrated skilled performance. Among external influences, Langan-Fox et al. (2002) noted that interruptions, goals, practice format and task characteristics influenced how someone acquired skilled performance. They indicated that spaced or continuous practice format may determine how soon the state of automaticity is achieved. The interval between practice sessions may markedly affect performance. Workplace interruptions and expectations to handle two or more incompatible tasks at the same time may adversely affect stage one and stage two of skill acquisition. Nature of task, whether it is novel, complex or familiar, has a similar implication of using cognitive resources and may impair performance (Ackerman 1988).

The major implication of Langan-Fox et al.'s (2002) skilled performance learning model is it views skill acquisition and proficiency development as a process in which several factors influence how soon an individual can achieve a skilled performance state. This model might also suggest that in addition to task characteristics and practice amount, several other internal and external factors must be addressed to accelerate skill acquisition.

These skill acquisition theories provided congruent accounts of the final state of automaticity of performance expressed as *autonomous performance* (Fitt & Posner 1967) or *procedural performance* (Anderson 1982). This final stage is characterised by speed and accuracy, as indicated in Ackerman (1988). Langan-Fox et al. (2002) termed this state as *skilled performance*. Cognitive literature views automaticity as one of the characteristics exhibited by highly proficient workers and experts who are considered the individuals who deliver superior skilled performance (Dreyfus 2004).

2.3 PROFICIENCY

There is considerable overlap between the literature on expertise and proficiency. The existing literature on proficiency is mainly derived from classic expertise theories or skill acquisition theories such as those proposed by Dreyfus and Dreyfus (Dreyfus & Dreyfus 1986, 2004, 2005), Ericsson (Ericsson 2000, 2002, 2003, 2004, 2006a, 2007, 2008, 2009c; Ericsson et al. 1993; Ericsson & Charness 1994; Ericsson, Prietula & Cokely 2007), Benner (1984, 2004), Chi (Chi 2006; Chi, Glaser & Rees 1982; Chi, Glaser & Farr 1988; Chi, Glaser & Rees 1981, 1982; Glaser & Chi 1988), and Hoffman (Hoffman et al. 2008, 2009, 2014; Hoffman & Andrews 2012; Hoffman, Andrews & Feltovich 2012; Hoffman, Andrews, et al. 2010; Hoffman, Feltovich, et al. 2010), among others. In general, proficiency is an indicator of a level of mastery in a given task, skill, or function, i.e., how good someone is in that domain. In this section, the literature on proficiency acquisition and development is reviewed.

2.3.1 Novice-to-expert transition

A review of the literature suggests that novice-to-expert transition could be viewed as staged progression. While the basic idea of such transition is that experts are relative to the novice, the goal of such an approach is 'to understand how we can enable less skilled or experienced persons to become more skilled...' (Chi 2006, p. 23). Classic studies defined stage-like progressions towards automaticity of skills (Fitt & Posner 1967; Anderson 1982; Ackerman 1988). Later researchers have developed more refined details of the stages towards proficiency. Among them, Shuell (1986, p. 364) noticed that 'as an individual acquires knowledge, his or her knowledge structure gradually evolves in qualitative as well as quantitative ways'. Subsequently, classic studies indicated a qualitative shift in traits as novice learners moved towards higher proficiency (Benner 1984; Dreyfus & Dreyfus 1986). Similarly, Hoffman (1998, p. 84) supported this qualitative shifts: 'The distinction between "novice" versus "expert" implies that development can involve both qualitative shifts and stabilizations in knowledge and performance'. This implies that the novice-to-expert transition process could be viewed as being made up of several stages.

Theorists have used different development parameters for level-like shifts, for example, the transformation of skills as second nature (automaticity), as well as implicit knowledge (Alexander 2003a; Spiro et al. 2003). Some studies have established that it is possible to qualitatively define proficiency levels in terms of skills and knowledge exhibited by professionals on-the-job. The most significant studies in this regard were carried out by Dreyfus and Dreyfus (Dreyfus & Dreyfus 1986, 2004, 2005), popularly known as *Dreyfus and Dreyfus model*. They contended that an individual passes through five stages: novice, advanced beginner, competent, proficient and expert. As one progresses through the stages, the approach in solving problems become more intuitive. Benner (2004) attempted to define levels of proficiency on the Dreyfus and Dreyfus model in terms of certain attributes of expected performance at each level in the context of nursing professions, demonstrating that progression could be reasonably explained using stages specified by the Dreyfus and Dreyfus model. Peña (2010) and Khan and Ramachandran (2012) applied the Dreyfus and Dreyfus model in the context of clinical and healthcare jobs and asserted that there is a level-like progression which can be demarcated qualitatively in terms of job attributes.

Some researchers maintained that task performance could be an indicator of different stages (Chi 2006; Merrill 2006; Schreiber et al. 2009). According to this premise, the novice completes simple versions of tasks during training, and as skill levels increase, s/he can move to tasks that are more complex. Progressively, s/he becomes skilful at relatively more complex tasks. The learner could address several cues at the same time. The literature indicates that measurement of task performance must reflect this gradual acquisition of skill. Merrill (2006, p. 269) stated that proficiency measurement requires one to 'detect increments in performance demonstrating gradually increased skill in completing a whole complex task or solving a problem'.

Another group of researchers took a measurement approach to define proficiency levels in terms of some measurable attributes of jobs. For example, Chi (2006) proposed that proficiency levels could be roughly measured using inputs such as academic qualification, years of experience on the task, peer feedback or even profession-related tests. Schreiber et al. (2009) developed metrics for measurement of pilot proficiency using simulators and postulated that it is possible to develop an objective measure of performance in complex jobs that require a range of judgement and meta-skills. Recently, Kim (2012, 2015) proposed a different approach: measurement in terms of knowledge structures across different levels of learning progress. The author defined a set of measures indicating the levels of the features of knowledge structure. Relations between the measures and the features of knowledge structures were determined based on theoretical assumptions, as well as empirical evidence. A similar approach was suggested by Dörfler, Baracskai and Velencei (2009), who used knowledge as the demarcation for levels to explain the stages or levels of expertise.

The notion of stages conveys the idea of progression being a process. Both foundational and more recent research studies support the view that developing a higher level of performance to proficiency and expertise can be viewed as a process. Studies by Lajoie (2003) focused on transitions and trajectories to increase expertise. In characterising this progression, Lajoie (2003, p. 22) noted that 'becoming an expert is a transitional process'. At the same time, researchers have maintained that expertise is not the ultimate goal rather it is a 'nonlinear process state' (Moon, Kim & You 2013, p. 228). A certain amount of quantity of knowledge, skills or behaviour does not mean expertise. Bransford et al. (2004) also maintained that expertise is not a finished product; rather it is a continuing process. Expertise is not a defined stage; rather expertise grows out of interactions with the environment. The literature has viewed expertise as a continuous process of adjusting knowledge, re-learning, changing mental representation as one interacts with situations, reflects upon it, and use pattern recognition and correct one's way of thinking (Alexander 2003a). In terms of the continuous process towards adjustments, Sternberg (1999, p. 359) contended that developing expertise involves 'the ongoing process of the acquisition and consolidation of a set of skills needed for a high level of mastery in one or more domains of life performance'. In a dynamic world, abilities are not always static. Alexander (2003b, p. 12) asserted that 'the journey toward expertise is unceasing. Even those who have attained the knowledge, strategic abilities, and interests indicative of expertise cannot sit idly by as the domain shifts under their feet'. Thus, it is reasonable to infer that expertise involves a constant evaluation of one's progress towards mastery.

2.3.2 Stages of proficiency

Dreyfus and Dreyfus (1986) observed numerous performers, mostly aircrew emergency staff and jet pilots to understand how they tackle direct problems. They proposed a model that was based on the premise that skill acquisition is a continuous process in which skills are transformed into performance by experience and mastery (proficiency). Dreyfus and Dreyfus (1986) observed that only experience with concrete situations produced higher levels of performance. They discovered that during skill acquisition, a learner passed through five levels of proficiency: novice, advanced beginner, competence, proficiency and expertise.

They identified few characteristics that varied gradually from one stage to the next, how they perceived the elements of the situations (components), how they recognised which part of the situation to pay attention to (perspective), how they made decisions to act in a particular way (decision), and finally, how much they were committed or involved with the task (commitment) (Dreyfus & Dreyfus 1986, 2004, 2005). They observed that perception shifted from context-free understanding of facts to more situational understanding. In terms of the progression of these characteristics, as someone moved up from novice stage, knowledge began to be treated in the context of the situation. Further, with experience, an individual became more selective in what elements of the situation were considered more important. In the beginning, novices were not able to recognise the relevance of their knowledge of the skill, but they started doing so as they moved to the next stage. The context was analysed analytically to begin and developed into a more holistic assessment at higher stages. They contend that there was an observable shift from analytical approaches to intuition-based approaches while making decisions. Decision-making was rational for all the learners except for the experts who made decisions intuitively. The degree of immersion increased from a detached commitment to highly involved, along with the understanding of the task, deciding and the outcomes (Dreyfus & Dreyfus 1986, 2004, 2005).

Based on these shifts, they developed the characteristics of five stages a learner passed through towards higher proficiency. It has proven to be an extremely useful model for depicting levels of expertise in any profession. Most significant of this research has been the work of Benner (2004, p. 194) who tested the applicability of the Dreyfus and Dreyfus model in nine studies spanning over 21 years and found that it was 'predictive and descriptive of distinct stages of skill acquisition in nursing practice'. The author described the nature of expertise at each stage that added richer perspectives to the Dreyfus and Dreyfus model. Lately, researchers have expanded and characterised each stage. A general description of the five stages based on the collective characteristics suggested not only by Dreyfus and Dreyfus (1986) but also by later researchers who applied this model in various professions, e.g., clinical (Peña 2010), healthcare (Khan & Ramachandran 2012); correctional services (Scobey 2006); education (Bedi 2003); and nursing (Ramsburg 2010) are as follows:

Novice: A novice is someone who does not know much about the new topic or domain. The only mechanism usually they have is some form of training. A novice is typically placed in training where s/he learns some facts about the skills and the rules to apply the skills. While applying these skills, the novice sees everything context-free. For every new thing, they need rules and maxims to solve it. Usually, they are trained to follow these rules without exceptions. At this stage, they do not have a contextual understanding of how to evaluate a situation and how to decide whether a given rule will be applicable in that situation. Therefore, the novice cannot discriminate between situations (Dreyfus & Dreyfus 1986, 2004, 2005).

Advanced beginner: The novice moves up as an advanced beginner as s/he starts gaining some experience in real situations. The advanced beginner starts grasping the concepts underlying the situations and starts comprehending the facts about situations. As they gain more experience, they start comparing and discriminating the situations. They can apply the rules in a structured setting, but they do not yet have the experience to tackle real-world situations. As the new situation is encountered, they tend to identify the unrecognised aspects of the situation, tend to apply the previously learned rules and try to relate to the situation. They develop some situational perception, but it is still very limited. The task involvement is increased. At this point, the performance is improved marginally (Dreyfus & Dreyfus 1986, 2004, 2005).

Competent: As the advanced beginner starts gaining more experience, s/he handles more situations. The performer starts developing an understanding of context-free elements and situational elements. They can now recognise various aspects of the problem, and they can set goals. They may not apply rules all the time depending on the situation, but they try to tackle situations in novel ways. At this point, they have a better contextual understanding whether a rule should be applied in a given situation. However, the decision-making is still analytical. A competent performer is highly involved with the task, as well as the outcome of the task (Dreyfus & Dreyfus 1986, 2004, 2005). The term competent has seen the appeal in training and instruction design for a long time as an indication of someone's qualification. However, Eraut (1994, p. 126) clarified that 'the Dreyfus definition of competence is based on how people approach their work, not on whether they should be judged as qualified to do it'.

Proficient: At this stage, the involvement of the performer with the task, as well as its outcome, is very high. The context is considered holistically, and among those, the proficient performer is able to make situational discriminations and pay attention to what is important and what is not. Pattern recognition is strengthened whereby s/he can recognise new unrecognised elements of a novel situation. S/he has very little dependence on the rules of familiar situations, but s/he may use maxims in novel situations. At this stage, the decision-making is very quick. Performance is improved drastically. In clinical practice, Khan and Ramachandran (2012, p. 5) observed a proficient person as one who was able to handle complex routine work unsupervised but may need supervision for non-routine complex tasks, and performance was usually based on experience. Benner (2004, p. 198) observed that there was a change in perception used by proficient performers regarding a situation. At this stage, they were deliberate about changing the strategies based on an understanding of the new situation.

Expert: This last stage in skill progression was seen to be acquired with concrete experience. Deep involvement with the understanding of the situation, task and its outcome resulted in highly contextual experiences. The learner developed deep tacit knowledge; a learner developed the intuitive grasp on situations. Thus, the decision-making became intuitive rather than analytical at this stage. At this stage, they also developed highly developed skills to make subtle discriminations between situation and knowledge used in different situations. Based on experience, they could even work out the solution for novel and never-seen-before problems (DiBello & Missildine 2011). Based on prior experience, they can even come up with a solution for new or never experienced before situations. Experts adopt a contextual approach to problem-solving and understand the relative, non-absolute nature of knowledge. Reflection comes naturally, and experts solve problems almost unconsciously. At this point, an expert's skills became automatic to the point that they were not even aware of it (Dreyfus & Dreyfus 1986, 2004, 2005).

Earlier researchers like Eraut (1994, p. 127) recognised the strength of this model was in 'the case it makes for tacit knowledge and intuition as critical features of professional expertise in 'unstructured problem areas''. Further, this model emphasised the process view which positioned progression towards the expertise as 'the way in which experts solve problems, rather than simply by the amount of knowledge that experts possess' (Ge & Hardré 2010, p. 24). Despite widespread simplicity and appeal of the Dreyfus and Dreyfus model, another school of thought questioned the validity of the same. For example, Day (2002) noted that it is difficult to apply five stages in professional settings because practitioners perform a range of tasks in their jobs and they will not fit into one stage for all the tasks they do. Thus, the most common objection raised was a representation that proficiency acquisition is a linear process independent of the influence of external factors and domain expertise (Grenier & Kehrhahn 2008). Another objection to this model was 'its failure to explain how someone becomes an expert and its stress on the importance of experience and not of its impact' (Farrington-Darby & Wilson 2006, p. 29). Other concerns included the absence of social structure in knowledge and skill acquisition, lack of objective quantification in regards to how to measure attainment of each stage or where a particular stage ends, and lack of operational definitions of intuition (See Peña 2010). Even though these staged skill acquisition models conceptually explains how an individual learns, 'one cannot accurately predict where people are in the skill-acquisition process' (Langan-Fox et al. 2002, p. 106).

The major implication of the Dreyfus and Dreyfus model was an evolution of the concept of scaling the proficiency in the form of stages so that suitable instructional design could be implemented for learning at different stages. Researchers have translated the stages into appropriate instructional methods to be used at each stage to move a novice through to higher stages of proficiency (Benner 2001; Clavarelli, Platte & Powers 2009). Despite its limitations, the Dreyfus and Dreyfus model appears to be a starting point in identifying the methods and strategies to develop the proficiency of a learner.

2.3.3 Proficiency scaling

While the Dreyfus and Dreyfus model explained the novice-to-expert transition in terms of stages, it was based on how people approach work. The second foundational view towards novice-to-expert transition was to quantify the level of proficiency at each stage somehow. Hoffman et al. (2014, p. 25) assumed proficiency scaling as a fundamental action that needs to happen in any accelerated proficiency studies 'to forge a domain – and organisationally appropriate scale for distinguishing levels of proficiency'.

Hoffman (1998) recognised the challenges in defining expertise and posit that the differentiation between novices and experts itself suggested the presence of some qualitative shifts of knowledge and performance between the two extremes of development continuum. He commented 'If one acknowledges that expertise develops, and that qualitative changes occur over the developmental period, then one must make some attempt at stage-like categorization, if only to motivate research' (Hoffman 1998, p. 84). If one can define novice and experts in terms of characteristics, knowledge and performance, remaining stages in this continuum of development can be retrieved from the literature. Hoffman et al. (2014, p. 26) contended that it was important to develop 'a scale that is both domain and organisationally appropriate, and that considers the full range of proficiency'. They believed that it was possible to scale proficiency by using various inputs such as interviews, age, seniority, experience, education, training, professional certifications, performance measures and social standing.

Based on the Middle Ages craft guilds in Europe, Hoffman (1998) proposed that novice-to-expert transition could be represented through seven stages, similar to gaining mastery in a craft (*Table 2-1*).

Table 2-1: Proficiency scaling proposed by Hoffman (1998)

Stage	Characteristics
Naïve	Completely ignorant about the domain.
Novice	A member in the domain who has minimal exposure to the domain.
Initiate	A novice who has started on the profession.
Apprentice	Someone who is taking up instructions beyond introductory level. S/he is working with and assisting an experienced person.
Journeyman	One who is executing orders and performs a day's work and duties unsupervised. S/he has achieved some level of competence, has become experienced and is a reliable worker.
Expert	A distinguished journeyman regarded for his/her accurate judgements, is efficient and delivers reliable performance. Special skills attained due to extensive experience and can deal effectively with rare or "tough" cases.
Master	A journeyman or expert who is also qualified to teach those at a lower level. Highly experienced experts whose judgments establish regulations, standards, or ideals. Equally regarded by other experts as the "real" expert in certain subdomains.

Source: adapted from Hoffman (1998)

Hoffman's (1998) progression was based on changing knowledge and skills that are associated with the experience. Macmillan (2015, p. 36) explained this approach as:

> Hoffman's Scheme, on the other hand, presumes a progression of knowledge and capabilities associated with different amounts of instruction and domain-specific experience. It describes relative levels of expertise or proficiency within a single knowledge domain. In doing so, it fulfils its traditional function as a means of describing the progression of increasing knowledge and skills as one moves, over many years, from the status of novice to a master in a specific field.

On similar lines, Jacobs (1997) proposed a 'taxonomy of human competence' which suggested that human competence could be scaled with designations such as novice, specialists, experienced specialist, expert, and master. The distinction was based on someone's ability to produce outcomes. At the same time, it was recognised that '*master*, *expert*, a *specialist*, or a *novice* are usually relative notions' (Jacobs 2003, p. 7). While, on the one hand, novices are the ones whose 'outcomes are less valuable or who produce no outcomes can have lower of competence' (Jacobs 2003, p.5), on the other hand, experts are those who 'achieve the most valuable outcomes in organisations'. Masters were considered the 'experts of the highest order' (Jacobs 2003, p. 5). The taxonomy of human competence (Jacobs 1997, 2001, 2003; Jacobs & Washington 2003) specified the definitions of novice, expert and master, which are almost similar to Hoffman (1998), while the definitions of *specialist* level and *experienced specialist* are closely aligned with the *apprentice* and *journeyman* levels of Hoffman (1998).

The major implication of this scaling was that it envisioned a full spectrum of proficiency and suggested that individuals at different stages of their career may possess a different level of proficiency (Hoffman 1998) or competence (Jacobs 1997, 2001, 2003). Thus, these scaling taxonomies did not propose proficiency as a specific stage in the Dreyfus and Dreyfus (1986, 2005, 2006) model. Rather it views that even a competent person has a certain level of proficiency in skills, tasks or job functions, though qualitatively and quantitatively (if it can be measured) less than a proficient performer. Moreover, the stage of journeyman (Hoffman 1998) or experienced specialist (Jacobs 1997, 2001, 2003) corresponds to the competent or proficient stages of Dreyfus and Dreyfus (1986, 2004, 2005). In subsequent research, Hoffman et al. (2014, p. 3) clarified about journeyman that 'they have practiced to the point where they can perform their duties unsupervised (literally, they can go on a journey)'. They further point out that:

> While there may be some requirements for more senior experts in select areas, there is more profound and continuing need for journeyman and senior journeymen to carry out the complex cognitive work effectively to ensure current and future success. (Hoffman et al. 2014, p. 3)

Some researchers criticised the lack of scientific rigour of Hoffman (1998) framework. For example, Farrington-Darby and Wilson (2006, p. 29) commented '[w]hat this classification does not provide is the process that has to occur to move between the classifications'. Hoffman (1998) suggested this model to advance the research thinking in the absence of any scientifically validated model. It should be noted that the implication of these stages is not really to create another staged view of proficiency; rather it is to introduce the concept of scaling of the proficiency at each stage of the progression, whether using the progression suggested by Dreyfus and Dreyfus (1986, 2004, 2005) or any other measurements.

While most of the classic studies focused either on novice-to-expert differences or purely on the construct of expertise, the mid-range proficiency levels have been ignored (Hoffman et al. 2014). Mid-range proficiency levels refer to journeyman (Hoffman 1998) or an experienced specialist that is proficient (Dreyfus & Dreyfus 1986, 2004, 2005; Jacobs 1997). The literature is so focused on novice-expert differences that it lacks development focus on the intermediate phases completely (Alexander 2003b). The mid-range of proficiency levels became important as researchers noticed that organisations started paying attention to the proficiency of employees: 'Proficiency … is the primary objective of both formal and informal learning undertakings in organisations' (Enos, Kehrhahn & Bell 2003, p. 371). While proficiency scaling in terms of stages is generally accepted in the literature, no literature was found that included evidence of methods to quantify the proficiency to distinguish one stage from another objectively or in measurable terms. To complicate the matters further, even among researchers, there is less agreement on performance measures in regards to whether to measure job performance in terms of tasks or behaviours or outcomes (Koopmans et al. 2011).

2.3.4 Proficiency

The prevalent view of proficiency is that it represents mastery of skills, tasks, knowledge or job function what someone acquires as a result of experience (Enos, Kehrhahn & Bell 2003, p. 371). Instead of differentiating between confusing constructs of competence, proficiency and expertise, Hoffman, Feltovich, et al. (2010, p. 28) viewed all such levels in terms of proficiency in which expertise is referred to as 'high proficiency'. From that standpoint, they appeared to suggest proficiency in knowledge and skills as a continuum along which novices, journeymen and experts can be placed. In that view, experts were believed to possess a large body of knowledge. Novices, on the other hand, were believed to have not reached as high a proficiency level as an expert, even though they could be highly experienced individuals in their domains. The researchers suggested the role of reasoning skills as a differentiator as: 'Proficiency is defined not just in terms of knowledge but also in terms of reasoning strategies and skills' (Hoffman, Feltovich, et al. 2010, p. 29). They maintain that proficiency can be understood by 'distinguishing experts (high and very high proficiency) from novices (very low proficiency)' (id. 32). Chi (2006, p. 22) supported a similar position of using the term *proficiency* to mean mastery in skills as 'expertise is a level of proficiency that novices can achieve'. That also meant that the notion of high proficiency, as suggested by Hoffman, Feltovich, et al. (2010), was akin to the stage of expertise in the Dreyfus and Dreyfus (1986, 2004, 2005) model. Researchers also viewed proficiency as a qualitative indication of expertise or mastery (Scobey 2006).

Proficiency has also been used as a measure of performance. In most studies, performance was considered as the final outcome as a result of the level of proficiency one exhibited. The higher the proficiency, the higher is the performance. Performance could be a task performance, outcome performance or job performance depending upon what is being measured for proficiency. Campbell (1990, 1999) was among the first to use proficiency as a measure of performance, though it was in the context of performance of specific tasks. He proposed *job-specific task proficiency* as a key determinant of an individual's performance, which communicated the sense of the ability of someone to do the task well. Several performance-related studies use the term *proficiency* in the context of the task performance in a job (Borman & Motowidlo 1993, 1997; Campbell & Wiernik 2015; Koopmans et al. 2011; Motowidlo, Borman & Schmit 1997; Motowidlo & Van Scotter 1994; Viswesvaran & Ones 2000; Viswesvaran 1993). In the context of job performance, Kanfer and Kantrowitz (2002, p. 30) observed that 'job proficiency is generally more narrowly defined as a task-relevant outcome'. They indicated that in some studies performance was measured with a cognitive ability that in turn was measured in terms of task proficiency. However, these instances limited the reference to proficiency in the context of job-specific tasks. One may be less proficient or highly proficient in a specific set of tasks (or skills). This calls upon the concept of proficiency scaling. If the proficiency level of an individual can be quantified, it may be possible to plot it on the proficiency scale to see where an individual is in the progression towards high proficiency.

As indicated before, another view suggested viewing proficiency as a specific stage, as indicated by the Dreyfus and Dreyfus model. Dreyfus (2004) stated that a proficient performer is deeply involved with the task. A proficient performer can identify the important part of tasks and pay requisite attention. A proficient person sees situations holistically in terms of various elements: 'With holistic understanding, decision-making is less labored since the professional has a perspective on which of the many attributes and aspects present are the important ones' (Benner 1984, pp. 13–34). As the situation changes, his/her deliberation, plan and assessment may change. With changing situations, s/he is able to see new patterns which deviate from normal. Decision-making is very quick and fluid because of his/her experience in a similar situation in the past. 'Action becomes easier and less stressful as the learner simply sees what needs to be done rather than using a calculative procedure to select one of several possible alternatives' (Dreyfus & Dreyfus 2005, p. 786). The proficient performer considers fewer options and will focus on a correct aspect of the problem (Benner 1984). Subsequently, Benner (2004) noted that nurses at the proficiency stage exhibited a situated understanding of their patients' responses: 'The nurse feels increasingly at home in the situation and can now recognise when she or he has a good sense of the situation' (id. 195). Dreyfus and Dreyfus (2005, p. 787) further clarified that 'the *proficient performer*, immersed in the world of skillful activity, *sees* what needs to be done, but *decides* how to do it'.

Alexander (2003b) further proposed a three-stage model of learning based on studies conducted in educational settings. She characterised proficiency as the interplay of knowledge, strategies and motivations. She observed that at the proficiency/expertise stage, performers demonstrated use of a broad and deep knowledge base on the topic or domain knowledge base, and at the same time, were seen using deeper processing strategies. It was also seen that they have high individual interest and engagement, as similar to the observation made by Dreyfus and Dreyfus (1986, 2004, 2005) regarding involvement with the task.

2.3.5 Expertise

In the novice-expert continuum, stage of expertise has invited the most attention among researchers in the field of cognitive psychology, training, learning, performance and business practices, leading to volumes of academic research by leading expertise researchers such as *The nature of expertise* (Chi, Glaser & Farr 1988), *Exploring expertise* (Williams, Faulkner & Fleck 1998), *Cambridge handbook of expertise and expert performance* (Ericsson et al. 2006), *Development of professional expertise* (Ericsson 2009a), and *Expertise out of context* (Hoffman 2012). Most of the expertise discussion in these publications are based on classic and seminal works dating back to the 1960s. The expertise researchers regard extensive classic and seminal works by leading researchers such as De Groot (1965; 1966), Chase and Simon (1973), Chi, Glaser and Rees (1982), Glaser and Chi (1988), Dreyfus and Dreyfus (1986) and Ericsson et al. (1993) as the foundation to most expertise theories which continue to be used in modern research.

According to Hoffman (1998), three dimensions can define expertise: (1) development of expertise; (2) the knowledge structures possessed by experts; and (3) the reasoning processes used by experts. On the other hand, Novak (2011) suggested that expertise could be viewed from four perspectives: (1) attributes; (2) cognition; (3) stages; and (4) community. The attribute perspective defines expertise based on years of studies in several fields, which revealed certain characteristics about how experts operate. The cognition perspective is based on cognitive studies of experts in fields like chess, music and sports. Such studies reveal how experts think and organise knowledge. The stage perspective represents expertise as a sort of progression of knowledge and skills. Lastly, the community perspective represents expertise as a quality that emerges from the interactions individuals have with people and their environment.

One stream of literature is almost entirely devoted to novice-expert differences. The pioneering research by De Groot (1965; 1966) on the differences in performance of novices and experts in the game of chess has motivated other studies (Chi, Glaser & Farr 1988). Subsequently, several studies revealed how experts were different from novices, and others have attempted to explain the general nature of expertise (Chi, Glaser & Rees 1981; Farrington-Darby & Wilson 2006; Schraagen 1993). Expertise is best understood by understanding what an expert does. In the proficiency scale, Hoffman (1998, p. 85) considered expert as a person who has special skills, extensive experience and ability to crack tough problems. From that perspective, expertise has been defined as 'the possession of a large body of knowledge and procedural skills' (Chi, Glaser & Rees 1982, p. 8). In their seminal work, Glaser and Chi (1988) made a point that knowledge structures, processing capability and problem solving are the collective ingredients to develop expertise. An argument for expertise being acquired and hence an outcome or goal of skill acquisition was posited by Chi (2006, p. 23) as 'presumably the more skilled person became expert-like from having acquired knowledge about a domain, that is, from learning and studying' and 'from deliberate practice'. Moreover, experts within their domains are considered to be skilled, competent and think in qualitatively different ways from novices (Anderson 2000; Chi, Glaser & Farr 1988).

In a study conducted by Klein (1998), he interviewed several first responding emergency workers such as firefighters, military officers, nurses and air traffic controllers who made decisions under stress. He noted that expertise or expert performance has the key attribute of pattern recognition which is an ability possessed by an expert to recognise aspects of a new situation based on the exhaustive repertoire of previous experience. Experts recognise patterns, select a course of action and then assess the course of action through mental simulation before executing it. Klein (1998) strongly emphasised that experts have well-developed intuitive capabilities. Thus, exclusivity was one feature of expertise that set it apart from any other construct in skill acquisition. This means expertise typically has been viewed as knowledge, skills, abilities and performance characteristics being possessed by only some people and usually are not common enough to be possessed by all (Dror 2011). These abilities may contain a range of skills such as superior well-organised knowledge, specific mental representations, cognitive skills, the ability to process a large amount of information, ability to identify patterns, ability to filter signal from noise and highly automatic skills (Dror 2011).

A continuum view of the novice-to-expert transition has usually been used to explain actions and characteristics of experts. On that continuum, Dreyfus and Dreyfus (2005) contended that an expert operates and behaves differently from a novice, advanced beginner, competent performer or proficient performer. An expert exhibits experience based deep understanding. 'An immense library of distinguishable situations is built upon the basis of experience' (Dreyfus & Dreyfus 1986, p. 32). Thus, experts treat knowledge in context, and they can recognise the relevance. Similar to the observation made by Klein (1998), Dreyfus and Dreyfus (2005) also made the observation that actions by an expert are driven by intuition and from tacit knowledge and usually are unconscious. They suggested that at the expert level, an individual relies on intuition and the analytical approach is only used in new situations or unrecognised problems not previously experienced. They appear to grasp the conceptual understanding and principles governing the situations intuitively. Thus, they have the ability to recognise the relevant features of new situations. Selectivity also eventuates because of experience, whereby an expert performer can selectively know quickly what needs to be achieved and how to achieve it. The experts can see alternative approaches in a given situation. An expert 'focuses on the accurate region of the problem without wasteful consideration of a larger range of unfruitful possibilities' (Benner 1984, p. 34). Therefore, an expert is able to make unobvious discriminations in situations that a proficient performer may not be able to make. Thus, the expert performer can adapt his/her approach based on the situation. Based on prior experience, the expert can even devise and implement a solution for situations they have never experienced before (DiBello & Missildine 2011).

At this stage, skill attains the automaticity, as indicated by Fitt and Posner (1967), Anderson (1981, 1982) and Ackerman (1988). Skill becomes so automatic sometimes that even an expert may not be aware of it. The performance of an expert at automaticity is fluid. Therefore, it is believed that the expert could move effortlessly between intuitive and analytical approaches and they have the ability to see the overall picture. Furthermore, reflection also characterises the expertise: 'Experts not only possess extensive domain knowledge through experience and proceduralisation, but also utilise self-regulatory knowledge in monitoring progress' (Ge & Hardré 2010, p. 25). However, experts are most critical reflections of their own assumptions, while considering a different course of actions, especially in time-critical situations (Klein 1998).

In almost all the expertise development models, expertise progression has been considered quite one-dimensional, especially in stage models. Such approaches viewed proficiency as a trait possessed by an individual. However, contemporary researchers appeared to recognise that expertise development depends on 'becoming socially embedded in the appropriate groups of experts so that one can acquire 'specialist tacit knowledge'' (Collins 2011, p. 255). Recognising the social aspect of expertise, Collins et al. (2006) and Collins (2011) proposed the construct of interactional expertise. They propose that there are two extra dimensions to expertise. One deals with the degree of exposure to tacit knowledge and the other deals with esotericity (specialised knowledge). They argued that those dimensions create 3-D *expertise space* in which expertise can be explored in a number of ways. The postulation by Collins (2011, p. 255) was based on the fundamental premise that '[t]acit knowledge can be acquired only by immersion in the society of those who already possess it'.

Furthermore, expertise in an organisational context appears to be more encompassing for the whole job itself rather than on representative tasks, as suggested in the expert performance model. On those lines, Cornford and Athanasou (1995, p. 15) suggested a concept of occupational expertise: 'People build up highly specialised knowledge about an operation, about a company, about equipment or solving particular problems'. Subsequently, professional expertise in the occupational space and practice oriented-professions (e.g., legal, consulting) have been studied (Billett 2010; Boshuizen 2003; Evers et al. 2011; van der Heijden 2002; Holt, Mackay & Smith 2004; Lajoie 2009; Mieg 2009; Mott 2000)

2.3.6 Expert performance

Among classic theories, the Fitt and Posner's (1967) model asserted the value of practice in developing automaticity during skill acquisition. However, Ericsson (2009b) believed that practice, as described by Fitt and Posner's (1967) model, was helpful in achieving automaticity only in everyday skills and was no way a mechanism to attain superior expert performance. While classic expertise studies characterised experts and expertise, (Ericsson et al. 1993) suggested a mechanism of achieving *expert performance* based on several studies in the domains like music, chess and sports. They maintained that the construct of expert performance was special. Ericsson and Charness (1994, p. 731) described expert level performance (or expert performance) as 'if someone is performing at least two standard deviations above the mean level in the population, that individual can be said to be performing at an expert level'. Such superior performance is achieved with a combination of high-level skills and domain-specific knowledge and skilled memory (Charness & Tuffiash 2008).

In studies in the domain of music and chess, the findings indicated that individuals normally used extensive training, deliberately and carefully designed professional practice and extended domain-related activities that improved their performance incrementally (Ericsson et al. 1993). The deliberate efforts included constant engagement in similar domain activities, exposure to new issues in his/her domain, and subject to the certain special type of practice called *deliberate practice*. Deliberate practice is not just practice or any other domain-related activity such as work or on-the-job training event (Ericsson & Charness 1994). Rather, deliberate practice is a highly individualised training on tasks selected by a qualified teacher to build expertise in an individual. The deliberate practice is based on the premise that 'expert performance requires the opportunity to find suitable training tasks that the performer can master sequentially.... typically monitored by a teacher or coach' (Ericsson 2006a, p. 692). The feedback from a designated coach is considered an important factor in deliberate practice. With such efforts, the individual may be able to increase expertise.

In several studies, Ericsson emphasised and characterised the nature of deliberate practice (Ericsson, Prietula & Cokely 2007; Ericsson 2000, 2002, 2003, 2004, 2006a, 2007, 2008, 2009c). In their studies, they identified four components in the deliberate practice model: focused goals which are determined by a teacher in order to improve a specific aspect of performance, concentration and effort, feedback from a teacher comparing actual to desired performance, and further opportunities for practice (Ericsson 2007, 2008, 2009c). Deliberate practice activities are designed to allow the repeated experience to allow learners to observe various critical aspects of tasks. Constant stretching and correcting of mistakes were central to the expert performance model because 'attempts for mastery require that the performer always try, by stretching performance beyond its current capabilities, to correct some specific weakness while preserving other successful aspects of function' (Ericsson 2006a, p. 700). Such stretching of skills leads to gradual changes in cognitive mechanisms leading to long-term skill retention. Ericsson (2014, p. 81) suggested that 'new cognitive mechanisms are gradually acquired during the extended period, and they mediate the superior performance, thus leading to qualitative differences in structure compared to untrained performance'. Ericsson (2000, 2002, 2003, 2004, 2006a, 2007, 2008, 2009c) further hypothesised that dramatic differences in performance between experts and non-experts could be attributed to the amount of deliberate practice. Thus, the acquired performance of an individual is a direct function of the amount of time engaged in deliberate practice activities.

In their earlier studies, Ericsson et al. (1993) confirmed that it takes 10,000 hours or ten years of intense training and deliberate practice to become an expert in almost anything. Since then, researchers have applied the concept of deliberate practice in other domains such as science, weather forecasting, engineering, military command and control, surgery and sports and have seen that the framework reasonably explained or supported the development of expertise (Ericsson & Ward 2007; Kirkman 2013; Roth 2009; Ward et al. 2007; van de Wiel & Van den Bossche 2013). Ericsson et al. (1993) hypothesised that true measurement of expert performance could happen only in laboratory settings by studying the reproducibility of superior performance on representative tasks. The expert performance, as suggested by the deliberate practice mechanism, is defined and measured on the representative and specific set of tasks on which reproducibility and superiority of the performance could be verified in the laboratory (Ericsson 2014).

Studies on expert performance have also faced criticism. Recent studies have reasoned that deliberate practice as the only method to achieve expertise is probably not realistic and cited some deficiencies of the approach. For instance, some of the deficiencies were that it discounted the effect of innate talent; it did not explain the performance in novel situations; it possibly ignored the effect of task complexity and task characteristics; and it exhibited a large variance of performance among individuals (Ackerman 2014; Gobet 2013; Hambrick, Altmann, et al. 2014; Hambrick, Oswald, et al. 2014; Kulasegaram, Grierson & Norman 2013; Lombardo & Deaner 2014). Most of the objections appear to stem from the issue that the deliberate practice approach was based on repetition of familiar or routine tasks in relatively closed and repetitive domains such as sports and music, in which standards of measurements are defined and finite. In a domain in which problems were novel or non-repetitive in nature, the applicability of this model is not well established.

On the contrary to the claims that deliberate practice was the only mechanism explaining expert performance, some studies indicated that more factors were contributing to expert performance (Kulasegaram, Grierson & Norman 2013; van de Wiel & Van den Bossche 2013). For example, experience stood out as a key differentiator in both Dreyfus and Dreyfus's (1986, 2004, 2005), as well as Hoffman's (1998) account of expertise. However, there has been conflicting evidence in regards to the contribution of experience towards expert performance. Contrary to common belief that experience leads to expertise, Ward et al. (2007) negated the sole effect of experience in gaining expert or superior performance in a study involving 203 male soccer players between 8 and 18 years of age. The participants consisted of experienced elite players from professional clubs, while sub-elite players were recruited from local schools. The study found that accumulated weekly hours in practice most consistently discriminated between skill levels, rather than the experience of the players. Ericsson (2006a, p. 685) supported this observation by saying that '[e]xtensive experience in a domain does not, however, invariably lead to expert levels of achievement ... further improvement depend [*sic*] on deliberate efforts to change particular aspects of performance'. However, van de Wiel and Van den Bossche's (2013) study involving 17 residents undergoing an internal medicine program and 28 experienced physicians in internal medicine appeared to contradict these claims. In this study, the researcher tried to examine the effect of work-related deliberate practice on performance. They found that deliberate engagement in work-related activities was not related to case test performance of the experienced physicians. However, work experience showed a clear positive relationship with the performance of the resident students.

These impracticalities and the long period of ten years have been viewed as a daunting obstacle in the organisation (Fadde & Klein 2010, 2012; Kirkman 2013). Ericsson maintained that there was probably no shorter or faster way to expert performance stating that 'researchers have not uncovered some simple strategies that would allow non-experts to rapidly acquire expert performance' (Ericsson & Charness 1994, p. 737). Despite the criticism to the ten-year rule, there is only limited evidence to the contrary showing the possibility to reduce the ten-year period (Lombardo & Deaner 2014). Nevertheless, deliberate practice and expert-performance characteristics have guided scaled versions of the training approaches for specific skills (Fadde 2013, 2016; Ward et al. 2007). A major implication of this expert performance approach and deliberate practice framework was to identify the representative tasks and then design training activities with focused, deliberate practice in a certain sequence to develop expertise. The deliberate practice framework placed value on the sequence of exercises, the amount of deliberate practice, feedback and coaching mechanisms. Another implication was the role of deliberate personal efforts by an individual in terms of a disciplined, deliberate practice, as well as training efforts on achieving the expert performance.

2.4 ACCELERATED PROFICIENCY

The literature review has suggested that over the past few decades the research focus has been on skill acquisition, development of workplace proficiency and higher-level expertise. However, changing organisational challenges and attempts to apply principles derived from expertise studies appears to have raised concerns about the length of the proficiency acquisition process. Apparently, in recent years, generally after 2000 and specifically after 2010, accelerating proficiency has become an important topic.

2.4.1 Accelerating proficiency

Developing employees to the desired level of proficiency is a key goal of organisations for their sustainability. 'Proficiency is critical to performance in complex work contexts' (Hoffman, Feltovich, et al. 2010). In a work context, proficiency has been defined as a level where a practitioner is able to perform like a journeyman

(Kuchenbrod 2016). Hoffman et al. (2014, p. 24) defined journeyman as 'a person who can perform a day's labor unsupervised, although working under orders. An experienced and reliable worker, or one who has achieved a level of competence'. A reliable performance is expected from a person with journeyman's proficiency. Employees in organisations are expected to meet the minimum standards of performance. Therefore, organisations expect a minimum journeyman level of proficiency from their employees. Organisations, however, continuously striving to develop peoples' skills to the next level of proficiency due to new business challenges and competition. For some critical functions or roles in organisations, such as CEO's position, there may be need to develop individuals to a very high level of proficiency as determined by the nature of the challenges faced, such as a CEO's position. Such brilliant individuals may be experts in their domains. However, not everyone needs to be an expert, and possibly could not be an expert. Hoffman, Andrews and Feltovich (2012, p. 8) supported that:

> We do not assume that every organisation needs to have every employee be expert at every task. Instead, we are recognizing that for the majority of employees achieving a degree of competence to become journeymen is just fine. Hence our general reference is to accelerated proficiency.

From a practical standpoint, the business challenge is to bring people to a certain level of proficiency so that they can do their job to desired standards. Hoffman, Feltovich, et al. (2010) called this effort as *accelerated proficiency* and defined it as the 'phenomenon of achieving higher levels of proficiency in less time' (p. 9) and dealt with 'how to train and train quickly to higher levels of proficiency' (p. 8). The level of proficiency is the desired level decided by organisations for the job. Once the desired level of proficiency is defined, the next challenge is to reach to that proficiency in a shorter time. Hoffman, Andrews and Feltovich (2012, p. 8) considered that accelerated proficiency deals with 'achievement of knowledge and skill across the proficiency spectrum, all the way from apprentice to expert levels' in a shortest possible time. In business language, doing so is referred to as reducing time-to-proficiency (Rosenbaum & Williams 2004).

Studies on time-to-proficiency date back to the late 1980's. Carpenter et al. (1989) and Faneuff et al. (1990) were among the first to develop a time-to-proficiency model in a military context for recording aviator proficiency. In their study involving avionics communication specialists, Carpenter et al. (1989) measured time-to-proficiency in terms of performance in a selected set of tasks. They defined time-to-proficiency as 'the length of time it takes to bring people with different attributes (especially mental aptitude) to targeted levels of task performance' (Carpenter et al. 1989, p. 1). They correlated productivity, attrition, cost and aptitude in their model with the time-to-proficiency. Based on the model, they found that time-to-proficiency metrics were viable performance measurement methods in the job which 'provides sufficient information for the modeling of productivity' (Carpenter et al. 1989, p. 1). In a different application of the same concept, Pinder and Schroeder (1987) conducted a time-to-proficiency study which involved 354 managers from eight companies in Canada who were surveyed regarding their time-to-proficiency after job transfers. They conceived time-to-proficiency as 'the length of time that elapses between the individual's movement into a new job and ascendancy of that individual to a level of performance at which a balance between inducements and contributions exists' (id. 337). Inducements were the investments made in the person when s/he started on a new job, while contributions were his/her productivity on the new job. In this study, time-to-proficiency was expressed in the context of productivity and contributions to the job instead of a certain set of tasks. This definition reveals the key implication that while someone is working towards desired proficiency and trying to be productive in a new job; their performance has a financial impact on the business, thus making it a compelling reason to monitor time-to-proficiency in a given job.

Hoffman et al. (2014, p. 169) referred to time-to-proficiency in terms of career stages as the time taken by an individual to reach a desired level of proficiency. The career stages they most frequently referred to were journeyman and senior journeyman. The journeyman career stage exhibited characteristics like being reliable, experienced, able to work unsupervised, and having achieved a certain level of competence. These characteristics, in general, though not entirely, lined up well with the proficiency stage of Dreyfus and Dreyfus's (2005) model. Hoffman et al. (2014, p. 169) explained reducing time-to-proficiency in terms of an S-curve of proficiency acquisition, as shown in *Figure 2-2*. The proficiency scales show the stages of initiator, apprentice, journeyman and expert. They further broke the journeyman and expert stages into three different levels to indicate seniority, given that time is plotted in terms of career. The basic inference drawn from this graph is that there could be some methods or mechanisms that can accelerate the time-to-proficiency, at least at the journeyman level.

Figure 2-2: Accelerated proficiency growth curve and time-to-proficiency

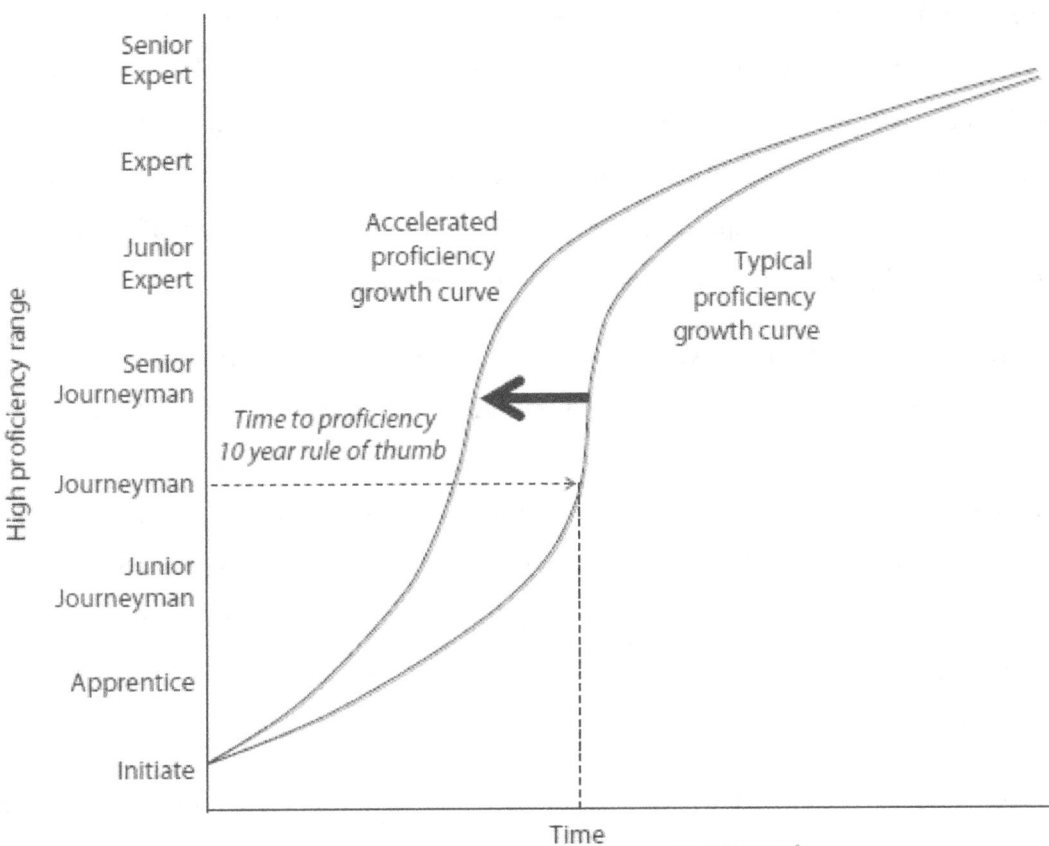

Source: *adapted from Hoffman et al. (2014)*

Few studies have focused on how much time it takes for someone to reach high proficiency (expertise), and they were mostly situated within classic studies on expertise or expert performance. Ericsson and Charness (1994) proposed, '[t]o measure the duration of the acquisition process, we analyze the length of time it takes for best individuals to attain the highest levels of performance within a domain'. Measurement of time taken to acquire high proficiency has long intrigued researchers. Chase and Simon (1973) found that several other domains exhibit the patterns of achieving high proficiency in ten years, similar to the observations made in the domain of chess. Since then, the ten-year rule to achieve expertise has been empirically tested by researchers (Hayes 1989; Simonton 1997). The most extensive work on this has been carried out by Ericsson et al. (1993), who analysed the effect of deliberate practice by comparing three groups of 30 under-training violinists and two groups of 24 expert and amateur pianists. Through extensive modelling and measurements, they concluded that it required about ten thousand hours or ten years of intense training and deliberate practice activities to attain expertise in almost anything. However, this estimate of ten years was for attaining an elite performance on a specific set of tasks or skills, mainly in a closed domain where standards of performance are well established. In a study involving 215 modern writers, their best works since the time they wrote their first publication were evaluated (Kaufman & Kaufman 2007). They found that the several famous writers required ten years to reach a point of writing to achieve a well-regarded publication, which required, in addition, an even longer preparation time. Nevertheless, they also stated that 'it takes 10 years to become not just an "expert" but a "world-class" expert' (id. 115). However, Hoffman, Feltovich, et al. (2010, p. 61) criticised the ten years of deliberate practice as a rule to gain high level of proficiency: 'Our reason for calling out the ostensive limitations of the "approach" is that if expertise is achieved only after deliberate practice (the 10-year rule of thumb), then acceleration would not be possible'.

While all of these studies refer to the ten year period as time-to-expertise at world-class status, there are only a few studies which report measurements of time-to-proficiency (Carpenter et al. 1989; Faneuff et al. 1990). An air force communication specialist's time-to-proficiency was noted in the range of 18 months to 36 months depending upon their aptitude scores (Carpenter et al. 1989). In another study involving 300 call centre agents, Borton (2007) noted that time-to-proficiency of the agents was more than six months. More recently, a survey conducted with chief sales officers of 1,200 companies worldwide by Accenture (2013) indicated that time-to-proficiency of 73% of the new sales representative workforce was approximately one year or more.

Some researchers have speculated that in some professions such as military and air force time-to-proficiency was very long. Hence a need to accelerate proficiency was recognised as: '[In the US Air Force] it still ordinarily takes many years to achieve proficiency. Therefore, there would be great advantages if the USAF could establish regimens of training that could accelerate the achievement of that proficiency' (Hoffman, Andrews & Feltovich 2012, p. 1). Market pressure, particularly over the last decade, has warranted accelerating the expertise cycle as a necessity (Clark 2013). Wray and Wallace (2011, p. 243) appealed, 'A more realistic aspiration is to create conditions encouraging all individuals to proceed at the maximum pace possible for them, both in training settings and workplace practice'.

Some researchers pointed out financial reasons of accelerating proficiency: 'If any time could be shaved off the "10000 clock," there would be potentially significant saving of money and time, an increase in overall organisational capability...' (Hoffman et al. 2014, p. 169). However, several nonfinancial reasons such as impact of non-proficiency in critical professions have also led researchers to investigate the concept of accelerating proficiency. For example, in a study involving firefighting commanders, lack of events to gain experience and become proficient was perceived to endanger life and property when those events occur which require proficient people to handle them (Kuchenbrod 2016). The need for acceleration of proficiency has been explained in the literature for sectors such as the military, sports, utility, research, biotech and information technology sectors (see examples in Hoffman et al. 2014). However, the phenomenon and process of accelerated proficiency remained inadequately explained. The literature lacks a richer understanding of how and why business dynamics dictate the need for accelerated proficiency and what benefits it could accrue. Hoffman, Andrews and Feltovich (2012, p. 9) specified a set of research questions for future time-to-proficiency research that they believed were the gaps and problems for which there were no direct answers in the literature:

> What is it within the work itself that takes time to master? What is it about the nature of the cognition within the work that requires time to achieve high levels of proficiency?... What might be the payoff if this problem were solved, say, by reducing the time to achieve journeyman level skill by some significant amount (e.g., from 4 years to 2)? (Hoffman, Andrews & Feltovich 2012, p. 9)

The literature provides speculations and assumptions, as opposed to concrete cases, to understand the business dynamics and challenges that drive the need for accelerated proficiency. These apparent gaps in the literature, therefore, require further investigation.

2.4.2 Theoretical issues

The literature on the topic of accelerated proficiency is in nascent phases. A thorough literature review suggested that there was no specific theory or model of that could explain the true nature of accelerated proficiency or accelerated expertise (more so in the natural settings of organisations). In a recent synthesis of several decades of research on expertise and accelerated expertise, Hoffman et al. (2014, p. 132) agreed to this observation:

> A considerable number of theories or approaches are manifestly pertinent to the topic of accelerated proficiency. But on close examination, not all of them fit well with what we know about expertise, and not all of them fit well with the complex and ever changing tasks that characterize the "real world".

They observed that two theories — cognitive transformation theory (CTT) and cognitive flexibility theory (CFT) — appeared to explain certain aspects of acquiring and accelerating proficiency: 'Both try to achieve proficiency, but in different ways' (Hoffman, Feltovich, et al. 2010).

Spiro et al. (1992, p. 9) believed the unlearning was a key component of learning: 'We now know that the path from novicehood to expertise is not one of monotonic progress, but rather requires a stage of *undoing* the results of earlier learning before further progress can be made'. Researchers noticed that as individuals go through cognitive development, they keep getting fixated on the mental model (Feltovich, Spiro & Coulson 1997). Extending further, Klein and Baxter (2009) developed CTT and noted that cognitive skills, unlike behaviour skills, depend heavily on the mental model. Mental models (or knowledge structures or schemata) are models to organise one's knowledge. Klein and Baxter (2009) believed that cognitive skills were not about adding anything more to the existing mental models, but it was about *sense making* to see and think about things differently. To learn a cognitive skill, one needed to reorganise his/her knowledge structure, which did not happen with the usual components of learning – diagnosis, learning objectives, practice, feedback, etc. They believed that for cognitive skills it is difficult to diagnose the subtle aspects of cognitive skills. Instead, they proposed that to help people reorganise existing mental models, learners have to first unlearn some of their existing flawed models. Therefore, to develop and accelerate proficiency, it is necessary to figure out ways to unlearn and reject flawed mental models. To build and accelerate proficiency, Klein and Baxter (2009, p. 7) stated that training instructions need to 'diagnose limitations in mental models, design interventions to help students appreciate the flaws in their mental models, and provide experiences to enable trainees to discover more useful and accurate mental models'. CTT emphasised that it is important to design systems which allow learners to recognise their flaws in their current mental models and then discard flawed models in favour of less flawed models.

CTT is one of the theories with several implications on developing and accelerating expertise. In a review, Hoffman et al. (2008) concluded that CTT explained the mechanisms to accelerate the proficiency and beyond. 'Cognitive transformation theory describes the changes to knowledge and reasoning that proficient workers need to undergo in order to make the jump from mere proficiency to superior levels of expertise' (Hoffman et al. 2008, p. 5.2). Using a similar concept, in multiple operational simulation experiments conducted by DiBello et al. (DiBello, Missildine & Struttman 2009; DiBello & Missildine 2008, 2011, 2013), it was shown that when performers were exposed to multiple cycles of failures, their flawed mental models were revealed. The rapid failure cycles helped them reorganise their mental models. The fundamental premise of their approach was to develop 'cognitive agility' (DiBello & Missildine 2011, p. 17) based on a concept of 'disequilibration', which involved showing learners their flawed mental model, whereby they get to unlearn their previous model, reorganise the new mental model and develop a sustainable change in their behaviour in shorter time (DiBello, Missildine & Struttman 2009, pp. 27–28). The mechanism observed in these studies is explained as: 'Only when something traumatic occurred, such as a failure, would the experts reexamine their mental models and replace questionable aspects' (Klein & Borders 2016, p. 269). Therefore 'unlearning the flawed mental model' appears to be a key strategy to develop and accelerate adaptive expertise. Some of the methods to accelerate proficiency that share theoretical underpinning of CTT are simulation-based training, tough cases, desirable difficulties, scenario-based training and time-compression.

In their original studies, Spiro et al. (1987, 1988) noticed that knowledge acquisition was accelerated in ill-structured domains when instructions supported learners to develop flexible mental models. Based on their empirical results, Spiro et al. (1987, 1988, 1990, 1992) viewed expertise in ill-structured domains as the ability to develop flexible mental models, and spontaneously change one's mental model adaptively to respond to changing situational demands. This changed mental model enabled them to apply knowledge from multiple perspectives depending on the situation. Based on this premise, CFT was developed focusing on the nature of learning in complex and ill-structured domains and concerned about the transfer of knowledge and skills beyond initial learning situations (Spiro & Jehng 1990). The fundamental mechanism suggested by CFT was to build "cognitive flexibility" in learners so that they understand deeply and then apply flexibly. Cognitive flexibility was emphasised as one of the most basic requirements to accelerate proficiency. As Spiro et al. (1992, p. 7) put it: 'A learner who has developed "cognitive flexibility" will be able to utilize conceptual knowledge in an adaptive fashion'. CFT advocated presenting content to learners from several different perspectives and themes. This allowed learners to present their knowledge in multiple dimensions rather than in a single conceptual dimension. The core of CFT was to use multiple mental and pedagogical representations, promote multiple alternative systems of linkage among knowledge elements, and promote abstraction of functional and conceptual understanding and the need for participatory learning. It also emphasised not to over-simplify the content, rather to support context-dependent knowledge. CFT advocated a constructivist view and specified using case-based learning for knowledge construction from highly interconnected knowledge sources in which all ranges of complexity may exist (Hoffman et al. 2014). Studies conducted by Spiro et al. (1987), Coulson, Feltovich and Spiro (1997), Jonassen (1992) and Jonassen et al. (1997) suggested that learners studying the material designed using cognitive flexibility theory were better able to transfer the principles to the novel, unrelated cases. Spiro et al. (2003) contended that by suitably designing instructions using hypermedia based on CFT principles, they could accelerate the experience of learners in complex learning. CFT as the theoretical framework has also showed up in case-based learning scenario-based simulations and games.

Both CTT and CFT appeared to explain certain aspects of accelerated proficiency. Hoffman et al. (2008, p. 5.2) stated that:

> Core ideas of cognitive flexibility theory (what makes problems difficult for learners and the simplistic understandings that result for those learners) and cognitive transformation theory (the need for unlearning experiences) are certainly pertinent to shaping any program of accelerated learning.

Hoffman, Feltovich, et al. (2010, p. 139) suggested that both theories could be merged to form a new theory for accelerated proficiency because they are complementary to each other. However, none of them appears to describe the phenomenon of accelerated proficiency completely. From the scarce literature on this topic, it appears that researchers are yet to develop a better understanding of the process of accelerated proficiency because there is no comprehensive theory yet. Hoffman and Andrews (2012, p. 5) raised the importance of crystallising understanding of the concept of accelerated proficiency:

> There are theoretical and practical issues with regard to what we mean by accelerated learning and whether the training and scientific communities are conceptualizing this problem as a topic demanding programmatic research. As such, concepts of accelerated learning and accelerated proficiency bring in a host of interesting questions, issues, and challenges in the area of instructional design, training, transfer, retention, the role of feedback, mentoring, and others. (Hoffman & Andrews 2012, p. 5)

2.4.3 Challenges to accelerate proficiency

Current methods of accelerating proficiency in the literature are primarily grounded in the domain of learning. Therefore, the role of training in accelerating proficiency and the challenges associated with such role is reviewed in this sub-section. From the literature review, two challenges have become evident in regards to accelerating proficiency. First, the literature has suggested a lack of understanding on the actual mechanisms of how someone gains proficiency, despite a large amount of research on the higher end of expertise. Second, the literature has suggested challenges in regards to methods and solutions to accelerate the acquisition of proficiency. The first challenge is expressed as: 'One also needs to understand how expertise is acquired, how it can be taught, and how new employees can be presented with appropriate experience and management activities' (van der Heijden 2002, p. 55). Among other things, understanding the mechanisms of learning and how they interact to develop a novice into an expert is extremely crucial to develop suitable instructional design and training interventions to ensure acceleration of novice-to-expert development (Welch 2008). The actual process of how one becomes proficient using training or other methods remains under-explored in the literature, as pointed out by Lajoie (2003). The gap identified by researchers two decades ago, still persists today. For instance, some researchers noted: 'Most studies can't explain how the expertise reaches to a specific level or stage by multiple mechanisms. Accordingly we have to develop specific and realistic model for how expertise develops' (Moon, Kim & You 2013, p. 226). There is another aspect to this gap. The classic studies focused either on a range of issues related to novice-expert differences (Chi, Glaser & Farr 1988) or on the development of higher end expertise (Ericsson et al. 1993). However, developing and accelerating proficiency to the stages of journeyman and senior journeyman, in between extreme ends of novice and expert, have not received much attention (Alexander 2003b; Hoffman et al. 2014). These mid-range proficiency stages have been positioned as the most important stages 'considering the significant impact of the journeyman stage and the need for hastening performance in that stage' in organisations (Jung, Kim & Reigeluth 2016, p. 58). However, there are scarce empirical studies on how to accelerate proficiency, particularly at the mid-range of the journeyman and senior journeyman proficiency levels.

Methods for effective skill acquisition training and learning interventions have continued to be the focus of researchers and organisations alike (Salas et al. 2012). For decades, the literature has positioned the value of training, learning and development interventions in improving the speed of learning, improving performance and acquiring skills required to do the job. As Lajoie (2003, p. 23) suggested '[t]he road to competence can be shortened if systematic studies of expertise lead to improvements in instruction and assessment'. Researchers have attempted to explore the mechanisms of accelerating proficiency or expertise from classical studies. However, there is a growing body of arguments over the past decade questioning the ability of traditional training models to develop and accelerate proficiency in complex domains. Hoffman et al. (2009,

p. 19) appealed that 'traditional learning methods that focus on cursory exposure and short-term results might be insufficient to accelerate the achievement of proficiency'. Traditional, Instructor-led, classroom-based training posed some challenges to shorten time-to-proficiency due to several reasons. Some of the reasons are lengthy training programs required to develop complex skills (Andrew & Fitzerald 2010); longer training design cycle (Arnold, Ringquist & Prien 1998); merely textbook problem-solving capabilities (Mayer 1986; Brown, Collins & Duguid 1989; Perkins & Soloman 1989); classroom methodologies disconnected from the workplace realities (Vaughan 2008); and the need to re-learn the same tasks in the workplace way (Bransford & Schwartz 2004).

More recently, Arnold and Collier (2013, p. 2) observed issues with traditional training methods: 'Traditional training methods, such as on-the-job training and expert-led lecture/discussion schemes, have shown little capability to accelerate this expertise development process'. For example, evidence showed that traditional pedagogies such as lecturing and demonstrating solutions to problems, very often result in students being capable of solving textbook problems but unable to apply the knowledge to solve real-life problems (Hung 2009).

To add to this challenge, the complexity in the workplace could influence how soon an employee reaches target proficiency and could be a determining factor that leads to variations in performance on the same task among several performers. Hoffman, Feltovich, et al. (2010, p. 17) pointed out that training notions need to be changed in view of increased complexity: 'The workers in sociotechnical systems must be trained to be adaptive, so that they can cope with the ever changing world and ever-changing workplace.... and workers must be trained faster'. Complexity raises the emphasis on adaptive expertise as a key component of accelerated proficiency, which allows an individual to be able to handle novel and unfamiliar problems (Hesketh & Ivancic 2002). However, traditional training methods did not appear to be helpful in developing adaptive expertise: 'Traditional methods are appropriate for training routine expertise and are designed to develop automatic behavioral responses to performance requirements that are familiar to the performer' (Shadrick & Lussier 2009, p. 289).

Complexity brings another challenge on training development as well. According to Andrews and Fitzgerald (2010, p. 3) complexity may add time to learn by stating that, 'if the content to be learned is complex, we must allow considerable time, sometimes years, for the acquisition of that skill or knowledge, and we must spend considerable non-time resources'. Consequently, there is more content to be developed and the duration of such training programs tended to become long. Some studies to investigate methods to accelerate training development noted that 'what training departments need are sound methods for shortening the cycle time of the training development process, while not sacrificing validity and quality of the output' (Arnold, Ringquist & Prien 1998, p. 23). Sharing similar views, van Merriënboer, Clark and de Croock (2002, p. 39) made an appeal that training needed to focus on 'development of training programs for learner who need to learn and transfer highly complex cognitive skills or "competencies" to an increasingly varied set of real-world context and settings'.

Another school of thought have recognised experience as a critical piece of proficiency and accelerating the same (Kuchenbrod 2016). The proficient person uses intuition, which comes out of his/her past experience (Dreyfus & Dreyfus 2005). This experience typically is acquired from real-world assignments and workplace tasks (Eraut 1994, 2004, 2007a, 2007b). According to Sheckley and Keeton (1999, p. 28):

> Individuals develop proficiency by working in challenging and supportive environments, self-monitoring, engaging in deliberate practice, and solving ill-defined problems. The key becomes how to increase the learner's experience in the shortest amount of time yet ensure the learner ultimately attains domain mastery.

Then the question arises how to accelerate that experience in a short period of time. That experience generally comes through on-the-job assignments and tasks, through a training curriculum that is designed to incorporate this experience or using the workplace to deliver the training (Billett 2004). Klein (1998) reasoned that training is just a supplement to gain expertise and cannot be a substitute for real-world experience. Accepting that premise, Grossman, Spencer and Salas (2014, p. 315) also appealed that 'beyond the formal training settings, another important area in need of future research is how training opportunities can be extended into the work environment'. Thus, an important aspect of methods for accelerating proficiency appears to be extending training to the workplace. Hoffman et al. (2009) suggested that the training design should be such that '[t]he modes and means of training should engage real work practice–the job challenges, context, and duties to the greatest extent possible'. However, Lesgold (2001) cautioned about the lack of opportunities for practice on non-routine problems in the workplace:

> The real world mostly provides opportunities to do the routine. Expertise involving the non-routine is harder to get from everyday work experience because the right situations occur rarely and often are handled by established experts when they do occur, not by students (Lesgold 2001, p. 967).

Cross (2013) highlighted the importance of workplace learning:

> Companies that focus on shortening the time employees [sic] complete formal, explicit learning are looking at a drop in the bucket. Improving the effectiveness of experiential, tacit learning adds much more to the bottom line. [http://www.internetalliance.com]

The literature appears to provide approaches favouring, as well as approaches rejecting workplace-training methods. Recognising that traditional training methods, whether classroom-based or workplace-based do not appear to answer the challenge of accelerating proficiency, some studies have observed that training design for accelerating proficiency may require different methods. Fadde (2007, p. 373) recognised in his studies that such methods may require 'instructional designers to create efficient instructional tasks'. This gap continues to persist, as evident by the concerns raised by Fadde (2016, p. 1, 13):

> The goal of accelerating expertise [proficiency] can leave researchers and trainers in human factors, naturalistic decision making, sports science, and expertise studies concerned about seemingly insufficient application of expert performance theories, findings and methods for training macrocognitive aspects of human performance (p. 1).... The theories, findings, and methods of expert performance research need to be translated into focused workplace training programs that meet the challenges of duration, curriculum development, resource optimization, and buy in from on-the-ground practitioners (p. 13).

Section 2.5 reviews studies on methods that have been reported in the literature towards accelerating proficiency.

2.5 METHODS OF ACCELERATING PROFICIENCY

In this section, the literature is reviewed for methods and techniques that appear to provide some empirical evidence or support to accelerate proficiency. Both classic and recent studies have been reviewed for methods of acceleration. Most of the methods that have provided evidence in the literature towards accelerating proficiency have some form of synergy or similar theoretical basis. In general, several HRD methods are used in the workplace to develop employees and to prepare them with the skills/competencies required to perform their job. Among others, the studies on structured on-the-job training (S-OJT) provided encouraging evidence of accelerating employee proficiency (sub-section 2.5.1). Another trend in accelerating proficiency involved modelling the experts in terms of capturing their thinking, strategies and behaviours through cognitive task analysis (CTA) (sub-section 2.5.2). Most studies advocated developing curriculum based on elements revealed by CTA methods to train novices or transfer that knowledge quickly. Another trend in methods to accelerate proficiency suggested using simulations-based and games-based methods to provide exposure and practice to novices in a highly time-compressed fashion (sub-section 2.5.3). In a similar trend, another set of methods suggests a convergence of use of scenarios, cases and problems which have shown evidence in accelerating proficiency by subjecting the performer towards multi-dimensional understanding, developing adaptive expertise, developing flexibility and challenging their mental models, and showing them ways to un-learn or reorganise their mental models (sub-section 2.5.4). Key techniques to accelerate proficiency include using desirable difficulties, tough cases, difficult problems and failures presented in time-compressed fashion.

A completely different approach suggested for accelerating the acquisition of complex skills is by focusing on isolating representative part-task, providing practice and accelerated expertise on those part-tasks and then integrate those part-tasks inside the whole-task context (sub-section 2.5.5). Further, methods like knowledge capture and transfer to new employees (sub-section 2.5.6) and using technology (sub-section 2.5.7) were also observed in some research studies claiming to accelerate proficiency of employees. Some studies suggested accelerated learning methods claiming that these methods contribute towards accelerating proficiency (sub-section 2.5.8). Finally, a range of methods suggested using workplace activities including cognitive apprenticeship, immersive activities and structured on-the-job training (sub-section 2.5.9). The studies using these methods are reviewed in the following sub-sections. Note: Some of the methods apply to training settings, as well as workplace settings.

2.5.1 HRD methods of employee development in the workplace

The HRD literature approaches workplace training/learning methods from a theoretical orientation put forward by notable philosophers: behaviourism (Thorndike, Watson, Hull, Tolman, Skinner), cognitivism (Kohler, Piaget, Bruner, Gagne), humanism (Buhler, Maslow, Rogers), social learning (Bandura, Rotter) and constructivism (Dewy, Lave, Piaget, Vygotsky). Workplace learning and training methods in HRD mostly fall under two schools of thought. Some researchers agree to an informal work-based approach (Piskurich 1993), while some prefer a more structured approach to on-the-job learning (Jacobs & Jones 1995; Rothwell & Kazanas 2004).

In the first school of thought, some leading studies by Cseh, Watkins and Marsick (1999), Watkins and Marsick (1992) and Marsick and Watkins (1997, 2015, 2001) proposed informal learning and incidental learning as the core mechanism of workplace learning. Informal learning is something that happens uncontrolled in the workplace. Incidental learning is a by-product of other interventions. Cseh, Watkins and Marsick (1999) described workplace learning through a model of informal and incidental learning. In a study conducted with 84 managers at a fortune 500 company, Enos, Kehrhahn and Bell (2003) found that the primary mechanism that developed proficiency of managers was informal learning, which allowed them to transfer learning quickly to real-world situations. Some researchers have pointed out the value of the social aspect of learning from each other as an important component of informal learning (Eraut 2004, 2007; Marsick et al. 2017). Lately, studies have proposed situated learning in the workplace and learning through communities of practices as key workplace learning methods that emphasise informal learning through social interactions in the workplace and learning from each other (Carter & Adkins 2017; Farnsworth, Kleanthous & Wenger-Trayner 2016; Mills 2011; Wenger 2000).

However, several studies have maintained the workplace was not a place that is conducive to learning and posed several barriers that hampered learning (Hager 1998; Kooken, Ley & De Hoog 2007; Schulz & Roßnagel 2010). Brooker and Butler (1997) conducted a study at six industrial sites to explore perceptions of trainees and trainers towards the workplace as a learning context. It was found that both trainers and trainees considered the workplace more as a production place than a learning place, and that learning was more disruptive when carried out in the workplace. On the contrary, Billett (1996) challenged this viewpoint thin the workplace is an informal, unstructured place for learning to happen. He contended that workplace activities are highly goal-oriented, structured, organised and measured, which in fact should accelerate learning and performance in the workplace. In another study, Billett (2006) concluded that workplace activities could be organised and sequenced as a curriculum or a learning pathway, in such a way that overall trajectory to performance could be made more systematic. Though the study did not lead to evidence of acceleration, it emphasises an important aspect of structured workplace learning, use of experiential learning, and learning through work.

HR practitioners value experiential learning (Kolb 1984) and action learning (Pedler 2011; Revans 1982) as a means to develop expertise and improve performance. Experiential learning includes learning from experience, context, non-routine conditions, the tacit dimension of knowledge, reflection and critical reflection, informal and incidental learning (Garrick 1998). Andresen, Boud and Cohen (2000, p. 208) define 'the ultimate goal of experiential learning involves the learner's own appropriation of something that is to them personally significant and meaningful (sometimes spoken in terms of the learning being "true to the lived experience of learners")'. Garrick (1998, p. 4) viewed informal learning also as experiential learning itself because 'experience of the learner occupies the central place in all considerations of teaching and learning'. Studies on the transfer of learning also contended value of experiential learning (Bates, Holton III & Seyler 1997; Holton III, Bates & Ruona 2000). While experiential learning methods appealed for the involvement of learners during learning, action learning, on the other hand, appeal for the participation of learners in real scenarios. Participation, sharing with each other, learning from each other and group learning are some of the key elements of action learning methods. Miller (2003) conducted a study of 400 people at a hospital, which demonstrated the use of action learning as a primary mechanism for workplace learning for 35 managers. Further, as discussed in the previous sub-section, Fadde and Klein (2010, 2012) suggested that action-learning activities could accelerate performance in natural settings.

The second school of thought on HRD emphasised a more structured approach to workplace learning. In a study conducted at a large food manufacturing plant with 17 learners, Billett (2002a) proposed guided participation in work activities, guided learning at work and guided learning transfer. His method advocated learning through undertaking everyday work activities, organising and sequencing of workplace experiences, access to routine and non-routine practice, monitoring learners' progress on a pathway of activities, providing goals with work practice, modelling the tasks to be performed, demonstrating procedures, coaching with an activity, providing opportunities to participate, observe and listen, and opportunities to reflect and abstract situation. In such studies, mentoring or coaching has been seen as a central mechanism of workplace learning which has provided some weak empirical evidence towards improving career outcomes for employees (Allen & Eby 2007; Allen et al. 2004; Billett 2003; Ramaswami & Dreher 2007). Based on the core principle of mentoring in the context of complex tasks or jobs, the cognitive apprenticeship method has shown evidence of accelerating expertise (Boling & Beatty 2010; Cash et al. 1996; Collins, Brown & Newman 1988; Collins 1990; Dennen & Burner 2008; Dennen 2004; Jin & Corbett 2011; Kuo et al. 2012; Woolley & Jarvis 2007).

Among the various HRD methods, structured on-the-job training (S-OJT) has emerged as the most promising method in organisations for experiential learning (Jacobs & Jones 1995). This method develops the expertise of new employees with the help of mentoring/coaching from experienced employees (Jacobs 2014a). This is a structured process of defining, tracking, monitoring and managing OJT. The S-OJT approach incorporated analysis of work activities, checklists and mentor sign-off. In an early study in clinical practice, the positive effect on S-OJT in the workplace was shown to improve customer satisfaction without having to take people away from the workplace (Sullivan, Brechin & Lacoste 1999). The key attribute of this approach appears to be a reduction in time-to-proficiency. In a study conducted by Jacobs and Bu-Rahmah (2012) at a petroleum company in the Middle East, the authors applied S-OJT to train new engineers. The new engineers were put under a pool of pre-qualified mentors for various tasks. They noted that 53 months of time normally required to advance an engineer to the desired performance was reduced to 36 months using S-OJT. Among other benefits, the S-OJT approach has reported a reduction in training times. For instance: '[t]he results related to training efficiency suggest that S-OJT usually takes less time to conduct and it achieves the training objectives when compared to unstructured OJT, classroom training, and blended versions of the training' (Jacobs 2014a, p. 281).

Further, Jacobs (2014a) reported nine case studies, which showed that S-OJT could accelerate proficiency in several different kinds of jobs that required skills ranging from low to high complexity, have predictable or pre-defined outcomes and for which well-documented procedures were available. Several studies have reported using S-OJT to reduce training time and improve training efficiency for jobs ranging from low complexity such as assembly jobs (Jacobs 1994), mid-level complexity such as manufacturing-related jobs (Gorman, Moore, Blake & Phillips, 2004) and hospital/healthcare related jobs (Mafi & Jacobs 2001), and high-level complexity jobs such as oil/gas sector related jobs (Jacobs & Bu-Rahmah 2012). Although there are several studies to manage and track S-OJT systematically, no literature was found that explained techniques to shorten the S-OJT cycle, which may still extend to several months in complex jobs (Jacobs & Bu-Rahmah 2012).

The HRD literature has long been inclined towards training and development as the core activity towards developing the expertise of employees in the workplace (Jacobs & Jones 1995). However, Billett (2014) has contended that most of the learning in the workplace occurs outside the boundaries of intentional mentoring and other structured HRD interventions. He argued that the processes of observation and imitation play a key role in workplace learning. Thus, the nature of workplace activities determines the pace at which learning happens. Further, work environment plays an important role in accelerating proficiency. From the literature review, it is evident that accelerating proficiency in the workplace could be a complex phenomenon. However, existing literature on proficiency lacks explanation of influencing conditions on proficiency development, as well as acceleration (van der Heijden 2002). In a meta-analysis to investigate instructional interventions to accelerate the novice-expert transition, Welch (2008, p. 108) concluded that one needs to examine if the work environment indeed supports shortening the novice-to-expert transition. Most expertise and proficiency theories have discounted the influence of a range of contextual factors such as job environment, nature of job, and dynamism of business environment. For instance, in a study aimed at understanding the expertise development process of 11 instructional design students, Ge and Hardré (2010, p. 24) identified several factors that influenced the development of expertise. They found that despite a large body of research on expertise 'little research has focused on the interactions of internal and external factors influencing novices' expertise development'. Therefore, the methods and solutions for accelerating proficiency have to consider the workplace dynamics, environment and other influencing factors (Moon, Kim & You 2013).

The role of managers in shaping the workplace environment and dynamics, and hence, developing or accelerating employee proficiency, cannot be underestimated. From a HRD perspective, managers are play a large role in enabling their employees with workplace learning (Beattie 2006; Gratton 2016; McLaughlin 2016; Yen, Trede & Patterson 2016). Despite the advances in work-based learning (Morris & Blaney 2010) or learning through work (Billett & Choy 2013; Billett 2010, 2014; Chan 2013), it seems that managers do not know how to support such learning. Woodall (2000) found that despite recognition of the importance of the workplace as an important place for learning, managers typically did not know much about work-based learning interventions and a systematic approach to workplace learning was lacking. Similarly, Hughes (2004) noted that, while workplace learning is expected to be influenced by supervisors, there was no noticeable attempt by supervisors to enable their staff to learn. Marsick and Volpe (1999) acknowledged that business practitioners know a little about how informal learning can be best supported, encouraged and developed.

Therefore, at a holistic level, HRD studies have indicated that to develop performance in the workplace, organisations must become learning organisations (Marquardt 1996; Matthews 1999; Watkins & Marsick 1993). As the originators of the concept of learning organisations, Senge (1994a, 1994b) and Senge et al. (1994) proposed personal mastery, mental models, shared vision, team learning, and system thinking as key ingredients of making an organisation a learning organisation. Further, Kaiser and Holton III (1998) proposed a learning organisational performance model which emphasised that learning outcomes at the individual, team and organisation level lead to performance outcomes.

Overall, the HRD literature has explored several workplace learning theories and methods. It has been established that HRD research typically does not seem to make acceleration of proficiency, performance or expertise as a primary goal or a strategic initiative. With the exception of the studies on S-OJT, none of the HDR studies reviewed could provide direct evidence of accelerating performance, proficiency or expertise in the workplace. However, studies on cognitive psychology and experimental psychological (as reviewed in the following sub-sections) have proposed viable methods and strategies for accelerating employee proficiency.

2.5.2 Cognitive task analysis (CTA) methods

Researchers have indicated that the key to expertise development is first to elicit this knowledge structure or mental models and then teach that to novices to develop expertise (Lajoie 2003). Lajoie (2003) suggested observing explicit exemplars or models of expertise from experts and then mapping them to create a trajectory that can help novices to develop similar competencies. She maintained that '[t]he transition from student to expert professional can be accelerated when a trajectory for change is plotted and made visible to learners' (Lajoie 2003, p. 24). She also proposed that cognitive task analysis (CTA) can help reveal that trajectory to the expertise. However, it depends on how well expertise can be modelled by an expert. Past studies have confirmed that experts developed automaticity, which was usually 'implicit or unconscious' (Clark & Estes 1996, p. 407) as a result of repeated use of declarative knowledge which developed into production knowledge (Anderson 2000). At the stage of automaticity, experts were believed to be so intuitive or unconscious about the decisions they made that they sometimes cannot fully articulate why they do what they do (Logan 1988). Early researchers developed CTA to capture these unconscious processes of how experts operate, think, behave and process a task. These methods revealed the cognitive structures and processes involved in performing a task (Clark & Estes 1996). Expert knowledge often takes different forms that enable different performances at different stages of expertise. Therefore, different CTA methods were introduced which varied in process and intent. In an earlier study, Merkelbach and Schraagen (1994) presented three frameworks, namely task modelling, knowledge modelling and cognitive modelling to develop an integrated view of how experts perform tasks, think and approach problems, handle challenging situations and decide their plan of action. Over the years, studies have introduced over 100 different methods to conduct CTA (Clark, Feldon, et al. 2008; Clark 2014). Major methods include hierarchical task analysis; goals, operators, methods and selections; knowledge analysis and documentation system; precursor or reason for action, result and interpretation of result; integrated task analysis model; critical decision method; work domain analysis; concept mapping; and think-aloud protocols among others (Clark, Feldon, et al. 2008; Clark, Feldon & Yates 2011; Hoffman & Lintern 2006).

The most popular study that combined CTA-based training design and simulation-based training together is the one using the Sherlock (1 & 2) intelligent tutoring system. This classic study conducted jointly by researchers at the University of Pittsburgh and US Airforce, has been noted in several publications such as Katz, Hall & Lesgold (1997); Lajoie & Lesgold (1992); Gott, Lesgold & Kane (1996); Gott, Lesgold & Kane (1996); Lajoie & Lesgold (1992); Lesgold et al. (1988); and Lesgold (1991). Though conducted in the late 1980's and 1990's, these studies have continued to be influential towards specifying the cognitive principles used in modern day time-compressed simulations. This intelligent computer-based coach provided experience to the learners on 'the most difficult aspects of cognitively-intense jobs in a simulated work environment' (Gott, Lesgold & Kane 1996, p. 2). This system packed meaningful problem-solving cases within a brief period of time. The cases were developed from actual real-world problem-solving process, and decisions flow captured using CTA methods from the experts troubleshooting F-15 aircraft electronic problems. The model of the system, the knowledge representations used by experts to solve the problem and cues/decisions they used to solve the problem were programmed. The cases progressed based on actions inputs by the novice learners while they were solving the apparent problems. The system incorporated not only on-demand coaching and feedback (critique of the student's activity) but also during task reflection and post-performance reflection, when necessary. In the end, the system also presented the experts' solutions to the same problems so that learners could learn from the experts (Lesgold 2001). To demonstrate this system's potential in accelerating proficiency, they tested three control groups of 54 F-15 avionics repair technicians. One group comprised master technicians with proven experience, while the second group was a control group which was comprised of untutored technicians and the third group was the experimental group who were tutored with the Sherlock system. The technicians were presented novel problems after they had practised a sequence of cases. They found that new learners using the Sherlock system were far more successful in troubleshooting novel problems than the experienced technicians. They suggested that those learners used their newly developed mental models and troubleshooting task schemata as 'interpretive structures' and 'flexible blueprints to guide their performance' to solve novel problems (Gott, Lesgold & Kane 1996, p. 5). They showed that novice technicians could score comparable troubleshooting proficiency scores to that of master technicians with over four years of job experience in just 20 hours of CTA-driven coaching over the three weeks. Gott and Lesgold (2000) reasoned that on-the-job experience takes years to attain and the job mostly provides routine opportunities, whereas the Sherlock system compressed that time by providing meaningful cases within a compressed timeframe.

Traditional studies have employed CTA methods to elicit the knowledge and information from experts and then designing training for the novices. While the primary goal of such studies was to investigate the effectiveness of training, it was seen that in some cases it also accelerated proficiency. For example, Schaafstal et al. (2000) conducted a study in 21 navy technicians responsible for repairing electronic equipment. The technicians formed two groups: one went through a regular traditional training course, while other group attended a course of troubleshooting designed using CTA methods. Both groups were given the same set of faults to troubleshoot. They were evaluated for the quality of the solution, systematicity of reasoning and functional understanding. It was observed that the technicians attending CTA-based course solved twice as many problems compared to the group who took the standard course. The findings of that study implied that learners took less time to reach to required performance thresholds, while their effectiveness was higher.

One study involving 26 new interns with similar backgrounds at the department of surgery were divided into two groups: one attending a standard "see-do-teach" course and the other group attending a CTA-based course. At the end of the respective courses, both groups appeared in the same practical and knowledge tests. It was noticed that the group with the CTA-based training required fewer attempts to find the vein (which means fewer needle punctures to locate the vein) and also showed a trend towards less time to complete the procedure (Velmahos et al. 2004). This study showed that time-to-training could be reduced, while at the same time accuracy and efficiency of the learners could be improved using CTA. The study also demonstrated that two and half months later the group of students who attended the CTA-based course retained their competence, even in a clinical stress environment. Retaining competence in the workplace and ability to perform to the same standards also implies that CTA may have potential to accelerate proficiency. On similar lines, Kirschenbaum, McInnis and Correll (2009) reported using the CTA method for training submarine sonar technicians. They reported that new sonar technicians exhibited faster acquisition of skills during training, as well as higher level of proficiency on the job. Training times were reduced by up to six months, and the technicians were able to start their on-the-job training sooner and carry out their work more effectively.

Incidentally, it is seen that CTA could be applied in critical and life-saving professions, which demand high accuracy and efficiency, especially medicine and surgery. The success of the CTA method in these fields is attributed to its ability to capture an accurate account of an expert's thinking process over the traditional self-reported techniques. This was demonstrated by several studies conducted by Clark. Clark, Pugh, et al. (2008) conducted a study with 11 trauma surgeons responsible for administrating emergency treatment in urban settings and war settings. The authors selected a task of insertion of a femoral artery shunt. Nine of the urban trauma surgeons unaided described the procedure. One Iraq-returned surgeon was interviewed using CTA methods. The eleventh surgeon, with experience in both settings, was used as the gold standard for comparative purposes. It was found that the account of surgeons matched 68% when using the CTA-based interview versus 31% without CTA support. This study demonstrated that CTA was far more successful in obtaining an accurate account of knowledge from experts. Subsequent papers by Clark supported evidence that experts not using CTA methods for interviews omitted nearly 70% of the necessary decision steps (Clark, Feldon, et al. 2008; Clark et al. 2011). Other studies using different surgical procedures found similar results in that experts omitted over 70% of the decision steps (Sullivan et al. 2014; Yates, Sullivan & Clark 2012). This evidence suggested that experts' cognitive processes can be accurately adapted in training materials which allow more effective expertise development. A significant acceleration to better performance was observed with training courses designed with CTA (Campbell, J et al. 2011; Clark et al. 2010) .

CTA methods were found to be complementary to other methods of curriculum development. Clark, Feldon, et al. (2008) asserted that CTA and 4C/ID models leveraged each other's strengths towards the development of expertise. As a note, 4C/ID (four components instructional design) model purports breaking a complex work into smaller recurrent part-tasks which can be practice independently, identifying just-in-time information that is required before and during part-task practice, integrating part-tasks into a concrete whole-tasks, and providing supportive information for non-recurrent portion of tasks (van Merriënboer, Clark & de Croock 2002). A study by Tjiam et al. (2012) supported the claim that CTA and 4C/ID models can be complementary to each other. In this study, 12 urologists who were experts at performing nephrostomy procedures were interviewed using CTA-based interviews to create a blueprint of the procedures. This information was then used to design simulation-based training using the 4C/ID approach, which allowed integrating part-task practice into the whole-task of performing the surgery. The more prevailing trend seen in the literature is that of using CTA methods to design simulation-based training or scenario-based training (Cannon-Bowers et al. 2013; Geissler et al. 2012; Munro & Clark 2013). In the context of the systems engineers' jobs, Squires et al. (2011) used a combination of CTA methods to develop competency maps or taxonomies of expertise in complex system engineering jobs. These competencies were then used to design an 'experience accelerator' simulator to shorten time-to-competence of systems engineers. In a recent study, Patterson et al. (2013) recruited fourteen paediatricians at a children's hospital. They were interviewed using critical decision methods (CDM) and were asked to describe a challenging incident they handled which involved diagnosis of sepsis. Scenarios were designed based on the cues expert physicians described that they used to recognise sepsis. These cues were then integrated into rich scenarios, and novice physicians were trained through scenario-based simulation. This method claimed to accelerate the expertise curve of novices.

The literature appears to place CTA-based methods as one of the forefront methods to accelerate the trajectory towards proficiency and expertise. It is apparent that CTA has become a standard method to identify 'the opportunities to improve performance through new forms of training, user interfaces, or decision aids' (Roth & O'Hara 2014, p. 320). The studies mentioned above have clearly shown innovative use of

CTA, providing evidence that when used appropriately with other expertise development techniques, CTA has the most potential in accelerating proficiency.

It appears that apart from high-risk professions such as medical, fire control and military, the applications of CTA methods in business settings is lacking, more so towards accelerating time-to-proficiency in the workplace. One possible explanation could be that CTA methods are very effort intensive endeavours. For instance, Clark and Estes (1996) indicated that efforts to design one-day CTA-based course from a standard two days long course were roughly 30 times. However, the financial benefits appear to outweigh such time-intensive efforts. For example, in the same study, Clark and Estes (1996) indicated that using the CTA-based design, the 'new course resulted in a 50% savings in training time on the part of the trainee managers'. In a meta-analysis of training literature, R Lee (2004) and Tofel-Grehl and Feldon (2013) reported an average of 53% to 87% post-training performance gain if training was designed using CTA. In addition, there have been some advances in using tools and software to rapidly conduct CTA (Zachary et al. 2012).

The key issue with the CTA-based method is its focus on tasks only. However, work in organisations is performed amidst several other variables, such as the environment and other influencing factors, which CTA-based methods do not address. In acknowledgement of this issue, a more encompassing approach called *cognitive work analysis* (CWA) was proposed by Rasmussen, Pejtersen and Goodstein (1994). The multi-stage framework was evolved to analyse how work is accomplished in complicated socio-technical systems. Socio-technical systems are the ones that rely heavily on the social process of communication and cooperation. This method involved conducting a range of analyses including work domain analysis (general characteristics and functional purposes of the system), control task analysis (tasks relevant to functional purposes of the system), analysis of possible strategies (to address the factors that may prevent a task from happening), team analysis, social and organisational analysis (interactions among people and with constraints), and analysis of workers' competencies (knowledge, training, skills and experience) to understand all possible interactions between work, worker and work elements (Ashoori & Burns 2013; Naikar, Lintern & Sanderson 2002; Naikar 2011; Roth & O'Hara 2014). Unlike CTA, there is no evidence of application of CWA towards accelerating performance despite several reviews and experimental studies being carried out (Demir, Abou-Jaoude & Kumral 2017; Naikar 2017).

2.5.3 Time-compressed simulations-based methods

On similar lines of the Sherlock training system, Fletcher (2010) demonstrated that using an automated troubleshooting expert system developed by DARPA, novice technicians solved 97% of the problems with 90% rated excellent compared to experienced technicians who produced 85% of the problem solved with 60% of the solutions rated excellent (see Hoffman et al. 2014). Studies on such intelligent systems have hypothesised that adaptive learning experience leads to accelerated performance. Implications of the studies on these coached-practice environments (e.g., Sherlock) in terms of strategies to accelerate expertise primarily included using authentic scenarios and difficult problems, making use of situated learning in a work context, employing models of expertise using CTA and coached cognitive apprenticeship principles, incorporating on-demand feedback, and making learners learn by doing and by reflection (Lesgold & Nahemow 2001; Lesgold 2001). These findings also indicated that simulation and feedback played an important role in accelerating proficiency. In a recent synthesis, Hoffman et al. (2014, p. 102) concluded that '[f]rom the Sherlock project, we know that it is possible to time-compress the experience-feedback cycle for acceleration from apprentice to journeyman proficiency levels'. The literature further suggested that time-compression was the most basic method to accelerate proficiency:

> All of the methods used in training for rapidization and for accelerated proficiency depend on one or another form of time (or experience) compression. One form is that of packing more varieties of experience into the training and not merely shortening the training.... A second sense of time compression is to truncate events that transpire within a scenario… (Hoffman et al. 2014, p. 118)

In other words, time-compression is achieved by developing a library of real and 'tough cases' and presenting them to learners within an accelerated time frame. 'Tough cases' are the challenging and difficult cases encountered in work. The literature also suggested various other ways such as simulation-based training, scenario-based training, game-based learning, scenario-based simulation and such variations to achieve time-compression.

The convergence of scenario-based learning with simulation-based learning has seen computer-based simulations replaced with expert-system based simulations. Recently, Arnold and Collier (2013) proposed simulating the experience through a web-based expert system which was designed based on a corpus of cases to accelerate expertise of financial knowledge workers. In that system, they developed a library of cases by interviewing the experts, understanding how they made the decisions in those cases and then tied those rationales to known financial principles. The new employees were trained through a web-based system which presented them the cases in a piecemeal fashion and asked learners to make decisions at different points in a case. Learners were able to compare their rationale with that of the experts, which acted as a feedback loop. Arnold and Collier (2013, p. 19) claimed that their research 'demonstrates the feasibility of one such methodology for using technology to accelerate experiential knowledge acquisition'. Further, recent studies have shown computer-based, expert-systems based and web-based intelligent tutoring systems using simulation-based training (Darzi et al. 2011; Sottilare & Goldberg 2012).

In complex domains, such as engineering, some researchers have proposed complex simulations shown to accelerate proficiency. In the 1980s, in the context of high-risk jobs such as air combat manoeuvring and air traffic controllers, time-compression was demonstrated by a technique called *above-real-time training* (ART). This method was based on the concept that learners are required to perform tasks to the same performance criteria as the real environment but the events or the sensory cues were presented to them in high-fidelity simulation at a faster rate than the actual real-time speed. Guckenberger, Uliano and Lane (1993) demonstrated a 50% time saving while training the high-performance skills like gunnery tasks in a tank and emergency procedures of F-16 aircraft using ART versus traditional real-time methods. They cited another study by Vidulich, Yeh and Schneider (1983) in which the technique had seen the application in training air traffic controllers. The controllers were found to be better at identifying the aircraft turn point in actual practice after they were trained with a simulator, which used an aeroplane approaching a speed 20 times faster than the actual speed. Guckenberger, Uliano and Lane (1993, p. 7) maintained that 'a new task that is practiced and learned in accelerated time (i.e., a difficult task) would require the learner to expend more than normal attention and effort, and hence accelerate the development of automaticity patterns'. Similar to the concept of 'tough cases', this method encompassed making training environment slightly more difficult than the real-world (like sports or athletics). Similar results were repeated in a study by Donderi et al. (2012) in which a PC-based simulation of fighter plane chase scenarios was used with 54 participants. The screen resolution was varied, and speed of simulation was increased in the second session. They found that post-test scores were significantly higher by using high-speed simulation. The studies on 'contextual interference' suggested that using more difficult tasks than actual difficulty levels, led to better long-term retention of skills (Paas & van Gog 2009).

Gamification has also emerged as a form of simulation which employs games or game-type concepts to replicate reality and provide close-to-reality experiences to the learners 'to accelerate the dialogue between knowledge and practice for efficient learning without risk of failure in real life' (Smeds 2003, p. 107). Learning by trial-and-error is a risky endeavour, especially for life-critical jobs. The idea of games, gamification, serious games through simulation or scenario-based games, is to create an immersive experience that engages learners and allows experiments by learners and trial and error among a range of variables to allow learners exposure to different situations. 'Well-constructed game-based scenarios can effectively compress several years of experience into a much smaller amount of learning time' (Higgins 2015, p. 8). A form of gamification and scenario-based training in the workplace is *decision-making exercises* (DMXs), as indicated by Klein (2003), and is used to accelerate complex decision-making in the workplace without taking professionals out of their job. In a study conducted by Harris-Thompson, Malek and Wiggins (2010) among board operators in oil and gas process control, they involved 17 CTA-based interviews to gather expert stories on critical, non-routine incidents. They analysed those scenarios and developed piecemeal scenarios called DMXs out of it. Appropriate additional data, as well as fabricated noise (irrelevant data similar to actual situation), were embedded into the piecemeal scenarios. The exercises were designed as paper-and-pen exercises feeding piece-meal information of a scenario to the new board operators as it would unfold in the real situation, but in time-compressed fashion. The learners were required to make decisions within specified time-frames based on the information available at a given moment. The study asserted that it was possible to accelerate cognitive skills and natural decision-making of professionals in natural settings.

As a corollary, the in some studies, CTA method was used in gamification while extending methods like tactical decision games (Schmitt 1996) or decision-making exercises (Klein 1993, 1998, 2003) by seeking expert view or rationale for their decisions. Demonstrating such forms of gamification, Hintze (2008) evolved a technique called *ShadowBox*, which allows novices to follow the thinking of experts. He conducted an experimental study among 43 fire department officers. They were divided into three groups: control, expert and experimental. Experts had more than 15 years' experience, while the control and experimental group represented new employees. The method employed interpretation of pre-design scenarios and comparing the interpretations with that of the experts. The method employed the expert modelling as a way to allow trainees to discover what experts believed was important in a situation and how they focused their attention (Borders et al. 2015; Klein & Borders 2016; Klein, Hintze & Saab 2013). This method used the CTA method for knowledge elicitation and to capture how experts viewed and solved a given situation. However, during the facilitation, expert presence was not required. This method appeared to accelerate the decision-making of the novice fire control officers. In other studies, Klein and Borders (2016, p. 270) applied the technique of *ShadowBox* in a study in the defence setting on 59 commissioned and non-commissioned officers of the army. They were divided into two groups: one had access to the expert to seek feedback, while the other group did not have any such option. Both groups were exposed to four challenging scenarios, and their responses to the actions they would take were recorded. The findings showed that for groups who received feedback from experts, their choices and ranking of course of actions matched those of the experts. The researchers concluded that 'it is possible to train cognitive skills in a reasonably short amount of time and in a way that can scale up' (Klein & Borders 2016, p. 276). They claimed: 'ShadowBox training can be seen as a platform for achieving rapidized training, higher levels of proficiency (accelerated proficiency), better transfer (rapidised transposition), and facilitated retention' (Klein & Borders (2016, p. 270).

As an alternative, Vandergriff (2012) proposed a model called *adaptive course model* (ACM) which employed scenario-based tactical decision games presented to learners under time constraints and uncertainty. Learners were required to solve the problem and justify the solution. ACM tended to add on to the experience of the learner. The focus was on the ability to quickly review the problem, prepare a solution and suggest a course of action. The model involved group discussions as an additional technique. The games were presented to the learners in progressively increasing difficulty. Employing experiential learning and a recognition-primed decision-making (RPD) process, this model was believed to accelerate decision-making skills.

While computer-based simulations were grounded in expertise, development principles were used for problem-solving, troubleshooting, diagnostic type of problem domains. However, for business problem solving, a different approach is needed. The literature indicated that immersive strategies showed promise in accelerating proficiency in the workplace for skills like naturalistic decision-making or leadership because it can deliver valuable experiences sooner than they may be experienced on the job. Such immersive strategies included simulation, game-based learning, tabletop exercises, interactive stories, board games and alternate reality games. Some researchers used immersive simulated games to accelerate leadership skills which incorporate storytelling and real-time feedback from leaders (Backus et al. 2010). These games involved a 'series of turns to allow players to try different game strategies and learn from them' (id. 147). Extending gamification further, Grossman et al. (2013) specified that decision-making expertise could be accelerated using simulation-based games in the workplace, among other strategies.

In an earlier study conducted by DiBello (1996), they demonstrated a time-compressed full-scale business scenario called OpSim (operational simulation) as a technique to accelerate higher-order skills in actual business settings. The shop floor workers acquired mastery in a computer-based material management system within two months, as opposed to the usual 18 to 24 months. In a subsequent study at a biotech firm, DiBello, Missildine and Struttman (2009) simulated time-compressed replica of business operations. They simulated business activities to be carried out in the normal course of six months into a few "game months" with the same target as actual business activities. The researchers reported that they could provide transferable expertise to the workplace, and the organisation realised the benefits of accelerated expertise that were gained over a few days rather than several years. DiBello and Missildine (2008) reported similar results in another study. DiBello and Missildine (2011) extended the operational simulation methodology into the virtual world using immersive computer technology. They maintained that a technology-enhanced immersive virtual world provided a 'number of opportunities for enhanced accelerated learning, and the rehearsal and planning of complex strategies and tactical plans' (DiBello & Missildine 2011, p. 19). Their simulation was based on the theory of showing learners their flawed mental model and helping them to un-learn it and then reorganising the new mental model that allowed them to acquire a sustainable change in their behaviour in a shorter time (DiBello & Missildine 2011, p. 17). Another premise of their approach was that expertise development required repeated encounters with highly challenging problems, active problem-solving and immediate performance feedback (DiBello & Missildine 2011, p. 17). To accelerate expertise, they proposed that providing multiple failures on 'tough cases' within a compressed time-frame allowed learners to recognise their flawed mental model quickly.

The *Production and Control Journal* dedicated one full issue to studies on simulation for accelerated learning in production settings which spanned the food supply chain, electrical engineering, production planning, project management and corporate management, problem-solving and change management (see Smeds 2003). In other complex jobs, such as engineering, serious simulations have also been introduced. Slootmaker et al. (2014, p. 563) called this as '*scenario-based serious games* are games where learners are placed in complex problem spaces, which mimic real world situations'. Robinson and Pennotti (2013, p. 2) designed multiple simulations exposing engineers responsible for designing complex systems to different challenges of complexity, confusion, decision-making and leadership. They observed that '[e]ngineers at different levels of experience, who have been immersed in these simulations, have demonstrated insights usually associated with time on the job. This raises the possibility that useful experience might be acquired at the dramatically reduced time, cost and risk' (Robinson & Pennotti 2013, p. 2).

The results of most of the simulation studies conducted have shown improved performance, and in several cases, accelerated performance. Researchers have reported that learners need fewer real-world hours by using simulators and overall experience was accelerated (Brudnicki, Ethier & Chastain 2007; Butler 2012; Clavarelli, Platte & Powers 2009; Robinson & Pennotti 2013). That also meant that learners spent more time in the simulator than traditional course learners did. For those reasons, Ward, Williams and Hancock (2006) commented that simulation-based training may not necessarily be a time-efficient method of training. However, when the goal is accelerating proficiency, training duration may be less of a consideration. The simulation also played a role in manufacturing events which were known to be rare.

2.5.4 Case-based and scenario-based methods

Researchers have maintained that learning around scenarios, cases or problems provided the contextual experience of real-world, or as close to the real-world, is key to gaining a higher level of expertise (Clark & Mayer 2013). Popularly known as scenario-based learning (SBL), the variations of these methods are known as problem-based learning, project-based learning, and case-based learning. These methods situate knowledge in a real-world context. 'After all, expertise is based on experience. With a well-designed program of SBL you can compress experience spanning years in the work environment, into a few hours of training time' (Clark 2009, p. 84). These techniques have attempted to provide a real-world experience or equivalent to novices to begin the process of getting them to think like experts. The learning started with a real-life or close to real-life problem or scenario and participants learned how to analyse a problem, identify relevant facts and generate hypotheses, identify necessary information/knowledge for solving the problem and make reasonable judgements about solving the problem (Buch & Wolff 2000). These interventions, due to their real-world context and appropriate guidance to solve problems, held significant potential to accelerate expertise (Jonassen & Hung 2008). Fundamentally, all of these approaches have created learning interventions around well-constructed problems from the real-world which learners were required to solve (Clark & Mayer 2013; Jonassen & Hernandez-Serrano 2002; Thomsen et al. 2010). This approach was seen to be the only feasible method in which risks of the actual job were not permissible.

However, the key idea to accelerate proficiency is time-compression of scenarios. While scenario-based methods hold the potential to accelerate proficiency, if the cases chosen are not representative of reality, the training becomes disconnected from the workplace when learning is complex in nature (Vaughan 2008). Selecting the right problems was identified as a key determinant of the effectiveness of these methods (Jonassen & Hung 2008). Two kinds of problems have been suggested in the literature. Bjork (2013) suggested adding 'desirable difficulties' into training as a problem. Desirable difficulties were useful failures, bugs or mistakes intentionally introduced into the learning that makes a learner struggle. The desirable difficulties, though they impeded the initial rate of skill acquisition, were seen to accelerate the transfer of abilities to solve tougher problems. Studies using the desirable difficulties approach have been conducted for many years. Doane et al. (1996) performed an experiment in which they gave difficult problems of discrimination to one group of participants and simpler problems to another group. At a later stage when both groups were given a block of difficult problems to discriminate, they found that learners who started with difficult problems first, outperformed compared to the control group learners who start with simpler problems first. On those lines, Pandy et al. (2004) demonstrated the *How People Learn* (HPL) framework (Bransford et al. 2004) could accelerate the learning of engineering students. They advocated challenge-based instruction accelerate expertise development. 'These findings indicate that challenge-based instruction, when combined with an intellectually engaging curriculum and principled instructional design, can accelerate the trajectory of novice-to-expert development in bioengineering education' (Pandy et al. 2004, p. 220).

On the other hand, for developing higher-level proficiency, a concept of 'tough case time compression' is suggested which involved creating a library of tough cases and then exposing the learners to the tough cases within a short time (Hoffman et al. 2010, p. 14). This involved exposing learners to tough or difficult cases which allowed them to recognise their flawed mental models. 'Accelerated proficiency can be achieved through the use of case-based instruction and realistic tough cases with focus on errors and "desirable difficulties"' (Hoffman, Feltovich, et al. 2010). In a recent research study, Soule (2016) tested the hypothesis that difficult cases could accelerate the expertise of the learner. He concluded that expertise in complex decision-making was accelerated because tough cases triggered both experiential and social cognitive learning in the single process. He also asserted that learning involved in tough cases was 'substantial experiential, social, emotional, and practical features' (Soule 2016, p. 172).

Collectively, the literature review indicates that desirable difficulties appeared to accelerate post-training transfer of beginners, the tough cases, on the other hand, appeared to accelerate proficiency on the higher end of the scale. The tough cases suggest developing adaptive expertise in handling non-routine, novel and unfamiliar situations (Hesketh & Ivancic 2002). To represent expertise to handle unfamiliar novel problems, early researchers developed a construct of adaptive expertise and differentiated it from routine expertise (Hatano & Inagaki 1986). 'Adaptive experts not only have knowledge that is well organised, but also display the ability to transfer their knowledge, skills, beliefs, and attitudes to new situations' (Pandy et al. 2004, p. 211). Adaptive experts developed some form of conceptual skills with which they were more effective in novel situations than non-routine experts (VanLehn & Chi 2012). The adaptive experts built extra knowledge about the task domain (such as the mental model of structure and function of a system) that helped them solve novel problems in the new domain. Important components of adaptive expertise were conceptual abstraction, knowledge structures, and representation and pattern recognition (Feldon 2006).

Adaptive expertise becomes important from the point of accelerating proficiency as: 'Transfer, or the ability to use knowledge flexibly and effectively across application areas, is an important component of proficiency' (Hoffman et al. 2014, p. 4). Based on the assumption that adaptive expertise would take longer to achieve, researchers maintained that '[t]raining must promote flexibility and adaptability' to address complexity (Hoffman et al. 2008, p. 5.3). Adaptive expertise methods have been suggested as key methods to accelerate proficiency. Schwartz et al. (2005) established that knowledge representation accelerated the rate at which an expert solved novel problems. That is why it was believed that the key aspect of developing adaptability and flexibility was to prepare learners for significant complexity. That was the fundamental premise of CFT (Spiro et al. 1992) and CTT (Klein & Baxter 2009).

One example of accelerating expertise in a complex situation was using tough cases to develop adaptive performance is demonstrated in a program called *think like a commander* (TLAC). For example, Shadrick, Lussier and Fultz (2007) reported an experiment in which they subjected 143 army officers to three challenging and dynamic tactical problems. Officers were exposed to several scenarios in a compressed time-frame; they were coached on how an expert would think in the same scenario, and learners were allowed to correct their mental model and decision-making. A key focus of this program was to provide officers with the ability to evaluate rapidly changing situations through deliberate practice on several scenarios and develop an understanding of an expert tactician's thinking pattern. Shadrick, Lussier and Fultz (2007, p. 5) found that officers trained through TLAC performed better in adaptive thinking skills than the officers having lived the real-world experience. They concluded that 'deliberately training complex cognitive skills may be substantially more effective and efficient than the experiential learning methods that take place in live and virtual environments' (id. 5). That method was believed to accelerate officers' proficiency in making tactical decisions, as reported in a number of studies by Shadrick et al. (Shadrick & Lussier 2009). The approach suggested that practice activities allowed the subjects to ingrain the task and to perform the task under a variety of conditions that led to developing the ability to perform the task with little or no conscious attention, as opposed to the trial-and-error method of the real-world (id. 18).

A similar approach was taken by van den Bosch, Helsdingen and de Beer (2004) in a study in which they developed a number of scenarios about air defence and trainees who were provided a range of information to make decisions, defend their positions and explain their plans in a given situation. In three different studies, adaptive flexibility was found to be a predictor of performance, as well as acceleration. The first study involved 140 expert and novice business people solving complex problems in a business simulation of a chocolate factory (Güss et al. 2017). The second study involved 14 US SWAT officers who were monitored for their in-event real-time decision-making under real situations (Harris et al. 2017). The third study involved 23 expert and novice authorised firearms officers during armed confrontations (Boulton & Cole 2016). These three studies proposed exposing performers to a range of varied real scenarios that would lead to developing adaptive flexibility, which in turn accelerates expertise.

Bransford and Schwartz (2009, p. 765) contended that a learner's preparation to absorb new information and develop performance to new standards also was a determining factor for adaptive expertise development and helping them "work smarter". In the context of adaptive expertise, developing conceptual skills and principles of domains to prepare learners for future roles and demands was another area which had implications on accelerating proficiency. In a case study involving 44 college students with an algebra background but no background on statistics, VanLehn and Chi (2012) conducted an experiment. The participants were divided into two groups. The first group were given domain principles of probability with the help of an intelligent tutoring system and asked to solve some problems. They were not allowed to go to the next domain principle until they solved a given problem. The other group were asked to solve problems whichever way they wanted. Then, both groups were taught physics principles. Researchers found that the group which was taught explicit problem-solving strategy in probability showed improved performance in the physics task domain over the other group of students who were not provided such principle-based knowledge. They concluded that when students were taught using principle-based learning, and students were taught to focus on conceptual skills rather than the procedures of a domain, it tended to accelerate the rate at which they learned a new task domain. They stated that *acceleration of future learning* (AFL) occurred when prior knowledge increased the rate at which some students learn, relative to others (id. 31). Future learning was also believed to be accelerated by teaching students the metacognitive skills and learning-to-learn skills, note taking, and explanations, as VanLehn and Chi (2012, p. 32) contended: 'These are domain-independent skills (e.g., selfmonitoring, note taking, self-explanation), in that they can in principle accelerate the learning of almost any content'.

Clark and Feldon (2008) suggested some training strategies to build adaptive expertise: application environment, motivation, increasing novelty, variable practice, and targeted feedback. Clark (2006) supported that by providing varied practice and declarative knowledge that allowed the learners to adopt a procedure to handle a novel situation. Some researchers have recommended using training design strategies as advance organisers, analogies, guided discovery, error-based training, metacognitive instruction, learner control, and mastery-oriented learning (Smith et al. 1997). In a review of the training literature, Lazzara et al. (2010) recommended eight training strategies which worked well for adaptive expertise, including: cue-recognition training, sense-making training, planning and forecasting, meta-cognition skills training, error-based training, and guided self or team correction.

The research on adaptive expertise suggested that such methods might accelerate proficiency. Furthermore, it also suggested the applicability of the concepts from CTT and CFT to develop adaptive expertise.

2.5.5 Representative part-task approach

Most of the methods available in the literature are whole-task methods, in which a particular task is taught as a whole (van Merriënboer, Clark & de Croock 2002). However, a new method of representative part-task approach was evolved by Van Merriënboer & Kester (2008), which extended their previous work on whole-task. The key idea of the part-task technique is to isolate a specific sub-skill and teach within a whole-task to build skills on the part-task. In a study conducted by Klein et al. (1997) among 30 US Marin corps squad leaders, they interviewed several fire ground commanders and workers in a number of other high-risk professions in dynamic situations to understand how professionals make decisions and how they evaluate options. He found that experts typically made decisions by recognising the aspects of a new situation by comparing it to the previous situation. He called this as *recognition primed decision Making* (RPD) (Klein 1993). In later studies, Klein isolated the pattern recognition sub-skill as a representative part-task and then used that to accelerate the decision-making of a novice (Klein et al. 1997; Klein 1997, 1998).

Fadde (2007) extended this recognition technique using principles of expertise studies such as Ericsson and Charness (1994) and developed an approach called *expertise-based training* (XBT). He maintained that any complex skills like intuitive decision-making can be broken into sub-skills or sub-tasks such as detection, categorization, and prediction, situational awareness and pattern recognition. Once decoupled, one can then develop targeted instructional design activities in workplace settings to accelerate those sub-skills (Fadde 2009a). Fadde (2007) applied this approach to baseball and called the method *temporal occlusion* in which part-task practice of pitch recognition skills were taught using video-based or computer-based simulation. Once the sub-skill of pitch recognition was mastered in video-based or computer-based training, the skill was integrated into real drill practice by having a player to shout out aloud the incoming pitch. The XBT approach involved designing instructional interventions on repurposing those tasks which have been identified as differentiators between experts and novices (Fadde 2009c). In these interventions, the sub-skills that led to expertise were systematically targeted using a part-task approach which could accelerate the performers towards a higher level of proficiency in whole-tasks.

In several studies, mainly in baseball and similar sports, evidence of using this approach were shown (Fadde 2007, 2009b, 2009c, 2010, 2012, 2013). A similar approach has been reported in soccer (Belling, Suss & Ward 2014a); baseball (Belling, Sada & Ward 2015); tennis (Williams et al. 2002); and cricket (Müller & Abernethy 2014). Particularly, the XBT approach has seen applications in high-performance sports (Fadde (2016), classroom teaching (Fadde & Sullivan 2013), online masters programs (Tokmak, Baturay & Fadde 2013) and nursing education (Razer, Blair & Fadde 2015).

In an early study, Starkes and Lindley (1994, p. 218) demonstrated that decision-making time of baseball players was reduced by approximately 540 milliseconds just in six video sessions. This time is enough for them to anticipate an opponent's move or making their own decisions. Subsequently, several of the studies showed that representative tasks can be trained using video simulations or computer-based programs which can be run in workplace settings (Belling, Sada & Ward 2015; Belling, Suss & Ward 2014a, 2014b; Fadde 2007, 2009a, 2012, 2013). A computer or video-based training on representative tasks was believed to be accelerating situational awareness of novices. Recently, the literature has reported the application of the XBT approach using video for accelerating proficiency of science teachers (Sancar-Tokmak 2013). Another variation of this strategy was to integrate model-based feedback via video-simulation. In a university education setting, a study conducted by Fadde (2012) on 55 university students reported that the participants in a group which received video-based training annotated with expert feedback aligned more with the content expert than did participants in the control group who did not receive such training.

The key implication of representative part-task methods is to isolate representative sub-skills and then put focused, deliberate activities in the workplace or in training settings to conduct practice on those sub-skills to allow the learners to use it in a whole-task manner as part of the larger work.

2.5.6 Knowledge capture methods

Accelerating knowledge acquisition is one key goal identified by researchers. Hoffman, Feltovich, et al. (2010, p. 28) reasoned that '[t]o accelerate proficiency, one must accelerate the acquisition of knowledge that is extensive and highly organized'. Alongside training interventions, knowledge capture and sharing in organisations helped new professionals to make quick decisions and accelerate their own expertise. In a study conducted among 100 top-level executives and next-in-line executives in Fortune 500 companies, Baxter (2013) demonstrated that proficiency or expertise in complex workplace skills like strategic thinking, situational awareness, and decision-making, could be accelerated by capturing and using tacit knowledge. She demonstrated that tacit knowledge could be captured through knowledge elicitation methods such as in-depth interviews of senior professionals on how they made a decision in a case. This study demonstrated another use of CTA to capture knowledge and quickly transfer to junior practitioners, as opposed to the traditional approach of designing training programs. The captured knowledge was then transformed into scenarios and presented to professionals to practice decision-making and receive feedback from senior professionals.

In two separate studies, one using a case study on 19 employees at a call centre (McQueen & Chen 2010) and the other using in-depth interviews with 15 client-facing consultants at a levy-fund company (McQueen & Janson 2016), it was found that scripting the tacit knowledge led to accelerating the speed to proficiency in handling clients. Hoffman et al. (2008) supported knowledge capture and sharing as a method to accelerate proficiency. However, they also cautioned that 'knowledge management by knowledge capture and knowledge repositories is only a part of the solution to workforce problems' (p. 3.6).

2.5.7 Technology-based methods

Most modern-day simulation methods use some form of technology. Some technologies are used in the workplace and in training to improve performance. Performance support systems and automation is also argued as a means of accelerating proficiency (Hoffman et al. 2014). A multitude of modern technologies have been used to accelerate expertise in controlled environments in a handful of studies. For example, Raphael et al. (2009) presented an 'adaptive performance trainer' system that involves modelling an expert in terms of 'psychophysiological profile' of expertise in the form of an EEG signature and other physiological metrics that change during the stages of learning. The system provides continuous psychophysical monitoring and feedback to the trainee and customising the training based on that feedback. This approach has been demonstrated to accelerate skill acquisition in marksmen training (Behneman et al. 2012).

Technology offers distinct advantages in accelerating learning and allows learners to learn more content in a short time. Sottilare and Goldberg (2012) proposed that a technology-based tutoring system could minimise intrinsic cognitive load by appropriately selecting the problems of appropriate difficulty, while presenting information that increases the germane load (domain-specific activities) as per cognitive load theory (CLT). Such a system could use multiple representations of information or content to apply to flexible mental models, as per CFT. Lastly, such a system can be designed which would allow learners to recognise their flaws in their current mental models and then discard flawed models in favour or less flawed models, as per CTT. More contemporary techniques, such as blended learning and a blend of online and face-to-face training, are believed to accelerate learning. For example, in a controlled group study, Patchan et al. (2015) found that students learned basic and additional content at a considerably higher rate when blended learning was used via online technologies. While the literature indicates that technology supports learning flexibly and accelerates learning, Jipp (2016, p. 92) argued the opposite view that automation of information hinders expertise development because such automation does not put any load on working memory.

2.5.8 Accelerated learning methods

One concept that is interrelated with accelerated proficiency is that of accelerated learning. In the literature *accelerated learning* is often used synonymously with the intent of accelerating proficiency and accelerating expertise. Two schools of thoughts have emerged. In more traditional terms, Adams, Karthaus and Rehak (2011, p. 1) described it as: 'Accelerated learning allows a shortened timeframe for learning with a comparative amount of material learned and retained'. Historically, accelerated learning has been considered as a set of techniques to enable students to think fast and learn more (Rose 2000). Over the years, accelerated learning has become a buzzword. The literature review indicated a range of claims and methods towards accelerating learning. For instance: brain-based learning (Smith & Call 1999); blended online learning (Patchan et al. 2015); accelerated fast-track training programs (Trekles & Sims 2013); social learning and involvement (Meier 2000); experiential learning (Abston & Rhodes 2013); intelligent computer-based tutoring (Sottilare & Goldberg 2012); electrocardiograph feedback to accelerate learning (Berka et al. 2010); and as extreme as direct current stimulation to the brain (McKinley et al. 2013). However, none of the accelerated learning viewpoints appear to match.

In the context of this thesis, some studies have attempted to accelerate learning of employees and teams in the workplace (Lynn, Akgün & Keskin 2003; Seow et al. 2005). In an organisational context, accelerated learning means to learn some task in a shorter time and be able to produce results. Andrews and Fitzgerald (2010, p. 5) expressed accelerated learning in terms of its goal to 'speed up knowledge acquisition in ways that are not detrimental to learning'. Hoffman, Feltovich, et al. (2010) asserted that accelerated learning means several things including the idea of training people to the minimal level of proficiency in a shorter time; getting individuals to achieve higher levels of proficiency at a faster rate; and making learning less prone to decay. In a subsequent development, Hoffman, Andrews and Feltovich (2012) considered accelerated learning as an umbrella concept, of which accelerated proficiency is a sub-set:

> "Accelerated learning" refers not only to the idea of hastening the achievement of basic-level proficiency; it reaches across the proficiency scale to the question of how to accelerate the achievement of expertise, and whether that is even possible. (Hoffman, Andrews & Feltovich 2012, p. 8)

The traditional view of accelerated learning, and the one submitted by Hoffman (Hoffman, Feltovich, et al. 2010; Hoffman & Andrews 2012; Hoffman, Andrews & Feltovich 2012) do not seem to intersect with each other. Accelerated learning continues to be part of any accelerated proficiency discussions for the lack of any clear-cut distinction or characterisation. Whether to accelerate learning or accelerate proficiency, several approaches have been suggested as leverage points for acceleration: tapping the right theories; studying how mentors do it; initiating a tough-case time compression; implementing blocked practice sequenced by complexity and readiness level; introducing problem-based learning with reduced scaffolding; mentoring; using task variants; developing team skills; requiring appropriately timed meaningful corrective feedback; playing computer games, utilising simulation and immersion; using scenario-based training; presenting case-based instructions with desirable difficulties; compressing a library of tough cases in a short time; presenting decision-making exercises; providing virtual reality or operational simulation; stretching of skills; building knowledge structures; and implementing cognitive tutoring systems (Andrews & Fitzgerald 2010; Hoffman et al. 2008, 2009, 2014; Hoffman, Andrews & Feltovich 2012; Hoffman & Andrews 2012; Hoffman, Feltovich, et al. 2010). On those lines, Jung, Kim and Reigeluth (2016) presented instructional guidelines to accelerate proficiency of journeymen built upon the deliberate performance model (as explained in next sub-section) of Fadde and Klein (2010, 2012).

2.5.9 Workplace training/learning methods

On-the-job training has been a way to impart necessary experience and practice to a new employee to meet job expectations. Hoffman et al. (2008, p. 7.4) observed that '[o]n-the-job training is the first, and often only, strategy corporations rely on for learning—indeed, as much as 60% of all training is on-the-job training'. Extending training into the workplace is challenging because workplaces are considered as unstructured entities. Rosenbaum and Williams (2004) noted that 70% to 80% of learning happens on the job through unstructured activities that hamper speed to proficiency. Contrary to this, Billett (2004) negated the common arguments of viewing workplace learning as an unstructured or informal entity. Rather, he believed that 'workplace activities and interactions are highly structured and regulated' (Billett 2004, p. 314). He further stressed that workplace participatory activities engaged professionals in developing competence leading to making workplaces as a legitimate learning environment.

While the previous methods discussed were implanted through some training intervention (mostly in a classroom or controlled setting), accelerating proficiency in the workplace is a key challenge for organisations. In their seminal work, Collins, Brown and Newman (1989) developed a method of direct modelling of experts in performing complex cognitive tasks. They called the approach *cognitive apprenticeship* and defined it as 'learning through guided experience on cognitive and metacognitive, rather than physical, skills and processes' (Collins, Brown & Newman 1989, p. 456). Fundamentally, the cognitive apprenticeship challenged the traditional apprenticeship model's ability in delivering cognitive skills in situated settings. When using cognitive skills such as decision-making or performing other complex tasks, most of the thinking is internal to the performer. While in traditional apprenticeship, the learner builds his skills under a mentor by direct observation, and it becomes challenging when cognitive skills are involved. The main premise of the cognitive apprenticeship model was to make thinking visible through actions or other means: 'Applying apprenticeship methods to largely cognitive skills require [*sic*] the externalization of processes that are usually carried out internally' (Collins, Brown & Newman 1987, p. 4). From a process standpoint, the methodology involved breaking larger or more complex tasks into smaller tasks which were within the *zone of proximal development* (Vygotsky 1978) or within the reach of the learner, and then support and offer guidance in situated settings on authentic and representative tasks, rather than classroom type tasks.

The cognitive apprenticeship process consisted of six key components: modelling, coaching, scaffolding (and fading), articulation, reflection, and exploration. Modelling involved revealing knowledge structures used by an expert and having him/her to externalise the process, actions or thinking. This included factual or conceptual knowledge, heuristics and strategies. Coaching involved observing learners and offering them prompts, feedback and questions. Scaffolding involved support, suggestions or cues provided during the task execution to the learner. Reflection involved bringing moments when learners could compare their processes with that of an expert. Articulation involved learners to explain, summarise and clarify or ask questions. Lastly, exploration involved making learners explore new goals and formulate new tests for their hypotheses (Druckman & Bjork 1991; Woolley & Jarvis 2007, p. 75). The cognitive apprenticeship model also incorporates several approaches including a model of expertise, collaborative learning, communities of practice and mentoring (Dennen & Burner 2008; Lajoie 2009).

Cash et al. (1996) studied the effect of cognitive apprenticeship in 28 college students taking up automotive air-conditioning training courses. Students were divided into two groups. They were measured at three time periods. The group receiving experimental treatment of cognitive apprenticeship scored significantly higher than the other group. They found that compared to the classroom-based methodology, cognitive apprenticeship resulted in a more effective acquisition of technical concepts and troubleshooting skills. Stalmeijer et al. (2013) in a study of 17 clinical teachers also confirmed that clinical teaching practice followed cognitive apprenticeship.

Though applied in several educational settings, the main implication of the cognitive apprenticeship model is its application during everyday practice in the workplace. In business studies, Backus et al. (2010) suggested two methods to accelerate leadership development: (1) immersive learning such as simulations; and (2) cognitive apprenticeship. They contended that cognitive apprenticeship offered an immersive solution considering the dynamics of the workplace. In a review of research studies on six components of cognitive apprenticeship, Dennen and Burner (2008, p. 436) affirmed that cognitive apprenticeship matches with how learning happens in the workplace:

> Empirical studies have confirmed much of what theories have suggested: (1) that the cognitive apprenticeship model is an accurate description of how learning occurs naturally as part of everyday life and social interactions, and (2) that the instructional strategies that have been extracted from these observations of everyday life can be designed into more formal learning contexts with positive effect.

Recently, Kuchenbrod (2016) used CTA and the DACUM (design a curriculum) process to accelerate the expertise of live-burn instructors in the firefighting domain. Their method involved using CTA-type analysis with subject matter experts to capture the necessary skills required for the occupation, identifying a required proficiency level for each skill and then designing a curriculum for proficiency. Using the learner's self-assessment and demonstration of the skills to the desired proficiency quickly moved the learner to the next skills, thus, leading to shorter time-to-proficiency for the job. The key implication of cognitive apprenticeship and guided mentoring was its ability to provide authentic and highly job-specific learning and experience to the performer. Such authentic learning appears to accelerate learning. Trekles and Sims (2013) stated:

> When learners engage in authentic learning situations, they have the opportunity to synthesize all of the skills and concepts that they have learned thus far, allowing them to develop practice that in turn leads to the development of more extensive and complex schemata and expertise regarding the topic of study. (Trekles & Sims 2013, sec. method, para 1)

A variation of the cognitive apprenticeship is seen as an approach popularly known as *structured on-the-job training* (S-OJT), which was reviewed in sub-section 2.5.1 in the workplace (Jacobs 2014a). Evidence suggests that technology can be used to design all of the six components of cognitive apprenticeship (modelling, coaching, scaffolding (and fading), articulation, reflection, and exploration) as described in previous paragraphs. The demonstration on the coached-practice environment and computer-based intelligent tutoring systems such as the Sherlock system were examples of the technology-assisted cognitive apprenticeship model (Collins 1990; Gott 1988; Katz, Hall & Lesgold 1997; Lesgold et al. 1988; Lesgold 1991). Graesser, McNamara & VanLehn (2005) designed a computer-based learning environment which supported self-explanation and coaching students in metacognitive strategies. The study demonstrated that a deeper level of metacognitive skills could be developed using computer-based systems. In the last two decades, several researchers demonstrated the use of cognitive apprenticeship through computer-based, technology-based or web-based solution to provide expert guidance to the performers (Boling & Beatty 2010; Hausmann, van de Sande & VanLehn 2008; Hong et al. 2007; Jin & Corbett 2011; Kuo et al. 2012; Lesgold & Nahemow 2001; Mitrovic, Ohlsson & Barrow 2013; Ong & Ramachandran 2003; Sottilare & Goldberg 2012). Thus, the literature suggests that cognitive apprenticeship methods, either as they are or through technology, are a powerful accelerator of proficiency.

The deliberate practice mechanism, as proposed by Ericsson et al. (1993), has been investigated for its applicability to the workplace also. In a study involving 100 sales agents working for 10 German insurance companies, Sonnentag and Kleine (2000) found that workplace activities such as extensive preparation of task accomplishment, gathering information from domain experts, or seeking feedback can be used to develop performance through deliberate practice. They noted that performance was directly associated with the amount of time spent on the deliberate practice of those work-related activities. They implied that the deliberate practice mechanism can also be used in work settings which include a range of usual job activities and tasks. However, they also cautioned about the complexity of work performance as 'a number of factors in addition to deliberate practice that might impact an individual's work performance.... these factors override the effects of deliberate practice' (Sonnentag & Kleine 2000, p. 90).

On the contrary to this attempt to apply deliberate practice mechanism in business settings, Fadde and Klein (2010, 2012) argued that professionals and business personnel do not have the time and luxury to engage in a narrow set of skills and years to engage in the focused, deliberate practice besides their regular roles. Another aspect is that job rotation — reassignments to different roles and other job duties — precludes the conscientious deliberate practice on specific skill sets at workplace settings (Hoffman et al. 2014). Therefore, deliberate practice mechanisms may not work for organisations and in particular in the job involving knowledge work. Hoffman, Feltovich, et al. (2010, p. 402) quoted Gary Klein's perspective: 'Deliberate practice usually involves motor or perceptual-motor skills, whereas most of the skills needed in business and industry involve cognitive work'.

To address this challenge, Fadde and Klein (2010, 2012) proposed a framework called *deliberate performance*, also called *action learning activities*, based on routine day-to-day workplace events as the opportunities for professional and business people to accelerate expertise in domain-specific tacit knowledge and intuitive expertise. They intended to incorporate tacit knowledge to develop expertise-based intuition and to base activities on everyday situations that were authentic to the particular workplace and job performance and were mostly self-guided. They suggested doing so by engaging the individuals in routine work activities using on-the-job or just-in-time training opportunities. They proposed it as 'an instructional method designed to accelerate the process by making it more systematic, that is, more drill-like (in the fashion of deliberate practice)' (Fadde & Klein 2012, p. 12). This expertise in natural settings could be accelerated using four types of deliberate performance exercises: estimation, experimentation, extrapolation and explanation (Fadde & Klein 2010). Estimation of time and resources needed to complete a task or project was an important skill that increased awareness of the individual. Experimentation was trying new ways to do the things allowing professions to apply induction, deduction and abduction processes. Extrapolation referred to deliberate exercises that allowed professions to reuse their previously learned information or experiences. The last exercise they recommended was an explanation, which includes a group analysis of a recent event or project. Fadde and Klein (2010) positioned this feedback and coaching were deemed essential components of deliberate performance. Recently, Jung, Kim and Reigeluth (2016) developed instructional guidelines based on the deliberate performance model and proposed four phases – development plan, action, reflection on action and remedies to accelerate the proficiency of journeymen. However, there are no studies confirming this framework to-date.

Professionals normally learn and accelerate their skill acquisition while handling real assignments, challenging tasks and projects and practising on their job (Eraut 1994, 2004, 2007a, 2007b). Learning at work is an expectation and a necessity, rather than a good-to-have protocol: 'Competent professionals are busy with everyday tasks. Thus, learning for journeymen mostly takes place by participating in projects' (Jung, Kim & Reigeluth 2016, p. 61). In preliminary findings, Attri and Wu (2015, p. 13) noted that 'rather than waiting for workplace to provide experiences, if designers can leverage day-to-day routine at workplace, systematically design experiences and pack those in a compressed timeframe, the time-to-proficiency could be accelerated.' However, workplace learning is subject to opportunities and may offer only routine situations. Lesgold (2001) cautioned about the lack of opportunities for practice on non-routine problems in the workplace: 'The real world mostly provides opportunities to do the routine. Expertise involving the non-routine is harder to get from everyday work experience because the right situations occur rarely ...' (Lesgold 2001, p. 967). This lack of opportunity to practice rare problems poses issues in accelerating proficiency. Conversely, simply doing the job may not accelerate proficiency unless there is certain deliberate planning associated with it. Hoffman, Andrews, et al. (2010, p. 399) stated that working on the job is not enough to accelerate proficiency:

> Simply "working at a job" does not promote progression along the proficiency continuum. Unless there is continuous deliberate practice at difficult tasks, the only thing one can do "on the job" is forget and actually experience degradation of skill.

The literature review suggests that most of the methods of workplace learning and training have been used with the goal of *building* proficiency rather than the goal of *accelerating* it. Though researchers have appealed, there are insufficient studies regarding how the work environment supports or hampers accelerating proficiency in the workplace in business settings.

2.6 CONCLUSION ON RESEARCH ISSUES

Section 2.2 reviewed the major perspectives on job performance. The review indicated that job performance was a complex multi-dimensional phenomenon. A linkage between learning and skill acquisition with performance was established and classic theories of skilled performance were reviewed. The section concluded that theories of stages of skill acquisition, despite their limitations, were still relevant in explaining the progression of skills in the context of novice-to-expert transitions. Section 2.3 reviewed the literature on novice-to-expert transitions including the stage models of proficiency which explained staged progression towards a higher level of proficiency. The gap on insufficient coverage on mid-level proficiency was found to be a concern for developing proficiency of employees in organisations. A gap was also noted regarding the lack of measurements of progression in stages, indication of start and end of a stage and scales of proficiency in various stages. It was noted that the literature does not specify how such scaling was being carried out in organisations. Finally, the literature on classic studies on expertise and expert performance were reviewed. It was pointed out that the nature of expertise was different from the construct of proficiency warranted in the workplace.

Section 2.4 reviewed the recent advances on the concept of accelerated proficiency. The literature on definition and construct of accelerated proficiency and time-to-proficiency was reviewed. Theoretical issues were highlighted in regards to the lack of appropriate theory to explain accelerated proficiency. It was observed that in the absence of any unified theory, the true nature of accelerated proficiency, more so in organisations, was not elaborated in the literature sufficiently. This section also reviewed the challenges reported in the literature regarding traditional methods to accelerate the proficiency. Section 2.5 reviewed the proven methods to accelerate proficiency. Several old and new studies were reviewed. The section concluded that most of the methods reported in the literature were training-oriented methods. While there was a legitimate need to extend training methods into the workplace, the literature provided only a few methods that could be applied to workplace settings.

The review in the preceding sections recognised the fact that time-to-proficiency was generally very long, and hence it called for methods to shorten it. For instance, the leading authority on accelerated proficiency, Hoffman, Andrews and Feltovich (2012, p. 9) recognised this need:

> This empirical fact about expertise (i.e., that it takes a long time) sets the stage for an effort at demonstrating the acceleration of the achievement of proficiency – an effort that sets out to address a number of inter-related questions concerning the path to expertise... Our vision is that methods for accelerating the achievement of proficiency, and even extraordinary expertise, might be taken to new levels such that one can accelerate the achievement of proficiency across the journeyman-to-expert span post-hiring.

However, the basic question about the possibility of acceleration, as well as methods of acceleration, appears to be under-researched, particularly in workplace settings. Notably, Hoffman, Andrews and Feltovich (2012, p. 9) raised a question which was not well addressed in literature at the time of their study:

> Can the achievement of journeyman-level skill be accelerated? What might be the payoff if this problem were solved, say, by reducing the time to achieve journeyman level skill by some significant amount (e.g., from 4 years to 2)?

To answer these questions, they recently synthesised a range of methods from existing literature in their latest publication *Accelerated Expertise* (Hoffman et al. 2014). In this publication, they suggested investing in 'research projects that would contribute to attempts to accelerate accelerated learning, likely focusing on the progression for journeyman to senior journeyman, or from senior journeyman to junior expert' (id. 169-170), with goals such as: '(1) Facilitating the achievement of high proficiency, especially accelerating across the apprentice to senior journeyman levels of proficiency … (3) Producing applications' (id. 173).

In summary, there are several gaps identified by this literature review regarding outstanding issues raised by recent researchers that are either under-researched or not researched yet. This study attempts to address two gaps in the literature: (1) understanding the true nature of proficiency and accelerated proficiency in the workplace, including the understanding of market forces that drive such need in organisations; and (2) workplace methods that are used to accelerate proficiency of the workforce in organisational settings and the payoffs it may bring. Further, the literature review did not lead to any framework or model that could be applied to explain the concept of accelerated proficiency reasonably well in workplace settings or one which could actually be implemented to accelerate workforce proficiency. In both the scholarly literature and practitioner literature alike, no systematic attempt was found to develop a model for accelerated proficiency. In the absence of any framework to guide business professionals, instructional designers, and learning specialists to accelerate time-to-proficiency of employees, this study was designed to help fill this gap.

Based on the literature review and gaps highlighted, it is noted that there was a lack of research on accelerating proficiency in natural settings in the workplace. Therefore, this study has been situated in organisational settings. While mainstream academic/scholarly literature showed insufficient coverage of workplace methods to accelerate proficiency in organisational settings, the practitioner literature, such as magazines, institutional reports, consulting blogs, industry awards and corporate white papers, continue to uphold several success stories and methods to reduce time-to-proficiency in business settings (Emily & Krob 2014; PetroSkills 2009; PTC 2005; Rosenbaum 2014; WalkMe 2013). Therefore, one of the aims of this research was to explore such methods already implemented in various organisations with a successful reduction in time-to-proficiency (i.e., metrics to measure acceleration in proficiency) and bring these methods to mainstream academic research.

Based on the above gaps, a central research problem and question was formed: **How can organisations accelerate time-to-proficiency of their employees in the workplace?** Three research questions were developed to answer this central question. The overall scope, intent, aims, questions and objectives of this research study are summarised in *Table 2-2*.

Table 2-2: Summary of research questions and research objective

Business problem		
The business challenge this study aimed to solve is that organisations are struggling with long time-to-proficiency of their workforce in certain job roles.		
Intents/aims		
To explore and understand the meaning practitioners place on the concept of accelerated proficiency in the workplace. To understand what makes the need for accelerating proficiency critical for organisations and what benefits they draw from reducing time-to-proficiency. To identify practices, strategies, methods and processes that have been proven to reduce time-to-proficiency successfully in different contexts.		
Central research question		
How can organisations accelerate time-to-proficiency of the employees in the workplace?		
Research questions		
Research question #1	Meaning of accelerated proficiency	What does the concept of accelerating proficiency or accelerating time-to-proficiency mean to organisations?
Research question #2	Driving factors and benefits of reduced time-to-proficiency	What business factors drive the need for reducing time-to-proficiency of the workforce and how do organisations benefit from achieving it?
Research question #3	Practices and strategies to accelerate proficiency	What core practices and strategies do business leaders and practitioners adopt to achieve shorter time-to-proficiency of the workforce in a given job?
Research objective		
The objective of this research is to develop a conceptual model and/or framework of proven practices or strategies that practitioners can use to reduce time-to-proficiency of the workforce in various settings.		

Chapter 3 RESEARCH METHODOLOGY

3.1 INTRODUCTION

Chapter 2 reviewed the major theoretical issues in the literature. Three research questions were developed from the identified gaps in the literature and are addressed in this study. Essentially, this research strove to contribute towards solving a critical business problem of long time-to-proficiency of the workforce in any given job. This research study explored the meaning of accelerated proficiency as seen by organisations, the business need for shorter time-to-proficiency and its benefits. Further, the study explored the business practices used by project leaders to reduce time-to-proficiency in different settings successfully. The research questions and intent of the study are summarised in *Table 3-1*.

Table 3-1: Summary of research questions and research objective

Business problem		
The business challenge this study aimed to solve is that organisations are struggling with long time-to-proficiency of their workforce in certain job roles.		
Intents/aims		
To explore and understand the meaning practitioners place on the concept of accelerated proficiency in the workplace. To understand what makes the need for accelerating proficiency critical for organisations and what benefits they draw from reducing time-to-proficiency. To identify practices, strategies, methods and processes that have been proven to reduce time-to-proficiency successfully in different contexts.		
Central research question		
How can organisations accelerate time-to-proficiency of the employees in the workplace?		
Research questions		
Research question #1	Meaning of accelerated proficiency	What does the concept of accelerating proficiency or accelerating time-to-proficiency mean to organisations?
Research question #2	Driving factors and benefits of reduced time-to-proficiency	What business factors drive the need for reducing time-to-proficiency of the workforce and how do organisations benefit from achieving it?
Research question #3	Practices and strategies to accelerate proficiency	What core practices and strategies do business leaders and practitioners adopt to achieve shorter time-to-proficiency of the workforce in a given job?
Research objective		
The objective of this research is to develop a conceptual model and/or framework of proven practices or strategies that practitioners can use to reduce time-to-proficiency of the workforce in various settings.		

The purpose of this chapter is to present the methodology used to conduct this study. Methodologies were chosen for this study to ensure that outcomes were practice-oriented and relevant to the real-world in contributing towards a greater understanding of the concept and process of accelerated proficiency in organisational and business contexts. This chapter discusses the justification of the approaches used, describes the research process adopted, explains the sampling strategies and methods to recruit the participants, outlines the methods to collect data and methods to analyse the data, and finally, enumerates the methods used to ensure validation and reliability of the study. This chapter is organised as follows:

Section 3.2 describes the inquiry framework and research process used in this research. This section justifies the use of the pragmatism paradigm and qualitative approach. Section 3.3 describes the sampling strategies adopted in this study. The process of searching, connecting and selecting the participants is explained. The distribution profile of the participants is also presented. Section 3.4 details the three phases of data collection process adopted in this study. The process of in-depth interviews and interview protocol is also explained. Section 3.5 enumerates the main data processing and management strategies employed in this study to handle the large amount of data collected. Further, the process of classifying the project cases is described. Section 3.6 details the distribution profile of the project cases collected in this study. Section 3.7 gives details the data analysis process and techniques used in this study. Section 3.8 lists various techniques and methods employed to ensure validity and reliability of the study. Section 3.9 summarises the ethical considerations and protocols used in this study.

3.2 RESEARCH DESIGN

The study is positioned in the 'pragmatic paradigm' using a qualitative approach due to its potential practical implications. In the following sub-sections, the rationale of these choices is explained.

3.2.1 Inquiry framework and research process

The research process in this study was guided by an inquiry framework consisting of six blocks—ontology, epistemology, theoretical perspective, methodology, methods and sources, as shown in *Figure 3-1*. This framework is adapted from the frameworks suggested by Crotty (1998), Creswell (2007, 2014) and Hay (2002). This framework informed the design of this research study in terms of methodologies, sampling strategies, methods for data collection and analysis, and sources from which to seek the data. This framework specified that ontology, epistemology theoretical perspective, methodology, methods, and sources are a series of steps that a researcher should define. These steps are: how the researcher views reality (ontology), the position s/he takes relative to the sources of reality to acquire knowledge about that reality (epistemology), what is the context within which s/he places her/his research process (theoretical perspective), what plan or process s/he uses to best uncover the reality (methodology), what techniques or procedures s/he uses to gather and analyse the data (methods), and then finally, the data s/he seeks to obtain that knowledge (sources) (Crotty 1998; Hay 2002; Creswell 2007).

In his original framework, Crotty (1998) suggested that four blocks—epistemology, theoretical perspective, methodology and methods—make a research process and all the decisions embodied in a research study. He postulated that there is a logical connection between these four building blocks in such a way that epistemology informs theoretical perspective, which in turns defines methodological decisions and in turn, dictates the methods appropriate for the research study (Crotty 1998, p. 4). Later, Creswell (2007, 2014) and Hay (2002) contended that ontology should be the first block before epistemology, which Crotty (1998) argued was implicit with epistemology. Later applications of those adapted models included a block named *sources* to inform data collection. To develop a research process, Crotty (1998, p. 2) proposed four questions researchers need to ask to design the building blocks of research: 'What *methods* do we propose to use? What *methodology* governs our choice and use of methods? What *theoretical perspective* lies behind the methodology in question? What *epistemology* informs this theoretical perspective?' Subsequently, Hay (2002, p. 63) supported a similar logical relationship stating that 'relationship is directional in the sense that ontology logically precedes epistemology which logically precedes methodology'. He proposed three questions researchers need to ask in a research design: 'Ontology: What is out there to know? Epistemology: What and how can we know about it? Methodology: How can we go about acquiring that knowledge?' (Hay 2002, p. 64). In this study, the above views were combined into an adapted inquiry framework, as shown in Figure 3-1.

Figure 3-1: Inquiry framework used for present research study

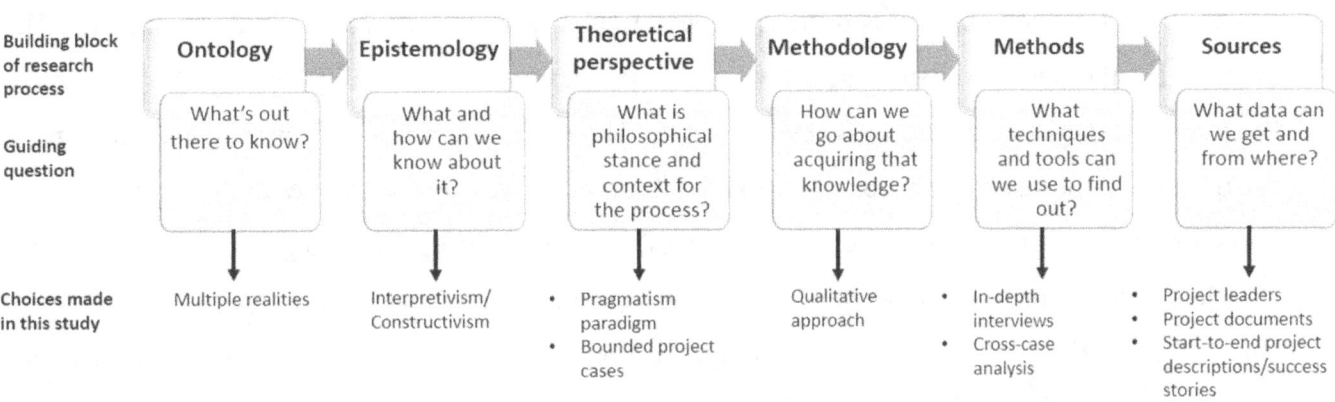

Source: adapted from Crotty (1998), Hay (2002) and Creswell (2007)

The blocks of the adapted framework and the stands taken in this research study are explained here:

1. **Ontological stand**: The first building block of this inquiry framework is *ontology*, which represents 'nature of reality' as seen by a researcher (Creswell 2007, p. 17). It is the researcher's viewpoint of what s/he believes is available to know about. The researcher's ontological stand indicates his/her assumptions about the nature of the social world which is being investigated and how the researcher defines reality. One side of a continuum is realism, which means there is only one natural reality in the world waiting to be discovered independently of the human mind and interactions. The other end of the continuum is relativism, which is the belief that there are multiple realities and each reality is constructed by the human differently through interactions with other people. Researchers like (Creswell 2007, 2014) and Hay (2002) based their research approach on Crotty (1998), who postulated that the researcher's stance mostly decides whether research is qualitative, quantitative or mixed. In the present study, the researcher assumed that the way accelerated proficiency is manifested in an organisation and the way proficiency is accelerated in a given context are realities worth knowing about. However, there may not be one reality to that effect (i.e., only one specific type of strategy works in every organisation irrespective of the nature of the organisation). Different business challenges and different organisational contexts will lead to using different ways to reduce time-to-proficiency. Therefore, the ontological stand in this study is that there are multiple realities that exist, which this research study attempts to find out.

2. **Epistemological stand:** The second building block of this inquiry framework is *epistemology,* which is 'how we know what we know' (Crotty 1998, p. 8). This is also viewed as the 'relationship between the researcher and being researched' (Creswell 2007, p. 17). A researcher's epistemology stand indicates whether s/he is part of the knowledge sought or is external to it. Epistemology is viewed as a continuum in which one end is positivism/objectivism, which assumes that findings are true. The other end is the interpretivist/constructionism, which means that the reality needs to be interpreted through the experience of people (Creswell 2007). The purpose of defining epistemology is to make it explicit what kind of knowledge is possible about a phenomenon and how do we know that we know enough about it. Altogether, the intent of ontology and epistemology is differentiated as: 'While ontology embodies understanding *what is*, epistemology tries to understand *what it means to know'* (Gray 2014, p. 19). In the present study, it is assumed that the people in different organisations work differently. Thus, the meaning they associate with accelerated proficiency and strategies to achieve it are highly contextual. Therefore, the meaning of the same strategies in different contexts required different interpretations. This epistemological stand called for a largely interpretivist or

constructionist approach in this study to interpret a wide range of meanings people place to this phenomenon. This is explained in detail in sub-section 3.2.3

3. **Theoretical perspective:** The third building block of this inquiry framework is the *theoretical perspective,* which is 'the philosophical stance informing the methodology and thus providing a context for the process and grounding its logic and criteria' (Crotty 1998, p. 3). It is viewed as a 'statement of the assumptions brought to the research task and reflected in the methodology as we understand and employ it' (id. 7). The set of beliefs, values, and assumptions regarding nature and conduct of the research among a community of researchers is called a *paradigm* (Kuhn 1996, p. 10) or *worldview* (Guba 1990). Paradigm sets the intent, motivation, and expectations for the research in terms of 'what should be studied, how research should be done, how results should be interpreted' (Bryman 1988, p. 4). In this study, the research problem addressed is what works in the workplace towards shortening time-to-proficiency. This is the only reality that matters. This dictates a pragmatic paradigm viewpoint. Briefly speaking, pragmatic paradigm considers "what works" as the ultimate reality and does not subscribe to one absolute reality viewpoint.

Most of the performance improvement initiatives like reducing time-to-proficiency in organisations are typically run as bounded projects with a definite start and end and specific goals (Dooley, Lupton & O'Sullivan 2005; Turner & Müller 2003). Therefore, "what works" is embedded into project stories. The concept and process of accelerated proficiency and strategies to reduce time-to-proficiency are best understood as project-based success stories, thus informing the choice of the bounded project case as the sampling unit. This perspective also informed the purposive and criterion sampling to recruit the participants with pertinent experience in executing such projects. This is described in detail in section 3.3.

4. **Methodological choices:** The fourth building block in this inquiry framework is *methodology,* which is 'the strategy, plan of action, process or design lying behind the choice and use of particular methods and linking the choice and use of methods to the desired outcomes' (Crotty 1998, p. 3). The process of research itself is referred to as methodology. A researcher's methodological stand is also considered as a continuum in which on one side is a quantitative methodology and on the other side is the qualitative methodology. Using a quantitative methodology allows the researcher to discover facts, causal relationships, what works, and outcomes. On the other hand, using a qualitative approach allows the researcher to understand the deeper meaning of a phenomenon or issue in terms of how and why. In the present study, ontological and epistemological stands suggested largely an interpretive and hence, qualitative approach, since the topic explored was a relatively new

phenomenon in the workplace and relatively unexplored topic in the literature. Therefore, an exploratory approach was called for in this study. As opposed to a quantitative approach, a qualitative methodology was better positioned to reveal the deeper meaning project leaders placed on this phenomenon.

5. **Methods:** The fifth building block in this inquiry framework is *methods,* which are 'the techniques or procedures used to gather and analyse data related to some research question or hypothesis' (Crotty 1998, p. 3). In the present study, all of the above stands led to the selection of in-depth interviews as the most appropriate method to explore experiences and viewpoints of project leaders and to develop an understanding of the overall context, factors, situations and rich experiences of the practitioners. Further, the theoretical perspective informed using in-depth interviews, which were structured as start-to-end success stories or project case descriptions. The data analysis approach of the cross-case analysis was informed by data collection to compare the bounded project cases across various contexts to make contextual sense of the phenomenon. This is described in detail in section 3.4.

6. **Sources:** Some adaptations in previous studies have added a last building block of *sources* into the research process (Grix 2002, p. 180; Vachette 2016, p. 11). In the present study, the theoretical perspective informed using bounded project cases as data collection instruments. Thus, the data required for this study were the start-to-end project success stories. Project leaders are generally assigned to lead every such project in organisations, and they have the most in-depth and first-hand knowledge of the project. Therefore, the potential sources for gathering data were the project leaders who have successfully completed projects to accelerate time-to-proficiency and secondary sources were the associated project case documents. This informed the participant characteristics, recruitment and selection appropriate to the goals of the research. This is described in detail in sections 3.3 and 3.4.

3.2.2 Justification for pragmatic paradigm

While there are several paradigms (e.g., positivism, post-positivism/realism, critical theory, interpretivist/constructionism and pragmatism), this study has been positioned into the pragmatism paradigm to support usability of the research output and to use the most appropriate methods to conduct the research. The choice of paradigm governed the choices of methods for the study. The theoretical perspective, as explained in sub-section 3.2.1 informed choosing pragmatic paradigm. Three primary reasons for choosing the pragmatic paradigm were: (1) focus of the research questions on the business reality of "what works"; (2)

usability/usefulness of research outcome; and (3) choice of methods appropriate to create usable knowledge.

What works

The principal research question was to explore the strategies in terms of "what works" and has been proven to work successfully in terms of shortening time-to-proficiency. In this research study, the researcher took the philosophical stand that project leaders in organisations develop, apply and test certain methods or strategies to reduce time-to-proficiency just like experimental scientists. The outcome of those experiments is the 'reality' and 'truth' in a given context. Johnson and Onwuegbuzie (2004, p. 18) supported this argument stating that 'workable knowledge' created in jobs is 'analogous to experimental and scientific inquiry' which leads to outcomes which are real and true in that organisational context. However, different contexts may lead to different realities, an outcome which requires a much deeper understanding of various realities. A positivist paradigm would have assumed only one objective reality waiting to be discovered (Swanson 2005). Thus, a positivistic paradigm was not expected to lead to a deeper understanding of the phenomenon warranted by the research question in this study. As such, the critical theory paradigm also would not have served the goal of the research either because there was no historical view available to compare or critique the time-to-proficiency strategies against (Guba & Lincoln 1994). On the other hand, however, in a study positioned in the interpretivism or constructionism paradigm, this would have led to a deeper understanding of multiple realities in terms of how project leaders were shortening time-to-proficiency in each context (Swanson 2005). However, the caveat regarding this paradigmatic position is that only understanding the concept and process of accelerated proficiency was not sufficient (Guba & Lincoln 1994). In the present study, the real value of understanding this phenomenon was to understand how practitioners achieved it in terms of the practical strategies that really "worked". Another kind of paradigm called pragmatism enabled this value, particularly for practice-oriented research. Tashakkori and Teddlie (2003, p. 713) defined pragmatism as a 'paradigm that debunks concepts such as "truth" and "reality" and focuses instead on "what works" as the truth regarding the research questions under investigation'. Hence, the pragmatic paradigm's philosophical stand aligned well with the researcher's view of reality in business organisations in this study and was a natural choice.

Usability/usefulness of outcome

The objective of this research study was to develop a conceptual model or framework that works and something practitioners and business leaders can use in their context with reasonable success to reduce time-to-proficiency. This research study's objective was far-reaching than just describing the nature and meaning of accelerated proficiency. In this study, the researcher started with the premise that a business research study plays a powerful role when it translates "what works" into guidelines for practitioners that can solve business problems. Past studies have supported this, as creating such kind of knowledge is a key advantage of the pragmatism paradigm:

> The knowledge character within pragmatism is thus not restricted to explanations (key form of positivism) and understanding (key form of interpretivism). Other knowledge forms such as prescriptive (giving guidelines), normative (exhibiting values) and prospective (suggesting possibilities) are essential in pragmatism. (Goldkuhl 2012, p. 144)

In line with this concept, some researchers even positioned pragmatic thinking as: 'To pragmatists, scientific knowledge is useful when it helps people to better cope with the world or to create better organisations' (Fendt, Kaminska-Labbé & Sachs 2008, p. 478). Thus, the usability and usefulness of the outcomes the researchers aimed for was a determinant in choosing the pragmatic paradigm. It was encouraged by the fact that applied and practice-oriented usefulness of the pragmatic paradigm has been shown in past research in organisational studies (Wicks & Freeman 1998); information sciences (Goldkuhl 2008); strategic tourism studies (Pansiri 2005) and sports psychology (Giacobbi Jr, Poczwardowski & Hager 2005).

This research objective is aligned to appeal by Rorty (1999, p. xxvi) that instead of the traditional aim of trying to describe reality accurately, the research's aim should be of usefulness to the people. In a business context, useful is what the outcome of the research does for the organisation, people, project and business results. The researcher's central research question is how organisations can reduce time-to-proficiency, which has significant business value. Swanson (2007) maintained that organisational researchers have a pragmatic view of outcomes in terms of business results and ask high consequence questions: 'Will the organisation perform better? Will the process perform better? Will the individuals perform better? Has performance increased (system level and financial performance)? Have people learned (knowledge and expertise learning)?' (Swanson 2005, p. 17).

Choice of methods

Paradigms like positivism, critical theory and interpretivism specify how reality should be viewed and understood. However, the challenge is that naturalistic situations, such as the workplace, may not fit into one of these views and the method specified by each of these orientations may not necessarily be the best fit for natural settings. The appeal of the pragmatic paradigm fundamentally has been that it allowed researchers to choose any data collection and analysis method appropriate to answer the question at hand. While doing so, this paradigm allows the researcher to be flexible and not biased due to any philosophical loyalty to any paradigm. The research design and other decisions in the pragmatic paradigm are made based on 'what works best' when answering the questions under study (Creswell & Clark 2011, p. 23). The "what works" philosophy also guided the researcher to use bounded project cases as a sampling unit to primarily gather the success stories of how organisations successfully reduced time-to-proficiency (what worked). When a study is positioned in the pragmatism paradigm, research focuses on the quality of the knowledge, as well as the usefulness of the knowledge which is somewhat limited while using other paradigms. Further, Wicks and Freeman (1998, p. 130) supported the usefulness of the pragmatic paradigm:

> For the pragmatist, the criterion of usefulness applies across two dimensions that the positivist views as sharply distinct: epistemological (is this information credible, well-founded, reliable?) and normative (does this help advance our projects?). This criterion allows the pragmatist to make judgments about research where the positivist and antipositivist could not.

At the same time, the success stories collected in this study needed to be interpreted. This called for a purely qualitative approach, as suggested by Goldkuhl (2012), despite popular notion of the pragmatic paradigm mainly being used for mixed-method research (Johnson & Onwuegbuzie 2004). The pragmatic paradigm in this study informed using the type of data analysis methods, which are not limited to a particular epistemological stand. Therefore, the frameworks by Miles, Huberman and Saldana (2014), Boyatzis (1998) and Braun and Clarke (2006, 2013) were considered appropriate for this research because they are grounded in the pragmatism paradigm and do not subscribe to any specific genre or epistemological assumption.

In summary, the intent, research questions and research objectives of this research study are best expressed using the pragmatism paradigm, hence the choice of this paradigm to best meet the research goals.

3.2.3 Justification of qualitative research approach

The business challenge of accelerating proficiency is considered a relatively new phenomenon and much needs to be understood about the process, factors, meaning and characteristics encompassing accelerated proficiency. Qualitative research is considered the most appropriate approach in such cases where 'very little is known about the problem' (Domegan & Fleming 2007, p. 24). Researchers supported that 'qualitative methods are often used when the field of research is yet not well understood or unknown and aim at generating new hypotheses and theories' (Kohlbacher 2006, para. 47).

The ontological and epistemological stands explained in sub-section 3.2.1 together informed the choice of the qualitative research approach adopted for this study. The qualitative approach is justified based on the aims of the study to develop a comprehensive understanding of the concept and process of accelerated proficiency, as seen by the project leaders who have shortened time-to-proficiency successfully, understanding how they implemented different strategies in their contexts, and understanding factors and characteristics that influenced accelerated proficiency. A qualitative research approach best meets the intent of this study:

> Qualitative research focuses on understanding the intervention or phenomenon and exploring questions like ''why was this effective or not?'' and ''how is this helpful for learning?'' The intent of the qualitative research is to contribute to understanding. (Sargeant 2012, p. 1)

Project leaders are normally involved intensively in planning and constantly monitoring project progress. Such intense, rich and lived experience can only be captured by in-depth interviews of such individuals with the qualitative research approach. The meaning of these experiences must be understood and interpreted within organisational space of processes, systems and goals among which project leaders work. Such an interactional space is not quantifiable. A qualitative approach is best suited because 'it attempts to make sense of, or to interpret, phenomena in terms of the meaning people bring to them' (Denzin & Lincoln 2017, p. 3).

Mechanisms and strategies to accelerate proficiency of the workforce may vary from organisation to organisation and may even vary among different jobs within the same organisation, making it a highly contextual complex phenomenon. It was important to know why some strategies worked in one context and not in others. Mason (2002, p. 1) stated that qualitative research has 'unrivalled capacity to constitute compelling arguments about *how things work in particular contexts'*. Besides, in today's world, it becomes very important for organisations to be able to understand, and hence, control the situational and environmental factors that influence speed-to-proficiency. Such situational understanding can be gained only through qualitative research (Maxwell 2008).

The decision of using the qualitative research approach in this study corroborate five goals which Maxwell (2008, p. 221) specified as being ideal for qualitative research:

> 1. Understanding the meaning that participants in a study give to the events, situations and actions that they are involved with; and of the accounts they give of their lives and experiences; 2. Understanding the particular context within which the participants act, and the influence this context has on their actions; 3. Identifying unanticipated phenomena and influences, and generating new, grounded theories about them; 4. Understanding the process by which events and actions take place; 5. Developing causal explanations.

3.3 SAMPLING AND PARTICIPANT SELECTION

In this research study, a five-step process was utilised to recruit participants: (1) developing the profile of ideal participants; (2) searching for an ideal profile; (3) connecting to potential participants; (4) applying criteria-based selection; and finally (5) contacting and inviting the candidates to participate in the study. 85 individuals participated in this research study. The participants were selected by using purposive sampling, maximum deviation sampling and criterion sampling. The sampling strategies adopted in this research study are described in the following sub-sections.

3.3.1 Purposive sampling

A limited number of experts were expected to possess "know-how" in the area of accelerated proficiency. Therefore, purposive sampling was used in this study, which involved choosing participants according to the needs of the research who could provide 'information-rich cases' suitable for the endeavour (Morse 1991,

2000; Patton 2002). The information-rich cases are those cases 'from which one can learn a great deal about issues of central importance to the purpose of the research' (Patton 2002, p. 230). The most important criteria for recruitment of participants in this study was that participant must have specific experience in reducing time-to-proficiency of the workforce in organisations. Before selecting the participants, the evidence for experience was checked. Evidence included:

- Mention of leading a project related to accelerated proficiency or time-to-proficiency, explicitly in written media (e.g., industry reports, interviews, company newsletters, conference presentations, webinars, books, journal or magazine article authorship, white papers, blog posts, etc.)
- Recognitions earned (e.g., industry awards, nominations, etc.) or association/affiliation with a society, forum, client, company or organisation whose charter or work relates to accelerated proficiency.
- Employment or association with the organisations or companies known to have run projects specific to accelerated time-to-proficiency.
- Self-acclaimed experience on a project or consulting achievement related to accelerated proficiency or time-to-proficiency in the media (e.g., a LinkedIn resume, internet profiles, academic CVs, responses to research questionnaires, personal communication, etc.)

The purposive sampling allowed preliminary scrutiny of the evidence to ascertain the breadth and depth of experience of a prospective participant before recruiting the individual for the research.

3.3.2 Search for ideal participants

The participants in this study were expected to be project leaders and business practitioners working in global corporations. Internet searches and social media channels were primarily used to find the prospective global participants. Sappleton (2013) contended that online methods of participant recruitment may even surpass traditional methods. As a first step, a list of potential keywords was prepared, which included variants of time-to-proficiency, time-to-expertise, time-to-competence, speed-to-proficiency, time-to-full productivity, accelerating performance, accelerating proficiency, accelerating expertise, accelerated learning, rapid skill acquisition, and rapid training. As a second step, a comprehensive search was conducted through the Google search engine to locate potential participants. This search led to identification of several practitioners who appeared in blogs, institutional reports, project reports, seminars and conference presentations, white papers, business books, business case studies and featured articles in magazines such as *Chief Learning Officer, Training Industry magazine, Training magazine, Performance Improvement magazine, T+D magazine,*

Harvard Business Review, etc. As some researchers have maintained, such grey literature holds powerful avenues for locating participants with pertinent experience (Marsland & Wilson 2000).

As a third step, a subscription to the premium LinkedIn professionals' online database (that is, the Facebook for professionals) was purchased, a database which has more than 500 million members in over 200 countries [Source: https://press.linkedin.com/about-linkedin]. Several research studies have used the LinkedIn database with reasonable success (Robinson, Sinar & Winter 2013). The LinkedIn profile typically contains self-declared expertise areas, projects, links to blogs, publications, names of companies served and contact information. The participants located in Google were searched in this database. Additionally, a systematic, criteria-based and keyword-based search in the LinkedIn database located potential experts with the project experience useful or relevant to this research topic. As a fourth step, researchers who have conducted practice-oriented research on accelerated proficiency were also located from scholarly publication databases and were scrutinised for their experience and relevance to the research topic.

Using a combination of these strategies generated a list of 549 potential participants who appeared to have pertinent experience in the area relevant to the research.

3.3.3 Connection with potential participants

Most of the 549 potential participants were busy corporate professionals in large organisations or consultants running their own businesses. They were globally distributed. The logistics of contacting such a widespread research sample was a formidable challenge. Online communication was the only feasible option. However, online recruiting had its own challenges. In a world of increasing cyber threats and online scams, well-known professionals are highly sceptical about whom they are talking to and how soon they can trust the sender of unsolicited e-mail. Past studies have shown that reaching out to busy professionals over the internet via a traditional approach of sending mass impersonal mailers was not a guarantee of successful participation (Dabbish & Kraut 2006; Meho 2006; Sappleton & Lourenço 2016). Recognising the challenge of recruiting and reaching out to participants over the web, James & Busher (2006, p. 417) advised the researchers to 'think very carefully about how they build relationships of trust with participants they cannot see and may never meet'. Establishing credibility with the participant even before contacting him/her through online media was an important consideration in this study to successfully recruiting a participant from a small cohort of a known population.

For this study, ongoing informal conversations were initiated with potential participants to build a personal connection before sending any invitations or mailers to participate. That approach was intended to foster rapport, mutual trust and credibility at the same time. Several researchers have argued that a trusting relationship between the researcher and participant can ensure trustworthiness of the qualitative research (Krueger & Casey 2015; Rossman & Rallis 2012). Thus, a combination of networking, communication, outreach and interpersonal strategies were utilised with satisfactory results. Networking through LinkedIn was established with potential participants. Once they were in the network, they were in touch with regular updates and postings the researcher put on the LinkedIn profile regarding the research. Online presence of the research was created through SlideShare and Twitter, and a blog was set up on this research topic, with potential participants invited to subscribe the same. Conversely, blogs of potential participants, if any, were located. The researcher read their blog posts and commented on their blogs to trigger intellectual exchanges. Lastly, the researcher attended the industry's largest training conference, ASTD, which is attended by 9,000 people, and over 300 speakers from 80 countries. [Source: http://www.webvent.tv/uploads/assets/264/document/HowtoLeadaDelegationtoICE2014.pdf]. During the conference, the researcher personally participated in forums and connected with several business leaders who appeared to have experience in the topic of this research.

All of the above techniques collectively led to better connections, trust and credibility with the potential participants. This whole process of outreach required six months to a year to establish grounds for sending an invitation for research participation.

3.3.4 Selection and invitation of target participants

During the pre-invitation interactions and conversations, the researcher gained more insight into the nature of each potential participant's experience and his/her suitability for the research study. The list of 549 potential participants was refined down to 371-targeted participants who possessed requisite experience relevant to the study, as seen from the evidence criteria mentioned in sub-section 3.3.1 (Morse 1991). This study had the risk of poor response or under-participation because the strategies to shorten time-to-proficiency were presumably considered highly strategic and confidential information by some companies due to its competitive value (P Koehler 2015, pers. comm., 30 March). Therefore, this research study targeted all 371 qualified participants to avoid the risk of a low response rate. This population represented participants from a range of organisational settings, thus leading to diversity and maximum variation sampling in this study (Kuzel 1999; Lincoln & Guba 1985; Patton 2002; Sandelowski 1995). Maximum sampling variation is used to 'to document variations that have emerged in adapting to different conditions' (Lincoln & Guba 1985, p. 200).

3.3.5 Participation rate

The participants who expressed their interest directly received an electronic survey form to capture their demographics and experience pertinent to the research if that information was not available from the original sources. Among the 371 participants, 45 participants were unreachable through e-mails (bounced) or any other social media, and hence, were not included in the sample. The remaining 326 participants comprised the eligible known population within the constraints of the criteria used and the search method employed to identify such population. They were the candidates that were contacted/invited for research participation. Out of the 326 targeted participants, 296 were contacted. Overall, 178 participants responded to the request for participation; 118 participants did not respond despite numerous reminders. Time constraints also impacted the process. The participation process for 30 participants was not completed. Of the 178 responding individuals, 37 participants explicitly declined participation. Among all, 19 participants did not meet the criteria during subsequent conversations. Among the 141 participants who favourably responded, 21 hibernated after the first or second contact, and no interview took place. *Table 3-2* summarises the participant turnout in the study.

Table 3-2: Response rate and participation rate in the study

	# of potential participants	% distribution
Total targeted contactable participants	326	100%
Participation process not completed	30	11%
No response	118	36%
Responded	178	54%
Declined participation	37	11%
Hibernated after the first contact	21	6%
Total subjects participated	**85**	**26%**

3.3.6 Distribution profile of participants

85 subjects participated in the research, which represented a response rate of 29% of the targeted 326 participants. The 85 participants comprised the total number for all three stages of data collection. The distribution profiles of the participants are provided in *Table 3-3*. Detailed participant demographic characteristics and profiles of the participants are provided in Appendix 1. In summary:

- The participants were from seven countries, with 77% of the participants from the USA.
- The participants were recruited from 24 different industries (self-declared as per the LinkedIn form), with the highest number of participants engaged in professional training and management consulting professions.

- The career positions of participants varied greatly, from retired experienced professionals to the president of companies. The majority of the participants were CEOs, consultants, or an equivalent. The mean number of years of experience was more than 20 years, and the majority of the participants had more than 11 years of experience.
- Most of the participants were highly educated, with 35% holding doctoral degrees and 39% holding masters degrees.
- The gender composition of the participants was 75% male and 25% female.

Table 3-3: Distribution profile of research participants

Country		
USA	66	77%
Australia	5	6%
Netherlands	5	6%
UK	4	5%
Singapore	3	4%
UAE	1	1%
Philippines	1	1%
Total	**85**	**100%**

Current Industry (self-declared)		
Professional training & coaching	18	20%
Management consulting	13	15%
Education management	7	8%
Computer software	6	7%
Higher education	6	7%
Semiconductors	6	7%
Research	5	6%
E-learning	5	6%
Information technology & services	3	4%
Oil & energy	2	2%
Financial services	2	2%
Oil & energy	1	1%
Military	1	1%
Broadcast media	1	1%
Public relations & communications	1	1%
Electrical/Electronic manufacturing	1	1%
Education technology	1	1%
Banking	1	1%
Management consulting	1	1%
Internet	1	1%
Human resources	1	1%
Information services	1	1%
Unknown	1	1%
Total	**85**	**100%**

Current Position / Title		
President / CEO / MD / Founder	27	32%
Researcher / Scientist / Academician / Author	13	15%
Consultant	12	13%
Program / Training manager	10	12%
Director / VP	9	11%
Trainer / Facilitator / Instructional designer	6	7%
CLO / CKO	5	6%
Leadership / HRD specialist	2	2%
Retired	1	1%
Total	**85**	**100%**

Education		
Doctorate	29	35%
Masters	34	39%
Bachelors	16	19%
No information	6	7%
Total	**85**	**100%**

Experience range		
0 to 10	3	4%
11 to 20	24	27%
21 to 30	22	26%
31 to 40	24	29%
41 to 50	7	8%
Unknown	5	6%
Total	**85**	**100%**

Gender		
Female	21	25%
Male	64	75%
Total	**85**	**100%**

3.3.7 Sampling unit/unit of analysis: Bounded project cases

The sampling unit and unit of analysis chosen for this study was a bounded project case. For this study, the term *bounded project cases* describes a case (i.e., a success story of a phenomenon in bounded context) which has a defined start and end (i.e., a project), and it is bounded (i.e., its boundaries are defined in terms of scope) (Merriam & Tisdell 2016; Miles, Huberman & Saldana 2014; Turner & Müller 2003).

The selection of this sampling unit is informed by the theoretical perspective used in this study that traditionally organisations, in an attempt to drive highly focused operational improvements or changes, setup project-based initiatives by pulling together a temporary team (Dooley, Lupton & O'Sullivan 2005; Turner & Müller 2003). Projects are typically 'undertaken to create lasting outcome' even though '[t]he temporary nature of projects indicates that a project has a definite beginning and end' (Project Management Institute 2013, p. 2). The literature suggested that time-to-proficiency initiatives/efforts/improvements in organisations were also executed as projects with a defined start, end and targeted outcome (Pollock, Wick & Jefferson 2015; Thompson 2017). Therefore, the nature of accelerated proficiency and success strategies to reduce time-to-proficiency is best understood by understanding start-to-end project case descriptions and success stories. The intent of choosing this sampling unit was to collect such success stories systematically in which project leaders reduced time-to-proficiency successfully and achieved substantial reduction using a certain set of strategies which this research intended to establish. Further, the bounded project case, as a sampling unit, allowed for deeper analysis with qualitative research methods, as suggested by Miles, Huberman and Saldana (2014, p. 11) that 'the emphasis is on the specific *case*, a focused and bounded phenomenon embedded in its context. The influence of local context is not stripped away but are taken into account'.

Sampling unit or unit of analysis informed the participant selection in turn (Gabriel & Griffiths 2004). This sampling unit specified a constraint that the participant for the phase-2 data collection must be a project leader, project owner, project designer or some senior project team member who had the rich and first-hand details of all aspects of the project. Besides, choosing the bounded project case as the sampling unit allowed structuring and conducting the interview with business professionals in the same language and terminology which they used in day-to-day work within their organisations (Davies & Hobday 2011).

3.4 DATA COLLECTION

The data collection occurred in three phases: informal interviews with practice leaders (phase-1); in-depth semi-structured interviews with project leaders (phase-2); and expert focus groups using the Delphi method with select experts (phase-3). The data collection phases and how they were used in the data analysis is shown in *Figure 3-2*. The primary method for data collection in this study was in-depth interviews. Interviews were conducted over four modes: phone or technology-mediated, face-to-face, questionnaire interview, and e-mail interview.

The interested participants were categorised into two categories depending on whether they possessed specific project experience or broader domain experience - *practice leaders* and *project leaders* (see sub-section 3.4.1 and sub-section 3.4.2), who were interviewed in phase-1 and phase-2 of the data collection, respectively.

Figure 3-2: The process of three-phase data collection

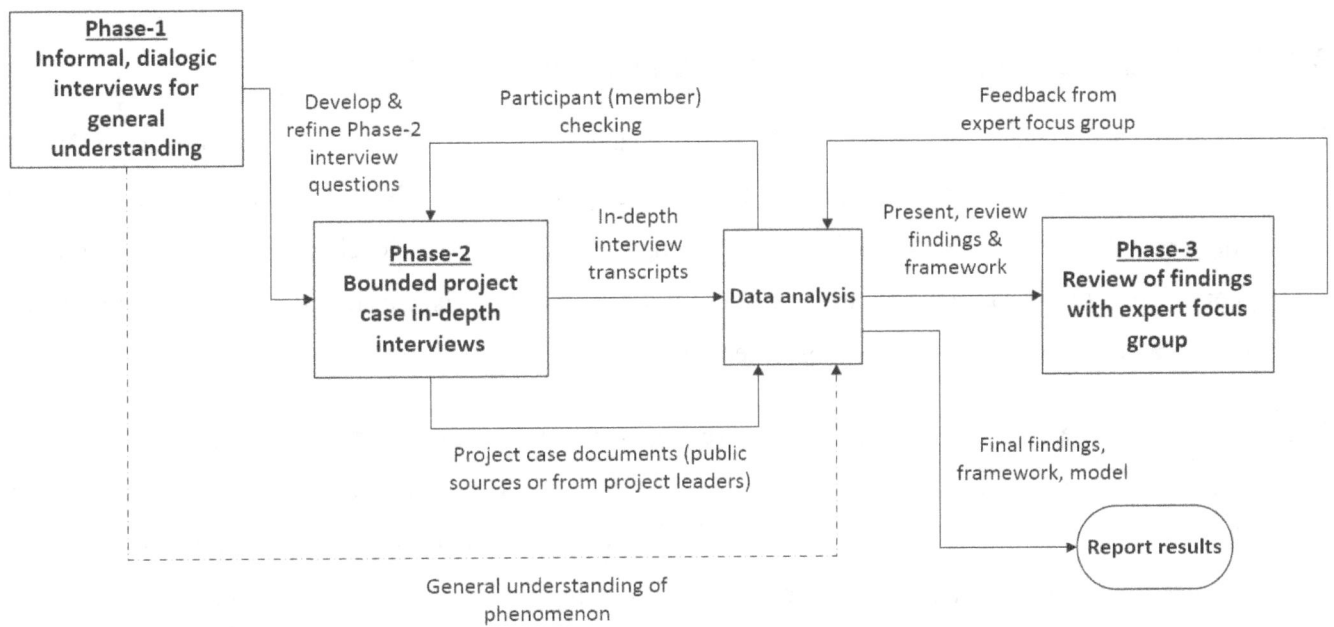

Source: *developed for this research study*

Table 3-4 summarises the distribution of participants and outcome from each phase of the data collection. Each of the phases is described briefly in the following sub-sections.

Table 3-4: Participant distribution and outcomes of three-phase data collection process

	Phase-1	Phase-2	Phase-3
Who	Practice leaders with broader experience	Project leaders with specific project experience	Practitioners and experts
Goal	General understanding of the phenomenon	Collect success stories in the form of bounded project cases	Review findings of the study
Method	Informal, dialogues, conversational interviews	Semi-structured in-depth interviews	Expert focus group using one-round of "feedforward" Delphi
Population	25	62	5
Number of interviews	24	61	None
Bounded project cases	None	66	None
Associated documents	13	50	None

3.4.1 Phase-1 interviews for general understanding

The phase-1 interviews were conducted with the practice leaders who were the participants who had indicated broader domain experience on the topic of accelerated proficiency. Their experience spanned across overseeing several projects and/or overall understanding of the challenge of accelerating time-to-proficiency of the people in the organisations. 25 participants out of 85 were categorised as practice leaders (note: two of the practice leaders also participated as project leaders).

The purpose of phase-1 interviews was to acquire a general understanding and the issues in the field of accelerated proficiency from their broad experience and knowledge. These interviews were exploratory in nature that took the form of dialogues in which participants and researcher together explored and developed the shared meaning of various terms or concepts. Phenomenology researchers have long suggested the value of using such informal, conversational interviews when a process or phenomenon is new or unexplored (Seidman 2013). The interviews with practice leaders revealed several aspects not originally known at the beginning of the study and formed the basis of framing/refining interview questions for phase-2 with the project leaders. Telephone conversations and Skype were utilised for twenty-two interviews, while two were e-mail interviews. During this phase, thirteen documents were also gathered from the participants to enhance the understanding.

3.4.2 Phase-2 interviews for collection of bounded project cases

Phase-2 was the main phase of data collection. The goal of this phase was to get a detailed description of successful bounded project cases in which time-to-proficiency was reduced successfully. The participants categorised as project leaders were interviewed in this phase. Project leaders were the participants who had indicated specific experience in designing, implementing or leading projects related to shortening of time-to-proficiency. The insights gained in phase-1 of interviews informed the design of the semi-structured phase-2 interview questions. A bounded project case was used as the sampling unit in this phase. Each project leader who consented to participate in the study was asked to provide one project case in detail. Most commonly, the improvement projects, such as Six Sigma improvement projects, are structured quite similarly and is usually structured around five phases: define (goal), measure (how far it is off), analyse (why it is off), improve (new solution) and control (monitor or compare) (Ramly & Yaw 2012, p. 359; Thawani 2004, p. 658). This structure is shown in *Figure 3-3*.

Figure 3-3: Five stages of a typical improvement or problem-solving project

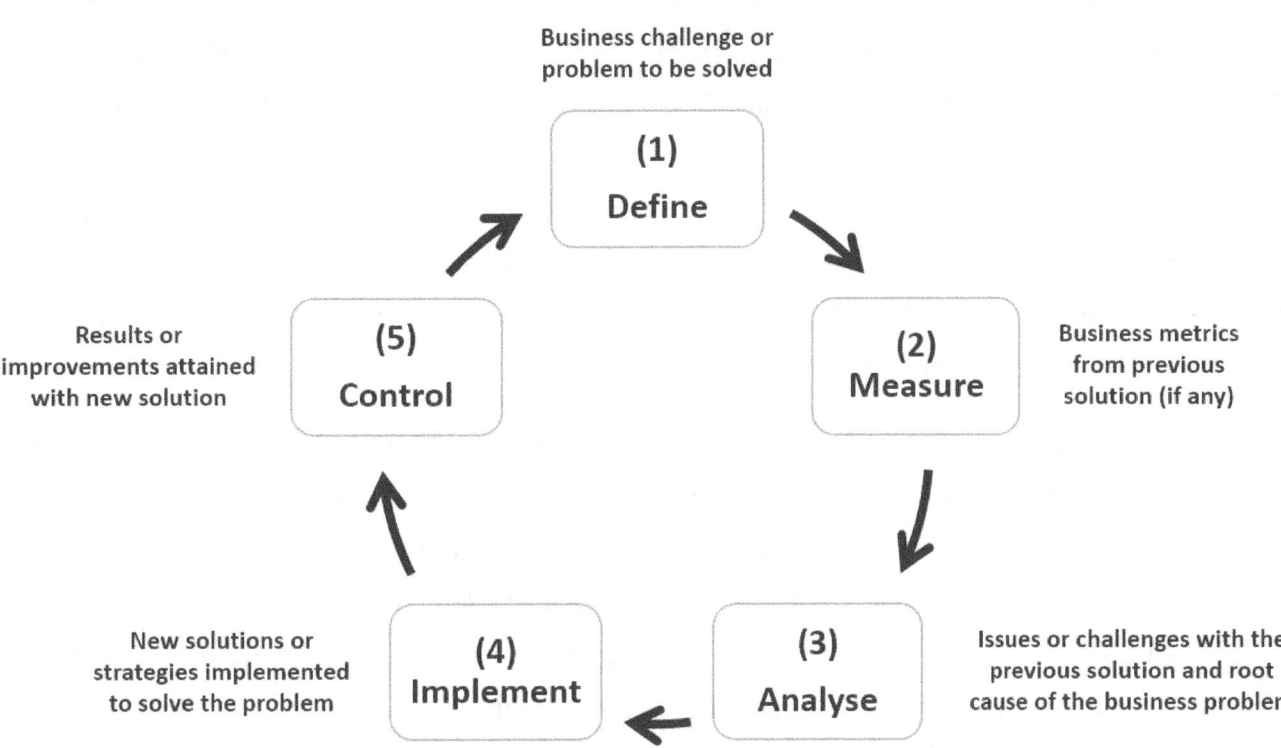

Source: developed for this research study

In short, a business challenge is defined which may be causing a negative impact (e.g., long time-to-proficiency) in an earlier solution. Measures are put in place to gather and analyse the data (e.g., actual time-to-proficiency) to identify the root cause of the problem in the earlier solutions. Improvement strategies or new solutions are then implemented. The results or improvements of the new solutions are monitored. Any deviation from goals is fed back to the process, and suitable adjustment is made in improvement strategies. Accordingly, interviews were structured around five core elements which essentially described a story in a project as follows: (1) business challenge or problem of time-to-proficiency to be solved; (2) description of the previous solution in place (if any) to reduce time-to-proficiency and previous results (business metrics); (3) issues or challenges with the previous solution and root cause of the problem; (4) description of the new solutions or strategies implemented to reduce time-to-proficiency; and (5) the results in terms of reduction in time-to-proficiency (quantitative, qualitative or anecdotal results).

These interviews structured around bounded project case descriptions allowed consistent data, and hence added to the data quality and completeness. The approach was also consistent with what Miles, Huberman and Saldana (2014, p. 154) called a pre-structured case which is used in a study 'where time is limited, and research questions are well specified, the pre-structured case is a way to focus and streamline data collection and analyses that are "quick and clean" and will more likely provide trustworthy results' (id. 155). Besides, this approach allowed easy cross-case analysis to compare the bounded projects cases across several variables to understand commonality, differences, transferability and generalisability (Bower et al. 2015; Miles, Huberman & Saldana 2014; Stake 2006; Vohra 2014; Yin 2014). The interview questions/guide designed on this structure is given in Appendix 3. The research question map to the interview questions is provided in Appendix 43. Each question was tied to an element in the bounded project case structure 'indicating the concepts contained in the research questions' (Phellas, Bloch & Seale 2011, p. 186). 66 start-to-end project cases were collected. The detailed distribution of the project cases is discussed in section 3.6, while the profile of each case is provided in Appendix 2.

Many of the professionals who became participants had published success stories in the form of blogs, agency reports or case coverage in online media or articles in magazines. Such documents pertaining to the project cases were collected either indirectly from public sources or directly from the participant consistent with approaches used by several researchers (Charmaz 2014; Hardman 2013; Plummer 2004; Prior 2003). Those documents supplemented the interview data. These data (published success stories) were used to validate the information shared by participants in the interview. Corresponding to 66 cases gathered at this stage, 50 documents were collected in addition to the interview transcripts.

3.4.3 Phase-3 expert focus group for review of findings

The purpose of this phase was to conduct a focus group of experts to review the findings of the research study and conceptual model developed during data analysis and seek the feedback on validity, transferability and utilisation of the findings. Ten project leaders were invited from the phase-2 participants from different backgrounds and industries to participate in an expert focus group review. The experts were selected based on their demonstrated leadership, diversity of business sectors and the probability of receiving responses.

Among them, five participants actually participated in the focus group. Their profiles are summarised in *Table 3-5*.

The model and findings were presented to the focus group as a thirty-page document using one round of the Delphi method. The goal of this one round of 'feed-forward' Delphi method was to elicit inputs from these experts by 'presenting to respondents the information about emerging consensus derived from the prior interviews' (Gordon 1994, p. 5). This method of using one round of Delphi method has been considered sufficient in the literature when validating research outcomes (Hartman & Baldwin 1995). To use this method in the present study, the questions were prepared to verify the results, to understand the boundaries of the research, and to understand where these results can be extended. An online internet-based form was used to collect the responses, the success of which has been demonstrated in many studies (Cabaniss 2001; Gordon 1994; Schmidt 1997). The experts were asked some specific questions and to provide their comments.

Table 3-5: Profile of participants in expert focus group

	Expert 1	Expert 2	Expert 3	Expert 4	Expert 5
Current organisation	$100+ billion hi-tech company	Consulting firm	$100+ billion medical technology co.	Consulting firm	Consulting firm
Current business domain	Technology equipment	Business consulting	Healthcare	Business consulting	Business consulting
Position / Title	Program manager	Program manager	Project leader	Director /VP	CLO/CKO
Experience range	21-30 years	21-30 years	21-30 years	20-30 years	20-30 years
Education	Master's	Master's	Master's	Master's	Doctorate
Gender	Male	Male	Male	Male	Male
Location	USA	USA	USA	UK	USA

3.4.4 In-depth interviews

Three types of interviews were incorporated into the research design to collect data from the participants: (1) in-depth qualitative interviews; (2) questionnaire interviews; and (3) e-mail interviews. The primary method used for data collection was in-depth interviews to understand this new phenomenon in rich detail. 76 participants participated via in-depth interviews. While three interviews took place in-person in face-to-face settings, 73 of those were audio-based (phone or otherwise) or technology-based (internet, video). Refer to the *Table 3-6* for the participation rate in various data collection methods and modes.

Table 3-6: Participation rate in various data collection methods and modes

Mode	Methods	Number of participants	%
Audio-based	Audio-conference / phone	53	63%
Technology-based	Internet-based (e.g., Webex)	12	13%
	Video-based (e.g., Skype)	8	10%
In-person	Face-to-face interview	3	4%
Questionnaire	Questionnaire (web-based)	4	5%
	Questionnaire (attachment in e-mail)	2	2%
	E-mail interview	3	4%
	Total	85	100%

The 85 responding and consenting participants were geographically dispersed in different countries across a wide global area. Phone or technology-mediated interviews were the most appropriate options (Salmons 2010). Past research studies have established that phone interviews and technology-mediated interviews are equally effective as face-to-face interviews (Kazmer & Xie 2008; Mann & Stewart 2000; Phellas, Bloch & Seale 2011; Sturges & Hanrahan 2004). In this study, technology-mediated and phone interviews were accepted well because most of the professionals used these methods for their routine communications in the workplace. Where possible this study used internet-mediated communication technologies such as Skype, WebEx, Adobe Connect, and GoToMeetings, which allowed multi-channel data sharing of video, documents and presentations during the interviews (Salmons 2012). Reasonable adjustments were made in time zones, convenience and methods for the interviews based on needs. The researcher used his personal experience of conducting business using these methods to exert appropriate sensitivity to language, clarifications, and communication style for effective interview outcomes.

Some organisations/participants considered their strategies as competitive advantages and put control mechanisms in place (like a review by the legal department). Therefore, on the request of participants, alternative written data collection methods were included in the research design to allow those participants to participate. This arrangement was in accordance with the observation that 'one should let the participants choose as much as possible: let them choose the medium when possible, and within the medium let participants have as much choice as is methodologically feasible' (Kazmer & Xie 2008, p. 273). A written questionnaire interview was designed with the same set of open-ended questions used in the in-depth interviews and was structured similarly based on recommendations by Harris and Brown (2010). Six participants used this method to participate in the research study. Past studies indicated that such interviews through questionnaire allowed participants enough time to check their records and provide an enriched description at their convenience (Adamson et al. 2004; Phellas, Bloch & Seale 2011). The questionnaire interview template is provided in Appendix 4. An excerpt of one of the questionnaire interviews is provided in Appendix 5.

Similarly, the research design also included a method that allowed asking questions from participants via multiple e-mail exchanges if their schedules did not allow them time to complete the questionnaire. Seven interviews via e-mail interview mode were conducted. Meho (2006) used this method in certain settings and defined this mode as 'online, asynchronous, in-depth interviewing, which is usually conducted via e-mail, is, *unlike e-mail surveys,* semistructured in nature and involves multiple e-mail exchanges between the interviewer and interviewee over an extended period of time' (p. 1284). Similar to questionnaire interviews, the e-mail interview has been seen in past studies as providing enriched responses (Bampton & Cowton 2002; Mann & Stewart 2000).

3.4.5 Interview protocol

An interview guide with a tentative set of questions was prepared based on the research questions (see Appendix 43), and the questions were appropriately sequenced (see Appendix 3). The interview guide and protocols were prepared considering guidelines from earlier researchers such as Jacob and Furgerson (2012). The phone-mediated and technology-mediated interviews followed guidelines by Burke and Miller (2001) and Curasi (2001). The interview was piloted with one participant and questions were refined in subsequent interviews. The candidates identified to be contacted were invited to express their interest in the research and express their availability for participation and interview. A sample invitation letter used for the study is given in Appendix 6. An information sheet was included in the e-mail as well (see Appendix 7). The participation in the research was voluntary. Participants were able to express their interest by clicking a web link which opened up the electronic consent form designed using SurveyMonkey and Qualtrics survey management system (see Appendix 8 and Appendix 9). Participants were also able to confirm the consent by replying to e-mail instead of signing a paper-based form. As Meho (2006, p. 1288) stated 'simply replying via e-mail affirmatively to an invitation to participate by stating in the message that the consent form was read and agreed to' is informed consent. Consenting selected participants for the interviews were contacted and a convenient location and time was set. Participants' were asked about their choice of preferred technology, mode or interview channel during informed consent (Heijmans, van Lieshout & Wensing 2015).

An expectation-setting e-mail was sent prior to the interview (see Appendix 10) along with a copy of the tentative questions for the interview that would follow. This approach guided the participants towards the research objectives (Berry 1999; Kvale 1996; Seidman 2013). Englander (2012, p. 27) indicated that such an approach could result in the collection of richer data because 'it can aid the researcher in getting a richer description during the interview without the researcher having to ask too many questions'. During the actual interview, most participants came well prepared with answers. Some of them even opened up the associated project notes on their computers during the interview. Some participants shared the screen via Webex and walked the researcher through the approach they used during the project in detail.

In order to get better-quality outcomes, the interviews were conducted mainly in a semi-structured and semi-directive way. A directive style of questioning was used when needed. Participants were asked open-ended questions to allow them to describe the details because rich information and elaboration of strategies were key to the success of this research. During the interview, notes were taken as hand-sketched concept maps (also called mindmaps or cognitive maps). These concept maps captured during the interviews ensured quick, efficient and visual summaries of the interview produced during the interview. A sample concept map created during one of the interviews is provided in Appendix 11. These maps elaborated on an initial relationship, clarify certain dependencies and to summarise the interview take-away at the end, which acted as confirmation from the participants (Brightman 2003). These concept maps were updated before starting the data coding as a reflexive exercise and for subsequent data analysis of themes (see updated concept map in Appendix 12).

Interviews were digitally recorded with the permission of the participants. A 'thank you' e-mail, along with a concept map or high-level interview summary was sent acknowledging each participant's contribution. Post-interview, the richness of the data was reviewed to identify any gaps in data sufficiency, identify any unanswered questions to follow-up, mark any unusual or deviant cases for further exploration and to note any interesting aspects for probing in the subsequent interviews. Guest, MacQueen and Namey (2011, p. 26) reminded the importance of initial data: 'The goal is to assess the effectiveness of the questions in eliciting desired information'. The appropriate adjustments or additions in probing questions were made in subsequent interviews to improve the richness of the data.

3.5 DATA PROCESSING AND MANAGEMENT

The scale of this study involved data for 85 interviews. Collectively, it amounted to 2,000 pages of transcripts, over 50 documents, and approximately 85 concept maps and project case summaries. This large size of qualitative data was properly processed and prepared in the manner stressed by Miles, Huberman and Saldana (2014, p. 71). Data processing included the following tasks: prepare post-interview summaries; develop or refine concept maps; capture initial impressions, themes and observations; review data quality and sufficiency; transcribe interviews; anonymise the documents and interviews; organise and manage the research documents; organise the notes and memos and classify project cases. A large amount of data was organised and managed carefully using NVivo software. A comprehensive research tracker was maintained (See Appendix 15). The 66 projects collected in this study came from a range of organisations, business sectors and industries. To assist in data analysis, these projects were classified using standard industry classification systems. Project classification is explained in sub-section 3.5.3.

3.5.1 Data processing

An interview/project case summary template was created which was filled immediately after an interview was completed. These summaries captured the main points quickly and reduced the multi-page transcripts of a case into a one-page summary before a new set of data arrived. This technique of handling a large volume of data using case summary was demonstrated by Knafl and Ayres (1996). A sample of interview/project case summary is given in Appendix 13. The rough concept maps jotted down during the interviews were entered into XMind software. The documented cognitive maps captured the ideas and concepts visually to enhance the understanding. Appendix 12 provides the refined concept map thus generated for one of the interviews.

Transcription of interviews was very important in this study. As researchers have maintained, 'transcription is a pivotal aspect of qualitative inquiry' (Oliver, Serovich & Mason 2005, p. 1273). This also determined data quality and data analysis. The recorded interviews were transcribed professionally by a company that guaranteed 98% transcription accuracy for a wide range of English accents. The informational content of interviews was important in the present study due to the nature of the questions posed. Therefore, the recorded interviews were transcribed as denaturalised (clean verbatim) rather than naturalised (which captures every utterance in detail) (Oliver, Serovich & Mason 2005, p. 1276). The transcriptions were read multiple times, as suggested by Hagens, Dobrow and Chafe (2009), to make corrections that enhanced the accuracy and quality of the data. The transcripts were anonymised, and any personal or professional references that potentially identified the participant or his/her organisation, or the project, were removed. Each practice leader and project leader was identified by a pseudonym. Each project case was given an identification (ID) number, as well as a title (evolved by the researcher) based on the goals of the project. Further, Guest, MacQueen and Namey (2011, p. 29) appeal to systematically catalogue the data so that a systematic approach to analysis can be used. Thus, the data were appropriated and catalogued, irrelevant data were marked but not discarded, incomplete data were flagged for follow-ups, and data were indexed and labelled in NVivo and Excel spreadsheets.

3.5.2 Data management

A large volume of data tends to impair the data coding, as well as data analysis quality (Miles & Huberman 1994, p. 45). NVivo 11 professional version was used for organising and managing the data (St John & Johnson 2000). All the audio recordings, transcribed interviews, documents, memos, journals, concept maps and codebooks were managed in NVivo. This strategy allowed integrating data collection, data management and data analysis in the same place. A master tracker was maintained for all the interview activities. The master tracker was used as a checklist as a 'data accounting log' (Miles, Huberman & Saldana 2014, p. 122). This ensured itemisation of each source and that each data piece was properly collected and accounted for. An excerpt of the 74-column, 371-row matrix is shown in Appendix 15. The data were kept in a password-protected 256-bit hardware encrypted hard-drive. This ensured the highest possible level of data security.

3.5.3 Classification of project cases

All the project cases collected in this study required classification based on the context. Mason (2006, p. 18) defined context as:

> Depending upon the focus of the enquiry, contexts might for example be: places or spaces; localities; physical environments; virtual environments; visual environments; bodily environments; sets of experiences; sets of processes; sets of relationships; commitments; networks; legal and administrative forms of organisation and practice; transport infrastructures; 'public' or 'wider' patterns of behaviour; family, local, global or virtual cultures; traditions; values; imaginaries; memories; fears; conflicts and animosities; affections and desires; time; history.... Context means *associated surroundings* and the concept of 'association' is crucial here.

Four broad categories of contextual variables were identified from interview project case summaries that characterised the project cases. These contextual variables were used for cross-case comparison of project cases. (1) Sectors: Economic, business or industry; (2) Nature of the job role; (3) Critical-to-success (CTS) skills: primary skills for the job; and (4) Complexity levels: the complexity of the skill or the job role or both. A classification framework was developed for this study and shown in *Figure 3-4*.

Figure 3-4: Project case data classification framework

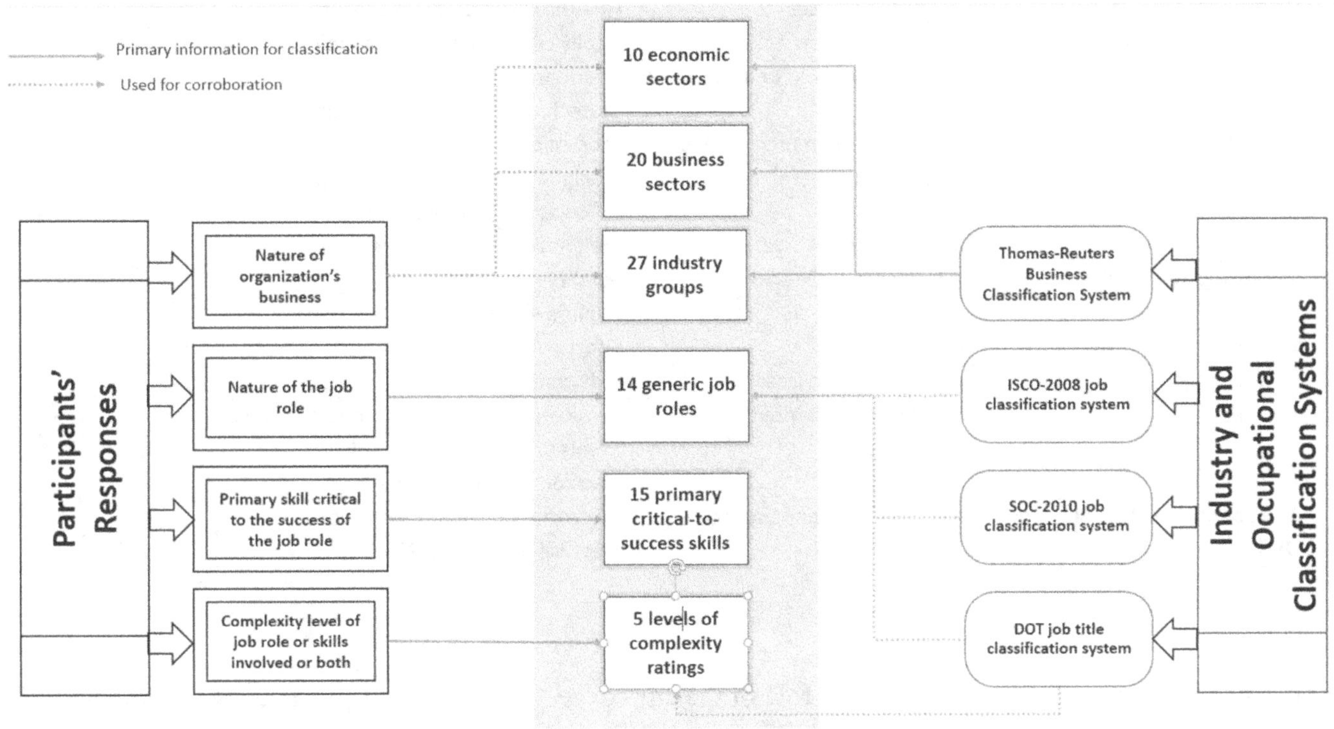

Source: developed for this research study

Thomson Reuters' 2012 version of Business Classification (TRBC) system was used to classify economic, business and industry sectors of the project cases (Thomson Reuters 2012). The project cases distribution by economic sectors, business sectors and industry groups is shown in *Table 3-7*. Government and Military sectors were added to the map because commercial systems like Thomson-Reuters do not have those sectors in the system.

Table 3-7: Project cases by economic sector, business sector and industry group

Economic Sector (TRBC)	Business Sector (TRBC)	Industry Group (TRBC)	No. of projects
Basic materials	Chemicals	Chemicals	1
	Mineral resources	Metals & mining	2
Consumer non-cyclicals	Automobiles & auto parts	Automobiles & auto parts	2
	Cyclical consumer services	Media & publishing	1
		Hotels & entertainment services	1
	Food & beverages	Food & tobacco	2
	Retailers	Other specialty retailers	2
Energy	Energy - fossil fuels	Oil & gas	6
		Oil & gas related equipment and services	2
Financials	Banking & investment services	Investment banking & investment services	4
		Banking services	2

		Insurance	Insurance	3
		Real Estate	Real estate operations	1
Healthcare		Healthcare services	Healthcare providers & services	3
			Healthcare equipment & supplies	1
		Pharmaceuticals & medical research	Pharmaceuticals	2
			Biotechnology & medical research	2
Industrials		Industrial & commercial services	Professional & commercial services	3
		Industrial goods	Machinery, equipment & components	2
			Aerospace & defense	1
		Transportation	Freight & logistics services	1
Military/ government		Government / military	Military	2
			Public services	1
Sports		Sports	Sports	1
Technology		Software & it services	Software & it services	3
		Technology equipment	Semiconductors & semiconductor equipment	8
			Communications & networking	3
			Electronic equipment & parts	1
Telecommunication services		Telecommunications services	Telecommunications services	2
Utility		Utilities	Electrical utilities & IPPS	1
			Total	**66**

Participants provided the nature of the job role of the employees whose time-to-proficiency was the focus in the project case under discussion. These generic job roles were condensed and refined into fourteen categories using a basic premise that all sales-related jobs, irrespective of business sector, had similar goals related to sales (i.e., to sell a certain quantity and make certain revenue). Mapping was corroborated and with International Standard Classification of Occupations (ISCO-2008), Standard Occupational Classification (SOC-2010) and Department of Labor's Dictionary of Titles (DOT) (Mannetje & Kromhout 2003). The detailed mapping of jobs between the three different occupational classification systems with their generic job types is provided in Appendix 16. Project case distribution by nature of the job is given in *Table 3-8*.

In each project, participants were asked to identify one crucial primary skill which was *critical-to-success* (CTS) of that job role based on the responsibility and goals of the job role. For example, in certain technical or engineering job roles assigned to repair capital equipment, the ability to do complex troubleshooting was the primary success skill, whereas, in other technical or engineering jobs where roles meet to handle the setup of a factory, the project execution skills were the CTS skills. Fifteen such CTS skills were identified, as listed in *Table 3-9*.

The complexity rating was derived from participant accounts considering the complexity of the job role itself or the complexity of the CTS skills involved. A matrix of case vs. complexity quote from each case was created (see Appendix 17). A preliminary five-level complexity rating was also assigned to each project: very high, medium-high, medium, medium-low and low, which were then corroborated with a three-digit complexity code, assigned by Dictionary of Titles (DOT) for each job title based on a combination of data, people or things related to the skills required to do that job (Mannetje & Kromhout 2003, p. 421). Refer to Appendix 18 for the three-digit complexity code system of DOT. The distribution of project cases by complexity level is given in *Table 3-10*.

Table 3-8: Project cases by nature of job role

Generic nature of job role	No. of Project cases
Technical or engineering	22
Sales - non-technical	9
Scientific or development	6
Customer service helpdesk	4
Managerial, supervisory	4
Strategic management, leadership	4
Sales - technical	3
Production, manufacturing	3
Medical, healthcare	3
Financial services	2
Training or education	2
Warehouse	1
Assembly, repair	1
Management consulting	1
Sports, athletics	1
Total	**66**

Table 3-9: Project cases by critical-to-success (CTS) skill

Critical-to-success skills	No. of project cases
Sales and negotiation	12
Complex troubleshooting	12
Technical problem solving	7
Innovation and design	6
Strategic thinking	4
Supervisory	4
Helpdesk support	4
Project execution	3
Precision machining	3
Medical and psychological care	3
Financial analysis	2
Teaching and training	2
Perceptual and physical skills	1
Data processing	1
Business analysis	1
Assembly	1
Total	**66**

Table 3-10: Project cases by complexity levels

Complexity Rating	No. of project cases
High	10
Medium-high	24
Medium	10
Medium-low	16
Low	6
Total	**66**

3.5.4 Criterion sampling of bounded project cases

In this study, the researcher's goal was to collect project cases structured as start-to-end project cases structured around five phases as per Figure 3-3 described in sub-section 3.4.2. Further, the project case had to be related to shortening time-to-proficiency exclusively. Therefore, before the data analysis was conducted, it was very important to validate if all the project cases met the intent of the research question under investigation. Patton (2002, p. 238) called this approach 'criterion sampling' which is meant 'to review and study all cases that meet some predetermined criterion of importance, a strategy common in quality assurance efforts'. Accordingly, the purpose of criterion sampling was to enhance the quality of the study. Three criteria determined the appropriateness and adequacy of a project case to answer the research question:

Criteria 1: Project goals are explicitly to reduce time-to-proficiency in business settings: The main goal of the project must be reducing time-to-proficiency in business settings. In case the main goal with which the project started was not to reduce the time-to-proficiency, then the time-to-proficiency as a byproduct of the project is acceptable. The project must be situated in business settings.

Criteria 2: Project produces one of the direct indicators of reduction in time-to-proficiency: The results must be directly related to time-to-proficiency reduction.

Criteria 3: Project description has three essential structural elements: For a reasonably representative description of a project story, it must have at least three of the five phases of an improvement project structure as per sub-section 3.4.2 to allow comparability across other project cases: (1) business challenge; (2) solutions put together; and (3) the business results obtained. For a new initiative/project, at the minimum, these three elements are certain to be there if the initiative/project was executed as a project.

The results of all the project cases were analysed systematically against these criteria. Combinations of these criteria indicated that six of the 66 projects did not meet the criteria. The process of applying above criteria and matrix of project cases not meeting the criteria is shown in Appendix 19.

3.6 DISTRIBUTION PROFILE OF SELECTED PROJECT CASES

Based on the criteria described in sub-section 3.5.4, 60 project cases were selected for analysis. These project cases represented the context of the wide range in almost every economic sector listed in TRBC, while covering a wide range of business sectors or industry groups, represented several job role types and skills, and spanned across all levels of complexities. The distribution analysis of the 60 selected project cases is shown in *Table 3-11*. The project characteristics are detailed in Appendix 2. The distribution suggests some important observations:

- More than 85% of the project cases were conducted in the USA, while four other countries represented the remaining 15% of the project cases.
- Project cases represented nine of the ten economic sectors in the Thomason-Reuters classification system. Project cases belonging to the cyclical economic sector did not pass the selection criteria. The technology and financial sectors represented the larger portion of project cases (23%). Basic materials, telecommunication services and utilities represented sectors with few project cases. This could be because of the limited reach to participants with required experience in these sectors or those sectors are yet to understand the benefits of initiatives/projects setup to accelerate proficiency.
- Project cases represented 20 business sectors of the 28 sectors in the Thomason-Reuters classification. The largest number of project cases came from the technology equipment business sector (20%), which is driven primarily by time-to-market pressures of new products. The next largest number of cases came from the energy business sectors.

- Project cases represented 28 of 54 industry groups in the Thomason-Reuters classification system. The industry groups such as semiconductor and semiconductor equipment represented the largest number of project cases (13%), followed by oil & gas and investment banking. Projects were seen relatively uniformly distributed across the remaining industry groups.
- Job roles like technical and engineering represented 35% of the project cases, followed by technical sales in 13% of the project cases.
- Skills like troubleshooting (20%), sales and negotiation (18%) and technical problem-solving (10%) characterised the majority of projects.
- The largest number of projects cases exhibited medium-high (37%) complexity.

Table 3-11: Distribution of project cases by contextual variables

Economic Sector (TRBC)		
Technology	14	23%
Financials	10	17%
Healthcare	8	13%
Industrials	7	12%
Energy	7	12%
Consumer non-cyclicals	5	8%
Basic materials	3	5%
Military/government	3	5%
Telecommunication services	2	3%
Utility	1	2%
Total	**60**	**100%**

Business Sector (TRBC)		
Technology equipment	12	20%
Energy - fossil fuels	7	12%
Healthcare services	6	10%
Pharmaceuticals & medical research	4	7%
Insurance	4	7%
Industrial & commercial services	3	5%
Government / military	3	5%
Industrial goods	3	5%
Telecommunications services	3	5%
Software & it services	2	3%
Mineral resources	2	3%
Retailers	2	3%
Real estate	2	3%
Transportation	1	2%
Chemicals	1	2%
Automobiles & auto parts	1	2%
Utilities	1	2%
Cyclical consumer services	1	2%
Food & beverages	1	2%
Technology equipment	1	2%
Total	**60**	**100%**

Industry Group (TRBC)		
Semiconductors & semiconductor equipment	8	13%
Oil & gas	5	8%
Investment banking & investment services	4	7%
Communications & networking	3	5%
Professional & commercial services	3	5%
Healthcare providers & services	3	5%
Insurance	3	5%
Pharmaceuticals	2	3%
Oil & gas related equipment and services	2	3%
Telecommunications services	2	3%
Banking services	2	3%
Other specialty retailers	2	3%
Biotechnology & medical research	2	3%
Software & it services	2	3%
Machinery, equipment & components	2	3%
Military	2	3%
Real estate operations	2	3%
Electronic equipment & parts	1	2%
Healthcare equipment & supplies	1	2%
Chemicals -	1	2%
Public services	1	2%
Hotels & entertainment services	1	2%
Electrical utilities & IPPS	1	2%
Aerospace & defense	1	2%
Food & tobacco	1	2%
Freight & logistics services	1	2%
Automobiles & auto parts	1	2%
Semiconductors & semiconductor equipment	1	2%
Total	**60**	**100%**

Complexity rating		
High	9	15%
Medium-high	22	37%
Medium	9	15%
Medium-low	14	23%
Low	6	10%
Total	**60**	**100%**

Primary job role		
Technical or engineering	21	35%
Sales - non-technical	8	13%
Scientific or Development	5	8%
Customer service helpdesk	4	7%
Strategic management, leadership	4	7%
Managerial, supervisory	3	5%
Sales - technical	3	5%
Medical, healthcare	3	5%
Production, manufacturing	3	5%
Financial services	2	3%
Warehouse	1	2%
Training or Education	1	2%
Assembly, repair	1	2%
Management consulting	1	2%
Total	**60**	**100%**

Critical-to-success skills		
Complex troubleshooting	12	20%
Sales and negotiation	11	18%
Technical problem-solving	6	10%
Innovation and design	5	8%
Strategic thinking	4	7%
Helpdesk support	4	7%
Supervisory	3	5%
Project execution	3	5%
Precision machining	3	5%
Medical and psychological care	3	5%
Financial analysis	2	3%
Business analysis	1	2%
Teaching and training	1	2%
Assembly	1	2%
Data processing	1	2%
Total	**60**	**100%**

Countries		
USA	51	85%
Netherlands	3	5%
Singapore	3	5%
Australia	2	3%
Thailand	1	2%
Total	**60**	**100%**

3.7   DATA ANALYSIS PROCESS AND METHODS

This study used thematic analysis (Braun & Clarke 2006, 2013) to identify patterns and themes within the framework of matrix analysis approach (Miles, Huberman & Saldana 2014) to perform the cross-case analysis. Additionally, the pragmatic orientation of 'what works' allowed using other supplementary data analysis techniques such as template analysis, conceptual maps, thematic networks and thematic maps in conjunction with thematic analysis to unravel the deeper meaning. Doing so made it congruent with the concept of using multiple data analysis methods to improve understanding of the participants' perspective and add new perspectives (Leech & Onwuegbuzie 2007). The methodological underpinning of the data analysis process used in this study is described below, and the major steps are briefly explained.

3.7.1   Thematic analysis

A combination of thematic analysis methods suggested by Braun and Clarke (2006, 2013) and Boyatzis (1998) were applied when identifying the themes and patterns in this study. This thematic analysis method was used within the umbrella of Miles, Huberman and Saldana's (2014) matrix analysis framework. Braun and Clarke (2006, p. 79) positioned thematic analysis as 'a method for identifying, analysing and reporting patterns (themes) within data'. Though it is called analysis, in actual practice researchers position thematic analysis as 'not another qualitative method but a process that can be used with most, if not all, qualitative methods' (Boyatzis 1998, p. 4). The process of thematic analysis does not subscribe to a specific epistemological stand, thus making it a preferred choice in the pragmatic paradigm (Braun & Clarke 2006, p. 81). Further, thematic analysis is grounded in the data, just like grounded theory. 'A thematic analysis process analyses the data without engaging pre-existing themes, which means that it can be adapted to any research that relies only upon participants' clarifications' (Alhojailan 2012, p. 42). As a result, thematic analysis was found suitable for a new unexplored topic of accelerated proficiency, where no prior theoretical underpinning existed. Besides, the thematic analysis process offered great flexibility to analyse a large corpus of data obtained in this study (Namey & Johnson 2007).

For subsequent discussion, terms used in the thematic analysis are clarified due to a different meaning associated with these terms in different research approaches.

Code: Code is a label assigned to a chunk of data. The code is 'the most basic segment, or element, of the raw data or information that can be assessed in a meaningful way regarding the phenomenon' (Boyatzis 1998, p. 63). The code can be assigned to anything interesting, a data segment, a chunk, even a word or to mark a theme (Braun & Clarke 2006).

Theme: Theme is a 'pattern found in the information that at the minimum describes and organises possible observations or at the maximum interpret aspects of the phenomenon' (Boyatzis 1998, p. 4). 'A theme captures something important about the data in relation to the research question, and represents some level of patterned response or meaning within the data set' (Braun & Clarke 2006, p. 82). Identifying patterns in data may lead to identifying a potential theme.

Overarching theme: The overarching themes 'organise and structure the analysis; they tend not to contain codes or data, but instead simply capture an idea encapsulated in a number of themes' (Braun & Clarke 2013, p. 231). An overarching theme may have several themes underneath it with certain hierarchical or non-hierarchical relationships (Braun & Clarke 2006, p. 89).

Sub-theme: 'Sub-themes are essentially themes-within-a theme. They can be useful for giving structure to a particularly large and complex theme, and also for demonstrating the hierarchy of meaning within the data' (Braun & Clarke 2006, p. 92). 'subthemes capture and develop notable *specific* aspects of the central organizing concept of one theme' (Braun & Clarke 2013, p. 231).

Category: Category is another name for the theme in context of this thesis (Miles, Huberman & Saldana 2014)

3.7.2 Miles and Huberman matrix analysis approach

In the present study, comparative data analysis was conducted using the matrix analysis approach specified by Miles and Huberman (1994) and Miles, Huberman and Saldana (2014). The matrix analysis approach arranges themes and data of bounded project cases in the form of a matrix (a table of columns and rows to arrange the data for easy viewing in one place) to understand the dynamics of the project cases within itself and then across the project cases by stacking rows of data from other project cases. The main purpose of matrices is to understand 'a phenomenon of some sort occurring in a bounded context' (id. 28). Thus, the sampling strategy of bounded project cases informed the choice of the Miles, Huberman and Saldana's (2014) framework. Furthermore, the research study assumed its position within the pragmatic paradigm. Miles and Huberman's matrix thematic approach, positioned as *'pragmatic realists'* (id. 7), deals with data analysis from a pragmatic angle, as it does not subscribe to 'any one particular genre of qualitative research' (id. 9) such as case study methodology, ethnography, or phenomenology. This approach of data analysis kept these divides aside and provided an orderly set of techniques to the qualitative researcher to conduct systematic and rigorous data analysis.

In this method, the interpretative analysis is conducted in three stages that run concurrently with the data collection: (1) data condensation; (2) data display; (3) drawing and verifying conclusions. In the data condensation stage, the corpus of data from interview transcripts, interview notes, concept maps and documents was reviewed. Steps such as summaries, data coding, and developing themes and writing analytic memos were taken in this stage. In this model, coding is considered as analysis itself which 'sharpens, sorts, focuses, discards, and organises data in such a way that "final" conclusions can be drawn and verified' (id. 13). Thematic analysis on the data was performed at this stage using the techniques of Braun and Clarke (2006, 2013) and drew some guidelines from Boyatzis (1998) and Guest, MacQueen and Namey (2011). Using thematic analysis, the patterns were explained in terms of the meaning of the participant's actions.

In the data display stage, information was organised to display in the form of matrix displays, network displays, diagrams and concept maps, etc., which allowed the researcher to draw conclusions. At this stage, the key focus was: 'How do all the codes and themes relate to each other? What is the big picture, and how does it relate to each theme or code? Where does one begin to tell the story?' (Miles & Huberman 1994, p. 69). To compare the bounded project cases, matrices were used as the main mechanism to order and display the information. Graphics and networks were also used as the ways to display the analysis, if that best communicated the data.

In the third stage, drawing and verifying conclusions, the main actions involved were noting patterns, building causal explanations (cause and effect), developing prepositions, drawing conclusions and testing the conclusions for their 'plausibility, sturdiness and confirmability – that is, their validity' (id. 14). In this approach, conclusion drawing is considered as the initial activity and emphasis is on validating those conclusions, thereby providing credibility to the research. Though called stages, everything was concurrent, recursive, moved back-and-forth and there were no linear steps involved. The cyclic process is described as:

> The coding of data, for example *(data condensation)*, leads to new ideas on what should go into a matrix *(data display)*. Entering the data requires further data condensation. As the matrix fills up, preliminary *conclusions* are drawn, but they lead to the decision, for example, to add another column to the matrix to *test* the conclusion. (Miles, Huberman & Saldana 2014, p. 14)

The overall process of data analysis adopted in this study is shown in *Figure 3-5*. Though it appears linear, in actual practice every process step led to the iteration of the previous step continuously throughput the data analysis.

Figure 3-5: Data analysis process adopted in this study

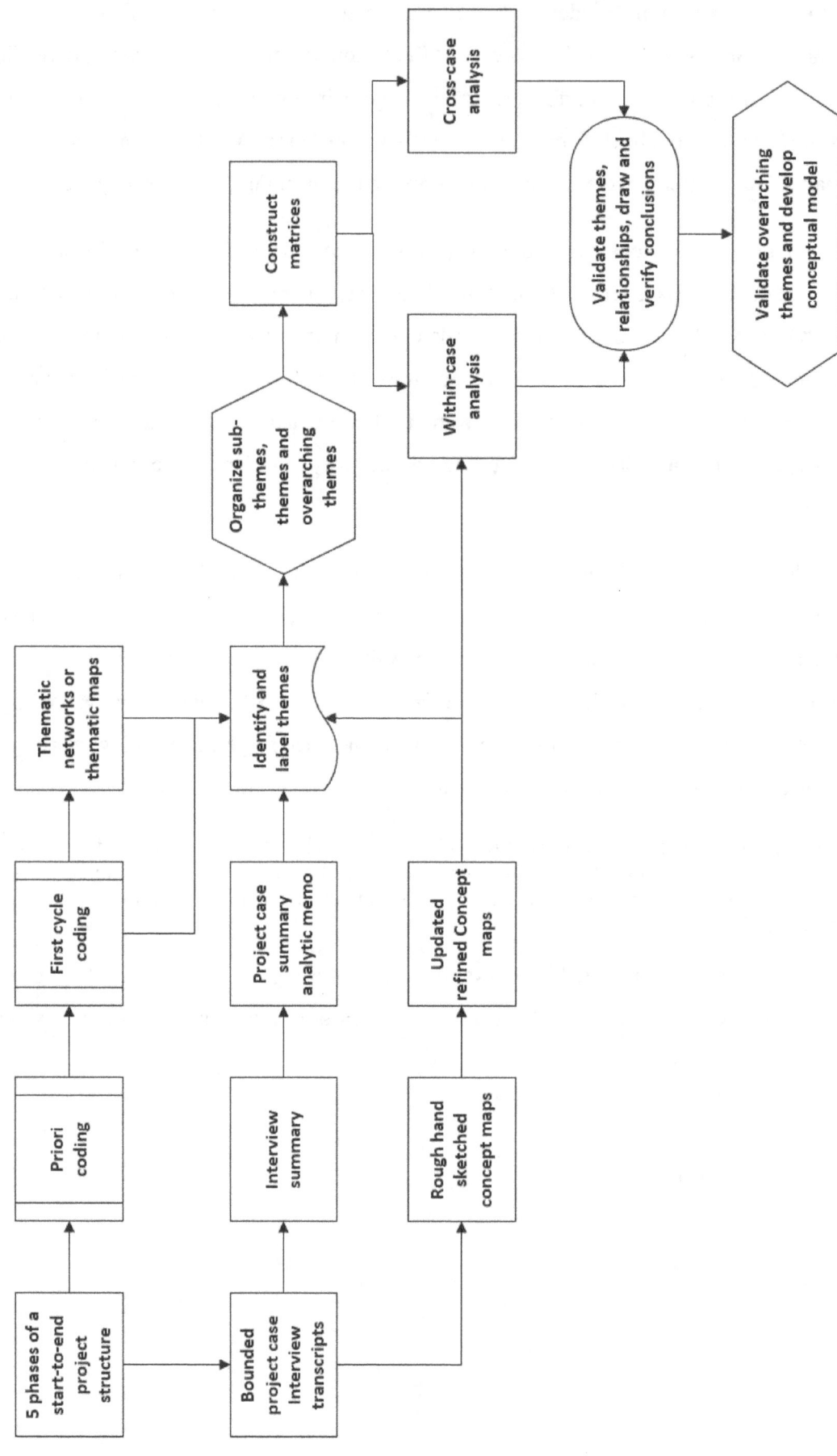

Source: developed for this research study

3.7.3 Concept maps to identify themes

This step refers to the 'updated refined concept map' and 'identify and label themes' in the data analysis process shown in *Figure 3-5*. In several studies, concept maps were established as useful tools to reduce data, identify themes quickly and provide a strong foundation for coding process (Burgess-Allen & Owen-Smith 2010; Daley 2004; Wheeldon & Faubert 2009). On these lines, concept maps or cognitive maps were used in this study as an analytic tool to analyse a case in its entirety and build a broad overview of each of the project cases, thus leading to 'within-case analysis' (Miles, Huberman & Saldana 2014, p. 101). Since concept maps were developed for each interview, comparison of concept maps was logically used as the first step to identify patterns that repeated and strengthened across multiple interviews. Based on rough concept maps drawn during the interviews, refined visual maps of the interviews were developed to understand the big picture and clarify the dynamics of each project case separately, as shown in *Figure 3-6* and *Figure 3-7*. Concept mapping led to an improved understanding of the overall project cases. Certain notable dependencies, relationships, determinants, factors, and philosophies, otherwise not evident in the running narrative without detailed coding, were labelled using concept maps (Miles, Huberman & Saldana 2014, p. 188). Also, the concept maps supplemented and enhanced the interview summaries. That was congruent with the triangulation strategy of using multiple methods to collect rich, high-quality data (Denzin 2009).

Concept maps were used as the first instrument for data condensation, coding, exploring and identifying the patterns, defining themes and presenting the data analysis (Brightman 2003). To explain the process, *Figure 3-6* and *Figure 3-7* present concept maps of interviews with two different participants. A pattern appeared from the comparison of both concept maps: MANAGER'S INVOLVEMENT (blue box). On closer examination, the concept maps also generated a sub-theme that was METHODS TO INVOLVE (green box). If MANAGER'S INVOLVEMENT is a strategy to reduce time-to-proficiency, then sub-themes acted as containers for methods, techniques or ways to implement that strategy that enriched the details of the main themes. The concept map of each interview transcript was compared similarly. In both concept maps, another pattern appeared: ENVIRONMENT (purple box), which had a strong dependence on the MANAGER'S INVOLVEMENT theme. Such relationships were further compared, contrasted, checked, verified and explained with concept maps of other interviews. Finally, MANAGER'S INVOLVEMENT formed as the sub-theme to an overarching theme of SETTING UP PROFICIENCY ECO-SYSTEM (not shown in these concept maps) and their relationships were identified.

Figure 3-6: Concept map #1 of an interview showing themes related to manager's involvement

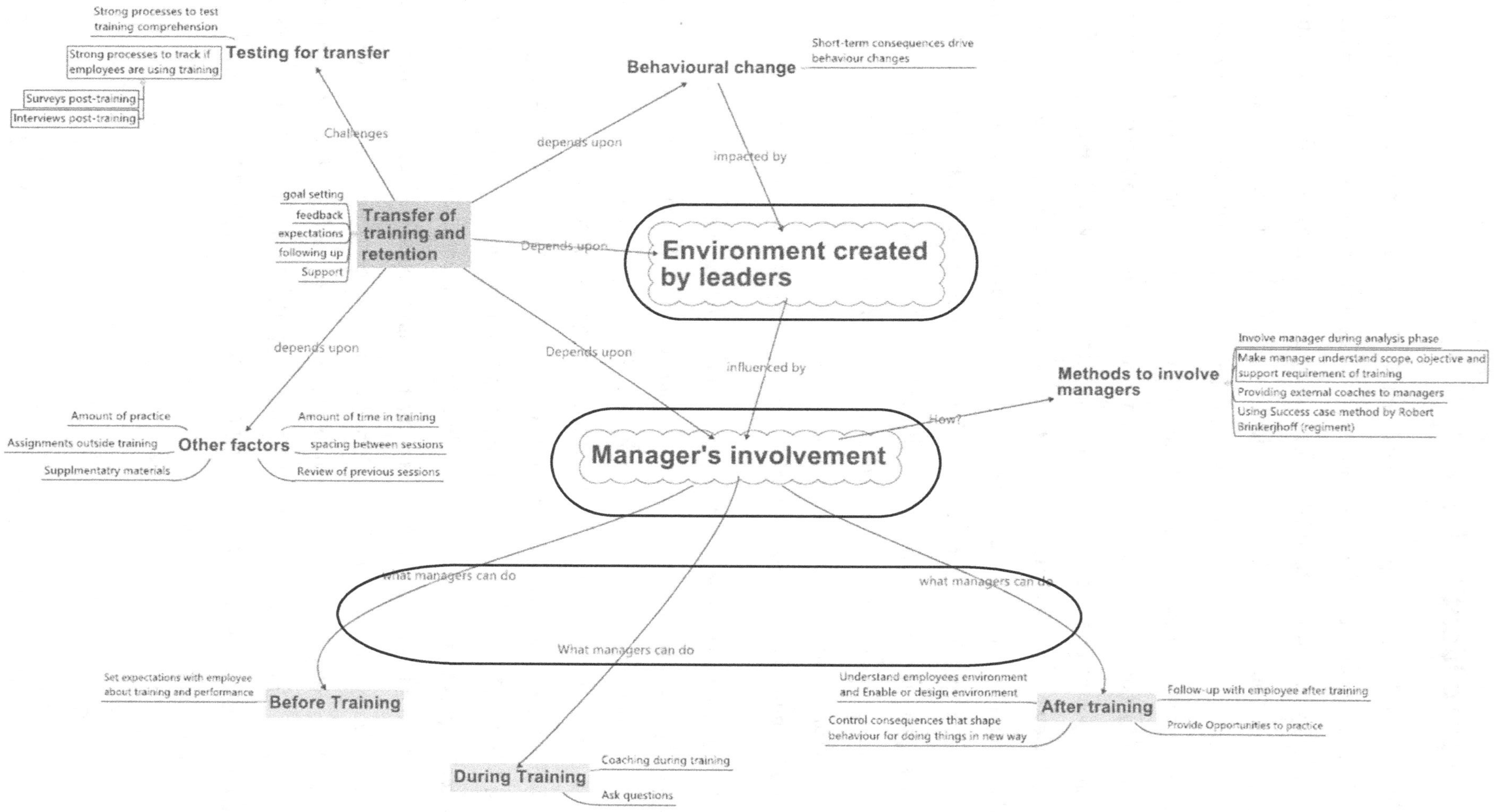

- **Transfer of training and retention**
  - Challenges
    - **Testing for transfer**
      - Strong processes to test training comprehension
      - Strong processes to track if employees are using training
        - Surveys post-training
        - Interviews post-training
  - depends upon
    - goal setting
    - feedback
    - expectations
    - following up
    - Support
  - depends upon
    - **Other factors**
      - Amount of time in training
      - spacing between sessions
      - Review of previous sessions
      - Amount of practice
      - Assignments outside training
      - Supplimentary materials
  - Depends upon → **Environment created by leaders**
    - impacted by ← **Behavioural change**
      - Short term consequences drive behaviour changes
  - Depends upon → **Manager's involvement**
    - influenced by ← Environment created by leaders
    - How? → **Methods to involve managers**
      - Involve manager during analysis phase
      - Make manager understand scope, objective and support requirement of training
      - Providing external coaches to managers
      - Using Success case method by Robert Brinkerhoff (regiment)
    - what managers can do → **After training**
      - Follow-up with employee after training
      - Provide Opportunities to practice
      - Understand employees environment and Enable or design environment
      - Control consequences that shape behaviour for doing things in new way
    - What managers can do → **During Training**
      - Coaching during training
      - Ask questions
    - what managers can do → **Before Training**
      - Set expectations with employee about training and performance

Source: developed for this research study

Figure 3-7: Concept map #2 of another interview showing themes related to manager's involvement

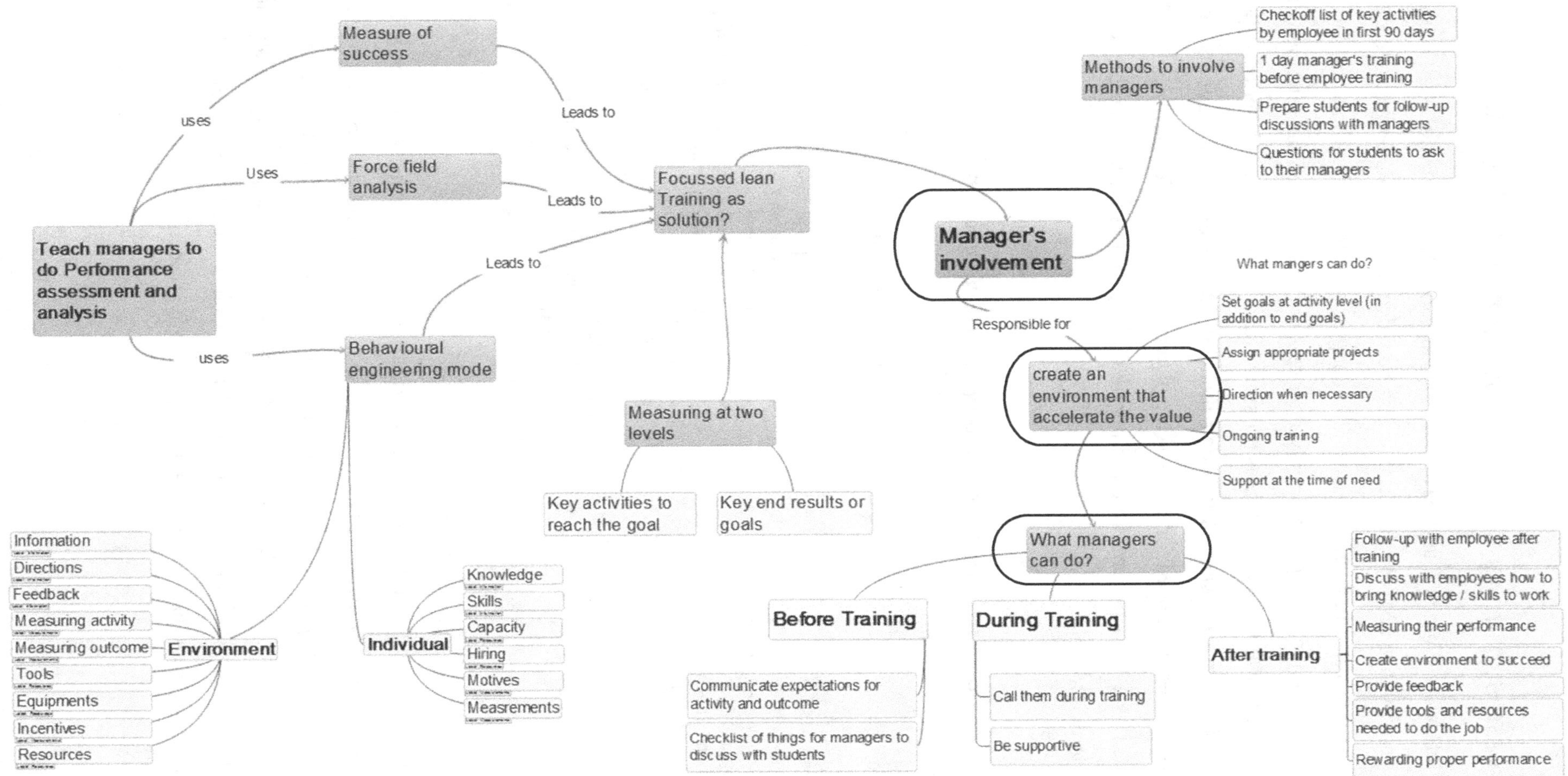

Source: developed for this research study

3.7.4 Project case summary and analytic memos to identify themes

This step refers to the 'interview summary' and 'project case summary analytic memo' steps shown in *Figure 3-5*. Miles, Huberman and Saldana (2014) advised that in a bounded case-oriented approach, the researcher should look at detailed case profiles in terms of issues, challenges, solutions, situations and factors. Then a detailed profile of each case should be compared with other cases. To this effect, the interview/project case summary for each project case was written as soon as possible after the interviews. Refer to Appendix 13 for a sample of an interview/project case summary which included two fields: 'new patterns' and 'patterns repeated'. These summaries were reviewed for any striking patterns. For example, *Figure 3-8* highlights how 'structured OJT' emerged as a 'new pattern' in one interview (Box 1) and came to be marked as 'pattern repeated' in later interviews (Box 2).

Figure 3-8: Patterns captured in project case summary memos

Box 1. Excerpt of project case summary: Diana, Project leader No. 11	Box 2. Excerpt of project case summary: Maximum, Project leader No. 36
New Patterns • Structured OJT • Re-organise the information • Reading converted to doing Patterns Repeated • Mentorship / Coaching • Learning by doing	New Patterns • Pre-training performance support system • Case-based learning • Skill management tracking • Tiered structure (i.e., low cognitive skills, high cognitive skills, etc.) • Online e-learning • Field coaching and on-the-job learning Patterns Repeated • Self-guided / self-paced learning • Structured OJT

After the concept maps were completed, the project case summaries were further extended and elaborated with the analytic memo based on any theme or significant (big) ideas that emerged from a concept map. An example of the project case summary analytic memo is shown in Appendix 14. The analytic memo followed this general structure: big ideas; key determinants and factors; key strategies; questions to explore; contradictions/outliers (where applicable). This structured approach allowed the capture of the essential major ideas in each project in a way that was comparable across the projects.

3.7.5 A priori coding using Template Analysis (TA)

This step refers to 'priori coding' block of data analysis process shown in *Figure 3-5*. In this study, before performing inductive data-driven coding, a priori deductive coding was applied as per the approach of deducting coding technique called *Template Analysis,* as suggested by Crabtree and Miller (1992, 1999) and King (2004, 2012). Since the interview questions were structured based on a typical bounded start-to-end project cases, the interview transcripts were expected to have these pre-designated data segments somewhere in the transcript. These data segments were marked with a pre-defined codes tied to interview questions, as suggested by Coffey and Atkinson (1996, p. 34) that 'in fact, the first pass at generating themes often comes from the questions in an interview protocol' (cited in Ryan & Bernard 2003, p. 88). The first two columns in the *Table 3-12* are taken from the interview guide (see Appendix 3). Using priori codes, all the bounded project cases were reduced to several comparable pre-defined data segments in NVivo. The data segments from a given a priori code could then be assembled or collated at the same place for further analysis (Waring & Wainwright 2008). These were tentative codes, some of which were found useful, while some were refined based on emergent data (Brooks et al. 2015).

Table 3-12: A priori thematic codes developed for the study

question	Segments of interview transcripts	A priori code defined
Context of the project	Company business / context	ORGANISATION BUSINESS
	Nature of Job role	JOB ROLE
	Nature of primary skills	PRIMARY SKILLS
	Skill or job role complexity	SKILL JOB COMPLEXITY
Business challenge	Goal of project	PROJECT GOAL
	Business reason	BUSINESS DRIVERS
Old model and challenges (Solution before)	Previous solution, strategies	BEFORE – STRATEGIES / MODEL
	Root cause/ challenges	ROOT CAUSE FOR LONG TTP
New model and solution (Solution after)	New solution / strategies	AFTER – STRATEGIES / MODEL
	Guiding Philosophy	PHILOSOPHY / BELIEF
Results & effectiveness	Effectiveness	PROJECT RESULTS
	Proficiency indicators	PROFICIENCY METRICS
	Measure of proficiency	
	Proficiency definition	PROFICIENCY DEFINITION
	Determinants/Factors	DETERMINANT & FACTORS (Enabler-disablers)
Transferability	Transferability	TRANSFERABILITY

3.7.6 First cycle coding

This step refers to the 'first cycle coding' block of data analysis process shown *Figure 3-5*. In this study, all the interviews and documents were coded using NVivo software. Once the priori codes were applied to the interview transcripts and documents, the next inductive coding was used, in which codes emerged purely from the data. Coding was an act of data condensation in which a label or tag was added to the meaningful text segments that stand out and that have a commonality.

Figure 3-9: Example demonstrating process of first cycle coding

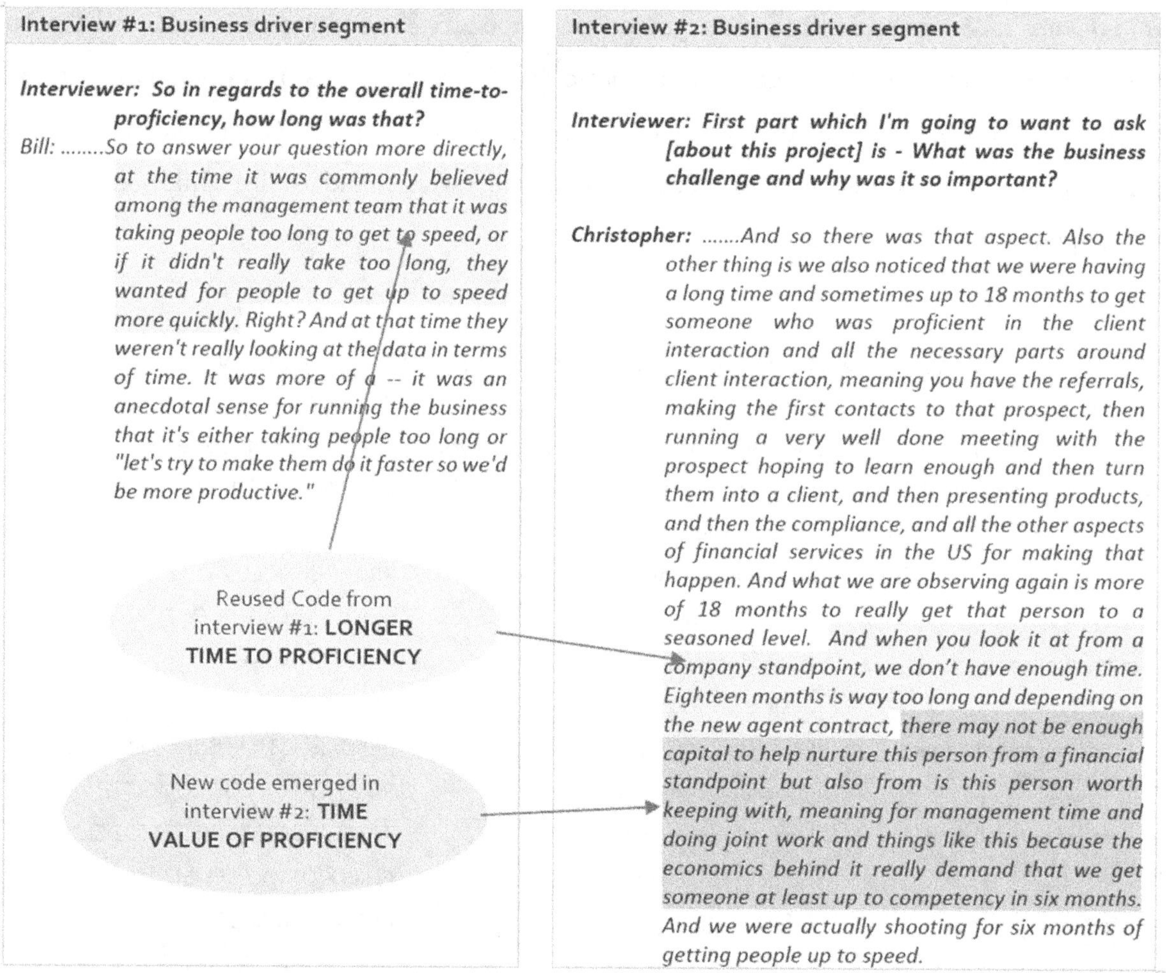

Interview #1: Business driver segment

Interviewer: So in regards to the overall time-to-proficiency, how long was that?
Bill: ....So to answer your question more directly, at the time it was commonly believed among the management team that it was taking people too long to get to speed, or if it didn't really take too long, they wanted for people to get up to speed more quickly. Right? And at that time they weren't really looking at the data in terms of time. It was more of a -- it was an anecdotal sense for running the business that it's either taking people too long or "let's try to make them do it faster so we'd be more productive."

Reused Code from interview #1: **LONGER TIME TO PROFICIENCY**

New code emerged in interview #2: **TIME VALUE OF PROFICIENCY**

Interview #2: Business driver segment

Interviewer: First part which I'm going to want to ask [about this project] is - What was the business challenge and why was it so important?

Christopher: ....And so there was that aspect. Also the other thing is we also noticed that we were having a long time and sometimes up to 18 months to get someone who was proficient in the client interaction and all the necessary parts around client interaction, meaning you have the referrals, making the first contacts to that prospect, then running a very well done meeting with the prospect hoping to learn enough and then turn them into a client, and then presenting products, and then the compliance, and all the other aspects of financial services in the US for making that happen. And what we are observing again is more of 18 months to really get that person to a seasoned level. And when you look it at from a company standpoint, we don't have enough time. Eighteen months is way too long and depending on the new agent contract, there may not be enough capital to help nurture this person from a financial standpoint but also from is this person worth keeping with, meaning for management time and doing joint work and things like this because the economics behind it really demand that we get someone at least up to competency in six months. And we were actually shooting for six months of getting people up to speed.

Source: developed for this research study

In the coding process, codes were assigned to identify recurring patterns in the data which appeared meaningful. Then the themes (or sub-themes) were identified by clustering the similar codes appropriately. The relationship between the themes was analysed and concepts or theory were developed from the analytic meaning of those relationships (Miles, Huberman & Saldana 2014, p. 73). The process of emergent first cycle coding is demonstrated in *Figure 3-9,* in which a previously identified code LONGER TIME-TO-PROFICIENCY was reused in interview #2, while a new code TIME VALUE OF PROFICIENCY was identified in the interview #2. The old codes were revisited, expanded, renamed, broken into multiple codes, merged with others or even discarded. Various perspectives were used to develop the code which included context, situation, ways of thinking, perspectives, processes, activities, events, strategies, and relationships, among others, as suggested by Bogdan and Biklen (2006).

3.7.7 Thematic network to analyse themes for relationships

This step refers to the 'thematic network or thematic maps' block of data analysis process shown in *Figure 3-5*. Several researchers proposed essentially similar techniques but with different names such as thematic networks (Attride-Stirling 2001, p. 288), thematic maps (Braun & Clarke 2013, p. 232), causal networks (Miles, Huberman & Saldana 2014, p. 235) and concept maps (Daley 2004), among several other names. Fundamentally, each technique specified to create visual representation of the themes. On those lines, visual maps or networks were used to explore the relationship among first cycle codes, as well as sub-themes, themes and overarching themes. Most iterations were handwritten sketches for the major code clusters or significant themes. As the analysis progressed, several refinements were done in each visual map. The new clusters, new relationships, new dependencies and new themes were uncovered through such mapping. *Figure 3-10* shows the thematic maps/network of one key theme of PURPOSEFUL SOCIAL INTERCONNECTIVITY @ WORK. Based on several such maps, a hierarchical map of major sub-themes, themes and overarching themes was created to answer each research question.

Appendix 21 shows a larger thematic network of themes representing 24 strategies to analyse the relationship among themes to form/group the overarching themes.

Figure 3-10: Example of a thematic map of the theme 'purposeful social interconnectivity'

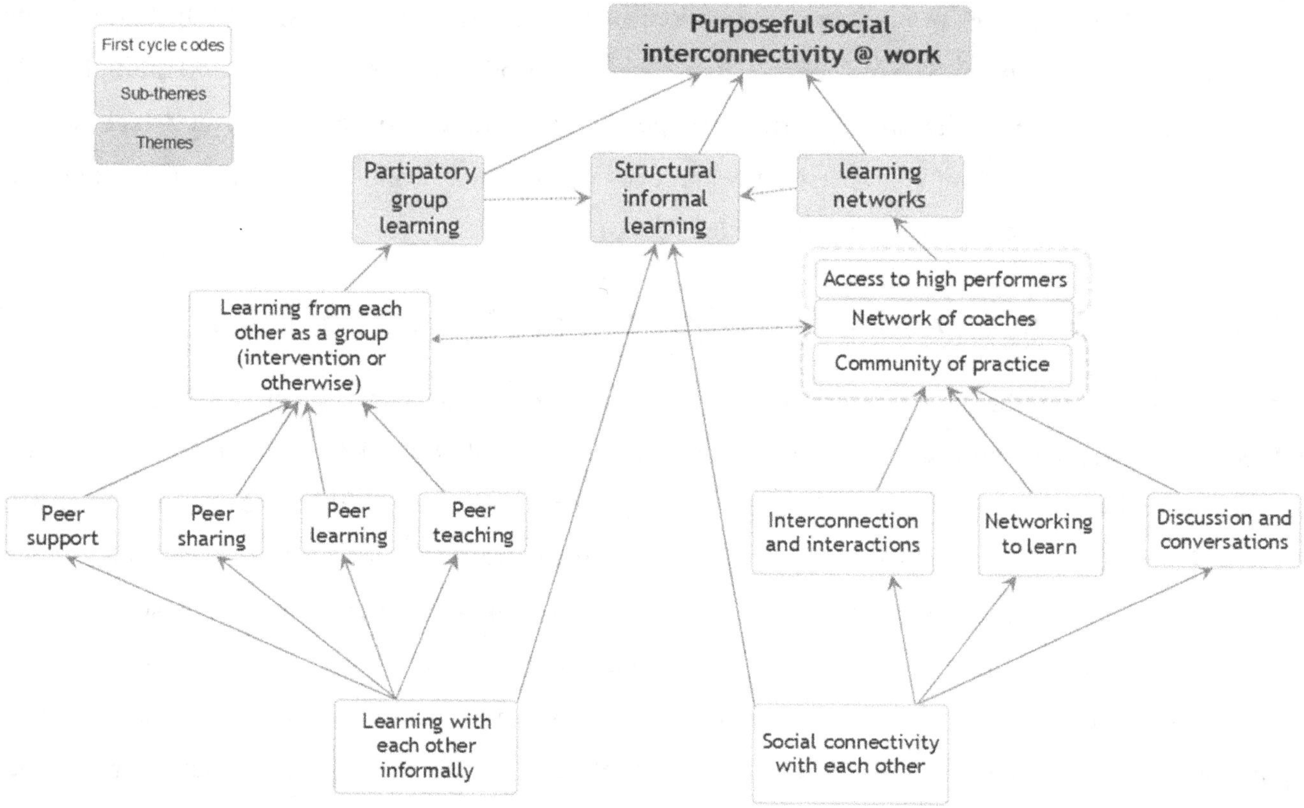

Source: developed for this research study

3.7.8 Organising sub-themes, themes and overarching themes

This step refers to the 'organising sub-themes, themes and overarching themes' block of data analysis process shown in *Figure 3-5*. At this stage, the goal was to recognise if there was any central organising concept among the cluster of codes that connected them together. Each theme had a 'central organising concept, which tells us something about the content of the data that's *meaningful*, something about how, and in what way, that concept appears in the data; it tells us something meaningful in relation to the research question' (Braun & Clarke 2013, p. 224). This organising concept could indicate the presence of explanation, relationship, specific configuration or even an issue. At a high level, the theme may shape up as 'categories or themes, causes/explanation, relationships among people and theoretical constructs' (Miles, Huberman & Saldana 2014, p. 87). Once a *candidate* theme (a potential or provisional theme) was identified from a cluster of first cycle codes, the cluster was labelled with 'explanatory or inferential codes' to create a meaningful and 'parsimonious unit of analysis' (id. 86). This study used most of the guidelines specified by Ryan and

Bernard (2003, p. 89) to identify the themes based on repetition of the patterns and terms and the prevalence of the code (count of code presence). This also involved assessing to see whether a given code was rich enough that it could be a marked as a theme under which other similar codes should be grouped (Charmaz 2014).

The analytic memo in Appendix 20 shows an example of the process used to develop four themes, namely: TIME-RELATED PRESSURE, SPEED-RELATED COMPETITIVENESS, SKILL-RELATED DEFICIENCIES and COST OR FINANCIAL IMPLICATIONS by clustering 19 first cycle codes by using different perspectives. Further analysis led to the formation of BUSINESS DRIVERS as an overarching theme, which together with the other two overarching themes of MAGNITUDE & SCALE and BUSINESS BENEFITS answered research questions #3. The hierarchical map of the thematic coding is shown in *Figure 3-11*. In this example, there was no sub-theme. However, when such analysis was conducted on a full corpus of data, several codes were clustered to form the sub-themes. Appendix 39 shows the full thematic map (except sub-themes) for all three research questions, which is described in Chapter 4. It was an active process of interacting with the data and with the codes from the researcher's eye, while staying grounded to the data and seeing what emerged out of it (Braun & Clarke 2013, p. 225). The reflection on the approach, relationships observed and the outcome of this process was captured in the analytic memo.

Figure 3-11: Clustering of first cycle codes to form themes, sub-themes and overarching themes

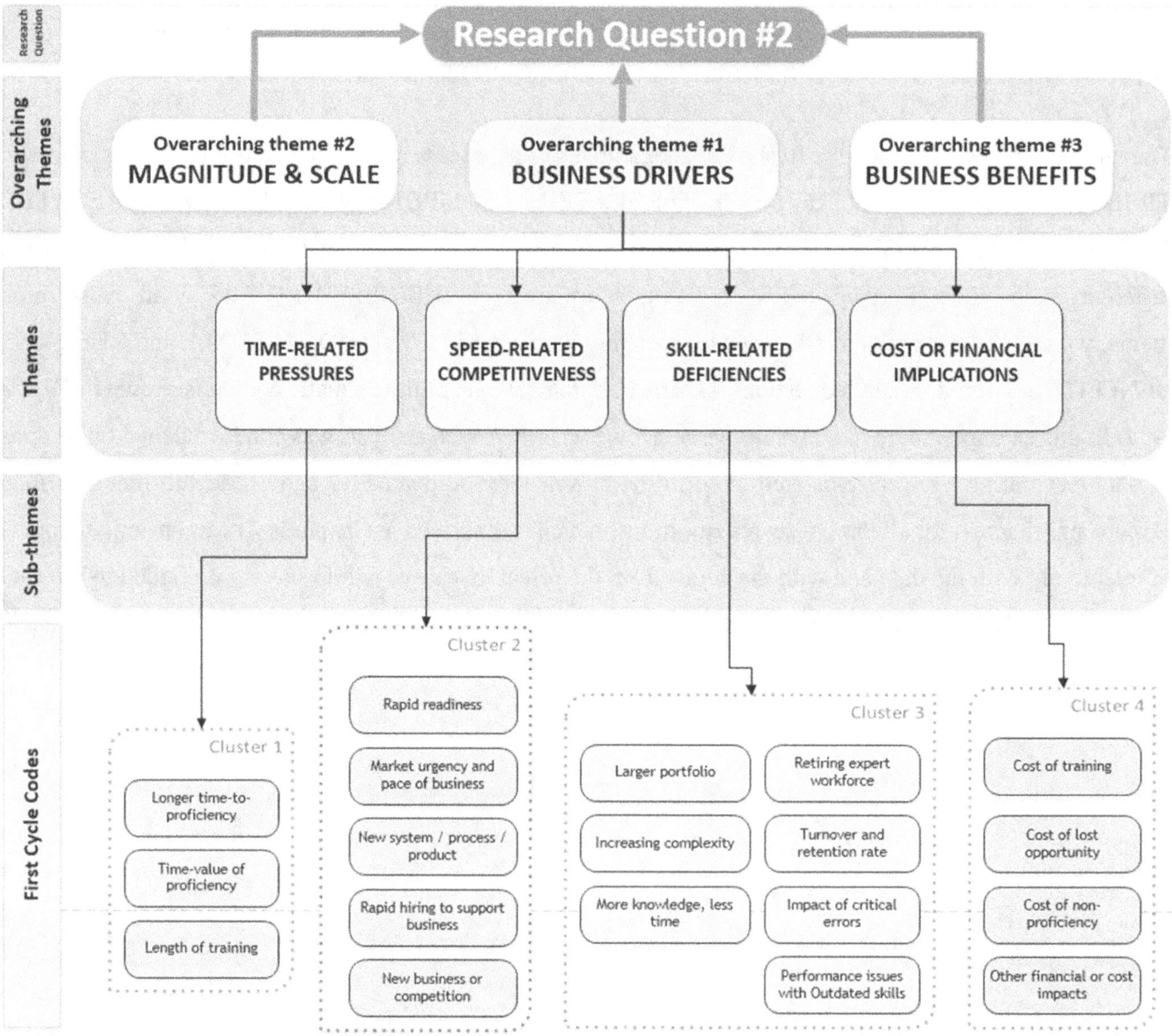

Research Question #2

Overarching Themes
- Overarching theme #2: **MAGNITUDE & SCALE**
- Overarching theme #1: **BUSINESS DRIVERS**
- Overarching theme #3: **BUSINESS BENEFITS**

Themes
- TIME-RELATED PRESSURES
- SPEED-RELATED COMPETITIVENESS
- SKILL-RELATED DEFICIENCIES
- COST OR FINANCIAL IMPLICATIONS

Sub-themes / First Cycle Codes

Cluster 1:
- Longer time-to-proficiency
- Time-value of proficiency
- Length of training

Cluster 2:
- Rapid readiness
- Market urgency and pace of business
- New system / process / product
- Rapid hiring to support business
- New business or competition

Cluster 3:
- Larger portfolio
- Increasing complexity
- More knowledge, less time
- Retiring expert workforce
- Turnover and retention rate
- Impact of critical errors
- Performance issues with Outdated skills

Cluster 4:
- Cost of training
- Cost of lost opportunity
- Cost of non-proficiency
- Other financial or cost impacts

Source: developed for this research study

3.7.9 Constructing matrices

This step refers to the 'constructing matrices' block of data analysis process shown in *Figure 3-5*. While each case was summarised using the project case summary memo, as well as the concept map individually, to perform cross-case analysis, all that information along with the themes were transferred to the matrices. Past studies suggested the usefulness of matrices: 'Guided by themes and questions identified in the study; matrices provide a visual display of the data, including extracted themes. Such matrices simplify the data for researchers' discussions, while the case summaries provide more details on the data' (White, Oelke & Friesen 2012, p. 247). Miles and Huberman (1994, p. 137) suggested to '[u]se supplementary displays such as matrices to further condense and examine the concept maps – especially if you contemplate cross-case analysis'.

Constructing matrices was the heart of this research study. The primary purpose of these matrices was to validate the within-case analysis and to perform the cross-case analysis. This involved transferring the themes and major codes or categories identified in previous steps to a suitably constructed multi-row and multi-column matrix designed based on the guidelines of Miles, Huberman and Saldana (2014). Five types of matrices were developed in Microsoft Excel to perform the thematic analysis: partially-ordered meta-matrix, checklist matrices, case-ordered matrices, case-ordered descriptive meta-matrix, and conceptual clustered matrix.

Table 3-13 lists an excerpt of major matrices used for the study. This list is not exhaustive, just a partial list of several matrices that were created during the data analysis. Creating, changing, re-designing and discarding matrices was an iterative process and in the process over 50 different matrices were constructed. Some of the matrices were as large as 1,000 rows x 200 columns. Space limitation would not permit reproduction of any of those here. However, small excerpts of some of the key matrices are given in the appendices where possible.

Table 3-13: Summary of major matrices constructed in this study

Category	Type of matrix	Matrix title	Description	How constructed	Analytical purpose	Appendix
Case profile matrix	Partially-ordered meta-matrix	Project cases classification by contextual variables	Mapping of project cases with contextual variables (sectors, job role, skills, complexity)	Size: 60 rows x 10 columns. Rows: project cases. Columns: Economic sector, business sector, industry group, ISCO-2008 job classification, SOC-2008 job classification, DOT titles, Generic job role, primary critical-to-success skill, complexity rating. Allied information like DOT complexity codes and reasons. Sorting: By any column	Case classification and distribution across contextual variables. Define contextual variables of each case for subsequent analysis of themes vs. contextual variables. Sorting by any variable to cluster projects together for a given variable value (e.g., all projects in technology sector).	Appendix 2
Organisational context	Case-ordered matrices	Project cases vs. business context	Summary of organisational business environment, challenge, context at one place with quotes	Size: 60 rows x 3 columns. Rows: project cases. Columns: Summary of the CONTEXT (priori code) and corresponding quotes. Sorting: None	Document business landscape such as nature of company, nature of business, business environment, job type of the target group and business challenge. Analyse relationship of business context with the strategies used in those contexts (e.g., how does the companies facing attrition challenge view need for accelerating TTP).	Appendix 23
Business drivers	Case-ordered matrices	Project cases vs. business drivers	Summary of business drivers in each project that led to need for a shorter time-to-proficiency	Size: 60 rows x 5 columns. Rows: project cases. Columns: First cycle codes categorised as TIME, SPEED, SKILL, FINANCIAL with quotes and analytic comments. Sorting: by each column	Analyse the relationship among different drivers (e.g., if time-related pressures manifest always with speed-related competitive advantages). Analyse pattern how different drivers manifest or associated with different contextual variables of a project case (e.g., does speed-related drivers always show up in technology jobs?)	Appendix 24
TTP improvement indicators	Checklist Matrix	Case vs type of TTP measures	Quick checklist of type of indicator for time-to-proficiency improvement	Size: 60 rows x 9 columns. Rows: project cases. Columns: Category of indicator for TTP reduction	Project case validation by type of result. Relationship between set of strategies with type of results.	Appendix 26
Reduction in TTP results	Case-ordered matrices	Project cases vs. reduction in TTP	Actual TTP results attained in each project compared to baseline	Size: 60 rows x 6 columns. Rows: Project cases. Columns: Type of results by category (direct or indirect) and sub-categories	Relationship of set of strategies to the type and extent of reduction in TTP. Evidence that strategies discovered in this study indeed work.	Appendix 27

Business benefits	Case-ordered matrices	Case vs. business benefits matrix	Business benefits attained from each project case	Size: 60 rows x 1 column Rows: project cases Columns: concise statement of business relates by category (productivity, cost savings etc.) Sorting: by project cases and by type of business gain	Trends of business benefits attained in TTP initiatives/projects over and above reduction in time-to-proficiency.	Appendix 28
Proficiency measures	Case-ordered matrices	Project case vs. proficiency measures	Measures of proficiency in different project cases or contexts	Size: 60 rows x 3 columns matrix Rows: project cases Columns: 1st cycle codes from the text labelled with priori codes PROFICIENCY MEASURES and corresponding quotes Sorting: By proficiency measure	Categorise proficiency measures in high-level thematic clusters. How the type of measures varies by changing contextual variables (e.g., in what kind of complexity the proficiency is measured by comparative performance).	Appendix 29
Analytic memos	Conceptually clustered matrix	Project cases vs. project case summary	Project case summary template converted to table by project cases	Size: 60 rows x X columns (X varied based on items) Rows: project cases Columns: big ideas, key determinants, key strategies, questions to follow, contradictions Sorting: By project cases	Dynamics of the project and first pass on the overall story of the project case. Cluster projects with similar big ideas or similar determinants together and understand common themes among project cases. Combine or partition the matrix into sub-matrices.	Appendix 22
Code matrix	Conceptually clustered matrix	Theses or codes hierarchy vs. project cases	Major themes arranged by project cases	Size: A 908 rows x 60 columns matrix Rows: Themes and codes by hierarchy levels Columns: project cases Sorting: by any of the project characteristics like business sector, industry, nature of job, etc.	Within-case analysis by reading the columns (e.g., How different themes manifest themselves to explain the project dynamics). Cross-case analysis by reading a theme across all the project case columns to see how it manifests at different level across all the project cases. How different themes manifest themselves by changing various contextual variables (e.g., if a given theme occurs only in one type of industry.)	Appendix 30
Theme prevalence	Conceptually clustered matrix	Themes or codes by levels vs. prevalence % of the code	Degree of prevalence (counting of code presence) of a code/theme across project cases and contextual variables	Size: A 908 rows x 248 columns matrix Rows: Themes and codes by hierarchy levels Columns: Computed % of prevalence by each project cases and % prevalence grouped by contextual variables. Filter: By hierarchical level of theme	Analyse degree of prevalence of themes (at each level) across all project cases and across all contextual variables (e.g., which themes are strongly prevalent across and which themes are weakly prevalent.)	Appendix 35

Chapter 3 — Research Methodology

pg. 147

3.7.10 Within-case analysis

This step refers to the 'within-case analysis' block of data analysis process shown in *Figure 3-5*. In the within-case analysis, one row of a given project case was picked and read all the way across to all the columns to see possible relationships across the different component variables of the same project case. The goal was to understand dynamics of a project case thoroughly based on various characteristics, variables and contexts and to understand full start-to-end project success story. The full picture included a snapshot of business challenges; inefficiencies of previous models; factors and determinants; philosophical stands; proficiency measures; inputs; processes, methods, techniques and practices used in each of the projects; and the project results. Several thematic networks, as well as concept maps, were drawn to represent the project case dynamics. This analysis of projects was first focused on one project in its entirety. The next project case analysis led to certain insights that led the researcher reviewing the previously analysed case or cases to redefine or redraft or change something in the light of new learning. As Miles, Huberman and Saldana (2014, p. 292) put it, this as 'progressive focusing' in which 'constant comparisons' lead to 'structural corroborations'. During this process, the logical relationship created in previous projects were tested in a subsequent project case, and additional characteristics that emerged were noted.

3.7.11 Cross-case analysis

This step refers to the 'cross-case analysis' block of data analysis process shown in *Figure 3-5*. In the present study, project cases were collected across different contexts such as different organisations, industries, business environment, job types, complexity levels and countries. Comparison of themes among different contexts were made. This was basically stacking up of all the single case displays on a very large virtual sheet. In the cross-case analysis, each variable or each theme was picked one-at-a-time and then read vertically along that column through all the project cases. Variations of key themes from one project case to another were noted. Constant comparison of each theme, set of themes or variable/s across all the project validated themes was conducted, and some themes were refined or collapsed or expanded, while some were merged. Several display forms were constructed before reaching a useful view, which enabled the drawing of meaningful conclusions. From the larger matrix, sub-matrices were created in which individual projects were compared to other projects to see if a given theme appeared across all the projects or some of them. Then the projects were grouped by contextual variables such as economic sector, business sector, generic job role, nature of primary skill and complexity level. The sub-matrices were used to analyse the patterns of the themes across these contextual variables to see the association and relationships. This was an iterative process going back-and-forth between data, codes, themes, concept maps and matrices.

An excerpt of the matrix is shown in Appendix 22 (note: the appendix does not show all the columns due to space constraints). This matrix lists project cases in the rows, while columns are designed from major elements of the analytic memo (i.e., big ideas, key determinants, key strategies, questions to follow, contradiction, etc.). Reading in a given column- strategies, for example - the repetition of strategies became noticeable. Just a quick scan (colour coded in three colours) suggested three potential patterns of SOCIAL CONNECTIVITY/INTERACTIONS, PERFORMANCE SUPPORT SYSTEMS, and SCENARIOS-BASED. Thus, the comparison across projects led to understand the repetition and breadth of a theme that drives the decision to rearrange themes and revalidate relationship as an iterative process. Appendix 25 shows a matrix for the BUSINESS DRIVERS theme ordered by complexity rating. Appendix 36 shows another matrix for an overarching theme of ANALYSIS STRATEGIES developed in earlier stages of the study, in which the first column is major themes, while the cells indicate the sub-themes ordered by complexity rating to see which themes prevail at a certain type of complexity.

3.7.12 Validation of themes, relationships and conclusions

The two steps 'validate themes, relationships, draw and verify conclusions' and 'validate overarching themes and develop conceptual model' indicated in *Figure 3-5* were not separate steps but recursive back-and-forth validation that occurred throughout the analysis. The themes were validated with a participant account in the interview, and major themes were reviewed during the member check. Briefly stating, this study specifically followed techniques enlisted by Miles, Huberman and Saldana (2014), that is: checking for representativeness, checking for researcher effects, conducting triangulation, weighing the evidence, checking the meaning of outlier, using extreme cases, following up surprises, looking for negative evidence, making if-then tests, replicating findings, and checking for rival explanation and getting feedback from participants, verifying interpretation by participants, utilising peer review, and constantly comparing earlier data with later data using different bases for comparison.

3.8 VALIDITY AND RELIABILITY METHODS

3.8.1 Framework for assessing trustworthiness

The most comprehensive and well-regarded criteria of quality or "rigor" is the idea of trustworthiness (Lincoln & Guba 1985), which depicts the overall quality of the research, i.e., data quality, data analysis quality and relevance or applicability of findings. Lincoln and Guba (1985) proposed that four principles can depict trustworthiness of a qualitative study: credibility, transferability (or applicability), dependability (or consistency) and confirmability (or neutrality). This research study follows nomenclature proposed by Miles, Huberman and Saldana (2014, pp. 311–315) who grouped various criteria known with different names from different researchers into five groups. The first three criteria were used during research design, data collection and analysis and the last two criteria were mainly used to assess the generalisability of the findings.

Objectivity/confirmability: The idea of confirmability is the degree of neutrality or the extent to which the findings were shaped by the respondents only and not by research bias, motivation or interest (Krefting 1991). 'Confirmability requires one to show the way in which interpretations have been arrived at via the inquiry' (Koch 2006, p. 92). This is a measure of objectivity and repeatability of a qualitative study. For those reasons, Miles, Huberman and Saldana (2014) combined objectivity and confirmability into one group, and the terms are used interchangeably throughout this thesis. Guba and Lincoln (1992) expressed the opinion that research has achieved confirmability when it meets credibility, transferability and dependability standards. In the present study, methods of maintaining decision trails (sub-section 3.8.6) and reflexivity journals (sub-section 3.8.11) were used to enhance confirmability of interpretation.

Reliability/dependability/auditability: Similarly, different researchers referred to the idea of consistency and reproducibility of findings with different terms like reliability, dependability and auditability. Dependability refers to findings being consistent and could be repeated with similar studies, similar subjects or similar contexts. It is defined as a measure of whether or not the results are consistent with the data collected (Sandelowski 1986). Dependability in qualitative research has been seen akin to reliability in quantitative research (Clonts 1992; Seale 1999). Due to same underlying meaning Miles, Huberman and Saldana (2014) combined those terms into one group and terms are used interchangeably throughout this thesis. In the present study, methods of maintaining audit trails (sub-section 3.8.6), peer reviews (sub-section 3.8.8) and expert focus group (sub-section 3.8.9) were used to ensure the reliability of the study.

Internal validity/credibility/authenticity: Different researchers proposed different terms like internal validity, credibility and authenticity to communicate the same intent of whether or not findings are true. Credibility corresponds to confidence in the truth of the findings. In other words, it is internal validity to represent how closely research matches what the researcher actually heard and observed and whether or not findings make sense to the participants or other people (Zucker 2009). Lincoln and Guba (1985) considered credibility to be the most important factor in establishing trustworthiness. In the present study, methods of sampling adequacy (sub-section 3.8.2), data triangulation (sub-section 3.8.3), data analysis triangulation (sub-section 3.8.4) and member checking (sub-section 3.8.7) were used to enhance credibility.

External validity/transferability/fittingness: While qualitative research is considered powerful in revealing the situated meaning in a particular context, the same situated meaning often contributes to the lack of generalizability, as 'they are seen as 'too local' or 'too contextual' to be able to underpin generalisation or theorization' (Mason 2006, p. 17). Mason (2006, p. 17) further suggests importance of understanding the phenomenon across contexts as: 'Going on to understand how they [the phenomena] are played out across a range of different contexts makes possible the development of cross-contextual generalizations'. External validity raises questions about the extent to which the findings can be generalised and if they could be applied to other contexts or another group of people. The criteria of external validity/transferability/fittingness ask: 'Are they [findings] transferable to other contexts? Do they fit? How far they can be generalised?' (Miles, Huberman & Saldana 2014, p. 314). Some researchers used the term *replicability* to explain the same intent: 'It is the probability that results obtained in the original study will be predictive of what will occur in similar research' (Rocco & Hatcher 2011, p. 202). In the present study, methods of prevalence analysis (sub-section 3.8.5), peer reviews (sub-section 3.8.8), expert focus group (sub-section 3.8.9), and rich/thick description (sub-section 3.8.10) were used to establish transferability of research findings.

Utilisation/applicability/action orientation: From a pragmatic standpoint, the quality of outcome (i.e., results/findings) also becomes crucial in terms of 'Does it work?' Miles, Huberman and Saldana's (2014, p. 314) grouping of utilisation/applicability/action orientation adds a level of meaning as: 'Even if a study's findings are valid and transferable, we still need to know what the study does for its participants – both researchers and researched – and for its consumers'. This criterion expands the perspective from transferability to ask if 'the actions taken actually help solve a problem' (id. 315). In the present study, methods of peer reviews (sub-section 3.8.8) and expert focus group (sub-section 3.8.9) were used to assess the applicability of the findings.

In this study, attention was paid to ensure quality of the data (i.e., sampling diversity and data triangulation), quality of the data analysis (i.e., data analysis triangulation, prevalence analysis (counting of code presence), audit and decision trails, member checking, and reflexivity) and quality of the outcomes (i.e., peer reviews, expert focus group review, and thick and rich description). The sub-sections below describe the methods used to address the above validity and reliability criteria. The five considerations for validation and reliability methods were built into the research design and research process right from the beginning of the study, as suggested by Patton (2014), Guest, MacQueen and Namey (2011) and Morse et al. (2002), who supported:

> We argue that strategies for ensuring rigor must be built into the qualitative research process per se. These strategies include investigator responsiveness, methodological coherence, theoretical sampling and sampling adequacy, an active analytic stance, and saturation. (Morse et al. 2002, p. 9)

3.8.2   Sampling adequacy

Sandelowski and Barroso (2007) maintained that numbers are important in ensuring adequacy of the sampling strategy. However, in a qualitative study, there is no simple answer to how much sampling is adequate. In a review of over 2,500 studies, M Mason (2010, para. 41) reported that 85% of qualitative studies used fewer than 50 participants. Charmaz (2006, 2014) guided that 25 participants provide a reasonably good sample required for saturation in a qualitative study. Compared to those estimates, this study used 85 participants, generating a total 66 project cases spanned across seven countries, 10 economic sectors, 20 business sectors, 14 job types, 16 skill types, and 5 complexity levels. The diversity of the sample used in this study is in congruence with the recommendation of Miles, Huberman and Saldana (2014, p. 314) that to establish transferability one needs to ensure that 'sampling is theoretically diverse enough to encourage broader applicability when relevant'. Table 3-3 lists diverse distribution of participants and Table 3-11 lists diverse distribution of project cases analysed in this study.

3.8.3 Data triangulation

Triangulation (methodological, data, theory, and investigator) is an approach to the generalisation of the discoveries and a way to acquire additional knowledge (Denzin 2009) and to enrich the analysis rather than proving that one's analysis is right (Braun & Clarke 2013, p. 286). In this study, the data triangulation was attempted by searching additional documents like write-ups, case studies, presentations, blog posts, white papers, and magazine articles related to the project case under discussion explaining the project cases itself or the approaches used by the project leaders. Over 50 documents collected in this study were included in the data analysis consistent with the approach suggested by several researchers (Charmaz 2014; Hardman 2013; Plummer 2004; Prior 2003). Several of these documents, such as blogs and case notes, were authored by the participants themselves. Suter (2012, p. 350) supported this approach of using documentation in the analysis: 'It would not be uncommon, for example, to analyze transcribed interviews along with observational field notes and documents authored by the respondents themselves'. The codes generated from the interviews were cross-checked with those of the documents to verify assertions made by the participants in their interviews. Appendix 34 provides an excerpt of some of the codes taken from the interview of a participant and the documents related to the same project case. There were instances in which documents supplemented or complemented what the participants said. There was no instance in which documents contradicted the statements or strategies shared during the interview. Thus, this check 'provides converging evidence' (Suter 2012, p. 366). Once the data triangulation supported the assertions, the documents and interview codes were merged under the corresponding project case to enrich the details and strengthen the codes.

3.8.4 Data analysis triangulation

Some researchers have emphasised conducting data analysis at several levels using multiple methods (Lauri 2011; Leech & Onwuegbuzie 2007; Michel 2008). On those lines, the pragmatic paradigm allowed the researcher to choose the appropriate methods based on the goals and end outcome of the research study. The approach used in this study is described as:

Within-method complementary (i.e., seeking elaboration, enhancement, illustration, clarification of the results from one analytical tool with results from another tool); within-method triangulation (i.e., seeking convergence and corroboration of results from different analytical methods used on the same data); within-method expansion (i.e., seeking to expand the breadth and range of inferences by using different analytical tools for different data components); and within method development (i.e., using the results from one analytical approach to help inform results from another analytical approach). (Leech & Onwuegbuzie 2007, pp. 579–580)

In this study, multiple supplementary techniques, such as matrix analysis, thematic analysis, concept maps, thematic maps, thematic networks, template analysis, within-case and cross-case comparative analysis were used to enhance data analysis and to improve the representation of participants' experience. For example, the themes reported in the concept maps were corroborated with the themes noticed in the project case summary memo, as well as in the first cycle coding. The relationships between themes were checked with the concept and thematic maps, as well as through matrix display. These techniques together improved the validity of the data analysis.

3.8.5 Prevalence Analysis

The code presence feature of NVivo software was used to create code matrix that counted how many project cases showed a given code (or theme) among the total number of project cases being analysed. Prevalence analysis (counting of code presence) was done at two dimensions: by hierarchical level of the code or theme and grouping it by each contextual variable. The purpose of this analysis was to understand if a given theme was seen in all or some project cases and if it was seen across all or some values of a given contextual variable. Some examples of using this method of prevalence analysis are seen in studies by Clarke and Kitzinger (2004) (cited in Braun & Clarke 2006, p. 82) and Burke & Ambass-Shisanya (n.d.) (cited in Guest, MacQueen & Namey 2011, p. 174). In the present study, this approach led the researcher to assess the generalisability of the research findings and the model. Thematic prevalence of overarching themes of practices is given in Appendix 35.

3.8.6 Audit trail and decision trails

A study and its findings are said to be auditable and dependable when other researchers can use raw data, data reduction products and process notes of the researcher and arrive at similar conclusions with similar data and situation/s (Sandelowski 1986). 'The qualitative researcher has an obligation to be methodical in reporting sufficient details of data collection and the processes of analysis to permit others to judge the quality of the resulting product' (Patton 1999, p. 1191). Leaving such audit trails of theoretical, methodological, and analytical decisions improve rigour by ensuring trustworthiness of the research (Koch 2006; Sandelowski & Barroso 2007; Sandelowski 1986). In this study, an audit trail was maintained which involved maintaining and preserving all transcripts, notes, audio/video recordings and other datasets, etc., which ensure proceedings and developments in the research process can be assessed. All the handwritten notes, hand-made concept maps and interview notes, etc., were scanned and converted into electronic format to keep as audit trail evidence and prevent any loss of data. The interview summaries and observations were captured in OneNote. A version control system was used regularly to maintain revisions of each file that was used in the research (including the NVivo coding). Code structures and summaries were exported in date-indexed folders with appropriate revision to trace back incremental or drastic changes made over a period so that they could be verified.

Confirmability was ensured by linking the findings to the raw data and by ensuring that interpretations were not a result of the researcher's own viewpoints and assumptions (Charmaz 2006, 2014; Shenton 2004). In this study, memos and journals were used to keep track of how theory or interpretation emerged from data confirming the research findings and grounding them in the evidence. The researcher captured personal positions, impressions, how s/he changed decisions and what led to such changes in master trackers, and as well as in NVivo memo as a decision trail (Koch 2006). As a demonstration, the analytic memo in Appendix 20 and analytic/comments column in Appendix 24, Appendix 25, Appendix 31 and Appendix 32 shows how the decisions were made. Analytical memos were written whenever there was a change in method or scope.

3.8.7 Member (participant) checking

Lincoln and Guba (1985, p. 314) called member check as 'the most critical technique for establishing credibility'. In this study, to keep the findings authentic and internally valid, the member check process was used in several ways such as checking the interview transcripts, checking the researcher's interpretation of the data and taking an aggregate model back to some participants to see how well they see themselves in it (Creswell 2014). During the interview, the researcher summarised the overall takeaway from the interview and reaffirmed with the participant. Reviewing interview transcripts with participants did not lead to desired results because some participants demanded heavy editing of their transcription of how they spoke and rather wanted to re-write in formal written English. Therefore, the approach was changed and concept map of the interview or the high-level notes were shared instead with some of the participants. Hagens, Dobrow and Chafe (2009) and Creswell (2014) advised the researchers to use other, less problematic means to verify and improve the precision of the transcriptions such as taking some findings or specific descriptions or themes back to participants to determine accuracy. Another member checking was carried out during the post-analysis phase by providing participants with higher-level details of the final findings, conceptual model and themes, and were provided a questionnaire seeking their feedback (see Appendix 33). Specific feedback was also sought on transferability aspects of the findings. That was in congruence with the argument that transferability is established when 'a range of readers report that the findings are consistent with their own experiences' (Miles, Huberman & Saldana 2014, p. 314). The suggestions received from the participants were incorporated into the overall plan.

3.8.8 Peer reviews

Ziyani, Ehlers and King (2004, p. 13) contended that techniques such as peer debriefing and peer evaluation enhanced the credibility of the research findings. To do so, firstly, the preliminary and final findings of this study were regularly discussed with a highly experienced organisational learning consultant. He provided several inputs for validation of the findings and additional exploration actions. For example, one of their inputs was to redraft 'time to proficiency drivers' to 'business drivers', which made better sense and much wider acceptability (G Hughes 2017, pers. comm., 10 Feb). Secondly, this study was peer-reviewed by three industry practitioners/managers during data analysis and the final findings. Inputs were received to make the terms used in this study more acceptable in practice such as: 'I suggest you use the term *exemplary performers* rather than *star* performers' (C Jennings 2017, pers. comm., 16 January). Thirdly, the findings of this study were reviewed toward the final phases by two highly published and eminent research professors in the area of accelerated proficiency, with comments such as: 'You have discovered the limitations of organisational mindsets' (R Hoffman 2017, pers. comm., 10 May). Fourthly, continuous reviews with the research supervisor, a practising management consultant, guided the direction of the study and relevance of the findings. Fifthly, this study was presented at seven international conferences, among which four were double-blind reviewed, and two were doctoral colloquiums. Written feedback was received from review committees, and also other experienced peers commented on the relevance of the findings to their context and critique of the methodology used. Creswell and Miller (2000; 2013) highly recommended this method of using different levels of peer debriefing so that the study resonates with a larger audience. Finally, experienced professors were specifically invited during presentation sessions for well-rounded feedback. Such methods of peer review to confirm the validity of the finding and to confirm generalizability were supported by several researchers (Clonts 1992; Lincoln & Guba 1986; Morse et al. 2002; Patton 1990, 2002, 2014).

3.8.9 Expert focus group

During phase-3 of the data collection, the final findings and the conceptual model were presented to a focus group consisting of renowned project leaders and training experts from different industries to understand the relevance of the research findings and to identify the areas where the research could be extended (see sub-section 3.4.3). For this purpose, one round of the Delphi method was used to elicit inputs from these experts, because:

> The Delphi is based upon the assumption of safety in numbers (i.e., several people are less likely to arrive at a wrong decision than a single individual). Decisions are then strengthened by reasoned argument in which assumptions are challenged, thus helping to enhance validity. (Hasson, Keeney & McKenna 2000, p. 1013)

Several researchers have contended Delphi as a key method for enhancing the validity of the research (Gordon 1994; Hartman & Baldwin 1995; Hasson, Keeney & McKenna 2000; Hsu & Sandford 2007; Skulmoski, Hartman & Krahn 2007). A 30-page online document was used to conduct one round of Delphi, as suggested by some researchers who received effective results from using such a method (Cabaniss 2001; Gordon 1994; Schmidt 1997). Feedback from experts was sought on eight different aspects of the conceptual model and framework developed in this study. The detailed feedback against these eight aspects is summarised in Appendix 36. The experts commented: 'This work reflects how I think about accelerating time to proficiency as a learning design leader' [Expert 1]. 'It aligns closely with the model I have worked on and developed (advocated in other places)' [Expert 4]. '[I give] 9.5 of 10 - very similar to my approach' [Expert 5]. The experts agreed that the model appears to have high utilisation and application and at the same time rich enough to guide practitioners to implement it practically. Thus, the research meets the generalizability guidelines indicated by Mason (2002, p. 8) in that '[q]ualitative research should produce explanations or arguments which are generalizable in some way, or have some demonstrable wider resonance'.

3.8.10 Thick and rich description

Miles, Huberman and Saldana (2014, p. 314) suggested transferability or fittingness of the findings to other contexts can be established if '[t]he findings include enough "thick description" for readers to assess the potential transferability and appropriateness for their own settings'. In this thesis, chapter 4 has been developed in such a way to create a rich description of themes and findings. Apart from that, this thesis described the participants, settings, and contexts in thick and rich details so that readers can make decisions about the applicability of the findings in their own settings. As Rocco and Hatcher (2011, pp. 201–202) asserted:

> The researcher is obligated to provide thick description of the site, the informants, and all the characteristics of the data and the process of study so that the audience is able to judge whether the meaning of the results might (*might!*) apply to his or her situation' (italics in original).

Following this, an attempt has been made to describe the findings in Chapter 4 and discussion in Chapter 5 in detail, and as vividly as possible. Creswell and Miller (2000, p. 129) posited that 'credibility is established through the lens of readers who read a narrative account and are transported into a setting or situation'. To do so, one project case was explained and described by applying the conceptual framework developed in this study and is shown in Appendix 37. This approach enhanced the applicability of the research findings to describe the initiatives/projects setup to reduce time-to-proficiency in different contexts.

3.8.11 Reflexivity for credibility and controlling researcher's bias

Reflexivity is 'articulating the researcher's personal views and insights about the phenomenon explored' (Dowling 2006, p. 17). The researcher is intimately involved in the process of producing knowledge in a research study. S/he is engaged in the co-construction of meanings with participants. There are high possibilities that researcher's bias, prior knowledge and viewpoints will affect interpretation. Instead of ignoring such biases, they should be acknowledged and made explicit through memos and in the research methodology. Creswell and Miller (2000) specified that the goal should be to understand how subjectivity of the researcher shaped the analysis rather than trying to make the study more objective. Reflexivity is central to qualitative research as a tool to understand that subjectivity. Reflexivity is considered necessary in the pragmatic paradigm in order to avoid any sort of distortion of how the researcher views the data (McGhee, Marland & Atkinson 2007, p. 334). In this study, the researcher used reflexivity with the simple act of making his thought process explicit through personal memos. Elliott and Lazenbatt (2005, p. 51) supported this strategy by appealing that a 'general approach to enhance confidence in interpretative research findings is by providing evidence of how the researcher's own *a priori* assumptions may have shaped the data collection and analysis'. The researcher continuously wrote reflexive journals (see Appendix 38 for examples) about his thoughts and questions during the data analysis in an attempt to determine to what extent his own experience, terminology, wording or perspective might have influenced the coding, concepts and model, as suggested by Charmaz (2014).

3.9 ETHICAL CONSIDERATIONS

3.9.1 Informed consent

The first step of informed consent is the acceptance of the invitation to participate. The invitation letter explained the aims and objectives of the research in detail. The information sheet explained the expected time commitment and mode of data collection. The invitation or information sheet included a link to the electronic consent form for expressing the interest, as well as consent. This informed consent form included clauses that indicated:

- That their participation in the research was at their own volition and was purely voluntarily.
- That they had the right to withdraw from the research without any implications to them.
- That their names and other details would be completely anonymous and confidential and would not be shared with anyone.
- That data gathered in the research would be kept by the University for seven years.

- That the data collected would be secured in password-protected and encrypted hard drives, which are accessible only to the researcher.

The research did not commence until receipt of this electronic or signed consent of the participants was received. It was made clear to the potential participants that their participation was purely voluntary. Care was taken that no potential participant was troubled in any manner related to the research agenda when they declined the invitation to participate. The researcher also made his professional agenda and position clear to the potential participants how the findings would be used and reported (Reed 1995). The participants were allowed to undertake a thorough assessment of any implication to their organisation's intellectual property, non-disclosure restrictions and competition clauses. This research study was approved by Human Research Ethics Committee of Southern Cross University per approval number ECN-14-232. The participants were informed of this ethics clearance by the university.

3.9.2 Confidentiality

The study adhered to standards of privacy, confidentiality and anonymity specified in the *Australian code for responsible conduct of research* (Australian Government 2007a) and *National statement on ethical conduct in human research* (Australian Government 2007b). A researcher's duty is to maintain the anonymity of the participants (Fink 2000). All the interview transcripts were thoroughly checked and re-read to remove references to any names, organisations or any other identifiable information, and pseudonyms were assigned to maintain anonymity. Only the researcher had access to the data collected or shared by the participant, and it was stored in a password-protected hard drive encrypted with 256-bit hardware encryption, commercially represented as the most secure data encryption in the market. This ensured participant privacy. All data shared by the participant and their identities were kept confidential.

3.10 CHAPTER SUMMARY

This research study was conducted to address three research questions. The exploration of the concept and process of accelerated proficiency required an in-depth understanding of the meaning of this phenomenon. A qualitative approach was selected for the study, positioned in the pragmatism paradigm. Purposive and criterion sampling were used. 85 participants were recruited in this study. The data collection was planned in three phases. The first phase of the data collection involved a general understanding of the phenomenon and issues with industry experts. The second phase involved collecting bounded project cases of success stories of how project leaders in various settings reduced time-to-proficiency. The third phase involved reviewing findings of the study with an expert focus group. In-depth interviews over the phone and the internet were the main methods of data collection, while web-based and e-mail interviews were used as alternate methods.

In Phase-2 of the data collection, 66 successful projects were collected from project leaders. By applying specific criteria, 60 project cases were selected for analysis. The collected data were coded and analysed using matrix analysis and thematic analysis approaches. Within-case and cross-case analysis were also performed. To address the research questions, sub-themes, themes and overarching themes were defined, and relationships among them were established. Various methods for ensuring validity and reliability were employed to enhance the study on five dimensions: objectivity, reliability, credibility, transferability, and applicability. The next chapter describes the findings of this study.

Chapter 4   RESEARCH FINDINGS

4.1   INTRODUCTION

Chapter 3 described the methodology adopted in this research study to explore the three research questions established in Chapter 2. In this chapter, findings of the data analysis of 60 selected project cases are presented. The research objective and questions discussed in previous chapters are revisited in *Table 4-1* to re-cap before the findings of the study are introduced.

Table 4-1: Summary of research questions and research objective

Business problem		
The business challenge this study aimed to solve is that organisations are struggling with long time-to-proficiency of their workforce in certain job roles.		
Intents/aims		
To explore and understand the meaning practitioners place on the concept of accelerated proficiency in the workplace. To understand what makes need for accelerating proficiency critical for organisations and what benefits they draw from reducing time-to-proficiency. To identify practices, strategies, methods and processes that have been proven to reduce time-to-proficiency successfully in different contexts.		
Central research question		
How can organisations accelerate time-to-proficiency of the employees in the workplace?		
Research questions		
Research question #1	Meaning of accelerated proficiency	What does the concept of accelerating proficiency or accelerating time-to-proficiency mean to organisations?
Research question #2	Driving factors and benefits of reduced time-to-proficiency	What business factors drive the need for reducing time-to-proficiency of the workforce and how do organisations benefit from achieving it?
Research question #3	Practices and strategies to accelerate proficiency	What core practices and strategies do business leaders and practitioners adopt to achieve shorter time-to-proficiency of the workforce in a given job?
Research objective		
The objective of this research is to develop a conceptual model and/or framework of proven practices or strategies that practitioners can use to reduce time-to-proficiency of the workforce in various settings.		

To ease the readability and presentation of the findings, this chapter is organised in three parts: **Part 1**: provides a summary of the overarching themes with thematic maps to develop a high-level picture. **Part 2**:

provides the details of each of the emergent themes noted during the analysis with appropriate quotes. **Part 3**: provides analysis of the results of project cases in terms of time-to-proficiency.

4.2 THEMATIC STRUCTURE OF EMERGENT THEMES IN DATA ANALYSIS

In this chapter, three terms are used as fundamental terminology to describe the findings as per the thematic analysis notions: **themes, sub-themes and overarching** (Braun & Clarke 2006, 2013). As a re-call, the theme is a pattern found in the data that captures something important in the data in relation to the research question, which describes and organises possible observations or interpret the aspects of the phenomenon. The overarching theme captures the idea encapsulated in the themes and organises the analysis. This may be considered as a higher-level category of themes. A theme may have sub-themes, which are the themes within-a-theme developed by the clustering of codes (and represent notable specific aspects of one theme and also provides structure and hierarchy of meaning) (Braun & Clarke 2006, 2013).

This data analysis spanned across 60 qualified project cases in a range of contexts. 42 emergent themes were identified, which is rather a large number of themes due to scale, sampling size and contextual coverage of the study. These emergent themes described key aspects of the three research questions. These emergent themes, were then grouped under 11 overarching themes to organise the analysis. The 11 overarching themes collectively answered the three research questions. The complete thematic map for all the three research questions explored in this study is provided in *Table 4-2*.

For ease of understanding, the thematic structure of the large number of themes and overarching themes, the thematic description is explained in two parts:

- **Part-1** provides only the summary of the 11 overarching themes, mostly without quotes, but supplemented with conceptual maps and thematic tables.
- **Part-2** describes each emergent theme in detail with key elements noted in each theme with quotes.

Table 4-2: Thematic structure of emergent themes noted in data analysis

	Overarching themes		Emergent themes
Research question #1: What does the concept of accelerating proficiency or accelerating time-to-proficiency mean to organisations?			
C1	Proficiency	C1.1	Proficiency refers to meeting established performance thresholds for a job role.
		C1.2	Consistency is the hallmark of the state of proficiency of a job role.
		C1.3	Proficiency is measured by business outcomes of the job role or observable actions linked to outcomes.
		C1.4	Proficiency is not just about learning an isolated skill, task or activity in a job
C2	Accelerated proficiency	C2.1	Accelerated proficiency is measured in terms of reduction in time-to-proficiency.
		C2.2	A clear definition of proficiency for a job role is the most critical requirement to baseline, monitor and shorten time-to-proficiency.
		C2.3	Accelerated proficiency is not accelerated learning or accelerated training.
		C2.4	Training alone rarely leads to accelerating proficiency, it requires solutions beyond training.
Research question #2: What business factors drive the need for reducing time-to-proficiency of the workforce and how do organisations benefit from achieving it?			
D1	Magnitude and scale (of time-to-proficiency business problem)	D1.1	Magnitude of time-to-proficiency problem
		D1.2	Scale of time-to-proficiency problem
D2	Business drivers (for accelerating proficiency)	D2.1	Time-related pressures
		D2.2	Speed-related competitiveness
		D2.3	Skill-related deficiency
		D2.4	Cost or financial implications
D3	Business benefits (of reduced time-to-proficiency)	D3.1	Business gains
		D3.2	Improvement in operational metrics
		D3.3	Improvement in productivity
		D3.4	Cost savings
Research question #3: What core practices and strategies do business leaders and practitioners adopt to achieve shorter time-to-proficiency of the workforce in a given job?			
P1	Defining business-driven proficiency measures	P1.1	Starting with end in mind: upfront definition and measures of proficiency in terms of business outcomes and link it to business needs.
		P1.2	Baseline and establish time-to-proficiency targets based on business drivers.
P2	Developing a proficiency reference map	P2.1	Conduct upfront comprehensive work analysis drawn from the outcomes.
		P2.2	Profile capabilities and capacities of the job performers.
		P2.3	Model success behaviours of exemplary performers.
		P2.4	Understand job operating conditions and environmental influences.
		P2.5	Analyse roadblocks and hindrances that lead to longer time-to-proficiency.
P3	Sequencing an efficient proficiency path	P3.1	Segment tasks and activities based on characteristics from analytics.
		P3.2	Create logical sequence of experiences as a complete path.
		P3.3	Optimise the proficiency path for efficiency and time saving.

P4	**Manufacturing accelerated contextual experiences**	P4.1	Assign performers on authentic job activities that allow practice on generating job-specific outcomes.
		P4.2	Embed learning into the work and focus on doing the job rather than topic-wise learning.
		P4.3	Expose performers to multiple cycles of deliberate and purposeful failures at a rapid rate or in a compressed time-frame.
		P4.4	Compress hard-to-obtain experiences on known situations in highly contextualised realistic cases, gamified scenarios and representative simulations.
		P4.5	Strengthen generic, transferable, principle-based, fundamental skills to handle unfamiliar or unknown situations.
P5	**Promoting an active emotional immersion**	P5.1	Active engagement and emotional immersion with the tasks and situations similar to the workplace.
		P5.2	Provide immediate feedback and allow moments of focused reflection.
		P5.3	Assess performers through job-specific, continuous, multi-level assessment beyond a training intervention.
P6	**Setting up a proficiency eco-system**	P6.1	Create enabling and supportive environment.
		P6.2	Structured involvement, accountability, support and reinforcement from manager.
		P6.3	Institute a structured mentoring and coaching process at workplace.
		P6.4	Design opportunities for purpose-driven social connectivity and structured informal learning in the workplace.
		P6.5	Deploy on-demand performance support systems embedded in workflow and learning.
		P6.6	Leverage subject matter experts strategically.

CHAPTER 4

PART-1: OVERARCHING THEMES

Summary of 11 overarching themes (practices)

4.3 RESEARCH QUESTION #1: MEANING OF ACCELERATED PROFICIENCY

The first research question that was explored is: **What does accelerating proficiency or accelerating time-to-proficiency mean to organisations?**

In response to this research question, eight emergent themes were identified which were grouped into two overarching themes to organise the analysis (using the notation specified by Braun & Clarke 2013). This grouping is shown in *Table 4-3*. The overarching theme C1—'Proficiency', grouped emergent themes explaining the characteristics of proficiency at workplace, while the overarching theme C2—'Accelerated proficiency', grouped the emergent themes explaining the characteristics of the concept of accelerated proficiency. A conceptual map showing relationships between sub-themes, themes and overarching themes based on the data analysis was developed, as shown in *Figure 4-1*.

Table 4-3: Thematic structure of overarching themes noted in research question #1

Overarching theme			Emergent themes
C1	Proficiency	C1.1	Proficiency refers to meeting established performance thresholds for a job role.
		C1.2	Consistency is the hallmark of the state of proficiency of a job role.
		C1.3	Proficiency is measured by business outcomes of the job role or observable actions linked to outcomes.
		C1.4	Proficiency is not just about learning an isolated skill, task or activity in a job
C2	Accelerated proficiency	C2.1	Accelerated proficiency is measured in terms of reduction in time-to-proficiency.
		C2.2	A clear definition of proficiency for a job role is the most critical requirement to baseline, monitor and shorten time-to-proficiency.
		C2.3	Accelerated proficiency is not accelerated learning or accelerated training.
		C2.4	Training alone rarely leads to accelerating proficiency, it requires solutions beyond training.

4.3.1 Overarching theme C1: Proficiency

The project leaders in this study described how they view and define proficiency in the workplace. An analysis led to the identification of four emergent themes, as shown in *Table 4-3*, labelled as C1.1—'Proficiency refers to meeting established performance thresholds for a job role', C1.2—'Consistency is the hallmark of the state of proficiency of a job role', C1.3—'Proficiency is measured by business outcomes of the job role or observable actions linked to outcomes', and C1.4—'Proficiency is not just about learning an isolated skill, task or activity in a job', which were grouped under the overarching theme C1—'Proficiency'. The four emergent themes characterised the nature of proficiency in a job role.

The data on overarching theme C1—'Proficiency' suggested that project leaders who successfully reduced time-to-proficiency in their settings viewed proficiency as the state at which an individual achieves a consistent performance, meeting pre-defined standards of the job role consistently and maintaining it. Most of the leaders measured proficiency in terms of business outcomes or the observable actions that closely represented or led to business outcomes. In both cases, producing business outcomes rather than doing tasks or activities were the hallmark of the state of proficiency. Project leaders also differentiated that proficiency was not just about learning an isolated skill, task or activity in a job and they further differentiated it from the constructs such as competence and competency. See sub-section 4.6.1 for a detailed description of each of the four emergent themes under this overarching theme.

4.3.2 Overarching theme C2: Accelerated proficiency

The project leaders in this study described how they view and define the concept of accelerated proficiency in the workplace. An analysis led to identification of four emergent themes, as shown in Table 4-3, labelled as C2.1—'Accelerated proficiency is measured in terms of reduction in time-to-proficiency'; C2.2— 'A clear definition of proficiency for a job role is the most critical requirement to baseline, monitor and shorten time-to-proficiency'; C2.3—'Accelerated proficiency is not accelerated learning or accelerated training'; and C2.4—' Training alone rarely leads to accelerating proficiency, it requires solutions beyond training', which were grouped under the overarching theme C2—'Accelerated proficiency'. The four emergent themes characterised the nature of the concept of accelerated proficiency in the workplace.

Data on overarching theme C2—'Accelerated proficiency' showed that defining proficiency was a key requirement to accelerate it in the first place. Project leaders considered a lack of a clear and crisp definition of proficiency upfront as the biggest hindrance to accelerating proficiency. Project leaders driving such initiatives/projects specified that accelerated proficiency, as a goal, was not to accelerate learning of some content or learning more content in a short time or shortening training duration. Time-to-proficiency appeared to have a clear meaning that could be implemented with metrics to measure acceleration in proficiency or measure success of accelerated proficiency projects. Finally, training was considered important for improving performance, but training alone was not viewed as a solution to shorten time-to-proficiency. Project leaders advocated several non-training solutions to be integrated with training solutions to achieve shorter time-to-proficiency. See sub-section 4.6.2 for a detailed description of each of the four emergent themes under this overarching theme.

4.3.3 Conclusion of research question #1

The investigation of research question #1 led to the identification of eight emergent themes which characterised how organisations defined and measured proficiency and how they viewed the concept of accelerated proficiency in various contexts. These eight emergent themes were grouped under two overarching themes: 'proficiency' and 'accelerated proficiency' to organise the analysis and collectively answer research question #1. Proficiency was seen as consistently meeting the minimum specified performance thresholds defined for a job role in terms of business outcomes and observable behaviours. Accelerated proficiency was seen as conscious effort measured in terms of time-to-proficiency to reach that state of consistent performance in shorter time.

Figure 4-1: Concept map of overarching themes C1 and C2 (meaning of proficiency and accelerated proficiency)

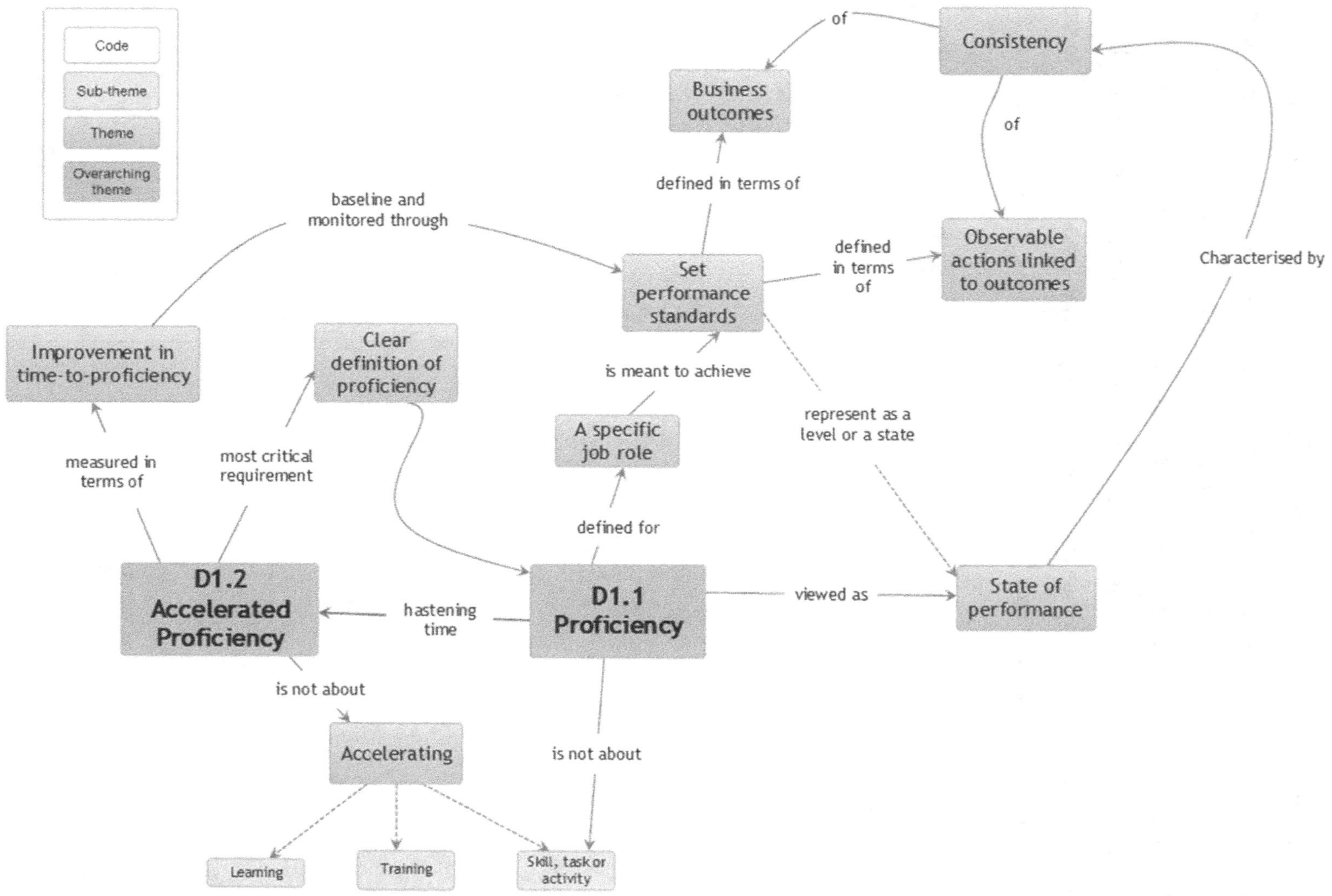

Source: developed for this research study

Figure 4-2: Conceptual map of overarching theme D1, D2 and D3 (drivers for accelerating proficiency and benefits of reduced time-proficiency)

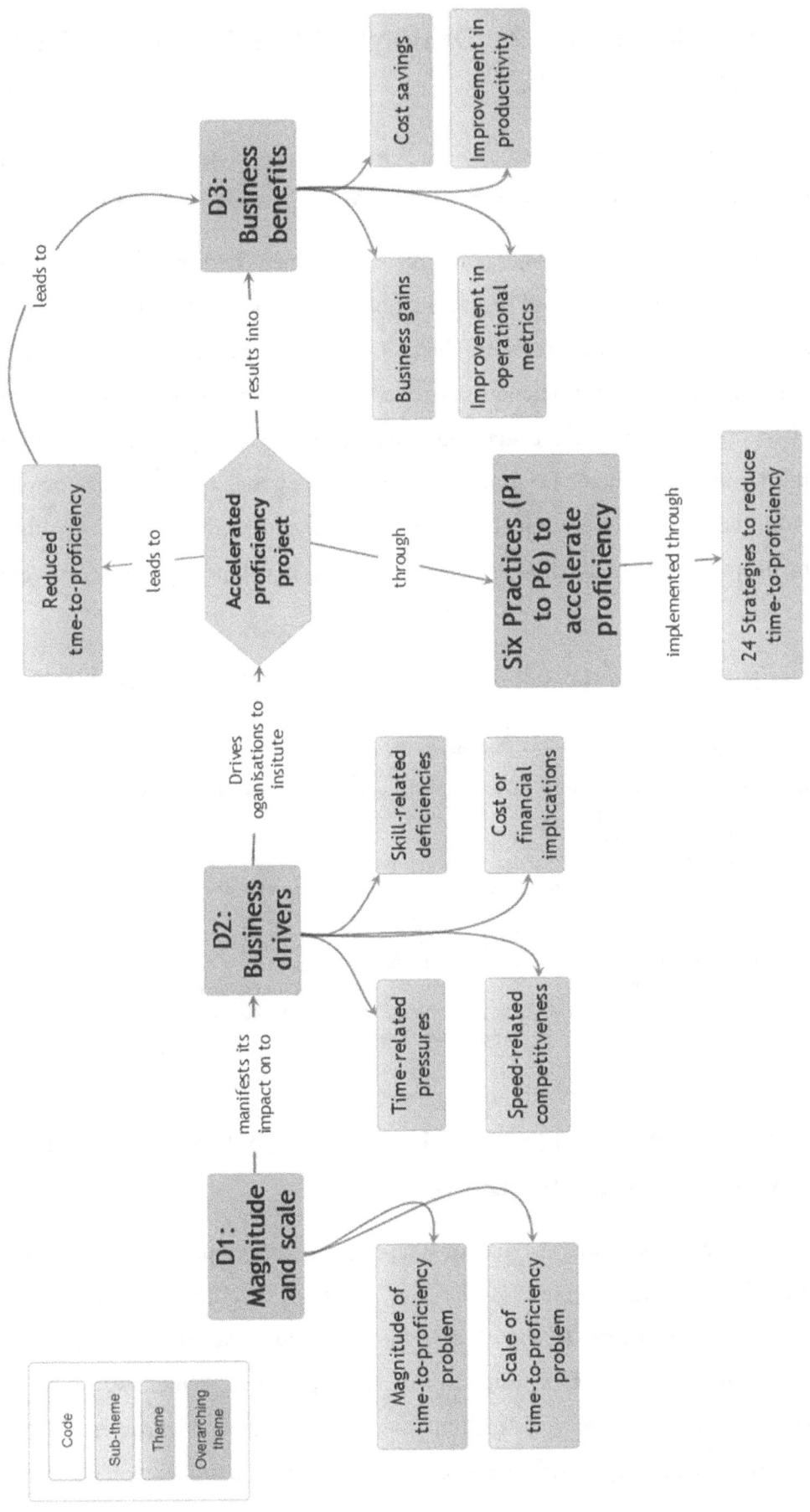

Source: developed for this research study

4.4 RESEARCH QUESTION #2: DRIVING FACTORS AND BENEFITS OF REDUCED TIME-TO-PROFICIENCY

This section proposes answers to research question #2: **What business factors drive the need for reducing time-to-proficiency of the workforce and how do organisations benefit from achieving it?**

In response to this research question, 10 emergent themes were identified which were grouped into three overarching themes to organise the analysis (using the notation specified by Braun & Clarke 2013). This grouping is shown in Table 4-4. The overarching theme D1 grouped emergent themes explaining the size and range of the problem of time-to-proficiency. The overarching theme D2 grouped the emergent themes explaining market or organisational forces that make it necessary for organisations to shorten time-to-proficiency. The third overarching theme D3 grouped the overarching themes explaining the type of business benefits attained from shorter time-to-proficiency. A conceptual map showing the relationship between sub-themes, themes and overarching themes based on data analysis was developed, as shown in *Figure 4-2* above.

Table 4-4: Thematic structure of overarching themes noted in research question #2

Overarching themes		Themes	
D1	Magnitude and scale (of time-to-proficiency business problem)	D1.1	Magnitude of time-to-proficiency problem
		D1.2	Scale of time-to-proficiency problem
D2	Business drivers (for accelerating proficiency)	D2.1	Time-related pressures
		D2.2	Speed-related competitiveness
		D2.3	Skill-related deficiency
		D2.4	Cost or financial implications
D3	Business benefits (of reduced time-to-proficiency)	D3.1	Business gains
		D3.2	Improvement in operational metrics
		D3.3	Improvement in productivity
		D3.4	Cost savings

4.4.1 Overarching theme D1: Magnitude and scale of time-to-proficiency business problem

The project cases in this study described the size of time-to-proficiency business problem in each context differently. An analysis of trends in time-to-proficiency numbers specified in each project case led to identification of two emergent themes, as shown in Table 4-4, labelled as D1.1—'Magnitude of time-to-proficiency problem' and D1.2—'Scale of time-to-proficiency problem', which were grouped under the overarching theme D1—'Magnitude and scale (of time-to-proficiency business problem)'. Magnitude (how long is the time-to-proficiency of one person in a given job role) and scale (how much is time-to-proficiency of overall staff serving same job role) in a given context collectively described the impact of the business problem. For example, the magnitude of 16 weeks of time-to-proficiency is far less in scale for a given job role with 10 people compared to the same 16 weeks of magnitude for 100 people performing the same job role. The data analysis indicated that collectively magnitude and scale of the problem make a compelling reason for organisations to work on this problem. One project leader commented:

> *They [the organisation] have something like 3,000 people in development and engineering, and they knew they had to grow with 1,200 more within a year. And they knew that it took approximately 3 years before people were up to speed and it should go back to approximately 1 year ...* (Teresa, Project leader 58)

Data analysis indicated that such a large scale problem was not only impactful for the organisation but also impacted the individual in terms of self-worth, confidence and career progression. The analysis suggested that time-to-proficiency was so long in magnitude and far out in most of the jobs that it was worth doing something about it. As one project leader summarised:

> *There is a universal problem all businesses have and if they work on their problem they can make significant gains, which is just what you are saying that people simply aren't getting up the speed as fast they can and it's very, very expensive when they're not. And basically it's the basic business case that we've started with is that every minute someone isn't fully up to speed is costing you money and it's worth doing something about it. It's probably the most significant issue.* (Stephen, Project leader 53)

See sub-section 4.7.1 for detailed descriptions of each of the four emergent themes under this overarching theme.

4.4.2 Overarching theme D2: Business drivers for accelerating time-to-proficiency

Each project case was seen to be driven by different business needs which were captured in a matrix, as shown in Appendix 24. The analysis led to the identification of four emergent themes, as shown in Table 4-4, labelled as D2.1—'Time-related pressures'; D2.2—Speed-related competitiveness; D2.3—'Skill-related deficiency'; and D2.4—'Cost or financial implications', which were then grouped under an overarching theme D2— 'Business drivers'. These four business factors as emergent themes led organisations to actively think about shortening time-to-proficiency.

The business programs on accelerated proficiency most commonly appeared to be driven by skill-related drivers and then time-related drivers or speed-related drivers. The prevalence analysis (counting the code presence) showed that skill-related drivers were the main trigger for forcing organisations to implement initiatives/projects to accelerate proficiency. The next major drivers were time-related and speed-related drivers. The study indicated that factors like time-to-market, competitiveness and market leadership mattered more than the money they could save. Cost-related drivers were not seen as the main or primary drivers. It was also noted that the skill-related drivers were more prevalent in management, manufacturing and highly technical jobs which faced high competition, required a high level of skills from people and faced faster obsolescence of skills. Those drivers were also prevalent in jobs driven by regulatory pressures, such as oil & gas and medicine research, in which skill deficiencies were stated as damaging to the business. Time- and speed-related drivers were seen as next most prevalent drivers, predominantly in technical, engineering and scientific jobs due to time-to-market and competitive pressures. The cost-related drivers were more prevalent in the technical sales jobs due to the direct impact on revenue in such jobs.

Further, none of the business drivers appeared in isolation; rather there was a chain connection between various business drivers. As seen in the comments of one project leader:

> In Project Case No. 29, a large aircraft engine manufacturer faced an unacceptably long time-to-proficiency of the computer numerical control (CNC) machinists manufacturing highly sophisticated engine parts. They were required to develop proficiency in precision manufacturing skills in shorter time. Skill-related deficiencies were seen as '*a severe skill shortage*' in the industry for those specific job skills. This shortage led the organisation to hire people at a rapid pace to support the business. '*Massive recruitment efforts yielded few potential employees.*' The need to bring new employees up to speed was driven by speed-related competitiveness like customer expectations and time-to-market. '*[T]he longer that it takes somebody to learn, the more difficult it is to complete our process and ship to the customer on time.*' The skill-related drivers were amplified by the need for precision work involved in the job and the need to prepare employees to a proficiency level of error-free work. '*The sooner people are fully competent to perform job, new employee becomes more safe and productive.*' Though not the primary drivers, the usual cost-related drivers of the organisation came up in this project case due to the impact of non-proficiency on production and opportunity cost lost during the waiting period. '*In addition, the company wanted to reduce costs (including recruitment costs)*'. [All quotes from Hogdan, Project leader 29).

See sub-sections 4.7.2 and 4.6.1 for detailed descriptions of each of the four emergent themes under this overarching theme.

4.4.3 Overarching theme D3: Business benefits of reduced time-to-proficiency

Appendix 28 summarises business benefits by project cases. Analysis of business results of each project case led to the identification of four emergent themes, as shown in Table 4-4, labelled as D3.1—'Business gains', D3.2—'Improvement in operational metrics', D3.3—'Improvement in productivity', and D3.4—'Cost savings', which were then grouped into the overarching theme D3—'Business benefits'. These four emergent themes represented the gains organisations accrue out of reduced time-to-proficiency. It was observed that shortening a long time-to-proficiency automatically led to cost savings, and hence, was invariably realised in every business project. There were gains in business (such as market share), improvement in operational metrics and improvement in productivity.

See sub-sections 4.7.3 and 4.6.1 for a detailed description of each of the four emergent themes under this overarching theme.

4.4.4 Conclusion of research question #2

The investigation of research question #2 led to the identification of 10 emergent themes. These themes explored and described the magnitude and scale of time-to-proficiency business problem, business factors that drove the need for shorter time-to-proficiency and the business gains of shorter time-to-proficiency. The 10 emergent themes were grouped under three overarching themes to organise the analysis, which answered research question #2 collectively. The magnitude and scale of the business problem of time-to-proficiency was seen to be so large that it could not be ignored. This magnitude and scale showed impact in terms of four business factors: time-related pressures, speed-related competitiveness, skill-related deficiency and cost or financial implications that led organisations to institute business projects to reduce time-to-proficiency. The skill-related deficiencies were main drivers. Cost-related implications showed up as cost savings as a result of any business project on accelerated proficiency. Most business projects led to business gains, improvement in operational metrics and improvement in productivity in addition to cost savings.

4.5 RESEARCH QUESTION #3: PRACTICES AND STRATEGIES TO ACCELERATE PROFICIENCY

This section explores the answer to research question #3: **What core practices and strategies do business leaders and practitioners adopt to achieve shorter time-to-proficiency of the workforce in a given job?**

To answer this research question, all 60 project cases were compared with each other and analysed for strategies on how organisations have reduced time-to-proficiency in their organisational context. The analysis led the identification of 24 emergent themes that run through the data that explained the "strategies" shared by project leaders in terms of how they reduced time-to-proficiency in the workplace. This was a large number due to the sample size and coverage of the study. Thus, these 24 emergent themes representing strategies were grouped under six broad overarching themes (using the notation specified by Braun and Clarke 2013) to organise and present the analysis. This grouping is shown in *Table 4-5*. The six overarching themes (practices) are described in this part, while the 24 emergent themes are described in part-2 of this chapter.

From the nature of overarching themes, it was seen that each overarching theme in this question represented a business "practice". For the remainder of the thesis, research question #3 is addressed as:

Overarching theme ↔ business-level "Practices" adopted by leaders

Themes ↔ "Strategies" to implement business practices

The description will use the terms 'overarching theme/theme' to preserve the guidelines of thematic analysis, while using interchangeably the terms 'practices/strategies' respectively to more appropriately address this research question. Where necessary, both terms are used if required to describe the intent. Conceptual maps showing the relationship between sub-themes, themes and overarching themes based on data analysis were developed for each overarching theme and are shown in Figure 4-3, Figure 4-4, Figure 4-5, Figure 4-6, Figure 4-7 and Figure 4-8, which are presented in the following sub-sections.

Table 4-5: Thematic structure of overarching themes in research question #3

	Overarching themes (business practices)		Emergent themes (strategies)
P1	Defining business-driven proficiency measures	P1.1	Starting with end in mind: upfront definition and measures of proficiency in terms of business outcomes and link it to business needs.
		P1.2	Baseline and establish time-to-proficiency targets based on business drivers.
P2	Developing a proficiency reference map	P2.1	Conduct upfront comprehensive work analysis drawn from the outcomes.
		P2.2	Profile capabilities and capacities of the job performers.
		P2.3	Model success behaviours of exemplary performers.
		P2.4	Understand job operating conditions and environmental influences.
		P2.5	Analyse roadblocks and hindrances that lead to longer time-to-proficiency.
P3	Sequencing an efficient proficiency path	P3.1	Segment tasks and activities based on characteristics from analytics.
		P3.2	Create logical sequence of experiences as a complete path.
		P3.3	Optimise the proficiency path for efficiency and time saving.
P4	Manufacturing accelerated contextual experiences	P4.1	Assign performers on authentic job activities that allow practice on generating job-specific outcomes.
		P4.2	Embed learning into the work and focus on doing the job rather than topic-wise learning.
		P4.3	Expose performers to multiple cycles of deliberate and purposeful failures at a rapid rate or in a compressed time-frame.
		P4.4	Compress hard-to-obtain experiences on known situations in highly contextualised realistic cases, gamified scenarios and representative simulations.
		P4.5	Strengthen generic, transferable, principle-based, fundamental skills to handle unfamiliar or unknown situations.
P5	Promoting an active emotional immersion	P5.1	Active engagement and emotional immersion with the tasks and situations similar to the workplace.
		P5.2	Provide immediate feedback and allow moments of focused reflection.
		P5.3	Assess performers through job-specific, continuous, multi-level assessment beyond a training intervention.
P6	Setting up a proficiency eco-system	P6.1	Create enabling and supportive environment.
		P6.2	Structured involvement, accountability, support and reinforcement from manager.
		P6.3	Institute a structured mentoring and coaching process at workplace.
		P6.4	Design opportunities for purpose-driven social connectivity and structured informal learning in the workplace.
		P6.5	Deploy on-demand performance support systems embedded in workflow and learning.
		P6.6	Leverage subject matter experts strategically.

Figure 4-3: Concept map of overarching theme (practice) P1: Defining business-driven proficiency measures

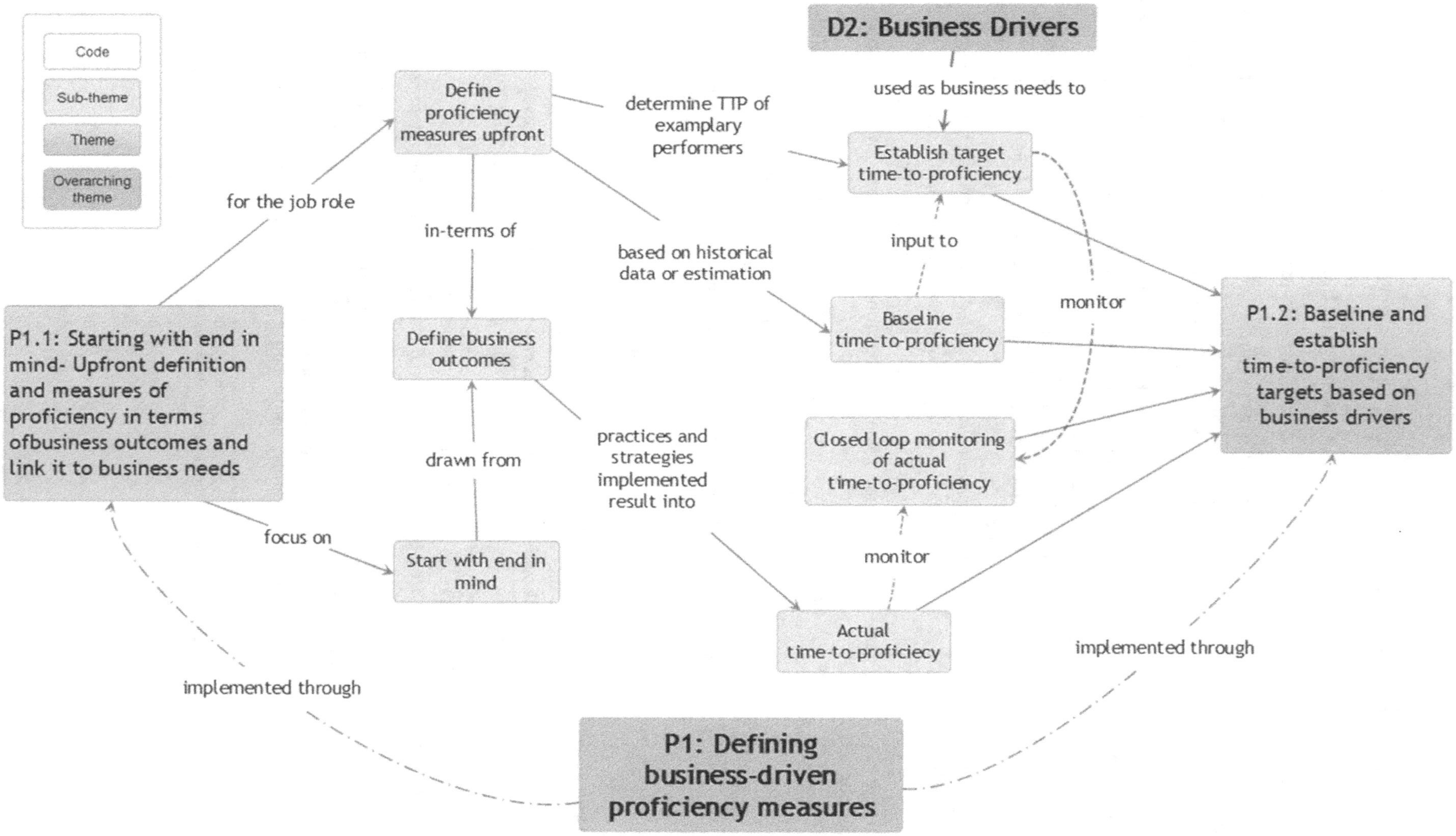

Source: developed for this research study

Chapter 4 – Research Findings   pg. 176

Figure 4-4: Conceptual map of overarching theme (practice) P2: Developing a proficiency reference map

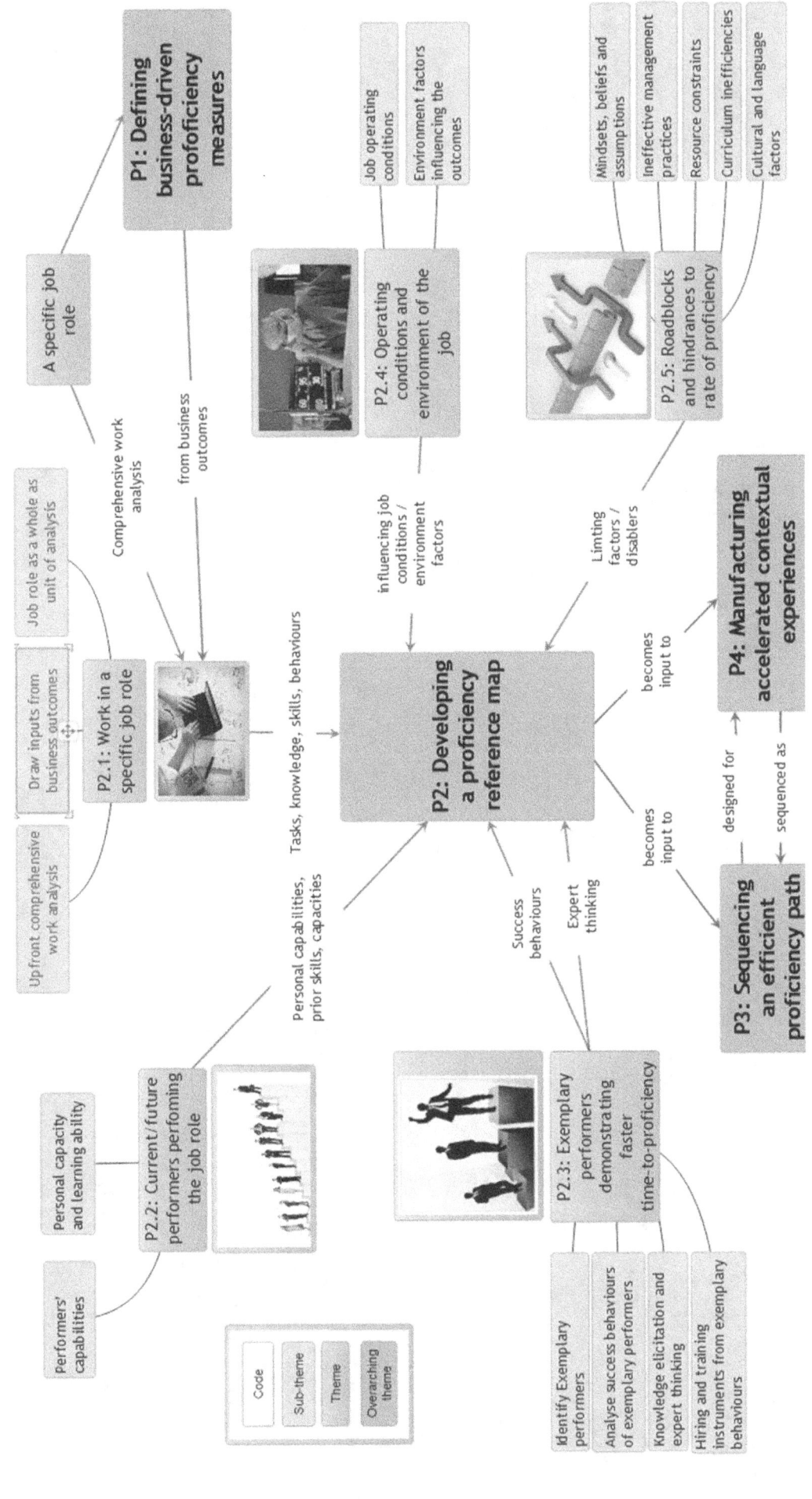

Source: developed for this research study

Figure 4-5: Concept map of overarching theme (practice) P3: Creating an efficient proficiency path

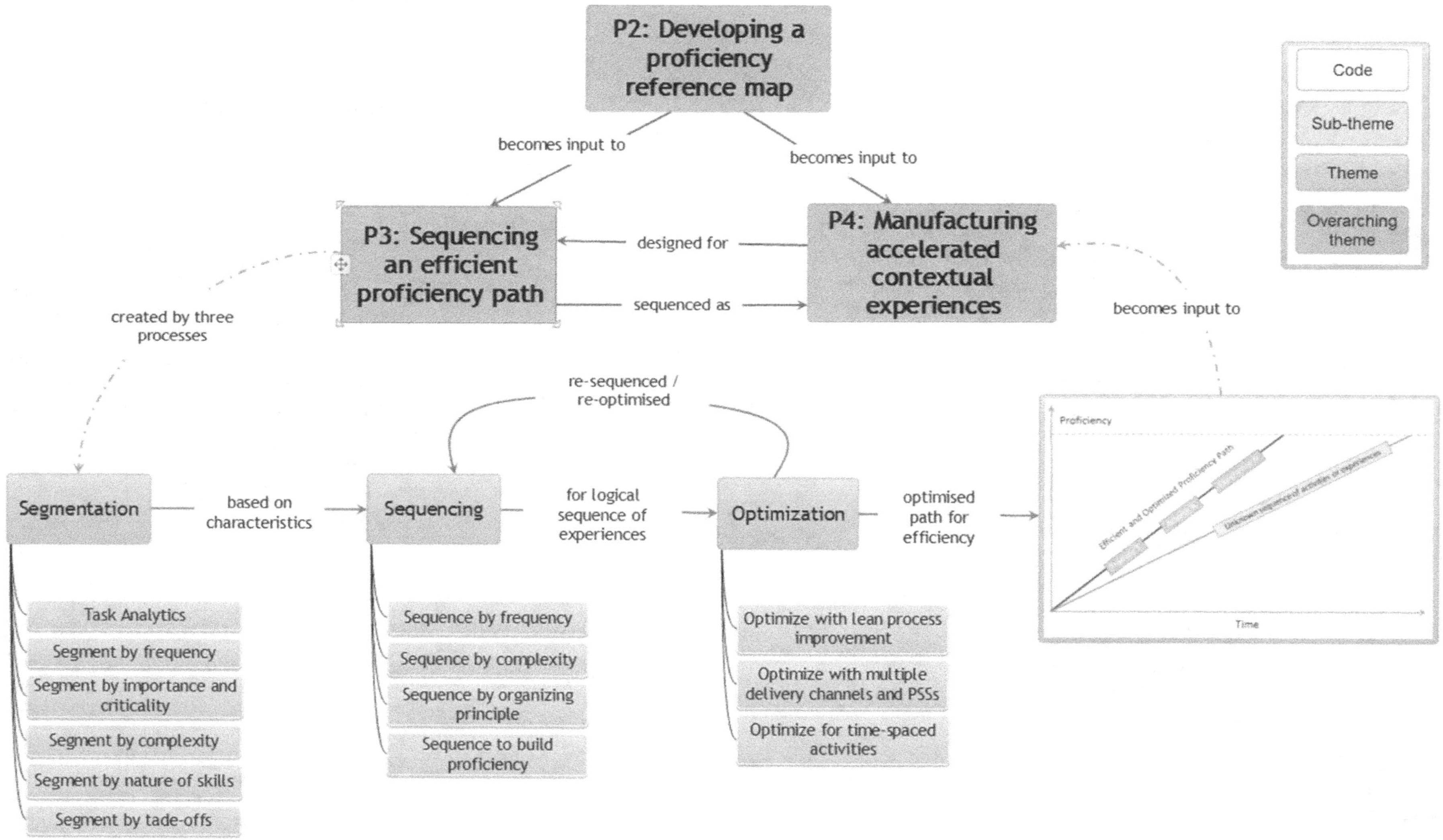

Source: developed for this research study

Chapter 4 – Research Findings

Figure 4-6: Conceptual map of overarching theme (practice) P4: Manufacturing accelerated contextual experiences

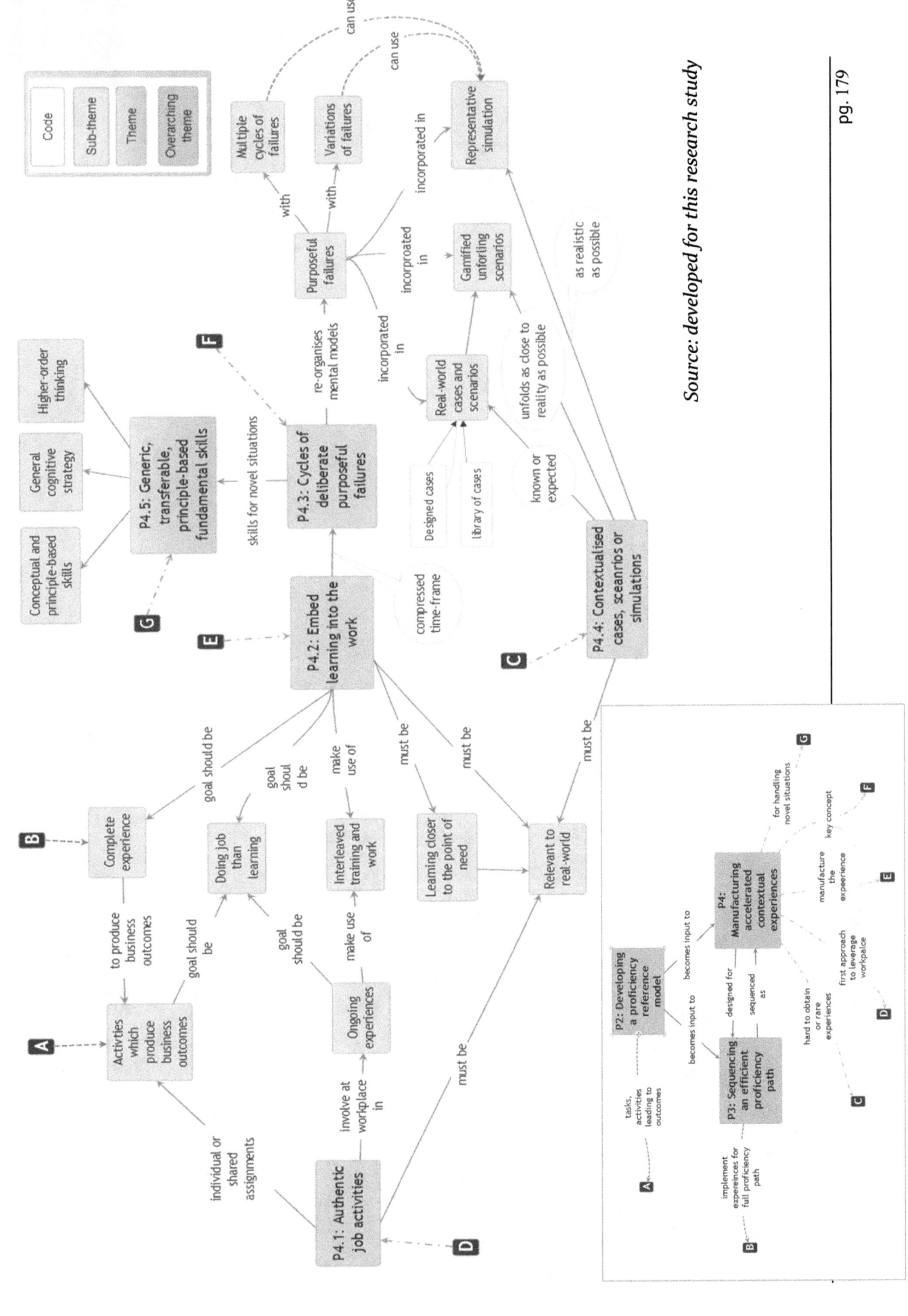

Source: developed for this research study

pg. 179

Figure 4-7: Concept map of overarching theme (practice) P5: Promoting an active emotional immersion

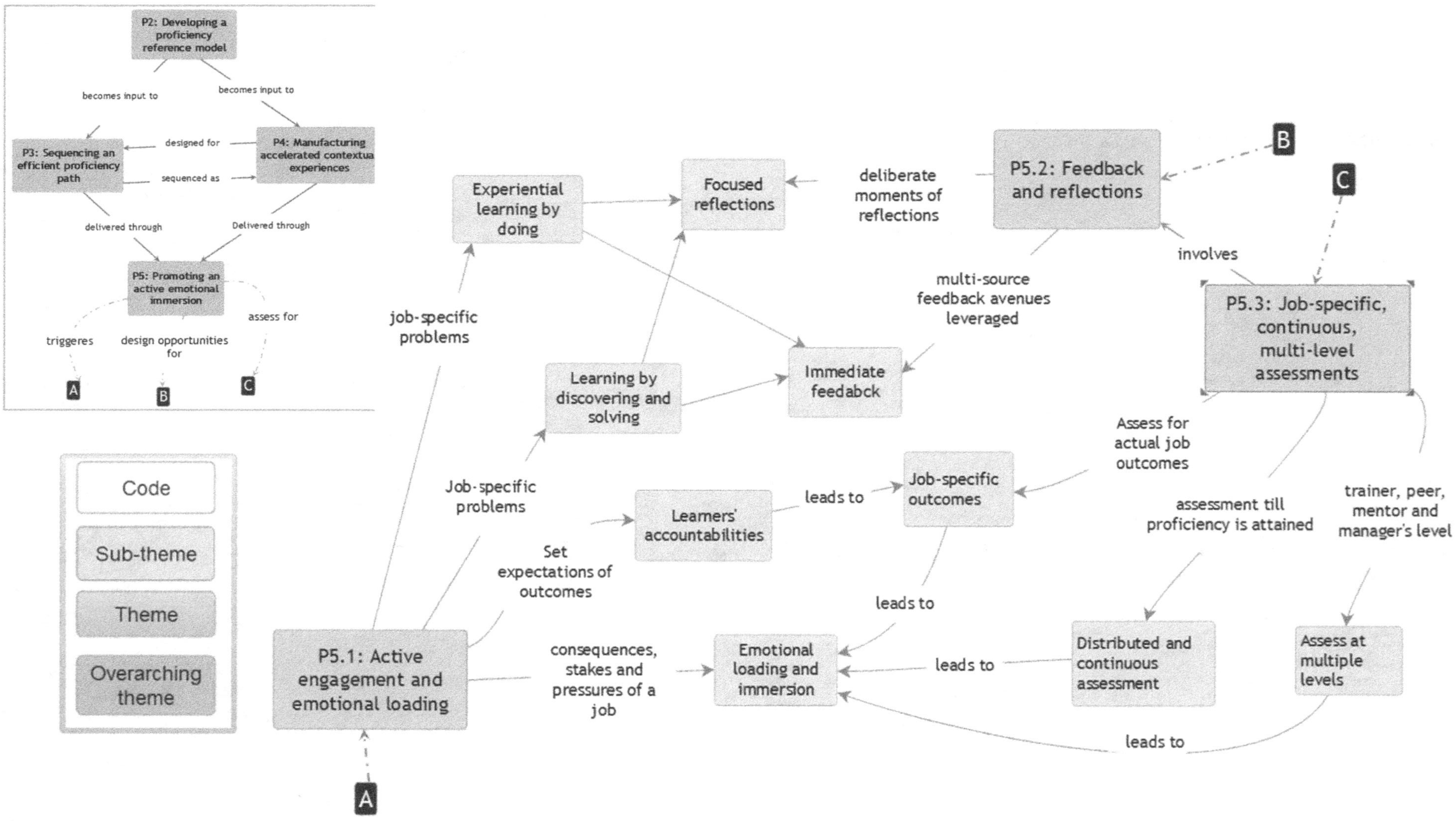

Source: developed for this research study

Chapter 4 – Research Findings   pg. 180

Figure 4-8: Concept map of overarching theme (practice) P6: Setting up a proficiency eco-system

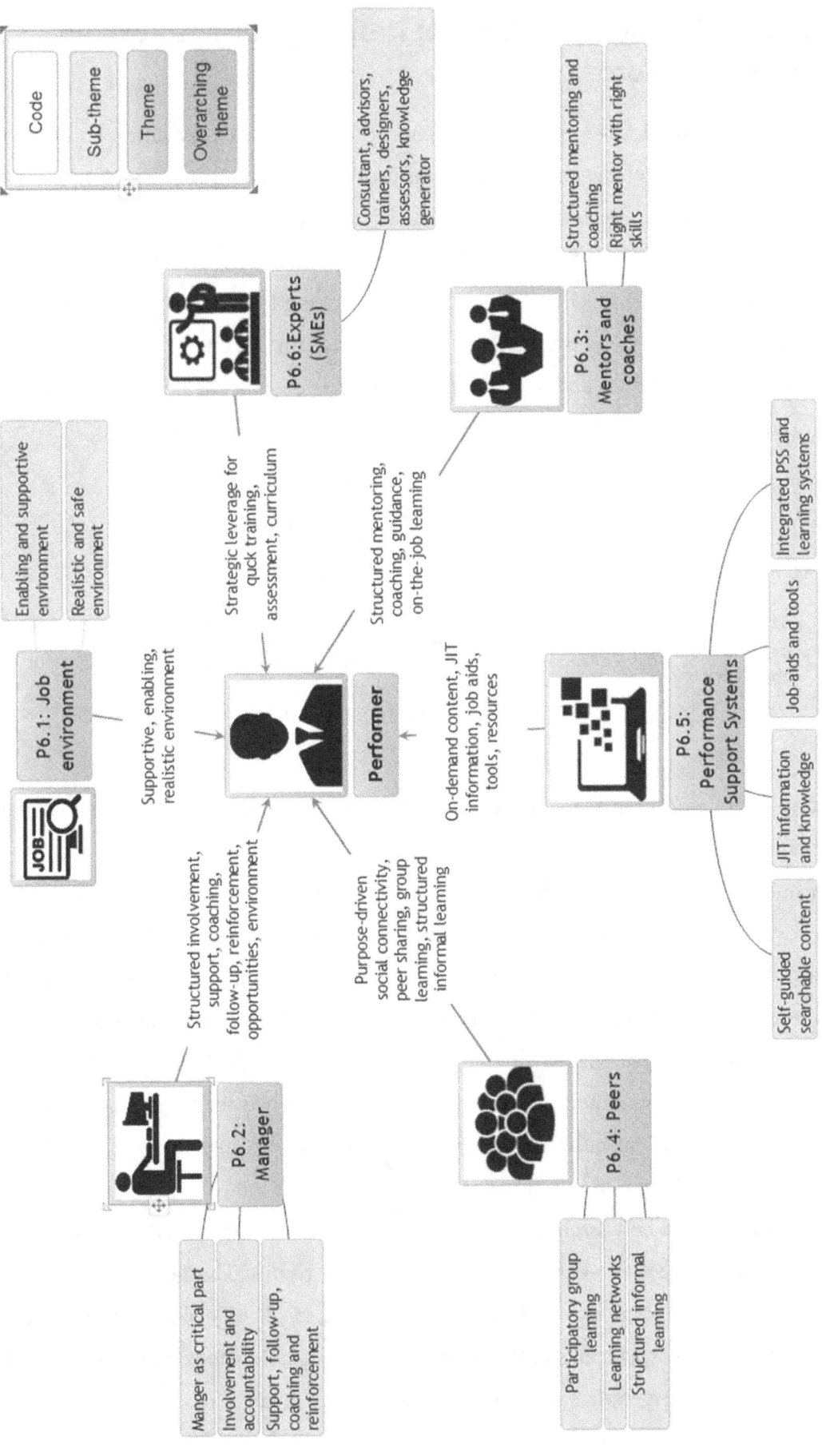

Source: developed for this research study

4.5.1 Overarching theme (practice) P1: Defining business-driven proficiency measures

Two emergent themes (strategies) P1.1—'Starting with end in mind: Upfront definition and measures of proficiency in terms of business outcomes and link it to business needs' and P1.2—'Baseline and establish time-to-proficiency targets based on business drivers' that addressed upfront definition and establishing baselines and targets were grouped under the overarching theme (practice) P1—'Defining business-driven proficiency measures', as shown in *Table 4-6*. The grouped overarching theme (practice) P1 was prevalent in 93% of the project cases based on the prevalence of themes underneath. A conceptual model based on the relationship between sub-themes, themes and overarching themes was developed, as shown in *Figure 4-3*.

Table 4-6: Thematic structure of overarching theme (practice) P1: defining business-driven proficiency measures

Overarching theme (business practice)		Emergent themes (strategies)
P1: Defining business-driven proficiency measures	P1.1	Starting with end in mind: Upfront definition and measures of proficiency in terms of business outcomes and link it to business needs
	P1.2	Baseline and establish time-to-proficiency targets based on business drivers

The overarching theme (practice) P1 represented the concept of defining proficiency and its measures upfront in terms of business outcomes designated for the job role rather than in terms of activities or tasks. With a clear definition upfront, project leaders baselined, as well as set reasonable targets for time-to-proficiency. The project leaders advocated to choose job role as the unit of analysis and define proficiency for the job role upfront. Most of project leaders defined proficiency in terms of business outcomes expected from the job role rather than in terms of activities and tasks. Project leaders tended to use historical data and estimation to baseline time-to-proficiency. They established a strong linkage of proficiency definition with the business goals to put all the efforts in the same direction. Therefore, they established the target time-to-proficiency based on business needs indicated by business drivers (found in research question #2). Having a clear definition of proficiency allowed them to measure time-to-proficiency of the exemplary performers which was data used as input to establish new target time-to-proficiency. They continuously monitored the actual time-to-proficiency and made corrections in the strategies based on the results. The data indicated that project leaders were working backwards from required business outcomes to identify skills and the knowledge required to achieve them, which was seen to lead to a shorter list of inputs. See sub-section 4.8.1 for a detailed description of each of the four emergent themes under this overarching theme.

4.5.2 Overarching theme (practice) P2: Developing a proficiency reference map

Five emergent themes (strategies) P2.1—'Conduct upfront comprehensive work analysis drawn from the outcomes', P2.2—'Profile capabilities and capacities of the job performers', P2.3—'Model success behaviours of exemplary performers', P2.4—'Understand job operating conditions and environment influences', and P2.5—'Analyse roadblocks and hindrances that lead to longer time-to-proficiency' were grouped under the overarching theme (practice) P2—'Developing a proficiency reference map', as shown in *Table 4-7*. The grouped overarching theme (practice) P2 was prevalent in 93% of the project cases based on the prevalence of themes underneath. A conceptual model based on the relationship between sub-themes, themes and overarching themes was developed, as shown in *Figure 4-4*.

Table 4-7: Thematic structure of overarching theme (practice) P2: developing proficiency reference map

Overarching theme (business practice)		Emergent themes (strategies)
P2: Developing proficiency reference map	P2.1	Conduct upfront comprehensive work analysis drawn from the outcomes
	P2.2	Profile capabilities and capacities of the job performers
	P2.3	Model success behaviours of exemplary performers
	P2.4	Understand job operating conditions and environment influences
	P2.5	Analyse roadblocks and hindrances that lead to longer time-to-proficiency

The overarching theme (practice) P2 representing a practice of developing a complete proficiency map included comprehensive work analysis, performer analysis and environmental analysis. Data analysis indicated that after defining proficiency measures and setting up new targets for desired time-to-proficiency, the majority of project leaders developed a reference map for two things: (1) all the inputs that were required to produce the desired outputs in a given job role; and (2) all the known factors influencing one's ability positively or negatively to produce these outcomes. Inputs were those things which were required to produce successful business outcomes such as tasks required to be carried out in a given job role, skills and knowledge to do those tasks, successful behaviours to do the tasks effectively and efficiently, and assessment of capabilities and capacities of performers to do such tasks. The influencing factors included environmental factors, job conditions and roadblocks that influence the deceleration or acceleration of proficiency. The data analysis suggested that from this map, data project leaders identified the *levers* that could be manipulated to achieve outcomes in a much a shorter time. As indicated by one project leader:

These will identify what are the key inputs, what are the key outputs, the level of difficulty of acquiring this particular set of capabilities, what resources are available and what constraints are there and what subtleties you have to take into account. (Harry, Project leader 18)

The project leaders who successfully shortened the time-to-proficiency first performed a comprehensive work analysis, which included task analysis as a subset to understand the total requirements to do a given job role. The important focus of project leaders appeared to be identifying the relationships of tasks, skills, behaviours among themselves and with the outcomes to fully understand how a job role produces desired outcomes. Project leaders conducted the analysis starting from the desired outcomes going backwards to build a full map of tasks, knowledge, skills and behaviour needed to produce the desired business outcomes. Two types of analyses were seen to be conducted on the performers themselves. Several project leaders appeared to profile the capabilities and capacities of performers. Almost all of them also analysed the success behaviour of exemplary performers who had already demonstrated faster time-to-proficiency. Replicating this success behaviour in the rest of the workforce led to shorter time-to-proficiency for the overall workforce serving that job role. The findings also indicated that project leaders tended to execute a detailed analysis of influencing operating conditions and environmental factors of the job, as well as limiting factors and roadblocks that hampered accelerated proficiency. Such detailed inventories formed the proficiency reference map which then became a reference to design appropriate experiences and solutions to shorten time-to-proficiency. See sub-section 4.8.2 for a detailed description of each of the four emergent themes grouped under P2.

4.5.3 Overarching theme (practice) P3: Sequencing an efficient proficiency path

Five Emergent themes (strategies) P3.1—'Segment tasks and activities based on characteristics from analytics', P3.2—'Create logical sequence of experiences as a complete path', and P3.3—'Optimise the proficiency path for efficiency and time saving' were grouped under the overarching theme (practice) of P3—'Sequencing an efficient proficiency path', as shown in *Table 4-8*. The grouped overarching theme (practice) P3 was prevalent in 88% of the project cases based on the prevalence of themes underneath. A conceptual model based on the relationship between sub-themes, themes and overarching themes was developed, as shown in *Figure 4-5*.

Table 4-8: Thematic structure of overarching theme (practice) P3: sequencing an efficient proficiency path

Overarching theme (business practice)		Emergent themes (strategies)
P3: Sequencing an efficient proficiency path	P3.1	Segment tasks and activities based on characteristics from analytics
	P3.2	Create logical sequence of experiences as a complete path
	P3.3	Optimise the proficiency path for efficiency and time saving

The overarching theme was (practice) P3 representing a practice of sequencing an efficient proficiency path. The data analysis suggested that almost all of the project leaders sequenced learning activities and on-the-job assignments to provide the most optimal path to the performers. Optimal and effective sequencing appeared to be the key to accelerating proficiency. Project leaders referred to this concept with names such as *learning path, learning sequence, performance path*, and *pathway* etc. This represented the path of a job role from day one to until the desired proficiency was achieved, as suggested by comments such as:

> *Our definition of a learning path is every learning activity that happens from day one to proficiency.... A robust learning path goes beyond a single course or curriculum to ensure the proficiency definition is achieved.* (Stephen, Project leader 53)

> *So the idea there was not just a matter of helping to get people to learn how to adapt to a new role and do it very quickly, but overall improve their performance. So I started calling these Performance Paths as a result.* (Patrick, Project leader 40)

The concept is termed *proficiency path* in this study. Proficiency path thus represented the blueprint of how to get a performer from a certain low level of proficiency to full proficiency most efficiently and effectively in the shortest possible time. Most project leaders were creating an efficient proficiency path using three processes concurrently: (1) segmentation; (2) sequencing, and (3) optimisation, with each of them based on certain criteria. The analysis indicated a key philosophy adopted by most of the project leaders that the mastery of all skills or knowledge was not required to produce a given outcome, or at least was not required to be learned upfront. Also, not all skills included in a training program were so equally frequent, critical or important for a given job that acquiring all of them at once was required. Thus, project leaders used the technique to segment and categorise tasks, skills, events, activities, etc., based on characteristics such as frequency, complexity, criticality and nature of skills through data analytics. Project leaders were seen to focus on two things: first, the things that mattered the most at the job towards producing desired outcomes; and second, the most frequent events (i.e., tasks, skills or tools) that a performer was surely going to encounter at his job.

Segmentation prioritised what was essential. Based on segmentation, a logical sequence of experiences in the form of the complete path was developed. Sequencing involved creating an appropriate order in which things should be learned, done or exposed in a given job role that overall length of the sequence is shorter. The sequencing was done based on frequency, complexity and organising principles, and finally, sequenced to build proficiency. The data analysis suggested that correctly and effectively organised sequence was the single most important factor that had the greatest impact on shortening time-to-proficiency.

This sequence was optimised for efficiency and saving time by removing waste and non-value activities, and by using multiple channels of delivery and time-spacing activities. The project leaders focused on cutting waste out of the path, removing non-value-added activities, taking time out and using various channels to choose a most time-efficient option. By doing so, they made it efficient until expected time-to-proficiency met the targeted time-to-proficiency. The goal of time-efficient optimisation was not delivering content quickly but was to make performers start demonstrating the desired performance in a shorter time. *'It wasn't about how efficiently or how quickly can we deliver content, it is really about the performance of the individual'* (Stephen, Project leader 53). Such an optimisation finally led to a major reduction in time-to-proficiency because time was being cut from the overall path to proficiency. The data analysis indicated that sequencing and optimisation were mostly being done concurrently. It was seen that segmentation, sequencing and optimisation together led to a highly efficient and effective proficiency path. The study revealed that several criteria project leaders used this in their projects to segment, sequence and optimise a full proficiency path. See sub-sub-section 4.8.3 for detailed description of each of the four emergent themes under this overarching theme.

4.5.4 Overarching theme (practice) P4: Manufacturing accelerated contextual experiences

Five Emergent themes (strategies) P4.1—'Assign performers on authentic job activities that allow practice on generating job-specific outcomes', P4.2—'Embed learning into the work and focus on doing the job rather than topic-wise learning', P4.3—'Expose performers to multiple cycles of deliberate and purposeful failures at a rapid rate or in a compressed time-frame', P4.4—'Compress hard-to-obtain experiences on known situations in highly contextualised realistic cases, gamified scenarios and representative simulations', and P4.5—'Strengthen generic, transferable, principle-based, fundamental skills to handle unfamiliar or unknown situations' were grouped under the overarching theme (practice) of P4—'Manufacturing accelerated contextual experiences', as shown in *Table 4-9*. The grouped overarching theme (practice) P4 was prevalent in 97% of the project cases based on the prevalence of themes underneath. A conceptual model based on the relationship between sub-themes, themes and overarching themes was developed, as shown in *Figure 4-6*.

Table 4-9: Thematic structure of overarching theme (practice) P4: manufacturing accelerated contextual experiences

Overarching theme (business practice)		Emergent themes (strategies)
P4: Manufacturing accelerated contextual experiences	P4.1	Assign performers on authentic job activities that allow practice on generating job-specific outcomes
	P4.2	Embed learning into the work and focus on doing the job rather than topic-wise learning
	P4.3	Expose performers to multiple cycles of deliberate and purposeful failures at a rapid rate or in a compressed time-frame
	P4.4	Compress hard-to-obtain experiences on known situations in highly contextualised Realistic cases, gamified scenarios and representative simulations
	P4.5	Strengthen generic, transferable, principle-based, fundamental skills to handle unfamiliar or unknown situations

In the previously described overarching theme (practice) P2, proficiency reference maps dictated what was needed for a performer to become proficient. Project leaders advocated learning the expertise to produce desired outcomes that were the hallmark of the state of proficiency. In the next overarching theme (practice) P3, proficiency paths dictated the most efficient sequence in which performer would become proficient. Then the overarching theme (practice) P4 represented the practice of deliberately manufacturing (or assembling) contextual experienced needed by a performer to become proficient at an accelerated rate. The foremost strategy project leaders used was to assign performers on authentic job activities that allowed practice on generating job-specific outcomes. The assignments were deliberately laid out for that experience to happen according to the proficiency path sequence. It was seen that project leaders consistently leveraged jobs if job assignments provided better and faster ways to demonstrate how to produce those outcomes. In the event that the job did not offer an early opportunity for such experience, instead of waiting for that experience to occur, project leaders resorted to manufacturing those experiences purposely in the context of the job itself. A project leader expressed this philosophy as:

> *So in effect, what happens is people learn in most jobs as a result of the happenstance or coincidence of events that happen around them, and they learn based on what the universe decides to provide them in terms of experiences in a very happenstance fashion.... So why would you want to wait for the universe to give you those experiences when it decides to? Why don't we manufacture them and compress them in 6 months rather than wait for the universe to haphazardly deliver them over two years.... let's focus on learning by doing but let's do it in such a way that we facilitate experiences in a structured sequence and let's not just wait for the universe to provide those experiences in a haphazard fashion.... the variety can take a long time to happen if you're just waiting for the universe, which is why you want to structure and format those experiences so you can deliver them more quickly or have people have those experiences. (Mathews, Practice leader 16G)*

To build those experiences, project leaders manufactured experiences by using a combination of job assignment and workplace training interventions. Few project cases also used classroom training. These contextual experiences carried similar contexts, challenges, expectations, failures and emotional loading, as would unfold in a real job. Project leaders suggested embedding learning to work together in such a way that the focus was on doing the job, rather than on learning. To accelerate proficiency, performers in several project cases were exposed to multiple cycles of deliberate and purposeful failures at a rapid rate. Hard-to-obtain experiences on known situations were delivered in highly contextualised realistic cases, gamified scenarios and representative simulations. However, not all situations or experiences could be accommodated in a training event of reasonable length. To accelerate proficiency in handling unfamiliar or unknown situations, data analysis indicated that project leaders developed the performers with generic, transferable, and principle-based fundamental skills. See sub-section 4.8.4 for a detailed description of each of the four emergent themes under this overarching theme.

4.5.5 Overarching theme (practice) P5: Promoting an active emotional immersion

Three Emergent themes (strategies) P5.1—'Active engagement and emotional immersion with the tasks and situations similar to the workplace', P5.2—'Provide immediate feedback and allow moments of focused reflection', and P5.3—'Assess performers through job-specific, continuous, multi-level assessment beyond a training intervention' were grouped under overarching theme (practice) of P5— 'Promoting an active emotional immersion', as shown in *Table 4-10*. The grouped overarching theme (practice) P5 was prevalent in 98% of the project cases based on the prevalence of themes underneath. A conceptual model based on the relationship between sub-themes, themes and overarching themes was developed, as shown in *Figure 4-7*.

Table 4-10: Thematic structure of overarching theme (practice) P5: promoting an active emotional immersion

Overarching theme (business practice)		Emergent themes (strategies)
P5: Promoting an active emotional immersion	P5.1	Active engagement and emotional immersion with the tasks and situations similar to the workplace
	P5.2	Provide immediate feedback and allow moments of focused reflection
	P5.3	Assess performers through job-specific, continuous, multi-level assessment beyond a training intervention

This overarching theme (practice) P5 signified the presence of active engagement, emotional loading and immersive experience at the same time to accelerate proficiency, thus calling it as *active emotional immersion*. The study findings indicated that contextual experiences, in a training intervention or at the job, contributed towards accelerating proficiency when performers were actively immersed in the task with similar challenges they encountered in the workplace. Project leaders suggested that by creating emotional loading similar to the actual job led to accelerating proficiency significantly. Providing immediate feedback during skill acquisition ensured almost instant behavioural change and higher retention rates. In several project cases, project leaders deliberately designed the moments of focused reflection, before, during and after the skill acquisition to deepen the skill learning.

The analysis also noted that assessments were not a one-time paper-pen event. Rather, the assessment was instituted in such a way that it was job-specific, conducted continuously at certain intervals and conducted at several levels such as trainer, mentor and manager level. One project leader expressed the intent of those practices:

> *Now if they're learning stuff in the workplace, chances are there's a lot more emotion involved. It's more real. It's more immediate. There are other people directly involved. There are consequences of failure or success. All of those things put an emotional loading on whatever is learned and that means that learning will stick more. So in that sense, there's a pretty good chance that it will stick better if it's learned at the point of work rather than in a classroom. But it's not because it's formal or informal, it's because of the way those memories are encoded and the richness of the sensory experience that's going on when that encoding happens.* (Mathews, Practice leader 16G)

See sub-section 4.8.5 for a detailed description of each of the four emergent themes under this overarching theme.

4.5.6 Overarching theme (practice) P6: Setting up a proficiency eco-system

Six Emergent themes (strategies) P6.1—'Create enabling and supportive environment', P6.2—'Structured involvement, accountability, support and reinforcement from manager', P6.3—'Institute a structured mentoring and coaching process at workplace', P6.4—'Design opportunities for purpose-driven social connectivity and structured informal learning in the workplace', P6.5—'Deploy on-demand performance support systems embedded in workflow and learning', and P6.6—'Leverage subject matter experts strategically' were grouped under the overarching theme (practice) of P6—'Setting up a proficiency eco-system', as shown in *Table 4-11*. The grouped overarching theme (practice) P6 was prevalent in 95% of the project cases based on the prevalence of themes underneath. A conceptual model based on the relationship between sub-themes, themes and overarching themes was developed, as shown in *Figure 4-8*.

The analysis suggested that key elements surrounding the performer, namely managers, peers, mentors, resources and environment had a profound impact on how soon a performer produced the desired outcomes necessary to reach proficiency. This eco-system is called the *proficiency eco-system* to represent the idea of an eco-system within which proficiency was positively developed and accelerated. The overarching theme (practice) P6 grouped six emergent themes (strategies) referring to setting up such an eco-system that provides the necessary support, coaching, environment, tools and resources from peers, mentors, managers and subject matter experts to the performer.

Table 4-11: Thematic structure of overarching theme (practice) P6: setting up a proficiency eco-system

Overarching theme (business practice)		Emergent themes (strategies)
P6: Setting up a proficiency eco-system	P6.1	Create enabling and supportive environment
	P6.2	Structured involvement, accountability, support and reinforcement from manager
	P6.3	Institute a structured mentoring and coaching process at workplace
	P6.4	Design opportunities for purpose-driven social connectivity and structured informal learning in the workplace
	P6.5	Deploy on-demand performance support systems embedded in workflow and learning
	P6.6	Leverage subject matter experts strategically

The findings indicated that having an eco-system to enable accelerated proficiency required creating an enabling and supportive environment. A manager's structured involvement, support, coaching, and reinforcement with the right opportunities was seen as the central and most critical influences on accelerating the time taken by an employee to reach proficiency. Further, structuring mentoring activities and the coaching process in the workplace influenced the rate of acceleration of a novice while learning from a mentor. Project leaders highlighted that purpose-driven social connectivity and interactions in the workplace through participatory group learning, forming learning networks and targeted informal learning was a big multiplier of the rate of proficiency acceleration. In several project cases, provision of on-demand performance support systems such as self-learning content, searchable knowledge base, and job-aids embedded in the workflow altogether eliminated the need for lengthy, non-valued added training. Lastly, the eco-system leveraged subject matter experts strategically for faster delivery of learning, effective coaching, designing realistic training and conducting assessments without requiring lengthy instructional design and traditional training processes. While the previous five practices could be addressed by strategies from training and learning domains in some shape or form, designing an efficient and supportive eco-system appeared to be the most important business practice to accelerating proficiency. It was noted in the study that when a good proficiency eco-system was put in place, the effectiveness of other practices increased significantly. See sub-section 4.8.6 for a detailed description of each of the four emergent themes under this overarching theme.

4.5.7   Conclusion of research question #3

The data analysis of research question #3 led to the identification of 24 emergent themes representing strategies that project leaders implemented in most of the project cases to reduce time-to-proficiency successfully. These themes were grouped into six overarching themes (practices) representing the business practices adopted by project leaders across the board. *Table 4-12* lists all six practices with the prevalence (counting of code presence) across all project cases. All six practices represented strongly in almost all of the project cases. None of the projects showed only one or two overarching themes (practices) in isolation; rather all the six practices were present to varying degree. Further, almost all of the project cases showed that several of the 24 emergent themes (strategies) were present in their solution for accelerated proficiency. Thus, none of the overarching themes (practices) or emergent themes (strategies) in isolation may be able to accelerate time-to-proficiency. This prevalence analysis also shows that all of the overarching themes (practices) were orchestrated together to attain shorter time-to-proficiency.

The thematic maps in Figure 4-3, Figure 4-4, Figure 4-5, Figure 4-6, Figure 4-7 and Figure 4-8, revealed input-output interactions among overarching themes (practices) P1 to P6. These relationships are shown in *Figure 4-9*. The concept map developed from the analysis indicated that accelerated proficiency solutions work as a system. The 24 emergent themes (strategies) further guided the methods and techniques used by project leaders to implement the core practices in their respective projects.

Table 4-12: Prevalence of six overarching themes (practices) across project cases

Overarching themes (business practices)		Prevalence
P1	Defining business-driven proficiency measures	93%
P2	Developing a reference model of proficiency	93%
P3	Sequencing an efficient proficiency path	88%
P4	Manufacturing accelerated contextual experiences	97%
P5	Promoting active and emotional immersion	98%
P6	Setting up a proficiency eco-system	95%

As seen in prevalence percentage in *Table 4-12*, all six overarching themes (practices) were present in almost all of the project cases. No project showed one or two overarching themes (practices) in isolation. Further, almost all of the project cases showed that several of the 24 themes were present in their solution for accelerated proficiency. Thus, none of the overarching themes (practices) or emergent themes (strategies) by themselves or in isolation appeared to accelerate time-to-proficiency. Thematic maps of the overarching themes (practices) indicated that there were input-output interactions among these themes. Thus, to accelerate proficiency, the presence of all the overarching themes (practices) may be expected. However, not all the emergent themes (strategies) were present in all of the projects.

Figure 4-9: Concept map of interactions among overarching themes (practices)

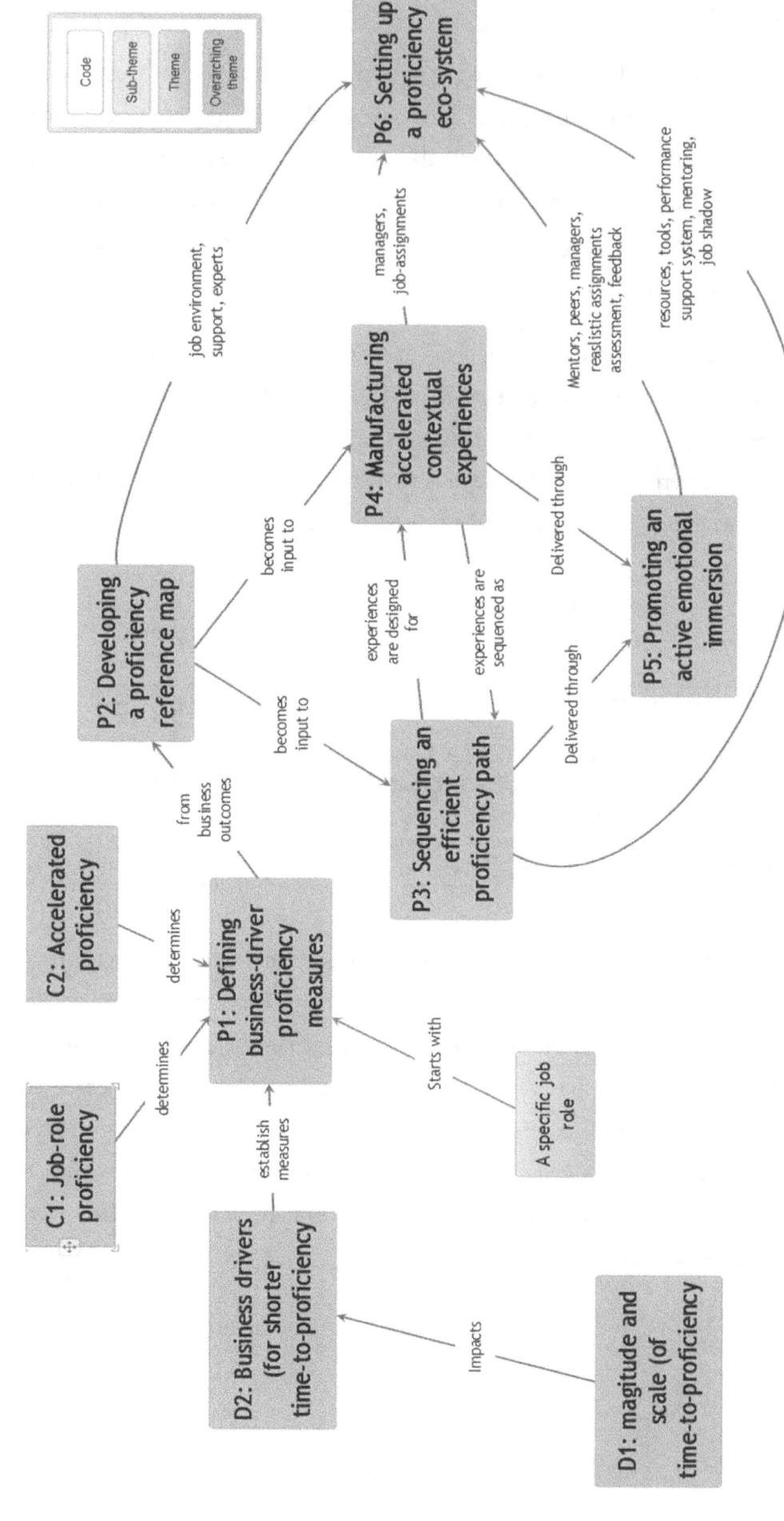

Source: developed for this research study

CHAPTER 4

PART-2: EMERGENT THEMES

Detailed description of 42 emergent themes (strategies) with participant quotes

4.6 RESEARCH QUESTION #1: MEANING OF ACCELERATED PROFICIENCY

The first research question that was explored is: **What does accelerating proficiency or accelerating time-to-proficiency mean to organisations?** In response, eight emergent themes emerged and are described below.

4.6.1 Emergent themes grouped under C1: Proficiency

1) Emergent theme C1.1: Proficiency refers to meeting established performance thresholds for a job role

The data analysis suggested that the majority of the project leaders viewed proficiency as a state in which an individual displayed performance that met the threshold performance set by the organisation for a given job role:

> *A performer who meets certain thresholds of business metrics was identified by the business as having achieved proficiency.* (Sam, Project leader 56)

> *Proficiency is defined as a required level of performance in terms of measurable result and observable actions.* (Stephen, Project leader 53)

Project leaders viewed proficiency as a non-negotiable state – the performer was either above the set level or s/he was not. They also suggested that there was no other in-between state important enough for a business to track. This point was evident from the comments of some project leaders:

> *You either did it right and got checked off, or you did it wrong, and you did not get checked off.* (Diana, Project leader 11)

> *It's simply do they achieve the specification for the task? And it is kind of you have to do it through the 100% standard; it has to be 100% correct. If you are less than 100% then you did not do it.* (Johnson, Project leader 22)

2) Emergent theme C1.2: Consistency is the hallmark of the state of proficiency of a job role

The data suggested that meeting standards consistently and repeatedly was deemed as proficiency (or proficient performance). Merely achieving performance once was not deemed proficiency. A project leader commented:

> *Because they can hit those performance objectives one time, we would not consider that proficiency. We want to see a pattern [of consistency]. Again, there are three times that they are evaluated against those metrics, and if they consistently hit those thresholds, then we would say that they are proficient.* (Sam, Project leader 56)

3) Emergent theme C1.3: Proficiency is measured by business outcomes of the job role or observable actions linked to outcomes

The data analysis suggested codes for 15 proficiency indicators in the interview transcripts of 60 project cases. These indicators were then grouped into three sub-themes representing the type of proficiency measure: (1) measurable business outcomes; (2) observable actions; and (3) controlled performance. The data analysis indicated that most project leaders (95%) defined and measured proficiency of a job role in terms of measurable business outcomes (such as meeting customer satisfaction) or in terms of those observable actions (such as work-output meeting the specifications) that closely represented those business outcomes. Some project leaders expressed this observation as:

> *A performer who meets certain thresholds of business metrics was identified by the business as having achieved proficiency.* (Sam, Project leader 56)

> *Proficiency is defined as a required level of performance in terms of measurable result and observable actions.* (Stephen, Project leader 53)

> *The measurable results and observable actions that define proficiency (the ability to perform independently to an appropriate level of quality for the position).* (Stephen, Project leader 53)

The key is meeting the expectations of the job role consistently. The results of sub-theme level analysis and project case distribution are shown in *Table 4-3*. More than half (53%) of the project cases primarily measured proficiency in a job role in terms of measurable business outcomes, for example, business results, customer satisfaction scores, key performance indicators, work performance specs, individual productivity or work quality score. This measurement method was seen in those project cases where measurable business outcomes were feasible or were the norms. Some project leaders expressed:

> *People have to get to this level of performance – they have to produce this much [outputs] with this much [inputs] with this reject rate [specifications].* (Stephen, Project leader 53)

> *We have to focus on things that matter – metrics that matter for the organisations.* (Matt, Project leader 33)

> *People have to be at this level of performance in order for them to be here [proficient] and to be working and productive, and that's how we'll define proficiency. It's a level of performance.* (Stephen, Project leader 53)

A project leader further explained with an example:

> *For a chemical manufacturer, it's making the right products and the right quantity with a minimum of waste and making it in a timely fashion so that it can be delivered to the customer according to the expectation ... if that reactor operator is at full proficiency or not is when you would take a sample of the batch and do a quality assurance test, if at every step along the way the batch fell within specification, then you'll have confidence that the reactor operator was demonstrating full proficiency.* (Richardson, Project leader 45)

Observable actions, which closely represented the business outcomes as the measure of proficiency, were utilised by 42% of the project leaders. Measurements were expressed in terms of measurements of activities, comparison with experienced peers doing the same work, evidence of authentic work immediately, the number of repetitions performed on a task, and verifiable and observable behaviour or action. This method appeared to be applicable to the project cases where some sort of benchmark existed or where activities were representative of the outcomes that would be achieved by performing those activities. Some project leaders expressed the intent of such measures as:

> *We can describe what that looks like and what's going on and that really is proficiency for that particular role.* (Stephen, Project leader 53)

As an example, proficiency of a technical support executive responsible for troubleshooting computer software was measured by a comparative performance:

> *Be proficient enough that they're performing at the same level as someone who's already been doing the job for a number of months.* (Jason, Project leader 21)

It was seen that a small percentage of project leaders (5%) used performance in a controlled representative environment as the only indicator of proficiency, particularly if it was not feasible to measure the results, or results were not available immediately (e.g., business strategy role).

The data analysis also suggested that there was not always one single indicator of measuring proficiency. On average, project cases in this study showed that proficiency was measured using two or three different indicators, while business outcomes-related indicators were invariably the primary measurements. For example, proficiency of customer service executives selling investment products over the phone was measured using three different indicators. As a project leader stated:

> *Productivity was measured by calls per hour.... 9.6 calls per hour (productivity measures); how well the phone calls met the set of criteria that were defined by the team (customer satisfaction scores) ; At the end of the four weeks you had to be at the same performance level as the current average of the performance level of experienced people on the floor (comparison to experienced performers).* (Billy, Project leader 2)

For the remainder of the thesis, any reference to *producing desired business outcomes will* connote referring to the state of proficiency.

Table 4-13: Three categories of indicators of proficiency measures reported in project cases

Sub-themes for proficiency measures	% of project cases	Indicator of proficiency	Representative quotes
Measurable business outcomes	53%	Business results	Every machine is delivered at the expected date at the customer. (Teresa, Project leader 58) The number of actual sales that they make, and then the commissions that they generate. (Rodridge, Project Leader 47)
		Customer satisfaction scores	A 90% or higher CSAT (customer satisfaction) score. (Mike, Project leader 36)
		Key performance indicators (KPIs) improvements	To reduce downtime - to get outages corrected more quickly. (Mayer, Project leader 9)
		Performance specs	Met the colour specifications and met the customers' needs. (Richardson, Project Leader 45)
		Productivity	Complete at least 20 parts to desired proficiency as rated by their trainer. (Hogdan, Project Leader 29)
Observable actions	42%	Quality and quantity of activities	How many referrals did you get, number of contacts and then your success to get new appointments with that referral, the number of fact find meetings you're doing, your discovery meetings, the number of points in the analysis that you've completed, then making your recommendations. (Christen, Project Leader 6)
		Comparison to experienced performers	Comparing them to an agent who we consider proficient, they would be at 80% of what those metrics were. (Hallmark, Project Leader 17)
		Evidence from authentic work	Quality assurance auditors would review the work to determine if those claims have been processed accurately enough. (Liza, Project Leader 13)
		Number of repetitions	They will need to have 10 repetitions of completing this task. (Richardson, Project Leader 45)
		Verifiable observable behaviours	To stand up and actually discuss the action plan, how they look at the data or what they want to do next. (Mohammad, Project Leader 39)
Controlled performance	5%	% of skill mastered	It was defined through the use of a skills matrix for tasks that were desired. (Mille, Project Leader 38)
		Pre- and post-performance in training	We try to do pre- and post-testing with our clients that they could work on their own. (Bella, Project Leader 28)
		Proficiency scores	Needed to accumulate enough points where we determine was an acceptable level of sales performance. (Matt, Project Leader 33)
		Simulated performance	How long did it take them time one versus time two versus time three? (White, Project Leader 63)
		Testing at regular intervals	We also looked a year down the road and how rapidly they were able to be able to take on far more complex and challenging situations than they were with people who have been through situation. (Aloha, Project Leader 19)

4) Emergent theme C1.4: Proficiency is not just about learning an isolated skill, task or activity in a job

Project leaders emphasised that proficiency is a state or level of performance. They differentiated it from being good in some skills, knowledge or attitude or ability to perform some activities, steps or tasks. One project leader supported this view by stating:

> *People have to be at this level of performance in order for them to be [proficient] here and to be working and productive. And that's how we'll define proficiency. It's a level of performance as opposed to I've got to know something.... It's not about acquiring skills, knowledge and attitudes, but rather about how these building blocks are successfully used on the job to produce required results.* (Stephen, Project leader 53)

Another project leader used an analogy to differentiate proficiency from the steps and activities involved in performing a task:

> *If the proficiency is [to] make a delicious sandwich, then steps in that process would be the bread and the meat and the condiments and spread the right quantity of condiments on the bread. And lay out the right quantity of meat and cheese and lettuce and what have you. So, those are steps, those are not the proficiencies. The proficiency is make a delicious sandwich* (Richardson, Project leader 45)

The study findings indicated that in organisations, proficiency and competence were viewed as markedly different constructs. Competence was viewed as a combination of knowledge, skills and attitudes necessary to do the task or job. However, competence was not seen by project leaders as someone's ability to produce consistent business outcomes. Some comments from project leaders supported this distinction:

> *Competence is much more related to the knowledge and skills and to some extent the attitude of the person that we're talking about, but just because someone is competent doesn't mean they can do the job when they're given it at their desk.* (Connan, Practice Leader 5G)

Project leaders also differentiated a related term of competency from proficiency.

> *We're saying competencies are not the same thing [as proficiency]. Competencies are those skills, knowledge and attitude kind of stuff.* (Stephen, Project leader 53)
>
> *Proficiency definitions include key business measures which are usually left out of competency statements. This makes them far easier to measure.* (Stephen, Project leader 53)

Project leaders also indicated that developing someone to be proficient is not the same as making someone an expert in something. Some project leaders stated:

> *I think in most organisations while there could still be some experts that are required, not everybody has to be an expert, but they should be proficient.* (Andrew, Practice leader 2G)
>
> *Developing people to experts is a much different thing than developing people to be proficient at something.* (Ron, Project leader 48)

4.6.2 Emergent themes grouped under C2: Accelerated proficiency

1) Emergent theme C2.1: Accelerated proficiency is measured in terms of reduction in time-to-proficiency.

The data analysis suggested that the accelerated proficiency phenomenon was about bringing people to the desired state of performance quickly. Various project leaders expressed a sense of acceleration of proficiency with a range of connotations such as compressing, accelerating, speeding up, ramping up, up-to-speed, rapidly, quickly or shortening. Project leaders described accelerated proficiency as:

> *People get to a higher level of proficiency more quickly than people did before.* (Robinson, Practice leader 19G)

> *The idea is, how do we get new people coming into that level [of performance] as fast as we can.* (Stephen, Project leader 53)

Project leaders expressed their ideas about accelerated proficiency in a measurable business metric, namely time-to-proficiency. Most project leaders viewed time-to-proficiency as the time taken by an individual in a given job role from the start of the job to reach the state of desired performance. That view was evident from comments such as:

> *We define time-to-proficiency as when does the performance of an individual meet all of the thresholds this business identified as a meets expectation performer.* (Sam, Project leader 56)

> *And so the time-to-competence [or time-to-proficiency] is from the time they start their on-the-job training... until the step four is signed off on, all the steps have been signed off on by their trainer and their production leader and the learner.* (Hogdan, Project leader 29)

> *We typically talk about [time-to-proficiency as] how long it takes for people to become 80% proficient.* (Reese, Practice leader 14G)

The data analysis showed that the term *time-to-proficiency* appeared to have a very clear meaning to business people. The definition of *proficiency* was mostly used to track time-to-proficiency. Project leaders commented that:

> *I had a very clear definition of time-to-proficiency and that was, how long would it take for someone to be able to do 9.6 calls per hour.* (Billy, Project leader 2)

> *TTP (time-to-proficiency) was determined by the business using the same criteria they use in evaluating incumbent performers. It consisted of 11 key metrics and measures. A performer who meets certain thresholds was identified by the business as having achieved proficiency.* (Sam, Project leader 56)

2) Emergent theme C2.2: A clear definition of proficiency for a job role is the most critical requirement to baseline, monitor and shorten time-to-proficiency.

The project leaders were unanimous regarding the importance of clearly defining proficiency and its measures upfront. This definition served as a way to drive agreement across the teams and tools to track proficiency. For instance:

> *You have to really be careful to define what those results are .... That number one is: you have to define what the results look like.* (Dickenson, Project leader 12)

> *First of all, we have to define what we mean by proficiency ... What do you need to be able to do to show that you're proficient and able to do this? So that was the first step. And actually that in itself became very valuable, because that became a great set of expectations of what people should be able to do.* (McDonalds, Project leader 32)

> *The proficiency definition also served as the ongoing assessment tool.* (Stephen, Project leader 53)

> *We then took those same metrics and we started to apply those to the graduates of the new program to see if we were able to get them to achieve time-to-proficiency at a faster pace.* (Sam, Project leader 56)

While acknowledging the importance of the definition, the project leaders also pointed out that people in organisations struggle to define proficiency clearly. In the absence of a clear definition, organisations did not know if their employees in a given role had attained proficiency or not. Some project leaders emphasised this issue:

> *Most organisations can't actually tell you what they mean by proficiency, and they only have a very general idea of on average, how long does it take? .... So, if you're serious about reducing the time-to-proficiency, then you have to get clear about what that means, and then you have to start tracking it, so that you can apply process improvement principles.* (Reynold, Project leader 49)

> *People have such a poor understanding what proficiency was, is that [sic] they didn't even agree on that. So it's hard to find time-to-proficiency if you don't agree on what proficiency is.* (Stephen, Project leader 53)

> *A training project needs to start out by describing in behavioural terms exactly what proficiency looks like, and there's the problem. A lot of people don't take the time to really describe what proficiency looks like in behavioural terms. Once you do that, you have to have a plan to measure to make sure when you've gotten people to proficiency. I think most people fail on those two counts, first of all.* (Dickenson, Project leader 12)

3) Emergent theme C2.3: Accelerated proficiency is not accelerated learning or accelerated training.

The analysis suggested that accelerated proficiency is about enabling people to be able to reach the same level of mastery in attaining business performance, irrespective of their speed of learning. Project leaders clarified that accelerated proficiency is not about speeding up the learning curve of a certain individual or it is not learning or training a given content in a shorter time. One project leader commented:

> *We might have to put in a coach, we might have to let the person repeat some things, we might let that person do a remedial loop, but they can achieve the same level of mastery. That's where time-to-proficiency could mislead people sometimes. Sometimes, not all human beings can learn quickly.* (Dickenson, Project leader 12)

The goal of accelerated proficiency was seen as reducing the total time taken to reach the state of proficiency, rather than reducing the training duration alone. Project leaders indicated that reducing training duration was not the goal of their accelerated proficiency projects, though the shorter duration of training came out to be a by-product in most of the project cases. In the majority of the project cases, achieving the state of proficiency took several times more time than the duration of the training interventions used. For example, one project leader stated:

> *Do the week's program in a day and that's not we're talking about, we're talking about the 18 months' target moving that down to 12 months.* (Stephen, Project leader 53)

In some project cases, it was noted that if proficiency to initial operating readiness was important, shorter training was used as a strategy with the goal of having the people to start producing business specific outcomes sooner:

> *'How quickly can I teach you?' Because what we found was, we could do an initial program that would at least get you the basics, to get in front of the computer within roughly about two to four weeks.* (Christian, Project leader 5)

Furthermore, the analysis suggests that the goal of accelerated proficiency is not to shorten the transaction time or activity time to appear to be doing work faster. For example, it is not about how soon someone makes a sale to a given customer or how fast someone closes the sales cycle; rather it is about how soon someone reaches to the mark where s/he produces set sales targets consistently. For instance:

> *[Proficiency is that] I should be able to do 80% of my job.... It may take me longer to do them right, but I can still get it done.* (Kieve, Project leader 24)

4) Emergent theme C2.4: Training alone rarely leads to accelerating proficient performance, it requires solutions beyond training.

The data indicated that the journey towards proficiency was much more than training events or learning interventions. One project leader commented:

> *The real answer to compressing time-to-competence is that one has to look outside of the training – look at what's wrapped around it.* (Charlie, Project leader 4)

Almost all the participants advocated that training alone was not the solution to accelerate proficiency. Project leaders viewed training as one of many solutions, and they used a range of non-training solutions as well, which altogether appeared to reduce time-to-proficiency. Several project leaders commented:

> *Training isn't the answer in every situation, and for many situations, you need a very different strategy as the main approach to getting people to the point when they are competent.* (Todd, Project leader 57)

> *Training is usually one of the more insignificant ones [solutions].* (Dickenson, Project leader 12)

> *Training very rarely will result in desired performance; that it takes a number of different interventions, all woven together to produce an outcome.* (Harry, Project leader 18)

> *When you think about really learning to do something to a level of performance or a level of proficiency, it takes a lot more than that [training] and that's what people kind of fall short...* (Stephen, Project leader 53)

In the instances where training was designed, the focus was on making performers produce the desired business outcomes that mattered most to the organisation. Training did not seem to end until that state was achieved. It appears that their focus was not so much on making the performers learn something:

> *You really need to be clear about what's the business point, not what people need to learn, but what needs to happen for the business, or how do they need to perform.* (Reynold, Project leader 49)

> *Completion of [traditional] training is specifically the moment that the trainer conveys all the information. But in this model [of accelerated proficiency], training is complete only when the learner has achieved proficiency... It was less about how much time have we covered and how many PowerPoint slides have been – and it was much more focused on how to help this learner become proficient in their job as quickly as possible so that they are contributing to the overall roles of the organisation... It's not that the training was content-free by any means, but it was all focused on an account on the reactor operator performing at the level I need as measured by making batches quickly and efficiently without errors and making sellable products.* (Richardson, Project leader 45)

In that perspective that training was considered as a small part of the overall solution, the traditional instructional design processes appeared to have rendered outcomes that were not required or not immediately useful, and in some cases, they even caused a bottleneck that slowed down the rate of proficiency. One project leader shared an insightful reflection of how organisations care less about traditional training modalities if the goal is shortening time-to-proficiency:

> *[It was] liberating [for me] in some way, not to have to abide by those sort of cultural norms or [traditional] training development and instructional design that I was so familiar with. All that really matters was for the employee[to] make the product within specification in a timely fashion to meet the customers' needs. At no point in the process was any stakeholder interested really in what instructional design methodologies do they use or any of those things that we often in our field that we often judge ourselves about. That just was not of importance to the stakeholders in this case. It was 'I want to get product out the door to our customers'. It has their specifications and that's really what matters. That's what drives our organisation and that's what we care about. I had to learn to let go of many things that I held dear as just not what was important to the project.... I'll consider that technical language from a training or learning and development standpoint but I did not introduce that type of language or those constructs to my team. There was no explicit attempt to link what we were doing for developing task analysis to what I would call those academic constructs that you just named. Just the language would not have been familiar to the members of the team and I don't think it would have helped them arrive more quickly at the set of proficiency statements ... And no one really was interested in a lot of the metrics we've developed for ourselves in the training industry because that's not why the paint company was in business.* (Richardson, Project leader 45)

Some project leaders indicated that the dynamics inside the training process were not representative of what happens in the real world in terms of pressure, consequences, goals and experience:

> *Retention happens when there's a good emotional loading on it.... Now, it's difficult to get that emotional loading onto something in a training room ... most things that happen in a training room are fairly ordinary. People are sitting there, absorbing stuff, talking about stuff and it's not an emotional rollercoaster, let's put it that way.* (Mathews, Practice leader 16G)

Project leaders strongly iterated that performance during a training event was a false indicator of an individual's proficiency. They also recognised that not all of the performance seen in any training event would transfer to the job towards accelerating proficiency. Some project leaders supported this by stating that:

> *Performance during the acquisition process is misleading, and in many situations, that's the only thing that people [responsible for training] are going to see - the performance during training.* (Robert, Practice leader 4G)

> *In traditional training what people do is to go inside a competency [list] and then start saying how do we train each of these competencies. I'm going to use a competency, let's do a training program...* (Stephen, Project leader 53)

However, the value of training in skill acquisition and knowledge acquisition was not undermined by any project leader. Some of them even believed that the primary goal of a training intervention should be to reduce time-to-proficiency. Otherwise it may not be useful:

> *The training has only one value, and that is to improve skills and knowledge. That's all it does.* (Harry, Project leader 18)

If training isn't shortening the time, then maybe they shouldn't be doing it. It should always shorten the time. (Diana, Project leader 11)

4.7 RESEARCH QUESTION #2: DRIVING FACTORS AND BENEFITS OF REDUCED TIME-TO-PROFICIENCY

This section proposes answers to research question #2: **What business factors drive the need for reducing time-to-proficiency of the workforce and how do organisations benefit from achieving it?** In response, 10 emergent themes emerged and are described below.

4.7.1 Emergent themes grouped under D1: Magnitude and scale of time-to-proficiency business problem

1) Emergent theme D1.1: Magnitude of time-to-proficiency problem

All 60 projects were compared to each other and categorised by job type, economic sector, business sector or industry group to understand the pattern of the scale of the problem in different contexts. *Table 4-14* groups the project cases by job nature. The data analysis shows that the magnitude of time-to-proficiency was significantly large across all the job role types. While sale and managerial jobs required about three months to one and half years to reach proficiency in 11 projects, the technical or engineering jobs required two months to several years, as seen in 16 projects. Further, scientific or development jobs took six months to three years to become fully proficient, as observed in four projects. Assembly and production-related jobs took lesser time from one week to five months to become proficient, as suggested by four projects. Just the training programs alone typically took as low as one week to as high as 18 weeks of classroom time across different job types.

Table 4-14: Magnitude of time-to-proficiency across primary job nature

Categories of Primary job nature	No. of project cases	Magnitude of time-to-proficiency	Magnitude of training duration
Technical or engineering	16	2 months to several years	5 to 18 weeks
Sales - non-technical	5	3 months to 1.5 years	1 to 10 weeks
Scientific or development	4	6 months to 3 years	No data
Customer service helpdesk	4	1.5 months to 1 year	4 to 12 weeks
Sales - technical	3	Unknown to 1.5 years	No data
Managerial, supervisory	3	1 month to 14 months	4 to 13 weeks
Strategic management, leadership	3	1 year to very long	No data
Medical, healthcare	3	3 months to 1 year	
Production, manufacturing	3	1 month to 5 months	
Financial services	2	5 months to 3 years	15 weeks
Training or education	1	1-2 years	No data
Assembly, repair	1	1 week	

Similarly, when projects are arranged by economic sectors, the technology sector (13 projects) showed time-to-proficiency from two months to three years, while basic materials sector (three projects) appeared to have a very long cycle to proficiency. Training duration was as short as one week in the financial and economic sectors, and as long as 18 weeks in the industrial sector. Major observations are summarised in *Table 4-15*.

Table 4-15: Magnitude of time-to-proficiency across economic sectors

Economic sectors	No. of project cases	Magnitude of time-to-proficiency	Magnitude of training duration
Technology	13	2 months to 3 years	5 to 13 weeks
Financials	9	1.5 months to 1 year	1 to 15 weeks
Healthcare	7	Unknown to 2 years	No data
Consumer non-cyclicals	5	1 week to 14 months	4 to 13 weeks
Energy	4	1 month to several years	No data
Industrials	4	5 months to 1.5 years	18 weeks
Basic materials	3	1.5 to 2 years, 8-20 years' event frequency	No data
Telecommunication services	2	3 months to 1 year	
Military/ government	2	1 to 3 years	
Utilities	1	2 years	

The theme D1.1—'Magnitude of time-to-proficiency problem' suggested that time-to-proficiency of most jobs across several economic sectors was not in days, rather it was as long as 3 years in some project cases. Duration of training programs used to develop proficiency of workforce ranged up to 18 weeks. Variations for the time-to-proficiency were due to different job goals, context organisational work culture, team composition and other factors which were not necessarily the same even for the same job nature across different organisations.

2) Emergent theme D1.2: Scale of time-to-proficiency problem

The theme D1.2—'Scale of time-to-proficiency problem' suggested that in several of the project cases, the magnitude of time-to-proficiency in a given job role when multiplied over the entire target group of employees in that job role, led to hundreds of person-years. For instance, in project case 36, a large business process outsourcing company noticed that for a job role comprised of 600 people, the magnitude of time-to-proficiency was one year. Scaled to the entire group of people led to 600 person-years worth of time, indicating compelling reasons to address this problem. The project leader commented:

> *It was probably about close to three months of training before they were able to get on the phone... Three months is a long, long time ... So there were three months in sort of training and then it was taking them an additional nine months to reach that score ... So then, it would take them about another year to basically start reaching those high scores. So it was too long. So what would happen was the financial institution would grade the business process outsourcer, would grade them on those scores. If in two-quarters you are below these*

numbers, we have the right to cancel the contract. (Mike, Project leader 36)

In another project, project case 1, at a large semiconductor equipment company, almost 20 engineers were required to undergo a certification program every year in which the magnitude of time-to-certification was a minimum of 53 weeks. Scaled to the total number of engineers per year, it amounted to 20 person-years worth of time, or 100 person-years in five years. The project leader commented:

> *So in my current program, training takes 13 weeks [total] for five different modules [courses] and then each module has 10 weeks of an average waiting time [in-between each module]. I have five modules, so it totals around 53 weeks or basically a year for the engineer to get certified.* (Benny, Project leader 1)

4.7.2 Emergent themes grouped under D2: Business drivers for accelerating time-to-proficiency

1) Emergent theme D2.1: Time-related pressures

23 (38%) of the project cases showed this theme D2.1—'Time-related pressures'. This theme represented those drivers in which operational metrics were consciously measured in the unit of time. Examples were time-to-market pressures, longer time-to-proficiency and longer training duration:

> *People simply aren't getting up the speed as fast they can and it's very, very expensive when they're not [coming up to speed quickly]... the basic business case that we've started with is that every minute someone isn't fully up to speed is costing you money and it's worth doing something about it.* (Stephen, Project leader 53)

> *The only thing that counts within [this company] is time-to-market for the project. Every machine is delivered at the expected date at the customer. They never put up with even 1 day delay in shipping the machine...* (Teresa, Project leader 58)

2) Emergent theme D2.2: Speed-related competitiveness

24 (38%) of the project cases showed this theme D2.2—'Speed-related competitiveness'. This theme included those operational metrics in which speed was perceived as a measure of success. Examples were customer pressures to deliver fast; market urgencies to produce fast; business ramp-up speed, the speed of launch of new product, service or business; and the need for rapid operational readiness and rapid hiring sprints:

> *... demand for this service was very high with investors, this online brokers firm was hiring new service and sales people every single week. Almost every single week. In some cases, you might have new 30 or 40 people per week or per month being hired in this continuous cycles of new employees to support the growth and of course to support any turnover that occurs in the normal customer service and sales business.* (Billy, Project leader 2)

> *... for them to go to their other clients and tell them "We lost this contract because we're not able to ramp up people fast enough to get to the satisfaction scores that this company is requesting of us" is going to look really bad to the rest of the clients.* (Mike, Project leader 36)

3) Emergent theme D2.3: Skill-related deficiencies

More than half of the project cases, 32 (53%), showed this theme D2.3—'Skill-related deficiencies'. This theme included those needs that arise because of a lack of workforce skills or lack of qualified workforce. Examples were attrition and retirement, new hires replacing expert workforce, and performance issues due to a lack of skills and obsolete skills:

> *People are reaching retirement age so they were going to begin losing the institutional knowledge of their senior personnel in short order, and that the time frame that it took to get people up to speed, the new engineers up to speed and learn the ins and outs of what the utility did, what each department did. The amount of time necessary to follow that path, they were going to lose people sooner than the people would get up to speed.* (Tony, Project leader 60)

4) Emergent theme D2.4: Cost or financial implications

20 (33%) of the project cases showed this theme D2.4—'Cost or financial implications'. This theme included those factors and impacts which were measured in the unit of money. Examples were the cost of training, the cost of someone not being proficient, as indicated by errors and mistakes, the cost of opportunity lost while someone was not proficient, and other regulatory pressures that cost the company severely if not observed, such as safety:

> *The real costs of achieving proficient job performance in complex jobs come after training is done. These costs are substantial, but are rarely measured. We all know they exist—and they can be huge. These costs show up as: sub-par productivity, mistakes, dissatisfied customers, time spent getting help from others, manager's time reviewing and correcting work, attrition, due to people feeling unprepared or overwhelmed by their jobs……. If we can reduce the time it takes to become expert or at least proficient performers, we can save our organisations a lot of money, increase retention rates, reduce errors, and improve customer satisfaction.* (McDonalds, Project leader 32)

4.7.3 Emergent theme grouped under D3: Business benefits of reduced time-to-proficiency

1) Emergent theme D3.1: Business gains

This theme D3.1—'Business gains' represented gains such as increased market share, shorter sales cycle, increased profit, revenue, competitiveness, readiness of staff, improved sales and higher customer satisfaction realised as a result of shorter time-to-proficiency. For example, in project case 44, the organisation *'shortened the sales cycle substantially and increased market share'* (Ricky, Project leader 44). Some project leaders cited benefits such as:

- $1.8M additional net profit per seller;
- client cited phenomenal results;
- onboarding of 400 new staff in shorter time;
- stock increased by 5X, market cap increased by 3X and no debt;
- improved sales and internal efficiencies; and

- high customer satisfaction.

2) Emergent theme D3.2: Cost savings

This theme D3.2—'Cost savings' represented cost savings from shorter time-to-proficiency, shorter training duration and less travel required, and cost savings aggregated on a larger population. For example, in project case 56, *'the organisation saved $5.68M in 2 years'* (Sam, Project leader 56). Some project leaders cited benefits such as:

- cost avoidance of $145K in 1 year;
- saved millions of dollars for 600 people;
- reduced cost by 24%; and
- saved travel expenses by 40%.

3) Emergent theme D3.3: Improvement in operational metrics

This theme D3.3—'Improvement in operational metrics' represented an increase in staff retention, need for fewer staff, high training capacity with shorter courses, and improvement in skill scores of the staff. For example, in project case 53, *'employee retention improved from 55% to 95%'* (Stephen, Project Leader 53). Some benefits cited by other project leaders were:

- needed 40% fewer staff to execute the program; and
- cut manager-to-employee ratio by 50% (1 to 20 ratio to 1 to 40 ratio).

4) Emergent theme D3.4: Improvement in productivity

This theme D3.4—'Improvement in productivity' represented an improvement in processing rate, reduction in errors, improved output, availability of staff, efficiency and saving of time. For example, in project case 21, the organisation realised productivity improvement from 45% to 95% in terms of the number of faults troubleshooted. Some benefits cited by project leaders were:

- 53% drop in misdirected calls;
- improved by 66% (3 defects to 1 defect per week);
- 10% increase in efficiency compared to past graduates;
- 26% higher quota attainment over 6 quarters; and
- saved 45,500 hours of 1,250 people per year.

The data analysis noted that all four themes D3.1, D3.2, D.3.3 and D3.4 were uniform across all project cases with no specific strong prevalence of one kind. In fact, each project realised more than one type of business benefit. For example, in project case 3, a high-tech semiconductor equipment company in the fast-paced technology business was pressed hard to keep customers' production running and keep equipment uptime commitments. The business benefits of reducing time-to-proficiency were reported by the project leader as:

Customer satisfaction: '*Another side benefit of this whole thing is that your customer satisfaction goes up. Because the people that are working on the [equipment] actually know how to work on the things that actually happen on the tool, so the customer will have a higher degree of confidence in the individual's ability*'. (Rustom, Project leader 46)

Operational metrics: '*So overall that benefit is probably we've reduced our training load by about 75%. So that's the direct impact that we've seen*'. (Rustom, Project leader 46)

Cost savings: '*We've also done cost avoidance savings that are somewhere in the probably around 8-10 million dollars, I believe that*'. (Rustom, Project leader 46)

4.8 RESEARCH QUESTION #3: PRACTICES AND STRATEGIES TO ACCELERATE PROFICIENCY

This section explores research question #3: **What core practices and strategies do business leaders and practitioners adopt to achieve shorter time-to-proficiency of the workforce in a given job?**

In response, 24 emergent themes (strategies) emerged and are described below.

4.8.1 Emergent themes (strategies) grouped under P1: Defining business-driven proficiency measures

1) Emergent theme (strategy) P1.1: Starting with end in mind: upfront definition and measures of proficiency in terms of business outcomes and link it to business needs

Emergent theme (strategy) P1.1 indicated that defining proficiency and its measures upfront was the most crucial requirement to accelerate it in the first place. From all the project cases analysed in this study, it was seen that time-to-proficiency was so far out that just defining it in a crisp and measurable fashion could lead to deliberate and conscious efforts to reduce it. Defining proficiency upfront appeared to align management efforts in the same direction. Proficiency was greatly accelerated when proficiency was defined in terms of desired business outcomes expected from the job rather than skills, knowledge or activities required to do the job. It was observed that most practitioners were inclined towards using business outcome-based measurements. By keeping the end in mind, project leaders established a strong linkage of the proficiency definition with the business goals that allowed them much more clarity on how to reach in shorter time. That in turn appeared to lead to a much shorter or leaner list of skills, knowledge and behaviours required to accomplish those end results, and being much leaner or shorter. That shorter list led to shorter time to prepare people to a level where they could produce the desired business outcomes. Some project leaders' comments expressed the intent of this theme:

> *So the first step was to bring in experts and define, okay, what are the criteria for being able to handle a case effectively. And what do you need to be able to do to show that you're proficient and able to do this? ... And actually that in itself became very valuable, because that became a great set of expectations of what people*

> *should be able to do.* (McDonalds, Project leader 32)

> *But if you have clarity about what outcomes need to be produced and work backwards and backwards to the knowledge and skills, you get a much leaner approach if you think of lean factory ... if we start from the inputs [knowledge, skills etc.] first... the level of expertise required will appear to be much more complex than if we start from the outcomes and work backwards to those inputs ...* (Ellis, Project leader 14)

2) Emergent theme (strategy) P1.2: Baseline and establish time-to-proficiency targets based on business drivers

Emergent theme (strategy) P1.2 indicated that after defining proficiency measures, the next most important aspect project leaders focused on was to baseline the current time-to-proficiency. Project leaders used some historical data or estimation to do so. To establish new target time-to-proficiency, project leaders mentioned the use of several inputs. Among those were business drivers (D2.2 as discovered in research question #2) such as targeted time-to-market, expected timelines for readiness or dates for business ramp-up and the current average time-to-proficiency of exemplary performers. Project leaders suggested a continuous closed loop monitoring of actual time-to-proficiency by comparing it against established time-to-proficiency targets. The study results showed that this process drove any corrections or change in strategies:

> *The third step involved quantifying the current time-to-proficiency to provide a baseline for improvement. This was done through reviewing historical data and interviewing key staff and managers.* (Stephen, Project leader 53)

> *So we have to figure out what are the business results we want and that's how we define the proficiency, and then we look at how quickly it takes for people to get to that on average in a baseline and then [we asked], can we increase that?* (McDonalds, Project leader 32)

> *When we began to build the new version of the program, we immediately put a process in place to measure the graduates of the old program and how long it took them to achieve time-to-proficiency [baseline]. And then of course as we launched our new program, we then took those same [time-to-proficiency] metrics, and we started to apply those to the graduates of the new program to see if we were able to get them to achieve time-to-proficiency at a faster pace.* (Sam, Project leader 56)

4.8.2 Emergent themes (strategies) grouped under P2: Developing a proficiency reference map

1) Emergent theme (strategy) P2.1: Conduct upfront comprehensive work analysis drawn from the outcomes.

Emergent theme (strategy) P2.1 emerged from ideas of performing comprehensive work analysis (not just task analysis) using the job role as a unit of analysis. One key point was that successful project cases used job role as a unit of analysis rather than the analysis of one employee. The goal of this work analysis mostly had been to map out how the outcomes were being achieved in a job role within the influence of other enabling or disabling variables. Part of this understanding was to identify the relationships between behaviour, skills and tasks, and in turn, their relationship to business outcomes. Based on various project case accounts, it was observed that the overall comprehensive work analysis included things such as what tasks a performer was required to do in a given job role (to achieve targeted outcomes), what s/he needed to know to do those tasks, what skills s/he needed to apply to complete the task and what behaviours s/he needed to exhibit to do the task effectively and to attain desired outcomes. Most of the project leaders had drawn tasks, skills, knowledge, behaviours and other requirements from the business outcomes to become proficient. Some project leaders' comments described certain elements of this theme:

> *The main thing is that you are really breaking down the job and you begin with what are the outcomes that are required, and work backwards from that ... The most important thing is that you begin with the outcomes of the job. You have to break down the job, so that you have an excellent portrait of what the job is ... Begin with the job. You'll identify what needs to be done both from an outcome point of view and a process point of view.* (Harry, Project leader 18)

> *Work analysis looks at the total amount of work that has to be carried out... it looks at the overall goals that need to be accomplished for a particular work to be carried out and that is broader than just the one particular individual who does certain things in a certain way.* (Martin, Project leader 31)

> *So the question is "What is the connection between that dependent variable [outcome] and the behaviour of the individual?"... Why is that behaviour manifesting itself and how does that behaviour really relate to the achievement of the goal within that task.* (Mike, Project leader 36)

2) Emergent theme (strategy) P2.2: Profile capabilities and capacities of target performers

Emergent theme (strategy) P2.2 revealed that in addition to analysing the skills, tasks, knowledge, and behaviours required to accomplish the goals of a given job role, project leaders also attempted to understand the current capabilities and prior skills of the performers. Project leaders suggested that capabilities of the current performers and yet-to-be-hired performers was a factor in speeding up time-to-proficiency that gave them a head start and cut short time on unnecessary things or skills performers already possessed. They also attributed variations in speed to proficiency among individuals performing the same job to their personal capacity and learning ability, and advocated profiling it. The information on current capabilities, experience and skill assessment, inventory of prior skills and assessment of learning capacities or any other individual differences among performers potentially impacting speed to proficiency were noted and constituted as the inputs to the proficiency reference map. A project leader indicated that:

> *Obviously, the time-to-proficiency for any of these technical things will be affected by the level of proficiency I brought in at the beginning.* (Reynold, Project leader 49)

3) Emergent theme (strategy) P2.3: Model success behaviours of exemplary performers

Emergent theme (strategy) P2.3 emerged from the ideas of identifying the exemplary performers, understanding and modelling their success behaviours and replicating those behaviours in the rest of the workforce. Almost all of the project cases showed that understanding exemplary performers' success behaviour was central to a good proficiency reference map. Project leaders identified the exemplary performers in a given job role who had produced business accomplishments to the desired proficiency in a shorter time than their peers. Then their success behaviours were analysed to see how they produced those results in shorter time. Project leaders stressed that they focused on differentiating characteristics such as attitude or behaviour that separated exemplary performers rather than skills or knowledge they possessed. It was seen in the analysis that most of the project leaders identified specific observable and verifiable success behaviours as the primary approach and did not advocate any detailed task-based analysis or complex knowledge elicitation. Almost all the project leaders then attempted to accelerate proficiency of the remaining workforce by replicating those success behaviours through training or otherwise. It was seen that they did not need any massive training program to do so. In most cases it was just on-the-job mentoring, knowledge sharing, checklists or instruction sheets. Some project leaders explained this:

> *This method is based on capturing the performance profile of your stars and then using this information to quickly enable significant improvement in the results produced by the remainder of your workforce... The most effective and efficient way to capture models of optimal performance is to work with your current stars. These are the individuals who have established approaches to their work that consistently produce the desired accomplishments at a high level.... Many times these individuals have developed rich mental models of what success looks like and ways of predicting a successful outcome.... So one of the ways to accelerate that kind of performance-centric expertise is to provide these rich models of how the current high performers succeed because that provides the context and the clarity to let others improve their performance more rapidly.... driving improved business results by replicating the accomplishments of your star performers. The advantage of this approach is that it is derived from the current performance of your star employee. Therefore, you know it is possible within your current structure and culture. It also has the advantage of being cost-effective and quick.* (Ellis, Project leader 14)

> *We basically map out what are the behaviours that are contributing to the success of each one of those top performers within each segment of the job.... we map out what are the different components of this job... then we map out the behaviours of the top performers against each one of those tasks. What you get there is you start seeing patterns and you start seeing different things that emerge from that analysis and at that point you're able to distil that into a model of the superhuman customer service representative.* (Mike, Project leader 36)

> *The way we do that is to examine who are successful performers; determine what their characteristics are, not the skills and knowledge, but their characteristics... We have to look at what is their attitude, how they operate, what are their behaviours and what are the success factors that make them successful.* (Harry, Project leader 18)

> *It turns out we didn't have to develop the other ten operators' knowledge of chemistry to the same level of the star performer. We just had to have them shift what screen they were monitoring and make adjustments earlier in the process.* (Ellis, Project leader 14)

The analysis indicated that only some project leaders used sophisticated techniques such as cognitive task analysis, knowledge elicitation, critical decision or critical mistake methods, think-aloud or similar protocols. Those were seen when the project involved complex jobs in which thinking strategies and decision-making strategies were important outcomes of the job. In such project cases, the goal was to understand what an exemplary performer thought, how and why s/he thought so, what his/her mental representations were and what core concepts or strategies s/he was using to perform the job. Then that information was used to design training programs for the remaining workforce:

> *Interviewees defined the primary tasks for their positions and prioritised which tasks required the most judgement and decision-making. We asked each interviewee to recall a critical, non-routine situation in which he/she was the primary decision maker. This specific incident provided us with a salient example to discuss and revealed the expertise required to perform in this environment.* (Dany, Project leader 8)

> *If you make the expert knowledge more explicit and train that directly to the novice in a certain way, then their proficiency could be accelerated... Our approach was to look at how experts would troubleshoot and then try to train that and get it across to the students to see if we could make them experts as it were in the faster time -- in a short amount of time, so that they could troubleshoot in a better fashion.* (Martin, Project leader 31)

Some project leaders relied just on this theme to develop the overall proficiency reference map of skills, knowledge and behaviours of exemplary performers which they used to design their hiring checklists, training courses and assessment instruments:

> *I have a reference model of what the super-duper customer service is. That's the kind of person I'm going to screen for. That's the kind of person I'm going to be selecting for. That's the kind of person I'm going to be onboarding. That's the kind of person I'm going to be coaching, and that's the kind of person I'm going to be motivating and evaluating... once I know the sort of performance that I need from a top performer you will create the simulations that can be used for screening the individuals who apply for the job.* (Mike, Project leader 36)

4) Emergent theme (strategy) P2.4: Identify job operating conditions and environment factors that influence outcomes

Emergent theme (strategy) 2.4 was drawn from ideas of identifying operating conditions of the job and identifying environment factors that may influence time-to-proficiency. Project leaders across several project cases attempted to understand the job operating conditions and also identified the environment factors that potentially influenced the outcomes and the constraints within which outcomes were to be achieved. Such constraints included organisational processes, procedures, organisational design and mandatory regulatory practices, all of which a new solution to accelerated proficiency was required to adhere to or work within. The analysis suggested that many of the project leaders considered operating conditions and environment factors exerting a profound impact on the rate at which proficiency was acquired. This was suggested by comments from some of the project leaders:

> *Time-to-proficiency, I would actually say, is more dependent on the environmental factors than the learning factors ... probably 70% or more [performance problems] are the result of environmental factors stopping performance rather than competency factors.* (Mathews, Practice leader 16G)

> *It stands everywhere from understanding the organisational processes and procedures and build that into the training in conjunction with the skills and knowledge with which they needed to operate in the field at a certain level.* (Tony, Project leader 60)

5) Emergent theme (strategy) P2.5: Analyse roadblocks and hindrances leading to longer time-to-proficiency

Emergent theme (strategy) P2.5 was suggested by ideas of thoroughly analysing roadblocks to time-to-proficiency. The study results indicated that inhibitors and hindrances severely affected time-to-proficiency.

Project leaders appeared to be unanimous that such roadblocks must be analysed first and solutions must be put in play first before investing in the factors that can accelerate proficiency. The findings indicated that simply eliminating roadblocks, barriers, hindrances or any such limiting factors may lead to accelerated proficiency without doing anything else. The findings indicated that mindsets, beliefs and assumptions people held in the workplace limited the rate at which new changes and new behaviours were adopted in some project cases. In other project cases, management factors such as inefficient management practices, lack of communication, feedback, lack of performance management systems, and managers' non-involvement were identified as factors that severely slowed time-to-proficiency. Some project cases showed that resource constraints such as availability of training instructors, technology to support the job and headcounts for a given job hired to handle a given workload were the factors that hindered faster readiness of the workforce. Cultural and language factors also were seen as hindrances when time-to-proficiency depended on working across the boundaries of several countries. Most important of all, in almost all the project cases, curriculum inefficiencies were limiting factors that lengthened time-to-proficiency rather than reducing it. Project cases showed inefficiencies such as massive and irrelevant content, unstructured training, long training courses and information overloads, which hampered the achievement of proficiency. Some additional factors like rigid business protocols, organisational policies and cultural barriers were also noticed. Some project leaders addressed this issue:

> *You've got to think about 'What are the driving forces? What are the restraining ones? ... And then what's getting in the way of them becoming proficient?' Deal with all of that.* (Knox, Practice leader 12G)

> *We do a risk assessment at the beginning to understand what could stand in the way of them becoming proficient in their role and we have a scientific risk assessment we do, and then we bring forth resources in our methodology that are consistent with the risk factors that have been identified.* (Reese, Practice leader 14G)

> *A large amount of that content in the training program is what I would call informational and knowledge content. It's about, how does the system work or how does this – it's about – it might be about a process, or it's informational. Now actually a classroom is probably the most inefficient and ineffective way in order to deliver that information.* (Charlie, Project leader 4)

4.8.3   Emergent themes (strategies) grouped under P3: Sequencing an efficient proficiency path

1)   Emergent theme (strategy) P3.1: Segment tasks and activities for trends based on analytics

Emergent theme (strategy) P3.1 combines the idea of segmenting tasks by characteristics such as frequency, complexity, importance, criticality, nature of skills and other variables to assess the relative significance of tasks, activities and events. The study findings indicated that project leaders leveraged data analytics like historical records or other activity logs to understand the characteristics of the skills, activities, events or tasks in terms of what happened frequently, what was complex, what was critical and important, and what was difficult or error-prone. This segmentation led to identifying the occurrence rate of events, tasks and activities; usage rate of skills, tools or products; and offerings or demand of products or services and similar characteristics. For example, some project leaders noticed that usually 80% of the most important and most frequent events in the workplace in a job role were being addressed with just 20% of the skills.

Another key criterion most project leaders used for segmentation was to identify critical and important tasks that were of high value, or caused high impact or were error-prone, including rare events with known critical impact. Some project leaders also segmented tasks by complexity to decide how a training program should progress, the level of scaffolding and fading, the level of support needed by the performer, and the time required to perform a task. In some project cases, it was seen that the objective criteria of frequency or complexity were not feasible, and tasks were segmented according to the nature of the skills involved (e.g., skills required to complete activities such as creating plans vs. skills to produce outcomes such as making a sale) or skills based on phases in the process. The findings indicated that there were situations which demanded certain trade-offs that had a bearing on the amount of overall skills to be included in a program. For example, the trade-off of what to hire for and what to train for led to a reduction in time-to-proficiency, particularly if people with the right skills were hired. All these decisions together determined an efficient structure leading towards shorter time-to-proficiency. Project leaders made comments like:

> *You're allowed to focus on the more important things and not have to worry about everything else that was in the old version of the program. That I think is probably our greatest asset in getting towards time-to-proficiency.* (Sam, Project leader 56)
>
> *In these two years, this is how often those events occurred and this is the amount of times the events occurred on top of each other... we could actually start analysing and doing histograms of the actual event versus frequency and event versus hours so that we actually start to get an understanding of what the engineers were actually doing.* (Rustom, Project leader 46)
>
> *What we found when we did the analysis of this product is that of about 150 individual items that we teach, 80% of the service events were contained within 20 tasks.* (Rustom, Project leader 46)
>
> *You only help the learners to train on the most important things they need to do their job.... In order to identify the important learning, it is to ask the same question: What are the areas with the highest value? What is the areas of the errors that you want to anticipate?* (Rayman, Project leader 42)
>
> *What are the things that we really should be just hiring for, versus the things that we should be training to once they get here?* (Christian, Project leader 5)
>
> *What knowledge should be available and what can be done via training or probably can't be done via training.* (Teresa, Project leader 58)

2) Emergent theme (strategy) P3.2: Create a logical sequence of experiences in the form of a complete path

Emergent theme (strategy) P3.2 emerged from ideas of sequencing tasks and activities by different variables such as task frequency, complexity, themes, practice areas, interleaving, time targets and the cycle of repetitions. The data analysis suggested that to reduce time-to-proficiency, most of the project leaders sequenced learning activities and the manufactured experiences using many different logics such as by tasks characteristics (e.g., frequency, complexity, importance, impact, etc.); by some organising principle or central themes; or by methods that ensure proficiency development. The ultimate goal of choosing the right kind of sequencing was to progress the performer to desired proficiency faster. The majority of the participants suggested ordering the experiences in the form of a progression that allows the worker to have frequent practice, repetitions and multiple exposures to a task. Another guiding criterion noticed was arranging tasks in increasing order of complexity, which dictated starting with simpler or less complex tasks and progressing to more complex tasks, while scaffolding or support was reduced progressively so that performers were made to practice by themselves. Complexity was also manifested by moving from a controlled-classroom experience to much more complex real-world experiences. In most project cases, frequency and complexity were considered together. The next guiding criterion used by project leaders was sequencing tasks or activities around some central organising principle such as workflow, product cycles, key principles, practice areas or themes.

The data analysis showed that another key guiding criterion was to sequence the tasks to build proficiency. Several project leaders were seen developing proficiency by exposing performers through spirals of repetitions that allowed them not only to practice new skills but also to integrate and practice the skills learned previously. Another pattern showed sequencing of interleaved learning tasks, job shadow assignments and mentored sessions in a way that developed robust proficiency. Finally, some project cases suggested individualising the sequence based on prior skills of the performers, bypassing unnecessary competencies, thus shortening time to learning. Some project leaders stated:

> *That was another factor we took into account and the learning order is which parts of this process could we give the trainee frequent exposure to so that they have more practice opportunities and to develop that proficiency more quickly.* (Richardson, Project leader 45)
>
> *Then we tried to organise them so that they were around themes, like around specific practices that people were doing in the lab.* (Diana, Project leader 11)
>
> *A way to really accelerate time-to-development in the technical disciplines would be to organise it around problems, use the problem as the organising principle, and then teach them whatever they have to know about the software, the hardware, the troubleshooting, etc.* (Reynold, Project leader 49)
>
> *So we have the systematic process of working some cases from the very beginning, increasing the complexity, decreasing the amount of support over time as they got better and better in doing these, getting across the key principles but applying them in context of the cases at the teachable moment, so they understood how the principles apply in context.* (McDonalds, Project leader 32)
>
> *Then when you move on and you add something else to the practice, then you bring what you practised before so you are practising what you did before and what you are doing next. If you add something new you do the same thing... So you are always circling back, circling back, circling back and integrating, circling back and integrating.* (Mike, Project leader 36)
>
> *Then you can begin to reduce the amount of time that that person would have to take in a complete program because you're eliminating things that they already know or that they can already do.* (Davidson, Project leader 10)

> *So in order to accelerate time-to-proficiency, you're starting to get individualised learning programs depending on people's ability to absorb that program.* (Mathews, Practice leader 16G)

3) Emergent theme (strategy) P3.3: Optimise the proficiency path for efficiency and time saving

Emergent theme (strategy) P3.3 emerged around ideas about optimising the path by removing waste or non-value-added activities, using time-efficient multiple delivery channels, leveraging performance support systems and creating efficiency with time distributed spaced-practice. Most of the project leaders appeared to converge into a philosophy that learning and proficiency are processes; therefore, process improvement thinking could be applied as a guiding criterion to eliminate the waste, overlap, redundancies, repetitive content and non-value added activities that do not lead to desired proficiency goals.

The analysis suggested another guiding criterion used by project leaders was that proficiency path was optimised in many project cases by using a mixture of multiple delivery channels such as classroom training, e-learning, job shadow, self-reading, technologies, performance support systems, etc., not so for variety but for time efficiency; for example, something that does not necessary need massive time. Project leaders tried to choose the most efficient method that could cut as much time as possible from the proficiency path, but still could lead performers to the desired outcomes in shorter time. Some project cases also evidenced the use of performance support systems to eliminate the need of training interventions altogether. Some project leaders converted larger tasks or activities and lessons into smaller chunks, distributed those over a period of time, delivered using performance support systems, technology or just-in-time systems. These small segments of learning were used just-in-time during other contextual activities such as job shadow. The findings showed that during optimisations project leaders were cognizant of where one activity could lead to achieving several goals or several activities could lead to only one goal. The findings also indicated that an optimised sequence did not always mean a shorter training duration; rather, in some cases the training duration was prolonged to accommodate necessary job shadow opportunities, participation in ongoing projects and spaced practice. Balancing most of the requisite elements allowed a highly efficient and lean proficiency path to be evolved, which focused on the critical and most essential activities required to become proficient in the job and produce desired business outcomes in shorter time. Some project leaders stated:

> *Learning is a process rather than a one-time event. Once you map out a learning process, you can apply process improvement tools to reduce time, waste, and variability.* (Stephen, Project leader 53)

> *When you build the reference model you actually know that these are the only things that a super customer representative needs to do... you are eliminating the waste you are eliminating the irrelevant activities out of the process... when you do have that ideal reference model you are able to get rid of the waste, so you get rid of that baggage that is holding people down.* (Mike, Project leader 36)

> *I think the more that you can offer modalities for people to get information or have questions answered quickly, the greater the chance are that you can shorten that time-to-proficiency cycle.* (Sam, Project leader 56)

> *The right kind of performance support for certain tasks can eliminate training entirely.* (Reynold, Project leader

49)

> *We do that also again via very short learning moments. Everything should be done fast and short and should hardly take any time.* (Teresa, Project leader 58)

> *There might be five things to do for one proficiency statement and there might one thing you do for another or there might five proficiencies they are involved in, so it's not – you're not trying to create this one to one wiring diagram of proficiency and learning activities.* (Stephen, Project leader 53)

4.8.4 Emergent themes (strategies) grouped under P4: Manufacturing accelerated contextual experiences

1) Emergent theme (strategy) P4.1: Assign performers on authentic job activities that allow meaningful practice in generating job-specific outcomes

Emergent theme (strategy) P4.1 emerged from the idea of assigning performers on activities which lead to business outcomes. Project leaders noted that the key to achieving proficiency sooner was to learn to produce the required business outcomes in the job. In most of the project cases, they engaged performers to work independently or on a shared basis on those job assignments in which they directly contributed towards producing desired outcomes. In the absence of such direct or shared assignments, performers participated in ongoing opportunities such as projects, tasks or assignments where they can observe how to produce outcomes and apply their skills. The study noted that rather than completing tasks, the focus of those assignments was to make performers see how to use different skills to achieve job outcomes. Some project leaders stated:

> *They do simulations and role plays, they have to produce plans, they create artefacts, they have to go online and find competition, they have to develop prices, there are many things they do. But these are things they'll do on the job too.* (Harry, Project leader 18)

> *So if there was an attack [network intrusion on server] happening, or if there was an event happening, we still would get them over there just so they could be in the middle of it.* (Christian, Project leader 5)

> *... and then in the afternoon was when they were starting to do whole length seeing prospects for the first time and so on and so forth.* (Christen, Project leader 6)

2) Emergent theme (strategy) P4.2: Embed learning into the work and focus on doing the job rather than topic-wise learning

Emergent theme (strategy) P4.2 is based on the idea of doing the work than learning, learning closer to the point of need, learning highly relevant to the real world, focusing on complete proficiency path, and interleaved training and work assignments. The study results indicated that a long period might be required before someone gets realistic experience at the job in which it is necessary to develop proficiency that can deliver consistent business outcomes. In such situations, project leaders expressed that instead of waiting for the universe to provide opportunities (Mathews, Project leader 16G), they manufactured or deliberately designed those experiences for attaining proficiency in a compressed timeframe. Project leaders manufactured or leveraged the contextual experiences in the workplace in the context of the job. Participants believed that ultimate context in the workplace was the work and the results as stated: *'Learning needs to be contextualised, because working in a company is the real context, working the real products is the real context'* (Dan, Practice leader 6G). They leveraged all learning resources, projects, opportunities and training options such as self-learning, classroom or on-the-job activities or a combination of all to manufacture these experiences as close to the job as possible.

Several project leaders advocated that to accelerate proficiency, organisations first needed to diffuse the barrier between work and learning. Almost all the project leaders emphatically stressed that they embedded learning into the job in such a way that focus was placed on doing the job rather than doing topic-by-topic or task-by-task learning. Performers were challenged to learn from actual use cases encountered in the job using the tools and workflows used in the job. This also meant that they focused on producing outcomes, rather than just performing some tasks. It appeared that people gained proficiency faster by doing real and challenging work rather than any classroom training.

Other ways project leaders embedded learning and work together was to interweave training sessions and work assignments, which allowed authentic learning through on-the-job practice. The majority of project leaders tried to keep the delivery of learning closer to the point of need and in the context of the job in order to accelerate proficiency. Performers were made to work on things that were essential to producing outcomes. The data analysis indicated that business practitioners looked beyond training interventions and considered the complete experience out of training to do the job. Complete experience meant to show how to produce the results in an actual workplace. They focused on the before and after phases of the training intervention rather than just during the intervention:

> *The barrier between training and work should be taken away and learning and working should more and more becoming just integrated process, and you're always learning as you're working and you're always working as you're learning.* (McDonalds, Project leader 32)
>
> *And the only thing you do is you only help the learners to train on the most important things they need to do their job. The focus has got to be on doing the job and not the training.* (Rayman, Project leader 43)
>
> *Upon completion of the boot camp, associates are moved into their business units where they will spend the next nine months gaining hands-on sales experience in parallel with their continued classroom learning. This on-the-job experience component is meant to reinforce the sales and technical competencies developed throughout the program, while allowing the associates to apply new skills in a controlled environment.* (Elisa, Project leader 30)
>
> *If you can bring the learning as closer to the point of need as possible, that's likely to accelerate the opportunity.* (Charlie, Project leader 4)
>
> *Your training itself should be near the job so that it's not training, rather on the first day of training you're starting your job and you learn how to do the job.* (Harry, Project leader 18)
>
> *Now I am not learning how to use SAP as an example or any other ERP. I'm learning how to, as a procurement person, to minimise the cost to the business for which I'm going to get a bonus by using a tool.* (Ellis, Project leader 14)

They're going to get training and they're going to get deployed in the ongoing project to apply the skills and it is basically one single cycle.... We built the training and the experience into the training itself that it's almost ongoing in a daily basis so that they get the practical application of what they get the clients from virtually within the same, if you will, the same week in which it is taught to them. (Tony, Project leader 60)

Although they were in the classroom, they would go out in the field to do application. They were constantly going out to the field to observe, see the calls taken, which really actually contributed to them having the better understanding what the expectations of the customers were. (Hallmark, Project leader 17)

Design the complete experience, which means you pay attention to what happens before and afterwards ... So your learning experience starts before you ever go to class, and continues long after you're back on the job... when we think about the complete experience, we've got to think about much, much more than the formal training that occurs, and engineer the things so that it all hangs together if we really want to accelerate time-to-performance. (Reynold, Project leader 49)

3) Emergent theme (strategy) P4.3: Expose performers to multiple cycles of deliberate and purposeful failures at a rapid rate or in a compressed timeframe

Emergent theme (strategy) P4.3 is organised around the ideas of incorporating deliberate, planned, goal-driven, purposeful failures, mistakes and variations. Failures, mistakes or errors appear to challenge workers' ways of thinking, make them understand flaws in their current ways of thinking or mental models and then make them ready to re-build new mental models. A direct relationship appeared to exist between how fast someone was exposed to failure and how soon they could acquire proficiency in that domain.

Project leaders chose the failures (or mistakes, errors, bugs, etc.) which had the potential to provide intense experiences to people, made a contribution towards building proficiency and had significant value in compressing the experience into a short time. Several project leaders reasoned that this then exposed performers to multiple iterations of those purposeful failures in a compressed timeframe. Some project leaders made it explicit in that the rate of proficiency acquisition was accelerated if performers were exposed to failures at a rapid pace. One project leader mentioned *'So you want to cycle through as many of those as possible'* (White, Project leader 62). Another project leader supported it as *'...and it has to be rapid cycles'* (Bella, Project leader 28). The study data also revealed that deliberate and expected mistakes incorporated during learning served the same purpose as failures when performers were exposed to several iterations of trials or attempts. As an alternative to failure cycles, project leaders suggested including a range of variations and a variety of cases, bugs, simulations and errors in learning activities. Combinations of those strategies appeared to have a significant impact on time-to-proficiency. Some project leaders stated:

What we could do we could insert certain faults into the equipment, deliberately insert faults, and then we could ask them to troubleshoot that fault. (Martin, Project leader 31)

And the key driver to reorganisation is getting opportunities to assimilate your model of the domain to a situation, see if it works or not, and see the ways that it doesn't work, and it does work and keep iteratively refining it. We call it 'cycle of failure' but it is iterative refinement or iterative reorganisation. (Bella, Project leader 28)

> *The idea is that it doesn't matter how long you've been exposed to tasks; it matters how many times your mental model has failed around that task. So it really depends on how many cycles you've gone through of approaching a task, having your way of understanding it, not work out and then reorganising your cognition to understand it in a more complex way.* (White, Project leader 62)

> *Faster we can get people up where they can make those mistakes in a non-threatening situation, the less likely it's going to happen on the actual process with potentially tracked results.* (Davidson, Project leader 10)

> *You do need to have a variety of activities, a variety of jobs, a variety of tasks, and a variety of formal learning as well in order to cover all the bases over a period of time. So if you don't give them that variety, they're not going to become proficient. But the more variety you give them and the quicker you can give it to them within reason, then they will become proficient more quickly.* (Mathews, Practice Leader 16G)

> *When we create this taxonomy of cases, we make sure we include the variations in there so that the people get experienced with all of those in a systematic way.... I want to make sure that I stayed on these variations, make sure that by the time they've done it, they've done all these different types of things, and these ones is about more multiple times to be able to develop those proficiencies.* (McDonalds, Project leader 32)

4) Emergent theme (strategy) P4.4: Compress hard-to-obtain experiences on known situations in highly contextualised realistic cases, gamified scenarios and representative simulations

Emergent theme (strategy) P4.4 represented the ideas of using real-world scenarios and cases, gamifying the scenarios and representative simulation to accelerate proficiency in hard-to-obtain experiences. Hard-to-obtain experiences were low-frequency or rare or infeasible to use in real-life to develop proficiency (e.g., underground fire). Project leaders in almost every project exposed performers to difficult real-world cases from the past or designed something that was likely to happen in the future. Some project leaders in the domains where knowledge was relatively static and stayed relevant with time suggested maintaining a library of cases if experiences were rare or difficult to access. In the absence of real-life cases, project leaders incorporated deliberate but productive or desirable failures in training. Study participants expressed that proficiency on known but low-frequency events could be built faster by exposing performers to this kind of situations using gamified scenarios and representative simulations. Several project leaders used the approach to gamify the scenarios in a training intervention to expose performers to realistic challenges as it would unfold in the real job.

In several project cases, scenarios were unfolded to the performer in a piece-meal fashion, or in the form of stages, progressively like a story as it had happened in real-life. Such a mechanism helped to expose performers to near-reality situations, and they used their observation, problem-solving and thinking skills to the level as would be required to solve the problem in real-life. Almost every project leader identified simulation as one of the most impactful strategies to shorten time-to-proficiency on rare events. Operational simulation appeared to be the most common strategy across the board. The operational simulation involved designing representative simulation, role-playing, or situations to allow performers to practice the skills as much as they needed to build proficiency as close to reality as possible. Several project leaders commented:

So our entire simulation methodology is built around the premise that you need to expose people to tough problems and situations to have them cycle through the kinds of encounters and situations that create complex decision-making.... And that simulation methodology works well in that way too, where it will increase your time-to-proficiency by compressing the failure cycle you go through to adopt a new way of thinking in an organisation. (White, Project leader 62)

There was an opportunity to practice what they were being taught by being given actual business cases to work on in a collaborative framework, so, not just hypothetical lecture or business cases, but actual cases that they could then work and solve altogether. (Elisa, Project leader 30)

They typically have come from actual scenarios that have occurred in the past. The ones that have all been developed to reflect events that both occurred and were not potentially handled well. (Davidson, Project leader 10)

What we've done is we've turned that model on its side and we 'game-ified' into a scenario-based approach... And so they just took those scenarios and put them into a game format. (Jason, Project leader 21)

Another technique was taking the story and creating vignettes with dilemmas that less experienced employees had to decide how to solve, including determining what was required, who would they speak with, and potential second and third-order consequences. (Aloha, Project leader 19)

We have them answer that question and then have a discussion around that and then proceed in the scenario. The intent is that you're giving them more information, there's probably some escalation within the scenario, so they should be getting a number of data points back together on making some decisions. (Dany, Project leader 8)

So that was completely simulated in the classroom so that they first prepared for it, they looked at meters, they talked about how they needed to handle various things, then they ran the simulation and they saw what happened in the simulation and then they debriefed it in terms of what they would need to do differently and things that would need to do differently communication. (Abigail, Project leader 16)

5) Emergent theme (strategy) P4.5: Strengthen generic, transferable, principle-based, fundamental skills to handle unfamiliar or unknown situations

Emergent theme (strategy) P4.5 emerged from the idea of equipping performers with conceptual, principle-based, universal skills and higher-order thinking skills. Every project leader indicated that there was a limitation on how many scenarios performers could be exposed to at a given time. In some project cases that dealt with rapidly changing domains, leaders anticipated new, unfamiliar and never-seen-before situations for the workforce. In such cases, project leaders focused on designing interventions around the most generic fundamental skills, as well as core principles and concepts. Perfomers could apply such core principles in most of the familiar and unfamiliar situations encountered in the job. Project leaders tended to make learning experiences pragmatic and problem-based and they focused on developing critical thinking and general cognitive strategy that performers could apply to solve problems, even in unfamiliar situations. The data analysis suggested that many project cases leveraged situations that could drive a deeper level of thinking, questioning, higher-order thinking skills and problem-solving skills. Some project leaders commented:

> *If someone is an expert on a machine and they learn how to work this machine perfectly, and then that machine is set aside and a new machine comes, then they will be at a complete loss and will be a – it will take them a long time to fill up. But if they have learned how to approach working with the machine to achieve X and how the machines of this nature function, then it will be really easy for them to change from one machine to the next.* (Abigail, Project leader 16)

> *There are basically a series of fundamental skills and knowledge that would be applicable to almost all situations and this is where we changed the training to make sure it was more principle-based training than it was process or procedure-based... As people learn the principles, they begin to learn how to apply them in different situations. You try and give them as many diverse applications as possible for that knowledge and skill.* (Tony, Project leader 60)

> *The development of detailed mental model of how complex piece of machinery works, is then important, because it allows you to reason about it more consciously, reason about things that can go wrong around and how do you deal with new unexpected unfamiliar errors in the system.* (Merrill, Practice leader 15G)

> *What we tried to do was to teach them certain skills that would enable them to deal with any kind of fault no matter how frequent it occurred or not... now you're asking them to think through what are the issues and the problems associated with this? What's the mental framework which you need to apply? What are the constructs that you need to apply to this particular situation that was slightly different than the previous one?* (Martin, Project leader 31)

4.8.5 Emergent themes (strategies) grouped under P5: Promoting an active emotional immersion

1) Emergent theme (strategy) P5.1: Active engagement and emotional loading from the tasks and situations similar to the workplace

The main things project leaders pointed out were that people learn a task by experiencing the task themselves, learn by doing and learn by engaging themselves in the task actively. In most of the project cases, active engagement of the performer with the task was increased by having performers produce or discover something relevant to job outcomes or solve job-specific problems. Project leaders observed that, by doing so, learning occurred at a faster rate and transferred to the workplace quickly. Several project leaders pointed out that results were produced in real jobs at accelerated speed because real jobs drove a very high level of emotional loading with consequences and stakes involved. As opposed to the traditional approach of keeping emotions out of training, they incorporated emotions and emotional loading similar to what a real workplace challenge would drive. That included similar pressures, stakes, consequences, time constraints, performance specifications and team dynamics to what would occur while doing the task in the real job. Project leaders suggested setting correct expectations and accountabilities with the performers so that they themselves own their results in a similar way they are accountable for the actual job. Part of this was to give them a full idea where they stand, how much progress they were making and how close they were to the goal. Some project leaders expressed this approach as:

> *There has to be an immersion in the learning to actually accelerate it. I think experiential learning is a really good way to accelerate it to basically throw them in, give them some information, let them learn and then have them come back and talk about.* (Meline, Project leader 35)

> *We end up putting in aspects that we feel like are relevant, we have to engage participants in a task that's full of what we call "symbolic density". We like them to be engaged in tasks that will trigger various ways of thinking about the issue and is mimicking what they're doing in real-life or mimicking what we want them to be doing in the future.* (White, Project leader 62)

> *One was the gamification which caused a high level of engagement from the learners on a regular basis.*

> *Nobody could check out, nobody could fall asleep, nobody could not participate because that was the training.* (Jason, Project leader 21)

> *As a rule, it is all about discovery. There can be troubleshooting, problem-solving, discovery – the main idea is that they are doing something to discover something.* (Rayman, Project leader 43)

> *You're pulling their learning towards the goal by having them solve the problem and now they've come to this realisation through an activity process, rather than through a series of recommendations from an outsider.* (White, Project leader 63)

> *Rather than using a "watch and learn" job-shadowing model, each associate is expected to take an active role in contributing to the bottom line of her team.* (Elisa, Project leader 30)

> *From a practical point of view, making sure that structured training is experiential and contains designed opportunities to reflect the situations that people are going to encounter in the workplace. It certainly accelerates performance. The opportunities of reflection has to be built into day-to-day work after the training as well.* (Charlie, Project leader 4)

2) Emergent theme (strategy) P5.2: Provide immediate feedback and allow for moments of focused reflection

Almost all the project leaders highlighted that when participating in the real experience, faster and sustained transfer of learning to the workplace required immediate feedback and focused reflection, both during and after the experience. The study findings indicated that acquiring proficiency needed immediate feedback to correct the behaviours and mistakes and reinforce the learning, both during training and in the workplace. Project cases leveraged feedback from multiple sources such as trainers, peers, managers, simulators or even pre-recorded by experts. Project leaders emphasised that providing immediate feedback had an important bearing on learning the right behaviours which influenced the rate of proficiency significantly:

> *Feedback is probably the most important that we do in terms of guiding their performance towards the goal. So we have very rigorous feedback that's almost always tied directly to performance.* (White, Project leader 63)

> *That really once the exercise starts as long as the feedback is very instantaneous and immediate and granular they don't need anything else. They just need to know how they are doing in relation to a goal.* (Bella, Project leader 28)

The other sub-theme this strategy suggested, 'focused reflection', utilised focused and targeted reflection geared towards certain goals. Project leaders systematically planned and deliberately built moments of reflection into the learning, as well as during the feedback loop. Most of the project leaders had used focused reflection before, during and after an intense learning intervention. They mentioned that the reflections before the skill acquisition prepared the performers to absorb the skill effectively, while reflection during the skill acquisition affected the rate at which the worker acquired a new skill and internalised it. The reflection after the skill acquisition allowed performers to integrate skills in their day-to-day jobs. Some project leaders claimed:

> *If you're going to learn by doing, you need to reflect in order to abstract the principle that you can apply to next time ... a core learning process is doing, extracting the principles or the key learnings from that and then apply it the next time. So if you can set up a way to do that in a systematic way and focused, that really speeds*

up the process too as opposed to just leaving it to. And individual may or may not reflect effectively or focus on the right things.... from an instructional perspective, you can guide them to focus and reflect on the most important things that we know so that experts are going to help them be better when they do, that's going to be powerful, so targeted reflection. (McDonalds, Project leader 32)

So reflection before action means that the participants take time before the scenario that stimulation as I'm calling it. They take times beforehand to think about okay, based on some other things that we've been doing today, what are some things that are going to absolute key for us to succeed in this upcoming simulation which is really simulating what happens in our plant. And then they take time for each person reflects then they share their thoughts and ideas and discuss that, and then you start the simulation. (Abigail, Project leader 16)

This is a "learning during" tool that is used in the moment for teams that are doing work together to learn from each other and improve the very next time they do it or improve on the job what they're doing ... And together then the team would go through these four questions. So, "What was supposed to happen?" "What actually happened?" "Why are they different" and "What can we learn from this and do different right now?". (Kenny, Project leader 25)

3) Emergent theme (strategy) P5.3: Assess performers through job-specific, continuous, multi-level assessments beyond training interventions

The analysis revealed that almost all the project leaders suggested that to accelerate proficiency, assessment was implemented not just as a one-time paper-pen or practical test during or at the end of the training intervention. Rather, assessments were embedded, continuous, distributed, job-specific and conducted at several different levels. One project leader suggested:

When you put together these learning activities that are job-based, you need to identify how you know when someone has performed it to an acceptable level, you'll also provide an opportunity for other people that might be used in this process like coaches to be able to determine whether this person has in fact learned the competency to the level that was identified from an evaluation standpoint. (Connan, Practice leader 5G)

Various elements suggested in the above quotes were represented by the emergent theme (strategy) P5.3. Primarily, assessments standards were exactly the same as standards for the job, which drove performers to produce job-specific outcomes or deliverables. In some project cases the performers were required to meet the given performance specs for the outcomes. The non-negotiable assessment goals meant stake and consequences to performers, which kept them emotionally and actively immersed with the tasks. In several project cases, assessments were conducted at regular frequency, which allowed project leaders to track where and when someone reached the desired proficiency level. Assessments were conducted at various stages such as pre-assessment of performers, end of training assessment, post-training assessment and on-the-job monitoring or assessment until desired proficiency was achieved.

Another pattern observed was that to accelerate proficiency, assessments were carried out at multiple levels, for example, self-assessment, peer-assessment, trainer's assessment, mentor's assessment, and supervisor's assessment. Almost all the project cases showed two key approaches: first, sign-off by mentors or coaches was key to check for workplace proficiency; and second, continuous assessment at the manager's level was also found to be critical in this study because the manager ultimately was responsible for assigning the right assignments to his/her people for measuring and reporting time-to-proficiency. In some project cases, on-the-job assessments were conducted using manager-employee reviews, regular performance reviews or other job metrics that are monitored at certain intervals. No matter how the assessment was implemented in each project case, the immediate feedback from the assessment was invariably used in each project for the performers to correct certain behaviours or adopt new strategies. Some project leaders stated:

> *But definitely the key parameter is defining a non-negotiable goal because that really pulls their learning.* (White, Project leader 62)
>
> *Instead of administering a multiple-choice test on what makes a good proposal, assess a proposal that sellers create as part of the training.* (Matt, Project leader 33)
>
> *It happened three times after the training program ended. So there would be a thirty-day evaluation, a sixty-day evaluation and then a ninety-day evaluation.* (Thomson, Project leader 59)
>
> *And then putting the onus for signing off on proficiency back to the managing supervisor, with some very clear guidelines for what proficiency means.* (Reynold, Project leader 49)
>
> *There were goals every week, and each week those goals increased ... at the end of every week, the new hires received their quality and productivity scores and then met with the trainers to review their performance and to talk about how to improve that.* (Billy, Project leader 2)

4.8.6 Emergent themes (strategies) grouped under P6: Setting up a proficiency eco-system

1) Emergent theme (strategy) P6.1: Create enabling and supportive environment

Emergent theme (strategy) P6.1 emerged from the ideas of enabling and a supportive environment which is realistic and safe. The data analysis showed that project leaders were cognizant of effects of dynamics of the environmental elements such as teams, peers, managers, processes and resources on the rate of proficiency acquisition. The study findings suggested that a supportive environment was an essential element of the proficiency eco-system and appeared to be a must-have condition to shorten time-to-proficiency. In most of the project cases, the emphasis was seen to be on designing an environment that addressed environmental or limiting factors with a negative influence on time-to-proficiency which were identified in the proficiency reference map. Some project leaders supported this by saying that:

> *To accelerate time-to-proficiency, one of the things that a lot of people will not think about is the environment those people are in ... I would say it's far more dependent on the environment they're within and how supportive that environment is and all the rest of it. And by supportive I mean management culture, the management service they are delivered, the amount of information they've got, the performance support they've got, the tools, the flexible working, all of the engagements stuff. All of that stuff will have a much bigger impact on time-to-proficiency because see, one of the biggest factors of time-to-proficiency is someone fully engaged in what they are there to do.* (Mathews, Practice leader 16G)
>
> *Does our environment support the quality, quantity, time, cost and improvement of the time-to-performance? Then we take a look at the information we give people, do they have the proper equipment like the right software or the right hardware? Do they have the time to do what we expect them to do? ... It would also be difficult to assess if the individual had the right motives, capacity and knowledge and skills to do the job if the environmental factors of information, resources, and incentives are not sufficiently present.* (Rodridge, Project

leader 47)

2) Emergent theme (strategy) P6.2: Structured involvement, accountability, support and reinforcement from manager

The data analysis indicated that managers were the most critical element of the eco-system because they were the ones who were responsible for creating the environment for employees to learn, providing opportunities to practice skills and setting up the proficiency goals for people and then monitoring or assessing whether goals were being met or not. The analysis also emphasised that managers were the biggest enablers or the biggest barriers to shortening time-to-proficiency. It was seen that the project leaders involved managers in a very structured fashion before, during and after any training program or plan for accelerated proficiency for the employees. They reported that this involvement was crucial in preparing people, and setting and clarifying expectations before they were sent to training.

Some project leaders used pre-training involvement of managers to seek sponsorship and support for the program, holding managers accountable to create an environment and to define expected outcomes for the employees. Managers were equipped with the right tools, knowledge, and information to support and coach their staff and to reinforce their employees' behaviours to produce desired outcomes. The study indicated that successful time-to-proficiency project cases relied heavily on managers' support and follow-up during or after the training interventions. In most of the successful project cases, the project leaders had line managers to be accountable for monitoring the progress of their employees at the job and ensure that they provided opportunities and assignments to employees as per the sequence of proficiency path. Project leaders highlighted that a manager's reinforcement and monitoring of behaviours of his/her people had a great impact on how soon people used new skills/behaviours and reached proficiency. The study findings showed that the manager's role was critical in managing, monitoring, supporting and correcting the performance of the employee at the job. The role of a manager in reviewing an employee's performance made the manager a central element to the proficiency eco-system across all the project cases. Some project leaders supported this by claiming that:

> *In order to successfully compress time-to-competence, we need to have managers who really understand that they have a huge impact on the way their people perform. Managers need to understand that they can put people through good training courses, but these people will not become proficient faster unless they (the managers) provide them with the necessary support after they return to the workplace. They need to provide the opportunity to practice; the opportunity to reflect and discuss where things are going well and where things aren't and focus on those that aren't going well, and fix them. (Charlie, Project leader 4)*

> *So management has a big factor to play in time-to-proficiency because management by and large is responsible for the environment that people are operating within, most of it – not all of it but most of it. A team leader has a huge impact on the environment around people when they are doing their job.... the quality of the management service they receive from their manager has a huge impact on time-to-proficiency, and the management service is a big component of the environment. (Mathews, Practice leader 16G)*

> *On the converse side, when the manager expresses his or her support for the training, especially before the training, then you get an acceleration of the amount of time-to-proficiency. Getting the manager alignment right, getting the manager engagement correct is absolutely critical to getting people up to speed quickly...when the manager expresses his or her support for the training, especially before the training, then you get an acceleration of the amount of time-to-proficiency.* (Reynold, Project leader 49)

> *But what's most important is that leader is engaging the employee go through training, they're talking about the training beforehand, they're setting expectations about the training, they're asking the employee as they're going through the training how it's going, they're asking them questions about it, and then they're following up with them.* (Rickky, Practice Leader 18G)

> *Regular review with the supervisor was critical to the success of this program and it was something that had not been part of any previous training practice in the plant.... 100% success of reducing the time-to-proficiency is of these regular reviews of the supervisor.* (Richardson, Project leader 45)

3) Emergent theme (strategy) P6.3: Institute a structured mentoring and coaching process at workplace

The Emergent theme (strategy) P6.3 was based on structured mentoring and focused coaching from a mentor with the right skills. This theme appeared to represent the most significant elements of a proficiency eco-system which allowed performers to learn the job quickly and start being productive in shorter time. The data analysis of project cases established that experiencing the job under someone qualified allowed much faster proficiency, as opposed to learning the same task in the classroom. Study participants referred such approach with several terms like cognitive apprenticeship, guided mentorship model, structured on-the-job training, and facilitated practice.

The mentoring involved the performer first observing the mentor doing a task, then the performer doing the same task under the mentor's observation, and eventually doing it individually, at which point the mentor qualified him/her as proficient in the given task or aspect of the job. The idea mainly stressed in all the project cases that mentoring was targeted, focused and based on proficiency goals. In several project cases, organisations put their performers in a high support and monitoring period immediately after a training event. During this high support period, training and on-the-job experience ran in parallel. Performers were made to try applying new skills in the actual job and practice the expertise to produce outcomes. Project leaders emphasised that to successfully shorten time-to-proficiency through structured mentoring, pairing performers to the right mentors was crucial. The mentors were selected carefully. Organisations that relied heavily on structured mentoring practices to accelerate proficiency, prepared their mentors well with tools, techniques and skills to mentor and coach the new people. Project leaders suggested:

> *Step two is, they went into the lab and they observed their mentor doing whatever their thing was. And then step three was, they actually did it with their mentor so they both did the practice together. And then step four was their mentor observed them doing the process and providing feedback. And step five was, they checked them off. And they said, "Yes this person is ready" so it's like a performance test in step five.* (Diana, Project leader 11)

> *So these four weeks were the high support environment during which the eight of new hires were taking phone*

calls and answering customer e-mails in an environment where they could pair up and do it together, and in an environment where there were two trainers available to help them with their customer interactions. (Billy, Project leader 2)

Trainers should have been selected based on specific criteria, have received some formal instruction and qualification on how to be a trainer, and are required to use specific steps to deliver the training. (Ron, Project leader 46)

4) Emergent theme (strategy) P6.4: Design opportunities for purpose-driven social connectivity and structured informal learning in the workplace

Project leaders pointed out that in the workplace people work in teams and produce results as a group. They learn socially and informally by doing work with each other, talking to each other, sharing with others, supporting each other and teaching each other. Emergent theme (strategy) P6.4 was formed based on strategies used by several project leaders to harness the power of social and informal learning in the workplace through deliberate actions, making social interactions purpose-driven and putting the structure around informal learning avenues to accelerate the proficiency of teams in the workplace.

Project leaders in this study leveraged participatory, group or collective learning through usual team interactions. Highly immersive learning experiences through group interactions were created in which performers were interacting, talking and discovering with each other. Such experiences appeared to have used multi-directional learning from each through peer learning, peer support, peer sharing, and peer teaching, whereby everyone was responsible for their own learning while they were given a purpose to accomplish. Project leaders strongly advocated setting up learning networks as communities of practice created to drive purpose-driven discussions, conversations, interactions and interactions among the performers. Such social connectivity allowed multi-dimensional social learning by reaching out to peers and seeking help from each other when they encountered an unfamiliar problem. In several project cases, project leaders had set up learning networks that allowed new performers access to high performers who may had solved a similar problem and could quickly guide the performers. The data analysis suggested that this approach accelerated knowledge acquisition by new people significantly.

Project leaders indicated that they observed that people learned most of their job informally, rather than through formal training programs. Project leaders put a certain level of structure around informal learning by establishing expectations, clarifying intended outcomes and setting up a sequence beforehand (if possible) to make sure it was goal-directed. These purpose-driven social interactions and structured informal learning appeared to act as multipliers of acceleration not only for one person but for the group. As suggested by the following comments:

We came at this from the angle that most people learn most of what they know through doing, through experiential learning, through informal learning and experiential or social; in other words, talking with colleagues or actually just doing it and having the experience. (Mathews, Practice leader 16G)

I think that powerful accelerator of skill acquisition is when you get multiple people to learn from each other in the development of the skill or competency. Learning together and acquiring skills together, to me, is a multiplier. It can help accelerate your acquisition of a particular skill. (Kenny, Project leader 26)

The people already know a lot and if we can give them a mechanism to gather the knowledge and share with others it potentially can replace formal learning or formal training. (Teresa, Project leader 58)

A community of practice provides a context for people to reflect, reinforce and extend their knowledge by discussing it with each other. (McDonalds, Project leader 32)

It created a tight and broad network of people that they could depend on to get things done, to ask questions, to problem solve together. (Elisa, Project leader 30)

More about building social networks that allow learners to connect with master performers and learn from the master performer rather than focusing strictly on formal learning events. (Sam, Project leader 56)

So that's the sequence and that is a way to in effect control informal learning. Your first step if you want to control informal learning is to understand what your outcomes are. In other words, there's a control point there. And then you design some activities which could be an actual activity or a social experience that will probably get those learnings. Send them off on the activity but while they're off on the activity, you've got to let go of control. (Mathews, Practice leader 16G)

5) Emergent theme (strategy) P6.5: Deploy on-demand performance support systems embedded in workflow and learning

Emergent theme (strategy) P6.5 emerged based on the observations that across all the project cases, performance support systems (PSS) embedded into day-to-day workflow of the job role was established to be an important strategy to reduce time-to-proficiency. This theme was formed from four sub-themes, each suggesting a different kind of on-demand performance support system. The analysis indicated that performance support systems were used primarily to make information, knowledge and learning available at the teachable moment during the job so that people apply the content in the context of the job. Such contextual application contributed towards shorter time-to-proficiency.

It was seen from each project case description that project leaders provided performers with self-guided online searchable content instead of lengthy informational training. Self-guided content allowed performers to learn at their own pace and they did not have to wait for the formal training class to learn the content. Instead of massive upfront learning of certain content or tasks, performance support systems were implemented to allow accessing information or knowledge just-in-time (JIT) fashion at the point of need.

PSS were seen to accelerate the initial readiness of the performer. Some project cases used JIT systems as simple as instant chat messenger, allowing them to access a larger pool of people to draw from. In most project cases, a range of job-aids was deployed that appeared to shorten time-to-proficiency. These included checklists, task sheets, decision support systems, flow charts and procedures to name a few. Some project leaders indicated that properly designed job-aids could eliminate the need for training altogether. Some project leaders were seen using new trends in technologies such as mobile coaching or mobile learning and similar platforms that delivered PSS and learning in an integrated fashion. Examples included sending regular practice reminders or quizzes through mobile phones and constant monitoring of employee progress via mobile apps. Mechanism of on-demand access and support from managers, peers, and team members through PSS also made much difference to the speed to proficiency. Some comments suggested:

> *If people could get questions answered at point of need, that will accelerate their competency on-the-job way faster.* (Meline, Project leader 35)

> *How you can shorten the time-to-competence is to look at your training and take away or change the channel of delivery of that informational content, that knowledge content... And let's take all that content delivery out and make that available to people beforehand, they can read it in their own time as part of their own workflow, they can do that. So that's just an efficiency measure, which I think certainly helped us just to reduce the time that was spent in terms of training and compress that time.* (Charlie, Project leader 4)

> *The support could be performance support, which is the idea of giving people the information they need at the moment they need it as much as possible, so that they reference as they are doing things.* (McDonalds, Project leader 32)

> *And it could be a model, it could be an algorithm, it could be a decision table, it could be a number of different kinds of job-aids but you're always looking to create job-aids if possible because it just consolidates the information. And again by doing that you also speed up the learning process.* (Connan, Practice leader 5G)

> *Certainly providing checklist within the [anonymous] model is to help reduce time-to-competence by taking away some of the need to put people through formal training.* (Charlie, Project leader 4)

> *By integrating the learning material (such as scenario-based questions) into the business procedures, the EPSS becomes a powerful online learning platform.* (Todd, Project leader 57)

6) Emergent theme (strategy) P6.6: Leverage subject matter experts strategically

This emergent theme (strategy) originated from an observation in the analysis that the organisations that successfully reduced time-to-proficiency looked across their available pool of subject matter experts (SMEs) and leveraged them in many different ways, beyond usual mentoring, job-shadowing and knowledge elicitation processes. By strategically using experts allowed project leaders to cut the time out from the processes, which otherwise under the regime of dedicated training departments used to require greater time. The involvement included elements such as precisely defining proficiency with experts, rapid training development without massive content development, knowledge sharing in short quick chunks, JIT training bypassing lengthy instructional design processes, experience-rich facilitation sessions and job-specific assessments. Some project leaders supported this practice by saying:

> *To decrease training time and to increase time-to-proficiency is that the subject matter experts learns how to make fast and efficient training.* (Teresa, Project leader 58)

> *In conjunction with those as subject matter experts, SMEs, to draw out what would be the fundamental skills necessary to operate as a more experienced engineer and then define, ascertain, assess the skill level of the new engineers and build the training to bridge.* (Thomson, Project leader 59)

> *We also had subject matter experts' teams for each therapeutic area that were the go-to person if that study team needed somebody to hold their hands through doing some of the work introduction.* (Meline, Project leader 35)

> *Every competency has a competence team and a competence leader who is responsible to bring that competence to a higher level.* (Teresa, Project leader 58)

CHAPTER 4

PART-3: ANALYSIS OF TIME-TO-PROFICIENCY RESULTS OF PROJECT CASES

4.9 ANALYSIS OF RESULTS OF TIME-TO-PROFICIENCY REDUCTION IN PROJECT CASES

The selected 60 project cases included in this study were all success cases in regards to a substantial reduction of time-to-proficiency or related indicators. Previous sections presented the collective analysis of new practices and strategies implemented by project leaders in various project cases to attain successful reduction of time-to-proficiency. Each project case was required to provide data on how results were measured and data on success indicators before and after the implementation of practices/strategies that could establish if project leaders were indeed successful in reducing time-to-proficiency (addressing the pragmatic goal of "does it work?"). This section presents the analysis that was conducted on these success indicators to understand the level of success of the practices/strategies reported in this study. The success indicators reported by project leaders were segmented into direct or indirect results. The distribution of project cases is summarised in *Table 4-16*.

4.9.1 Indicators of reduction in time-to-proficiency

54 (90%) of the project cases reported results with direct indicators. The direct indicators of success were represented by a reduction in time-to-proficiency of people, reduction in time-to-readiness of a business operation or reduction in training duration at the training course level. Only six (10%) of the project cases did not report any direct results because the consultants or the project leader did not have any access to the client or results anymore. Project leaders had a positive feeling of the end results being good in those cases. In those cases, project leaders reported results using indirect indicators such as improvements in performance compared to experienced staff, the percentage of population crossing desired thresholds and visible evidence of the improved rate of learning. Those observations suggested that the strategies reported in each project case worked in the majority of their contexts towards shortening time-to-proficiency.

Some observations based on *Table 4-16* are:

- Of the 60 project cases, 24 (41%) project cases were about shortening time-to-proficiency of people in a job role, while 13 (25%) project cases addressed the time-to-proficiency problem at the group, business or organisational level to get ready for certain new business, process or operation, expressed in terms of time-to-readiness.
- Of the 60 project cases, 7 (12%) project cases reported results only as training duration reduction because proficiency was being developed primarily in training settings. This shows that only a relatively small number of programs were geared towards shortening time-to-proficiency with

training, thus affirming an earlier postulation that time-to-proficiency is more than just reducing the duration of the training program.

- While 6 (10%) project cases did not report direct results, their indirect results indicated positive trends towards acceleration. Also, 20 (33%) project cases reported indirect results alongside the direct results, thus legitimating the use of indirect results as an indication of acceleration.

Table 4-16: Distribution of success indicators

Indicator type	No of projects	Sub-indicator	When used	Reported as the only indicator	Reported with more than one indicator
Direct indicators	54 projects (90%)	Time to proficiency	If the time to proficiency of the people in a job role is reduced compared to a baseline	24 (41%)	32 (55%)
		Time-to-readiness	If the time to readiness of given operation (process, product, system, equipment, business unit, group-wise certification, etc.) is reduced compared to expected time	13 (25%)	15 (25%)
		Training program duration	If the duration of training program (where it is primary vehicle to develop proficiency) is reduced compared to duration before	7 (12%)	17 (28%)
Indirect indicators	6 projects (10%)	Comparative performance	If new people are performing comparable to experienced staff, means time-to-proficiency of new people is relatively shorter than previous staff	1 (2%)	6 (10%)
		Proficient population	If % of proficient people increased at the end of the project, means time-to-proficiency of the group is shortened	1 (2%)	1 (2%)
		Rate of learning	If time to learning representative tasks is reduced compared to average indications before	3 (5%)	16 (36%)

4.9.2 Effectiveness of practices/strategies in reducing time-to-proficiency

Detailed results arranged by each project case are provided in Appendix 27. The results were reported in one or more of above six indicators. The results were reported mostly in comparison to a baseline number established for that indicator before the new practices/strategies (as shared by the project leaders) were implemented. Comparing the data before and after the implementation of new practices/strategies, the following observations were made:

- Compared to the baseline established at the beginning of each project case, the new practices/strategies shared by project leaders in the interviews reduced time-to-proficiency of people to as low as 20% and up to as high as 83%, depending on the context. This significant variation was due to the diverse contexts included in this study.

- Compared to the estimates established at the beginning of each project case, the new practices/strategies shared by project leaders reduced the time-to-readiness of a business or operation by as low as 50% and up to as high as 90%, depending on the context. This significant variation was also due to the diverse contexts included in this study.

- Compared to the baseline training program duration at the beginning of each project case, the new practices/strategies shared by project leaders reduced training program duration by as low as 20% and up to as high as 80%, depending on the context. This significant variation was due to the nature of the training program and also diverse contexts included in this study. Of the 60 project cases, 28% realised reduced training duration as a side benefit in addition to the main result of reduced time-to-proficiency.

- To reach the performance comparable to that of experienced peers already serving a given job role, the new performers took 34% less time to reach that performance compared to the new performers who came to the same job before implementation of new practices/strategies shared by the project leaders.

- Compared to 35%, performers in a given job role being deemed proficient in performing the job role at the beginning of the project cases, within eight weeks of implementation of new practices/strategies, the number of proficient performers increased to 55%.

This comparable evidence suggests the practices/strategies shared by the project leaders indeed worked in their isolated settings. Accordingly, the aggregated themes and overarching themes (practices) drawn from the individual successful project cases are likely to have similar success in reducing time-to-proficiency.

4.10 CHAPTER SUMMARY

In this chapter, the findings from the data analysis were presented. This research study explored three research questions. 42 emergent themes grouped under 11 overarching themes were formed during the data analysis. The first research question addressed how organisations and project leaders viewed the concept of accelerated proficiency. The study revealed two overarching themes representing proficiency and accelerated proficiency. Eight themes represented the characteristics of proficiency and accelerated proficiency. The second research question explored in this study was the importance of shorter time-to-proficiency and the benefits accrued from reduced time-to-proficiency. Data analysis of this section revealed eight themes grouped under three overarching themes. The magnitude and scale of the problem of time-to-proficiency were seen to be substantial. Four themes were discovered explaining the imperatives that drive organisations to institute time-to-proficiency projects. These included time-related pressures, speed-related competitiveness, skill-related deficiencies, cost or financial implications. Four themes of business benefits emerged which included business gains, improvement in operational metrics, improvement in productivity and cost savings. The third research question explored in this research study was practices and strategies that have been proven successful in various organisations in shortening time-to-proficiency of the workforce. The data analysis revealed that without exception, organisations deployed six practices to shorten time-to-proficiency as a system. These six practices represented 24 strategies that practitioners and project leaders have implemented to drive a reduction in time-to-proficiency.

The following chapter (chapter 5) concludes the study. Specifically, it discusses the findings presented in this chapter, compares them with the literature and derives major postulations, as well as describes the conceptual model that emerged from the findings. Implications of the findings discussed in this chapter are elaborated further in chapter 5.

Chapter 5 CONCLUSIONS & IMPLICATIONS

5.1 INTRODUCTION

A summary of Chapter 1 to Chapter 5 is presented here as a preamble to Chapter 5. Chapter 1 introduced the study on the business problem of longer time-to-proficiency of the workforce in the organisations and the concept and process of accelerated proficiency in the workplace. The chapter provided the background and rationale of the study. The chapter formed the central research problem and the research questions that were investigated in this study. The central research problem and business challenge, along with the research questions, are shown in *Table 5-1*.

Table 5-1: Summary of research questions and objective

Central research problem and business challenge		
The business challenge this study aimed to solve is that organisations are struggling with long time-to-proficiency of their workforce in certain job roles.		
Intent of the research study		
To explore and understand the meaning practitioners place on the concept of accelerated proficiency in the workplace. To understand what makes the need for accelerating proficiency critical for organisations and what benefits they draw from reducing time-to-proficiency. To identify practices, strategies, methods and processes that have been proven to reduce time-to-proficiency successfully in different contexts.		
Central research question		
How can organisations accelerate time-to-proficiency of the employees in the workplace?		
Research questions		
Research question #1	Meaning of accelerated proficiency	What does the concept of accelerating proficiency or accelerating time-to-proficiency mean to organisations?
Research question #2	Driving factors and benefits of reduced time-to-proficiency	What business factors drive the need for reducing time-to-proficiency of the workforce and how do organisations benefit from achieving it?
Research question #3	Practices and strategies to accelerate proficiency	What core practices and strategies do business leaders and practitioners adopt to achieve shorter time-to-proficiency of the workforce in a given job?
Research objective		
The objective of this research is to develop a conceptual model and/or framework of proven practices or strategies that practitioners can use to reduce time-to-proficiency of the workforce in various settings.		

Chapter 2 described the literature review in detail and positioned the literature in four major topics — (1) performance; (2) knowledge and skill acquisition; (3) expertise and proficiency; and (4) accelerated proficiency. Historical and contemporary studies were reviewed, and deficiencies inferred from the literature were explained. Chapter 3 described the research methodology adopted in this study to investigate the research questions. An adapted research process was explained which justified adopting the pragmatism paradigm and qualitative methodology approach to the study. The sampling strategy of using purposive sampling and criterion sampling was justified. The chapter then presented the data collection plan, which was conducted in three phases. The rationale and process of using in-depth interviews and other considerations were described. The chapter provided a detailed overview of the data analysis approaches used to conduct the matrix analysis and thematic analysis. Finally, the chapter explained the strategies observed throughout the study to ensure reliability and validity its findings. Chapter 4 presented the findings that were discovered from the data obtained from participants and analysed using the methods described in chapter 3 for each research question. Findings related to the three research questions were explained through 11 overarching themes formed based on the grouping, relationships and synergies of 42 themes. The themes were explained using concept maps, hierarchical thematic maps and quotes from the participants.

The purpose of this chapter is to discuss the findings presented in Chapter 4, compare the findings with the literature and identify the contributions made by the study. Further, this chapter also presents the emergent conceptual model of business practices and framework of successful strategies used by project leaders to shorten time-to-proficiency. The implications of the findings on theory, methodology and practice are also discussed. Finally, the chapter concludes with suggestions for future studies.

5.2 SUMMARY OF EMERGENT THEMES

In this study, three interrelated research questions were investigated to address the central research problem. In research question #1, participants' responses were analysed to understand the meaning they ascribed to the concept of accelerated proficiency. Eight themes emerged, which were grouped under two overarching themes, which characterised how proficiency and accelerated proficiency were viewed in the workplace. In research question #2, the business drivers that motivated organisations to institute initiatives/projects to accelerated proficiency were identified and categorised. The data analysis led to the identification of three overarching themes and ten themes that describe why it is important for organisations to shorten time-to-proficiency and how they benefit from reduced time-to-proficiency. The data were gathered to understand the business benefits of shortening time-to-proficiency. Research question #3 was the principal research question investigated in this study. The project cases were compared to understand how organisations reduced time-to-proficiency. The study revealed six overarching themes representing practices and 24 themes representing strategies that contributed towards shortening time-to-proficiency.

In total, 11 overarching themes were identified against the three research questions, which were described in Chapter 4. *Table 5-2* summarises the extent to which the extant literature addressed each of these overarching themes. The discussion in the following sections explains the findings and compares them with the existing literature. New contributions are also identified in the discussion.

Table 5-2: Comparison of emergent themes with the literature

Research question		Overarching themes	Addressed in extant literature
#1	C1	Proficiency	Some extent
	C2	Accelerated proficiency	Some extent
#2	D1	Magnitude and scale (of time-to-proficiency)	None
	D2	Business drivers (for accelerating proficiency)	Little extent
	D2	Business benefits (of reduced time-to-proficiency)	Some extent
#3	P1	Defining business-driven proficiency measures	Some extent
	P2	Developing proficiency reference map	Some extent
	P3	Creating efficient proficiency path	Some extent
	P4	Manufacturing accelerated contextual experiences	Largely consistent
	P5	Promoting an active emotional immersion	Some extent
	P6	Setting up proficiency eco-system	Largely consistent

5.3 DISCUSSION OF RESEARCH QUESTION #1

Research question #1 was: **What does the concept of accelerating proficiency or accelerating time-to-proficiency mean to organisations?** In response to this question, eight themes grouped under two overarching themes described or characterised proficiency and accelerated proficiency in the workplace. In *Table 5-3*, the themes from Chapter 4 are repeated for reference.

The two emergent overarching themes, proficiency and accelerated proficiency (see *Table 5-3*), revealed several aspects of the concepts. Major interpretations for each overarching theme and emergent theme are summarised, and the contribution of each to the existing body of knowledge is highlighted. The overarching theme C1 and C2 are related to each other, as was shown in the concept map in *Figure 4-1*. Overarching theme C1 defines the nature and boundaries of proficiency in a given role, while C2 defines the characteristics that govern the acceleration of this proficiency.

Table 5-3: Emergent themes from research question #1

Overarching theme			Emergent themes
C1	Proficiency	C1.1	Proficiency refers to meeting established performance thresholds for a job role.
		C1.2	Consistency is the hallmark of the state of proficiency of a job role.
		C1.3	Proficiency is measured by business outcomes of the job role or observable actions linked to outcomes.
		C1.4	Proficiency is not just about learning an isolated skill, task or activity in a job
C2	Accelerated proficiency	C2.1	Accelerated proficiency is measured in terms of reduction in time-to-proficiency.
		C2.2	A clear definition of proficiency for a job role is the most critical requirement to baseline, monitor and shorten time-to-proficiency.
		C2.3	Accelerated proficiency is not accelerated learning or accelerated training.
		C2.4	Training alone rarely leads to accelerating proficiency, it requires solutions beyond training.

5.3.1 Overarching theme C1: Proficiency

Theme C1.1— Proficiency refers to meeting established performance thresholds for a job role: This theme entails ideas of performance thresholds and the job role. Job role was an anchor in the concept of defining proficiency in the workplace. A job role is a specific set of responsibilities or expectations and more coherent than simply the title of a job; while a job may encompass several other things as well. Most of the practitioners appeared to view proficiency more in terms of how a given job role performed (i.e., all the individuals performing same job role collectively) rather than how an individual performed a task or activity in that job role. Thus, the high investment efforts on initiatives/projects setup to accelerate proficiency were focused on accelerating the outcomes at the job role level rather than at the individual level. Recently, there is more management focus on job role based performance tracking. From the management consulting firm Deloitte, Bersin (2013) indicated on his blog that 'in today's high performing companies, people now take on "roles" not "jobs"'. It is also contended by some that 'job roles better encapsulated the totality of performance' (Baker 2016). Every job role in an organisation is designed for a purpose, and thus, has defined and specific expectations in terms of outcomes, results and deliverables measured with some metrics. A performer justifies being in a job role because s/he produces outputs to those established standards. Practitioners refer proficiency as a state in which someone is 'independently productive' and is fully contributing (Rosenbaum & Williams 2004, p. 13). The productivity of an individual is measured with reference to the standards of performance defined for a given job role. The scholarly literature expressed this as the 'journeyman' stage at which 'an individual can handle day-to-day job independently, is experienced and reliable' (Hoffman 1998, p. 85).

A vast amount of literature emphasises progression towards proficiency in the form of several stages in which each stage is described with a qualitatively different proficiency in skills (Alexander 2003b; Benner 2004; Dreyfus & Dreyfus 2005, 2009; Hoffman 1998; Jacobs 1997, 2001, 2003; Jacobs & Washington 2003). On the contrary, in this study, organisations did not appear to obtain any advantage by putting labels on their employee's development or progression in the journey towards proficiency. None of the project leaders expressed any inclination towards characterising or labelling any other in-between stage before proficiency. Main concerns appeared to be whether an individual was operating in the state of proficiency or not. This theme provides some support to the observation Dall'Alba and Sandberg (2006) made that experience and the understanding of practice were the major determinants of any professional skill development, and it may not have level-like stages. This finding also raises the question on the usefulness of the meaning or representation of stages of skill/proficiency acquisition for the workplace. Though studies have either detected or forced-fit the characteristics of individual proficiency to the description of stages found in such models, it is not clear from those studies if there was any business benefit to the organisation or any development benefit to the individual (Benner 2004; Beta & Lidaka 2015; Ramsburg 2010; Scobey 2006). Nevertheless, this study raises important concerns regarding whether or not proficiency tracking in the workplace should rely on staged-transition models.

Theme C1.2—Consistency is the hallmark of the state of proficiency of a job role: This theme ties the idea of consistency to performance. This theme suggests that performance has to be consistent and repeatable for a certain period in order to represent proficiency. Thus, maintenance of performance, i.e., consistently being at that performance level is also a characteristic of proficiency in a job role. Consistency in producing business outcomes or deliverables was identified as the hallmark of the state of proficiency, as well as the key differentiator that separated a proficient performer from a non-proficient performer. Practitioners like Rosenbaum and Williams (2004, p. 14) posited that 'proficiency is when a new employee achieves a predetermined level of performance on a consistent basis'. Though there are not many studies in which the role of consistency is studied, consistency is seen as an expected attribute of proficiency in high-risk or life-threatening jobs. For instance, in a study involving 200 patients who underwent thoroscopic lobectomy surgery by two different surgeons, Li, Wang and Ferguson (2014) noticed that efficiency and consistency defined the proficiency of surgeons. They found that while the personal experience of more than 100 cases developed efficiency, 'attaining consistency requires 200 or more cases' (id. 1154). Consistency in the sports arena is valued in terms of pay-for-consistency in performance (Deutscher et al. 2017). The idea of consistency implied that proficiency is a level or a state that is described as a non-negotiable state. Irrespective of the mastery of constituent skills, primary concerns of the business managers in this study were whether an individual was operating at desired proficiency (i.e., producing desired business outcomes). As stated before, an individual is either operating in that state or not.

Theme C1.3—Proficiency is measured by business outcomes of the job role or observable actions linked to outcomes: This theme clarifies the nature of the performance threshold against which someone's proficiency is measured and against which consistency is monitored. This theme indicated that proficiency of the workforce in organisations is measured by business outcomes or by observable actions representative of (or leading to) business outcome. The success of a job role was mainly assessed with business outcomes (e.g., business results, KPIs, productivity, performance specs, customer satisfaction scores, etc.). This insight supports the premise of using accomplishments, results or work outcomes as a measure of human performance in the HPT framework (Binder 2017; Gander 2006). On the same lines, using an outcome-based view, leading practitioners stated that 'Proficiency can be defined in numbers of transactions, dollars sold, defect rates, customer satisfaction scores, or anything else that is measurable and related to results' (Rosenbaum & Williams 2004, p. 14). Supporting this view, Jacobs (2003, p. 5) indicated that '[p]eople whose outcomes are less valuable or who produce no outcomes can have lower levels of competence'. However, there are instances when it is not possible to measure the end business results or outcomes (e.g., strategy related jobs). In those situations, proficiency was measured in terms of observable actions (i.e., quality and quantity of activities, comparison with experienced peers, the number of repetitions, verifiable and observable behaviours, and evidence from authentic work). For example, an evidence of authentic work is producing a business report. Such observable behaviours can be translated to the outcomes. Pollock, Wick and Jefferson (2015) emphasised the value of actions that directly lead to the outcome as '"good performance," in the business sense, and deemed to be activity that produces high value outcomes at relatively low input cost.

However, these two insights in this theme offer a view contrary to the school of thought which maintains that individual performance should be measured in terms of behaviours and not results (Campbell & Wiernik 2015). The divide between behaviours and outcomes is created by some authors and researchers themselves to ease measurement of individual performance from the measurements of work performance, later being a sum total of several other factors (Baker 2016, p. 2). An outcome-based view, as emphasised by this theme also suggests that proficiency is a true measure of the ability of an individual in the workplace to produce desired outcomes amidst all the unknowns, environmental influences and other enabling or constraining factors, surrounding a job role. Thus, proficiency in the workplace is a much larger construct which signifies overall work performance (Griffin, Neal & Parker 2007). Studies in HRD acknowledge that such overall job or work proficiency include aspects of behavioural performance, task performance, contextual performance, team and organisational performance and also recognised the challenge to develop individuals to such levels (Campbell & Wiernik 2015; Dumas & Hanchane 2010; Houger 2006; Kanfer & Kantrowitz 2002; Khan, Khan & Khan 2011; Quartey 2012; Wallace 2006). The theme C1.3 revealed in this study provides more encompassing performance measures using the concept of job role proficiency.

Theme C1.4— Proficiency is not about learning a skill, task or activity in a job: This theme suggests that proficiency is about results rather than about demonstrating a skill, task or activity. Producing the outcomes in a job role required orchestration of many skills, tasks and activities at the same time among the complex influence of several other conditions. Thus, it was not a few isolated skills or tasks in which proficiency mattered to project leaders. In some studies, the performance researchers found that job-specific task proficiency was the most common measure and thus, was the central idea of an individual's job performance (Koopmans et al. 2011). Studies in HRD have used task performance as an outcome measure to ascertain competence or proficiency levels of an individual (Borman & Motowidlo 1993; Campbell 1990; Jacobs 1997, 2001, 2003; Viswesvaran & Ones 2000). In contrast, proficiency researchers considered over-reliance on the concept of task performance as a roadblock to accelerating proficiency, calling it as 'paradox of tasks' which created an 'artificial sense of linearity and separability' (Hoffman et al. 2014, p. 178). Task domains are probably still important for expertise building in closed domains (e.g., sports, music, etc.) or where there are a limited set of well-defined static tasks (Shanteau 2015). Admittedly, without knowledge, skills and behaviours and without the ability to perform required tasks, procedures or activities, it is not feasible to produce the desired outcomes. The closest relationship of knowledge and the outcome was suggested by Fred (2002, p. 43) who valued the outcomes that come out of learning knowledge: 'The proficiency threshold, therefore, is the exact moment when a worker can convert knowledge through action into the promised value for the customer'. However, being able to ultimately produce the designated results independently determines whether or not someone is proficient, and if not there yet, how soon s/he could be in that state. This observation supports the viewpoint of performance paradigm in HRD in terms of enhancing total individual performance not just by training interventions but also by other interventions (Clark 2008; Swanson & Holton 2001).

With lesser direct focus on isolated skills, tasks or activities, there was an observation made in this study that the project leaders were not much concerned about a terminological divide between a competent vs. proficient performer, which is generally a key concern of training designers discussed widely in literature (Khan & Ramachandran 2012). Instead, project leaders focused more on expressing performance in terms of business metrics and stayed focused on when someone attained that performance consistently, instead of labelling the name of the stage where someone was at a given point of time. Project leaders just considered terms like *competence* and *competency* as training specific terms and ruled out much consideration because their basic assumption was that training plays a very small part in the overall goal of shortening time-to-proficiency. While this study neither confirms nor refutes the usefulness of such constructs (or differentiation among such constructs) to the workplace, these might still hold value in describing development progression in studies focused on training curriculum (Alexander 2003b; Jacobs 2003; Kim 2015; Scobey 2006; Teodorescu 2006).

Construct of job-role proficiency: Beta and Lidaka (2015, p. 1961) indicated that state of proficiency has 'no clear-cut explanation of the word, which allows the use of different interpretations according to the application'. Supporting that, Kim (2015, p. 2) stated that 'missing accounts of the middle stages [of proficiency] leave the developmental process somewhat unclear'. Filling this gap and advancing further, the preceding discussion pointed out certain characteristics of what proficiency is and is not, as summarised in *Table 5-4*. This distinction makes this construct qualitatively different from the constructs of proficiency, as described in the existing literature such as job-specific task proficiency (Campbell et al. 1993), task performance (Borman & Motowidlo 1993), technical proficiency (Griffin, Neal & Parker 2007), human competence (Jacobs 1997, 2001, 2003), stage of proficiency (Dreyfus & Dreyfus 2005) and proficiency as a continuum (Hoffman 1998). This distinction set the premise that proficiency for a job role is much more than an individual's performance, and supports the existence of another construct of *job-role proficiency* to explain the state of consistent performance in terms of outcomes, results and accomplishments of the given job role and to differentiate it from task proficiency. Theoretically, the basis of the construct suggested in this study is similar to the one suggested by concept of work role performance employing role theory: 'It is possible to assess proficiency when the requirements of a work role are formalised because there is a clear standard against which these judgments can be made' (Griffin, Neal & Parker 2007, p. 329). The construct of job-role proficiency, as emerged above, specifies the characteristics and nature of the performance at the state of proficiency, thus filling the gap not addressed in other studies. The properties of this construct are shown in *Table 5-4*.

Table 5-4: Construct of job-role proficiency

What it is	What it is not
Job role level	Individual's task performance
State of performance	Learning a task or skill
Threshold performance standards	One-time performance
Consistency of performance	Implied progression of stages
Measured by business outcomes	
Measured by actions leading to outcomes	

5.3.2 Overarching theme C2: Accelerated proficiency

Theme C2.1— Accelerated proficiency is measured in terms of improvement in time-to-proficiency: This theme indicated that the only metrics to monitor acceleration in proficiency are based on measuring time-to-proficiency. In the project cases studied in this study, the time-to-proficiency was measured from the start of the job role. Time-to-proficiency did not always mean on-boarding time and did not apply only to newly hired employees (Rosenbaum 2014). It was equally applicable metrics for transfer from one job role to another. Therefore, the start of the job role was usually the starting point. Project leaders monitored proficiency measures to track when employees in a given job role had reached desired proficiency. Further, it was not measuring time-to-proficiency of one person, rather measurement was being carried out for the entire job role and usually averaged across all employees serving that job role (Borton 2007). Though the metric is very clear, it may not always be feasible to measure time-to-proficiency accurately, or some job roles simply do not offer any measurable metrics for proficiency, for example, jobs related to fire control, enforcement officers and business strategy.

Theme C2.2— A clear definition of proficiency for a job role is the most critical requirement to baseline, monitor and shorten time-to-proficiency: This theme emphasises that a clear proficiency definition was the core requirement to the acceleration of proficiency. The emphasis on a clear definition integrates all the other themes from C1.1 to C1.4 related to proficiency, which includes meeting pre-specified performance thresholds for the job role, being measured in terms of business outcomes, being represented as consistency of performance and not being expressed in terms of tasks or activities into the definition of this theme. On those lines, the *human performance technology* (HPT) model also suggests conducting comprehensive performance analysis and defining performance measures upfront for any performance improvement endeavour (Kang 2017). Similarly, defining proficiency state and its measures upfront is critical to shortening the time someone takes to reach this proficiency state. Clearer internal definition of proficiency leads to identifying that point in the historical data to baseline time-to-proficiency and also allows managers to track that point in the future, thus supporting the theme C2.1, as well towards measuring time-to-proficiency. Without an undebated definition agreed upon across all stakeholders, it is not feasible to dedicate efforts and investments and drive alignment among managers about what needs to be achieved. More than anything else, the findings indicated that a clear definition supports managers to plan the path to the proficiency of a set of individuals performing a job role (Rosenbaum 2014).

Theme C2.3—Accelerated proficiency is not accelerated learning or accelerated training: This theme differentiates accelerated proficiency from similarly worded topics such as *accelerated learning* and *accelerated training*. Hoffman et al. (2014, p. 13) proposed a more encompassing meaning of accelerated learning which included constructs such as *rapidised training, rapidised knowledge sharing, accelerated proficiency* and *facilitated retention* under the umbrella of accelerated learning. However, organisations appeared to view accelerated proficiency and accelerated learning to mean two different things.

Not accelerated learning. Theme C2.3 suggests that accelerated proficiency is a characteristically different construct from the traditional meaning of accelerated learning, which is speeding up the learning curve of a certain individual, i.e., learning a given content in a shorter time or learning more content in the same time (Imel 2002; Patchan et al. 2015; Radler & Bocianu 2017; Trekles & Sims 2013). People learn at different rates and with different styles. Controlling every individual's learning curve is not feasible, and that is not the intent of accelerated proficiency. Learning something quickly does not necessarily mean an individual would start producing consistent business results quickly too. For example, if a sales engineer's monthly quota were $1M, learning the details of the product features, sales processes and sales technique would not mean s/he could surely produce $1M consistently month after month. S/he would have to develop relationships, connections and leads and gain experience in all aspects of the job role to be able to produce that many sales every month. Such outcomes require more than just learning content, knowledge or skills. Thus, the effect of accelerating learning or learning more content in a short time may or may not always contribute towards shorter time-to-proficiency. In the context of accelerating proficiency, the value or the contribution of accelerated learning aligns with 'faster attainment of skill and knowledge, and an increase in on-the-job performance with better retention of learning', as conceptualised by Andrews and Fitzgerald (2010, p. 2). Further, accelerated proficiency refers to the performance of a job role as a whole and a group of people serving that role as a whole. Thus, it is not about the learning of one person unless it is achieved collectively for the entire group in a job (Bologa & Lupu 2007). Though overlapping in meaning, accelerated learning and accelerated proficiency represent different intents for business. This theme presents a new insight that may need further exploration and characterising the distinction between these constructs.

Not accelerated training. Theme C2.3 also differentiates the concept of accelerated proficiency from the intent of traditional concept of accelerated training or shortened training duration. In this study, it was seen that accelerated proficiency projects are generally not started with the intent of shortening training duration or *rapidised training,* i.e., 'the idea of training individuals to achieve some *minimal level of proficiency* at a rate faster than usual' (Hoffman et al. 2014, p. 13). Studies on S-OJT have viewed achieving desired performance in terms of reduction in training time towards initial readiness. For instance, studies on S-OJT have shown up to 10 times reduction in training time compared to unstructured OJT to develop initial readiness for a given job (Jacobs 2003, 2014a; Jacobs & Bu-Rahmah 2012). On the contrary, this theme indicated that attaining such initial operating readiness (Duguay & Korbut 2002) to put someone on-the-job to do basic duties is also not the goal of accelerated proficiency, though some project cases paid attention to this goal as well. Rather, the true goal of accelerated proficiency is to make someone fully productive and fully functioning on his or her job to produce outcomes designated for the job role (Rosenbaum & Williams 2004). Thus, shortening training duration is not an explicit goal of accelerated proficiency projects in organisations, though in almost every case, it was attained as a by-product. As such, accelerated training should be proposed as a byproduct of accelerated proficiency.

<u>Theme C2.4— Training alone rarely leads to accelerating proficiency, it requires solutions beyond training</u>: In this study, the overall role of formal training interventions in accelerating proficiency was seen

as relatively small. This theme positions training as one of the several possible solutions to accelerate proficiency, rather than the total solution in itself. This also indicated that the strategies to accelerated proficiency extend much beyond training or learning interventions. This is consistent with the basic premise of the human performance technology (HPT) framework discussed in the literature review chapter in section 2.2.1, that training is one of the several performance interventions (Stolovitch & Keeps 1999). Leading practitioners Pollock, Wick and Jefferson (2015, p. 41) asserted that performance is the result of the interaction of the worker, work, and workplace, but the '[t]raining impacts worker only'. Training is useful only if it focuses on developing performers to produce business results. However, most of the time training is just an event with the specific purpose to deliver necessary skills or behaviours, and usually, it has a specific assessment checkpoint that signals its end. Producing results or waiting till results are produced is usually not the goal of training interventions and is certainly not feasible.

Project leaders in this study appear to believe that dynamics inside a training intervention was not a true representation of workplace challenges and complexities. Chevalier (2004), Solderstrom and Bjork (2015) and Stolovitch (2000) argued that performance during training interventions could be a misleading indicator of proficiency and long-term learning of behaviours that should persist in the workplace. Unless the performers are prepared to produce business outcomes in a shorter time, training may not contribute towards accelerating proficiency. While modern studies emphasise on aligning training objectives with business needs and goals (Saks, Haccoun & Belcourt 2010; Salas et al. 2012), preparing performers towards proficiency in shorter time appears to be beyond the reach of any instructional design models, just because instructional design models tend to focus on knowledge, skills and behaviours. Baker (2017) argued that in modern organisations the assumption that a technically superior workforce is the key to organisational performance tended to gear all solutions to being skill-focused or training-focused. As seen in previous themes, achieving business outcomes to pre-established standards consistently within the complexity of the workplace require not only skills, knowledge and behaviours but also requires several other support mechanisms and interventions. This closely aligns with the practices of human performance technology (Kang 2017; Marker et al. 2014; Pershing 2006; Van Tiem, Moseley & Dessinger 2012; Wallace 2006). This theme also confirms observations made by Swanson and Holton (2001) and Dean (2016) with regard to the need to use several non-linear interventions in addition to learning interventions to attain desired performance.

Admittedly, training is a critical part of most performance improvement interventions (Clark 2008; Kraiger 2014). There are cases in which desired proficiency can be attained in training settings, or training is the only a viable, practical option; for example, job roles in which life and safety matter (military, pilots, surgeons, firefighters, etc.) and failure is no option in real situations (Hintze 2008; Jenkins et al. 2016; Klein & Borders

2016; Kuchenbrod 2016). Alternatively, training may be more feasible solutions in the job roles that are not readily measured in terms of immediate on-the-job outcomes (e.g., roles related to business strategy), or job roles are governed by some licensing or other regulatory norms (e.g., oil and gas related jobs). Such situations may necessitate training as a fail-safe mechanism or even a mandatory requirement (Crichton & Flin 2004). In the present study, the analysis of this theme suggested that project leaders did not end the training until the desired proficiency was attained. Thus, this theme closely aligns with the proficiency-based curriculum (Angelo et al. 2015; Lee, P 2011; Rosenthal et al. 2009; Wilcox et al. 2014), focused on mastery learning (Guskey 2009), which is the practice on a given task until proficiency is achieved, instead of 'seat time', which is spending predefined time on a given task (Nagel 2011).

Themes C1.4, C2.3 and C2.4 suggest that goals of accelerated proficiency are not described in terms of learning knowledge or skill. However, neither theme undermines nor negates the critical value that learning and training plays in acquiring knowledge, skills and proficiency. At the same time, themes C1.1, C1.2 and C1.3 set the boundaries of how success should be defined. There is no doubt that learning is an underlying process in all the endeavours undertaken by an individual in the workplace (Saks, Haccoun & Belcourt 2010; Salas et al. 2012). Nevertheless, what is being measured and how success is reported are matters of perspective. In summary, these themes describe the nature of accelerated proficiency in the workplace in terms of what it is and what it is not.

5.3.3 Propositions from research question #1: Meaning of accelerated proficiency

Based on interpretations of the eight themes, a new theoretical construct of *job-role proficiency* is proposed to explain the true nature of proficiency in the workplace. These themes also explain the nature of the concept of accelerated proficiency in the workplace. Collectively, Box 5-1 summarises the above characteristics as two propositions to answer research question #1.

Box 5-1: Propositions from research question #1

> Based on the analysis of the findings of the study, following are proposed answers for the research question #1 — What does the concept of accelerating proficiency or accelerating time-to-proficiency mean to organisations?
>
> ***Job-role proficiency*** denotes a state of performance at which performers produce business outcomes or deliverables consistently to the set performance thresholds expected from a given job role. It refers to achieving and maintaining one pre-established performance level and does not imply progression through different stages or levels of performance. It refers to the business performance of the job role and does not convey an individual's performance demonstrated on a task or skill.
>
> ***Accelerating proficiency*** means shortening the time someone takes in a given job role to reach to a state of consistent performance that meets the set thresholds. This is measured in time-to-proficiency. A clearer definition of job-role proficiency and its measures are the foremost critical requirement to the acceleration of proficiency. Accelerated proficiency is not about learning a body of content faster or shortening the training duration because the solution to a shorter time-to-proficiency lies beyond training interventions.

5.4 DISCUSSION OF RESEARCH QUESTION #2

The second research question explored in this study was: **Why is reducing time-to-proficiency of the workforce important to organisations and how do they benefit from achieving it?** Findings in research question #2 reported ten themes grouped into three overarching themes. These themes contributed towards understanding how critical time-to-proficiency problems are, the drivers that make accelerated proficiency a necessity in organisations and the business gains achieved by shortening time-to-proficiency. The themes discovered from the responses to question #2 are repeated from Chapter 4 and shown in *Table 5-5*.

Three emergent overarching themes, D1—'Magnitude and scale (of time-to-proficiency business problem)', D2—'Business drivers (for accelerating proficiency)' and D3—'Business benefits (of reduced time-to-proficiency)' were formed based on 10 themes. These three overarching themes showed cause-and-effect relationship among themselves, as shown in the concept map in *Figure 4-2* in chapter 4. The magnitude and scale shown in overarching theme D1 manifest itself as an impact on four different business drivers shown in overarching theme D2, which in turn trigger organisations to see the need for reducing time-to-proficiency. A project so instituted leads to business benefits, as indicated in overarching theme D3.

Table 5-5: Emergent themes from research question #2

	Overarching themes		Emergent themes
D1	Magnitude and scale (of time-to-proficiency business problem)	D1.1 D1.2	Magnitude of time-to-proficiency problem Scale of time-to-proficiency problem
D2	Business drivers (for accelerating proficiency)	D2.1 D2.2 D2.3 D2.4	Time-related pressures Speed-related competitiveness Skill-related deficiency Cost or financial implications
D3	Business benefits (of reduced time-to-proficiency)	D3.1 D3.2 D3.3 D3.4	Business gains Improvement in operational metrics Improvement in productivity Cost savings

5.4.1 Overarching theme D1: Magnitude and scale of time-to-proficiency business problem

Theme D1.1—Magnitude and scale (of time-to-proficiency business problem): This theme staged a compelling reason that drive organisations to attend to the business problem of long time-to-proficiency in any job role. The data for the magnitude of time-to-proficiency is evident from *Table 4-14*, *Table 4-15* and Appendix 27. From the data, it was also seen that magnitude of the time-to-proficiency may be as large as over three years in certain job roles just to become productive to required performance metrics. Most of the current literature suggested time taken to acquire elite expertise on representative tasks in closed domains, such as chess, to be up to ten years (Ericsson & Towne 2010; Ericsson 2002, 2003). However, this time refers to altogether a different journey towards notable expertise. In the present context, time-to-proficiency refers to the time taken by an employee to reach the point where s/he can do his or her job reliably and can produce consistent results. By nature of the measurement, this time is expected to be much shorter than the one suggested by expert performance studies (i.e., ten years). Yet, time-to-proficiency noted in theme D1.1 is significantly large. Though specific estimates are scarce in the literature, the actual time-to-proficiency across various job roles noted in this study confirmed that time-to-proficiency in certain jobs is significantly large, as noted by some practitioners' case studies and surveys (Accenture 2013; Borton 2007; Fred 2002; Pollock, Wick & Jefferson 2015, p. 285; Thompson 2017, p. 169).

Theme D1.2—Scale of time-to-proficiency problem: The magnitude of time-to-proficiency was found to be generally so large that organisations could not ignore its scale, particularly when its effect was multiplied across the workforce. The data for the scale was provided in *Table 4-14*, *Table 4-15* and Appendix 27. The data in this theme indicates that the time-to-proficiency problem may become larger in scale because a given role may be served by hundreds or thousands of people globally based on the size of the organisation. Previously, researchers have appealed that it is worth doing something about such long time-to-proficiency, though the impact of time-to-proficiency and its scale has not been studied before (Fadde 2016; Hoffman, Andrews & Feltovich 2012). This theme draws the attention of organisations toward the fact that it is not one person's time-to-proficiency, rather it multiplies across a job role and hence, it is a significantly sized business problem.

5.4.2 Overarching theme D2: Business drivers for accelerating proficiency

While the magnitude and scale of the problem are the triggers for organisations to think of shortening time-to-proficiency, the overarching theme D2–'Business drivers for accelerating proficiency' indicated that the real push comes from the impact of longer time-to-proficiency on the business. This impact was seen in four dimensions, as indicated by themes D2.1—'Time-related pressures', D2.2—'Speed-related competitiveness' and D2.3—'Skill-related deficiency'. These four drivers primarily drove the need for shorter time-to-proficiency in organisations. There were some cost implications of longer time-to-proficiency, as well as indicated by the theme D2.4—'Cost or financial implications'. However, the intent of saving costs or other financial gains were not shown to be the main trigger for organisations to institute initiatives/projects to reduce time-to-proficiency. This study confirmed that speculations made in the literature regarding the retiring workforce, complexity, changing nature of work, time-to-market pressures, competitiveness and business pressures, as the drivers for accelerating time-to-proficiency (Bruck 2015; Fred 2002; Hoffman et al. 2014; Langerak, Hultink & Griffin 2008; Lynn, Akgün & Keskin 2003). None of the observed business drivers appeared in isolation; rather there was a chain connection between various business drivers, with one impacting the other. In practice, all or several of the business drivers may drive the need for a shorter time-to-proficiency of the workforce.

5.4.3 Overarching theme D3: Business benefits of a shorter time-to-proficiency

Shorter time-to-proficiency leads to a mix of substantial business benefits represented by four themes D3.1—'Business gains', D3.2—'Improvement in operational metrics', D3.3—'Improvement in productivity', and D3.4—'Cost savings'. The theme of D3.4—'Cost savings' almost always resulted from shorter time-to-proficiency without even being the direct goal. The data for these benefits by project case is provided in Appendix 28. While previous studies have made speculative statements about the possible need and potential benefits of shortening time-to-proficiency, this study provided confirmed quantified ranges and qualitative indications of actual business benefits accrued in 60 project cases.

The general literature showed several case studies indicating financial and business benefits of training (Bartel 2000; Kirkpatrick & Kirkpatrick 2009; Phillips 2012). This study showed the financial and business benefits of reducing time-to-proficiency through training interventions or otherwise. For financial or cost gains, the findings in this study support previous studies which indicated substantial financial or cost benefits of shorter training duration and faster readiness of the workforce (Jacobs 2014a; Liu & Batt 2007; Sullivan, Brechin & Lacoste 1999) and from the reduction of time-to-proficiency (Borton 2007, p. 32; Pollock, Wick & Jefferson 2015, p. 285; Thompson 2017, p. 169). The major contribution this study makes to the body of knowledge and literature is a holistic business case with data obtained from 60 project cases, revealing several aspects of the magnitude and scale of the business problem, type of business drivers and range of business gains from shorter time-to-proficiency.

5.4.4 Propositions from research question #2: Driving factors and benefits

The interpretations of the ten themes explain the driving factors and benefits from shorter time-to-proficiency in the workplace. Collectively, Box 5-2 summarises these interpretations as one proposition to answer research question #2.

Box 5-2: Proposition from research question #2

> Based on the data analysis, following is the proposed answer for research question #2 — Why is reducing time-to-proficiency of the workforce important to organisations and how do they benefit from achieving it?
>
> The magnitude of time-to-proficiency in any job role is typically significantly large. This magnitude, when multiplied across all the individuals serving same job role becomes a business problem of such a large scale that organisations are not able to ignore its impacts. The impacts manifest in the form of time-related pressures, speed-related competitiveness, skill-related deficiencies or cost or financial implications. These business needs trigger organisations to institute initiatives/projects with a goal to shorten time-to-proficiency. Such initiatives/projects lead to substantial business gains and improvement in operational metrics. Saving cost and financial implications are not usually the primary drivers to institute such initiatives/projects. However, financial gains are invariably attained in every such initiative/project.

5.5 DISCUSSION OF RESEARCH QUESTION #3

The third research question this study explored was: **What core practices and strategies do business leaders and practitioners adopt to achieve shorter time-to-proficiency of the workforce in a given job?** The investigation revealed 24 themes grouped under six overarching themes. As the six overarching themes emerged, they were re-classed to be business *practices*, listed as P1 to P6 in *Table 5-6*. As the 24 themes emerged, they were re-classed to be *strategies*, listed as P1.1 to P6.6 in *Table 5-6*. The overarching themes contributed towards understanding high-level business practices followed by the practitioners, while the themes contributed towards understanding actual strategies implemented to put those practices into motion. Henceforth, these will be referred to as practices and strategies, respectively:

Overarching theme ↔ business-level "Practices" adopted by leaders

Themes ↔ "Strategies" to implement business practices

Table 5-6: Emergent themes from research question #3

	overarching themes (practices)		Emergent themes (strategies)
P1	Defining business-driven proficiency measures	P1.1	Starting with end in mind- Upfront definition and measures of proficiency in terms of business outcomes and link it to business needs.
		P1.2	Baseline and establish time-to-proficiency targets based on business drivers.
P2	Developing a proficiency reference map	P2.1	Conduct upfront comprehensive work analysis drawn from the outcomes.
		P2.2	Profile capabilities and capacities of the job performers.
		P2.3	Model success behaviours of exemplary performers.
		P2.4	Understand job operating conditions and environmental influences.
		P2.5	Analyse roadblocks and hindrances that lead to longer time-to-proficiency.
P3	Sequencing an efficient proficiency path	P3.1	Segment tasks and activities based on characteristics from analytics.
		P3.2	Create a logical sequence of experiences as a complete path.
		P3.3	Optimise the proficiency path for efficiency and time-saving.
P4	Manufacturing accelerated contextual experiences	P4.1	Assign performers on authentic job activities that allow practice on generating job-specific outcomes.
		P4.2	Embed learning into the work and focus on doing the job rather than topic-wise learning.
		P4.3	Expose performers to multiple cycles of deliberate and purposeful failures at a rapid rate or in a compressed time-frame.
		P4.4	Compress hard-to-obtain experiences on known situations in highly contextualised Realistic cases, gamified scenarios and representative simulations.
		P4.5	Strengthen generic, transferable, principle-based, fundamental skills to handle unfamiliar or unknown situations.
P5	Promoting an active emotional immersion	P5.1	Active engagement and emotional immersion with the tasks and situations similar to the workplace.
		P5.2	Provide immediate feedback and allow moments of focused reflection.
		P5.3	Assess performers through job-specific, continuous, multi-level assessment beyond a training intervention.
P6	Setting up a proficiency eco-system	P6.1	Create enabling and supportive environment.
		P6.2	Structured involvement, accountability, support and reinforcement from the manager.

	P6.3	Institute a structured mentoring and coaching process in the workplace.
	P6.4	Design opportunities for purpose-driven social connectivity and structured informal learning in the workplace.
	P6.5	Deploy on-demand performance support systems embedded in workflow and learning.
	P6.6	Leverage subject matter experts strategically.

The study findings related to this question indicated that business-level practices consisting of several systems, processes, elements and stakeholders were required to accelerate the proficiency of people serving a given job role. Further, formal training or even workplace training was a small part of the overall solution for accelerating proficiency. The job itself was seen as the primary mechanism, place and mode for reducing time-proficiency. The findings of this study suggest that none of the practices or strategies in isolation held the potential to shorten time-to-proficiency. All six practices and 24 strategies worked in tandem with each other as a system to reduce time-to-proficiency. The interactional relationship was shown in the concept map in *Figure 4-9* in Chapter 4. Though in the following sub-sections each practice and strategy is discussed independently and compared with relevant literature, the collective inference drawn from the findings of this study is that none of the six practices shortens time-to-proficiency without implementing other practices to a reasonable degree.

A thorough search of the literature did not locate any equivalent studies on accelerated proficiency. Further searches did not lead to any studies specifying any holistic model of accelerated proficiency. Therefore, there were no reference studies prior to this study to make direct comparisons. Individual practices and strategies are discussed in relation to sub-disciplines of business strategy, performance management, training and instructional design, workplace learning and human resource development. Where possible, an attempt was made to look for specific and explicit evidence of acceleration in proficiency. Otherwise, relevant evidence of general improvement in training effectiveness or learning or performance enhancement is mentioned.

5.5.1 Practice P1: Defining business-driven proficiency measures

Practice P1—'Defining business-driven proficiency measures' indicates that the key to reducing time-to-proficiency was how well the overall initiative/project at the organisation was linked to business needs. A time-to-proficiency project was seen starting with one or several of the four business needs – time-related pressures, speed-related competitiveness, skill-related deficiencies and cost or financial implications. When projects were started with such drivers, it automatically linked the project to business needs. This observation aligned with 'Starting with "Why?" (business outcomes) informs the answers to what and how' (Pollock,

Wick & Jefferson 2015, p. 43). The practice of defining business-driven proficiency measures was implemented through the following two strategies:

Strategy P1.1— Starting with end in mind—Upfront definition and measures of proficiency in terms of business outcomes and link it to business needs: The strategy P1.1 highlights that while defining measures of proficiency, the most important thing to keep in mind is "the end" itself. The end in most cases is the organisational business performance a job role is intended to deliver. Keeping the end in mind leads to the identification of most essential things required to produce the desired performance. Defining proficiency in crisp and measurable terms upfront is important from any project management standpoint for appropriate buy-in, agreement, alignment, investment and efforts to reduce time-to-proficiency (Project Management Institute 2013). In fact, data indicated that time-to-proficiency in any job role usually was so far out that defining the state clearly allowed managers to be conscious of what they were seeking. With a lack of measures of proficiency, it was not possible to know when someone had reached that point. Rosenbaum and Williams (2004, pp. 147, 169) suggested writing 'proficiency statements' in the form of business outcomes and linking the time-to-proficiency with the business needs. Thus, defining proficiency measures mainly in terms of business outcomes of the job role appeared to be the most crucial thing to address in the direction of shortening it. Studies on Gilbert's (1978) BEM model and performance improvement also suggested that accomplishments and outcomes should be the way to measure performance (Binder 2017). By doing so, individuals were held accountable to the same standards for which they were hired. This is consistent with the assertion from the 6-disciplines (6D) training methodology: 'Define the business outcomes *before* they embark on *any* learning initiative' (Pollock, Wick & Jefferson 2015, p. 39). However, it is not always possible to define measures in the form of business outcomes. In those cases, strategy P1.1 suggested the second category of measures based on the observable action that has direct linkage with the business outcomes to which it would lead (Pollock, Wick & Jefferson 2015; Rosenbaum & Williams 2004). In either case, starting from the end — the business outcomes of the job role — is the key.

Strategy P1.2—Baseline and establish time-to-proficiency targets based on business drivers: The strategy P1.2 suggests using a range of tools, data, logs, quantitative or qualitative methods and estimation to establish the baseline of time-to-proficiency. Rosenbaum (2014) specified baselining current time-to-proficiency as one of the steps in *Learning Paths* methodology, consistent with the observations in this study. The business drivers such as time-related pressures, speed-related competitiveness, skill-related deficiencies and cost or financial implications that triggered the need for the project may itself translate to new targets for time-to-proficiency. At every point in the time-to-proficiency project, actual time-to-proficiency was continuously monitored and compared with the target time-to-proficiency. Recent studies argued that by monitoring time-to-proficiency, strategies could implemented to shorten it (Li, Wang & Ferguson 2014)

Practice P1 summary and application: The themes regarding magnitude/scale and business drivers discovered in research question #2 drives time-to-proficiency targets and hence the need to institute a project to reduce time-to-proficiency to new targets. Practice P1 of defining business-driven proficiency measures reiterated and validated the themes discovered in research question #1 regarding characteristics and nature of proficiency and accelerated proficiency. This practice insists on using business metrics as the requirement to manage and track any project initiated to reduce time-to-proficiency. The outcome of this practice is an agreed set of metrics for performance that tie into the review of job performance and other components of performance tracking at the performer's level, team-level, business unit level and organisational level.

5.5.2 Practice P2: Developing a proficiency reference map

Practice P2—'Developing a proficiency reference map' indicates that an important practice to develop a proficiency reference map which identifies all the inputs that go into making a job role successful and all the conditions that impact how well these inputs translate into outcomes. A proficiency reference map was deemed the blueprint for success at the job and encompasses all the inputs and their relationships with each other that determine outcomes in a job role. That blueprint appeared to be the answer to the questions concerning how the desired business outcomes were being produced within the actual environment of the job role and under what conditions they were being produced and what was known to hamper them. Inputs included knowledge, skills, tasks, success behaviours, capacities and capabilities that were necessary to produce outcomes. Conditions included job operating conditions or environmental factors under which outcomes must be produced. Limiting factors included mindsets, beliefs, resources, and training inefficiencies, which tended to hamper the rate of proficiency. Some studies use a similar technique of drawing performance enablers/disablers from the mastery performance model, however, not in the context of shortening time-to-proficiency (Wallace 2006). This practice of developing proficiency reference was based on following five strategies:

Strategy P2.1—Conduct upfront comprehensive work analysis drawn from the outcomes: The strategy P2.1 calls for a comprehensive work analysis drawn from outcomes taking job role as a unit of analysis. The project leaders in the study deployed the analysis of work, the relationship of knowledge and skills with the tasks, relationships of tasks with the behaviours, and relationships of behaviours with the overall job role outcomes to develop an overall understanding how the outcomes were produced in a job role. These relationships were a blueprint map of knowledge concerning outcomes in a job role. At the job role level, this blueprint explicitly made visible the relationship between behaviour, skills or tasks and how those led to the final outcomes among the influence of other enabling or disabling variables. The work analysis, in the context of the findings of this study, suggested focusing on what needs to happen for the business and how it should happen. This strategy supports Langdon (2006), who emphasised that work analysis models, as typically advocated by models like HPT, focus on definition of results but lack focus on how work is executed to achieve those results. Langdon stated that work analysis is 'a clear and concise consensus of work that is not just results-driven but execution-defined and driven to results' (id. 931) to 'reflect and represent the totality of work performance' (id. 932). The six elements proposed by Langdon (2006) were outputs, consequences, inputs, conditions, process steps, and feedback. Similarly, in the present study, project leaders started from business outcomes and worked backwards to draw the tasks, skills, knowledge and behaviours to achieve those outcomes. Starting from the business outcomes appeared to lead to only those things that were absolutely required to produce those outcomes and generated a very lean list of essentials required to be mastered for the given job role.

The comprehensive work analysis suggested several things — what the performance measures of proficiency were, what tasks a performer was required to do to achieve those targeted outcomes, what s/he needed to know to do those tasks, what skills s/he needed to apply to complete the task and what behaviours s/he needed to exhibit to do the tasks effectively so as to attain desired outcomes, and what levers performers could manoeuvre to achieve outcomes effectively and efficiently. The scope of analysis covered in strategy P2.1 is similar to the combination of work and worker analysis specified by the HPT model for performance improvement (Van Tiem, Moseley & Dessinger 2012). Work analysis includes work flow, procedure, responsibilities and ergonomics, whereas worker analysis includes knowledge, skills, capacity, motivation and expectations. For example, Kang (2017) analysed 30 HPT cases from the literature and found that 23 cases reported performing work analysis, while 18 cases reported performing worker analysis.

Strategy P2.1 is consistent with the goals of job analysis or work analysis, which is considered as the core of HRD processes. As a distinction, job analysis involves looking at an individual job to identify individual tasks and duties involved, whereas work analysis involves looking at several jobs at the same time (Heron 2005). With the evolution of jobs, broader term work analysis is sometimes advocated (Sackett & Laczo 2003). Still, work analysis sometimes is considered as rigid and inflexible. Morgeson and Dierdorff (2011, p. 4) argued that, for work analysis, one should focus on work role requirements because it 'enables the explicit acknowledgement of connection to and among other role holders, as well as the embeddedness of roles in the broader work context'. Fundamentally taking job role as a unit of analysis, the entire focus was how the stated business outcomes were produced by a job role, as opposed to focusing on doing a task analysis (Dgedge et al. 2014) of how an individual does something.

From a human factor peresctive, system engineering approaches such as cognitive work analysis (CWA) considers a job as a system (Rasmussen, Pejtersen & Goodstein 1994). Studies on the CWA framework have advocated the use of multiple systematic analyses such as work domain analysis, control task analysis, analysis of possible strategies, team analysis, social and organisational analysis, analysis of workers' competencies, training, skills and experience (Ashoori & Burns 2013; Demir, Abou-Jaoude & Kumral 2017; Naikar 2017; Roth & Bisantz 2013). On similar lines, strategy P2.1 suggests performing comprehensive work analysis, analysis of performers, analysis of environmental constraints, and analysis of limiting factors to fully understand how a job role operates. However, the intent of CWA analysis is to understand capabilities and constraints while performing work with complicated systems. Unlike such time-intensive and multi-stage analyses, strategy P2.1 did not construe performing any time-consuming analysis. Some form of proficiency reference map may already exist for a job role; therefore, it may not need to redeveloped.

Strategy P2.2—Profile capabilities and capacities of the job performers: The strategy P2.2 gears the focus towards the performers. Even within the same job role, time-to-proficiency may vary considerably for different performers despite using the same set of strategies just because the personal capabilities and capacities of the performers in each job role are significantly different. Personal capabilities, prior skills, personal capacity and learning ability someone brought to a job had a great influence on the starting point for acceleration. If the capabilities of the current performers are understood and leveraged thoroughly before designing any solution, it is likely that the time they take to reach desired proficiency is shortened. Conversely, if the performers are hired for capabilities required to produce the outcome, they would just need to focus on new skills they do not have. Personal capability (like prior skills) and personal capacity (like learning ability) of the employees were included as key performance determinants in the behavioural engineering model (BEM) (Chevalier 2003) and 6-disciplines approach (Pollock, Wick & Jefferson 2015). The positive effect of prior experience and skills on raising the performance level of learners have been reported in the literature (Johnson 2016).

The usual practice in performance improvement interventions is to assess the performance of current performers in terms of how much they are producing relative to each other in the same job role (Kang 2017; Pershing 2006; Swanson 2007). In the present study, the strategy P2.2 focussed only on how much time they were taking to cross the performance threshold defined for the job role. This is understandable because goals of time-to-proficiency projects were not to improve or uplift the performance or productivity of the individuals unlike typical performance improvement projects. The comparison of relative time-to-proficiency among the performers also served the purpose of locating exemplary performers (see strategy P2.3) who were reaching desired performance levels in shorter time. For those reasons, the time-to-proficiency is baselined as a whole job role and not at an individual level.

Strategy P2.3—Model success behaviours of exemplary performers: The strategy P2.3 points towards another element of developing a proficiency reference map: knowing who the exemplary performers are who have crossed the threshold line of consistent performance in much shorter time compared to others in the same job role. The key was to identify them and understand what behaviours they exhibited that were different from an average performer that allowed them to reach desired performance in shorter time. In principle, at the same workplace, in the same job role, when some performers have already achieved shorter time-to-proficiency, it is feasible for other performers to do so as long as they also exhibit similar behaviours in the context of that job role. Lajoie (2003) proposed a similar approach to first understanding what experts know, gathering explicit exemplars or models of how experts teach novices, responses or examples from experts and then mapping that to create a trajectory that can help novices to develop similar competencies. In the business arena, Elliott and Folsom (2013) emphasised strongly that modelling the exemplary performers was key to shift the performance curve of the entire workforce and to raise performance levels (and potentially in a shorter time). They fundamentally stressed identifying the differentiating behaviours and replicating them to the remaining workforce, consistent with this strategy. The data analysis of strategy P2.3 indicated that time-to-proficiency was more dependent on the characteristics, attitudes and behaviours of exemplary performers than to their knowledge or skills (or even experience). Characteristics were variables that set them apart from average performers. Existing studies found that performance defined who the exemplary performers were, while their behaviour determined how they became high performers (Bish & Kabanoff 2014; Oldroyd & Morris 2012). The literature showed some trends in using exemplary performers as benchmarks to understand their characteristics (Semali & Buchko 2014).

A complete understanding of success behaviours of exemplary performers may lead to designing targeted interventions or even hiring for those behaviours for that job role (Jones-Moore 2016). Such approach led to an improvement in the time-to-proficiency, without having to put massive training solutions for the future workforce. Strategy P2.3 also suggested that a lengthy cumbersome training program was not required in most instances in order to transfer exemplary success behaviours to the rest of the workforce. It could be as simple as peer coaching, providing a new checklist or a simple set of instructions.

Some project leaders in this study used an extended version of this behavioural modelling in some complex or thinking-intensive jobs to model expert thinking (Clark, Feldon, et al. 2008; Clark, Feldon & Yates 2011). In such cases, several methods such as in-depth knowledge elicitation interviews, think-aloud protocol and observations of experts based on incidents, activity, tasks or decisions and other CTA-based methods were used to understand the cognitive model of experts. This is consistent with previous studies where CTA-based methods were used (Champion et al. 2014; Ericsson 2006b; Feldon et al. 2010; Seager et al. 2011; Velmahos et al. 2004). CTA-based methods have been used in some studies for job roles such as top executive positions (Baxter 2015), life-saving jobs (Klein & Borders 2016) or disaster response personnel (Crichton & Flin 2004). The departure point seen in the present study compared to previous studies is that corporate professionals do not have that much time (as well as specific skills) to conduct time-consuming, detailed

CTA analysis (Clark & Estes 1996). Instead, in most of the project cases in this study, it was seen that strategy P2.3 focussed on identifying success behaviours and then replicating those behaviours to the remaining workforce.

Strategy P2.4—Understand job operating conditions and environmental influences: The strategy 2.4 identified the job operating conditions and the influencing factors in the job environment that could impact time-to-proficiency positively or negatively. The analysis was performed to see how well they enabled or inhibited achieving desired outcomes at a faster rate. The data indicated that despite capabilities of the performers and all the other solutions in place some environmental factors at the job influenced time-to-proficiency profoundly. The factors may be organisational processes, procedures, organisational design, regulatory practices, rigid business protocols or organisational policies. In a study conducted by Yasin and Ali (2016) among 120 banking employees, it was found that work environment was the strongest predictor of the role efficacy (i.e., effectiveness, efficiency and proficiency of an individual in a role) of the employees. Hartt, Quiram and Marken (2016) found that 65% to 74% of performance issues in 327 performance improvement projects could be attributed to organisational or environmental factors alone. Similarly, the factors found in this study may have a positive or negative role in accelerating proficiency, and some factors may need to be taken into account just because they are just going to be there due to the nature of the business. A similar observation was made by Chevalier (2003) who suggested doing force field analysis of information, resources, incentives, motives, capacity, knowledge/skills in an attempt to understand which factors are enablers and which ones are inhibitors. Strategy P2.4 also support the guidelines of the HPT model which advocate conducting detailed environment analysis for performance improvement (Van Tiem, Moseley & Dessinger 2012). The three main analyses included in HPT are workplace analysis, work analysis and worker analysis. The workplace analysis included organisation, resources, tools, stakeholders and competition. For example, Kang (2017) found that out of 30 HPT cases that were analysed from the literature, workplace analysis was conducted in 80% of them.

Strategy P2.5—Analyse roadblocks and hindrances that lead to longer time-to-proficiency: The strategy P2.5 suggests a need to specifically understand the roadblocks and limiting factors that may hamper or negatively impact the speed with which someone gains experience to produce outcomes. Some of the factors noticed in this strategy were resource constraints, cultural barriers, mindsets, beliefs and assumptions people held in the workplace, inefficient management practices or even cumbersome ineffective training design. All of these factors limited the rate at which the new behaviours were adopted and the rate at which new skills were acquired. For example, data suggested that inefficiencies in previous training models in most of the project cases made the time-to-proficiency longer instead of reducing it. Thus, analysis of why current curriculum and training methods are not working is suggested as part of the upfront analysis. Simply eliminating roadblocks, barriers, hindrances or any limiting factors may significantly improve the changes to accelerate proficiency with minimal efforts. No amount of new solutions will work to accelerate proficiency until solutions or strategies are put in place to address these limiting factors and hurdles. Therefore, this strategy dictated that a proficiency reference map (which mapped out such factors) was crucial before investing in any solution to reduce time-to-proficiency. This strategy emphasises and reiterates analysing the limiting factors as suggested by the CWA, HPT and BEM frameworks (Gilbert 2013; Kang 2017; Pollock, Wick & Jefferson 2015; Van Tiem, Moseley & Dessinger 2012). As an observation, none of the participants explicitly recommended conducting training need analysis (TNA) because training was stated as not the only solution at the outset. However, in the cases where training was already determined to be the most appropriate solution to shorten time-to-proficiency, the proficiency reference map may have reduced to a TNA exercise such as job task analysis, person analysis and organisational analysis (Salas et al. 2012).

Practice P2 summary and application. Practice P2 of developing a proficiency reference map recommends a holistic assessment of the job role at three levels: work level, performer level and environment level. The core of this practice is drawing the enablers/disablers to shorten time-to-proficiency by modelling proficiency. The outcome of this practice is a well-documented or well-understood proficiency reference model which can be used for identifying the right people for the job, right performance and training interventions, designing right performance support systems, aligning management and putting up right support systems in place.

5.5.3   Practice P3: Sequencing an efficient proficiency path

The practice P3—'Sequencing an efficient proficiency path' is based on two principles: (1) The mastery of all the skills or knowledge is not required, or at least not required to be learned upfront, to produce a given business outcome; and (2) All the skills included in a training program or otherwise given to a learner are not equally frequent, critical or important for a given job role. This practice set the groundwork to focus on the most important things that matter to deliver a business outcome. There were three strategies P3.1, P3.2 and P3.3 that formed this practice, all of which were inseparable and worked concurrently almost at the same time. These are discussed as follows:

Strategy P3.1—Segment tasks and activities based on characteristics from analytics: The strategy P3.1 suggests the importance of focusing on the things that matter the most at the job towards producing desired outcomes and focusing on the most frequent events (e.g., tasks, skills, transactions, tools, and demand) that a performer is most likely to encounter at his/her job. In the project cases analysed in this study, project leaders used organisational data sources appropriately that led to a better understanding of the patterns and characteristics of the skills, activities, events or tasks in terms of what happened frequently, what was complex, what was critical and important, and what was difficult or error-prone. With this segmentation, it was possible to identify what was required and considered important to attain proficiency. This finding fills an important gap in the literature on behavioural task analysis and cognitive task analysis (CTA), whereby all the skills, tasks and activities suggested by or observed from a subject matter expert receive equal attention. This tendency may lead to a largely over-taught training program. Additionally, the strategy P3.1 suggests extending or supplementing task analysis with data-analytics-based segmentation. Such analysis of tasks or skills may reduce the overall inventory of skills or tasks to be mastered by the performers, thus leading to a shorter time-to-proficiency. This observation supports general trends in the literature that suggested using data-analytics-based instructional approaches (Johnson 2017). However, the current studies done on those lines are inclined towards using learning analytics of the assessment data gathered during or after the interventions (Menchaca, Guenaga & Solabarrieta 2016; Mokhtari, Rosemary & Edwards 2007; Mostafavi, Liu & Barnes 2015; Salas et al. 2016). In business settings, use of data-analytics are mostly focused on business performance (Gunasekaran et al. 2017). Suggesting another line of inquiry, the present study found that upfront data-analytics can significantly reduce the amount of knowledge, skills or content to learn and use in the real job and hence can be an important tool to shorten time-to-proficiency.

Strategy P3.2— Create a logical sequence of experiences as a complete path: The strategy P3.2 suggests the need to map or design the full journey to reach to the desired proficiency in terms of sequence, checkpoints and milestones. That requires establishing a sequence of essential and important things that must happen in certain logical and efficient order. The sequence was based on segmentation associated with strategy P3.1. Project leaders organised and sequenced how things should be experienced by the performers in such a way that allowed the opportunity to work on producing the desired outcomes. The experiences were sequenced by several criteria such as by tasks characteristics (e.g., frequency, complexity, importance, and impact); by some organising principle or central themes (e.g., process flow and product manufacturing sequence); or by methods that ensure proficiency development (e.g., interleaved job shadow with training sessions and spiral practice sessions). The range of criteria specified by this strategy support several separate studies such as sequence content/tasks by practice sessions (Healy 2007); sequence by content type (Koubek, Clarkston & Calvez 1994); sequence by experience level of learners (Kalyuga et al. 2003); sequence by type of skills (Dodd 2009); and sequence by increasing complexity (Bunderson 2011). Sequencing the tasks/activities appropriately was one of the key principles of cognitive apprenticeship advocating sequencing the tasks in an order of increasing complexity and from global to local skills (Boling & Beatty 2010; Collins 2002; Dennen & Burner 2008; Jin & Corbett 2011; Kuo et al. 2012; Lajoie 2009; Vihavainen, Paksula & Luukkainen 2011; Woolley & Jarvis 2007). Similarly, appropriate sequencing of workplace activities, mentoring sessions and job shadow sessions is also a core idea of structured OJT approach (Jacobs 2014a).

The concept of the full proficiency path, as seen in the present study, extends some of the propositions made by earlier researchers. For example, Lajoie (2003, 2009) in concept emphasised that to accelerate journey from novice to expert, the 'trajectory' to expertise must be established and made clear. Billett (2006, p. 38) proposed a concept of workplace learning pathway claiming that 'an ideal intended workplace curriculum comprises the identification and sequencing of work activities that represent the "course to be run"—that lead to full participation in the particular work-practice'. The overarching theme P3 provides strong evidence, as well as an operational framework to Billet and Lajoie's concept, on how this can be done practically. For instance, sports studies have shown the impact of development speed by an appropriate sequence of skills (Taghizadeh & Daneshfar 2014).

The approach of breaking the larger task into smaller parts and then sequencing based on complexity and recurrence was the fundamental premise of the 4C/1D model presented by van Merriënboer, Clark and de Croock (2002). Within the whole-task, clusters of part-tasks are sequenced appropriately based on complexity, as well as recurrence (frequency) to build performance as a whole (Paas & van Gog 2009). This model supported building the whole-task sequence from a training perspective so that performers could integrate the part-tasks efficiently (van Merriënboer, Clark & de Croock 2002; Van Merriënboer & Kester 2008). Similarly, in the present study, the strategy P3.2 emphasises developing a complete proficiency path that gives the full ability to performers to integrate the sub-skills to produce outcomes. While conceptually consistent with the part-task/whole-task approach, this theme extends that concept beyond training into workplace settings. Breaking a task into training tasks and then sequencing for training is probably a very small part of the overall proficiency path sequence designed for accelerating proficiency.

While this study suggests that sequence by complexity is a reasonable strategy to develop a proficient path meant to accelerate proficiency, some studies presented the opposite view. Studies on cognitive flexibility theory (CFT), desirable difficulties and others have suggested not to sequence tasks from easy to difficult, rather to mix the complexity levels and offer highly complex situations to learners first (Bjork & Linn 2006; Bjork 2013; Coulson, Feltovich & Spiro 1997; Spiro et al. 1992).

Strategy P3.3—Optimise the proficiency path for efficiency and time saving: The strategy P3.3 advocates optimising the sequence developed using strategy P3.2 to decrease the time taken by overall sequence and make it more efficient. If the sequence is designed correctly to develop proficiency efficiently, it may decrease the time taken by overall sequence, while ensuring that performers reach target proficiency of producing the results. This strategy suggested a few ways to optimise the sequence such as removing waste, time-efficient delivery channels, performance support systems and time-distributed practice sessions.

One of the ways the sequence was made efficient was by eliminating waste, overlap, redundancies, repetitive content and non-value added activities that did not lead to desired proficiency goals. Some practitioners have shown evidence of such a strategy (Rosenbaum & Williams 2004; Rosenbaum 2014). There is limited evidence of using process improvement tools like Lean Six Sigma, a methodology to remove wasteful activities from any process (see Furterer 2009), to improve the efficacy of curriculum, which is a relatively new area with a limited number of studies (Thomas et al. 2017). This strategy P3.3 provides an encouraging line of inquiry towards eliminating waste to streamline the path towards proficiency and improve efficiency.

If learning interventions were required as part of the sequence, learning was provided using multiple time-efficient channels. For example, delivering on-demand learning through the performance support system almost eliminated any time spent on such learning in classroom settings. The workplace needed something quick for their employees to keep moving. Instead of a block of information, they needed information or knowledge while doing the tasks, at the moment of need and needed it quickly. Performance support systems provided information, help and resources at the time of need while doing the job. If leveraged strategically and appropriately, performance support systems, such as decision support software, checklists, knowledge repository, searchable content, job aids and instant messengers, may eliminate the need for some of the training activities, which again means efficiency in the sequence. This is consistent with benefits of performance support systems, as indicated by some studies (Cagiltay 2006; Gottfredson & Mosher 2011; Mitchell 2014; Raybould 1995; Villachica, Stone & Endicott 2006).

This strategy iterated the necessity to use shorter chunks (or microlearning) which were distributed in time, not because of the reasons of retention as suggested by previous studies, but primarily because of the nature of the work and lack of time in the workplace. Still, the benefits of microlearning are consistent with the literature that supports using shorter segments of content or sessions for better retention (Hug, Lindner & Bruck 2006; Hug 2015; Souza et al. 2015; Zhamanov & Zhamapor 2013). Further, evidence suggests that spaced practice and interleaving led to a slow-down of forgetting, improved learning, increase rate of skill acquisition and resulted in long-term retention (Birnbaum et al. 2013; Karpicke & Bauernschmidt 2011; Sobel, Cepeda & Kapler 2011; Spruit, Band & Hamming 2015; Wang, Zhou & Shah 2014). Shorter segments also made it efficient to deliver information through technology-based platforms for quick access and immediate application. In addition, this strategy emphasises that applying learning close to the point of need in the context of the work, cuts the need for multiple repetition cycles and improves the speed of the proficiency path.

Practice P3 summary and application. The practice of developing an efficient proficiency path is a characteristically different practice than most of the existing practices on designing a personalised or non-personalised learning sequence (of things to learn or preferred order of topics) (Hong et al. 2007; Hsieh & Wang 2010; Janssen, Berlanga & Koper 2010; Zhao & Wan 2006). Some studies have advocated designing and optimising the learning path based on learner profiling and dynamic assessment to speed up content learning and providing multiple pathways (Mostafavi & Barnes 2016; Mostafavi, Liu & Barnes 2015; Muhammad et al. 2016; Tam, Lam & Fung 2014, 2014; Yang, Li & Lau 2014). However, the learning sequence suggested by these studies lean towards sequencing the learning objectives in the instructional interventions through a topic-based or task-based curriculum. Another variation is seen in professional practice studies in which professional competencies are sequenced with appropriate proficiency checks in the form of multi-tier certification (ten Cate 2013). While conceptually it may look similar to concepts in existing studies, the present study's proposition of designing a proficiency path is to: (1) conduct data analytics on activities and tasks performers have performed in the past; (2) use that data to segment characteristics of the events; (3) sequence the activities or tasks most efficiently from day one at the job role until the desired proficiency is achieved (which may be several months or years); and (4) optimise this sequence ensuring that performers reach that stage in the shortest possible time.

5.5.4 Practice P4: Manufacturing accelerated contextual experiences

Practice P4—'Manufacturing accelerated contextual experiences' acknowledges that accelerated proficiency is about gaining real and authentic experience in producing business outcomes at an accelerated rate. The main driver for gaining such an experience is the job itself. Just as a manufacturing plant may not always need to make all the parts to assemble a finished product, the organisation may choose to assemble the required experiences from the available activities or assignments. The organisation may assign an individual to available on-the-job assignments or may decide to design and provide training interventions in a compressed time-frame deliberately. This observation supports the *synthetic learning environment* method proposed by Cannon-Bowers and Bowers (2008). A similar assertion was made in a study with battlefield officers in which Shadrick and Lussier (2009) identified the recurring themes of cognitive behaviours among officers and then designed deliberate training methods on the line of the *Think Like a Commander* (TLAC) program to impart complex expertise and adaptive thinking. Fundamentally, they noticed that manufacturing 'crucible experiences' (id. 302) through 'deliberate focused training approach and research-based scenario development' (id. 303) in a compressed time-frame could 'accelerate the development of adaptable thinking that would otherwise require long time' (id. 302). Practice P4 emphasised to design and pack such deliberate but highly contextual experiences into a compressed time-frame by leveraging a combination of workplace and training interventions. This practice deals with accelerating proficiency in four kinds of situations:

1) Known work situations experienced in the workplace: those situations that occur in the workplace on a regular basis and the job offers plenty of opportunities for experience (Strategy P4.1 and P4.2).

2) Known work situation experienced in a compressed time-frame: those situations which do not happen often but must be mastered immediately (Strategy P4.3).

3) Hard-to-experience work situations experienced through simulations: those situations which are low-frequency, rare or hard to get exposure to and the job does not offer immediate opportunities for experience (Strategy P4.4).

4) Unanticipated work situations which are not fully known as yet, exposed through foundational skills (Strategy P4.5).

Known work situations experienced in the workplace

Strategy P4.1—Assign performers on authentic job activities that allow practice on generating job-specific outcomes: The strategy P4.1 deals with accelerating proficiency in known day-to-day work activities by using the job as the primary mechanism. This strategy suggests having performers to focus on producing the outcomes in the context of a job role using actual use cases, tools and workflows offered by the job. Project leaders in this study assigned performers on the assignments as soon as possible to navigate the challenges, constraints, and dynamics at the job that were known to affect the outcomes. This strategy suggested that learning to do the job and gain proficiency amidst uncertainties, ambiguities, pressures and randomness of a job was a necessity. By being involved in job assignments working independently or under someone's guidance, performers were made to notice how to use different skills in an integrated fashion to achieve job outcomes rather than practising skills or completing tasks in isolation. This approach is consistent with the whole-task approach that advocates integrating part-tasks into a whole-task (Kirschner & van Merriënboer 2007; Van Merriënboer & Kester 2008). The majority of participants did not emphasise much on the part-task approach but rather suggested using the whole-task approach to impart highly integrated and well-rounded skills to accomplish desired outcomes. The whole-task approach is achieved by using the workplace environment that provides highly purposeful and streamlined methods to drive performers towards producing outcomes that are the hallmark of gaining proficiency. This observation is consistent with the position Billett (2002b) took in regards to workplace assignments being highly structured and focused. This theme also indicates that, as much as possible, the job is leveraged as the first choice if job assignments provide a better and faster way to learn and demonstrate how to produce those outcomes rather than putting time and investment on designing cumbersome, lengthy training programs. This is consistent with the literature advocating authentic and situated on-the-job learning within realistic environments (Billett 2006; Eraut

2007a, 2007c; Fenwick 2003; Kooken, Ley & De Hoog 2007; Miller 2003; Tynjälä 2008). The key was to lay out the job assignments deliberately or to create opportunities out of ongoing job activities (in the sequence defined by proficiency path) with the goal of developing proficiency in producing desired business outcomes. In principle, it is similar to the concept of constructing workplace curriculum out of the learning pathway (Billett 2006).

Strategy P4.2—Embed learning into the work and focus on doing the job rather than topic-wise learning:
While the strategy 4.1 suggested assigning performers on to the actual work, the strategy 4.2 recognises the need to learn skills and knowledge to do the job. However, merely learning a topic-by-topic or task-by-task curriculum did not lead to reducing time-to-proficiency. Participants stressed that people gain proficiency faster by doing real challenging work rather than any classroom training. The strategy P4.2 deals with accelerating proficiency in known day-to-day work activities by embedding learning into the work assignments a performer is expected to do. In a thought-provoking question, Hentschel (2017) asked if skills or the job came first and recognised that in reality, the jobs build skills. The analysis indicated that when the focus was on doing the job, learning was automatically drawn out of those experiences anyway. That observation was consistent with the recent movement towards learning through work and day-to-day activities (Billett & Choy 2013; Billett 2014a). Interleaving learning or training sessions with work assignments provided a complete experience to the performer (Billett 2014b). In general, strategy P4.2 supports the existing literature, which is largely focused on the mechanisms of *workplace learning,* i.e., how learning happens in the workplace (Kooken, Ley & De Hoog 2007; Lizier 2015; Tynjälä 2008), while some studies specifically focused on *workplace proficiency,* i.e., how proficiency or expertise is acquired in the workplace (Fadde & Klein 2012; Jacobs & Bu-Rahmah 2012; Miller 2003; Sonnentag & Kleine 2000; van de Wiel & Van den Bossche 2013). Strategy P4.2 extends the concepts of workplace learning and workplace proficiency into *workplace accelerated proficiency,* i.e., how proficiency at workplace is accelerated by suggesting that learning should be embedded into the work with the goal to accomplish job outcomes (doing the job) rather than the goal to achieve the learning outcomes (topic-wise learning).

Known work situations experienced in compressed time-frame

Strategy P4.3—Expose performers to multiple cycles of deliberate and purposeful failures at a rapid rate or in a compressed time-frame: Strategy P4.3 deals with known situations and challenges of a given job role, mastery in which is critical to producing outcomes. The strategy P4.3 suggests that the more anticipated failures to which performers are exposed, the faster they acquire proficiency. Therefore, deliberate, planned, goal-driven, purposeful failures were incorporated into the learning process. Failures are the intense moments that challenge the understanding of performers, make them change strategies and therefore reorganise their ways of thinking and approaches to handling the same problem (DiBello, Missildine & Struttman 2009).

Project leaders chose those failures that ensured providing intense experiences that had significant value towards building proficiency. Failures allowed performers to understand flaws in their own way of thinking and then adopt new ways of thinking. Some participants indicated that they exposed performers to such failure moments multiple times. In some cases, they presented several different failures in a compressed time-frame. Multiple exposures to a wide range of failures within the short term appeared to lead to accelerated proficiency. This strategy is congruent with cognitive transformation theory (CTT), which supports that expertise can be significantly accelerated if the focus is on correcting the flawed mental models rather than filling gaps in knowledge (Klein & Baxter 2009). Furthermore, this strategy supports a similar philosophy used in a study by DiBello, Missildine and Struttman (2009) in which they demonstrated that by exposing workers to multiple failure cycles deliberately designed in a compressed time-frame, led to developing new mental models to handle novel situations.

Strategy P4.3 also suggests that another way of exposing performers to failures is to present deliberate, planned and productive mistakes as opportunities in a controlled environment. Bjork did extensive research on the concept of incorporating desirable or productive failures in learning (Bjork & Bjork 2011; Bjork & Linn 2006; Bjork 2013). They supported that failures that are incorporated must be purpose-driven and difficult but 'in a good way' to promote learning. Lorenzet, Salas and Tannenbaum (2005, p. 319) showed that errors in training increased the performance of the learners and concluded that 'organisations are likely to see a greater return on their training dollars by incorporating errors into training programs'. Usually, as part of the learning process, some mistakes or errors may occur inadvertently, which may also lead to trial-and-error by performers. While some studies highlighted the learning value of such unplanned errors or mistakes (Bauer 2008; Billett 2012; Keith & Frese 2008; Lipsett 2017; Lorenzet, Salas & Tannenbaum 2005; Tulis, Steuer & Dresel 2016), strategy P4.3 in this study did not suggest any evidence to confirm or disconfirm contributions of such mistakes towards shortening time-to-proficiency.

Literature review in section 2.5 suggested adaptive performance as a key focus of previous studies to accelerate proficiency. In three different studies, adaptive flexibility was found to be a predictor of performance as well as acceleration (Boulton & Cole 2016; Güss et al. 2017; Harris et al. 2017). All three studies proposed exposing performers to a range of varied real scenarios would lead to developing adaptive flexibility, which in turn accelerates expertise. Extending the results of these studies, strategy P4.3 suggests that exposing performers to multiple difficult failures or mistakes at a rapid rate would also develop their cognitive flexibility and adaptive expertise towards acceleration of proficiency, as suggested by cognitive flexibility theory (CTF) (Spiro et al. 1992), cognitive transformation theory (CTT) (Klein & Baxter 2009) and desirable failure theory (Bjork & Bjork 2011; Bjork & Linn 2006; Bjork 2013).

Hard-to-experience work situations experienced through simulations

Strategy P4.4—Compress hard-to-obtain experiences on known situations in highly contextualised realistic cases, gamified scenarios and representative simulations: Strategies P4.1 and P4.2 suggested exposing performers to necessary experience using workplace assignments. However, a long wait period may be required before someone gets an opportunity to be involved in a realistic experience at the job if the event happens infrequently (Lesgold & Nahemow 2001; Lesgold 2001; Shadrick, Lussier & Fultz 2007; Shadrick & Lussier 2009). Certain known problems occur at such a low rate that one needs to wait for those events to happen to gain the experience. In some cases, it would be unreasonable and undesirable to wish for a high occurrence rate of certain events (e.g., fire, flood, plane crash, etc.) in order to experience the event in the real-world (Kuchenbrod 2016). The data analysis of strategy P4.4 suggests that rather than waiting for an experience to occur at its own pace, project leaders manufactured those experiences deliberately with similar scenarios, contexts, challenges, emotional loadings and limitations, as would unfold in a real job. This strategy was used if experiences were rare, or if there were no feasible opportunities in the workplace to get exposure to, or if the nature of job demanded those skills for immediate success. In any case, this strategy did not construe delivering blocked, instructor-led, or classroom training per se, rather where possible strategies leveraged workplace and workplace challenges to impart deliberate training.

The fundamental premise the project leaders expressed was that people become proficient faster on rare problems by exposure to difficult real-world cases from the past or designing something that is likely to happen in the future. Hoffman et al. (2014, p. 105) stated 'one could do a form of time compression in which one taps into a corpus of cases that present opportunities for perceptual learning, and thereby "hasten expertise"'. The inference made from this strategy supports studies which expressed the role potential tough cases hold in accelerating expertise (Klein & Borders 2016; Klein, Hintze & Saab 2013; Soule 2016). Some project leaders used technology-driven systems to expose performers to cases or scenarios that could be delivered right in the workplace during the job. Consistent with this, a trend in using technology-driven case-based delivery systems to accelerate proficiency was noted in the literature (Arnold & Collier 2013; Darzi et al. 2011; Jonassen & Hernandez-Serrano 2002; Sottilare & Goldberg 2012).

One component of this strategy also suggested that if the scenarios were unfolded to the performer progressively in form of stages, or like a story as it had happened in real-life, it may have exposed performers to the near-reality situation. Through this they learned to develop their observation, problem-solving and thinking skills to the level required to solve the situation. That leads them to reorganise their thinking processes to handle the problem when it occurs (Jonassen & Hernandez-Serrano 2002). This observation supports evidence from the studies which reported accelerating proficiency by combining gamification, storytelling and simulation (Borders et al. 2015; Harris-Thompson, Malek & Wiggins 2010; Klein & Borders

2016; Klein, Hintze & Saab 2013; Slootmaker et al. 2014). Observations further supported evidence from other studies on using scenario-based training as a successful strategy to accelerate the experience of the performer and increase the transfer of learning to the workplace (Clark 2009; Kreutzer et al. 2016; Salas et al. 2009; Sottilare & Goldberg 2012; Thomsen et al. 2010).

Similarly, simulation is seen as a highly useful method in shortening time-to-proficiency on the events that do not provide enough opportunities in the real-world. The literature provided an abundance of evidence on accelerating proficiency using realistic simulation strategies (Brundage et al. 2014; Brydges et al. 2012; Butler 2012; Clavarelli, Platte & Powers 2009; Fiorella, Vogel-Walcutt & Fiore 2012; Lee 2011; Macdonald 2014; Patterson et al. 2013; Robinson & Pennotti 2013; Seto & Kern 2016). Operational simulation appeared to be the most common strategy in business settings. That involved designing representative simulations, role-plays, or situations to allow performers to practice the skills as much as they needed to build proficiency as close to reality as possible. This strategy is consistent with the literature in which operational simulation has been shown to be a promising method to compress the experience in a shorter time-frame (DiBello, Missildine & Struttman 2009; DiBello & Missildine 2008, 2011; Hoffman et al. 2014). DiBello and Missildine (2013) showed that project management experience could be shortened from years to a few weeks using intense strategic rehearsals through virtual worlds. Operational simulation addresses the idea of time-compression of experience, as Hoffman, Feltovich, et al. (2010, p. 110) contended: 'All of the methods used in training for rapidization and for accelerated proficiency depend on one or another form of time compression'.

Unanticipated unknown work situations

Strategy P4.5—Strengthen generic, transferable, principle-based, fundamental skills to handle unfamiliar or unknown situations: Proficiency was defined for a job role. Thus, a person deemed proficient based on performance standards today should continue to stay proficient in future despite changing dynamics, new situations, and changes in workplace processes, as long as performance standards are the same. Thus, proficient performers require skills to handle not only familiar problems known today, or potential/probable problems that could occur tomorrow, but also need to have the ability to handle unknown, never-seen-before situations proficiently. Project leaders in this study realised that strategies P4.4, particularly of using simulation could build proficiency only for familiar events. Further, within limited time and resources, it was not possible to expose performers to every possible combination of known or probable situations. Even if it were feasible, it would not help in some rapidly changing domains, where new, unfamiliar and never-seen-before situations are very common. Strategy P4.5 infers that the key to accelerating proficiency of performers to handle such novel situations was to build their generic and transferable skills, conceptual skills, thinking skills, and problem-solving and principle-based skills that they could apply to almost any situation, familiar or otherwise. King, Goodson and Rohani (2004, p. 1) recognised that higher-order thinking processes were fundamental skills which were 'activated when individuals encounter unfamiliar problems, uncertainties, questions, or dilemmas'. Similarly, Jacobs (2017) suggested that complex knowledge work in novel situations requires employees to develop skills such as solving a problem, making a decision, conducting an inspection, developing a design, and facilitating a work process.

The literature emphasised the need for developing conceptual skills as part of the learning (Bransford et al. 2004; Deslauriers, Schelew & Wieman 2011; Feldon 2006; Kwon, Rasmussen & Allen 2005). Several researchers identified this strategy with different constructs such as conceptual abstraction (Feldon 2006); conceptual expertise (Vanlehn & van de Sande 2009); knowledge structures (Koubek, Clarkston & Calvez 1994); knowledge representation (Schwartz et al. 2005); and conceptual maps (Spiro et al. 1992). This strategy P4.5 is also congruent with emphasis studies on adaptive expertise placed on developing transferable skills and conceptual knowledge. The literature reviewed in Chapter 2 showed that adaptive expertise was believed to be a key element of accelerating expertise (Lazzara et al. 2010; Mylopoulos et al. 2016; VanLehn & Chi 2012). VanLehn and Chi (2012) established that conceptual and principle-based skills were the key to accelerate future learning, thus preparing learners to handle future problems. While workplace interventions are mostly focused on procedural and cognitive skills on known transactions (Collins 2002; Jacobs 2014a), this strategy adds new insights on the importance of building universal skills in the workplace to accelerate proficiency for future unpredictable challenges.

Practice P4 summary and application. Though indirectly, this practice points towards developing adaptability and flexibility in the performers as a key to accelerate proficiency. Each of the five strategies constituting practice P4 addresses different aspects of providing adaptive and contextual experiences to the performers. Strategy P4.1 advocate using a wide range of projects and assignments at the job as the primary vehicle, while strategy P4.2 suggests embedding the learning into the job activities itself. Strategy P4.3 suggests exposing performers to as many known failures and mistakes as possible in a compressed timeframe, while strategy P4.4 emphasises to expose performers to hard-to-obtain experiences in a short time frame using a variety of simulations or scenarios. Strategy P4.5 reasons to build universal skills to handle unknown and novel situations. Overall, practice P4 directs to deliberate, manufacture or assemble the knowledge required to build an all rounded experience of producing outcomes in all sorts of situations. On a closer examination, it indicates that these strategies are also consistent with some of the principles of CFT (Spiro et al. 1992) and CTT (Klein & Baxter 2009).

5.5.5 Practice P5: Promoting an active emotional immersion

The practice P5—'Promoting an active emotional immersion' is based on the premise that results were produced in the workplace at high speed mainly because of a high level of emotional loading caused by pressures, consequences and stakes a given job carried. Thus, this practice exposed performers to actual workplace challenges that drove the same pressures, consequences, assessment and emotional involvement which were normally associated with that job role. Studies on the constructionist approach to learning (Lesgold 2004), workplace learning (Crouse, Doyle & Young 2011; Lizier 2015; Miller 2003; Tynjälä 2008) and situated learning (Billett 1994; Carter & Adkins 2017; Liew & Harrison 2017; Mills 2011) have made similar assertions on making learning active and realistic. However, performers are usually shielded for the duration of interventions from emotional immersion involvement that comes with doing the job (DiBello, Missildine & Struttman 2009). Contradicting the popular belief, there is also evidence that heavy workload, which generated an immense amount of pressure, in fact, led to much deeper learning (Bernsen, Segers & Tillema 2009). Supporting the latter observation, the practice P5 suggests getting performers immersed into the task actively and emotionally, and exposing them to challenges, pressures, assessment, stakes and consequences normally associated with the job to drive emotional loading. The idea is to drive performers to produce desired outcomes in the shortest time amidst usual unknowns and knowns of the job role to the extent possible. The contextual experiences manufactured through practice P4 and sequenced efficiently through practice P3 are delivered through practice P5 with a very high level of active emotional immersion. This practice uses three strategies, discussed as follows:

Strategy P5.1—Promote active engagement and emotional immersion with the tasks and situations similar to the workplace: The strategy P5.1 suggests that to shorten the time taken for learning to transfer to the workplace, learning experiences in any training program need to include similar kinds of pressures, emotional loading, stakes, consequences, time constraints, performance specifications and team dynamics, as would occur while doing the task in the real job. The strategy P5.1 recognises the emotional loading that comes with pressures, stakes and consequences of the job as an important contributor in shortening workplace proficiency. Some researchers have suggested that emotions are fundamental to every aspect of any work behaviours and central to the human experience (Davachi et al. 2010; Fineman 2003; Langan-Fox et al. 2002). In a series of studies which involved observing and interviewing several emergency response professionals responsible for making quick decisions in high-stress situations (like fire control), emotional loading like exposure to stress, time pressure or ambiguity and consequences contributed towards accelerating performance (Klein 1998). In another study involving newly hired machine operators and office technicians, Taris and Feij (2004) found a very high level of learning on the job when high time pressure was introduced, along with a high level of control. In a later study with home care employees, Taris and Schreurs (2009) found a significant effect of emotional demand of the task on the learning of new behaviours, provided there was a high level of control as well. On the same lines, contrary to the traditional tendency of keeping emotions out of the training or treating emotional loading 'uncontextually' (Nuutinen 2005, p. 290), this theme suggests incorporating emotions and emotional loading while delivering learning. When intense active immersion with the task or situation is created, the pace with which someone acquires experience to produce outcomes is multiplied. It also deepens long-term retention, which in turn impacts time-to-proficiency.

Another component of strategy P5.1 in this study is active engagement, which was increased by delivering training in such a way that allowed performers to produce something, discover something or solve something which was relevant to the job outcomes or job-specific problems. Active engagement with the task was increased by using immersive learning, which is based on job-relevant situations. Experiential learning by doing, solving and discovering has been shown to accelerate performance in several studies (Abston & Rhodes 2013; DuFour et al. 2016; Freeman et al. 2014; Girgis 2011; Jennings & Wargnier 2010; Lesgold 2001). In the context of leadership development, Backus et al. (2010, p. 145) proposed 'actively engage in real-world scenarios and make decisions that result in real-time consequences'. Studies contended that using active, intense and immersive experiences more often resulted in accelerating proficiency (DiBello, Missildine & Struttman 2009; DiBello & Missildine 2011; Grossman, Spencer & Salas 2014).

Strategy P5.2—Provide immediate feedback and allow moments of focused reflection: The strategy P5.2 supports active and emotional immersion in the situation through feedback and reflection. It is inferred from this strategy that feedback was more meaningful when it was immediate or instantaneous. Immediate feedback had an important bearing on learning the right behaviours that impacted the rate of proficiency significantly. Existing literature reinforces that immediate corrective feedback is a powerful accelerator of performance (Andrews & Fitzgerald 2010). Clark (2006, p. 179) suggested that immediate feedback cuts the time for subsequent correction 'well-designed immediate feedback prevents the learning of incorrect knowledge that must later be corrected'. While feedback from trainers and managers is expected, the literature also supports this theme that peer feedback can be leveraged to shorten the learning cycle (Hsu 2016; Jaime et al. 2016; Kreutzer et al. 2016; Lai 2016; Li & Gao 2016).

Strategy P5.2 suggests that the concrete briefing, with focused reflection before, during and after an intense learning activity, allowed internalising the learning faster and eventually led to shorter time-to-proficiency. Numerous reflection moments were planned and deliberately built into the learning, as well as into the feedback loop. Such deliberate actions, which included reflections and immediate feedback, allowed faster absorption of skills and appeared to accelerate performance. Previously, Jacobs (2017, p. 197) noted that '[k]nowledge work is about thinking and acting, and thinking about the actions taken to perform complex work should occur not only during the task, but also after the task has been completed'. The insights noted above are consistent with the literature that suggested structured reflections occur in professional practices such as nursing (Bulman & Schutz 2013; Driscoll 2007). Ge and Hardré (2010) proposed that the learning environment is designed to support expertise development in which scaffolding is incorporated to support reflection and peer feedback. This, in turn, supports metacognition and expertise development. Recently, Beta and Lidaka (2015, p. 1964) identified eight different kinds of reflections that hallmark proficiency of nurses: 'Diverse reflection competence is an inseparable component of proficiency'.

Strategy P5.3—Assess performers through job-specific, continuous, multi-level assessment beyond a training intervention: The strategy P5.3 points towards an important aspect of assessment to accelerate proficiency: assessment must drive the stake and consequences. For that to happen, it is seen in the analysis of this strategy that the assessment criteria, standards and the environment were similar to the actual job outputs being assessed. Such assessments are likely to drive a high level of emotional loading. Some studies supported realistic job-alike assessments using cases or simulations during training interventions. Bennett Jr, Schreiber and Andrews (2002) used job-specific performance assessment embedded in a simulator for near real-time air combat problem-solving. Gander (2006) suggested assessing performers on their role-based work outcomes, which are assessed using the taxonomy of proficiencies set up on a proficiency scale. Some researchers demonstrated proficiency assessment of a team together in simulated settings (Grage et al. 2011; Salas et al. 2008).

Another aspect of assessment noted in strategy P5.3 is that assessment was continuous monitoring of skills and outcomes even beyond training interventions and is continued to be done in the workplace. Studies conducted on Sherlock-I system presented an earlier example in support of continuous assessment while solving problems (Lajoie & Lesgold 1992). A study in dentistry showed recurrent and continuous evidence-based assessment to monitor proficiency throughout a training program (Marshall et al. 2016). Some studies suggested taking assessment outside the training boundaries. For example, Duan, Wu and Bautista (2011) used continuous assessment involving pre- and post-training and at two months' lag period. Some studies have pointed out flaws in trainer-based assessment as more focused on the progression of learning rather than progression or achievement of proficiency (Carter & Bathmaker 2017). Consistent with that strategy, P5.3 also indicated that assessment is not just a trainer's tool. Instead, proficiency assessments were carried out at multiple levels such as at peers' level, at trainers' level, at mentors' level and supervisors' level. Proficiency assessment at managers' level could be as simple as part of the standard performance review cycles and goal settings with the employee. Fundamentally, strategy P5.3 noted that assessment continues until someone reaches a state of proficiency. Thus, rather than a one-time paper-pen event, assessments that contribute to accelerating proficiency are embedded, continuous, distributed, job-specific and conducted at several different levels.

Practice P5 summary and application. The practice P5 of promoting an active emotional immersion establishes that active emotional immersion is created not just with the realistic and challenging job-alike situations, but also through realistic, continuous and multilevel assessments of proficiency. Immediate feedback from peers, managers and trainers creates that immersive involvement as the stakes and consequences are involved with the situations and assessment. Reflection allows performers to get fully involved with the task before, during and after the task. Collectively an intense experience as realistic as the job itself with similar unknown/known variables and dynamics of the workplace contributes towards accelerating proficiency. While all the strategies from this practice are consistent with the literature, this practice highlights the importance of emotional loading and continuous assessments towards accelerating time-to-proficiency.

5.5.6   Practice P6: Setting up a proficiency eco-system

Practice P6—'Setting up a proficiency eco-system' suggests that performers, apart from skills and knowledge and real-life experience, require support, environment, coaching and resources to produce the desired outcomes. Thus, based on the data analysis, the most critical and central component of accelerated proficiency practices was designing a highly supportive eco-system in which a job operated. A supportive eco-system included necessary on-the-job support, coaching, resources, and enablement needed by an employee to be successful in doing his job proficiently. Data shows that a well-designed and well-managed eco-system with the right kind of support and resources to the employee before, during and after the training, and most importantly in the workplace, greatly influenced the speed with which a group of employees attained proficiency. Bransford and Schwartz (2009) emphasised that an ecosystem was important to develop expertise and suggested to 'experiment with objects in one's environment, use technology to find and test information, and work with others in "distributed expertise" teams' (p. 765). This practice was based on six strategies, and is discussed as follows:

Strategy P6.1—Create enabling and supportive environment: The strategy P6.1 highlights that the job environment is an integral part of the eco-system that has both positive and negative impact on time-to-proficiency. Accelerated proficiency is all about being able to successfully produce the outcomes of the job among the dynamics of teams, peers, managers, processes and resources. Thus, the project leaders in this study designed the environment so that it addressed any resource, process or other restrictions within which a job was required to operate. Furthermore, the redesigned environment addressed limiting factors, such as mindset, beliefs, work practices, thinking, and culture, etc., that would potentially limit attaining proficiency faster.

The literature shows significant focus on designing an enabling and supportive environment which addresses not only the conditions of learning but also the bottlenecks, limiting factors and other challenges of the workplace environment (Bjork 2009; Choi, van Merriënboer & Paas 2014; Ge & Hardré 2010; Janssens et al. 2017; Kyndt, Dochy & Nijs 2009; Rikers, van Gog & Paas 2008). However, strategy P6.1 does not refer to classroom or learning environment; rather it suggests setting up the environment of the job which fosters speed to proficiency. Consistent with this, the BEM framework (Chevalier 2003; Gilbert 2013), HPT framework (Kang 2017; Van Tiem, Moseley & Dessinger 2004, 2012) and CWA approach (Fidel & Pejtersen 2004) advocated performing a detailed environmental analysis (similar to the ones suggested in this study) and then put the interventions and processes in place to address any environmental factors to support performance or improve speed to performance.

Strategy P6.2—Structured involvement, accountability, support and reinforcement from manager: The strategy P6.2 communicates the importance placed in this study on the role of managers. Most of the participants believed that the manager had the foremost impact on the rate of proficiency acceleration of his/her people. The results showed that managers were the ones responsible for creating the environment for employees to learn, providing opportunities to practice the skills and setting up the proficiency goals for his/her direct reports. HRD studies have emphasised a similar role of managers in employee development and workplace learning (Beattie 2006; Gratton 2016; McLaughlin 2016; Yen, Trede & Patterson 2016). Researchers recognised that managers were the primary agents who set-up the environment for workplace learning by providing opportunities to employees (Marsick & Watkins 2015). Therefore, it is inferred that unless managers are willing to set up explicit goals aligned to time-to-proficiency targets, it is almost impossible to shorten the time-to-proficiency. That is what makes managers the most critical part of the eco-system.

A managers' systematic involvement before, during and after training interventions was crucial to accelerating proficiency. Managers provided confidence to his/her people by talking to the employees before the training and by setting and clarifying expectations with his/her people. While performers were attending training, the manager's monitoring of progress made a profound impact because performers knew that they have accountabilities and their manager was fully involved in how they utilise their skills and how they produce results. Managers have a crucial role to follow-up with their employees, understand where they needed coaching and what kind of assignments and opportunities could be provided to strengthen the skills and behaviour they have learned (McLaughlin 2016). Managers' reinforcement and monitoring of behaviours after the training events had a significant impact on how soon people came up to speed and use new skills/behaviours (Coates 2007). In an ethnography study at two volunteer organisations involving semi-structured interviews of 60 officials, Beattie (2006) studied the role of a line manager in support of workplace learning. He confirmed that actions taken by managers and the support they provided to their employees had a positive impact on the workplace learning of the employees.

Another component of strategy P6.2 is that managers need to be equipped with the right tools, knowledge, and information to support and coach their staff and to reinforce their employees' behaviours to produce desired outcomes. Typically managers are not well-versed with how people learn and acquire proficiency in the workplace and they leave such affairs to training departments to handle. Such a disappointing lack of manager's involvement appears to be the foremost and the most crucial hurdle towards accelerating proficiency. Several researchers contended that managers needed to be equipped with skills to support their employees and facilitate learning (Kirby et al. 2003). Recognising the need to educate managers, Eraut (2004, p. 268) pointed out in a study that '[o]ur evidence suggests that management styles and local workplace climates affect learning, retention and quality improvement in similar ways. Hence, managers have to be educated and supported for this role'. While existing literature recognised that managers influenced performance greatly, evidence has also suggested the lack of necessary involvement and support from the manager (Hughes 2004; Marsick & Volpe 1999; Woodall 2000). Based on interviews during the first few months of the start of employment of six public-sector employees, Hughes (2004) noticed a disappointing non-involvement of managers in supporting new staff to learn the job. In contrast, when managers were involved, the rate of proficiency was accelerated significantly. In a longitudinal study spread over a 10-month period with 986 first line new leaders at a large global technology firm, Dragoni et al. (2014) found that when experienced senior leaders who were managers of those new leaders coached them with model behaviours, the rate of self-perceived role knowledge accelerated significantly. The literature has recognised the role of managers in performance assessment and management of the employees (Yen, Trede & Patterson 2016). However, how managers impact time-to-proficiency has not been addressed in the literature, which is a key insight suggested by this strategy.

Strategy P6.3—Institute a structured mentoring and coaching process at workplace: The strategy P6.3 represents another key element of the eco-system, which is mentors. The data on this strategy suggested that experiencing the job under someone qualified allowed faster proficiency, as opposed to learning the same task in the classroom. Depending on the activity of the proficiency path, performers were made to work with specific mentors and were assigned specific goals to accomplish. When mentoring was structured, tracked and driven by proficiency goals, it accelerated the time-to-proficiency. This strategy reiterates the application of guided and structured mentoring suggested by the vast amount of classic and seminal studies on cognitive apprenticeship, as reviewed in Chapter 2 (Cash et al. 1996; Collins, Brown & Newman 1989; Collins 2002;

Dennen & Burner 2008; Dennen 2004). Immediate coaching and access to multiple coaches in the workplace (peers, trainers, managers, mentors, etc.) while doing the task made the difference in accelerating proficiency. There were not one coach or mentors. Strategy P6.3 suggests structured mentoring as an important component of a supportive eco-system. The emphasis in this study is on formalising mentoring and putting a systematic structure around it. Strategy P6.3 is consistent with studies on goal-oriented structured mentoring, structured coaching, structured cognitive apprenticeship and structured OJT (Collins, Brown & Newman 1989; Dennen & Burner 2008; Jacobs & Bu-Rahmah 2012; Lajoie 2009). Though not directly considered acceleration of proficiency, some HRD studies have shown empirical evidence regarding the career development of employees (Allen & Eby 2007; Allen et al. 2004; Billett 2003; Ramaswami & Dreher 2007). Productivity and time benefits of structured mentorship including apprenticeship have been reported (US Department of Commerce 2016). While evaluating the learning curves of surgeons, Li, Wang & Ferguson (2014, p. 1154) concluded that 'the presence of mentorship may substantially shorten the time and case load required to achieve proficiency'. On similar lines, structured on-the-job training was believed to accelerate time-to-proficiency for low complexity tasks (Jacobs & Bu-Rahmah 2012; Jacobs 2014a). On the other hand, coaching and mentoring was shown to be one of the key elements that accelerated complex skills like natural decision-making (Grossman, Spencer & Salas 2014).

Recently, medical and healthcare studies reported improved performance and efficiency of residents by using goal-focused structured mentoring and coaching (Aho et al. 2015; Harvey, Ambler & Cahir 2017; Merritt et al. 2017). While human mentoring by experts is unparalleled, new studies have showed that technology-based cognitive apprenticeship with on-demand mentoring also accelerated proficiency (Hoffman & Ward 2015; Mitrovic, Ohlsson & Barrow 2013; Sottilare & Goldberg 2012; Woolley & Jarvis 2007).

Furthermore, strategy P6.3 showed that for accelerating the transfer of skills and behaviours, it is very important that mentors are selected carefully. The pairing of mentor and performer in the workplace is critical to the success of such a high support process. Therefore, to accelerate proficiency, pairing alone may not be sufficient. One component of this strategy is that mentors need to be prepared well and equipped with coaching tools (Alllen & Eby 2011; Hoffman, Feltovich, et al. 2010; Jacobs 2014a). Strategy P6.3 suggests that structured mentoring and coaching processes are very important to accelerate the people in their jobs, especially when organisations choose non-training methods.

Strategy P6.4—Design opportunities for purpose-driven social connectivity and structured informal learning in the workplace: The strategy P6.4 indicates that peers are another important element of the eco-system because people work in teams in the workplace. This strategy recognises that people learn from each other most of the time in the workplace through social interactions and informally. Project leaders using this strategy stressed that the pace of skill acquisition was seen to multiply when people learned and shared with each other. Thus, social interactions, participatory learning and group learning were powerful accelerators of proficiency of the job role as a whole. Participatory and group learning leverages usual team interactions in the workplace within the same dynamics in which a job role operates. Besides that, the community of learners or learning networks acts as a key support element to new performers to connect with each other and access the expert performers to seek help and knowledge (Farnsworth, Kleanthous & Wenger-Trayner 2016; Wenger 2000). As opposed to leaving these interactions and communities to evolve on their own, this strategy suggests designing purpose-driven social interconnectivity opportunities through deliberate actions such as meetings, forums, communities, online systems, messengers and formation of teams. That was in line with participatory learning, social learning and community of practice methodologies suggested by previous researchers (Billett & Choy 2013; Billett & Sweet 2015; Billett 2014a; Carter & Adkins 2017; Farnsworth, Kleanthous & Wenger-Trayner 2016; Mills 2011).

Natural social learning mechanisms of peer sharing peer feedback, debriefings, peer discussions, peer teaching and collaboration are powerful drivers of learning in the workplace (Adams, Karthaus & Rehak 2011; Kyndt, Dochy & Nijs 2009). Previous studies suggested that peer feedback could be a contributor towards a faster rate of proficiency (Hsu 2016; Jaime et al. 2016; Kreutzer et al. 2016; Lai 2016; Li & Gao 2016). However, strategy P6.4 extends the situated learning literature by suggesting to put structure around social connectivity and making it purpose-driven (Farnsworth, Kleanthous & Wenger-Trayner 2016; Mills 2011).

The key advantage of social interconnectivity is channelising the powerful informal learning that happens in the workplace. The literature suggested informal learning as a vast untapped reservoir (Cross 2007; Enos, Kehrhahn & Bell 2003; Eraut 2004; Marsick & Watkins 2015, 2001; Schulz & Roßnagel 2010). In a study of 2,800 telephone operators at a large US telecom company, Liu and Batt (2007) analysed monthly training hours and job performance over a five-month period. They found that workers with average pre-training proficiency achieved greater productivity gains over time through peer training and informal learning. However, Eraut (2004, p. 271) pointed out that there was a lack of management support of informal learning: 'Little attention is given to supporting the learning of subordinates, allocating and organising work, and creating a climate that promotes informal learning'. This strategy P6.4 proposed the solution to that concern by putting purpose-driven structure around pervasive informal learning activities. In a study by Noe, Tews and Michel (2017) involving 180 restaurant managers, it was noted that goal orientation led to more informal learning. Such goal orientation was used while designing a proficiency path in practice P3 with appropriate goals, processes, systems or checklists that are put in place to provide a certain level of structure to informal learning through social interconnectivity. This study supports previous studies with similar findings that deliberate and appropriate conditions need to be provided to make the best use of informal learning. Kyndt, Dochy and Nijs (2009, p. 381) also encouraged organisations to be 'creating occasions for feedback, such as working in teams, debriefings or peer feedback are essential for employees'. Essentially, social interconnectivity and informal learning provide support to performers almost instantly while doing the job, which leads to a faster speed to proficiency.

Strategy P6.5—Deploy on-demand performance support systems embedded in workflow and learning: The strategy P6.5 indicated that appropriately designed performance support systems (PSS) could eliminate the need for most training. Performance support systems are resources that provide support for just-in-time information, help and guidance, decisions support, on-demand learning or other aid in an attempt to quickly accomplish a task. Project leaders in the present study used PSS within training, in addition to training or place of training. However, the primary purpose was consistent with other studies: that is, to provide performers with on-demand content, information, job aids, JIT knowledge and learning resources close to the point of need and during the workflow (Gottfredson & Mosher 2011). Information and support at the time of need in the context of the job or task appeared to support acceleration, while keeping the focus of the performers on producing outcomes rather than learning the content. This strategy is consistent with the literature (Cagiltay 2006; Gal et al. 2017; Gannan 2002; Nguyen 2006; van Schaik, Pearson & Barker 2002). For example, Nguyen, Klein and Sullivan (2005) reported significant differences in performance by using PSS. Strategy P6.5 suggests that PSS could be a powerful contributor to accelerate proficiency. Some studies established that time on task was significantly reduced when PSSs were used in combination with training, as compared when using only PSS (Mitchell 2014). Some studies viewed PSS as performance interventions, and in certain cases they were the only interventions required for a given performance issue (Villachica, Stone & Endicott 2006).

Strategy P6.6—Leverage subject matter experts strategically: The strategy P6.6 suggested that subject matter experts around the workplace are very important supportive resources. Apart from using them as a mentor, as seen in strategy P6.3, subject matter experts were used in a range of ways such as consultant, course designer, just-in-time trainer, assessor, and curriculum reviewer, among many other possibilities. The value was in using them strategically where possible if it gave the advantage to shorten time-to-proficiency. For example, micro-learning sessions were delivered by subject matter experts almost on-demand, which put performers ready to do that part of the job almost instantly. On the contrary, recent studies have shown that SMEs were expensive. They suggested an alternative route of computer-driven mentoring to training new people on decision-making using a ShadowBox method (Borders et al. 2015; Klein & Borders 2016; Klein, Hintze & Saab 2013). In contrast, this strategy suggests that in fact using SMEs strategically could save much time towards proficiency when scaled across all the people in a job role. The literature has yet to explore how subject matter experts are leveraged for other roles to accelerate time-to-proficiency of the remaining workforce.

P6 summary and application: The data analysis positioned the proficiency eco-system as a gatekeeping condition for other practices to be able to reasonably contribute towards shortening time-to-proficiency. Forming a supportive eco-system of the shape and form described in the findings of this study is probably well outside the boundaries of a training department. This practice has been a missing piece of the puzzle on why even the best training strategies do not lead to a shortening of time-to-proficiency. This practice sees designing an eco-system as mostly an organisational-level endeavour, primarily driven by the managers of the employee and has to happen for the business unit as a whole for successful reduction of time-to-proficiency in a given job role.

5.5.7 Propositions from research question #3: Practices and strategies to accelerate proficiency

The process of accelerating proficiency in the workplace is explained through six practices at the business level which are implemented through 24 strategies. The answer to research question #3 is described as one research proposition consisting of six business practices, as summarised in Box 5-3.

Box 5-3: Propositions from research question #3

> Based on the data analysis, following are the answers to research Question #3: What core practices and strategies do business leaders and practitioners adopt to achieve shorter time-to-proficiency of the workforce in a given job?
>
> Proficiency of individuals in a given job role in the workplace is accelerated through six business-level practices/processes which all interact with each other in an input-output-feedback system. Job-role proficiency is positively accelerated when the six business practices are orchestrated together in the workplace as a closely-loop system.
>
> **Defining business-driven proficiency measures**: Any initiative/project setup with a goal to accelerate proficiency and shorten time-to-proficiency at workplace starts with defining proficiency measures based on business needs and then defining current and target time-to-proficiency. This practice specifies starting with the end in mind, defining proficiency and its measures upfront in terms of business outcomes and linking it to business needs. Managers baseline and establish time-to-proficiency targets based on business drivers.
>
> **Developing a proficiency reference map:** The second practice involves developing an overall proficiency reference map mapping out all the inputs required to produce the outcomes in a given job role and mapping out all the conditions and limitations that may influence attaining such outcomes in shorter time. This practice specifies conducting upfront comprehensive work analysis drawn from the outcomes; profiling capabilities and capacities of the job performers; modelling success behaviours of exemplary performers; understanding job operating conditions and environmental influences; and analysing roadblocks and hindrances that lead to longer time-to-proficiency.

Sequencing an efficient proficiency path: The third practice involves sequencing the needed experiences effectively and optimising the sequence to build proficiency in a shorter time and most efficient manner. This practice specifies segmenting tasks and activities based on characteristics from analytics; creating a logical sequence of experiences as a complete path; and optimising the proficiency path for efficiency and time-saving.

Manufacturing accelerated contextual experiences: The fourth practice involves assembling contextual experience for the inputs defined in the proficiency reference map either by leveraging job or by designing interventions. This practice specifies assigning performers on authentic job activities that allow practice on generating job-specific outcomes; embedding learning into work and focus on doing rather than learning; exposing performers to multiple cycles of deliberate and purposeful failures at a rapid rate or in a compressed time-frame; compressing hard-to-obtain experiences on known situations in highly contextualised realistic cases, gamified scenarios and representative simulations; and strengthening generic, transferable, principle-based, fundamental skills to handle unfamiliar or unknown situations.

Promoting an active emotional immersion: The fifth practice involves delivering contextual experiences in such a way that drive active engagement and high emotional loading for the performers. This practice specifies ensuring active engagement and emotional immersion with the tasks and situations similar to the workplace; providing immediate feedback and allow moments of focused reflection; and assessing performers through job-specific, continuous, multi-level assessment beyond a training intervention.

Setting up a proficiency eco-system: The sixth practice involves setting an eco-system around the performers on the job with timely support with resources. This practice specifies creating an enabling and supportive environment; structuring involvement, accountability, support and reinforcement from the manager; instituting a structured mentoring and coaching process in the workplace; designing opportunities for social connectivity and structured informal learning; deploying on-demand performance support systems embedded in workflow and learning; and leveraging subject matter experts strategically.

The six practices are implemented through 24 strategies. Each strategy has a definite purpose and addresses an important element of a given practice. Though a particular strategy may serve its intended purpose on its own, the real results of shorter time-to-proficiency are achieved when all the strategies within a practice are implemented as a process and when all the practices are implemented together as a system to attain meaningful improvement in time-to-proficiency.

5.6 CONCEPTUAL MODEL AND FRAMEWORK

Analysis of the data obtained related to research question #3 led to the identification of overarching themes and emergent themes that were subsequently recognised and re-called as practices and strategies, respectively. The overarching themes identified through qualitative data analysis represent the six core practices business leaders and project leaders appeared to follow without exception. Those business practices determined how proficiency was accelerated systematically. The themes underneath these overarching themes of practices represent the 24 high-level strategies that project leaders implemented in order to support the six core practices. The overarching themes (practices) and themes (strategies) under those practices led to the development of a conceptual model called the *accelerated proficiency model (APM)* and a framework called the *6/24 framework of strategies*. While the 6/24 framework of strategies is a list of six practices and twenty-four strategies in the form of a checklist that are deployed to shorten time-to-proficiency, the accelerated proficiency model depicts the interactions among six practices explaining the general process of managing and monitoring an initiative to shorten time-to-proficiency.

5.6.1 Conceptual model of practices to accelerate proficiency

The data analysis revealed that every project case exhibited six overarching themes to a strong degree that represented business level practices. The data analysis also suggested that each of these practices was being followed like a process. A standalone process typically 'process' some inputs and produce some outputs. Therefore, each practice is viewed as a process as well. Accordingly, in development of the conceptual map, these practices/processes are referred to as: (from P1) *business-driven proficiency measures*, (from P2) *proficiency reference map*, (from P3) *efficient proficiency path*, (from P4) *accelerated contextual experiences*, (from P5) *active emotional immersion*, and (from P6) *proficiency eco-system*. Each practice, when implemented on its own, acts like any other process that may contribute towards improving time-to-proficiency. However, the study findings did not reveal any evidence that implementing any one of the practices/processes in itself would improve time-to-proficiency. Rather, in all the project cases analysed in this study, all six practices/processes were prevalent to varying degrees.

Further, the qualitative data analysis and the concept map that emerged from the participant account, as shown in *Figure 4-9*, suggested that these practices/processes interacted with each other as an input-output system in a way that each practice/process takes certain inputs and requires certain steps to process these inputs into outputs. The best results in shortening time-to-proficiency are achieved when all of these six practices/processes are correctly orchestrated together as a change management 'system'. As a definition, '*system* is a set of objects together with relationships between the objects and between their attributes' (Hall & Fagen 1956, p. 18). Such a view expressed by most of the practitioners is understandable because most of the human resource development models and performance improvement concepts used in business have been described using input-output-feedback systems (Pershing 2006; Van Tiem, Moseley & Dessinger 2012). Researchers reasoned that 'performance cannot be described or improved without specifying its determinants, accounting for the sophisticated processes through which performance is expressed… and making some judgement about whether it has, in fact, improved' (Swanson 1999, p. 7). This viewpoint calls for a system theory to describe performance improvement that involves 'inputs, processes, outputs, and a feedback loop' (Swanson 1999, p. 6). A closed-loop system is represented by inputs, outputs, and a transfer function that transforms those inputs into outputs under some specific conditions or environment (Swanson 1999). The system uses a feedback mechanism to monitor if outputs met previously defined standards used as a reference for comparison. If the output does not meet the desired standards, then adjustments are made to inputs or the conditions until the desired output is achieved. On those lines, several classic and modern researchers contended that the field of performance and human resources was most appropriately represented by system theory (Jacobs 1989, 2014b; Swanson & Holton 2001; Yawson 2013). Such system representation has been the well-established norm for more than half a century to communicate input-output-feedback interactions (Chen 1975).

Accordingly, a systems approach is used in this study to develop the conceptual model of accelerated proficiency from the interpretation of the overarching themes established. This conceptual model represented input-output-feedback interactions among six practices/processes as a closed-loop system (Arnold & Wade 2015; Herrscher 2006). So, the conceptual model developed in this thesis is called *accelerated proficiency model* or APM. The conceptual model developed in this study is consistent with the literature emphasising system-based representation of performance improvement (Jacobs 2014b; Pershing 2006; Rothwell et al. 2000; Van Tiem, Moseley & Dessinger 2012). This conceptual model is shown in *Figure 5-1*. The components of this model based on the data analysis conducted are also explained below.

Magnitude, scale and business drivers: In this model, the magnitude of the problem of time-to-proficiency in a given job role and its scale multiplied to all the employees serving the same role manifest its impact on the business, as explained in sub-section 4.4.1. The impact is expressed in the form of business drivers such as time-related pressures, speed-related competitiveness, skill-related deficiencies or cost and financial implications. The larger the scale, the larger the impact seen on these drivers. These drivers then trigger organisations to see the need for a shorter time-to-proficiency. Once the need is recognised, a project team is typically put in place to run the project.

Business-driven proficiency measures: Once the impact is recognised on any aspect of the business, project efforts are initiated with defining the proficiency and establishing the measures, as explained in sub-section 4.5.1. The proficiency is defined mostly in terms of business outcomes or the observable action that represents the business outcome. Part of this process is to baseline current time-to-proficiency based on historical data or other estimations. The new targets for time-to-proficiency are established based on business needs driving the initiative/project or other organisational goals. The new target for time-to-proficiency becomes the reference of comparison for monitoring any improvement in time-to-proficiency in the project. These actions form the practice/process of *business-driven proficiency measures*.

Proficiency reference map: Next, a thorough analysis of the work, worker and work environment is conducted in order to produce a proficiency reference map. In this map, all the inputs required to produce these desired business outcomes are mapped out. These are the business outcomes which are identified through the process of business-driven proficiency measure. The goal of such a map is to understand what a performer needs and how the performer achieves desired outcomes of the job role within the constraints, limitations, and environmental conditions related to that job role. The first component of the analysis required to create the map is to develop a comprehensive list of inputs such as skills, knowledge, tasks and behaviours required to produce the outcomes, as explained in sub-section 4.5.2. The behaviours are basically the success behaviours demonstrated by the exemplary performers. The capabilities and capacities of the current performers or future performers are assessed. The environment of the job is scanned for operating conditions within which a job role is required to produce the outcomes. The limiting factors that may decelerate speed to outcomes are identified. These actions form the practice/process of the proficiency reference map. This map becomes the overall scope of an accelerated proficiency project. For all the inputs and factors identified in the proficiency reference map, appropriate solutions need to be deployed, which are broadly of two types:

1) The experiences to impart necessary knowledge, skills and behaviours in a manner necessary to produce the outcomes for the job role. These experiences are imparted with the combination of *efficient proficiency path*, *accelerated contextual experience* and *active emotional immersion*. Shown as a transfer function (in the grey box in the conceptual model above), these three practices/processes interact with each other to transform the inputs from the proficiency reference map into the experiences in the most efficient order, so that a performer can deliver the business outcomes in shortest possible time.

2) The enabling systems, resources, tools and processes to address the conditions, environmental factors and limiting factors that influence or come on the way to successfully produce the outcomes or influence the speed with which these outcomes are produced. This enabling support is provided by *proficiency eco-system*.

Efficient proficiency path: This practice/process inside the transfer function involves organising and sequencing the activities, tasks and experiences to create an efficient proficiency path, as explained in sub-section 4.5.3. The tasks and activities are segmented, sequenced and optimised to ensure focus on the most important things that matter, logical progression of activities that build proficiency, and cutting the non-value-added time away from the path. The optimised proficiency path enables performers to reach to the desired performance state most efficiently in the shortest possible time. The path represents the total journey until someone achieves desired proficiency.

Figure 5-1: Conceptual model of accelerated proficiency

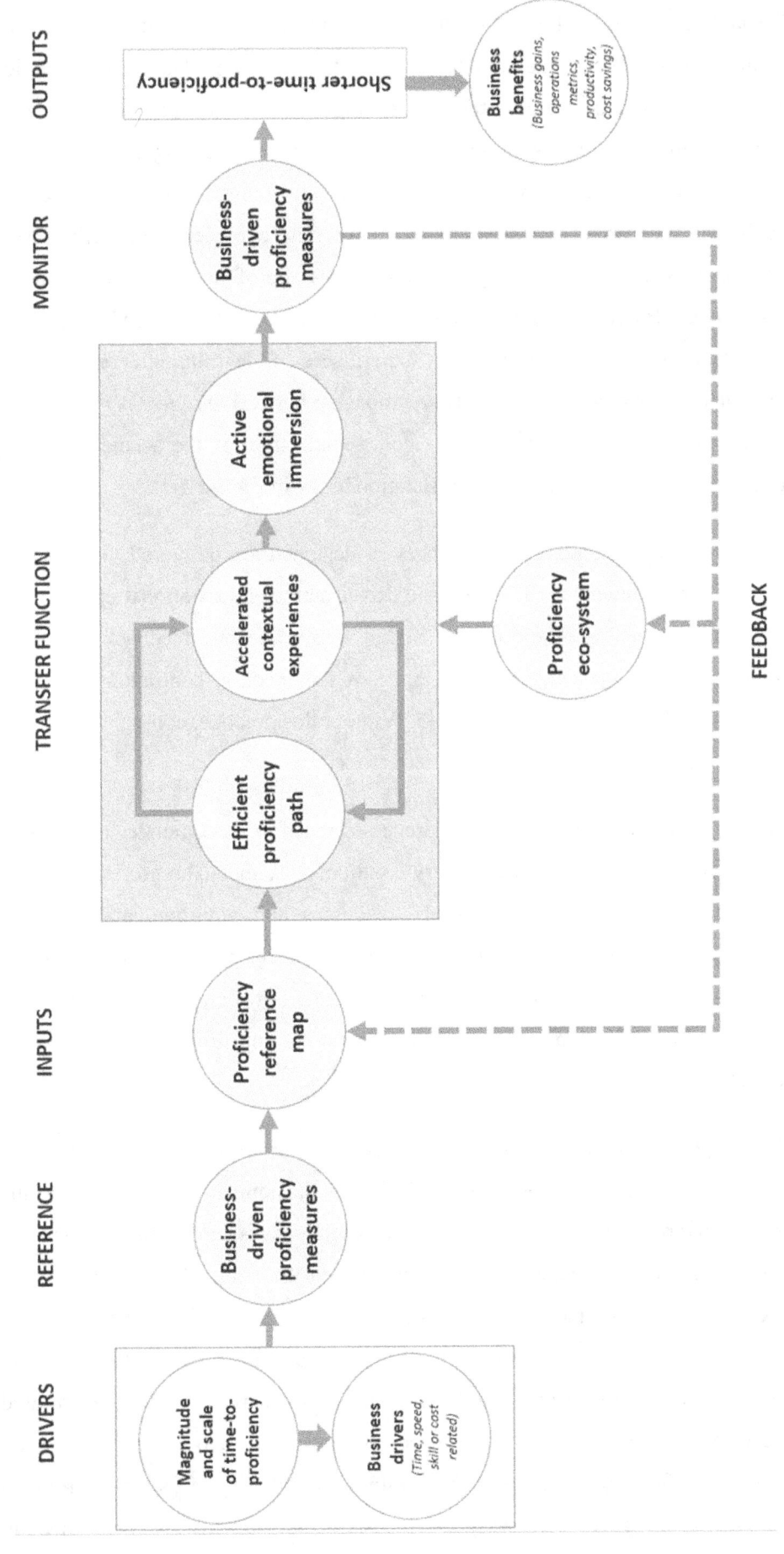

Source: developed for this research study

Accelerated proficiency experiences: This practice/process involves deliberate efforts to convert various components of the proficiency reference map into learning experiences, as explained in sub-section 4.5.4. The learning experiences are manufactured either by leveraging on-the-job activities or by designed focused training interventions in a compressed timeframe. This includes involving the performers on-the-job assignments, embedding the work and learning, focusing on doing the work rather than merely learning, using real-world scenarios and simulations, rapid failure cycles, and building the most fundamental and universal skills. During the segmentation phases of proficiency path creation, decisions are made regarding these experiences about what to be trained upon and what can be leveraged from the workplace. This has a bearing on how the proficiency experiences and learning interventions are finally delivered. Therefore, there is a cyclic back-and-forth relationship between *efficient proficiency path* and *accelerated contextual experiences*, as shown in the conceptualisation of the accelerated proficiency model, with bi-directional arrows inside the transfer function block in *Figure 5-1*.

Active emotional immersion: The learning experiences so designed are delivered in such a way that promotes an active emotional immersion. This practice drives active and emotional engagement of the performer through emotional loading on the tasks, coupled with immediate feedback and moments of reflection. Further, proficiency is tested through a range of job-specific, continuous and multi-level assessment strategies, as explained in sub-section 4.5.5. Without this practice, contextual experiences do not transform into business outcomes.

Proficiency eco-system: The earlier three practices/processes that form the transfer function lead to a shortened time-to-proficiency only if certain necessary conditions are met. The proficiency eco-system represents these enabling conditions, support, tools, resources and environmental advantages, as explained in sub-section 4.5.6. This practice/process addresses the decelerators that may hamper the rate of proficiency and strengthen the accelerators that support the rate of proficiency. An observation in this research indicated that without this supportive proficiency eco-system, time-to-proficiency could not possibly be accelerated.

Feedback loop: The outputs of the transfer function are measured or monitored against target time-to-proficiency with business-driven proficiency measures to identify the point at which performers in a given job have reached the desired proficiency level. New time-to-proficiency is compared with the target time-to-proficiency value. If time-to-proficiency still has not reached the goal, then the feedback loop, as shown in the accelerated proficiency model, drives re-assessment of the proficiency reference map and to the proficiency eco-system to investigate what new factors not known earlier might be inhibiting accelerated proficiency or what new accelerators not identified earlier may now be incorporated. Gaps may be some missing factors not identified in the proficiency reference map or the lack of appropriate support identified in the proficiency eco-system or it could be that the type of support provided is not congruent with the proficiency goals. Necessary corrections or adjustments are made in both of the practices. These adjustments may, in turn, require corresponding changes in the other three practices inside the transfer function. The feedback loop is put in place again. Eventually with appropriate correction and adjustment, desired time-to-proficiency is achieved.

Results/outcomes: The outcome of integration of the above components in the conceptual model leads to shorter time-to-proficiency. The outcome may depend on the degree of the orchestration of all the practices/processes. In addition to shorter time-to-proficiency, other benefits such as business gains, improved productivity, improved operational metrics and cost savings are also realised from these types of projects, as explained in sub-section 4.4.3.

5.6.2 Framework of strategies to shorten time-to-proficiency

The two levels of the hierarchy of overarching themes/practices and the themes/strategies formed a framework that provided a systematic list of actions that an organisation requires to shorten time-to-proficiency. This is shown in *Table 5-6*, and for quick reference is provided in Appendix 41. This framework is called the *6/24 framework of strategies*. While the framework appears as a checklist of practices and strategies, there are input-output-feedback relationships among these practices, as explained in the conceptual model in sub-section 5.6.1, and consequently among the strategies as well. Each strategy has input/output dependency on other strategies. Thus, none of the strategies by themselves may lead to shortening of time-to-proficiency. This checklist framework should be viewed as an operational depiction of the conceptual model of accelerated proficiency, as explained in the sub-section 5.6.1.

5.7 CONCLUSION ON RESEARCH FINDINGS

This section intends to conclude the findings of this research study.

5.7.1 Research question #1: meaning and nature of accelerated proficiency

In this study, participants described how they viewed accelerated proficiency in the workplace. Their responses led to the identification of two overarching themes and eight themes. One overarching theme described the characteristics of proficiency, while the other described the characteristics of accelerated proficiency. The sample size chosen in this study covered the project cases across 10 economic sectors and 20 business sectors. Thus, the understanding of accelerated proficiency phenomena developed in this study could be generalizable to a wide range of contexts and settings. The insight gained in this study advances the body of knowledge significantly and also provides ample pointers for future research.

The understanding of the phenomena of proficiency and accelerated proficiency developed in this study differs significantly from the current literature. A new construct of job-role proficiency emerged from the analysis to explain the true nature of proficiency in the workplace. The job-role proficiency, as suggested in this study, is a state of performance at which performers produce business outcomes or deliverables consistently to the set performance thresholds expected from a given job role. The investigation clarified that job-role proficiency does not imply different stages or levels of performance; rather it refers to achieving one pre-established performance level. It does not convey an individual's task-level performance, or learning/demonstrating a skill, or meeting specified thresholds at one time. The investigation suggested that attaining proficient performance by the workforce and attaining it in a shorter time as possible is a prime concern to organisations. Accelerated proficiency is an effort to shorten the time someone takes in a given job role to reach to a state of consistent performance that meets the set thresholds. This is measured in time-to-proficiency. It appeared that a clearer definition of job-role proficiency and its measures are the foremost critical requirement to the acceleration of proficiency. Investigations clarified that accelerated proficiency is not about learning content faster or shortening the training duration because the solution to a shorter time-to-proficiency lies much beyond training interventions.

5.7.2 Research question #2: driving factors and benefits of accelerated proficiency

A comprehensive analysis of triggers, drivers, importance and benefits of shorter time-to-proficiency was conducted with a large sample size of 60 project cases across the industries examined. The findings shed light on mechanisms of how organisations triggered the projects on reducing time-to-proficiency. The investigation revealed three overarching themes and nine themes that described why it was important for the organisations to find ways to shorten time-to-proficiency and what benefits they attain by doing so. The analysis indicated that the magnitude of time-to-proficiency in any job role is typically significantly large, to the tune of years in most cases. The study enumerated the ranges of time-to-proficiency in various business sectors and job roles. Investigations indicated that this magnitude, when multiplied across all the individuals serving the same job role, becomes a business problem of such a large scale that organisations are not able to ignore its impacts. One of the findings of the study is that the impact of magnitude and scale is usually so large that its impact manifests significantly on one or several of the four business drivers: time-related pressures, speed-related competitiveness, skill-related deficiencies, and cost/financial implications.

Other findings were that substantial business gains, improvement in productivity, improvement of operational metrics and cost-saving or financial gains are achieved when time-to-proficiency is shortened. The findings also clarified that reducing costs and financial implications are not usually the primary drivers that drive organisations to institute initiatives/projects to reduce time-to-proficiency. The thought process is driven by other market forces (e.g., competition, time-to-market, skill shortage). However, financial gains are invariably attained in every such initiative/project. In summary, the findings indicated that the time-to-proficiency business problem is too big for organisations to ignore and it is critical for organisations to address this business challenge because of the impact it has on the workforce, business metrics, profitability, and market competitiveness. The findings could also be generalised to several other contexts.

5.7.3 Research question #3: practices and strategies to accelerate proficiency

In this study, 60 project cases from different contexts were analysed and compared to identify the practices and strategies the project leaders adopted to reduce time-to-proficiency successfully. The crux of the findings is that path to proficiency acceleration is not one-dimension nor is it one strategy. Several organisational elements and functions need to work at the business level to make this happen. The data analysis revealed six core practices and 24 strategies that have been successful in shortening time-to-proficiency in various contexts. These practices are processes in themselves. These six practices/processes are: business-driven proficiency measures, proficiency reference map, efficient proficiency path, accelerated contextual experiences, active emotional immersion and proficiency eco-system. It is seen that there is an input-output-feedback relationship among these six practices, indicating that the practices must work as a system rather than in isolation, particularly if a significant time-to-proficiency reduction is to be achieved. The six practices manifested themselves in the form of 24 strategies that were used to implement these six practices. Each of these strategies in isolation may not hold the potential to shorten time-to-proficiency unless orchestrated together with other strategies as a system.

The magnitude/scale of time-to-proficiency problem and business drivers trigger the need for a shorter time-to-proficiency. The first important practice is to define proficiency measures upfront in terms of business outcomes and then use the same measures to baseline the time-to-proficiency. Business drivers that originally triggered the project govern setting up the target time-to-proficiency. A proficiency reference map is a comprehensive map of all the inputs, factors and conditions in a job role that describes how the business outcomes are being produced and what could accelerate or decelerate the speed to acquire that desired proficiency. A proficiency reference map acts as the input to the overall system. This map consists of work analysis (knowledge, skills, tasks, behaviours, etc.), personal capabilities and capacities of performers, success behaviours of the exemplary performers who achieved faster time-to-proficiency already, inventory of job conditions and environmental factors influencing the outcomes, and finally, all the limiting factors that hamper acceleration of performance in a given job role.

The inputs identified in the proficiency reference map are transformed into desired business outcomes through interactions of three practices — efficient proficiency path, accelerated contextual experiences and active emotional immersion. These three practices constitute a transfer function. A proficiency path is designed by sequencing the most important and essential activities (that lead to attaining business outcomes) appropriately and logically to build proficiency in a shorter time. The proficiency path is optimised by removing waste, using multiple time-efficient delivery channels, and using performance support systems to distribute shorter segments of learning in the context of the job. Next, those experiences are manufactured that then lead to producing outcomes. The key is to provide performers with the experience and knowledge of producing business outcomes, rather than making them learn some skills or perform tasks in isolation. The primary way is to leverage the job itself and to involve the performers in authentic on-the-job assignments. If the experience is not feasible to acquire at the job, the experiences are manufactured using interventions. These experiences are generally assembled quickly at the job, leveraging whatever is available rather than putting massive training programs and lengthy instructional design processes into place. Either way, highly contextual experience is provided in a compressed time-frame using real-world cases, unfolding scenarios and representative simulations in such a way that expose performers to several cycles of failures and mistakes. To handle novel situations, conceptual and principle-based skills of the performers are built. The performers are exposed to these experiences according to the proficiency path sequence. Thus, there is a cyclic adjustment of sequence and decisions on what to leverage from the job and what to design. The final sequence of manufactured contextual experiences is delivered in such a way that drive high active emotional loading onto the participants by having them to work on challenging assignments that include high-stakes consequences and pressures similar to the one exerted by the real job. Feedback and reflection are important elements of such active emotional immersion. Lastly, assessments of proficiency are job-specific, continuous and conducted at multiple levels including assessment by the manager until the desired proficiency is attained.

It is seen that inputs from the proficiency reference map are transformed into desired business outcomes only when necessary support and resources are provided in the form of a proficiency eco-system. The most critical practice revealed in this study is to set up an eco-system which provides support and coaching to the performers when needed. This eco-system consists of structured involvement and support of the manager, purposeful social connectivity and structured informal learning with peers, structured mentoring and coaching from senior experts in the workplace, resources and performance support system for on-demand and JIT support and leveraging the subject matter experts strategically. Proficiency eco-system thus appeared to be the necessary condition for other practices to contribute towards the acceleration of proficiency.

The actual time-to-proficiency is measured and monitored throughout and compared with target time-to-proficiency. A feedback loop determines the necessary adjustments required in the proficiency reference map and proficiency eco-system until the desired time-to-proficiency is attained. The key to these findings is thin the workplace assignment and the job itself is the primary mechanism for accelerating proficiency. Participants expressed that the solution to accelerating proficiency was much beyond training interventions. Formal training interventions take a very small part in the overall spectrum of strategies required to shorten time-to-proficiency. It is no longer a training challenge, but it is an organisational challenge, a business challenge and a managerial challenge. At various business levels, several strategies and systems need to be in place that enables and supports the acceleration of proficiency. Proficiency acceleration needs to be managed as a journey until it finishes within an eco-system in which managers, peers, mentors, exemplary performers, and performance support systems act as critical contributors.

This study generated a framework of six practices and 24 strategies which can be used as a checklist to implement the methods and strategies to accelerate time-to-proficiency of the workforce. A closed system conceptual model is developed from the six practices that explained the mechanisms and process to shorten time-to-proficiency. The large and diverse sample of project cases allowed the researcher to expect that the findings of this study could be highly generalizable across any context with varying degree of use of the six practices revealed.

5.8 CONTRIBUTIONS OF THE STUDY

The findings of this study have made some distinct contributions to the existing literature, body of knowledge, methodology and to practice and are summarised in *Table 5-7*. This study identified eleven overarching themes that characterised various aspects of accelerated proficiency against the research questions under investigation. The study contributed to the literature and body of knowledge through a new construct of job-role proficiency that explained the nature of proficiency in the workplace and differentiated it from other constructs such as individual performance and task proficiency. The study also contributed to the literature by clarifying the boundaries of accelerated proficiency and raising questions about the extent and applicability of training in accelerating proficiency.

This study further contributes to the literature by identifying the magnitude, scale, impact of slow rate of proficiency in the workplace and significance or benefits of accelerating it. The study adds new knowledge regarding the nature and types of drivers that trigger the need for shorter time-to-proficiency, along with the type and extent of business benefits these initiatives/projects can deliver. The findings of this study contributed to form six new constructs for the practices used by organisations to shorten time-to-proficiency. The study also supports the literature on several elements contained in these practices.

Finally, the study contributes to theory development for accelerated proficiency, a gap in the literature that was established in the literature review chapter. The conceptual model of accelerated proficiency contributes towards theory and mechanisms to accelerate proficiency in the workplace, while the 6/24 framework of strategies is a useful checklist for practitioners to implement the strategies that lead to shorter time-to-proficiency. This study, therefore, contributes significantly to advance what is known about accelerated proficiency and how to accelerate proficiency in the workplace.

Contributions made by this study to the methodology are explained in the next section 5.9.

Table 5-7: Contributions of this study

Areas	Contributions
Contribution to extant literature and body of knowledge	
Meaning of job-role proficiency and accelerated proficiency	New theoretical construct explained the nature of job role proficiency as seen by practitioners in the organisations. Contributed three groups of proficiency measures and 15 indicators used by organisations in different contexts for different job roles. Revealed the characteristics and the nature of accelerated proficiency. Distinguished from the constructs of accelerated learning and accelerated training. Specified extent of the role of training solutions to accelerating proficiency.
Driving factors and benefits of shorter time-to-proficiency	Described how organisations recognise the need for shorter time-to-proficiency. Established impact and importance of the business problem of time-to-proficiency by specifying a general range of magnitude and scale of time-to-proficiency in various contexts. Identified four types of business drivers in various contexts that trigger organisations to set up projects to reduce time-to-proficiency of the workforce. Classified four type of business benefits accrued by organisations by shortening time-to-proficiency. Specified range and level of business benefits in different contexts.
Core business-practices to shorten time-to-proficiency	Six new theoretical constructs as business practices to shorten time-to-proficiency. • New knowledge about the centrality of business-driven proficiency measures in terms of outcomes and mechanism to define time-to-proficiency targets. • New knowledge on using success behaviours of exemplary performers over time-consuming CTA methods. Supports existing studies on role of comprehensive work analysis, performer's analysis, environmental analysis and limiting factors analysis. • New knowledge on designing complete proficiency path through the 3-steps process of segmentation, sequencing and optimisation for highly efficient proficiency path. Supports existing studies on the role of sequencing and defining trajectory towards accelerating proficiency. • New knowledge about assembling the experiences as opposed to putting up massive training programs. Supports existing studies on the role of case-based, scenario-based, simulation-based approaches, failure cycles, desirable failures, embedding learning into work, learning through work and conceptual skills. Supports some postulations of cognitive transformation and cognitive flexibility theory towards accelerating proficiency. • New knowledge about using emotional loading with consequences, stakes and pressures to accelerate proficiency. Supports existing studies on role of active engagement, learning by doing/solving/discovering, emotional loading, feedback, reflection and assessment towards accelerating proficiency. • New knowledge about the critical role of eco-system as the main success practice, normally ignored while designing training programs. Supports existing studies on the role of manager's support, social connectivity, informal learning, performance support systems, subject matter experts, and mentoring towards accelerating proficiency.
Contribution to theory	
6/24 framework of strategies	The 2-level hierarchical framework of 6-practices and 24-strategies describes the theoretical bases, factors, determinants and methods to accelerate proficiency.

Accelerated proficiency Model	A conceptual model explaining the theory, dynamics, mechanism, process and practices to accelerate proficiency for the workforce in the organisations. Validated previous studies in HRD and performance improvement, which asserted system approach to performance improvement.
Contribution to methodology	
Social media to recruit participants	Demonstration of using social media and professional databases like LinkedIn to systematically search, connect and recruit a large number of participants with highly relevant experience even for the niche topics. Demonstration of using social media methods and outreach strategies to build credibility, rapport, trust, professional and personal connection to recruit participants.
Internet-mediated in-depth interviews	Evidence of using latest internet-mediated technologies to conduct cost-effective in-depth interviews around the globe, leading to rich data.
Bounded project cases as sampling unit and unit of analysis	Evidence of using bounded project cases as a sampling unit and unit of analysis to analyse the targeted improvement efforts that are generally run in organisations as projects.
Goal-oriented pragmatic approach to research	Demonstration of using the usual goal-oriented approach managers use in their day-to-day job with the pragmatic orientation of 'what works' to solve organisational problems through practice-based scholarly research.
Contribution to practice	
6/24 framework of strategies	The 2-level hierarchical framework of 6-practices and 24-strategies in the form of a checklist for practitioners to implement practices and strategies to shorten time-to-proficiency in the workplace.
60 success stories/ project cases	60 success stories, formatted as start-to-end bounded improvement projects cases, and could be used as case studies in academic courses.

5.9 CONTRIBUTIONS TO METHODOLOGY

This study used certain methods which contributed towards meaningful completion of this research study. These methods may have implications for future business research studies. In addition, this study provides evidence supporting the effectiveness of some of the existing methods employed in this area.

5.9.1 Using social media to recruit participants

As per the *New Ways of Working* report, social media is a powerful channel and expanding fast with mobile platforms penetrating every economy and across business operations (Branson et al. 2015). Trends reported in that report indicate that social media is the way to conduct business, training, consulting networking and marketing in the modern age (Branson et al. 2015). Thus, social media is expanding vigorously globally and across every walk of life. This study provides some encouraging evidence in how business researchers can use professional databases and social media to reach and connect with potential participants, particularly if participants are spread globally and are not previously known to the researcher. This study has employed several techniques to leverage the power of social media to locate, connect and recruit participants from seven countries.

The first technique this study demonstrated was the use of a professional database, such as LinkedIn, to source potential participants. Using LinkedIn, over 300 potential participants were located, though initially it was believed that there were only a handful of experts. Future researchers may leverage such databases to locate participants with the desired characteristics for their studies. A premium subscription to this database allowed searching capabilities with several variables to search from among 500 million professionals from 200 countries.

The second technique used in this research was to build the online presence of the research study. The researcher started new discussion forums on the topic of research. The responses to such discussion forums led to numerous conversations and greater connections. The researcher also started his own research blog to initiate the conversation about this new topic of research. A comprehensive slide set was designed and posted on SlideShare, the world's largest slide sharing social media site. Slides explained the scope, intent, goals, eligibility criteria, engagement protocol and contact details to participate. This was used as an online information sheet in subsequent communication. This site reached over 1,000 hits in a year. Such presence established credibility and reach to the desired set of participants.

The third technique this study demonstrated was building a personal connection with the potential participants. As part of this process, the researcher located the articles and blogs of the potential participants with pertinent experience who were actively writing on the topic of the research study. The researcher read their articles and blogs and commented on ideas to take the online discussion forward. Such online conversations led to further dialogue, debates and exchange of ideas, and eventually professional connections. Such exchanges eventually informed potential participants about the background of this research study and provided them with a channel to express their interest in participating.

5.9.2 Internet-mediated in-depth interviews

Over 95% of the interviews in this study were conducted using the phone or internet-mediated technologies, such as Skype, with 85 participants from seven countries. The scale and spread of this research study showed affirmative results towards strong evidence that internet-based interview methods are in fact powerful vehicles to obtain good reach, quality data and quality participation (Sturges & Hanrahan 2004). Thus, future researchers striving to reach global experts are encouraged to make more use of these multichannel, technology-mediated interviews. Such interviews provided the ability to record conversations, screen sharing and presentations, thus enriching the data collection further.

5.9.3 Bounded project cases as sampling unit and unit of analysis

Surtees (2014) used the project case-based data collection method in which she analysed various project cases. In this present study, the data collection was designed around a format that followed five essential elements of any project structure (define, measure, analyse, implement and control). It is seen that most of the improvement efforts and operational changes are run and managed as temporary projects, and an increasing number of firms are now using project-based teams and project-based organisations (Bakker et al. 2013; Bartsch, Ebers & Maurer 2012; Blindenbach-Driessen & Van Den Ende 2006; Gann & Salter 2000; Lundin et al. 2015). This study suggested that designing interviews and data collection protocols around a project-based structure is highly efficient if the goal is to compare one project to another project or one organisation's processes with another organisation. The advantage of this approach was evident in assigning a priori codes, systematically transfer the project information to comparable matrices and then use within-case and cross-case analysis to derive useful inferences. This methodology has implications for management researchers who either have large sample size available for comparability and generalizability or looking for alternatives to standard case study methodology, which may have some challenges of generalizability across different contexts (Salkind & Rainwater 2012; Yin 2014).

5.9.4 Goal-oriented pragmatic approach to research study

This study demonstrates that managers, business leaders and practitioners in organisations may be able to use goal-oriented methodologies to design research, collect data and conduct data analysis. Practitioners use goal-oriented project management approaches to conduct their day-to-day business in the workplace. Ounaies, Jamoussi and Ghezala (2013) expressed the goal-oriented business approach as keeping the end in mind. In a business context 'end' is expressed in terms of goal, objective, desired result or vision depending upon the operational focus (Berkem 2008; The Business Rules Group 2010). In this research study, the goal-oriented project management approach was used, which was also informed by the pragmatism paradigm to focus on 'what works'. In this study, the researcher used a set of reflective questions grounded in goal-orientation: What exactly are we trying to achieve here? What are the end goals? How does the success or the outcome of the end goal look like? What resources or constraints do we have to achieve the goals? What alternatives or options do I have? While keeping the focus on the goals of the research, these questions acted as 'reflective guidance' to the direction of the investigation (Dowling 2006). Merriam (1998) asserted that even though researchers are required to immerse in the process, every research study still needs to meet a larger goal at the end. Whether the end goal is to understand the problem or to use that knowledge to solve a problem, a research study project is no less than any business project. Therefore, a research project should require a 'businesslike' approach, which warrants a sharp focus on the end goal. Goals or purpose defined the direction of the study. McCaslin and Scott (2003, p. 453) stated the importance of setting the directions from the goals: 'Once that direction is established, we agree with Merriam (1991), that the focus should reside with the process allowing the data to emerge as they may'. Wolcott (1994, p. 387) stressed that researchers must 'learn to "think backward" from an intended end product to guide their thinking about the data they will need and how they will want to use it'.

Finally, this study demonstrated that the usual business and corporate focus on 'what works' can be used in a scholarly fashion to produce useful outcomes through research which indeed solve the real-world business problems encountered by organisations (Fendt, Kaminska-Labbé & Sachs 2008; Gray 2014). Such an orientation may allow business practitioners to focus on the end output of the applied research they intend to produce.

5.10 RECOMMENDATIONS TO PRACTITIONERS

This study produced two major implications for practice. First, the findings of this study indicate that practitioners would benefit from determining precisely what proficiency in a job role means. This study emphasised that proficiency is a state of consistently reproducible performance when an individual produces desired business outcomes consistently over a long period. Proficiency is about the success of a job role in total rather than success on a single task. The second key implication this study suggested for practice is that training is not the only solution to develop or accelerate proficiency. Training does not always lead to the proficiency in a job role. The data analysis indicated that many traditional training models were inefficient, and rather became a hindrance to accelerating proficiency. Shortening time-to-proficiency, therefore requires several solutions including training and non-training solutions.

Table 5-6 summarises the recommendations for practitioners in the form of a checklist consisting of top-level strategies to implement six core practices. The foremost recommendation to practitioners is to develop a definition of proficiency for a given role with as much clarity as possible (Practice P1). For most of the job roles, the time-to-proficiency is long. A clear definition of proficiency leads to goal-orientation, while aligning all the other elements of the organisation towards that goal. It is suggested that an organisation-wide alignment and agreement be sought from various stakeholders so that everyone knows what is being targeted. One agreed definition of proficiency across the stakeholders may align the resources and efforts in same direction. Practitioners are encouraged to avoid the tendency to define performance in terms of activities and tasks. Rather, proficiency should be defined and measured in terms of business outcomes as much as possible (Strategy P1.1). For example, if the success of a salesperson is measured in terms of a number of cold calls s/he made in a month, then the metrics for success (the desired state of proficiency) will be measured in terms of the number of calls made, which would have been an incorrect measure of proficiency. Instead, if the success metrics are specified in terms of revenue generated in a month, then the proficiency is likely to be measured for indications when an individual produces desired revenue for the company consistently. Historical data can be used to identify current (baseline) time-to-proficiency of individuals in a given job role (Strategy P1.2). A pressing business need should drive efforts focused on why organisations need to shorten time-to-proficiency.

If practitioners are serious about shortening time-to-proficiency, then the focus should be on the entire job role, as opposed to skills, knowledge or behaviours-type required to perform some tasks. A comprehensive reference model of proficiency is required to map inputs and factors that contribute positively or negatively towards developing and hampering proficiency, respectively (Practice P2). The general tendency is to start from tasks and then to develop a large list of knowledge, skills, etc., required to do those tasks, which may or may not lead to desired business outcomes. Rather this study's findings suggest starting from the outcomes and going backwards to identify the required knowledge and skills (Strategy P2.1).

By the law of averages, there are usually some exemplary performers in each team and in each job role who may be demonstrating shorter time-to-proficiency compared to rest of the workforce. Such exemplary performers should be identified (Strategy P2.3). Practitioners are strongly encouraged to thoroughly understand, identify and benchmark the success behaviours of such exemplary performers. Simply replicating these behaviours across the remaining workforce may significantly shorten time-to-proficiency. Before doing so, it is suggested that the manager should profile capabilities and capacities of the job performers serving on the given job role whose time-to-proficiency is under observance (Strategy P2.2). Similar profiling may be applied to incoming new performers. However, highly capable performers are not the only determining factor in driving down the time-to-proficiency. More than an individual's capabilities and skills, the environment plays a bigger role in hampering or accelerating speed to proficiency. Therefore, it is imperative to understand the conditions in which performers are required to operate and to analyse the environmental factors that may influence the speed of proficiency (Strategy P2.4). Practitioners should observe various roadblocks such as mindsets, beliefs, assumptions, management factors and even inefficiencies of current training models to identify what could potentially hamper speed to proficiency (Strategy P2.5).

The performers still need to acquire skills, knowledge and behaviours to perform the tasks required to do the job and actually acquire the experience to produce the real business outcomes that are the hallmark of attaining proficiency. As opposed to requiring massive content-heavy, instructor-centric training programs, practitioners are advised to assign performers onto authentic job activities and ongoing practical experiences in which they acquire the experience to produce the desired outcomes (Strategy P4.1). Proficiency is greatly accelerated during the actual job due to pressures, consequences, stakes and contextual immersion of the job-specific tasks. It is strongly recommended that focus should be placed on doing the job rather than learning (Strategy P4.2). Learning will result from this doing. Further, practitioners may consider how to provide experiences to the performers in the context of the overall job, particularly by interleaving training and work assignments and keeping the focus on the complete path to proficiency, i.e., leading to actually producing the outcomes defined for the job rather than just some tasks in isolation.

Not all experiences can be attained on-the-job, however, because then one has to wait for those events to occur to experience them. For those low-frequency experiences, it is recommended that suitable time-compressed experiences are manufactured either through leveraging the job environment or otherwise. The key to such experiences is to expose the performers to a rapid cycle of multiple purposeful failures (Strategy 4.3). The study noted that the more failures one experiences at a rapid rate, more is the rate of acquisition of proficiency. Such failures can be easily recreated by using actual real-world cases that have occurred before, gamifying the scenarios with realistic challenges and deliberate errors the way it would unfold in real-life, and using representative simulation as close as possible to the real environment (Strategy P4.4). Simulations could be on-the-equipment, simulators, operational mock-ups or role-playing the scenarios. Practitioners are advised to manufacture such experiences in a compressed time-frame.

Proficiency is about reproducible performance irrespective of the situation or problems. There will always be a limitation on the number of case scenarios or errors that can be incorporated into a given compressed training experience. To ensure consistent performance in novel situations, emphasis can be on developing employees with strong foundational conceptual skills, problem-solving and critical thinking skills that are principle-based, generic and transferable across unknown situations (Strategy P4.5).

After the experiences have been designed, either using workplace opportunities or manufactured compressed experiences through training interventions, these experiences must be sequenced efficiently. In fact, designing experiences and sequencing those experiences are bi-directional processes in which trade-offs are made regarding what to leverage, what to design and in what order to expose performers to those experiences. The normal tendency in traditional models of proficiency is to include every known aspect into some training program topic-by-topic hoping to position employees towards achieving proficiency. As opposed to the traditional view, this study found that organisations need to design a map of activities, opportunities, learning experiences and milestones representing the complete path of how one would reach desired proficiency in a desired time frame (Practice P3). It is recommended to classify the activities, tasks or events first, using data analytics, and then focus on the most frequent, critical and important activities that directly lead to producing outcomes (Strategy P3.1). The key to shorter time-to-proficiency is sequencing these activities and seeing that the tasks are sequenced efficiently and organised (Strategy P3.2) in such a way to take the waste and non-value added time out from the path by using process improvement philosophy (Strategy P3.3). In practice, time-efficiency is created by using several channels of delivering learning experiences and spreading those experiences over time. Multiple learning strategies and practice opportunities are recommended, rather than using the one teaching/learning method and one block of time.

A highly organised sequence will draw active and emotional engagement of the performer into the task (Practice P5). The more the performers become emotionally involved with a situation with job-like pressure, sense of consequences or stakes and accountabilities in a given assignment, the faster is the rate of acquiring skills. Tasks and situations that are contextually similar to workplace challenges (Strategy P5.1) enhance understanding. Mechanisms of immediate feedback through peers, trainers, managers or otherwise support learning. Further, designed moments of focused reflection during the entire cycle of skill acquisition (Strategy P5.2) enhance learning. Assessment is critical to monitor the proficiency of individuals. As opposed to one-time paper-pen type assessments, designers can incorporate assessments which are job relevant, i.e., tests the performers for producing the outcomes rather than doing the tasks. Assessment at several intervals continuously and much beyond any training intervention till they reach proficiency supports the worker's progress. Proficiency monitoring at various levels such as at trainer's level, manager's level, etc. (strategy P5.3), supports consistency of goals.

The central element of accelerating proficiency is setting up an eco-system that allows proficiency development and acceleration. The components and strategies described earlier would not work unless an enabling and supportive ecosystem is implemented (Practice P6). The manager's role in terms of his/her involvement, support, coaching and ownership is the centrepiece of the eco-system. Shortening time-to-proficiency is not the training department's job. Rather, the onus is on managers because they are the ones who are first responsible for creating a supportive and enabling environment in which proficiency grows (Strategy P6.1). Managers are the ones who provide the opportunities, assignments and reinforcement to achieve outcomes, monitor the workers, and finally review their performance. Business leaders are strongly urged to bring their managers into the process of defining proficiency of their employees, baseline time-to-proficiency, involve early in planning phases systematically, enable and equip them with tools or techniques they need to support and coach their employees, and hold them accountable for monitoring results of time-to-proficiency from their employees rather than assuming that they would do so (Strategy P6.2).

The study findings revealed that making someone learn to produce outcomes is a much faster approach than having him/her learn those things in the classroom. Practitioners are guided to make sure a structured mentoring and coaching process exists in which new people can learn and practice under a qualified mentor (Strategy P6.3). It is suggested that managers select the right mentors and then equip them with the right skills to mentor other people. Structured mentoring needs an outcome-driven focus so that people are put on the path that allows them to become proficient in producing desired outcomes. Managers play a critical role in putting such a process in motion. The study findings also indicated that social learning was a powerful multiplier that fostered proficiency in a given job role at an accelerated rate. Employees worked in teams and produced business results in the team. It is recommended that organisations pay attention to purpose-driven social connectivity where people work with each other, develop learning networks and develop connections with high performers (Strategy P6.4). In addition, while informal learning is considered to be happening on-the-fly, ad hoc and unmanageable, leaders can create a structure for informal learning experiences so that those avenues are used to drive proficiency. For example, a person assigned to shadow a senior employee in the field should be given a checklist of things to observe, ask or perform, thus putting a structure around informal learning that happens on-the-job. Since managers manage the teams, they play an important role in fostering and developing such purpose-driven social connectivity.

The study findings suggested that using the right performance support, such as knowledge repository, just-in-time information, checklists and technology-based tools, could eliminate the need for any formal training if orchestrated correctly. This study's findings supported the recommendation of implementing a range of performance systems and leveraging institutionalised systems that improve how quickly people get support at the point of need (Strategy P6.5). Finally, the study results indicated that successful organisations leverage their SMEs in the range of activities such as defining proficiency, designing training, designing assessments, and coaching people, among others. It is recommended that practitioners design into their processes how the experts are leveraged and used to accelerate the proficiency of new people, as opposed to just using them to instruct (Strategy P6.6).

As a concluding remark, accelerated proficiency appears to be a system in which various elements must work effectively with each other to shorten the time-to-proficiency. Practitioners are encouraged to avoid silos — training programs designed within closed boundaries of classrooms away from the job. Rather, they are urged to look at the challenge as a business problem which requires several solutions of training and non-training types of activities interwoven together to deliver shortened time-to-proficiency. It should be noted that though the checklist of strategies is shown as a list, there are complex interactions among practices and strategies in a closed-loop system, as seen in the conceptual model. Like any other system, there are several decisions and trade-offs involved and it is not necessary to implement every strategy in a given context for a given business challenge. Several existing systems, resources, methods and information sources can be used and leveraged or as a proxy to implement the six practices at a high level.

5.11 LIMITATIONS OF THE STUDY

As with any research, the limitations of this research study may affect the validity of the findings and generalizability. Three limitations were identified in this research study. The first limitation is in regards to the nature of the project case samples. The samples included in this study were the project cases that were already completed successfully. To ensure that the project cases demonstrated proven results in improving time-to-proficiency, the focus was on completed projects. The projects in organisations are typically executed by teams, and such teams are formed as a temporary endeavour to achieve specific goals. After the project goals are accomplished, the team is usually disintegrated and team members are assigned to other projects fitting their skills. Thus, not all team members for a given project could be located. Further, the teams are usually large, globally diverse and consist not only of one organisation but many vendors, consultants and organisations. Access to project teams, stakeholders and clients of the same projects was not possible. Therefore, locating individual team members of each project case was not feasible. This also meant that an in-depth understanding of few project cases using the case-study approach was not feasible after any of the project cases were completed. In this study, the primary source of data collection was the project leaders themselves who had conducted time-to-proficiency projects with evidence of success. The in-depth interviews were conducted mainly with the project leader(s) only, who usually have firsthand, in-depth knowledge about the project. The documents were collected from project leaders or public sources. Thus, the perspective on concepts, practices and strategies are purely based on the individual account of a given project case. The limitation of the project cases was that project cases lacked details and perspectives from other members of the project, stakeholders, customers and other entities, unlike the case-study methodology.

The second limitation is related to the amount of data collected. While there were initial concerns about a probable low rate of participation in this study due to the niche nature of the research topic, the study actually led to an overwhelming response from the practitioner community. Therefore, the study generated a large amount of data that was a challenge in itself to handle. In such a large data set, within a limited period, it was not feasible to analyse all the pertinent aspects and issues reported in the data. Thus, certain trade-offs were made not to analyse some issues. For example, aspects such as the role of technology, the role of organisational infrastructure, organisational culture, and size and scale of the organisations were not given attention while focusing on the main research questions. The data also reported a significant amount of information on training strategies that did not work towards accelerating proficiency. The study focused only on strategies that worked. Further, a large part of the training strategies that were reported as not being supportive of the goal of time-to-proficiency were excluded from the analysis.

The third limitation is related to the separation from any specific contextual settings. The 66 project cases collected in this study came from a range of business settings. No attempt was made to position the study in a particular context or business sector to develop a deeper understanding within that sector. The rationale for doing so was that since an overall general understanding of the accelerated proficiency phenomenon itself was lacking across the board, it was imperative to understand the phenomenon and generic model of accelerating proficiency. Despite these limitations, meaningful results were achieved against the three research questions and have subsequently led to suggestions for future research (as reported in the following section 5.12).

5.12 DIRECTIONS FOR FUTURE RESEARCH

The focus of the research questions placed certain boundaries and limitations on the aspects of what could and could not be studied in this thesis. Methodological choices limited the extent of the findings and aspects revealed in this study. While the qualitative approaches employed revealed some aspects, quantitative approaches may have suggested others. There are several possibilities suggested by this study that requires further analysis and investigation. However, these possibilities were beyond the scope of this research study. The limitation of this research study recognised key areas that future researchers can extend upon. Specifically, there are five major areas or topics on which further research can be carried out. These are: (1) building a sustainable theory of accelerated proficiency; (2) testing accelerated proficiency model; (3) analysing factors affecting accelerated proficiency; (4) developing guidelines for practitioners; and (5) case study of implementation.

5.12.1 Building theory of accelerated proficiency

From an organisational standpoint, no validated theory was found to assist practitioners in implementing programs and practices to shorten time-to-proficiency in the workplace. The current literature delves more into either basic readiness of novice workers on one side of the scale or developing the expertise of professionals at the higher end of the scale. This study attempted to create a knowledge base and model on the accelerated proficiency of workforce that has immediate business meaning. While this research study revealed several aspects of proficiency in the workplace and concepts to accelerate it, further research is warranted to understand each of the aspects in details. Though the sample size in this study was large enough for a qualitative study, the aspects revealed were subject to the experience and background of the participants recruited in the study. Access to practitioners from different domains or disciplines could have revealed further aspects. As such, future research studies may position their research studies in other contexts. Empirical and experimental studies on developing and accelerating expertise and high proficiency have been widely published, but further research is required on accelerating proficiency in practice and professions. It is suggested that further accelerated proficiency research could be either conducted from a holistic angle in terms of the application of the model into work settings or conduct in-depth research into each of the practices individually. Another potential area to investigate for future research could be to compare and contrast concepts of accelerated proficiency/accelerated expertise (as seen in the literature) versus the actual practice (Hoffman et al. 2014). A survey of practices/strategies as indicated by a review of previous studies could be carried out and administered with participants in an attempt to better understand the extent of usage and level of success of those practices/strategies in the workplace.

5.12.2 Testing and expanding accelerated proficiency model

While the model developed in this study is rich with details and guidance, it was developed based on the qualitative account of project cases gathered during the study. It is recommended that researchers test the model developed in this research using a quantitative research survey. The survey may be designed to understand the extent of practices used by other organisations that have already achieved shorter time-to-proficiency. The responses may be analysed to understand which of the six practices enumerated in this study contributed significantly to another success story. A six-hypothesis study may be appropriate. The researcher may be in a better position to test if all six of the practices need to be presented to shorten time-to-proficiency successfully. Future researchers may be able to test the interactions between the six practices, as depicted in the theoretical model. This study specified 24 strategies that organisations may use to implement the six practices. A detailed quantitative research can be carried out to test whether the specified strategies contributed towards accelerated proficiency. Such research may further establish an evidence-based framework of strategies to shorten time-to-proficiency.

5.12.3 Analysing factors affecting accelerated proficiency

The focus of this study was to understand the practices that contribute towards accelerating proficiency. This study did not address the factors that impact the rate of proficiency acquisition. Future research may be feasible using quantitative or qualitative studies to identify the factors that impact the implementation or success of the overall accelerated proficiency model. Factor analysis may enrich the theory and model of accelerated proficiency proposed in this research. Some factors appear to impact on the rate of proficiency acceleration. However, the exact nature of the effect and extent of the effect may be worth investigating. The first factor to consider is the scale and size of the organisation.

In this study, the focus was on contextual variables such as economy sector, business sector, an industry group, job role type and primary skills involved to address wider contexts. Therefore, the size and scale of an organisation were not the determining factors for the diversity of the samples. Future research studies may consider sampling organisations based on size and scale and do a comparative analysis of such practices. Future research may also investigate how many types of practices being used in large organisations are different from those used in smaller organisations. The second factor that could be studied is how technology contributes to accelerating proficiency and shortening time-to-proficiency. The organisations studied in this study were mostly large-scale, complex organisations, several of them with a global presence and widespread business operations. In such complex environments, developing and accelerating proficiency depends highly on infrastructural advantages and technologies in the workplace. Some participants mentioned the role of technologies and technology-based infrastructures such as knowledge management systems, Google-type search capabilities, mobile learning and mobile coaching and similar tools. There a timing issue in this regard. The initiatives/projects meant to reduce time-to-proficiency are typically run for two or more years before the results are available. That means there is an inherent obsolescence of methods or practices in any time-to-proficiency reduction case study. Therefore, some of the recent advances in technology towards accelerating time-to-proficiency may still be underway in some organisations, but results may not be available until one to two years after the study. This lag is challenging and may sometimes raise questions on contributions of the latest and greatest methodologies, practices and technologies. Therefore, the role of technology did not reveal any relationship or use case. However, this study acknowledged the potential effect of technologies given the convergence of learning, work and mentoring, networking and performance. Future studies may address this limitation by investigating how technology contributes to accelerating proficiency and shortening time-to-proficiency.

The third important factor inviting further academic attention is organisational infrastructure and culture. This study revealed six practices that were instrumental in accelerating proficiency across a range of contexts. However, some of the practices required tight collaboration between business managers and training department people. Further, any organisation operates in a pre-defined fashion determined by their business challenges, nature of business and culture. It is anticipated that just to accelerate proficiency of a given job role, the organisation would not start operating differently in a few weeks. Rather, they may invest in changing a few processes or instituting those processes within their current operational landscape. Such processes require investment and change management thought processes. Organisational dynamics, working culture, employee performance standards, willingness to adapt, pressures and criticality of the job, and availability of world-class infrastructure to the workforce may be acknowledged as noise in the model. The effect of these factors has not been considered or accounted for in this study. Future research studies may note this limitation and may study the role of organisational infrastructure and culture as an intermediate factor to accelerate proficiency. Finally, the fourth potential factor is about how buy-in and top management's support impacts the initiatives/projects setup to reduce time-to-proficiency. While this study recognises the strong buy-in and support from management as the critical factor for the success of any time-to-proficiency reduction initiatives, it did not explore how managers convince their top management to invest in such initiatives. In this study, it was noted that a deliberate planning and systematic processes were required if an organisation is serious about shortening time-to-proficiency. Initial setup and change management may invite heavy investment upfront. Though the goal of such initiatives is to compress time as much as possible, it does take a certain amount of time. For example, in one technology-related job, time-to-proficiency was shortened from three years to two years. Moreover, until after two years, the return on investment on a project and success of accelerated proficiency practices cannot be established. Thus, shortening time-to-proficiency could be several years, with outcomes of such projects not being immediately available. How to convince management of such wait times and to achieve buy-in to apply the accelerated proficiency model is a critical issue. Future researchers may address such upfront project planning processes.

5.12.4 Generating context-specific guidelines for practitioners

While an attempt has been made to provide a certain level of guidance to practitioners to implement the model through twenty-four strategies, the same strategy could be implemented differently by different organisations. The methods, tactics and techniques may be highly context-dependent. For example, the strategy of an on-demand performance support system may present differently in a job role of floor technician compared to a data analyst's job role. While this research provides generic guidelines at the practical and strategic levels that can steer the thought processes of business leaders, researchers in specific disciplines may extend to provide guidelines to method level in a given context. Such a research outcome may lead to a higher acceptability among practitioners.

5.12.5 Conducting case study of implementation

Future researchers may perform in-depth analysis of few case studies within the same organisation or across several organisations to validate the model proposed in this research. Though this research study validated the applicability of practices in various contexts, the value of this research will be realised when the model is actually implemented and tested in practice, which could lead to financial and business benefits anticipated from this research outcome. It is suggested that organisations or practitioners could take the model, identify the methods best meeting their business operations and needs, and implement the model in their own context. Such research could be a long-term research case study spanning from a few months to a few years depending upon the nature of the job. This outcome will establish an evidence-based empirical research model. Another way this research study could be extended is to consider a case-study based research project. In this method, researchers can use the model developed in this study as a reference and can audit processes and practices in a given organisation and map the specific methods being used to the general framework of strategies specified in this study. Such research could validate the model for transferability and generalizability purposes.

5.13 CHAPTER SUMMARY

This concluding chapter presented the discussion and implications of major findings for each of the three research questions. The first research question described the characteristics of the job role proficiency construct and accelerated proficiency phenomenon in the workplace. Two research propositions were drawn from this question. The second research question explained how and why accelerating proficiency is important to organisations. One research proposition was drawn from this research question. The third research question identified six practices/processes that explained how organisations can accelerate proficiency. This research question identified twenty-four strategies that are used by organisations to shorten time-to-proficiency. A conceptual model (called accelerated proficiency model or APM) was developed describing the interactions of the six practices/processes that govern how proficiency is accelerated in the workplace. From this research question, a two-level hierarchical framework consisting of six practices and twenty-four strategies (called the 6/24 framework of strategies) emerged. This study has advanced the literature and knowledge in the area of accelerated proficiency and has identified practices/strategies to shorten time-to-proficiency in the workplace. The findings of this research study are promising, with a range of implications and benefits to both theory and practice. The study outcomes contributed to the existing literature and body of knowledge on accelerated proficiency. Finally, this research study provided several possibilities for further academic and practice-based research.

REFERENCES

Abston, KA & Rhodes, MK 2013, 'Experiential learning in accelerated human resource management courses', *Developments in Business Simulation and Experiential Learning*, vol. 40, pp. 68–73, viewed 24 June 2017, <https://absel-ojs-ttu.tdl.org/absel/index.php/absel/article/download/19/17>.

Accenture 2013, *Top-Five Focus Areas for Improving Sales Effectiveness Initiatives*, viewed 24 June 2017, <https://www.accenture.com/t20150523T052741__w__/us-en/_acnmedia/Accenture/Conversion-Assets/DotCom/Documents/Global/PDF/Strategy_4/Accenture-Top-Five-Improvements-Sales-Effectiveness.pdf>.

Ackerman, PL 1988, 'Determinants of individual differences during skill acquisition: cognitive abilities and information processing', *Journal of Experimental Psychology General*, vol. 117, no. 3, pp. 288–318, http://dx.doi.org/10.1037/0096-3445.117.3.288.

―――― 1992, 'Predicting individual differences in complex skill acquisition: dynamics of ability determinants', *Journal of Applied Psychology*, vol. 77, no. 5, pp. 598–614, http://dx.doi.org/10.1037/0021-9010.77.5.598.

―――― 2014, 'Nonsense, common sense, and science of expert performance: talent and individual differences', *Intelligence*, vol. 45, no. 4, pp. 6–17, http://dx.doi.org/10.1016/j.intell.2013.04.009.

Adams, BD, Karthaus, C & Rehak, LA 2011, *Accelerated Learning and Retention: Literature Review and Workshop Review*, Report No. CR 2011-105, Defense R&D Canada, Toronto, Canada, viewed 24 June 2017, <http://www.dtic.mil/cgi-bin/GetTRDoc?AD=ADA574124>.

Adamson, J, Gooberman-Hill, R, Woolhead, G & Donovan, J 2004, "'Questerviews': and quantitative health services research using questionnaires in qualitative interviews as a method of integrating qualitative', *Journal of Health Services Research & Policy*, vol. 9, no. 3, pp. 139–45, http://dx.doi.org/10.1258/1355819041403268.

Afiouni, F 2007, 'Human resource management and knowledge management: a road map toward improving organisational performance', *Journal of American Academy of Business*, vol. 11, no. 2, pp. 124–130, viewed 24 June 2017, <http://www.academia.edu/download/31163403/HR_and_KM.pdf>.

Aho, JM, Ruparel, RK, Graham, E, Zendejas-Mummert, B, Heller, SF, Farley, DR & Bingener, J 2015, 'Mentor-guided self-directed learning affects resident practice', *Journal of Surgical Education*, vol. 72, no. 4, pp. 674–679, http://dx.doi.org/10.1016/j.jsurg.2015.01.008.

Albrecht, SL, Bakker, AB, Gruman, JA, Macey, WH & Saks, AM 2015, 'Employee engagement, human resource management practices and competitive advantage: an integrated approach', *Journal of Organisational Effectiveness: People and Performance*, vol. 2, no. 1, pp. 7–35, http://dx.doi.org/10.1108/JOEPP-08-2014-0042.

Alexander, PA 2003a, 'Can we get there from here?', *Educational Researcher*, vol. 32, no. 8, pp. 3–4, http://dx.doi.org/10.3102/0013189X032008003.

―――― 2003b, 'The development of expertise: the journey from acclimation to proficiency', *Educational Researcher*, vol. 32, no. 8, pp. 10–14, http://dx.doi.org/10.3102/0013189X032008010.

Alhojailan, MI 2012, 'Thematic analysis: a critical review of its process and evaluation', *WEI International European Academic Conference Proceedings*, Zagreb, Croatia, 14-17 October, West East Institute, West Chester, pp. 8–21, viewed 24 June 2017, <http://www.westeastinstitute.com/journals/wp-content/uploads/2013/02/4-Mohammed-Ibrahim-Alhojailan-Full-Paper-Thematic-Analysis-A-Critical-Review-Of-Its-Process-And-Evaluation.pdf>.

Alllen, TD & Eby, LT (eds.) 2011, *The Blackwell Handbook of Mentoring: A multiple Perspectives Approach*, Blackwell, Victoria, Australia, viewed 24 June 2017, <https://www.researchgate.net/publication/295660090>.

Allen, TD, Eby, LT, Poteet, ML, Lentz, E & Lima, L 2004, 'Career benefits associated with mentoring for protégés: a meta-analysis', *Journal of Applied Psychology*, vol. 89, no. 1, p. 127, http://dx.doi.org/10.1037/0021-9010.89.1.127.

Andresen, L, Boud, D & Cohen, R 2000, Experience-based learning, in G Foley (ed.), *Understanding Adult Education and Training*, Allen and Unwin, Crows Nest, pp. 225–239.

Anderson, JR 1981, *Acquisition of Cognitive Skill*, Report No. 81-1, Carnegie-Mellon University, viewed 24 June 2017, <http://www.dtic.mil/cgi-bin/GetTRDoc?AD=ADA103283>.

―――― 1982, 'Acquisition of cognitive skill', *Psychological Review*, vol. 89, no. 4, pp. 369–406, http://dx.doi.org/10.1037/0033-295X.89.4.369.

―――― 2000, *Learning and memory*, John Wiley, New York.

Andersson, AW, Jansson, A, Sandblad, B & Tschirner, S 2014, Recognizing complexity: visualization for skilled professionals in complex work situations, in A Ebert, G van der Veer, G Domik, N Gershon & I Scheler (eds.), *Building Bridges: HCI, Visualization, and Non-formal Modeling*, Lecture notes in computer science, vol 8345, Springer, Berlin Heidelberg, Germany, pp. 47–66, http://dx.doi.org/10.1007/978-3-642-54894-9_5.

Andrews, DH & Fitzgerald, P 2010, 'Accelerating learning of competence and increasing long-term learning retention', paper presented to the ITEC Conference, London, 18-20 May, viewed 24 June 2017, <http://www.dtic.mil/cgi-bin/GetTRDoc?AD=ADA522088>.

Angelo, RL, Ryu, RK, Pedowitz, RA, Beach, W, Burns, J, Dodds, J, Field, L, Getelman, M, Hobgood, R, McIntyre, L & others 2015, 'A proficiency-based progression training curriculum coupled with a model simulator results in the acquisition of a superior arthroscopic bankart skill set', *Arthroscopy: The Journal of Arthroscopic & Related Surgery*, vol. 31, no. 10, pp. 1854–1871, viewed 24 June 2017, <https://www.ucc.ie/en/media/academic/assertforhealth/assertdocs/1.1-s2.0-S0749806315005836-main.pdf>.

Anitha, J 2014, 'Determinants of employee engagement and their impact on employee performance', *International Journal of Productivity and Performance Management*, vol. 63, no. 3, pp. 308–323, http://dx.doi.org/10.1108/IJPPM-01-2013-0008.

Arnold, DE, Ringquist, JJ & Prien, K 1998, 'Reducing the cycle time of training and development in organisations', *Journal of Cycle Time Research*, pp. 21–30, viewed 24 June 2017, <http://citeseerx.ist.psu.edu/viewdoc/download?doi=10.1.1.508.9235&rep=rep1&type=pdf>.

Arnold, RD & Wade, JP 2015, 'A definition of systems thinking: a systems approach', *Procedia Computer Science*, vol. 44, pp. 669–678, http://dx.doi.org/10.1016/j.procs.2015.03.050.

Arnold, V & Collier, P 2013, 'INCASE: simulating experience to accelerate expertise development by knowledge workers', *Intelligent Systems in Accounting and Financial Management*, vol. 20, no. 1, pp. 1–21, http://dx.doi.org/10.1002/isaf.

Ashoori, M & Burns, C 2013, 'Team cognitive work analysis: structure and control tasks', *Journal of Cognitive Engineering and Decision Making*, vol. 7, no. 2, pp. 123–140, http://dx.doi.org/10.1177/1555343412445577.

Attri, RK 2014, 'Rethinking professional skill development in competitive corporate world: accelerating time-to-expertise of employees at workplace', in J Latzo (ed.), *Proceedings of Conference on Education and Human Development in Asia*, Hiroshima, PRESDA Foundation, Kitanagova, pp. 1–11, http://dx.doi.org/10.13140/RG.2.1.5125.7043.

Attri, RK & Wu, W 2015, 'Conceptual model of workplace training and learning strategies to shorten time-to-proficiency in complex skills: preliminary findings', paper presented to the 9th International Conference on Researching in Work and Learning (RWL), Singapore, 9-11 December, viewed 24 June 2017, <http://www.rwl2015.com/papers/Paper100.pdf>.

Attride-Stirling, J 2001, 'Thematic networks: an analytic tool for qualitative research', *Qualitative Research*, vol. 1, no. 3, pp. 385–405, http://dx.doi.org/10.1177/146879410100100307.

Australian Government 2007a, *Australian Code for the Responsible Conduct of Research*, Australian Government, viewed 24 June 2017, <https://www.nhmrc.gov.au/_files_nhmrc/file/publications/r39_australian_code_responsible_conduct_research_150811.pdf>

―――― 2007b, *National Statement on Ethical Conduct in Human Research*, National Health and Medical Research Council, Canberra, viewed 24 June 2017, <http://www.nhmrc.gov.au/guidelines/publications/e72>.

Avolio, BJ, Waldman, DA & McDaniel, MA 1990, 'Age and work performance in nonmanagerial jobs: the effects of experience and occupational type', *Academy of Management Journal*, vol. 33, no. 2, pp. 407–422, http://dx.doi.org/10.2307/256331.

Bachlechner, D, Kohlegger, M, Maier, R & Waldhart, G 2010, 'Taking pressure off knowledge workers with the help of situational applications-improving time-to-proficiency in knowledge work settings', in A Fred & J Filipe (eds.), *Proceedings of the International Conference on Knowledge Management and Information Sharing (KMIS-2010)*, Valencia, 25-28 October, SCITEPRESS Science and Technology, Setúbal, Portugal, pp. 378–381, http://dx.doi.org/10.5220/0003118203780381.

Backus, C, Keegan, K, Gluck, C & Gulick, LMV 2010, 'Accelerating leadership development via immersive learning and cognitive apprenticeship', *International Journal of Training and Development*, vol. 14, no. 2, pp. 144–148, http://dx.doi.org/10.1111/j.1468-2419.2010.00347.x.

Baker, T 2016, *The end of the job description: Shifting from a job-focus to a performance-focus*, Palgrave MacMillan, London, http://dx.doi.org/10.1007/978-1-137-58146-4.

―――― 2017, *Performance Management for Agile Organisations*, Springer, Cham, http://dx.doi.org/10.1007/978-3-319-40153-9.

Bakker, RM, Boros, S, Kenis, P & Oerlemans, LA 2013, 'It's only temporary: time frame and the dynamics of creative project teams', *British Journal of Management*, vol. 24, no. 3, pp. 383–397, http://dx.doi.org/10.1111/j.1467-8551.2012.00810.x.

Bampton, R & Cowton, CJ 2002, 'The e-interview', *Forum Qualitative Sozialforschung/Forum: Qualitative Social Research*, vol. 3, no. 2, viewed 24 June 2017, <http://www.qualitative-research.net/index.php/fqs/article/viewArticle/848/1842>.

Barnes, JL 1987, 'An international study of curricular organizers for the study of technology', PhD thesis, Virginia Tech, Blacksburg, viewed 13 March 2018, <https://vtechworks.lib.vt.edu/bitstream/handle/10919/37284/Barnes,J.pdf?sequence=1>.

Bartel, AP 2000, 'Measuring the employer's return on investments in training: evidence from the literature', *Industrial Relations: A Journal of Economy and Society*, vol. 39, no. 3, pp. 502–524, viewed 24 June 2017, <http://sis.ashesi.edu.gh/courseware/cms/file.php/57/aaLIBRARY/Training_Development/Bartel_-_employer_s_ROI_from_training_devpt.pdf>.

Bartsch, V, Ebers, M & Maurer, I 2012, 'Learning in project-based organisations: the role of project teams' social capital for overcoming barriers to learning', *International Journal of Project Management*, vol. 31, no. 2, pp. 239–251, http://dx.doi.org/10.1016/j.ijproman.2012.06.009.

Bates, R, Holton III, EF & Seyler, D 1997, 'Factors affecting transfer of training in an industrial setting', in R Torraco (ed.), *Proceedings of the Academy of Human Resource Development Annual Conference*, Atlanta, Academy of Human Resource Development, Baton Rouge, pp. 347–354.

Bauer, J 2008, 'Learning from errors at work: studies on nurses' engagement in error-related learning activities', PhD thesis, University at Regensburg, Regensburg, viewed 24 June 2017, <https://epub.uni-regensburg.de/10748/1/diss_veroeff_endversion.pdf>.

Baxter, HC 2013, 'Transferring specialized knowledge: accelerating the expertise development cycle', *Interservice Industry Training, Simulation and Education Conference (I/ITSEC)*, Orlando, 2-5 December, National Training and Simulation Association (NTSA), Arlington, viewed 24 June 2017, <http://ac.els-cdn.com/S2351978915003248/1-s2.0-S2351978915003248-main.pdf?_tid=cf441efa-6fc0-11e7-a40c-00000aab0f6b&acdnat=1500826136_7386e303f14ad6be5a585b89a0f44c22>.

―――― 2015, 'Specialized knowledge transfer: accelerating the expertise development cycle', *Procedia Manufacturing*, vol. 3, pp. 1465–1472, http://dx.doi.org/10.1016/j.promfg.2015.07.323.

Beattie, RS 2006, 'Line managers and workplace learning: learning from the voluntary sector', *Human Resource Development International*, vol. 9, no. 1, pp. 99–119, http://dx.doi.org/10.1080/13678860600563366.

Bedarkar, M & Pandita, D 2014, 'A study on the drivers of employee engagement impacting employee performance', *Procedia-Social and Behavioral Sciences*, vol. 133, pp. 106–115, http://dx.doi.org/10.1016/j.sbspro.2014.04.174.

Bedi, A 2003, 'Student profiling: the Dreyfus model revisited', *Education for Primary Care*, vol. 14, no. 3, pp. 360–363, viewed 24 June 2017, <https://www.researchgate.net/publication/293527610>.

Behneman, A, Berka, C, Stevens, R, Villa, B, Tan, V, Galloway, T, Johnson, R & Raphael, G 2012, 'Neurotechnology to accelerate learning: during marksmanship training', *IEEE Pulse*, vol. 3, no. 1, pp. 60–63, http://dx.doi.org/10.1109/MPUL.2011.2175641.

Belling, PK, Sada, J & Ward, P 2015, 'Assessing hitting skill in baseball using simulated and representative tasks', *12th International Naturalistic Decision Making Conference*, McLean, 9-12 June, The MITRE Corp, McLean, viewed 24 June 2017, <http://eprints.hud.ac.uk/24799/1/WardAssessing.pdf>.

Belling, PK, Suss, J & Ward, P 2014a, 'Advancing theory and application of cognitive research in sport: using representative tasks to explain and predict skilled anticipation, decision-making, and option-generation behavior', *Psychology of Sport and Exercise*, vol. 16, no. 1, pp. 45–59, http://dx.doi.org/10.1016/j.psychsport.2014.08.001.

_____ 2014b, 'Cognitive processes supporting recognition in complex and dynamic tasks', *Proceedings of the Human Factors and Ergonomics Society 58th Annual Meeting*, vol. 58, no. 1, pp. 290–294, http://dx.doi.org/10.1177/1541931214581060.

Benner, P 1984, *From novice to expert: excellence and power in clinical nursing practice*, Addison-Wesley, Palo Alto, http://dx.doi.org/10.1097/00000446-198412000-00025.

_____ 2001, *From novice to expert: excellence and power in clinical nursing practice*, Commemorative edn, Prentice Hall, London, http://dx.doi.org/10.1097/00000446-198412000-00025.

_____ 2004, 'Using the Dreyfus model of skill acquisition to describe and interpret skill acquisition and clinical judgment in nursing practice and education', *Bulletin of Science, Technology and Society*, vol. 24, no. 3, pp. 188–199, http://dx.doi.org/10.1177/0270467604265061.

Bennett Jr, W, Schreiber, BT & Andrews, DH 2002, 'Developing competency-based methods for near-real-time air combat problem solving assessment', *Computers in Human Behavior*, vol. 18, no. 6, pp. 773–782, http://dx.doi.org/10.1016/S0747-5632(02)00030-4.

Berka, C, Pojmani, N, Coyne, JJ, Cole, A & Denise, C 2010, Neurogaming: merging cognitive neuroscience & virtual simulation in an interactive training platform, in T Marek, W Kawwowski & Valerie Rice (eds.), *Advances in Understanding Human Performance: Neuroergonomics, Human Factors Design, and Special Populations*, CRC Press, Boca Raton, pp. 313–324, http://dx.doi.org/10.1201/ebk1439835012-33.

Berkem, B 2008, 'From the business motivation model (BMM) to service oriented architecture (SOA)', *Journal of Object Technology*, vol. 7, no. 8, pp. 57–70, http://dx.doi.org/10.5381/jot.2008.7.8.c6.

Bernsen, P, Segers, M & Tillema, HH 2009, 'Learning under pressure: learning strategies, workplace climate, and leadership style in the hospitality industry', *International Journal of Human Resources Development and Management*, vol. 9, no. 4, pp. 358–373, http://dx.doi.org/10.1504/IJHRDM.2009.025069.

Berry, R 1999, 'Collecting data by in-depth interviewing', *British Educational Research Association Annual Conference*, Brighton, 2-5 September, British Educational Research Association, London, viewed 24 June 2017, <http://www.leeds.ac.uk/educol/documents/000001172.htm>.

Bersin, J 2013, 'The end of a job as we know it,' blog post, 30 January, viewed 24 June 2017, <http://blog.bersin.com/the-end-of-a-job-as-we-know-it/>.

Beta, G & Lidaka, A 2015, 'The aspect of proficiency in the theoretical overview of pedagogical practice of nurses', *Procedia-Social and Behavioral Sciences*, vol. 174, no. 2015, pp. 1957–1965, http://dx.doi.org/10.1016/j.sbspro.2015.01.861.

Billett, S 1994, 'Situating learning in the workplace-having another look at apprenticeships', *Industrial and Commercial Training*, vol. 26, no. 11, pp. 9–16, http://dx.doi.org/10.1108/00197859410073745.

_____ 1996, 'Towards a model of workplace learning: the learning curriculum', *Studies in Continuing Education*, vol. 18, no. 1, pp. 43–58, http://dx.doi.org/10.1080/0158037960180103.

_____ 2002a, 'Critiquing workplace learning discourses: participation and continuity at work', *Studies in the Education of Adults*, vol. 34, no. 1, pp. 56–67, http://dx.doi.org/10.1080/02660830.2002.11661461.

_____ 2002b, 'Workplace pedagogic practices: a workplace study', *Lifelong Learning in Europe, VII*, vol. 2, pp. 94–103, viewed 24 June 2017, <http://citeseerx.ist.psu.edu/viewdoc/download?doi=10.1.1.603.7844&rep=rep1&type=pdf>.

_____ 2003, 'Workplace mentors: demands and benefits', *Journal of Workplace Learning*, vol. 15, no. 3, pp. 105–113, http://dx.doi.org/10.1102/13665620310468441.

_____ 2004, 'Workplace participatory practices: conceptualising workplaces as learning environments', *Journal of Workplace Learning*, vol. 16, no. 6, pp. 312–324, http://dx.doi.org/10.1108/13665620410550295.

_____ 2006, 'Constituting the workplace curriculum', *Journal of Curriculum Studies*, vol. 38, no. 1, pp. 31–48, http://dx.doi.org/10.1080/00220270500153781.

_____ 2010, The practices of learning through occupations, in S Billett (ed.), *Learning through practice*, Springer, Dordrecht, pp. 59–81, http://dx.doi.org/10.1007/978-90-481-3939-2_4.

_____ 2012, Errors and learning from errors at work, in J Bauer & C Harteis (eds.), *Human Fallibility: The Ambiguity of Errors for Work and Learning*, Springer, Dordrecht, pp. 17–32, viewed 24 June 2017, <http://www.academia.edu/download/45112925/billett_Errors_and_learning_from_errors_v3.pdf>.

_____ 2014a, 'Mimesis: learning through everyday activities and interactions at work', *Human Resource Development Review*, vol. 13, no. 4, pp. 462–482, http://dx.doi.org/10.1177/1534484314548275.

_____ 2014b, Interdependence on the boundaries between working and learning, in C Harteis et al. (eds.), *Discourses on Professional Learning*, Springer, Dordrecht, pp. 369–385, http://dx.doi.org/10.1007/978-94-007-7012-6_18.

Billett, S & Choy, S 2013, 'Learning through work: emerging perspectives and new challenges', *Journal of Workplace Learning*, vol. 25, no. 4, pp. 264–276, http://dx.doi.org/10.1108/13665621311316447.

Billett, S & Sweet, L 2015, Participatory practices at work: understanding and appraising healthcare students' learning through workplace, in J Cleland & S Durning (eds.), *Researching Medical Education*, John Wiley & Sons, Chichester, pp. 117–128, http://dx.doi.org/10.1002/9781118838983.ch11.

Binder, C 2017, 'What it really means to be accomplishment based', *Performance Improvement*, vol. 56, no. 4, pp. 20–25, http://dx.doi.org/10.1002/pfi.21702.

Birnbaum, MS, Kornell, N, Bjork, EL & Bjork, R a 2013, 'Why interleaving enhances inductive learning: the roles of discrimination and retrieval', *Memory & Cognition*, vol. 41, no. 3, pp. 392–402, http://dx.doi.org/10.3758/s13421-012-0272-7.

Bish, AJ & Kabanoff, B 2014, 'Star performers: task and contextual performance are components, but are they enough?', *Asia Pacific Journal of Human Resources*, vol. 52, no. 1, pp. 110–127, viewed 24 January 2017, <https://eprints.qut.edu.au/63849/3/Manuscript_Revised_changes_accepted_12-06-13_APHR.pdf>.

Bjork, EL & Bjork, RA 2011, Making things hard on yourself, but in a good way: creating desirable difficulties to enhance learning, in M Gernsbacher, R Pew, L Hough & J Pomerantz (eds.), *Psychology and the real world: Essays illustrating fundamental contributions to society*, Worth, New York, pp. 55–64, viewed 24 June 2017, <https://bjorklab.psych.ucla.edu/wp-content/uploads/sites/13/2016/04/EBjork_RBjork_2011.pdf>.

Bjork, RA 2009, Structuring the conditions of training to achieve elite performance: reflections on elite training programs and related themes in chapters 10-13, in K Ericsson (ed.), *Development of professional expertise: Toward measurement of expert performance and design of optimal learning environments*, Cambridge University Press, New York, pp. 312–329, http://dx.doi.org/10.1017/cbo9780511609817.017.

_____ 2013, Desirable difficulties perspective on learning, in H Pashler (ed.), *Encyclopedia of the mind*, SAGE, Thousand Oaks, pp. 243–245, http://dx.doi.org/10.4135/9781452257044.n88.

Bjork, RA & Linn, M 2006, 'The science of learning and the learning of science: introducing desirable difficulties', *APS Observer*, vol. 19, no. 3, pp. 6–7, viewed 24 June 2017, <https://www.researchgate.net/profile/Robert_Bjork/publication/237420547>.

Blindenbach-Driessen, F & Van Den Ende, J 2006, 'Innovation in project-based firms: the context dependency of success factors', *Research Policy*, vol. 35, no. 4, pp. 545–561, http://dx.doi.org/10.1016/j.respol.2006.02.005.

Bogdan, RC & Biklen, SK 2006, *Qualitative research in education: an introduction to theory and methods*, 5th edn, Pearson, Boston.

Boling, EC & Beatty, J 2010, 'Cognitive apprenticeship in computer-mediated feedback: creating a classroom environment to increase feedback and learning', *Journal of Educational Computing Research*, vol. 43, no. 1, pp. 47–65, http://dx.doi.org/10.2190/EC.43.1.d.

Bologa, R & Lupu, AR 2007, 'Accelerating the sharing of knowledge in order to speed up the process of enlarging software development teams - a practical example', in C Long, V Mladenov & Z Bojkovic (eds.), *Proceedings of the 6th WSEAS International Conference on Artificial Intelligence, Knowledge Engineering and Data Bases*, Corfu Island, Greece, 16-19 February, World Scientific and Engineering Academy and Society, pp. 90–95, viewed 24 June 2017, <http://www.wseas.us/e-library/conferences/2007corfu/papers/540-225.pdf>.

Booth, WC, Colomb, GG & Williams, JM 2008, *The craft of research*, 3rd ed., University of Chicago Press, Chicago, viewed 30 March 2018, <http://wp.vcu.edu/univ200choice/wp-content/uploads/sites/5337/2015/01/The-Craft-of-Research-From-Topics-to-Questions-by-Wayne-C.-Booth.pdf>.

Borders, J, Polander, N, Klein, G & Wright, C 2015, 'Shadowbox™: flexible training to impart the expert mindset', in T Ahram, W Karwowski & D Schmorrow (eds.), *6th International Conference on Applied Human Factors and Ergonomics (AHFE 2015) and the Affiliated Conferences, Procedia Manufacturing*, vol. 3, pp. 1574–1579, Las vegas, 26-30 July, Elsevier, http://dx.doi.org/10.1016/j.promfg.2015.07.444.

Borman, WC & Motowidlo, SJ 1993, Expanding the criterion domain to include elements of contextual performance, in E Schmitt & W Borman (eds.), *Personnel Selection in Organisations*, Jossey-Bass, San Francisco, pp. 71–98.

_____(eds.) 1997, *Organisational citizenship behavior and contextual performance: a special issue of human performance*, Kindle edn, Psychology Press, London, http://dx.doi.org/10.4324/9781315799254.

Borton, G 2007, 'Managing productivity: measuring the business impact of employee proficiency and the employee job life cycle', *Management Services*, no. 7, pp. 28–33, viewed 24 June 2017, <http://www.ims-productivity.com/user/custom/journal/2007/autumn/IMSaut07pg28-33.pdf>.

Van den Bosch, K, Helsdingen, AS & de Beer, MM 2004, 'Training critical thinking for tactical command', *The RTO Human Factors and Medicine Panel (HFM) Symposium: Advanced Technologies for Military Training*, Genoa, Research and Technology Organisation (RTO) of North Atlantic Treaty Organisation (NATO), Cedex, France, pp. 1–10, http://dx.doi.org/10.14339/RTO-MP-HFM-101.

Boshuizen, HPA 2003, Expertise development: how to bridge the gap between school and work, in P Boshuizen (ed.), *Expertise development: The transition between school and work*, Open University Netherlands, Heerlen, pp. 7–31, viewed 24 June 2017, <https://pure.tue.nl/ws/files/1776251/572181.pdf>.

Bott, JP, Svyantek, DJ, Goodman, SA & Bernal, DS 2003, 'Expanding the performance domain: who says nice guys finish last?', *The International Journal of Organisational Analysis*, vol. 11, no. 2, pp. 137–152, http://dx.doi.org/10.1108/eb028967.

Boulton, L & Cole, J 2016, 'Adaptive flexibility: examining the role of expertise in the decision making of authorized firearms officers during armed confrontation', *Journal of Cognitive Engineering and Decision Making*, vol. 10, no. 3, pp. 291–308, http://dx.doi.org/10.1177/1555343416646684.

Bower, M, Dalgarno, B, Kennedy, GE, Lee, MJ & Kenney, J 2015, 'Design and implementation factors in blended synchronous learning environments: outcomes from a cross-case analysis', *Computers & Education*, vol. 86, no. 8, pp. 1–17, http://dx.doi.org/10.1016/j.compedu.2015.03.006.

Boyatzis, R 1998, *Transforming qualitative information: thematic analysis and code development*, Sage, Thousand Oaks.

Bransford, JD, Brown, AL, Cocking, RR, Donovan, MS & Pellegrino, JW (eds.) 2004, *How people learn brain, mind, experience, and school*, Expanded edn, National Academy Press, Washington, D.C., http://dx.doi.org/10.17226/6160.

Bransford, JD & Schwartz, DL 2009, It takes expertise to make expertise: some thoughts about why and how and reflections on the themes in chapters 15-18, in K Ericsson (ed.), *Development of professional expertise: Toward measurement of expert performance and design of optimal learning environments*, Cambridge University Press, New York, pp. 432–448, http://dx.doi.org/10.1017/cbo9780511609817.023.

Branson, R, Bray, D, Huffington, A, Hunt-Morr, K, McCord, P, Oelwang, J, Schiller, C & Sheridan, R 2015, *New Ways of Woking*, The B Team/Virgin Unite, London.

Braun, V & Clarke, V 2006, 'Using thematic analysis in psychology', *Qualitative Research in Psychology*, vol. 3, no. 2, pp. 77–101, http://dx.doi.org/10.1191/1478088706qp063oa.

_____ 2013, *Successful qualitative research: a practical guide for beginners*, Sage, Thousand Oaks, viewed 24 June 2017, <http://eprints.uwe.ac.uk/21156/3/SQR%2520Chap%25201%2520Research%2520Repository.pdf>.

Brightman, J 2003, 'Mapping methods for qualitative data structuring (QDS)', paper presented to the Strategies in Qualitative Research: Methodological issues and practices using QSR NVivo and NUD*IST conference, London, 8-9 May, viewed 24 June 2017, <http://www.banxia.com/pdf/de/Map_for_qual_data_struct.pdf>.

Brooker, R & Butler, J 1997, 'The learning context within the workplace: as perceived by apprentices and their workplace trainers', *Journal of Vocational Education and Training*, vol. 49, no. 4, pp. 487–510, http://dx.doi.org/10.1080/13636829700200028.

Brooks, J, McCluskey, S, Turley, E & King, N 2015, 'The utility of template analysis in qualitative psychology research', *Qualitative Research in Psychology*, vol. 12, no. 2, pp. 202–222, http://dx.doi.org/10.1080/14780887.2014.955224.

Bruck, B 2007, 'Speed to proficiency: strategically using training to drive profitability,", viewed 24 June 2017, <http://www.q2learning.com/docs/WP-S2P.pdf>.

_____ 2015, *Speed to proficiency: creating a sustainable competitive advantage*, CreateSpace, USA, viewed 24 June 2017, <http://www.readings.com.au/products/20647385/speed-to-proficiency-creating-a-sustainable-competitive-advantage>.

Brudnicki, D, Ethier, B & Chastain, K 2007, *Application of Advanced Technologies for Training the next Generation of Air Traffic Controllers*, Case No. 06-0978, MITRE Corporation, Bedford, viewed 24 June 2017, <https://www.mitre.org/sites/default/files/pdf/06_0978.pdf>.

Brundage, D, Lekowski, R, Carr, J, Finn, A, Hicks, P, Mehta, N & Perham, B 2014, 'Utilizing high signal simulation training to educate and ensure competency in high risk/low frequency skills in a pediatric pacu', *Journal of PeriAnesthesia Nursing*, vol. 29, no. 5, p. e27, http://dx.doi.org/10.1016/j.jopan.2014.08.092.

Brydges, R, Nair, P, Ma, I, Shanks, D & Hatala, R 2012, 'Directed self-regulated learning versus instructor-regulated learning in simulation training', *Medical Education*, vol. 46, no. 7, pp. 648–656, http://dx.doi.org/10.1111/j.1365-2923.2012.04268.x.

Bryman, A 1988, *Quantity and quality in social research*, Routledge, New York, http://dx.doi.org/10.4324/9780203410028.

Buch, N & Wolff, T 2000, 'Classroom teaching through inquiry', *Journal of Professional Issues in Engineering Education and Practice*, vol. 126, no. 3, pp. 105–109, http://dx.doi.org/10.1061/(ASCE)1052-3928(2000)126:3(105).

Bulman, C & Schutz, S (eds.) 2013, *Reflective practice in nursing*, 5th ed., Wiley-Blackwell, Oxford, viewed 24 June 2017, <http://zu.edu.jo/UploadFile/Library/E_Books/Files/LibraryFile_151614_52.pdf>.

Bunderson, CV 2011, 'Developing a domain theory defining and exemplifying a learning theory of progressive attainments.', *Journal of Applied Measurement*, vol. 12, no. 1, pp. 25–48, viewed 24 June 2017, <https://www.ncbi.nlm.nih.gov/pubmed/21512212>.

Burgess-Allen, J & Owen-Smith, V 2010, 'Using mind mapping techniques for rapid qualitative data analysis in public participation processes', *Health Expectations*, vol. 13, no. 4, pp. 406–415, http://dx.doi.org/10.1111/j.1369-7625.2010.00594.x.

Burke, LA & Miller, MK 2001, 'Phone interviewing as a means of data collection: lessons learned and practical recommendations', *Forum Qualitative Sozialforschung/Forum: Qualitative Social Research*, vol. 2, no. 2, viewed 24 June 2017, <http://www.qualitative-research.net/index.php/fqs/article/%20view/959/2094>.

Butler, WM 2012, 'The impact of simulation-based learning in aircraft design on aerospace student preparedness for engineering practice: a mixed methods approach', PhD thesis, Virginia Polytechnic Institute and State University, Blacksburg, viewed <https://theses.lib.vt.edu/theses/available/etd-05082012-183206/unrestricted/Butler_WM_D_2012.pdf>.

Cabaniss, K 2001, 'Counseling and computer technology in the new millennium-an internet Delphi study', PhD thesis, Virginia Tech, Blacksburg, viewed 24 June 2017, <https://vtechworks.lib.vt.edu/bitstream/handle/10919/26377/1Cabaniss.pdf?sequence=1&isAllowed=y>.

Cagiltay, K 2006, 'Scaffolding strategies in electronic performance support systems: types and challenges', *Innovations in Education and Teaching International*, vol. 43, no. 1, pp. 93–103, http://dx.doi.org/10.1080/14703290500467673.

Campbell, J, Tirapelle, L, Yates, K, Clark, R, Inaba, K, Green, D, Plurad, D, Lam, L, Tang, A, Cestero, R & others 2011, 'The effectiveness of a cognitive task analysis informed curriculum to increase self-efficacy and improve performance for an open cricothyrotomy', *Journal of Surgical Education*, vol. 68, no. 5, pp. 403–407, http://dx.doi.org/10.1016/j.jsurg.2011.05.007.

Campbell, JP 1990, Modeling the performance prediction problem in industrial and organisational psychology, in M Dunnette & L Hough (eds.), *Handbook of industrial and organisational psychology, Vol. 1*, Consulting Psychologists Press, Palo Alto, pp. 687–732.

———— 1999, The definition and measurement of performance in the new age, in D Ilgen & E Pulakos (eds.), *The changing nature of performance: Implications for staffing, motivation, and development*, Jossey-Bass, San Francisco, pp. 399–429.

Campbell, JP, McCloy, RA, Oppler, SH & Sager, CE 1993, A theory of performance, in N Schmitt & W Borman (eds.), *Personnel selection in organisations*, Jossey-Bass, San Francisco, pp. 35–70.

Campbell, JP, McHenry, JJ & Wise, LL 1990, 'Modeling job performance in a population of jobs', *Personnel Psychology*, vol. 43, no. 2, pp. 313–575, http://dx.doi.org/10.1111/j.1744-6570.1990.tb01561.x.

Campbell, JP & Wiernik, BM 2015, 'The modeling and assessment of work performance', *Annual Review of Organisational Psychology and Organisational Behavior*, vol. 2, no. 1, pp. 47–74, http://dx.doi.org/10.1146/annurev-orgpsych-032414-111427.

Cannon-Bowers, JA, Bowers, CA, Stout, R, Ricci, K & Hildabrand, A 2013, 'Using cognitive task analysis to develop simulation-based training for medical tasks.', *Military Medicine*, vol. 178, no. 10 Suppl, pp. 15–21, http://dx.doi.org/10.7205/MILMED-D-13-00211.

Cannon-Bowers, JA, Bowers, CA 2008, Synthetic learning environments, in J Spector, M Merrill, J van Merriënboer & M Driscoll (eds.), *Handbook of research on educational communications and technology*, Lawrence Erlbaum Associates, New York, pp. 317–327, viewed 24 Jun 2017, <http://www.aect.org/edtech/edition3/ER5849x_C027.fm.pdf>.

Carpenter, MA, Monaco, SJ, O'Mara, FE & Teachout, MS 1989, *Time to Job Proficiency: A Preliminary Investigation of the Effects of Aptitude and Experience on Productive Capacity*, Report No. AFHRK-TP-88-17, Air Force Systems Command, Brooks Air Force Base, San Antonio, viewed 24 June 2017, <https://www.researchgate.net/publication/235105070>.

Carter, A & Bathmaker, A-M 2017, 'Prioritising progression over proficiency: limitations of teacher-based assessment within technician-level vocational education', *Journal of Further and Higher Education*, vol. 41, no. 4, pp. 460–474, http://dx.doi.org/10.1080/0309877X.2015.1135881.

Carter, TJ & Adkins, B 2017, Situated learning, communities of practice, and the social construction of knowledge, in V Wang (ed.), *Theory and Practice of Adult and Higher Education*, IAP, Charlotte, pp. 113–137.

Cash, JR, Behrmann, MB, Stadt, RW & Daniels, HM 1996, 'Effectiveness of cognitive apprenticeship instructional methods in college automotive technology classrooms', *Journal of Industrial Teacher's Education*, vol. 34, no. 2, pp. 29–49, viewed 24 June 2017, <http://scholar.lib.vt.edu/ejournals/JITE/v34n2/Cash.html>.

Ten Cate, O 2013, 'Nuts and bolts of entrustable professional activities', *Journal of Graduate Medical Education*, vol. 5, no. 1, pp. 157–158, http://dx.doi.org/10.4300/JGME-D-12-00380.1.

Champion, M, Jariwala, S, Ward, P & Cooke, NJ 2014, 'Using cognitive task analysis to investigate the contribution of informal education to developing cyber security expertise', *Proceedings of the Human Factors and Ergonomics Society 58th Annual Meeting*, Chicago, 27-31 October, SAGE, Thousand Oaks, pp. 310–314, http://dx.doi.org/10.1177/1541931214581064.

Chalofsky, N & Lincoln, C 1983, *Up the HRD ladder*, Addisison-Wesley, Reading.

Chan, S 2013, 'Learning through apprenticeship: belonging to a workplace, becoming and being', *Vocations and Learning*, vol. 6, no. 3, pp. 367–383, http://dx.doi.org/10.1007/s12186-013-9100-x.

Charmaz, K 2006, *Constructing grounded theory: A practical guide through qualitative analysis*, Sage, London, viewed 24 June 2017, <http://www.sxf.uevora.pt/wp-content/uploads/2013/03/Charmaz_2006.pdf>.

_____ 2014, *Constructing grounded theory: a practical guide through qualitative analysis*, 2nd ed., Sage, London, viewed 24 June 2017, <http://www.sxf.uevora.pt/wp-content/uploads/2013/03/Charmaz_2006.pdf>.

Charness, N & Tuffiash, M 2008, 'The role of expertise research and human factors in capturing, explaining, and producing superior performance', *Human Factors*, vol. 50, no. 3, pp. 427–32, http://dx.doi.org/10.1518/001872008X312206.

Chase, WG & Simon, HA 1973, 'Perception in chess', *Cognitive Psychology*, vol. 4, no. 1, pp. 55–81, http://dx.doi.org/10.1016/0010-0285(73)90004-2.

Chen, GK 1975, 'What is the systems approach?', *Interfaces*, vol. 6, no. 1, pp. 32–37, http://dx.doi.org/10.1287/inte.6.1.32.

Chevalier, R 2003, 'Updating the behavior engineering model', *Performance Improvement*, vol. 42, no. 5, pp. 8–14, http://dx.doi.org/10.1002/pfi.4930420504.

_____ 2004, 'The link between learning and performance', *Performance Improvement*, vol. 43, no. 4, pp. 40–44, http://dx.doi.org/10.1002/pfi.4140430410.

Chi, MT 2006, Two approaches to the study of experts' characteristics, in R Hoffman, N Charness & P Feltovich (eds.), *The Cambridge Handbook of Expertise and Expert Performance*, Cambridge University Press, New York, pp. 21–30, http://dx.doi.org/10.1017/CBO9780511816796.002.

Chi, MT, Glaser, R & Farr, M (eds.) 1988, *The nature of expertise*, Lawrence Erlbaum, Hillsdale, http://dx.doi.org/10.4324/9781315799681.

Chi, MT, Glaser, R & Rees, E 1981, *Expertise in Problem Solving*, Technical Report No. 5, University of Pittsburgh, Pittsburgh, viewed 24 June 2017, <http://www.dtic.mil/cgi-bin/GetTRDoc?AD=ADA100138>.

Chi, MT 1982, Expertise in problem solving, in R Sternberg (ed.), *Advances in psychology of human intelligence, Vol.1*, Erlbaum, Hillsdale, pp. 7-75, viewed 24 June 2017, <http://www.dtic.mil/cgi-bin/GetTRDoc?AD=ADA100138>.

Cho, Y & Yoon, SW 2010, 'Theory development and convergence of human resource fields: implications for human performance technology', *Performance Improvement Quarterly*, vol. 23, no. 3, pp. 39–56, http://dx.doi.org/10.1002/piq.20089.

Choi, H-H, van Merriënboer, JJG & Paas, F 2014, 'Effects of the physical environment on cognitive load and learning: towards a new model of cognitive load', *Educational Psychology Review*, vol. 26, no. 2, pp. 225–244, http://dx.doi.org/10.1007/s10648-014-9262-6.

Clark, RE 2014, Cognitive task analysis for expert-based instruction in healthcare, in J Spector, M Merrill, J Elen & M Bishop (eds.), *Handbook of Research on Educational Communications and Technology*, Springer, New York, pp. 541–551, http://dx.doi.org/ 10.1007/978-1-4614-3185-5_42.

Clark, RC 2008, *Building expertise: cognitive methods for training and performance improvement*, 3rd ed., Pfeiffer, San Francisco, http://dx.doi.org/10.1002/pfi.4140390213.

_____ 2009, 'Accelerating expertise with scenario-based learning', *T+D*, pp. 84–85, viewed 24 June 2017, <http://www.clarktraining.com/content/articles/ScenarioBasedLearning.pdf>.

_____ 2013, 'Accelerating expertise with scenario-based e-learning', *The Watercooler Newsletter*, viewed 24 June 2017, <http://www.watercoolernewsletter.com/accelerating-expertise-with-scenario-based-elearning//#.Um0wNXD-ok>.

_____ & Mayer, RE 2013, *Scenario-based e-learning: evidence-based guidelines for online workforce learning*, Pfeiffer, San Francisco.

Clark, RE 2006, How much and what type of guidance is optimal for learning from instruction?, in S Tobias & T Duffy (eds.), *Constructivist Theory Applied to Instruction: Success or Failure*, Routledge, New York, pp. 158–183, viewed 24 June 2017, <http://www.anitacrawley.net/Articles/2009How%20much%20and%20what%20type%20of%20guidance%20is%20optimal%20for%20learning%20from%20instruction.pdf>.

Clark, RE 2010, 'Recent neuroscience and cognitive research findings on cyber learning', paper presented to the AECT Annual Convention, Anaheim, 26-30 October, viewed 24 June 2017, <http://www.cogtech.usc.edu/publications/clark_aect_oct_28_2010.pdf>.

Clark, RE & Estes, F 1996, 'Cognitive task analysis for training', *International Journal of Education Research*, vol. 25, no. 5, pp. 403–417, http://dx.doi.org/10.1016/S0883-0355(97)81235-9.

Clark, RE & Feldon, DF 2008, 'Gel, adaptable expertise and transfer of training', [Working Paper], viewed 24 June 2017, <http://www.cogtech.usc.edu/publications/gel_and_adaptability.pdf>.

Clark, RE, Feldon, DF, van Merriënboer, JJG, Yates, KA & Early, S 2008, Cognitive task analysis, in J Spector, M Merrill, J van Merriënboer & M Driscoll (eds.), *Handbook of research on educational communications and technology*, Lawrence Erlbaum, Mahwah, pp. 577–593, viewed 24 June 2017, <http://www.learnlab.org/research/wiki/images/0/0b/Clarketal2007-CTAchapter.pdf>.

Clark, RE, Feldon, DF & Yates, K 2011, 'Using cognitive task analysis to capture expert knowledge and skills for research and instructional design', *Annual Meeting of the American Educational Research Association*, New Orleans, American Educational Research Association, Washington, DC.

Clark, RE, Pugh, CM, Yates, K & Sullivan, M 2008, *The Use of Cognitive Task Analysis and Simulators for after Action Review of Medical Events in Iraq*, Center for Cognitive Technology, University of California, Los Angeles, viewed 24 June 2017, <http://www.dtic.mil/cgi-bin/GetTRDoc?AD=ADA466686>.

Clark, RE, Pugh, CM, Yates, KA, Inaba, K, Green, DJ & Sullivan, ME 2011, 'The use of cognitive task analysis to improve instructional descriptions of procedures.', *The Journal of Surgical Research*, vol. 173, no. 1, pp. e37–42, http://dx.doi.org/10.1016/j.jss.2011.09.003.

Clark, RE, Yates, K, Early, S, Moulton, K, Silber, K & Foshay, R 2010, An analysis of the failure of electronic media and discovery-based learning: evidence for the performance benefits of guided training methods, in K Silber & R Foshay (eds.), *Handbook of Training and Improving Workplace Performance, Volume I: Instructional Design and Training Delivery*, Pfeiffer, San Francisco, pp. 263–287, http://dx.doi.org/10.1002/9780470592663.ch8.

Clavarelli, A, Platte, WL & Powers, JJ 2009, 'Teaching and assessing complex skills in simulation with application to rifle marksmanship training', *Interservice Industry Training, Simulation and Education Conference (I/ITSEC)*, Orlando, 30 November - 2 December, National Training and Simulation Association (NTSA), Arlington, viewed 24 June 2017, <http://www.dtic.mil/cgi-bin/GetTRDoc?AD=ADA535072>.

Clonts, JG 1992, 'The concept of reliability as it pertains to data from qualitative studies', paper presented to the Annual Meeting of the Southwest Educational Research Association, Houston, viewed 24 June 2017, <http://files.eric.ed.gov/fulltext/ED363628.pdf>.

Coates, DE 2007, 'Enhance the transfer of training', in J Brusino (ed.), *ASTD Infoline*, no. 0710, ASTD Press, Alexandria, viewed 24 June 2017, < https://www.2020insight.net/Docs4/IL0710-READ%20ONLY.PDF>.

Coffey, A & Atkinson, P 1996, *Making sense of qualitative data: complementary research strategies*, Sage, Thousand Oaks.

Collins, A 1990, Cognitive apprenticeship and instructional technology, in B Jones & L Idol (eds.), *Dimensions of Thinking and Cognitive Instruction*, Lawrence Erlbaum, Hillsdale, pp. 121-138, viewed 24 June 2017, <http://files.eric.ed.gov/fulltext/ED331465.pdf>.

———— 2002, Cognitive apprentice, in R Sawyer (ed.), *Cambridge Handbook of the Learning Sciences*, Cambridge University Press, New York, pp. 47–60, viewed 24 June 2017, <http://ocw.metu.edu.tr/pluginfile.php/9108/mod_resource/content/1/Collins.pdf>.

Collins, A, Brown, JS & Newman, SE 1987, *Cognitive Apprenticeship: Teaching the Craft of Reading, writing and Mathematics*, Technical Report No. 403, Center for the study of reading. University of Illinois, Urbana, Champaign, viewed 24 June 2017, <http://files.eric.ed.gov/fulltext/ED284181.pdf>.

————, Cognitive apprenticeship: teaching the craft of reading, writing and mathematics, in L Resnick (ed.), *Knowing, learning, and instruction: Essays in honor of Robert Glaser*, Lawrence Erlbaum, Hillsdale, pp. 453–494, viewed 24 June 2017, <http://www.dtic.mil/cgi-bin/GetTRDoc?AD=ADA178530>.

————1988, 'Cognitive apprenticeship: teaching the craft of reading, writing and mathematics', *Thinking: The Journal of Philosophy for Children*, vol. 8, no. 1, pp. 2–10, http://dx.doi.org/10.5840/thinking19888129.

Collins, H 2011, 'Three dimensions of expertise', *Phenomenology and the Cognitive Sciences*, vol. 12, no. 2, pp. 253–273, http://dx.doi.org/10.1007/s11097-011-9203-5.

Collins, H, Evans, R, Ribeiro, R & Hall, M 2006, 'Experiments with interactional expertise', *Studies in History and Philosophy of Science Part A*, vol. 37, no. 4, pp. 656–674, http://dx.doi.org/10.1016/j.shpsa.2006.09.005.

Cornford, I & Athanasou, J 1995, 'Developing expertise through training', *Industrial and Commercial Training*, vol. 27, no. 2, pp. 10–18, http://dx.doi.org/10.1108/00197859510082861.

Coulson, RL, Feltovich, PJ & Spiro, RJ 1997, 'Cognitive flexibility in medicine: an application to the recognition and understanding of hypertension', *Advances in Health Sciences Education*, vol. 2, no. 2, pp. 141–161, http://dx.doi.org/10.1023/A:1009780229455.

Crabtree, BF & Miller, WF 1992, A template approach to text analysis: developing and using codebooks, in B Crabtree & W Miller (eds.), *Doing Qualitative Research*, Sage, Newbury Park, pp. 93–109.

_____ (eds.) 1999, *Doing qualitative research*, Sage, Thousand Oaks.

Creswell, JW 2007, *Qualitative inquiry and research design: choosing among five approaches*, 2nd ed., Sage, Thousand Oaks, viewed 24 June 2017, <https://uk.sagepub.com/en-gb/asi/qualitative-inquiry-and-research-design/book235677>.

_____ 2013, *Research design: qualitative, quantitative, and mixed methods approaches*, 2nd edn, Sage, Thousand Oaks, viewed 24 June 2017, <http://www.ceil-conicet.gov.ar/wp-content/uploads/2015/10/Creswell-Cap-10.pdf>.

_____ 2014, *Research design: qualitative, quantitative, and mixed methods approaches*, 4th edn, Sage, Thousand Oaks.

Creswell, JW & Clark, VLP 2011, *Designing and conducting mixed methods research*, 2nd edn, Sage, Thousand Oaks.

Creswell, JW & Miller, DL 2000, 'Determining validity in qualitative inquiry', *Theory into Practice*, vol. 39, no. 3, pp. 124–130, http://dx.doi.org/10.1207/s15430421tip3903_2.

Crichton, M & Flin, R 2004, 'Identifying and training non-technical skills of nuclear emergency response teams', *Annals of Nuclear Energy*, vol. 31, no. 12, pp. 1317–1330, http://dx.doi.org/doi:10.1016/j.anucene.2004.03.011.

Cross, J 2007, *Informal learning: rediscovering the natural pathways that inspire innovation and performance*, Pfeiffer, San Francisco.

_____ 2013, 'How to shorten time-to-proficiency', blog post, 23 February, viewed 24 Jun 2017, <http://www.internettime.com/2013/02/how-to-shorten-time-to-proficiency/>.

Crossman, RM, Crossman, DC & Lovely, JE 2009, 'Human performance improvement', *Professional Safety*, vol. 54, no. 6, p. 63-72.

Crotty, M 1998, *The foundations of social research: meaning and perspective in the research process*, Sage, Thousand Oaks.

Crouse, P, Doyle, W & Young, JD 2011, 'Workplace learning strategies, barriers, facilitators and outcomes: a qualitative study among human resource management practitioners', *Human Resource Development International*, vol. 14, no. 1, pp. 39–55, http://dx.doi.org/10.1080/13678868.2011.542897.

Cseh, M, Watkins, KE & Marsick, V 1999, 'Re-conceptualizing Marsick and Watkins' model of informal and incidental learning in the workplace', in K Kuchinke (ed.), *Proceedings of the Academy of Human Resource Development Conference*, Washington D.C., Academy of Human Resource Development, Baton Rouge, pp. 349–356.

Curasi, CF 2001, 'A critical exploration of face-to-face interviewing vs computer-mediated interviewing', *International Journal of Market Research*, vol. 43, no. 4, p. 361, viewed 24 June 2017, <http://go.galegroup.com/ps/anonymous?id=GALE%7CA80011755>.

Custer, RL, Scarcella, JA & Stewart, BR 1999, 'The modified Delphi technique-a rotational modification', *Journal of Career and Technical Education*, vol. 15, no. 2, viewed 13 March 2018, <https://ejournals.lib.vt.edu/JCTE/article/view/702/1013>.

Cyphert, FR & Gant, WL 1971, 'The Delphi technique: a case study.', *Phi Delta Kappan*, vol. 52, no. 5, pp. 272–273.

Dabbish, LA & Kraut, RE 2006, 'Email overload at work: an analysis of factors associated with email strain', *Proceedings of the 20th Anniversary Conference on Computer Supported Cooperative Work (CSCW'06)*, Banff, 4-8 November, ACM, New York, pp. 431–440, http://dx.doi.org/10.1145/1180875.1180941.

Dailey, AL 1988, 'Faculty consensus at a multi-campus college through Delphi', *Community/Junior College Quarterly of Research and Practice*, vol. 12, no. 1, pp. 21–26.

Daley, BJ 2004, 'Using concept maps in qualitative research', in N Derbentseva, F Safayeni & A Cañas (eds.), *Proceedings of the First International Conference on Concept Mapping*, Pamplona, 14-17 September, Universidad Pública de Navarra, Pamlona, viewed 24 June 2017, <http://eprint.ihmc.us/60/1/cmc2004-060.pdf>.

Dalkey, NC 1972, The delphi method: an experimental study of group opinion, in N Dalkey, D Rourke, R Lewis & D Snyder (eds.), Studies in the quality of life: Delphi and decision-making, Lexington Books, Lexington, pp. 13–54.

Dall'Alba, G & Sandberg, J 2006, 'Unveiling professional development: a critical review of stage models', *Review of Educational Research*, vol. 76, no. 3, pp. 383–412, http://dx.doi.org/10.3102/00346543076003383.

Darzi, M, Hosseini, M, Liaei, AA, Manesh, ZM & Asghari, H 2011, 'Accelerating growth in high tech MSEs through tacit knowledge sharing using case-based recommender systems', viewed 24 June 2017, <http://old.ictrc.ir/Documents/Document0/Accelerating%20growth1.pdf>.

Davachi, L, Kiefer, T, Rock, D & Rock, L 2010, 'Learning that lasts through ages', *NeuroLeadership Journal*, vol. 3, no. 3, pp. 1–13, viewed 24 June 2017, <https://www.ahri.com.au/__data/assets/pdf_file/0016/16144/Learning-that-lasts-through-AGES.pdf>.

Davies, A & Hobday, M 2011, *The business of projects: managing innovation in complex products and systems*, Paperback edn, Cambridge University Press, Cambridge.

Day, J 2002, 'What is an expert?', *Radiography*, vol. 8, no. 2, pp. 63–70, viewed <http://www.blumehaiti.org/uploads/2/8/3/8/2838360/fallcelloday.pdf>.

Dean, PJ 2016, 'Tom Gilbert: engineering performance with or without training', *Performance Improvement*, vol. 55, no. 2, pp. 30–38, http://dx.doi.org/10.1002/pfi.21556.

Deloitte 2017, *Rewriting the rules for the digital age: 2017 Deloitte Global Human Capital Trends*, Deloitte University Press, UK, viewed 24 June 2017, <https://www2.deloitte.com/us/en/pages/human-capital/articles/introduction-human-capital-trends.html>.

Demir, S, Abou-Jaoude, E & Kumral, M 2017, 'Cognitive work analysis to comprehend operations and organisations in the mining industry', *International Journal of Mining Science and Technology*, col. 27, no. 4, pp. 605-609, http://dx.doi.org/10.1016/j.ijmst.2017.05.008.

Dennen, VP 2004, Cognitive apprenticeship in educational practice research on scaffolding, modeling, mentoring, and coaching as instructional strategies, in D Jonassen (ed.), *Handbook of research for educational communications and technology*, Lawrence Erlbaum, Mahwah, pp. 813–828, viewed 24 June 2017, <http://www.aect.org/edtech/ed1/31.pdf>.

Dennen, VP & Burner, KJ 2008, The cognitive apprenticeship model in educational practice, in J Spector, M Merrill, J van Merriënboer & M Driscoll (eds.), *Handbook of research on educational communications and technology*, Lawrence Erlbaum, Mahwah, pp. 425–439, viewed 24 June 2017, <http://www.aect.org/edtech/edition3/ER5849x_C034.fm.pdf>.

Denzin, NK (ed.) 2009, *The research act: a theoretical introduction to sociological methods*, Routledge, New York, http://dx.doi.org/10.2307/1318434.

Denzin, NK & Lincoln, YS (eds.) 2017, *The sage handbook of qualitative research*, 5th edn, Sage, Thousand Oaks.

Deslauriers, L, Schelew, E & Wieman, C 2011, 'Improved learning in a large-enrollment physics class', *Science*, vol. 332, no. 6031, pp. 862–864, http://dx.doi.org/10.1126/science.1201783.

Deterline, WA & Rosenberg, MJ 1992, *Performance technology: Success stories*, International Society for Performance Improvement, Washinton, D.C.

Deutscher, C, Gürtler, O, Prinz, J & Weimar, D 2017, 'The payoff to consistency in performance', *Economic Inquiry*, vol. 55, no. 2, pp. 1091–1103, http://dx.doi.org/10.1111/ecin.12415.

Dgedge, M, Mendoza, A, Necochea, E, Bossemeyer, D, Rajabo, M & Fullerton, J 2014, 'Assessment of the nursing skill mix in mozambique using a task analysis methodology', *Human Resources for Health*, vol. 12, no. 5, pp. 1-9, http://dx.doi.org/10.1186/1478-4491-12-5.

DiBello, L 1996, 'Providing multiple 'ways in' to expertise for learners with different backgrounds when it works and what it suggests about adult cognitive development', *Journal of Experimental & Theoretical Artificial Intelligence*, vol. 8, no. 3-4, pp. 229–257, http://dx.doi.org/10.1080/095281396147311.

DiBello, L & Missildine, W 2008, 'Information technologies and intuitive expertise: a method for implementing complex organisational change among new yorkcity transit authority's bus maintainers', *Cognition, Technology and Work*, vol. 12, no. 1, pp. 61–75, http://dx.doi.org/10.1007/s10111-008-0126-z.

_____ 2011, 'Future of immersive instructional design for the global knowledge economy: a case study of an IBM project management training in virtual worlds', *International Journal of Web Based Learning and Teaching Technologies*, vol. 6, no. 3, pp. 14–34, http://dx.doi.org/10.4018/jwltt,2011070102.

_____ 2013, The future of immersive instructional design for the global knowledge economy: a case study of an IBM project, in N Karacapilidis, M Raisinghani & E Ng (eds.), *Web-Based and Blended Educational Tools and Innovations*, Information Science Reference, Hershey, pp. 115–135.

DiBello, L, Missildine, W & Struttman, M 2009, 'Intuitive expertise and empowerment: the long-term impact of simulation training on changing accountabilities in a biotech firm', *Mind, Culture, and Activity*, vol. 16, no. 1, pp. 11–31, http://dx.doi.org/10.1080/10749030802363863.

Van Dijk, JA 1990, 'Delphi questionnaires versus individual and group interviews: a comparison case', *Technological Forecasting and Social Change*, vol. 37, no. 3, pp. 293–304.

Doane, SM, Alderton, DL, Sohn, YW & Pellegrino, JW 1996, 'Acquisition and transfer of skilled performance: are visual discrimination skills stimulus specific?', *Journal of Experimental Psychology: Human Perception and Performance*, vol. 22, no. 5, pp. 1218–1248, http://dx.doi.org/10.1037/0096-1523.22.5.1218.

Dodd, L 2009, 'Valuing investment in military command and control training: can we use intermediate decision-based measures?', *14th International Command and Control Research and Technology Symposium*, Washington, D.C., 15-17 June, Department of Defense, USA, viewed 24 June 2017, <https://pdfs.semanticscholar.org/681c/d5102b91fbbee2c7c8f586c432f781ca2b9a.pdf>.

Domegan, C & Fleming, D 2007, *Marketing research in Ireland: theory and practice*, 3rd edn, M.H. Gill & Co., Dublin.

Donderi, D, Niall, KK, Fish, K & Goldstein, B 2012, 'Above-real-time training (ARTT) improves transfer to a simulated flight control task', *Human Factors: The Journal of the Human Factors and Ergonomics Society*, vol. 54, no. 3, pp. 469–479, http://dx.doi.org/10.1177/0018720812439711.

Dooley, L, Lupton, G & O'Sullivan, D 2005, 'Multiple project management: a modern competitive necessity', *Journal of Manufacturing Technology Management*, vol. 16, no. 5, pp. 466–482, http://dx.doi.org/10.1108/17410380510600464.

Dörfler, V, Baracskai, Z & Velencei, J 2009, 'Knowledge levels: 3-D model of the levels of expertise', paper presented to The 68th Annual Meeting of the Academy of Management, Chicago, 7-11 August, viewed 24 June 2017, <http://www.viktordorfler.com/webdav/papers/KnowledgeLevels.pdf>.

Dowling, M 2006, 'Approaches to reflexivity in qualitative research', *Nurse Researcher*, vol. 13, no. 3, pp. 7–21, http://dx.doi.org/10.7748/nr2006.04.13.3.7.c5975.

Dragoni, L, Park, H, Soltis, J & Forte-Trammell, S 2014, 'Show and tell: how supervisors facilitate leader development among transitioning leaders', *Journal of Applied Psychology*, vol. 99, no. 1, pp. 66-86, http://dx.doi.org/10.1037/a0034452.

Dreyfus, HL & Dreyfus, SE 1986, *Mind over machine: the power of human intuition and expertise in the era of the computer*, The Free Press, New York, http://dx.doi.org/10.1109/mex.1987.4307079.

_____ 2004, 'The ethical implications of the five-stage skill-acquisition model', *Bulletin of Science, Technology and Society*, vol. 24, no. 3, pp. 251–264, http://dx.doi.org/10.1177/0270467604265023.

_____ 2005, 'Peripheral vision: expertise in real world contexts', *Organisation Studies*, vol. 26, no. 5, pp. 779–792, http://dx.doi.org/10.1177/0170840605053102.

_____ 2009, The relationship of theory and practice in the acquisition of skill, in P Benner, C Tanner & C Chesla (eds.), *Expertise in nursing practice: Caring, clinical judgment, and ethics*, Springer, New York, pp. 1–23, viewed 24 June 2017, <http://lghttp.48653.nexcesscdn.net/80223CF/springer-static/media/samplechapters/9780826125446/9780826125446_chapter.pdf>.

Dreyfus, SE 2004, 'The five-stage model of adult skill acquisition', *Bulletin of Science, Technology & Society*, vol. 24, no. 3, pp. 177–181, http://dx.doi.org/10.1177/0270467604264992.

Driscoll, J 2007, *Practising clinical supervision: a reflective approach for healthcare professionals*, 2nd edn, Elsevier Health Sciences, Edinburgh.

Dror, IE 2011, The paradox of human expertise: why experts get it wrong, in N Kapur (ed.), *The paradoxical brain*, Cambridge University Press, New York, pp. 177–188, http://dx.doi.org/10.1017/cbo9780511978098.011.

Druckman, D & Bjork, RA 1991, *In the mind's eye: enhancing human performance*, D Druckman & R Bjork (eds.), National Academies Press, Washington, D.C., http://dx.doi.org/10.17226/1580.

Duan, X, Wu, D & Bautista, AF 2011, 'Assessment of reaching proficiency in procedural skills: fiberoptic airway simulator training in novices', *Open Access Medical Statistics*, vol. 1, pp. 45–50, http://dx.doi.org/10.2147/OAMS.S24625.

DuFour, R, DuFour, R, Eaker, R & Many, T 2016, *Learning by doing*, Solution Tree Press, Bloomington, viewed 24 June 2017, <https://www.researchgate.net/profile/Richard_Felder/publication/279589632>.

Duguay, SM & Korbut, K a 2002, 'Designing a training program which delivers results quickly!', *Industrial and Commercial Training*, vol. 34, no. 6, pp. 223–228, http://dx.doi.org/10.1108/00197850210442458.

Dumas, A & Hanchane, S 2010, 'How does job-training increase firm performance? the case of morocco', *International Journal of Manpower*, vol. 31, no. 5, pp. 585–602, http://dx.doi.org/10.1108/01437721011066371.

Elliott, N & Lazenbatt, A 2005, 'How to recognise a 'quality' grounded theory research study', *The Australian Journal of Advanced Nursing*, vol. 22, no. 3, p. 48, viewed 24 June 2017, <http://www.ajan.com.au/vol22/vol22.3-8.pdf>.

Elliott, PH & Folsom, AC 2013, *Exemplary Performance: Driving Business Results by Benchmarking Your Star Performers*, John Wiley & Sons, San Francisco.

Emily, D & Krob, A 2014, 'Partnering to improve time to competency and proficiency', *Talent Development*, vol. 68, no. 8, pp. 40–44.

Englander, M 2012, 'The interview: data collection in descriptive phenomenological human scientific research', *Journal of Phenomenological Psychology*, vol. 43, no. 1, pp. 13–35, http://dx.doi.org/10.1163/156916212x632943.

Enos, MD, Kehrhahn, MT & Bell, A 2003, 'Informal learning and the transfer of learning: how managers develop proficiency', *Human Resource Development Quarterly*, vol. 14, no. 4, pp. 369–387, http://dx.doi.org/10.1002/hrdq.1074.

Eraut, M 1994, *Developing professional knowledge and competence*, Routledge, London, http://dx.doi.org/10.4324/9780203486016.

―――― 2004, 'Informal learning in the workplace', *Studies in Continuing Education*, vol. 26, no. 2, pp. 247–273, http://dx.doi.org/10.1080/158037042000225245.

―――― 2007a, 'Learning from other people in the workplace', *Oxford Review of Education*, vol. 33, no. 4, pp. 403–422, http://dx.doi.org/10.1080/03054980701425706.

―――― 2007b, How professionals learn through work, in N Jackson (ed.), *Learning to be Professional through a Higher Education E-Book*, Surrey Centre of Excellence in Professional Training and Education, University of Surrey, Surrey, Chapter A2, pp. 1–28, viewed 24 June 2017, <http://learningtobeprofessional.pbworks.com/f/CHAPTER+A2+MICHAEL+ERAUT.pdf>.

―――― 2007c, *Learning in the Workplace: Research Summary for House of Commons Committee*, House of Commons Committee, London.

Ericsson, K, Charness, N, Feltovich, P & Hoffman, R (eds.) 2006, *Cambridge handbook of expertise and expert performance*, Cambridge University Press, New York.

Ericsson, KA 2000, 'Expertise in interpreting: an expert-performance perspective', *Interpreting*, vol. 5, no. 2, pp. 187–220, http://dx.doi.org/10.1075/intp.5.2.08eri.

―――― 2002, Attaining excellence through deliberate practice: insights from the study of expert performance, in M Ferrari (ed.), *The Pursuit of Excellence Through Education*, Lawrence Erlbaum, Mahwah, pp. 21–55, http://dx.doi.org/10.1002/9780470690048.ch1.

_____ 2003, Development of elite performance and deliberate practice: an update from the perspective of the expert performance approach, in J Starkes & K Ericsson (eds.), *Expert Performance in Sports: Advances in Research on Sport Expertise*, Human Kinetics, Champaign, pp. 53–83, viewed 24 June 2017, <http://drjj5hc4fteph.cloudfront.net/Articles/2003%20Starkes%20and%20Ericsson%20Chapt%203.pdf>.

_____ 2004, 'Deliberate practice and the acquisition and maintenance of expert performance in medicine and related domains', *Academic Medicine*, vol. 79, no. 10, pp. 70–81, http://dx.doi.org/10.1097/00001888-200410001-00022.

_____ 2006a, The influence of experience and deliberate practice on the development of superior expert performance, in K Ericsson, N Charness, P Feltovich & R Hoffman (eds.), *The Cambridge Handbook of Expertise and Expert Performance*, Cambridge University Press, New York, pp. 683–704, http://dx.doi.org/10.1017/CBO9780511816796.038.

_____ 2006b, Protocol analysis and expert thought: concurrent verbalizations of thinking during experts' performance on representative tasks, in K Ericsson, N Charness, P Feltovich & R Hoffman (eds.), *The Cambridge Handbook of Expertise and Expert Performance*, Cambridge University Press, New York, pp. 223–242, http://dx.doi.org/10.1017/CBO9780511816796.013.

_____ 2007, 'Deliberate practice and the modifiability of body and mind: toward a science of the structure and acquisition of expert and elite performance', *International Journal of Sport Psychology*, vol. 38, no. 1, pp. 4–34, viewed 24 June 2017, <http://drjj5hc4fteph.cloudfront.net/Articles/2007 IJSP - Ericsson - Deliberate Practice target art.pdf>.

_____ 2008, 'Deliberate practice and acquisition of expert performance: a general overview', *Academic Emergency Medicine*, vol. 15, no. 11, pp. 988–94, http://dx.doi.org/10.1111/j.1553-2712.2008.00227.x.

_____ (eds.) 2009a, *Development of professional expertise: Toward measurement of expert performance and design of optimal learning environments*, Cambridge University Press, New York.

_____ 2009b, 'Discovering deliberate practice activities that overcome plateaus and limits on improvement of performance', in A Willamon, S Pretty & R Buck (eds.), *International Symposium on Performance Science*, Auckland, 15-18 December, European Association of Conservatoires (AEC), Utrecht, The Netherlands, pp. 11–21, viewed 24 June 2017, <http://www.performancescience.org/ISPS2009/Proceedings/Rows/003Ericsson.pdf>.

_____ 2009c, Enhancing the development of professional performance: implications from the study of deliberate practice, in K Ericsson (ed.), *Development of professional expertise: Toward measurement of expert performance and design of optimal learning environments*, Cambridge University Press, New York, pp. 405–431, http://dx.doi.org/10.1017/cbo9780511609817.022.

_____ 2014, 'Why expert performance is special and cannot be extrapolated from studies of performance in the general population: a response to criticisms', *Intelligence*, vol. 45, no. 4, pp. 81–103, http://dx.doi.org/10.1016/j.intell.2013.12.001.

Ericsson, KA & Charness, N 1994, 'Expert performance: its structure and acquisition', *American Psychologist*, vol. 49, no. 8, pp. 725–747, http://dx.doi.org/10.1037/0003-066X.49.8.725.

Ericsson, KA, Krampe, RTR, Tesch-romer, C, Ashworth, C, Carey, G, Grassia, J, Hastie, R, Heizmann, S, Kellogg, R, Levin, R, Lewis, C, Oliver, W, Poison, P, Rehder, R, Schlesinger, K, Schneider, V & Tesch-Römer, C 1993, 'The role of deliberate practice in the acquisition of expert performance', *Psychological Review*, vol. 100, no. 3, pp. 363–406, http://dx.doi.org/10.1037/0033-295X.100.3.363.

Ericsson, KA, Prietula, MJ & Cokely, ET 2007, 'The making of an expert', *Harvard Business Review*, vol. 85, nos. 7-8, pp. 114–121, 193, viewed 24 June 2017, <https://www.researchgate.net/publication/6196703>.

Ericsson, KA & Towne, TJ 2010, 'Expertise', *Wiley Interdisciplinary Reviews: Cognitive Science*, vol. 1, no. 3, pp. 404–416, http://dx.doi.org/10.1002/wcs.47.

Ericsson, KA & Ward, P 2007, 'Capturing the naturally occurring superior performance of experts in the laboratory: toward a science of expert and exceptional performance', *Current Directions in Psychological Science*, vol. 16, no. 6, pp. 346–350, http://dx.doi.org/10.1111/j.1467-8721.2007.00533.x.

Evers, AT, Kreijns, K, Heijden, BIJMVD & Gerrichhauzen, JTG 2011, 'An organisational and task perspective model aimed at enhancing teachers' professional development and occupational expertise', *Human Resource Development Review*, vol. 10, no. 2, pp. 151–179, http://dx.doi.org/10.1177/1534484310397852.

Fadde, P & Sullivan, P 2013, 'Using interactive video to develop preservice teachers' classroom awareness', *Contemporary Issues in Technology and Teacher Education*, vol. 13, no. 2, pp. 156–174, viewed <http://www.citejournal.org/volume-13/issue-2-13/general/using-interactive-video-to-develop-preservice-teachers-classroom-awareness/>.

Fadde, PJ 2007, 'Instructional design for advanced learners: training recognition skills to hasten expertise', *Educational Technology Research and Development*, vol. 57, no. 3, pp. 359–376, http://dx.doi.org/10.1007/s11423-007-9046-5.

―――― 2009a, Training complex psychomotor performance skills: a part-task approach, in K Silber & W Foshay (eds.), *Handbook of Training and Improving Workplace Performance, Volume I: Instructional Design and Training Delivery*, Pfeiffer, San Francisco, pp. 468–507, http://dx.doi.org/10.1002/9780470587089.ch14.

―――― 2009b, 'Training of expertise and expert performance', *Technology, Instructional, Cognition and Learning*, vol. 7, no. 2, pp. 77–81, viewed 24 June 2017, <http://web.coehs.siu.edu/Units/CI/Faculty/PFadde/Research/xbtintro.pdf>.

―――― 2009c, 'Expertise-based training: getting more learners over the bar in less time', *Technology, Instructional, Cognition and Learning*, vol. 7, no. 2, pp. 171–197, viewed 24 June 2017, <http://web.coehs.siu.edu/units/ci/faculty/pfadde/Research/xbttraining.pdf>.

―――― 2010, 'Look'ma, no hands: part-task training of perceptual-cognitive skills to accelerate psychomotor expertise', *The Interservice Industry Training, Simulation and Education Conference (I/ITSEC)*, Orlando, 29 November-2 December, National Training and Simulation Association (NTSA), Arlington, pp. 1–10, viewed 24 June 2017, <http://ntsa.metapress.com/index/A4018183135VJ842.pdf>.

―――― 2012, 'What's wrong with this picture? video-annotation with expert-model feedback as a method of accelerating novices' situation awareness', *The Interservice Industry Training, Simulation and Education Conference (I/ITSEC)*, London, 3-6 December, National Training and Simulation Association (NTSA), Arlington, viewed 24 June 2017, <http://www.peterfadde.com/Research/iitsec12.pdf>.

―――― 2013, 'Accelerating the acquisition of intuitive decision-making through expertise-based training (XBT)', paper presented to the The Interservice Industry Training, Simulation and Education Conference (I/ITSEC), Orlando, 2-5 December, National Training and Simulation Association (NTSA), Arlington, viewed 24 June 2017, <http://peterfadde.com/Research/iitsec13.pdf>.

―――― 2016, 'Instructional design for accelerated macrocognitive expertise in the baseball workplace', *Frontiers in Psychology*, vol. 7, no. 292, pp. 1–16, http://dx.doi.org/10.3389/fpsyg.2016.00292.

Fadde, PJ & Klein, G 2010, 'Deliberate performance: accelerating expertise in natural settings', *Performance Improvement*, vol. 49, no. 9, pp. 5–14, http://dx.doi.org/10.1002/pfi.

―――― 2012, 'Accelerating expertise using action learning activities', *Cognitive Technology*, vol. 17, no. 1, pp. 11–18, viewed 24 June 2017, <http://peterfadde.com/Research/cognitivetechnology12.pdf>.

Faneuff, RS, and Stone, BM, Curry, GL & Hageman, DC 1990, *Extending the Time to Proficiency Model for Simultaneous Application to Multiple Jobs*, Report No. AFHRL-TP-90-42, Air Force Systems Command Brooks Air Force Base, San Antonio, viewed 24 June 2017, <http://www.dtic.mil/docs/citations/ADA224759>.

Farnsworth, V, Kleanthous, I & Wenger-Trayner, E 2016, 'Communities of practice as a social theory of learning: a conversation with etienne wenger', *British Journal of Educational Studies*, vol. 64, no. 2, pp. 139–160, http://dx.doi.org/10.1080/00071005.2015.1133799.

Farrington-Darby, T & Wilson, JR 2006, 'The nature of expertise: a review', *Applied Ergonomics*, vol. 37, no. 1, pp. 17–32, http://dx.doi.org/10.1016/j.apergo.2005.09.001.

Feldon, DF 2006, 'The implications of research on expertise for curriculum and pedagogy', *Educational Psychology Review*, vol. 19, no. 2, pp. 91–110, http://dx.doi.org/10.1007/s10648-006-9009-0.

Feldon, DF, Timmerman, BC, Stowe, KA & Showman, R 2010, 'Translating expertise into effective instruction: the impacts of cognitive task analysis (cta) on lab report quality and student retention in the biological sciences', *Journal of Research in Science Teaching*, vol. 47, no. 10, pp. 1165–1185, http://dx.doi.org/10.1002/tea.20382.

Feltovich, PJ, Spiro, RJ & Coulson, RL 1997, Issues of expert flexibility in contexts characterized by complexity and change, in P Feltovich, K Ford & R Hoffman (eds.), *Expertise in context: Human and machine*, MIT Press,

Cambridge, pp. 125–146, viewed 24 June 2017, <http://www.academia.edu/download/29334639/Issues_of_Expert_Flexibility.pdf>.

Fendt, J, Kaminska-Labbé, R & Sachs, WM 2008, 'Producing and socializing relevant management knowledge: re-turn to pragmatism', *European Business Review*, vol. 20, no. 6, pp. 471–491, http://dx.doi.org/10.1108/09555340810913502.

Fenwick, T 2003, 'Innovation: examining workplace learning in new enterprises', *Journal of Workplace Learning*, vol. 15, no. 3, pp. 123–132, http://dx.doi.org/10.1108/13665620310468469.

Fidel, R & Pejtersen, AM 2004, 'From information behaviour research to the design of information systems: the cognitive work analysis framework', *Information Research: An International Electronic Journal*, vol. 10, no. 1, viewed 24 June 2017, <http://www.informationr.net/ir/10-1/paper210.html>.

Fineman, S 2003, *Understanding emotion at work*, Sage, London.

Fink, AS 2000, 'The role of the researcher in the qualitative research process a potential barrier to archiving qualitative data', *Forum Qualitative Sozialforschung/Forum: Qualitative Social Research*, vol. 1, no. 3, viewed 24 June 2017, <http://www.qualitative-research.net/index.php/fqs/article/view/1021/2201>.

Fiorella, L, Vogel-Walcutt, JJ & Fiore, S 2012, 'Differential impact of two types of metacognitive prompting provided during simulation-based training', *Computers in Human Behavior*, vol. 28, no. 2, pp. 696–702, http://dx.doi.org/10.1016/j.chb.2011.11.017.

Fischer, A, Greiff, S & Funke, J 2011, 'The process of solving complex problems keywords', *The Journal of Problem Solving*, vol. 4, no. 1, pp. 19–42, http://dx.doi.org/10.7771/1932-6246.1118.

Fitt, PM & Posner, M 1967, *Learning and skilled performance in human performance*, Brock-Cole, Belmont.

Fitt, PM 1964, Perceptual-motor skill learning, in A Melton (ed.), *Categories of human learning*, Academic Press, New York, pp. 243–285, viewed 24 Jun 2017, < http://www.sciencedirect.com/science/article/pii/B9781483231457500169>.

Fletcher, J 2010, *Phase 1 Iwar Test Results*, IDA Document No. D-4047, Institute for Defense Analyses, Alexandria, Virginia, viewed 24 June 2017, <http://www.dtic.mil/dtic/tr/fulltext/u2/a518737.pdf>.

Fred, CL 2002, *Breakaway: Deliver value to your customers—Fast!*, Jossey-Bass, San Francisco, viewed 24 June 2017, <http://www.wiley.com/WileyCDA/WileyTitle/productCd-0787961647.html>.

Freeman, S, Eddy, SL, McDonough, M, Smith, MK, Okoroafor, N, Jordt, H & Wenderoth, MP 2014, 'Active learning increases student performance in science, engineering, and mathematics.', *Proceedings of the National Academy of Sciences of the United States of America*, vol. 111, no. 23, pp. 8410–8415, http://dx.doi.org/10.1073/pnas.1319030111.

Furterer, SL (ed.) 2009, *Lean Six Sigma in service: applications and case studies*, CRC Press, Boca Raton.

Gabriel, Y & Griffiths, DS 2004, Stories in organisational research, in C Cassell and G Symon (ed.), *Essential guide to qualitative methods in organisational research*, Sage.

Gagne, RM & Briggs, LJ 1974, *Principles of instructional design*, Holt, Rinehart & Winston.

Gal, E, Meishar-tal, H, Non, RB, Ben-Basat, A & Paikin, L 2017, 'Applying tablet-based performance support application for technicians' training at the Israeli air force: a case study', *Performance Improvement Quarterly*, vol. 30, no. 2, pp. 121–136, http://dx.doi.org/10.1002/piq.21243.

Gander, SL 2006, 'Beyond mere competency: measuring proficiency with outcome proficiency indicator scales', *Performance Improvement*, vol. 45, no. 4, pp. 38–44, http://dx.doi.org/10.1002/pfi.2006.4930450409.

Gann, DM & Salter, AJ 2000, 'Innovation in project-based, service-enhanced firms: the construction of complex products and systems', *Research Policy*, vol. 29, no. 7, pp. 955–972, http://dx.doi.org/10.1016/S0048-7333(00)00114-1.

Gannan, T 2002, 'Train them less; support them more- the case for integrating online learning with business process guidance', in E McKay (ed.), *E-Learning Conference on Design and Development 2002: International Best Practice to Enhance Corporate Performance*, Melboune, RMIT Publishing, Melboune, pp. 1–8, viewed 24 June 2017, <http://search.informit.org/documentSummary;dn=747615798730397;res=IELBUS>.

Garrick, J 1998, Informal learning in the workplace: unmasking human resource development, Routledge, London, http://dx.doi.org/10.4324/9780203028926.

Ge, X & Hardré, PL 2010, 'Self-processes and learning environment as influences in the development of expertise in instructional design', *Learning Environments Research*, vol. 13, no. 1, pp. 23–41, http://dx.doi.org/10.1007/s10984-009-9064-9.

Geissler, N, Hoffmeier, A, Kotzsch, S, Trapp, S, Riemenschneider, N & Korb, W 2012, 'Cognitive task analysis-a relevant method for the development of simulation training in surgery', in D. de Waard, N. Merat, A Jamson, Y Barnard & O Carsten (eds.), *Human Factors of Systems and Technology*, pp. 307–315, http://dx.doi.org/10.7205/MILMED-D-13-00211.

Giacobbi Jr, PR, Poczwardowski, A & Hager, PF 2005, 'A pragmatic research philosophy for applied sport psychology', *The Sport Psychologist*, vol. 19, no. 1, pp. 18–31, viewed 24 June 2017, <http://digitalcommons.brockport.edu/cgi/viewcontent.cgi?article=1079&context=pes_facpub>.

Gilbert, TF 1978, 'Human competence—engineering worthy performance', *Performance Improvement*, vol. 17, no. 9, pp. 19–27, http://dx.doi.org/10.1002/pfi.4180170915.

⎯⎯⎯⎯⎯⎯ 2013, *Human Competence: Engineering Worthy Performance*, Tribute edn, Pfeiffer, San Francisco.

Gill, P, Stewart, K, Treasure, E & Chadwick, B 2008, 'Methods of data collection in qualitative research: interviews and focus groups', *British Dental Journal*, vol. 204, no. 6, pp. 291–295, http://dx.doi.org/10.1038/bdj.2008.192.

Gilley, J, England, S & Wesley, A 1998, Principles of Human Resource Management, Perseus Publishing.

Girgis, MM 2011, 'An active learning environment for enriching mathematical, conceptual, and problem-solving competencies', *118th ASEE Annual Conference & Exposition*, Vancouver, 26-29 June, American Society for Engineering Education (ASEE), Washington D.C., pp. 22.159.1–22.159.20, viewed 24 June 2017, <https://peer.asee.org/an-active-learning-environment-for-enriching-mathematical-conceptual-and-problem-solving-competencies.pdf>.

Glaser, R & Chi, MTH 1988, Overview, in M Chi, R Glaser & M Farr (eds.), *The nature of expertise*, Lawrence Erlbaum, Mahwah, pp. xv–xxviii.

Gobet, F 2013, 'Expertise vs. talent', *Talent Development & Excellence*, vol. 5, no. 1, pp. 75-86, viewed <http://citeseerx.ist.psu.edu/viewdoc/download?doi=10.1.1.297.2267&rep=rep1&type=pdf>.

Gok, A & Law, M 2017, 'Performance improvement in the literature', *Performance Improvement*, vol. 56, no. 1, pp. 14–20, http://dx.doi.org/10.1002/pfi.21675.

Goldkuhl, G 2008, 'What kind of pragmatism in information systems research', in P Ågerfalk, M Aakhus & M Lind (eds.), *Proceedings of the Inaugural Meeting of AIS Special Interest Group on Pragmatist IS Research*, Paris, 14 December, Sprouts, Atlanta, pp. 3–8, viewed 24 June 2017, <http://www.academia.edu/download/30818892/SIGPrag2008Proceedings.pdf#page=8>.

⎯⎯⎯⎯⎯⎯ 2012, 'Pragmatism vs interpretivism in qualitative information systems research', *European Journal of Information Systems*, vol. 21, no. 2, pp. 135–146, http://dx.doi.org/10.1057/ejis.2011.54.

Gordon, TJ 1994, The Delphi method, in J Glenn & T Gordon (eds.), *Futures research methodology - Version 3.0*, The Millennium Project, Washington, D.C., viewed 24 June 2017, <http://millennium-project.org/FRMv3_0/04-Delphi.pdf>.

Gorman, P, Moore, R, Blake, D & Phillips, MG 2004, 'An empirical study of the effectiveness of publicly-funded 'structured on-site training': implications for policy and practice', *Journal of Vocational Education and Training*, vol. 56, no. 3, pp. 387–408, viewed 30 March 2018, <https://www.researchgate.net/profile/Daniel_Blake4/publication/249032990>.

Gott, SP 1988, *Rediscovering Learning: Acquiring Expertise in Real World Problem Solving Tasks*, Report No. AL/HR-TR-1997-0009, United States Air Force Armstrong Laboratory, Brooks, viewed 24 June 2017, <http://www.dtic.mil/dtic/tr/fulltext/u2/a345016.pdf>.

Gott, SP, Lesgold, A & Kane, RS 1996, Tutoring for transfer of technical competence, in B Wilson (ed.), *Constructivist learning environments: Case studies in instructional design*, Education Technology, Englewood Cliffs, pp. 33–48, http://dx.doi.org/10.1037/e447862004-001.

Gott, SP & Lesgold, AM 2000, Competence in the workplace: how cognitive performance models and situated instruction can accelerate skill acquisition, in R Glaser (ed.), *Advances in instructional psychology: Educational design and cognitive science, Vol. 5*, Lawrence Erlbaum, Mahwah, pp. 239–327.

Gottfredson, C & Mosher, B 2011, *Innovative performance support: Strategies and practices for learning in the workflow*, McGraw Hill, New York.

Government Publishing Office 2013, *Pilot Certification and Qualification Requirements for Air Carrier*, No. 78, Government Publishing Office, USA.

Graesser, AC, McNamara, DS & VanLehn, K 2005, 'Scaffolding deep comprehension strategies through Point&Query, AutoTutor, and iSTART', *Educational Psychologist*, vol. 40, no. 4, pp. 225–234, viewed 24 June 2017, <http://www.learnlab.org/uploads/mypslc/publications/graesser%20mcnamara%20vanlehn%20ep%2005.pdf>.

Grage, S, Sullivan, JO, Andrews, A, Cannon-bowers, J, Haass, MJ, Mccarthy, J, Pfautz, S & Bindas, T 2011, 'A demonstration of human performance assessment concepts to facilitate expertise of submarine command decision making in an operational environment', paper presented to the Human Systems Integration Symposium 2011, Vienna, 31 October – 2 November, viewed 24 June 2017, <http://www.academia.edu/download/39411545/HSIS_Final_paper_Grage_Submission_09Sept2011_Rev2.doc>.

Gratton, L 2016, 'Rethinking the manager's role', *MIT Sloan Management Review*, vol. 58, no. 1, p. 8, viewed 24 June 2017, <http://sloanreview.mit.edu/article/technology-and-the-end-of-management/>.

Gratton, L & Scott, A 2016, *The 100-year life: living and working in an age of longevity*, Bloomsbury, London.

Gray, DE 2014, *Doing research in the real world*, 3rd ed., Sage, London, viewed 24 June 2017, <http://www.sagepub.in/upm-data/58626_Gray__Doing_Research_in_the_Real_World.pdf>.

Grenier, RS & Kehrhahn, M 2008, 'Toward an integrated model of expertise redevelopment and its implications for hrd', *Human Resource Development Review*, vol. 7, no. 2, pp. 198–217, http://dx.doi.org/10.1177/1534484308316653.

Griffin, MA, Neal, A & Parker, SK 2007, 'A new model of work role performance: positive behavior in uncertain and interdependent contexts', *Academy of Management Journal*, vol. 50, no. 2, pp. 327–347, http://dx.doi.org/10.5465/amj.2007.24634438.

Grix, J 2002, 'Introducing students to the generic terminology of social research', *Politics*, vol. 22, no. 3, pp. 175–186, http://dx.doi.org/10.1111/1467-9256.00173.

De Groot, A 1965, *Thought and choice in chess (translated from the Dutch original, 1946)*, Reprinted edn, G Baylor (ed.), Ishi Press, New York.

De Groot, A 1966, Perception and memory versus thought: some old ideas and recent findings, in B Kleinmuntz (ed.), *Problem solving*, John Wiley, New York, pp. 19–50.

Grossman, R, Salas, E, Pavlas, D & Rosen, MA 2013, 'Using instructional features to enhance demonstration-based training in management education', *Academy of Management Learning & Education*, vol. 12, no. 2, pp. 219–243, http://dx.doi.org/10.5465/amle.2011.0527.

Grossman, R, Spencer, JM & Salas, E 2014, Enhancing naturalistic decision making and accelerating expertise in the workplace: training strategies that work, in S Highhouse, R Dalal & E Salas (eds.), *Judgment and decision making at work*, Routledge, New York, pp. 277–325.

Guba, EG 1990, The alternative paradigm dialog, in E Guba (ed.), *The paradigm dialog*, Sage, Newbury Park, pp. 17–27, viewed 24 June 2017, <http://www.appstate.edu/~jacksonay/rcoe/guba.pdf>.

Guba, EG & Lincoln, YS 1992, *Effective evaluation: improving the usefulness of evaluation results through responsive and naturalistic approaches*, Reprint edn, Jossey-Bass, San Francisco.

_____ 1994, Competing paradigms in qualitative research, in N Denzin & Y Lincoln (eds.), *Handbook of Qualitative Research*, Sage, Thousand Oaks, pp. 105–117, viewed 24 June 2017, < http://kanagawa.lti.cs.cmu.edu/11780/sites/default/files/10-guba_lincoln_94.pdf>.

Guckenberger, D, Uliano, KC & Lane, NE 1993, *Teaching High-Performance Skills Using Above-Real-Time Training*, Contract Report No. 4528, National Aeronautics and Space Administration, Edwards, viewed 24 June 2017, <http://ntrs.nasa.gov/archive/nasa/casi.ntrs.nasa.gov/19940007155.pdf>.

Guerra-Lopez, I 2016, 'Setting clear direction and ensuring alignment', *Performance Improvement Quarterly*, vol. 28, no. 4, pp. 3–5, http://dx.doi.org/10.1002/piq.21212.

Guest, G, MacQueen, KM & Namey, EE 2011, *Applied thematic analysis*, Sage, Thousand Oaks.

Gunasekaran, A, Papadopoulos, T, Dubey, R, Wamba, SF, Childe, SJ, Hazen, B & Akter, S 2017, 'Big data and predictive analytics for supply chain and organisational performance', *Journal of Business Research*, vol. 70, pp. 308–317, http://dx.doi.org/10.1016.

Guskey, T 2009, 'Mastery learning,", viewed 24 June 2017, <http://www.education.com/reference/article/mastery-learning/>.

Güss, CD, Devore Edelstein, H, Badibanga, A & Bartow, S 2017, 'Comparing business experts and novices in complex problem solving', *Journal of Intelligence*, vol. 5, no. 2, art. 20, pp. 1-18, http://dx.doi.org/10.3390/jintelligence5020020.

Hagens, V, Dobrow, MJ & Chafe, R 2009, 'Interviewee transcript review: assessing the impact on qualitative research', *BMC Medical Research Methodology*, vol. 9, pp. 1–8, http://dx.doi.org/10.1186/1471-2288-9-47.

Hager, P 1998, Understanding workplace learning: general perspectives, in D Boud (ed.), *Current issues and new agendas in workplace learning*, NCVER, Australia, pp. 30–42, viewed 24 June 2017, <https://pdfs.semanticscholar.org/431b/4773d7fc8bb616ba50ea4acddbb0d5a56e43.pdf#page=30>.

Hall, AD & Fagen, RE 1956, 'Definition of system', *General Systems*, vol. 1, no. 1, pp. 18–28, viewed 24 June 2017, <http://www.isss.org/yearbook/1-C%20Hall%20&%20Fagen.pdf>.

Hambrick, DZ, Altmann, EM, Oswald, FL, Meinz, EJ, Gobet, F & Campitelli, G 2014, 'Accounting for expert performance: the devil is in the details', *Intelligence*, vol. 45, no. 4, pp. 112–114, http://dx.doi.org/10.1016/j.intell.2014.01.007.

Hambrick, DZ, Oswald, FL, Altmann, EM, Meinz, EJ, Gobet, F & Campitelli, G 2014, 'Deliberate practice: is that all it takes to become an expert?', *Intelligence*, vol. 45, no. 4, pp. 34–45, http://dx.doi.org/10.1016/j.intell.2013.04.001.

Hardman, H 2013, 'The validity of a grounded theory approach to research on democratization', *Qualitative Research*, vol. 13, no. 6, pp. 635–649, http://dx.doi.org/10.1177/1468794112445526.

Harris, KR, Eccles, DW, Freeman, C & Ward, P 2017, '"gun! gun! gun!': an exploration of law enforcement officers' decision-making and coping under stress during actual events', *Ergonomics*, vol. 60, no. 8, pp. 1112–1122, http://dx.doi.org/10.1080/00140139.2016.1260165.

Harris, LR & Brown, GTL 2010, 'Mixing interview and questionnaire methods: practical problems in aligning data', *Practical Assessment, Research & Evaluation*, vol. 15, no. 1, pp. 1–19, viewed 24 June 2017, <http://pareonline.net/getvn.asp?v=15&n=1>.

Harris-Thompson, D, Malek, D & Wiggins, S 2010, Shortening the expertise curve: identifying and developing cognitive skills in board operators, in D Kaber & G Boy (eds.), *Advances in Cognitive Ergonomics*, Advances in Human Factors and Ergonomics Series, CRC Press, Boca Raton, pp. 774–783, http://dx.doi.org/10.1201/ebk1439834916-c77.

Hartman, FT & Baldwin, A 1995, 'Using technology to improve delphi method', *Journal of Computing in Civil Engineering*, vol. 9, no. 4, pp. 244–249, http://dx.doi.org/10.1061/(ASCE)0887-3801(1995)9:4(244).

Hartt, D, Quiram, T & Marken, JA 2016, 'Where the performance issues are and are not: a meta-analytic examination', *Performance Improvement Quarterly*, vol. 29, no. 1, pp. 35–49, http://dx.doi.org/10.1002/piq.21213.

Harvey, M, Ambler, T & Cahir, J 2017, 'Spectrum approach to mentoring: an evidence-based approach to mentoring for academics working in higher education', *Teacher Development*, vol. 21, no. 1, pp. 160–174, http://dx.doi.org/10.1080/13664530.2016.1210537.

Harward, D 2017, 'Controlling variation in time to performance', *Training Industry Magazine*, vol. 10, no. 3, p. 55, viewed 24 June 2017, <http://www.nxtbook.com/nxtbooks/trainingindustry/tiq_20170506/index.php?startid=55#/54>.

Hasson, F, Keeney, S & McKenna, H 2000, 'Research guidelines for the delphi survey technique', *Journal of Advanced Nursing*, vol. 32, no. 4, pp. 1008–1015, http://dx.doi.org/10.1046/j.1365-2648.2000.t01-1-01567.x.

Hatano, G & Inagaki, K 1986, Two courses of expertise, in H Stevenson, H Azuma & K Hakuta (eds.), *Children development and education in Japan*, Freeman, New York, pp. 262–272, viewed 24 June 2017, <https://eprints.lib.hokudai.ac.jp/dspace/bitstream/2115/25206/1/6_P27-36.pdf>.

Hausmann, RG, van de Sande, B & VanLehn, K 2008, Shall we explain? augmenting learning from intelligent tutoring systems and peer collaboration, in B Woolf et al. (eds.), *Intelligent tutoring systems*, Springer-Verlag, Berlin Heidelberg, Germany, pp. 636–645, http://dx.doi.org/10.1007/978-3-540-69132-7_66.

Hay, C 2002, *Political analysis: a critical introduction*, Palgrave Macmillan, New York.

Hayes, JR 1989, *The complete problem solver*, 2nd edn, Erlbaum, Hillsdale.

Healy, A 2007, Transfer: specificity and generality, in H Roediger, Y Dudai & S Fitzpatrick (eds.), *Science of memory: Concepts*, Oxford University Press, New York, pp. 271–275.

Van der Heijden, BI 2002, 'Individual career initiatives and their influence upon professional expertise development throughout the career', *International Journal of Training and Development*, vol. 6, no. 2, pp. 54–79, http://dx.doi.org/10.1111/1468-2419.00150.

Heijmans, N, van Lieshout, J & Wensing, M 2015, 'Improving participation rates by providing choice of participation mode: two randomized controlled trials', *BMC Medical Research Methodology*, vol. 15, no. 1, pp. 1-10, http://dx.doi.org/10.1186/s12874-015-0021-2.

Helmer, O & Helmer-Hirschberg, O 1983, *Looking forward: a guide to futures research*, Sage, Thousand Oaks.

Hentschel, J 2017, 'Skills or jobs: which comes first?', *IZA World of Labor*, http://dx.doi.org/10.15185/izawol.339.

Heron, R 2005, *Job and work analysis: Guidelines on identifying jobs for persons with disabilities*, International Labour Organization, Geneva, viewed 24 March 2018, <http://www.ilo.org/wcmsp5/groups/public/@ed_emp/@ifp_skills/documents/publication/wcms_111484.pdf>.

Herrscher, EG 2006, 'What is the systems approach good for?', *Systemic Practice and Action Research*, vol. 19, no. 5, pp. 409–413, http://dx.doi.org/10.1007/s11213-006-9032-6.

Hesketh, B & Ivancic, K 2002, Enhancing performance through training, in S Sonnentag (ed.), *Psychological management of individual performance*, John Wiley, San Francisco, pp. 293–308, http://dx.doi.org/10.1002/0470013419.ch12.

Hesketh, B & Neal, A 1999, Technology and performance, in D Ilgen & E Pulakos (eds.), *The changing nature of performance: Implications for staffing, motivation, and development*, Jossey-Bass, San Francisco, pp. 21–55.

Higgins, N 2015, *Gamification: Accelerating Learning*, KBR Kellogg Brown and Root Pty Ltd, Kingston, ACT, Australia.

Hintze, NR 2008, 'First responder problem solving and decision making in today's asymmetrical environment', Naval Postgraduate School, Monterey, viewed 24 June 2017, <http://www.dtic.mil/cgi-bin/GetTRDoc?AD=ADA479926>.

Hoffman, RR 1998, How can expertise be defined? implications of research from cognitive psychology, in R Williams, W Faulkner & J Fleck (eds.), *Exploring expertise*, Palgrave Macmillan, Edinburgh, Scotland, pp. 81–100, http://dx.doi.org/10.1007/978-1-349-13693-3_4.

        2012, *Expertise out of context*, Psychology Press, New York.

Hoffman, RR & Andrews, DH 2012, 'Cognition and cognitive technology for research on accelerated learning and developing expertise', *Cognitive Technology*, vol. 17, no. 1, pp. 5–6, viewed 24 June 2017, <http://cmapsinternal.ihmc.us/rid=1LM7CN14D-1335H6-1B3K/CogTech%20for%20Accelerated%20Learning-2013.pdf>.

Hoffman, RR, Andrews, DH & Feltovich, PJ 2012, 'What is 'accelerated learning'?', *Cognitive Technology*, vol. 17, no. 1, pp. 7–10.

Hoffman, RR, Andrews, DH, Fiore, SM, Goldberg, S, Andre, T, Freeman, J, Fletcher, JD & Klein, G 2010, 'Accelerated learning: prospects, issues and applications', *Proceedings of the Human Factors and Ergonomics Society 54th Annual Meeting*, San Francisco, 27 September - 1 October, Sage, Thousand Oaks, pp. 399–402, http://dx.doi.org/10.1177/154193121005400427.

Hoffman, RR, Feltovich, PJ, Fiore, SM & Klein, G 2010, *Accelerated Proficiency and Facilitated Retention: Recommendations Based on an Integration of Research and Findings from a Working Meeting*, Report No. AFRL-RH-AZ-TR-2011-0001, Air Force Research Laboratory, Mesa, http://dx.doi.org/10.21236/ada536308.

Hoffman, RR, Feltovich, PJ, Fiore, S, Klein, G & Moon, B 2008, *Program on Technology Innovation: Accelerating the Achievement of Mission-Critical Expertise: A Research Roadmap*, Report No. 1016710, Electric Power Research Institute (EPRI), Palo Alto, viewed 24 June 2017, <http://perigeantechnologies.com/publications/AcceleratingAchievementofExpertise.pdf>.

Hoffman, RR, Feltovich, PJ, Fiore, SM, Klein, G & Ziebell, D 2009, 'Accelerated learning (?)', *IEEE Intelligent Systems*, vol. 24, no. 2, pp. 18–22, http://dx.doi.org/10.1109/MIS.2009.21.

Hoffman, RR & Lintern, G 2006, Eliciting and representing the knowledge of experts, in K Ericsson, N Charness, P Feltovich & R Hoffman (eds.), *Cambridge handbook of expertise and expert performance*, Cambridge University Press, New York, pp. 203–222, http://dx.doi.org/10.1017/CBO9780511816796.012.

Hoffman, RR & Ward, P 2015, 'Mentoring: a leverage point for intelligent systems?', *IEEE Intelligent Systems*, vol. 30, no. 5, pp. 78–84, http://dx.doi.org/10.1109/MIS.2015.86.

Hoffman, RR, Ward, P, Feltovich, PJ, DiBello, L, Fiore, SM & Andrews, DH 2014, *Accelerated Expertise: Training for high proficiency in a complex world*, Expertise: Research and Applications Series, Psychology Press, New York, http://dx.doi.org/10.4324/9780203797327.

Holt, D, Mackay, D & Smith, R 2004, 'Developing professional expertise in the knowledge economy: integrating industry-based learning with the academic curriculum in the field of information technology', *Asia-Pacific Journal of Cooperative Education*, vol. 5, no. 2, pp. 1–11, viewed 24 June 2017, <http://dro.deakin.edu.au/eserv/DU:30002681/holt-developingprofessionalexpertise-2004.pdf>.

Holton III, EF 1999, 'An integrated model of performance domains: bounding the theory and practice', *Performance Improvement Quarterly*, vol. 12, no. 3, pp. 95–118.

Holton III, EF, Bates, RA & Ruona, WE 2000, 'Development of a generalized learning transfer system inventory', *Human Resource Development Quarterly*, vol. 11, no. 4, pp. 333–360, viewed 24 March 2018, <http://www.nakahara-lab.net/temp/jyugyo/holton.pdf>.

Hong, CM, Chen, CM, Chang, MH & Chen, SC 2007, 'Intelligent web-based tutoring system with personalized learning path guidance', in J Spector, D Sampson, T Okamoto, Kinshuk, S Cerri, M Ueno & A Kashihara (eds.), *Seventh IEEE International Conference on Advanced Learning Technologies (ICALT 2007)*, Tokyo, 18-20 July, IEEE, Los Alamitos, pp. 512–516, http://dx.doi.org/10.1109/ICALT.2007.167.

Houger, VP 2006, 'Trends of employee performance collaborative effort between managers and employees', *Performance Improvement*, vol. 45, no. 5, pp. 26–31, http://dx.doi.org/10.1002/pfi.2006.4930450508.

Hsieh, TC & Wang, TI 2010, 'A mining-based approach on discovering courses pattern for constructing suitable learning path', *Expert Systems with Applications*, vol. 37, no. 6, pp. 4156–4167, http://dx.doi.org/10.1016/j.eswa.2009.11.007.

Hsu, CC & Sandford, BA 2007, 'The Delphi technique: making sense of consensus', *Practical Assessment, Research & Evaluation*, vol. 12, no. 10, pp. 1–8, viewed 24 June 2017, <http://pareonline.net/pdf/v12n10.pdf>.

Hsu, T-C 2016, 'Effects of a peer assessment system based on a grid-based knowledge classification approach on computer skills training', *Journal of Educational Technology & Society*, vol. 19, no. 4, pp. 100-111, viewed 24 June 2017, <http://www.ifets.info/download_pdf.php?j_id=74&a_id=1763>.

Hug, T 2015, Microlearning and mobile learning, in Z Yan (ed.), *Encyclopedia of Mobile Phone Behavior*, IGI Global, Hersey, pp. 490–505, http://dx.doi.org/10.4018/978-1-4666-8239-9.ch041.

Hug, T, Lindner, M & Bruck, PA (eds.) 2006, *Micromedia & E-Learning 2.0: Gaining the Big Picture: Proceedings of Microlearning Conference 2006*, Innsbruck, 25-27 June, Innsbruck University Press, Innsbruck, Austria, viewed 24 June 2017, <https://www.uibk.ac.at/iup/buch_pdfs/microlearning2006-druck.pdf>.

Hughes, C 2004, 'The supervisor's influence on workplace learning', *Studies in Continuing Education*, vol. 26, no. 2, pp. 275–287, http://dx.doi.org/10.1080/158037042000225254.

Humphress, R & Berge, ZL 2006, 'Justifying human performance improvement interventions', *Performance Improvement*, vol. 45, no. 7, pp. 13–22, http://dx.doi.org/DOI: 10.1002/pfi.2006.4930450704.

Hung, W 2009, 'The 9-step problem design process for problem-based learning: application of the 3c3r model', *Educational Research Review*, vol. 4, no. 2, pp. 118–141, http://dx.doi.org/10.1016/j.edurev.2008.12.001.

Hunter, JE 1986, 'Cognitive ability, cognitive aptitudes, job knowledge, and job performance', *Journal of Vocational Behavior*, vol. 29, no. 3, pp. 340–362, http://dx.doi.org/10.1016/0001-8791(86)90013-8.

Huselid, MA & Becker, BE 2011, 'Bridging micro and macro domains: workforce differentiation and strategic human resource management', *Journal of Management*, vol. 37, no. 2, pp. 421–428, http://dx.doi.org/10.1177/0149206310373400.

Illustrative Mathematics n.d., *Comparing speeds in graphs and equations*, viewed 30 March 2018, <https://www.illustrativemathematics.org/content-standards/tasks/57>.

Imel, S 2002, 'Accelerated learning in adult education and training and development', *Trends and Issue Alerts No. 33*, pp. 1–2, viewed 24 June 2017, <http://www.calpro-online.org/ERIC/docs/tia00101.pdf>.

Institute of Physics 2014, *Using speed-time graphs to find an equation*, viewed 30 March 2018, <http://practicalphysics.org/using-speed-time-graphs-find-equation.html>.

iTutor 2013, *Graph of the motion*, viewed 30 March 2018, <https://www.slideshare.net/itutor/motiongraph-of-the-motion>.

Jacob, SA & Furgerson, SP 2012, 'Writing interview protocols and conducting interviews: tips for students new to the field of qualitative research', *The Qualitative Report*, vol. 17, no. 42, pp. 1–10, viewed 24 June 2017, <http://www.nova.edu/ssss/QR/QR17/jacob.pdf>.

Jacobs, RL 1989, System theory applied to human resource development, in D Gradous (ed.), *System Theory Applied to Human Resource Development*, ASTD, Alexandria, pp. 27–60, http://dx.doi.org/10.1002/hrdq.3920010413.

_____ 1994, Comparing the training efficiency and product quality of unstructured and structured OJT, in J Phillips (ed.), *The return on investment in human resource development: cases on the economic benefits of HRD*, American Society for Training and Development, Alexandria.

_____ 1995, *Structured on-the-job training: Unleashing employee expertise in the workplace*, Berrett-Koehler, San Francisco.

_____ 1997, 'A taxonomy of employee development: toward an organisational culture of expertise', paper presented to the Proceedings of the Academy of Human Resource Development, Baton Rouge.

_____ 2001. Managing employee competence and human intelligence in global organisations. In F. Richter (ed.), *Maximizing Human Intelligence in Asia Business: The Sixth Generation Project*. Prentice-Hall, New York, pp. 44-54.

_____ 2003, *Structured on-the-job training: Unleashing employee expertise in the workplace*, 2nd edn, Berrett-Koehler, San Francisco.

_____ 2014a, Structured on-the-job training, in R Poell, T Rocco & G Roth (eds.), *The Routledge Companion to Human Resource Development*, Routledge, Oxon, pp. 272–284.

_____ 2014b, System theory and HRD, in N Chalofsky and T Rocco and M Morris (ed.), *Handbook of human resource development*, Wiley Online Library, Hoboken, pp. 21–39, http://dx.doi.org/10.1002/9781118839881.ch2.

_____ 2017, 'Knowledge work and human resource development', *Human Resource Development Review*, vol. 16, no. 2, pp. 176–202, http://dx.doi.org/10.1177/1534484317704293.

Jacobs, RL & Bu-Rahmah, MJ 2012, 'Developing employee expertise through structured on-the-job training (S-OJT): an introduction to this training approach and the KNPC experience', *Industrial and Commercial Training*, vol. 44, no. 2, pp. 75–84, http://dx.doi.org/10.1108/00197851211202902.

Jacobs, RL & Jones, MJ 1995, Structured on-the-job training: Unleashing employee expertise in the workplace, Berrett-Koehler, San Francisco.

Jacobs, R & Washington, C 2003, 'Employee development and organisational performance: a review of literature and directions for future research', *Human Resource Development International*, vol. 6, no. 3, pp. 343–354, http://dx.doi.org/10.1080/13678860110096211.

Jacobson, D 1999, 'Doing research in cyberspace', *Field Methods*, vol. 11, no. 2, pp. 127–145, viewed 30 March 2018, <http://biblioteca.cejamericas.org/bitstream/handle/2015/3853/Doing_Research_Cyberspace.pdf>.

Jaime, A, Blanco, JM, Dominguez, C, Sánchez, A, Heras, J & Usandizaga, I 2016, 'Spiral and project-based learning with peer assessment in a computer science project management course', *Journal of Science Education and Technology*, vol. 25, no. 3, pp. 439–449, http://dx.doi.org/0.1007/s10956-016-9604-x.

James, N & Busher, H 2006, 'Credibility, authenticity and voice: dilemmas in online interviewing', *Qualitative Research*, vol. 6, no. 3, pp. 403–420, http://dx.doi.org/10.1177/1468794106065010.

Janssen, J, Berlanga, AJ & Koper, R 2010, 'Evaluation of the learning path specification: lifelong learners' information needs', *Educational Technology & Society*, vol. 14, no. 3, pp. 218–230, viewed 24 June 2017, <http://www.ifets.info/journals/14_3/18.pdf>.

Janssens, L, Smet, K, Onghena, P & Kyndt, E 2017, 'The relationship between learning conditions in the workplace and informal learning outcomes: a study among police inspectors', *International Journal of Training and Development*, vol. 21, no. 2, pp. 92–112, http://dx.doi.org/doi: 10.1111/ijtd.12095.

Jenkins, JT, Currie, A, Sala, S & Kennedy, RH 2016, 'A multi-modal approach to training in laparoscopic colorectal surgery accelerates proficiency gain', *Surgical Endoscopy*, vol. 30, no. 7, pp. 3007–3013, http://dx.doi.org/10.1007/s00464-015-4591-1.

Jennings, C & Wargnier, J 2010, 'Experiential learning-a way to develop agile minds in the knowledge economy?', *Development and Learning in Organisations*, vol. 24, no. 3, pp. 14–16, http://dx.doi.org/10.1108/14777281011037245.

Jin, W & Corbett, A 2011, 'Effectiveness of cognitive apprenticeship learning (CAL) and cognitive tutors (CT) for problem solving using fundamental programming concepts', *Proceedings of the 42nd ACM Technical Symposium on Computer Science Education*, Dallas, 9-12 March, New York, pp. 305–310, viewed 24 June 2017, <http://ai2-s2-pdfs.s3.amazonaws.com/de6f/c3f6a0e8075b6f7b92411db100b23f740f78.pdf>.

Jipp, M 2016, 'Expertise development with different types of automation a function of different cognitive abilities', *Human Factors: The Journal of the Human Factors and Ergonomics Society*, vol. 58, no. 1, pp. 92–106, http://dx.doi.org/10.1177/0018720815604441.

Johnson, BA 2016, 'Impact of prior exposure to laboratory apparatus on acquisition of process skills and academic performance in chemistry at secondary schools in GIWA zone Nigeria', *American Journal of Educational Research*, vol. 4, no. 12, pp. 903–906, http://dx.doi.org/10.12691/education-4-12-8.

Johnson, RB & Onwuegbuzie, AJ 2004, 'Mixed methods research: a research paradigm whose time has come', *Educational Researcher*, vol. 33, no. 7, pp. 14–26, http://dx.doi.org/10.3102/0013189x033007014.

Johnson, TE 2017, Using data analytics to drive performance and instructional decision-making, in F Lai & J Legman (eds.), *Learning and Knowledge Analytics in Open Education*, Springer, Cham, pp. 21–30, http://dx.doi.org/10.1007/978-3-319-38956-1_3.

Jonassen, DH 1992, Cognitive flexibility theory and its implications for designing CBI, in S Dijkstra, H Krammer & J van Merrienboer (eds.), *Instructional models in computer-based learning environments*, Springer, Berlin Heidelberg, pp. 385–403, http://dx.doi.org/10.1007/978-3-662-02840-7_23.

Jonassen, DH, Dyer, D, Peters, K, Robinson, T, Harvey, D, King, M & Loughner, P 1997, Cognitive flexibility hypertexts on the web: engaging learners in meaning making, in B Khan (ed.), *Web-based instruction*, Education Technology, Englewood Cliffs, pp. 119–133, viewed 24 June 2017, <http://www.academia.edu/download/6676532/36489.pdf>.

Jonassen, DH & Hernandez-Serrano, J 2002, 'Case-based reasoning and instructional design: using stories to support problem solving', *Educational Technology Research and Development*, vol. 50, no. 2, pp. 65–77, http://dx.doi.org/10.1007/BF02504994.

Jonassen, DH & Hung, W 2008, 'All problems are not equal: implications for problem-based learning', *Interdisciplinary Journal of Problem Solving*, vol. 2, no. 2, pp. 10–13, http://dx.doi.org/10.7771/1541-5015.1080.

Jones-Moore, L 2016, 'A qualitative study of job competencies for healthcare social work administrators: an application of the short competency model process used to identify the behaviors and personal characteristics of exemplary performers', PhD thesis, University of Nevada, Las Vegas, viewed 24 June 2017, <http://digitalscholarship.unlv.edu/thesesdissertations/2687>.

Jung, E, Kim, M & Reigeluth, CM 2016, 'Learning in action: how competent professionals learn', *Performance Improvement Quarterly*, vol. 28, no. 4, pp. 55–69, http://dx.doi.org/10.1002/piq.21209.

Kaiser, S & Holton III, E 1998, 'The learning organisation as a performance improvement strategy', in R Torraco (ed.), *Proceedings of the Academy of Human Resource Development Conference*, Oak Brook, Academy of Human Resource Development, Baton Rouge, pp. 75–82.

Kalyuga, S, Ayres, P, Chandler, P & Sweller, J 2003, 'The expertise reversal effect', *Educational Psychologist*, vol. 38, no. 1, pp. 23–31.

Kanfer, R & Kantrowitz, TM 2002, Ability and non-ability predictors of job performance, in S. Sonnentag (ed.), *Psychological management of individual performance*, John Wiley, San Francisco, pp. 27–50, http://dx.doi.org/10.1002/0470013419.ch2.

Kang, S "Pil" 2017, 'What do hpt consultants do for performance analysis?', *TechTrends*, vol. 61, no. 1, pp. 32–45, http://dx.doi.org/10.1007/s11528-016-0129-1.

Karatepe, OM 2013, 'High-performance work practices and hotel employee performance: the mediation of work engagement', *International Journal of Hospitality Management*, vol. 32, pp. 132–140, http://dx.doi.org/DOI: 10.1016/j.ijhm.2012.05.003.

Karoly, LA 2007, *Forces Shaping the Future Us Workforce and Workplace: Implications for 21st Century Work*, Report No. CT-273, Rand Corporation, Santa Monica, viewed 24 June 2017, <http://www.rand.org/content/dam/rand/pubs/testimonies/2007/RAND_CT273.pdf>.

Karpicke, JD & Bauernschmidt, A 2011, 'Spaced retrieval: absolute spacing enhances learning regardless of relative spacing', *Journal of Experimental Psychology, Learning, Memory, and Cognition*, vol. 37, no. 5, pp. 1250–1257, http://dx.doi.org/10.1037/a0023436.

Katz, SN, Hall, E & Lesgold, A 1997, *Cognitive task analysis and intelligent computer-based training systems: lessons learned from coached practice environments in air force avionics*, Report No. TM 027360, University of Pittsburgh, Pittsburgh, viewed 24 June 2017, <https://archive.org/details/ERIC_ED411309>.

Kaufman, SB & Kaufman, JC 2007, 'Ten years to expertise, many more to greatness: an investigation of modern writers', *The Journal of Creative Behavior*, vol. 41, no. 2, pp. 114–124, http://dx.doi.org/10.1002/j.2162-6057.2007.tb01284.x.

Kazmer, MM & Xie, B 2008, 'Qualitative interviewing in internet studies: playing with the media, playing with the method', *Information, Communication & Society*, vol. 11, no. 2, pp. 257–278, http://dx.doi.org/10.1080/13691180801946333.

Keith, N & Frese, M 2008, 'Effectiveness of error management training: a meta-analysis', *The Journal of Applied Psychology*, vol. 93, no. 1, pp. 59–69, http://dx.doi.org/10.1037/0021-9010.93.1.59.

Khan, K & Ramachandran, S 2012, 'Conceptual framework for performance assessment: competency, competence and performance in the context of assessments in healthcare-deciphering the terminology', *Medical Teacher*, vol. 34, no. 11, pp. 920–928, http://dx.doi.org/10.3109/0142159X.2012.722707.

Khan, RAG, Khan, FA & Khan, MA 2011, 'Impact of training and development on organisational performance', *Global Journal of Management and Business Research*, vol. 11, no. 7, pp. 63–67, viewed 24 June 2017, <https://globaljournals.org/GJMBR_Volume11/8-Impact-of-Training-and-Development-on-Organisational-Performance.pdf>.

Kim, MK 2012, 'Theoretically grounded guidelines for assessing learning progress: cognitive changes in ill-structured complex problem-solving contexts', *Educational Technology Research and Development*, vol. 60, no. 4, pp. 601–622, http://dx.doi.org/10.1007/s11423-012-9247-4.

―――― 2015, 'Models of learning progress in solving complex problems: expertise development in teaching and learning', *Contemporary Educational Psychology*, vol. 42, no. 3, pp. 1–16, http://dx.doi.org/10.1016/j.cedpsych.2015.03.005.

King, F, Goodson, L & Rohani, F 2004, *Higher Order Thinking Skills*, Center for Advancement of Learning and Assessment - University College London, London, viewed 24 June 2017, <http://research.acer.edu.au/cgi/viewcontent.cgi?article=1004&context=resdev>.

King Jr, CL & Cennamo, K 2016, 'The use of Gilbert's behavior engineering model to identify barriers to technology integration in a public school', in G Chamblee & L Langub (eds.), *Society for Information Technology*

& *Teacher Education International Conference*, Savannah, Association for the Advancement of Computing in Education (AACE), Waynesville, pp. 1224–1228, viewed 24 June 2017, <https://www.learntechlib.org/d/171844>.

King, N 2004, Using templates in the thematic analysis of text, in C Cassell & G Symon (eds.), *Essential guide to qualitative methods in organisational research*, Sage, Thousand Oaks, pp. 256–70, http://dx.doi.org/10.4135/9781446280119.n21.

_____ 2012, Doing template analysis, in G Symon & C Cassell (eds.), *Qualitative organisational research: Core methods and current challenges*, Sage, London, p. 426-450.

Kirby, JR, Knapper, CK, Evans, CJ, Carty, AE & Gadula, C 2003, 'Approaches to learning at work and workplace climate', *International Journal of Training and Development*, vol. 7, no. 1, pp. 31–52, viewed 24 June 2017, <https://www.researchgate.net/profile/John_Kirby5/publication/228253877>.

Kirkman, MA 2013, 'Deliberate practice, domain-specific expertise, and implications for surgical education in current climes', *Journal of Surgical Education*, vol. 70, no. 3, pp. 309–317, http://dx.doi.org/10.1016/j.jsurg.2012.11.011.

Kirkpatrick, DL & Kirkpatrick, JD 2009, *Transferring Learning to Behavior: Using the Four Levels to Improve Performance*, Berrett-Koehler, Oakland.

Kirschenbaum, SS, McInnis, SL & Correll, KP 2009, Contrasting submarine speciality training: sonar and fire control, in K Ericsson (ed.), *Development of professional expertise*, Cambridge University Press, New York, pp. 271–285, http://dx.doi.org/10.1017/cbo9780511609817.015.

Kirschner, PA & van Merriënboer, JJG 2007, Ten steps to complex learning: a new approach to instruction and instructional design, in T Good (ed.), *21st century education: A reference handbook*, SAGE, Thousand Oaks, pp. 244–253, http://dx.doi.org/10.4135/9781412964012.n26.

Klein, G 1997, 'Developing expertise in decision making', *Thinking & Reasoning*, vol. 3, no. 4, pp. 337–352, http://dx.doi.org/ 10.1080/135467897394329.

Klein, GA 1993, A recognition-primed decision (RPD) model of rapid decision making, in G Klein, J Orasanu, R Calderwood & C Zsambok (eds.), *Decision Making in Action*, Norwood, Ablex, pp. 138–147, viewed 24 June 2017, <https://pdfs.semanticscholar.org/0672/092ecc507fb41d81e82d2986cf86c4bff14f.pdf>.

_____ 1998, *Sources of power: How people make decisions*, MIT Press, Cambridge.

_____ 2003, *Intuition at work: Why developing your gut instinct will make you better at what you do*, Currency Doubleday, New York.

Klein, GA & Baxter, HC 2009, Cognitive transformation theory: contrasting cognitive and behavioral learning, in D Schmorrow, J Cohn & D Nicholson (eds.), *The PSI handbook of virtual environment for training and education: Developments for the military and beyond, Volume 1, Education: Learning, requirements and metrics*, Praeger Security International, Santa Barbara, pp. 50–65, viewed 24 June 2017, <https://pdfs.semanticscholar.org/99f0/b9bdbce6432c3232fdeffeae0fddea7bcebd.pdf>.

Klein, GA & Borders, J 2016, 'The shadowbox approach to cognitive skills training an empirical evaluation', *Journal of Cognitive Engineering and Decision Making*, vol. 10, no. 3, pp. 268–280, http://dx.doi.org/10.1177/1555343416636515.

Klein, GA, Hintze, N & Saab, D 2013, 'Thinking inside the box: the shadowbox method for cognitive skill development', in H Chaudet, L Pellegrin & N Bonnardel (eds.), *Proceedings of the 11th International Conference on Naturalistic Decision Making*, Marseille, 21-24 May, Aepege Science Publishing, Paris, pp. 121–124, viewed 24 June 2017, <http://arpege-recherche.org/ndm11/papers/ndm11-121.pdf>.

Klein, GA, McCloskey, M, Pliske, R & Schmitt, J 1997, 'Decision skills training', *Proceedings of the Human Factors and Ergonomics Society 41st Annual Meeting*, Albuquerque, 22-26 September, SAGE, Los Angeles, pp. 182–185, http://dx.doi.org/10.1177/107118139704100142.

Knafl, KA & Ayres, L 1996, 'Managing large qualitative data sets in family research', *Journal of Family Nursing*, vol. 2, no. 4, pp. 350–364, http://dx.doi.org/10.1177/107484079600200402.

Koch, T 2006, 'Establishing rigour in qualitative research: the decision trail', *Journal of Advanced Nursing*, vol. 53, no. 1, pp. 91–100, http://dx.doi.org/10.1111/j.1365-2648.2006.03681.x.

Kohlbacher, F 2006, 'The use of qualitative content analysis in case study research', *Forum Qualitative Sozialforschung / Forum: Qualitative Social Research*, vol. 7, no. 1, pp. 1–22, viewed 24 June 2017, <http://www.qualitative-research.net/index.php/fqs/article/viewArticle/75>.

Kolb, D 1984, Experiential learning as the science of learning and development, Prentice Hall, Englewood Cliffs.

Koller, V, Harvey, S & Magnotta, M 2005, *Technology-Based Learning Strategies*, Contract No. AF-12526-02-30, Office of Policy Development and Research, Oakland, viewed 24 June 2017, <https://www.doleta.gov/reports/papers/tbl_paper_final.pdf>.

Kooken, J, Ley, T & De Hoog, R 2007, How do people learn in the workplace? investigating four workplace learning assumptions, in E Durval, R Lamma & M Wolpers (eds.), *Creating new learning experiences on a global scale: Proceedings of Second European Conference on Technology Enhanced Learning*, Crete, 17-20 September, Springer Verlag, Berlin Heidelberg, pp. 158–171, http://dx.doi.org/10.1007/978-3-540-75195-3_12.

Koopmans, L, Bernaards, CM, Hildebrandt, VH, Schaufeli, WB, de Vet Henrica, C & van der Beek, AJ 2011, 'Conceptual frameworks of individual work performance: a systematic review', *Journal of Occupational and Environmental Medicine*, vol. 53, no. 8, pp. 856–866, http://dx.doi.org/10.1097/JOM.0b013e318226a763.

Korotov, K 2007, Accelerated development of organisational talent, in V Vaiman & C Vance (eds.), *Smart Talent Management: Building Knowledge Assets for Competitive Advantage*, Dward Elgar, Cheltenham, pp. 139–157, http://dx.doi.org/10.4337/9781848442986.00015.

Koubek, RJ, Clarkston, TP & Calvez, V 1994, 'The training of knowledge structures for manufacturing tasks: an empirical study', *Ergonomics*, vol. 37, no. 4, pp. 765–780, http://dx.doi.org/10.1080/00140139408963687.

Kraiger, K 2014, 'Looking back and looking forward: trends in training and development research', *Human Resource Development Quarterly*, vol. 25, no. 4, pp. 401–408, http://dx.doi.org/10.1002/hrdq.21203.

Kraiger, K, Passmore, J & Rebelo, N 2014, The psychology of training, development, and performance improvement, in K Kraiger, J Passmore, N Santos & S Malvezzi (eds.), *The Wiley Blackwell Handbook of the Psychology of Training, Development, and Performance Improvement*, John Wiley, San Francisco, pp. 535–544, http://dx.doi.org/10.1002/9781118736982.ch1.

Krefting, L 1991, 'Rigor in qualitative research: the assessment of trustworthiness', *American Journal of Occupational Therapy*, vol. 45, no. 3, pp. 214–222, http://dx.doi.org/10.5014/ajot.45.3.214.

Kreutzer, C, Marks, M, Bowers, C & Murphy, C 2016, 'Enhancing surgical team performance with game-based training', *International Journal of Serious Games*, vol. 3, no. 1, http://dx.doi.org/10.17083/ijsg.v3i1.103.

Krueger, RA & Casey, MA 2015, *Focus groups: a practical guide for applied research*, 5th edn, Sage, Thousand Oaks.

Kuchenbrod, R 2016, 'Accelerating expertise to facilitate decision making in high-risk professions using the DACUM system', PhD thesis, Eastern Illinois University, Charleston, viewed 24 June 2017, <http://thekeep.eiu.edu/cgi/viewcontent.cgi?article=3462&context=theses>.

Kuhn, TS 1996, The structure of scientific revolutions, in O Neurath (ed.), *International Encyclopaedia of Unified Science (3rd edition)*, vol. 2, no. 2, University of Chicago Press, Chicago, http://dx.doi.org/10.7208/chicago/9780226458106.001.0001.

Kulasegaram, KM, Grierson, LEM & Norman, GR 2013, 'The roles of deliberate practice and innate ability in developing expertise: evidence and implications', *Medical Education*, vol. 47, no. 10, pp. 979–989, http://dx.doi.org/10.1111/medu.12260.

Kuo, F-R, Hwang, G-J, Chen, S-C & Chen, SY 2012, 'A cognitive apprenticeship approach to facilitating web-based collaborative problem solving.', *Journal of Educational Technology & Society*, vol. 15, no. 4, pp. 319–331, viewed 24 June 2017, <http://www.ifets.info/others/download_pdf.php?j_id=57&a_id=1305>.

Kuzel, AJ 1999, Sampling in qualitative inquiry, in B Crabtreee & W Miller (eds.), *Doing qualitative research*, SAGE, Thousand Oaks, CA, pp. 31–44.

Kvale, S 1996, *Interviews: an introduction to qualitative research and interviewing*, Sage, Thousand Oaks.

Kwon, ON, Rasmussen, C & Allen, K 2005, 'Students' retention of mathematical knowledge and skills in differential equations', *School Science and Mathematics*, vol. 105, no. 5, pp. 227–239, http://dx.doi.org/10.1111/j.1949-8594.2005.tb18163.x.

Kyndt, E, Dochy, F & Nijs, H 2009, 'Learning conditions for non-formal and informal workplace learning', *Journal of Workplace Learning*, vol. 21, no. 5, pp. 369–383, http://dx.doi.org/10.1108/13665620910966785.

Lai, C-Y 2016, 'Training nursing students' communication skills with online video peer assessment', *Computers & Education*, vol. 97, pp. 21–30, http://dx.doi.org/10.1016/j.compedu.2016.02.017.

Lajoie, SP 2003, 'Transitions and trajectories for studies of expertise', *Educational Researcher*, vol. 32, no. 8, pp. 21–25, http://dx.doi.org/10.3102/0013189X032008021.

―――― 2009, Developing professional expertise with a cognitive apprenticeship model: examples from avionics and medicine, in K Ericsson (ed.), *Development of professional expertise: Toward measurement of expert performance and design of optimal learning environments*, Cambridge University Press, New York, pp. 61–83, http://dx.doi.org/10.1017/cbo9780511609817.004.

Lajoie, SP & Lesgold, A 1992, 'Dynamic assessment of proficiency for solving procedural knowledge tasks', *Educational Psychologist*, vol. 27, no. 3, pp. 365–384, http://dx.doi.org/10.1207/s15326985ep2703_6.

Langan-Fox, J, Armstrong, K, Balvin, N & Anglim, J 2002, 'Process in skill acquisition: motivation, interruptions, memory, affective states, and metacognition', *Australian Psychologist*, vol. 37, no. 2, pp. 104–117, http://dx.doi.org/10.1080/00050060210001706746.

Langerak, F, Hultink, EJ & Griffin, A 2008, 'Exploring mediating and moderating influences on the links among cycle time, proficiency in entry timing, and new product profitability', *Journal of Product Innovation Management*, vol. 25, no. 4, pp. 370–385, http://dx.doi.org/10.1111/j.1540-5885.2008.00307.x.

Langdon, DG 2006, Using an HPT model to become management's partner, in J Pershing (ed.), *Handbook of human performance technology: Principles, practices, and potential*, Pfeiffer, San Francisco, pp. 924–946.

Lauri, M 2011, 'Triangulation of data analysis techniques', *Papers on Social Representations*, vol. 20, no. 2, pp. 34.1–34.15, viewed 24 June 2017, <http://www.psych.lse.ac.uk/psr/PSR2011/20_33.pdf>.

Lazzara, EH, Dietz, AS, Weaver, SJ, Pavlas, D, Heyne, K, Salas, E & Ramachandran, S 2010, 'Guidelines for training adaptive expertise', *Proceedings of the Human Factors and Ergonomics Society 54th Annual Meeting*, San Francisco, SAGE, 27 September - 1 October, pp. 2294–2298, http://dx.doi.org/10.1518/107118110X12829370266400.

Lee, PWY 2011, 'Structured proficiency based progression phacoemulsification training curriculum using virtual reality simulator technology', Masters thesis, Royal College of Surgeons in Ireland, Dublin, Ireland, viewed 24 June 2017, <http://epubs.rcsi.ie/cgi/viewcontent.cgi?article=1007&context=mchrestheses>.

Lee, RL 2004, 'The impact of cognitive task analysis on performance: a meta-analysis of comparative studies', PhD thesis, University of Southern California, Los Angeles.

Leech, NL & Onwuegbuzie, AJ 2007, 'An array of qualitative data analysis tools: a call for data analysis triangulation', *School Psychology Quarterly*, vol. 22, no. 4, pp. 557–584, http://dx.doi.org/10.1037/1045-3830.22.4.557.

Lesgold, AM 1991, *Methodological Foundations for Designing Intelligent Computer-Based Training*, Research Report No. N00014-89-J-1168, Office of Naval Research, Arlington, viewed 24 June 2017, <http://www.dtic.mil/dtic/tr/fulltext/u2/a257925.pdf>.

―――― 2001, 'The nature and methods of learning by doing', *American Psychologist*, vol. 56, no. 11, pp. 961–973, http://dx.doi.org/10.1037/0003-066X.56.11.964.

―――― 2004, 'Contextual requirements for constructivist learning', *International Journal of Educational Research*, vol. 41, no. 6, pp. 495–502, http://dx.doi.org/10.1016/j.ijer.2005.08.014.

Lesgold, AM, Lajoie, S, Bunzo, M & Eggan, G 1988, *Sherlock: A Coached Practice Environment for an Electronics Troubleshooting Job*, Report No. AD-A201-748, University of Pittsburg, Pittsburg, viewed 24 June 2017, <http://eric.ed.gov/?id=ED299450>.

Lesgold, AM & Nahemow, M 2001, Tools to assist learning by doing: achieving and assessing efficient technology for learning, in S Carver & D Klahr (eds.), *Cognition and instruction: Twenty-five years of progress*, Lawrence Erlbaum, Mahwah, pp. 307–345.

Levy, F 2010, *How Technology Changes Demands for Human Skills*, Working Paper No. 45, OECD Publishing, Paris, France, http://dx.doi.org/10.1787/5kmhds6czqzq-en.

Li, L & Gao, F 2016, 'The effect of peer assessment on project performance of students at different learning levels', *Assessment & Evaluation in Higher Education*, vol. 41, no. 6, pp. 885–900, viewed 24 June 2017, <http://scholarworks.bgsu.edu/cgi/viewcontent.cgi?article=1033&context=vcte_pub>.

Li, X, Wang, J & Ferguson, MK 2014, 'Competence versus mastery: the time course for developing proficiency in video-assisted thoracoscopic lobectomy', *The Journal of Thoracic and Cardiovascular Surgery*, vol. 147, no. 4, pp. 1150–4, http://dx.doi.org/10.1016/j.jtcvs.2013.11.036.

Liew, A & Harrison, J 2017, 'Using situated learning tools to improve student learning of accounting processes', *Proceedings of International Conference on Accounting and Finance (AT)*, Singapore, 5-6 June, Global Science and Technology Forum, Singapore, pp. 74–83, http://dx.doi.org/10.5176/2251-1997_af17.55.

Lincoln, YS & Guba, EG 1985, *Naturalistic inquiry*, Sage, Newbury Park.

――― 1986, But is it rigorous? trustworthiness and authenticity in naturalistic evaluation, in D Williams (ed.), *New directions for program evaluation*, Jossey-Bass, San Francisco, pp. 73–84, http://dx.doi.org/10.1002/ev.

LinkedIn 2017, *2017 Workplace Learning Report: How Modern L&D Professionals Are Tackling Top Challenges*, LinkedIn Solutions, Sunnyvale, viewed 24 June 2017, <http://www.linkedin.com>.

Linstone, HA & Turoff, M (eds.)1975, *The Delphi method*, Addison-Wesley Reading, MA, viewed 13 March 2018, <https://web.njit.edu/~turoff/pubs/delphibook/delphibook.pdf>.

Lipsett, PA 2017, 'Surgical training to proficiency: learning from errors', *JAMA Surgery*, vol. 152, no. 6, p. 588, http://dx.doi.org/10.1001/jamasurg.2017.0104.

Liu, X & Batt, R 2007, 'The economic pay-offs to informal training: evidence from routine service work', *Industrial and Labor Relations Review*, vol. 61, no. 1, pp. 75–89, http://dx.doi.org/10.1177/001979390706100104.

Lizier, A 2015, 'Learning in complex adaptive organisations', paper presented to the 9th International Conference on Researching in Work and Learning (RWL), Singapore, viewed 24 June 2017, <http://www.rwl2015.com/papers/Paper010.pdf>.

Logan, GD 1988, 'Toward an instance theory of automatization', *Psychological Review*, vol. 95, no. 4, pp. 492-527, http://dx.doi.org/10.1037//0033-295x.95.4.492.

Lombardo, MP & Deaner, RO 2014, 'You can't teach speed: sprinters falsify the deliberate practice model of expertise', *PeerJ*, vol. 2, art. e445, pp. 1-31, http://dx.doi.org/10.7717/peerj.445.

London, M & Mone, EM 1999, Continuous learning, in D Ilgen & E Pulakos (eds.), *The changing nature of performance: Implications for staffing, motivation, and development*, Jossey-Bass, San Francisco, pp. 119–153.

Lorenzet, SJ, Salas, E & Tannenbaum, SI 2005, 'Benefiting from mistakes: the impact of guided errors on learning, performance, and self-efficacy', *Human Resource Development Quarterly*, vol. 16, no. 3, pp. 301–322, http://dx.doi.org/10.1002/hrdq.1141.

Ludwig, B 1997, 'Predicting the future: have you considered using the Delphi methodology', *Journal of Extension*, vol. 35, no. 5, pp. 1–4, viewed 13 March 2018, <https://www.joe.org/joe/1997october/tt2.php>.

Lundin, RA, Arvidsson, N, Brady, T, Ekstedt, E, Midler, C & Sydow, J 2015, *Managing and working in project society: institutional challenges of temporary organisations*, Cambridge University Press, Cambridge, http://dx.doi.org/10.1017/cbo9781139939454.

Lynn, G & Kalay, F 2015, 'The effect of vision and role clarity on team performance', *Journal of Business Economics and Finance*, vol. 4, no. 3, pp. 473–499, http://dx.doi.org/10.17261/Pressacademia.2015313067.

Lynn, GS, Akgün, AE & Keskin, H 2003, 'Accelerated learning in new product development teams', *European Journal of Innovation Management*, vol. 6, no. 4, pp. 201–212, http://dx.doi.org/10.1108/14601060310500922.

Lynn, GS, Skov, RB & Abel, KD 1999, 'Practices that support team learning and their impact on speed to market and new product success', *Journal of Product Innovation Management*, vol. 16, no. 5, pp. 439–454, http://dx.doi.org/10.1111/1540-5885.1650439.

Macdonald, RL 2014, 'See one, simulate fifty, then do one?', *Journal of Neurosurgery*, vol. 121, no. 2, pp. 225-227, http://dx.doi.org/10.3171/2014.3.JNS132591.

Macmillan, PJ 2015, 'Thinking like an expert lawyer: measuring specialist legal expertise through think-aloud problem solving and verbal protocol analysis', PhD thesis, Bond University, Robina, Australia, viewed 24 June 2017, <http://epublications.bond.edu.au/cgi/viewcontent.cgi?article=1167&context=theses>.

Mafi, SL & Jacobs, RL 2001, 'Using the gap service-management model to the human resource development function in organisations', in O Aliaga (ed.), *Proceedings of the Annual Conference of the Academy of Human Resource Development*, Baton Rouge, Academy of Human Resource Development.

Mann, C & Stewart, F 2000, *Internet communication and qualitative research: a handbook for researching online*, Sage, London.

Mannetje, A & Kromhout, H 2003, 'The use of occupation and industry classifications in general population studies', *International Journal of Epidemiology*, vol. 32, no. 3, pp. 419–428, http://dx.doi.org/10.1093/ije/dyg080.

Marker, A, Villachica, SW, Stepich, D, Allen, D & Stanton, L 2014, 'An updated framework for human performance improvement in the workplace: the spiral hpi framework', *Performance Improvement*, vol. 53, no. 1, pp. 10–23, http://dx.doi.org/10.1002/pfi.21389.

Marks, A, Richards, J, Hagemann, V, Kluge, A & Ritzmann, S 2012, 'Flexibility under complexity: work contexts, task profiles and team processes of high responsibility teams', *Employee Relations*, vol. 34, no. 3, pp. 322–338, http://dx.doi.org/10.1108/01425451211217734.

Marquardt, MJ 1996, *Building the learning organisation*, McGraw Hill, New York.

Marshall, T, Straub-Morarend, C, Guzmán-Armstrong, S & Handoo, N 2016, 'Evidence-based dentistry: assessment to document progression to proficiency', *European Journal of Dental Education*, http://dx.doi.org/10.1111/eje.12202.

Marsick, VJ & Volpe, M 1999, 'The nature and need for informal learning', *Advances in Developing Human Resources*, vol. 1, no. 3, pp. 1–9, http://dx.doi.org/10.1177/152342239900100302.

Marsick, VJ & Watkins, K 1997, Lessons from informal and incidental learning, in J Burgoyne & M Reynolds (eds.), *Management learning: integrating perspectives in theory and practice*, Sage, London, http://dx.doi.org/10.4135/9781446250488.n18.

―――― 2015, *Informal and incidental learning in the workplace*, Routledge Revivals edn, Routledge, New York.

―――― 2001, 'Informal and incidental learning', *New Directions for Adult and Continuing Education*, vol. 2001, no. 89, pp. 25–34, viewed 24 June 2017, <http://gcc.upb.de/www/WI/WI2/wi2_lit.nsf/d2f7ed56380ef2fdc125683100441206/6f9731f184cd7b3dc12570c3006303ed/$FILE/Informal+workplace+learning_Marsick.pdf>.

Marsick, VJ, Watkins, KE, Scully-Russ, E & Nicolaides, A 2017, 'Rethinking informal and incidental learning in terms of complexity and the social context', Journal of Adult Learning, Knowledge and Innovation, vol. 1, no. 1, pp. 27–34, http://dx.doi.org/10.1556/2059.01.2016.003.

Marsland, N & Wilson, I 2000, *A Methodological Framework for Combining Quantitative and Qualitative Survey Methods*, Project No. R7033, DFID-funded Natural Resources Systems Programme, viewed 24 June 2017, <http://www.reading.ac.uk/ssc/n/SADC DVD/Resources/SSC Good Practice Guidelines/qqa.pdf>.

Mason, J 2002, *Qualitative researching*, 2nd edn, Sage, Thousand Oaks.

―――― 2006, 'Mixing methods in a qualitatively driven way', *Qualitative Research*, vol. 6, no. 1, pp. 9–25, http://dx.doi.org/10.1177/1468794106058866.

Mason, M 2010, 'Sample size and saturation in PhD studies using qualitative interviews', *Forum Qualitative Sozialforschung/Forum: Qualitative Social Research*, vol. 11, no. 3, viewed 24 June 2017, <http://www.qualitative-research.net/index.php/fqs/article/view/1428/3027>.

Matthews, P 1999, 'Workplace learning: developing an holistic model', *The Learning Organisation*, vol. 6, no. 1, pp. 18–29, http://dx.doi.org/10.1108/09696479910255684.

Maxwell, JA 2008, Designing a qualitative study, in L Bickman & D Rog (eds.), *The SAGE handbook of applied social research methods*, Sage, Thousand Oaks, pp. 214–253, http://dx.doi.org/10.4135/9781483348858.n7.

McCaslin, ML & Scott, KW 2003, 'The five-question method for framing a qualitative research study', *The Qualitative Report*, vol. 8, no. 3, pp. 447–461, viewed 24 June 2017, <http://nsuworks.nova.edu/cgi/viewcontent.cgi?article=1880&context=tqr>.

McDaniel, MA, Schmidt, FL & Hunter, JE 1988, 'Job experience correlates of job performance', *Journal of Applied Psychology*, vol. 73, no. 2, p. 327, http://dx.doi.org/10.1037/0021-9010.73.2.327.

McGhee, G, Marland, GR & Atkinson, J 2007, 'Grounded theory research: literature reviewing and reflexivity', *Journal of Advanced Nursing*, vol. 60, no. 3, pp. 334–42, http://dx.doi.org/10.1111/j.1365-2648.2007.04436.x.

McKinley, RA, McIntire, L, Bridges, N & Goodyear, C 2013, 'Acceleration of image analyst training with transcranial direct current stimulation', *Behavioral Neuroscience*, vol. 127, no. 6, pp. 936–946, http://dx.doi.org/10.1037/a0034975.

McLagan, PA 1989a, *Models for HRD Practice*, American Society for Training and Development, Alexandria.

⎯⎯⎯⎯⎯⎯ 1989b, 'Models for HRD practice', *Training & Development Journal*, vol. 43, no. 9, pp. 49–60.

McLaughlin, MF 2016, 'Managers coaching employees to improve performance: supports and barriers', PhD thesis, ProQuest, Ann Arbor, viewed 24 June 2017, < https://search.proquest.com/openview/f84533858510deea42fb2b4d4052a28c/1?pq-origsite=gscholar&cbl=18750&diss=y>.

McQueen, RJ & Chen, J 2010, 'Building script-based tacit knowledge in call centre trainees', *Knowledge Management Research & Practice*, vol. 8, no. 3, pp. 240–255, viewed 24 June 2017, <https://www.researchgate.net/profile/Jihong_Chen2/publication/47354229>.

McQueen, RJ & Janson, A 2016, 'Accelerating tacit knowledge building of client-facing consultants: can organisations better support these learning processes?', *The Learning Organisation*, vol. 23, no. 4, pp. 202–217, http://dx.doi.org/10.1108/TLO-07-2015-0035.

Meho, LI 2006, 'E-mail interviewing in qualitative research: a methodological discussion', *Journal of the American Society for Information Science and Technology*, vol. 57, no. 10, pp. 1284–1295, http://dx.doi.org/10.1002/asi.

Meier, D 2000, *The accelerated learning handbook: a creative guide to designing and delivering faster, more effective training programs*, McGraw-Hill, New York.

Menchaca, I, Guenaga, M & Solabarrieta, J 2016, 'Using learning analytics to assess project management skills on engineering degree courses', in F García-Peñalvo (ed.), *Proceedings of the Fourth International Conference on Technological Ecosystems for Enhancing Multiculturality*, Salamanca, Spain, 2-4 November, ACM, New York, pp. 369–376, http://dx.doi.org/10.1145/3012430.3012542.

Merkelbach, EJHM & Schraagen, JMC 1994, *A Framework for the Analysis of Cognitive Tasks*, Report No. TNO-TM 1994 B-13, TNO Human Factors Research, Soesterberg, The Netherlands, viewed 24 June 2017, <http://www.dtic.mil/docs/citations/ADA285345>.

Merriam, SB 1998, *Qualitative research and case study applications in education*, 2nd edn, Jossey-Bass, San Francisco.

Merriam, SB & Tisdell, EJ 2016, *Qualitative research: a guide to design and implementation*, 4th edn, Jossey-Bass, San Francisco.

Van Merriënboer, JJ & Kester, L 2008, Whole-task models in education, in J Spector, M Merrill, J van Merriënboer & M Driscoll (eds.), *Handbook of research on educational communications and technology*, Erlbaum/Routledge, Mahwah, pp. 441–456, viewed 24 June 2017, <https://www.researchgate.net/publication/268000667>.

Van Merriënboer, JJG, Clark, RE & de Croock, MBM 2002, 'Blueprints for complex learning: the 4c/id-model', *Educational Technology Research and Development*, vol. 50, no. 2, pp. 39–61, http://dx.doi.org/10.1007/BF02504993.

Merrill, MD 2006, Hypothesized performance on complex tasks as a function of scaled instructional strategies, in J Enen & R Clark (eds.), *Handling complexity in learning environments: Research and theory*, Elsevier, Amsterdam, pp. 265–282, viewed 24 June 2017, <http://www.mdavidmerrill.com/Papers/Scaled_Instructional_Strategies.pdf>.

Merritt, C, Gaines, SA, Smith, J & Santen, SA 2017, 'A novel curriculum to optimize emergency medicine residents' exposure to pediatrics', *Western Journal of Emergency Medicine*, vol. 18, no. 1, pp. 14-19, http://dx.doi.org/10.5811/westjem.2016.10.31248.

Michel, CM 2008, 'Implementing a forensic educational package for registered nurses in two emergency departments in western australia', PhD thesis, University of Notre Dame, Australia, viewed 24 June 2017, <http://researchonline.nd.edu.au/theses/28/>.

Mieg, HA 2009, 'Two factors of expertise? excellence and professionalism of environmental experts', *High Ability Studies*, vol. 20, no. 1, pp. 91–115, http://dx.doi.org/10.1080/13598130902860432.

Miles, MB & Huberman, AM 1994, *Qualitative Data Analysis: An Expanded Sourcebook*, 2nd edn, Sage, Thousand Oaks.

Miles, MB, Huberman, AM & Saldana, J 2014, *Qualitative Data Analysis: A Methods Sourcebook*, 3rd edn, Sage, Thousand Oaks.

Miller, P 2003, 'Workplace learning by action learning: a practical example', *Journal of Workplace Learning*, vol. 15, no. 1, pp. 14–23, http://dx.doi.org/10.1108/13665620310458785.

Mills, N 2011, 'Situated learning through social networking communities: the development of joint enterprise, mutual engagement, and a shared repertoire', *Calico Journal*, vol. 28, no. 2, pp. 345–368, viewed <10.1080/00071005.2015.1133799>.

Mitchell, C, Ray, RL & van Ark, B 2016, *CEO Challenge 2016: Building Capability*, Research Report No. R-1599-16-RR, The Conference Board, viewed 24 June 2017, <http://pages.conference-board.org/rs/225-WBZ-025/images/TCB-1599-CEO-Challenge-2016-Report-Oracle.pdf>.

Mitchell, MD 2014, 'Effectiveness of electronic performance support system and training in a higher education setting', PhD thesis, ProQuest, Ann Arbor, viewed 24 June 2017, < https://search.proquest.com/openview/b8fd77082542d8496fb06aa33e883c4a/1.pdf?pq-origsite=gscholar&cbl=18750&diss=y>.

Mitrovic, A, Ohlsson, S & Barrow, D 2013, 'The effect of positive feedback in a constraint-based intelligent tutoring system', *Computers & Education*, vol. 60, no. 1, pp. 264–272, http://dx.doi.org/10.1016/j.compedu.2012.07.002.

Mokhtari, K, Rosemary, CA & Edwards, PA 2007, 'Making instructional decisions based on data: what, how, and why', *The Reading Teacher*, vol. 61, no. 4, pp. 354–359, viewed 24 June 2017, <http://www.academia.edu/download/6697808/making_instructional_decisions.pdf>.

Moon, YK, Kim, EJ & You, Y-M 2013, 'Study on expertise development process based on Arête, *International Journal of Information and Education Technology*, vol. 3, no. 2, pp. 226–230, http://dx.doi.org/10.7763/IJIET.2013.V3.269.

Morf, M 1986, *Optimizing work performance: a look beyond the bottom line*, Praeger, New York.

Morgan, DL, Fellows, C & Guevara, H 2008, Emergent approaches to focus group research, in *Handbook of emergent methods*, Guildford Press, New York, pp. 189–205, viewed 24 June 2017, <https://www.researchgate.net/profile/David_Morgan19/publication/276293452>.

Morgan, DL & Lobe, B 2011, Online focus groups, in S Hesse-Biber (ed.), *The handbook of emergent technologies in social research*, Oxford University Press, Oxford, pp. 199–230, viewed 24 June 2017, <https://www.researchgate.net/publication/273809338>.

Morgan, DL & Spanish, MT 1984, 'Focus groups: a new tool for qualitative research', *Qualitative Sociology*, vol. 7, no. 3, pp. 253–270, http://dx.doi.org/10.1007/bf00987314.

Morgeson, FP & Dierdorff, EC 2011, Work analysis: from technique to theory, in S Zedcck (ed.), *APA handbook of industrial and organisational psychology*, American Psychological Association, Washington, DC, pp. 3–41, viewed 24 March 2018, <https://msu.edu/~morgeson/morgeson_dierdorff_2011.pdf>.

Morris, C & Blaney, D 2010, Work-based learning, in T Swanwick (ed.), *Understanding medical education: Evidence, theory and practice*, Wiley-Blackwell, Hoboken, pp. 69–82, http://dx.doi.org/10.1002/9781444320282.ch5.

Morse, JM 1991, Strategies for sampling, in J Morse (ed.), *Qualitative nursing research: a contemporary dialogue*, Sage, Newbury Park, pp. 127–145, http://dx.doi.org/10.4135/9781483349015.n16.

_____ 2000, 'Determining sample size', *Qualitative Health Research*, vol. 10, no. 1, pp. 3–5, http://dx.doi.org/10.1177/104973200129118183.

Morse, JM, Barrett, M, Mayan, M, Olson, K & Spiers, J 2002, 'Verification strategies for establishing reliability and validity in qualitative research', *International Journal of Qualitative Methods*, vol. 1, no. 2, pp. 13–22, http://dx.doi.org/10.1177/160940690200100202.

Mostafavi, B & Barnes, T 2016, 'Exploring the impact of data-driven tutoring methods on students' demonstrative knowledge in logic problem solving', in T Barnes, M Chi & M Feng (eds.), *Proceedings of the 9th International Conference on Educational Data Mining*, Raleigh, 29 Jun - 2 July, International Educational Data Mining Society (IEDMS), pp. 460–465, viewed 24 June 2017, <http://www.educationaldatamining.org/EDM2016/proceedings/paper_125.pdf>.

Mostafavi, B, Liu, Z & Barnes, T 2015, 'Data-driven proficiency profiling', *Proceedings of the 8th International Conference on Educational Data Mining*, Madrid, 26-29 June, International Educational Data Mining Society, pp. 335–341, viewed 24 June 2017, <http://files.eric.ed.gov/fulltext/ED560536.pdf>.

Motowidlo, SJ, Borman, WC & Schmit, MJ 1997, 'A theory of individual differences in task and contextual performance', *Human Performance*, vol. 10, no. 2, pp. 71–83, http://dx.doi.org/10.1207/s15327043hup1002_1.

Motowidlo, SJ & Van Scotter, JR 1994, 'Evidence that task performance should be distinguished from contextual performance', *Journal of Applied Psychology*, vol. 79, no. 4, pp. 475-480, http://dx.doi.org/10.1037//0021-9010.79.4.475.

Mott, V 2000, 'The development of professional expertise in the workplace', *New Directions for Adult and Continuing Education*, vol. 2000, no. 86, pp. 23–31, http://dx.doi.org/10.1002/ace.8603.

Muhammad, A, Zhou, Q, Beydoun, G, Xu, D & Shen, J 2016, 'Learning path adaptation in online learning systems', *2016 IEEE 20th International Conference on Computer Supported Cooperative Work in Design (CSCWD)*, Nanchang, 4-6 May, IEEE, Piscataway, pp. 421–426, http://dx.doi.org/10.1109/cscwd.2016.7566026.

Müller, S & Abernethy, B 2014, 'An expertise approach to training anticipation using temporal occlusion in a natural skill setting', *Technology, Instruction, Cognition and Learning*, vol. 9, no. 4, pp. 295–312, viewed 24 June 2017, <https://espace.library.uq.edu.au/view/UQ:353646/UQ353646_OA.pdf>.

Munro, A & Clark, RE 2013, 'Cognitive task analysis-based design and authoring software for simulation training.', *Military Medicine*, vol. 178, no. 10 Suppl, pp. 7–14, http://dx.doi.org/10.7205/MILMED-D-13-00265.

Murphy, KR 1989, 'Is the relationship between cognitive ability and job performance stable over time?', *Human Performance*, vol. 2, no. 3, pp. 183–200, http://dx.doi.org/10.1207/s15327043hup0203_3.

Mylopoulos, M, Brydges, R, Woods, NN, Manzone, J & Schwartz, DL 2016, 'Preparation for future learning: a missing competency in health professions education?', *Medical Education*, vol. 50, no. 1, pp. 115–123, http://dx.doi.org/10.1111/medu.12893.

Nadler, L, Wiggs, GD & Smith, S 1988, 'Managing human resource development', *R&D Management*, vol. 18, no. 3, pp. 289–289.

Nagel, D 2011, 'Beyond seat time: advancing proficiency-based learning', *The Journal: Transforming Education*, viewed 24 June 2017, <https://thejournal.com/articles/2011/08/10/beyond-seat-time-advancing-proficiency-based-learning.aspx>.

Naikar, N 2011, *Cognitive work analysis: foundations, extensions, and challenges*, Report No. DSTO-GD-0680, Defence Science and Technology Organisation (DTSO), Fisherman's Bend, Victoria, Australia, viewed 24 June 2017, <http://www.dtic.mil/dtic/tr/fulltext/u2/a564221.pdf>.

_____ 2017, 'Cognitive work analysis: an influential legacy extending beyond human factors and engineering', *Applied Ergonomics*, vol. 59, pp. 528–540, http://dx.doi.org/10.1016/j.apergo.2016.06.001.

Naikar, N, Lintern, G & Sanderson, P 2002, Cognitive work analysis for air defense applications in Australia, in M McNeese & M Vidulich (eds.), *Cognitive Systems Engineering in Military Aviation Environments: Avoiding Cogminutia Fragmentosa!*, Human Systems Information Analysis Center, Dayton, pp. 169–200, viewed 24 June 2017, <https://www.researchgate.net/profile/Gavan_Lintern2/publication/242410104>.

Namey, E annd GG annd LT & Johnson, L 2007, Data reduction techniques for large qualitative data sets, in G Guest &K MacQueen (eds.), *Handbook for team-based qualitative research*, AltaMira Press, Plymouth, pp. 137–163, viewed 24 June 2017, <http://www.dl.icdst.org/pdfs/files/77efc132c01b9e2be2c6feb1d037dc39.pdf>.

NC State University 2011, 'Lab notes: uniformly accelerated motion', viewed 30 March 2018, <http://www.webassign.net/question_assets/ncsuplsemech2/lab_2/manual.html>.

Nguyen, F 2006, 'What you already know does matter: expertise and electronic performance support systems', *Performance Improvement*, vol. 45, no. 4, pp. 9–12, http://dx.doi.org/10.1002/pfi.2006.4930450404.

Nguyen, F, Klein, JD & Sullivan, H 2005, 'A comparative study of electronic performance support systems', *Performance Improvement Quarterly*, vol. 18, no. 4, pp. 71–86, http://dx.doi.org/10.1111/j.1937-8327.2005.tb00351.x.

Niazi, BRAS 2011, 'Training and development strategy and its role in organisational performance', *Journal of Public Administration and Governance*, vol. 1, no. 2, pp. 42–57, http://dx.doi.org/10.5296/jpag.v1i2.862.

Noe, RA, Tews, MJ & Michel, JW 2017, 'Managers' informal learning: a trait activation theory perspective', *International Journal of Training and Development*, vol. 21, no. 1, pp. 1–17, http://dx.doi.org/10.1111/ijtd.12092.

Novak, D 2011, *The systematic development of expertise*, CreateSpace Independent Publishing Platform, USA.

Nuutinen, M 2005, 'Expert identity construct in analysing prerequisites for expertise development: a case study of nuclear power plant operators' on-the-job training', *Cognition, Technology and Work*, vol. 7, no. 4, pp. 288–305, http://dx.doi.org/10.1007/s10111-005-0013-9.

Oldroyd, JB & Morris, SS 2012, 'Catching falling stars: a human resource response to social capital's detrimental effect of information overload on star employees', *Academy of Management Review*, vol. 37, no. 3, pp. 396–418, http://dx.doi.org/10.5465/amr.2010.0403.

Oliver, RL & Anderson, E 1994, 'An empirical test of the consequences of behavior-and outcome-based sales control systems', *The Journal of Marketing*, vol. 58, no. 4, pp. 53–67, http://dx.doi.org/10.2307/1251916.

Oliver, D, Serovich, J & Mason, T 2005, 'Constraints and opportunities with interview transcription: towards reflection in qualitative research', *Social Forces*, vol. 84, no. 2, pp. 1273–1289, http://dx.doi.org/10.1353/sof.2006.0023.

Ong, J & Ramachandran, S 2003, *Intelligent Tutoring Systems: Using Ai to Improve Training Performance and Roi*, Stotler Henke Associate, Inc., San Mateo, viewed 24 June 2017, <http://stage.shai.com/wp-content/uploads/2014/12/ITS_using_AI_to_improve_training_performance_and_ROI.pdf>.

Ounaies, HZ, Jamoussi, Y & Ghezala, HB 2013, 'Business goal oriented approach for adaptive learning system', *International Journal of Computer Science Issues*, vol. 10, no. 2, pp. 759–763, viewed 24 June 2017, <http://citeseerx.ist.psu.edu/viewdoc/download?doi=10.1.1.697.3436&rep=rep1&type=pdf>.

Oyewole, S a, Farde, AM, Haight, JM & Okareh, OT 2011, 'Evaluation of complex and dynamic safety tasks in human learning using the act-r and soar skill acquisition theories', *Computers in Human Behavior*, vol. 27, no. 5, pp. 1984–1995, http://dx.doi.org/10.1016/j.chb.2011.05.005.

Paas, F & van Gog, T 2009, Principles for designing effective and efficient training of complex cognitive skills, in F Durso (ed.), *Reviews of Human Factors and Ergonomics*, SAGE, Thousand Oaks, pp. 166–194, http://dx.doi.org/10.1518/155723409X448053.

Pandy, MG, Petrosino, AJ, Austin, B a & Barr, RE 2004, 'Assessing adaptive expertise in undergraduate biomechanics', *Journal of Engineering Education*, vol. 93, no. 3, pp. 211–222, http://dx.doi.org/10.1002/j.2168-9830.2004.tb00808.x.

Pansiri, J 2005, 'Pragmatism: a methodological approach to researching strategic alliances in tourism', *Tourism and Hospitality Planning & Development*, vol. 2, no. 3, pp. 191–206, http://dx.doi.org/10.1080/14790530500399333.

Parker, SK & Turner, N 2002, Work design and individual work performance: research findings and an agenda for future inquiry, in S Sonnentag (ed.), *Psychological management of individual performance*, John Wiley, San Francisco, pp. 69–93, http://dx.doi.org/10.1002/0470013419.ch4.

Patchan, MM, Schunn, CD, Sieg, W & McLaughlin, D 2015, 'The effect of blended instruction on accelerated learning', *Technology, Pedagogy and Education*, vol. 25, no. 3, pp. 1–18, http://dx.doi.org/10.1080/1475939X.2015.1013977.

Patterson, M, Militello, LG, Taylor, R, Bunger, A, Wheeler, D, Klein, G & Geis, G 2013, 'Acceleration to expertise in healthcare: leveraging the critical decision method and simulation-based training', in H Chaudet, L

Pellegrin & N Bonnardel (eds.), *Proceedings of the 11th International Conference on Naturalistic Decision Making (NDM 2013)*, Marseille, France, 21-24 May, Arpege Science Publishing, Paris, France, pp. 233–236, viewed 24 June 2017, <http://arpege-recherche.org/ndm11/papers/ndm11-233.pdf>.

Patton, M 2015, Enhancing the quality and credibility of qualitative studies, in *Qualitative Research & Evaluation Methods*, 4th edn, SAGE, Thousand Oaks, pp. 652–676, viewed 24 June 2017, < https://us.sagepub.com/sites/default/files/upm-binaries/65227_Patton_Chapter_9.pdf>.

Patton, MQ 1990, *Qualitative evaluation and research methods*, 2nd edn, Sage, Thousand Oaks.

_____ 1999, 'Enhancing the quality and credibility of qualitative analysis', *Health Services Research*, vol. 34, no. 5 Pt 2, pp. 1189–1208, viewed 24 June 2017, <http://www.ncbi.nlm.nih.gov/pmc/articles/PMC1089059/pdf/hsresearch00022-0112.pdf>.

_____ 2002, *Qualitative research and evaluation methods*, 3rd edn, SAGE, Thousand Oaks.

Pedler, M 2011, Action learning in practice, 4th edn, Gower Publishing, Burlington.

Peña, A 2010, 'The Dreyfus model of clinical problem-solving skills acquisition: a critical perspective', *Medical Education Online*, vol. 15, no. 1, art. 4856, pp. 1-11, http://dx.doi.org/10.3402/meo.v15i0.4846.

Pershing, JA (ed.) 2006, *Handbook of human performance technology: principles, practices, and potential*, 3rd edn, Pfeiffer, San Francisco.

Pershing, JA, Abaci, S & Symonette, S 2016, 'A treatise on the field of human performance technology: the need for a scholars' guild', *Performance Improvement*, vol. 55, no. 7, pp. 6–14, http://dx.doi.org/10.1002/pfi.21604.

Pershing, JA, Lee, J-E & Cheng, J 2008, 'Current status, future trends, and issues in human performance technology, part 2: models, influential disciplines, and research and development', *Performance Improvement*, vol. 47, no. 2, pp. 7–15, http://dx.doi.org/10.1002/pfi.182.

PetroSkills 2009, 'Accelerating time to competence through accelerated development programs', Petro Skills, USA, viewed 24 June 2017, <https://www.yumpu.com/en/document/view/8813692/accelerating-time-to-competence-through-accelerated-petroskills>.

Phellas, C, Bloch, A & Seale, C 2011, Structured methods: interviews, questionnaires and observation, in C Seale (ed.), *Researching Society and Culture*, Sage, London, pp. 181–205, viewed 24 June 2017, <http://www.sagepub.in/upm-data/47370_Seale_Chapter_11.pdf>.

Phillips, JJ 2012, *Return on investment in training and performance improvement programs*, Routledge, New York.

Piercy, NF, Cravens, DW & Morgan, NA 1998, 'Salesforce performance and behaviour-based management processes in business-to-business sales organisations', *European Journal of Marketing*, vol. 32, no. 1/2, pp. 79–100, viewed 24 Jun 2017, <http://neil-a-morgan.com/wp-content/uploads/2016/01/Piercy-Cravens-Morgan-EJM-1998.pdf>.

_____ 1999, 'Relationships between sales management control, territory design, salesforce performance and sales organisation effectiveness', *British Journal of Management*, vol. 10, no. 2, pp. 95-111, http://dx.doi.org/10.1111/1467-8551.00113.

Pinder, CC & Schroeder, KG 1987, 'Time to proficiency following job transfers', *Academy of Management Journal*, vol. 30, no. 2, pp. 336–353, http://dx.doi.org/10.2307/256278.

Piskurich, GM 1993, Self-directed learning: A practical guide to design, development, and implementation, Jossey-Bass, San Francisco.

Plummer, K 2004, 'Using documents in social research', *Contemporary Sociology: A Journal of Reviews*, vol. 33, no. 3, pp. 382–383, viewed 24 June 2017, <https://www.researchgate.net/publication/249826106_Using_Documents_in_Social_Research>.

Pollock, RV, Wick, CW & Jefferson, A 2015, *The six disciplines of breakthrough learning: how to turn training and development into business results*, 3rd edn, John Wiley, San Francisco.

Prior, L 2003, *Using documents in social research*, Introducing qualitative methods series, SAGE, London.

Project Management Institute 2013, *Guide to the project management body of knowledge (PMBOK)*, 5th edn, Project Management Institute, NewTown Square.

PTC 2005, 'Precision learning programs: personalized curriculums that accelerate adoption, boost productivity', Single-Sourcing Solutions Sunnyvale, viewed 24 June 2017, <http://www.single-sourcing.com/products/arbortext/elearning/32047en_file1.pdf>.

Quartey, SH 2012, 'Effect of employee training on the perceived organisational performance: a case study of the print-media industry in ghana', *Human Resource Management (HRM)*, vol. 4, no. 15, viewed 24 June 2017, <https://www.academia.edu/6817560/>.

Qui'nones, MA, Ford, JK & Teachout, MS 1995, 'The relationship between work experience and job performance: a conceptual and meta-analytic review', *Personnel Psychology*, vol. 48, no. 4, pp. 887–910, http://dx.doi.org/10.1111/j.1744-6570.1995.tb01785.x.

Radler, D & Bocianu, I 2017, 'Accelerated teaching and learning: roles and challenges for learners and tutors', *The International Scientific Conference eLearning and Software for Education*, Bucharest, 27-28 April, ProQuest, Ann Arbor, pp. 601–608, http://dx.doi.org/10.12753/2066-026X-17-170.

Ramaswami, A & Dreher, GF 2007, The benefits associated with workplace mentoring relationships, in T Allen & L Eby (eds.), *The Blackwell handbook of mentoring: a multiple perspectives approach*, Blackwell, Victoria, Australia, pp. 211–232, viewed 24 June 2017, <https://www.researchgate.net/publication/295660090>.

Ramly, NN & Yaw, LK 2012, 'Six sigma DMAIC: process improvements towards better it customer support', *International Journal of E-Education, E-Business, E-Management and E-Learning*, vol. 2, no. 5, pp. 359-364, http://dx.doi.org/10.7763/IJEEEE.2012.V2.146.

Ramsburg, L 2010, 'An initial investigation of the applicability of the Dreyfus skill acquisition model to the professional development of nurse educators', PhD thesis, Marshall University Graduate College, Huntington, viewed 24 June 2017, <http://mds.marshall.edu/cgi/viewcontent.cgi?article=1371&context=etd>.

Raphael, G, Berka, C, Popovic, D, Chung, GKWK, Nagashima, SO, Behneman, A, Davis, G & Johnson, R 2009, 'Adaptive performance trainer (APT): interactive neuro-educational technology to increase the pace and efficiency of rifle marksmanship training', in S Constantine (ed.), *Proceedings of the 13th International Conference on Human-Computer Interaction*, San Diego, 19-24 July, Springer-Verlag, Berlin Heidelberg, Germany, viewed 24 June 2017, <http://www.researchgate.net/profile/Chris_Berka2/publication/236660610>.

Rasmussen, J, Pejtersen, AM & Goodstein, L 1994, *Cognitive systems engineering*, John Wiley, New York.

Raybould, B 1995, 'Performance support engineering: an emerging development methodology for enabling organisational learning', *Performance Improvement Quarterly*, vol. 8, no. 1, pp. 7–22, http://dx.doi.org/10.1111/j.1937-8327.1995.tb00658.x.

Razer, A, Blair, L & Fadde, P 2015, 'Accelerating expert noticing in classroom teaching, nursing, and academic coaching', paper presented to the Annual convention of Association for Educational Communications and Technology Conference, Indianapolis.

Reed, J 1995, Practitioner knowledge in practitioner research, in J Reed & S Procter (eds.), *Practitioner Research in Health Care*, Springer, San Diego, pp. 46–61, http://dx.doi.org/10.1007/978-1-4899-6627-8_3.

Revans, R 1982, *The Origins and Evolution of Action Learning*, Chartwell-Bratt, Bromley.

Rikers, RMJP, van Gog, T & Paas, F 2008, 'The effects of constructivist learning environments: a commentary', *Instructional Science*, vol. 36, no. 5-6, pp. 463–467, http://dx.doi.org/10.1007/s11251-008-9067-4.

Roberts, MJ 2001, *Developing a teaching case*, Abridged edn, Harvard Business School Publication, Brighton.

Robinson, DG & Robinson, JC 1995, Performance consulting: Moving beyond training, Berrett-Koehler Publishers, San Francisco.

Robinson, SD, Sinar, E & Winter, J 2013, 'Social media as a tool for research: a turnover application using LinkedIn', *The Industrial Organisational Psychologist*, vol. 52, no. 1, pp. 133–141, viewed 24 June 2017, <http://www.siop.org/tip/july14/pdfs/robinson.pdf>.

Robinson, W & Pennotti, M 2013, 'Accelerating experience with live simulation of designing complex systems', paper presented to the ASEE International Forum, Atlanta, Georgia, viewed 24 June 2017, <https://peer.asee.org/accelerating-experience-with-live-simulation-of-designing-complex-systems.pdf>.

Rocco, TS & Hatcher, TG 2011, *The Handbook of Scholarly Writing and Publishing*, T Rocco & T Hatcher (eds.), John Wiley, San Francisco.

Rorty, R 1999, *Philosophy and social hope*, Penguin, London, viewed 24 June 2017, <http://cdclv.unlv.edu/pragmatism/rorty_intro_hope.pdf>.

Rose, C 2000, *Master it faster: how to learn faster, make good decisions & think creatively*, Accelerated Learning Systems, Las Vegas, viewed 24 June 2017, <http://www.goodreads.com/book/show/1026903.Master_it_Faster>.

Rosenbaum, S 2014, How we bring employees up to speed in record time using leaning path methodology, in R Pollock, C Wick & A Jefferson (eds.), *The field guide to the 6Ds*, Wiley & Sons, San Francisco, CA, pp. 345–351.

Rosenbaum, S & Pollock, R 2015, 'Creating a conducive talent development and learning culture', paper presented to the ATD International Conference and Exposition, Orlando, FL, 17-23 May.

Rosenbaum, S & Williams, J 2004, *Learning paths: increase profits by reducing the time it takes employees to get up to speed*, Jossey-Bass, San Francisco, viewed 24 June 2017, <http://www.wiley.com/WileyCDA/WileyTitle/productCd-0787975346.html>.

Rosenthal, ME, Castellvi, AO, Goova, MT, Hollett, LA, Dale, J & Scott, DJ 2009, 'Pretraining on southwestern stations dcreases training time and cost for proficiency-based fundamentals of laparoscopic surgery training', *Journal of the American College of Surgeons*, vol. 209, no. 5, pp. 626–631, http://dx.doi.org/10.1016/j.jamcollsurg.2009.07.013.

Rossman, GB & Rallis, SF 2012, *Learning in the field: an introduction to qualitative research*, 3rd edn, Sage, Thousand Oaks.

Roth, MM & O'Hara, J 2014, 'Discussion panel: how to recognize a "good" cognitive task analysis?', *Proceedings of the Human Factors and Ergonomics Society 58th Annual Meeting*, Chicago, 27-31 October, SAGE, Thousand Oaks, pp. 320–324, http://dx.doi.org/10.1177/1541931214581066.

Roth, EM & Bisantz, AM 2013, Cognitive work analysis, in J Lee, A Kirlik, E Roth & A Bisantz (eds.), *The Oxford Handbook of Cognitive Engineering*, Oxford University Press, New York, http://dx.doi.org/10.1093/oxfordhb/9780199757183.013.0015.

Roth, R 2009, 'Acquiring and maintaining expert ability', [Unpublished Manuscript], viewed 24 June 2017, <http://www.r2research.com/Research_files/ExpertAbility_Roth_2009.pdf>.

Rothwell, WJ, Brock, MC, Dean, PJ & Rosenberg, MJ 2000, *ASTD Models for Human Performance Improvement: Roles, Competencies, and Outputs*, 2nd edn, W Rothwell (ed.), American Society for Training and Development (ASTD), Alexandria.

Rothwell, WJ & Kazanas, HC 2004, Improving on-the-job training: How to establish and operate a comprehensive OJT program, John Wiley & Sons, San Francisco.

Rummler, GA & Brache, AP 1995, *Improving performance: How to manage the white space on the organisation chart*, 2nd edn, Jossey-Bass, San Francisco.

Ryan, GW & Bernard, HR 2003, 'Techniques to identify themes', *Field Methods*, vol. 15, no. 1, pp. 85–109, http://dx.doi.org/10.1177/1525822X02239569.

Sackett, PR & Laczo, RM 2003, Job and work analysis, in D Freedheim (ed.), *Handbook of psychology – Vol 1*, Wiley, Hoboken, pp. 21-37, http://dx.doi.org/10.1002/0471264385.wei1202

Saks, A, Haccoun, R & Belcourt, M 2010, *Managing performance through training and development*, 5th ed., Nelson Education, Canada, viewed 24 June 2017, <https://www.amazon.com/Managing-Performance-Through-Training-Development/dp/0176507337>.

Salas, DJ, Baldiris, S, Fabregat, R & Graf, S 2016, 'Supporting the acquisition of scientific skills by the use of learning analytics', in D Chiu, I Marenzi, U Nanni, M Spaniol & M Temperini (eds.), *International Conference on Web-Based Learning*, Rome, 26-29 October, Springer, Cham, pp. 281–293, http://dx.doi.org/10.1007/978-3-319-47440-3_32.

Salas, E, Rosen, MA, Held, JD & Weissmuller, JJ 2008, 'Performance measurement in simulation-based training: a review and best practices', *Simulation & Gaming*, vol. 40, no. 3, pp. 328–376, http://dx.doi.org/10.1177/1046878108326734.

Salas, E, Rosen, MA, Weaver, SJ, Held, JD & Weissmuller, JJ 2009, 'Research on SBT leads to the development of guidelines applicable to diverse training scenarios', *Ergonomics in Design: The Quarterly of Human Factors Applications*, vol. 17, no. 4, pp. 12–18, http://dx.doi.org/10.1518/106480409X12587548298009.

Salas, E, Tannenbaum, SI, Kraiger, K & Smith-Jentsch, K a 2012, 'The science of training and development in organisations: what matters in practice', *Psychological Science in the Public Interest*, vol. 13, no. 2, pp. 74–101, http://dx.doi.org/10.1177/1529100612436661.

Salkind, NJ & Rainwater, T 2012, *Exploring research*, 8th ed., Prentice Hall, Upper Saddle River, viewed 24 June 2017, <http://dinus.ac.id/repository/docs/ajar/Neil_J._Salkind_2012_-_Exploring_Research_.pdf>.

Salmons, J 2010, *Online interviews in real time*, Sage, Thousand Oaks.

―――― 2012, Designing and conducting research with online interviews, in J Salmons (ed.), *Cases in Online Interview Research*, Sage, Thousand Oaks, pp. 1–30, http://dx.doi.org/10.4135/9781506335155.n1.

Sancar-Tokmak, H 2013, 'Effects of video-supported expertise-based training (XBT) on preservice science teachers' self-efficacy beliefs', *Eurasia Journal of Mathematics, Science & Technology Education*, vol. 9, no. 2, pp. 131–141, http://dx.doi.org/10.12973/eurasia.2013.924a.

Sandelowski, M 1986, 'The problem of rigor in qualitative research', *Advances in Nursing Science*, vol. 8, no. 3, pp. 27–37, http://dx.doi.org/10.1097/00012272-198604000-00005.

―――― 1995, 'Sample size in qualitative research', *Research in Nursing & Health*, vol. 18, no. 2, pp. 179–183, http://dx.doi.org/10.1002/nur.4770180211.

Sandelowski, M & Barroso, J 2007, *Handbook for synthesizing qualitative research*, Springer, Berlin, viewed 24 June 2017, <https://www.researchgate.net/file.PostFileLoader.html?id=568df1dd7c1920ffce8b4567&assetKey=AS%3A315125020463104%401452143067307>.

Sangrà, A, Vlachopoulos, D & Cabrera, N 2012, 'Building an inclusive definition of e-learning: an approach to the conceptual framework', *International Review of Research in Open and Distance Learning*, vol. 13, no. 2, pp. 145–159, viewed 24 May 2015, <http://www.irrodl.org/index.php/irrodl/article/view/1161/2146>.

Sappleton, N 2013, *Advancing research methods with new technologies*, IGI Global, Hershey.

Sappleton, N & Lourenço, F 2016, 'Email subject lines and response rates to invitations to participate in a web survey and a face-to-face interview: the sound of silence', *International Journal of Social Research Methodology*, vol. 17, no. 5, pp. 611–622, http://dx.doi.org/10.1080/13645579.2015.1078596.

Sargeant, J 2012, 'Qualitative research part ii: participants, analysis, and quality assurance', *Journal of Graduate Medical Education*, vol. 4, no. 1, pp. 1–3, http://dx.doi.org/10.4300/JGME-D-11-00307.1.

Schaafstal, AA, Schraagen, JM, van Berlo, M & van Berlo, M 2000, 'Cognitive task analysis and innovation of training: the case of structured troubleshooting', *Human Factors*, vol. 42, no. 1, pp. 75–86, http://dx.doi.org/10.1518/001872000779656570.

Schaffer, SP 2000, 'A review of organisational and human performance frameworks', *Performance Improvement Quarterly*, vol. 13, no. 3, pp. 220–243, http://dx.doi.org/10.1111/j.1937-8327.2000.tb00183.x.

Van Schaik, P, Pearson, R & Barker, P 2002, 'Designing electronic performance support systems to facilitate learning', *Innovations in Education and Teaching International*, vol. 39, no. 4, pp. 289–306, http://dx.doi.org/10.1080/13558000210161043.

Schmid, U, Ragni, M, Gonzalez, C & Funke, J 2011, 'The challenge of complexity for cognitive systems', *Cognitive Systems Research*, vol. 12, no. 3-4, pp. 211–218, http://dx.doi.org/10.1016/j.cogsys.2010.12.007.

Schmidt, RC 1997, 'Managing Delphi surveys using nonparametric statistical techniques', *Decision Sciences*, vol. 28, no. 3, pp. 763–774, http://dx.doi.org/10.1111/j.1540-5915.1997.tb01330.x.

Schmitt, J 1996, 'Designing good TDGS', *Marine Corps Gazette*, vol. 80, no. 5, pp. 96–97.

Schmutz, J & Manser, T do 2013, 'Do team processes really have an effect on clinical performance? a systematic literature review', *British Journal of Anaesthesia*, vol. 110, no. 4, pp. 529–544, http://dx.doi.org/10.1093/bja/aes513.

Schneider, W 1993, Acquiring expertise: determinants of exceptional performance, in K Heller, F Mönks & A Passow (eds.), *International handbook of research and development of giftedness and talent*, Pergamon Press, Elmsford, NY, pp. 311–324, viewed <https://opus.bibliothek.uni-wuerzburg.de/frontdoor/deliver/index/docId/7140/file/Schneider_W_OPUS_7140.pdf>.

Schraagen, JM 1993, 'How experts solve a novel problem in experimental design', *Cognitive Science*, vol. 17, no. 2, pp. 285–309, http://dx.doi.org/10.1207/s15516709cog1702_4.

Schreiber, BT, Bennett Jr, W, Colegrove, CM, Portrey, AM, Greschke, DA & Bell, HH 2009, Evaluating pilot performance, in K Ericsson (ed.), *Development of professional expertise*, Cambridge University Press, New York, pp. 247–270, http://dx.doi.org/10.1017/cbo9780511609817.014.

Schulz, M & Roßnagel, CS 2010, 'Informal workplace learning: an exploration of age differences in learning competence', *Learning and Instruction*, vol. 20, no. 5, pp. 383–399, http://dx.doi.org/10.1016/j.learninstruc.2009.03.003.

Schwartz, DL, Bransford, JD, Sears, D & others 2005, Efficiency and innovation in transfer, in J Mestre (ed.), *Transfer of learning from a modern multidisciplinary perspective*, Information Age., Greenwich, pp. 1–51.

Scobey, BW 2006, 'The journey to expertise: pathways to expert knowledge traveled by Texas juvenile probation officers', PhD thesis, Texas State University, San Marcos, viewed 24 June 2017, <https://digital.library.txstate.edu/bitstream/handle/10877/4267/fulltext.pdf?sequence=1>.

Seager, W, Ruskov, M, Sasse, MA & Oliveira, M 2011, 'Eliciting and modelling expertise for serious games in project management', *Entertainment Computing*, vol. 2, no. 2, pp. 75–80, http://dx.doi.org/10.1016/j.entcom.2011.01.002.

Seale, C 1999, 'Quality in qualitative research', *Qualitative Inquiry*, vol. 5, no. 4, pp. 465–478, viewed 24 June 2017, <http://citeseerx.ist.psu.edu/viewdoc/download?doi=10.1.1.460.3511&rep=rep1&type=pdf>.

Seidman, I 2013, *Interviewing as qualitative research: a guide for researchers in education and the social sciences*, 3rd ed., Teachers College Press, New York, viewed 24 June 2017, <http://homes.cs.washington.edu/~depstein/hcde596/papers/seidman_interview.pdf>.

Semali, LM & Buchko, OV 2014, 'Can leadership competencies differentiate exemplary performers from typical ones? a case study of the Hubert H. Humphrey fellowship program in USA', *Journal of International Education and Leadership Volume*, vol. 4, no. 2, pp. 1-18, viewed 24 June 2017, <http://www.jielusa.org/wp-content/uploads/2012/01/HumphreyFellowshipProgram.pdf>.

Senge, PM 1994a, *The fifth discipline fieldbook. New York: Transformation thinking*, Berkley Publishing Group, New York.

―――― 1994b, Building learning organisations, in *The training and development sourcebook*, Prentice Hall, Englewood Cliffs, pp. 3.67–3.74.

Senge, PM, Kleiner, A, Roberts, C, Ross, RB & Smith, BJ 1994, *The fifth discipline fieldbook: Strategies and tools for building a learning organisation*, Crown Business, New York.

Seow, C, Hughes, J, Moon, S, Birchall, D, Williams, S & Vrasidas, C 2005, 'Developing design principles for an e-learning programme for sme managers to support accelerated learning in the workplace', *Journal of Workplace Learning*, vol. 17, no. 5/6, pp. 370–384, http://dx.doi.org/10.1108/13665620510606788.

Seto, AH & Kern, MJ 2016, 'Simulator training: the bridge between 'primum non nocere' and 'learning by doing,'" *Catheterization and Cardiovascular Interventions*, vol. 87, no. 3, pp. 381–382, http://dx.doi.org/10.1002/ccd.26432.

Shadrick, SB & Lussier, JW 2009, Training complex cognitive skills: a theme-based approach to the development of battlefield skills, in K Ericsson (ed.), *Development of professional expertise: Toward measurement of expert performance and design of optimal learning environments*, Cambridge University Press, New York, pp. 286–311, http://dx.doi.org/10.1017/cbo9780511609817.016.

Shadrick, SB, Lussier, JW & Fultz, C 2007, *Accelerating the Development of Adaptive Performance: Validating the Think like a Commander Training*, Research Report No. 1868, U.S. Army Research Institute for the Behavioral and Social Sciences, Arlington, http://dx.doi.org/10.21236/ada464668.

Shanteau, J 2015, 'Why task domains (still) matter for understanding expertise', *Journal of Applied Research in Memory and Cognition*, vol. 4, no. 3, pp. 169–175, http://dx.doi.org/10.1016/j.jarmac.2015.07.0032211-3681.

Sheckley, B & Keeton, M 1999, *Ecologies that support and enhance adult learning*, College Park: University of Maryland College.

Shenton, AK 2004, 'Strategies for ensuring trustworthiness in qualitative research projects', *Education for Information*, vol. 22, no. 2, pp. 63–75, http://dx.doi.org/10.3233/efi-2004-22201.

Shiffrin, RM & Schneider, W 1977, 'Controlled and automatic human information processing: perceptual learning, automatic attending and a general theory', *Psychological Review*, vol. 84, no. 2, pp. 127–190, viewed 24 June 2017, <http://www.bryanburnham.net/wp-content/uploads/2014/01/Shiffrin-1977-Psychological-Review.pdf>.

Shuell, TJ 1986, 'Individual differences: changing conceptions in research and practice', *American Journal of Education*, vol. 94, no. 3, pp. 356–377, http://dx.doi.org/10.1086/443854.

Simonton, DK 1997, 'Creative productivity: a predictive and explanatory model of career trajectories and landmarks.', *Psychological Review*, vol. 104, no. 1, pp. 66-89, viewed 24 June 2017, <https://pdfs.semanticscholar.org/abb5/02a8b01b50790a44cf5438f01f9f5ac9bf42.pdf>.

Skulmoski, G, Hartman, F & Krahn, J 2007, 'The Delphi method for graduate research', *Journal of Information Technology Education*, vol. 6, pp. 1–21, viewed 24 June 2017, < http://jite.org/documents/Vol6/JiteContentsVol6.pdf>.

Slootmaker, A, Kurvers, H, Hummel, H & Koper, R 2014, 'Developing scenario-based serious games for complex cognitive skills acquisition: design, development and evaluation of the Emergo platform', *Journal of Universal Computer Science*, vol. 20, no. 4, pp. 561–582, http://dx.doi.org/10.3217/jucs-020-04-0561.

Smeds, R 2003, 'Simulation for accelerated learning and development in industrial management', *Production Planning & Control*, vol. 14, no. 2, pp. 107–110, http://dx.doi.org/10.1080/0953728031000107707.

Smith, A & Call, N 1999, *The alps approach: accelerated learning in primary schools: brain-based methods for accelerating motivation and achievement*, Network Educational Press, Stafford, viewed 24 June 2017, <http://capitadiscovery.co.uk/brighton-ac/items/1253656>.

Smith, EM, Ford, JK, Kozlowski & Quiñones, SWJ 1997, Building adaptive expertise: implications for training design strategies, in A Miguel & A Ehrenstein (eds.), *Training for a rapidly changing workplace: Applications of psychological research*, American Psychological Association, Washington, D.C., pp. 89–118, http://dx.doi.org/10.1037/10260-004.

Sobel, HS, Cepeda, NJ & Kapler, IV 2011, 'Spacing effects in real-world classroom vocabulary learning', *Applied Cognitive Psychology*, vol. 25, no. 5, pp. 763–767, http://dx.doi.org/10.1002/acp.1747.

Soderstrom, NC & Bjork, RA 2015, 'Learning versus performance: an integrative review', *Perspectives on Psychological Science*, vol. 10, no. 2, pp. 176–199, http://dx.doi.org/10.1177/1745691615569000.

Sonnentag, S & Frese, M 2002, Performance concepts and performance theory, in S Sonnentag (ed.), *Psychological management of individual performance*, John Wiley, New York, pp. 3–25, http://dx.doi.org/10.1002/0470013419.ch1.

Sonnentag, S & Kleine, BM 2000, 'Deliberate practice at work: a study with insurance agents', *Journal of Occupational and Organisational Psychology*, vol. 73, no. 1, pp. 87–102, http://dx.doi.org/10.1348/096317900166895.

Sottilare, R & Goldberg, B 2012, 'Designing adaptive computer-based tutoring systems to accelerate learning and facilitate retention', *Cognitive Technology*, vol. 17, no. 1, pp. 19–33, viewed 24 June 2017, <http://www.researchgate.net/profile/Bob_Sottilare/publication/267037687>.

Soule, RT 2016, 'The learning experience of tough cases: a descriptive case study', PhD thesis, The George Washington University, Ann Harbor, MI, viewed 24 June 2017, <http://pqdtopen.proquest.com/doc/1751007250.html?FMT=AI>.

Souza, MIF, Torres, T, de Carvalho, J, Evangelista, S & do Amaral, S 2015, 'Non-formal education for technology transfer in Embrapa: microlearning, microtraining and microcontent by mobile devices', *Proceedings of the 7th International Conference on Education and New Learning Technologies (EDULEARN15)*, Barcelona, 6-8 July, IATED, Valencia, pp. 5728–5736, viewed 24 June 2017, <https://www.researchgate.net/publication/280091194>.

Spiro, RJ, Collins, BP, Thota, JJ & Feltovich, PJ 2003, 'Cognitive flexibility theory: hypermedia for complex learning, adaptive knowledge application, and experience acceleration', *Educational Technology*, vol. 43, no. 5, pp. 5–10, viewed 24 June 2017, <https://eric.ed.gov/?id=EJ675158>.

Spiro, RJ, Coulson, RL, Feitovich, PJ & Anderson, DK 1988, *Cognitive Flexibility Theory: Advanced Knowledge Acquisition in Ill-Structured Domains*, Technical Report No. 441, University of Illinois, Champaign, viewed 24 June 2017, <http://files.eric.ed.gov/fulltext/ED302821.pdf>.

Spiro, RJ, Feltovich, PJ, Coulson, RL, Jacobson, M, Durgunoglu, A, Ravlin, S & Jehng, J-C 1992, *Knowledge Acquisition for Application: Cognitive Flexibility and Transfer of Training in Iii-Structured Domains*, ARI Research Note No. 92-21, United States Army Research Institute for the Behaviorai and Social Sciences, Alexandria, viewed 24 June 2017, <http://www.dtic.mil/dtic/tr/fulltext/u2/a250147.pdf>.

Spiro, RJ & Jehng, J-C 1990, Cognitive flexibility and hypertext: theory and technology for the nonlinear and multidimensional traversal of complex subject matter, in D Nix & R Spiro (eds.), *Cognition, education, and multimedia: Exploring ideas in high technology*, Erlbaum, Hilldale, pp. 163–205.

Spiro, RJ, Vispoel, WP, J G Schmitz, Samarapungavan, A & Boerger, AE 1987, *Knowledge Acquisition for Application: Cognitive Flexibility and Transfer in Complex Content Domains*, Report No. 409, University of Illinois, Champaign, viewed 24 June 2017, <http://files.eric.ed.gov/fulltext/ED287155.pdf>.

Spruit, EN, Band, GP & Hamming, JF 2015, 'Increasing efficiency of surgical training: effects of spacing practice on skill acquisition and retention in laparoscopy training', *Surgical Endoscopy*, vol. 29, no. 8, pp. 2235–2243, http://dx.doi.org/10.1007/s00464-014-3931-x.

Squires, A, Wade, J, Dominick, P & Gelosh, D 2011, *Building a Competency Taxonomy to Guide Experience Acceleration of Lead Program Systems Engineers*, ERIC No. ADA589178, Stevens Institute of Technology, Hoboken, viewed 24 June 2017, <http://www.dtic.mil/cgi-bin/GetTRDoc?AD=ADA589178>.

St John, W & Johnson, P 2000, 'The pros and cons of data analysis software for qualitative research', *Journal of Nursing Scholarship: An Official Publication of Sigma Theta Tau International Honor Society of Nursing / Sigma Theta Tau*, vol. 32, no. 4, pp. 393–7, http://dx.doi.org/10.1111/j.1547-5069.2000.00393.x.

Stake, RE 2006, *Multiple case study analysis*, The Guilford Press, New York, viewed 24 June 2017, <http://www.guilford.com/books/Multiple-Case-Study-Analysis/Robert-Stake/9781593852481>.

Stalmeijer, RE, Dolmans, DH, Snellen-Balendong, HA, van Santen-Hoeufft, M, Wolfhagen, IH & Scherpbier, AJ 2013, 'Clinical teaching based on principles of cognitive apprenticeship: views of experienced clinical teachers', *Academic Medicine*, vol. 88, no. 6, pp. 861–865, http://dx.doi.org/10.1097/ACM.0b013e31828fff12.

Starkes, JL & Lindley, S 1994, 'Can we hasten expertise by video simulations?', *Quest*, vol. 46, no. 2, pp. 211–222, http://dx.doi.org/10.1080/00336297.1994.10484122.

Sternberg, RJ 1999, 'Intelligence as developing expertise.', *Contemporary Educational Psychology*, vol. 24, no. 4, pp. 359–375, http://dx.doi.org/10.1006/ceps.1998.0998.

Stolovitch, HD 2000, 'Human performance technology: research and theory to practice', *Performance Improvement*, vol. 39, no. 4, pp. 7–16, http://dx.doi.org/10.1002/pfi.4140390407.

Stolovitch, H 2007, The development and evolution of human performance improvement, in R Reiser & L Dempsey (eds.), *Trends and issues in instructional design and technology*, Pearson, Upper Saddle River, pp. 134–146.

Stolovitch, HD & Keeps, EJ 1992, What is human performance technology?, in H Stolovich & E Keeps (eds.), *Handbook of human performance technology: A comprehensive guide for analyzing and solving performance problems in organisations*, Pfeiffer, San Francisco.

Stolovitch, HD & Keeps, EJ 1999, What is performance technology?, in H Stolovich & E Keeps (eds.), *Handbook of human performance technology. Improving individual and organisational performance worldwide.*, Jossey-Bass/Pfeiffer, San Francisco, pp. 3–23.

Sturges, JE & Hanrahan, KJ 2004, 'Comparing telephone and face-to-face qualitative interviewing: a research note', *Qualitative Research*, vol. 4, no. 1, pp. 107–118, http://dx.doi.org/10.1177/1468794104041110.

Sudnickas, T 2016, 'Different levels of performance evaluation-individual versus organisational', *Viesoji Politika Ir Administravimas*, vol. 15, no. 2, http://dx.doi.org/10.13165/VPA-16-15-2-01.

Sullivan, ME, Yates, KA, Inaba, K, Lam, L & Clark, RE 2014, 'The use of cognitive task analysis to reveal the instructional limitations of experts in the teaching of procedural skills', *Academic Medicine*, vol. 89, no. 5, pp. 811–816, http://dx.doi.org/10.1097/ACM.0000000000000224.

Sullivan, R, Brechin, S & Lacoste, M 1999, Structured on-the-job training: innovations in international health training, in R Jacobs (ed.), *Linking HRD Programs with Organisational Strategy*, American Society for Training and Development (ASTD), Washington, D.C., pp. 155–179, viewed 24 June 2017, <http://reprolineplus.org/system/files/resources/astd_ojt.pdf>.

Surtees, J 2014, 'Interorganisational innovation and collaboration in the uk medical device sector', PhD thesis, Aston University, Birmingham, viewed 24 June 2017, <http://eprints.aston.ac.uk/28864/1/Surtees_Jennifer_R.L_2016.pdf>.

Suter, WN 2012, *Introduction to educational research: a critical thinking approach*, 2nd edn, Sage, Thousand Oaks, http://dx.doi.org/10.4135/9781483384443.

Swanson, RA 1994, *Analysis for improving performance: tools for diagnosing organizations and documenting workplace expertise*, Berrett-Koehler, Oakland.

―――― 1995, 'Human resource development: performance is the key', *Human Resource Development Quarterly*, vol. 6, no. 2, pp. 207–213, viewed 24 March 2018, <http://www.richardswanson.com/publications/Swanson(1995)HRDPerform.pdf>.

―――― 1999, The foundations of performance improvement and implications for practice, in R Torraco (ed.), *The theory and practice of performance improvement*, Berrett-Koehler, San Francisco, pp. 1–25, http://dx.doi.org/10.1177/152342239900100102.

―――― 2005, The process of framing research in organisations, in R Swanson & E Holton (eds.), *Research in organisations: Foundations and methods in inquiry*, Berrett-Koehler, San Francisco, pp. 11–26, viewed on 24 June 2017, <https://www.bkconnection.com/static/Research_in_Organisations_EXCERPT.pdf>.

―――― 2007, *Analysis for improving performance: tools for diagnosing organisations and documenting workplace expertise*, Berrett-Koehler, Oakland, viewed 24 June 2017, <http://www.bkconnection.com/static/Analysis-For-Improving-Performance_EXCERPT.pdf>.

Swanson, RA & Arnold, DE 1996, 'Part one: what is the purpose of human resource development? the purpose of human resource development is to improve organisational performance', *New Directions for Adult and Continuing Education*, vol. 1996, no. 72, pp. 13–19, http://dx.doi.org/10.1002/ace.36719967204.

Swanson, RA & Holton, EF 2001, *Foundations of human resource development*, Berrett-Koehler, Oakland, viewed 24 June 2017, <https://www.bkconnection.com/static/Foundations_of_Human_Resource_Development_EXCERPT.pdf>.

Taghizadeh, F & Daneshfar, A 2014, 'Sequencing skills in teaching table tennis: inter-task transfer of learning', *International Journal of Sport Studies*, vol. 4, no. 1, pp. 631–634, viewed 24 June 2017, <http://ijssjournal.com/fulltext/paper-09012016125242.pdf>.

Tam, V, Lam, EY & Fung, S 2014, 'A new framework of concept clustering and learning path optimization to develop the next-generation e-learning systems', *Journal of Computers in Education*, vol. 1, no. 4, pp. 335–352, http://dx.doi.org/10.1007/s40692-014-0016-8.

Taris, TW & Feij, JA 2004, 'Learning and strain among newcomers: a three-wave study on the effects of job demands and job control', *The Journal of Psychology*, vol. 138, no. 6, pp. 543–563, http://dx.doi.org/10.3200/JRLP.138.6.543-563.

Taris, TW & Schreurs, PJ 2009, 'Explaining worker strain and learning: how important are emotional job demands?', *Anxiety, Stress & Coping*, vol. 22, no. 3, pp. 245–262, http://dx.doi.org/10.1080/10615800802460401.

Tashakkori, A & Teddlie, C (eds.) 2003, *Sage handbook of mixed methods in social & behavioral research*, Sage, Thousand Oaks, http://dx.doi.org/10.4135/9781506335193.

Teodorescu, T 2006, 'Competence versus competency: what is the difference?', *Performance Improvement*, vol. 45, no. 10, pp. 27–30, http://dx.doi.org/10.1002/pfi.027.

Thawani, S 2004, 'Six sigma—strategy for organisational excellence', *Total Quality Management & Business Excellence*, vol. 15, no. 5-6, pp. 655–664, http://dx.doi.org/10.1080/14783360410001680143.

The Business Rules Group 2010, *The Business Motivation Model: Business Governance in a Volatile World*, Release 1.4, The Business Rules Group, viewed 24 June 2017, <http://www.businessrulesgroup.org/second_paper/BRG-BMM.pdf>.

Thomas, A, Thomas, A, Antony, J, Antony, J, Haven-Tang, C, Haven-Tang, C, Francis, M, Francis, M, Fisher, R & Fisher, R 2017, 'Implementing lean six sigma into curriculum design and delivery-a case study in higher education', *International Journal of Productivity and Performance Management*, vol. 66, no. 5, pp. 577–597, http://dx.doi.org/10.1108/IJPPM-08-2016-0176.

Thompson, KS 2017, Training's impact on time-to-proficiency for new bankers in a financial services organisation, in S Frasard & P Frederick (eds.), *Training Initiatives and Strategies for the Modern Workforce*, IGI Global, Hershey, pp. 169–185, http://dx.doi.org/10.4018/978-1-5225-1808-2.ch009.

Thomsen, BC, Renaud, CC, Savory, SJ, Romans, EJ, Mitrofanov, O, Rio, M, Day, SE, Kenyon, AJ & Mitchell, JE 2010, 'Introducing scenario based learning: experiences from an undergraduate electronic and electrical engineering course', *IEEE Education Engineering Conference EDUCON 2010*, Madrid, 14-16 April, IEEE, Piscataway, pp. 953–958, http://dx.doi.org/10.1109/EDUCON.2010.5492474.

Thomson Reuters 2012, *Thomson Reuters Business Classification (TRBC)*, Thomson Reuter, New York, viewed 24 June 2017, <http://financial.thomsonreuters.com/en/products/data-analytics/market-data/indices/trbc-indices.html>.

Van Tiem, D, Moseley, JL & Dessinger, JC 2012, *Fundamentals of performance improvement: optimizing results through people, process, and organisations*, 3rd edn, Pfeiffer, San Francisco.

Van Tiem, DM, Moseley, JL & Dessinger, JC 2004, *Fundamentals of performance technology: a guide to improving people process and performance*, International Society for Performance Improvement, Washington DC, http://dx.doi.org/10.1002/pfi.4140400313.

Tims, M, Bakker, AB, Derks, D & van Rhenen, W 2013, 'Job crafting at the team and individual level: implications for work engagement and performance', *Group & Organisation Management*, vol. 38, no. 4, pp. 427–454, http://dx.doi.org/10.1177/1059601113492421.

Tjiam, IM, Schout, BMA, Hendrikx, AJM, Scherpbier, AJJM, Witjes, JA & van Merriënboer, JJG 2012, 'Designing simulator-based training: an approach integrating cognitive task analysis and four-component instructional design.', *Medical Teacher*, vol. 34, no. 10, pp. e698–707, http://dx.doi.org/10.3109/0142159X.2012.687480.

Tofel-Grehl, C & Feldon, DF 2013, 'Cognitive task analysis-based training: a meta-analysis of studies', *Journal of Cognitive Engineering and Decision Making*, vol. 7, no. 3, pp. 293–304, http://dx.doi.org/10.1177/1555343412474821.

Tokmak, HS, Baturay, HM & Fadde, P 2013, 'Applying the context, input, process, product evaluation model for evaluation, research, and redesign of an online master's program', *The International Review of Research in Open and Distributed Learning*, vol. 14, no. 3, pp. 273–293, http://dx.doi.org/10.19173/irrodl.v14i3.1485.

Training Magazine 2016, '2016 training industry report', *Training Magazine*, vol. 53, no. 6, pp. 28–41, viewed 24 June 2017, <https://trainingmag.com/sites/default/files/images/Training_Industry_Report_2016.pdf>.

Trekles, AM & Sims, R 2013, 'Designing instruction for speed: qualitative insights into instructional design for accelerated online graduate coursework', *Online Journal of Distance Learning Administration*, vol. 16, no. 3, viewed 24 June 2017, <http://www.westga.edu/~distance/ojdla/winter164/trekles_sims164.html>.

Tulis, M, Steuer, G & Dresel, M 2016, 'Learning from errors: a model of individual processes', *Frontline Learning Research*, vol. 4, no. 2, pp. 12–26, http://dx.doi.org/10.14786/flr.v4i2.168.

Turner, JR & Müller, R 2003, 'On the nature of the project as a temporary organisation', *International Journal of Project Management*, vol. 21, no. 1, pp. 1–8, http://dx.doi.org/10.1016/s0263-7863(02)00020-0.

TutorVista 2018, *Dependent variable on a graph*, viewed 30 March 2018, <https://www.tutorvista.com/content/math/dependent-variable-on-a-graph/>.

Tynjälä, P 2008, 'Perspectives into learning in the workplace', *Educational Research Review*, vol. 3, no. 2, pp. 130–154, http://dx.doi.org/10.1016/j.edurev.2007.12.001.

US Department of Commerce 2016, *The Benefits and Costs of Apprenticeships: A Business Perspective*, ERIC Document No. ED572260, US Department of Commerce, viewed 24 Jun 2017, <http://files.eric.ed.gov/fulltext/ED572260.pdf>.

Vachette, A 2016, 'Networked disaster governance in Vanuatu: the anatomy of an inclusive and integrated system to build resilience in a small island developing', PhD thesis, James Cook University, Australia, viewed 24 June 2017, <http://researchonline.jcu.edu.au/46161/>.

Vandergriff, DE 2012, *Raising the bar: creating and nurturing adaptability to deal with the changing face of war*, Center for Defense Information, Washington, D.C.

VanLehn, K & Chi, M 2012, Adaptive expertise as acceleration of future learning, in P Durlach & A Tresgold (eds.), *Adaptive technologies for training and education*, Cambridge University Press, New York, pp. 28–46, http://dx.doi.org/10.1017/cbo9781139049580.005.

Vanlehn, K & van de Sande, B 2009, Acquiring conceptual expertise from modeling: the case of elementary physics, in K Ericsson (ed.), *The development of professional performance: toward measurement of expert performance and design of optimal learning environments*, Cambridge University Press, Cambridge, pp. 356–378, viewed <http://www.public.asu.edu/~kvanlehn/Not%20Stringent/PDF/09KVL_BvdS.pdf>.

Vaughan, K 2008, *Workplace Learning: A Literature Review*, The New Zealand Engineering Food & Manufacturing Industry Training Organisation Incorporated, Auckland, viewed 24 June 2017, <https://www.akoaotearoa.ac.nz/download/ng/file/group-189/n1575-workplace-learning-a-literature-review.pdf>.

Velmahos, GC, Toutouzas, KG, Sillin, LF, Chan, L, Clark, RE, Theodorou, D & Maupin, F 2004, 'Cognitive task analysis for teaching technical skills in an inanimate surgical skills laboratory', *The American Journal of Surgery*, vol. 187, no. 1, pp. 114–119, http://dx.doi.org/10.1016/j.amjsurg.2002.12.005.

Vidulich, M, Yeh, Y-Y & Schneider, W 1983, 'Time-compressed components for air-intercept control skills', *Proceedings of the Human Factors Society Annual Meeting*, vol. 27, no. 2, pp. 161–164, http://dx.doi.org/10.1177/154193128302700211.

Vihavainen, A, Paksula, M & Luukkainen, M 2011, 'Extreme apprenticeship method in teaching programming for beginners', *Proceedings of the 42nd ACM Technical Symposium on Computer Science Education*, Dallas, 9-12 March, ACM, New York, pp. 93–98, viewed 24 Jun 2017, <http://moodle2.beitberl.ac.il/pluginfile.php/136972/mod_forum/attachment/55467/p93.pdf>.

Villachica, SW, Stone, DL & Endicott, J 2006, Performance support systems, in J Pershing (ed.), *Handbook of human performance technology: Principles, practices, and potential*, Pfeiffer, San Francisco, pp. 539–566.

Viswesvaran, C 1993, *Modeling Job Performance: Is There a General Factor?*, University of Iowa, Iowa, viewed 24 June 2017, <http://www.dtic.mil/dtic/tr/fulltext/u2/a294282.pdf>.

Viswesvaran, C & Ones, DS 2000, 'Perspectives on models of job performance', *International Journal of Selection and Assessment*, vol. 8, no. 4, pp. 216–226, viewed 24 June 2017, <https://www.researchgate.net/profile/Deniz_Ones/publication/229645528>.

Vohra, V 2014, 'Using the multiple case study design to decipher contextual leadership behaviors in Indian organisations', *Electronic Journal of Business Research Methods*, vol. 12, no. 1, pp. 54–65, viewed 24 June 2017, <http://www.ejbrm.com/issue/download.html?idArticle=334>.

Vygotsky, LS 1978, *Mind in society: the development of higher mental process*, Harvard University Press, Cambridge.

WalkMe 2013, 'Express train: how to accelerate employee time to competence,", viewed 24 June 2017, <http://trainingstation.walkme.com/wp-content/uploads/2013/05/Express-Train.pdf>.

Wallace, GW 2006, Modeling mastery performance and systematically deriving the enablers for performance improvement, in J Pershing (ed.), *Handbook of human performance technology: Principles, practices, and potential*, Pfeiffer, San Francisco, viewed 24 June 2017, <http://widyo.staff.gunadarma.ac.id/Downloads/files/20372/HANDBOOK+OF+HPT_THIRD+EDITION.pdf#page=284>.

Wang, Z, Zhou, R & Shah, P 2014, 'Spaced cognitive training promotes training transfer', *Frontiers in Human Neuroscience*, vol. 8, art. 217, pp. 1-8, http://dx.doi.org/10.3389/fnhum.2014.00217.

Ward, P, Hodges, NJ, Starkes, JL & Williams, AM 2007, 'The road to excellence: deliberate practice and the development of expertise', *High Ability Studies*, vol. 18, no. 2, pp. 119–153, http://dx.doi.org/10.1080/13598130701709715.

Ward, P, Williams, AM & Hancock, PA 2006, Simulation for performance and training, in K Ericsson, N Charness, P Feltovich & R Hoffman (eds.), *Development of expertise and expert performance*, Cambridge University Press, New York, pp. 243–262, http://dx.doi.org/10.1017/cbo9780511816796.014.

Waring, T & Wainwright, D 2008, 'Issues and challenges in the use of template analysis: two comparative case studies from the field', *The Electronic Journal of Business Research Methods*, vol. 6, no. 1, pp. 85–94, viewed 24 June 2017, <http://www.ejbrm.com/issue/download.html?idArticle=187>.

Watkins, KE & Marsick, VJ 1992, 'Towards a theory of informal and incidental learning in organisations', *International Journal of Lifelong Education*, vol. 11, no. 4, pp. 287–300.

_____ 1993, *Sculpting the learning organisation: Lessons in the art and science of systemic change*, Jossey-Bass, San Francisco.

Welch, SK 2008, 'A metasynthesis of the transition from novice to expert: can instructional interventions shorten the process?', PhD thesis, ProQuest, Ann Arbor, viewed 24 June 2017, <https://search.proquest.com/docview/304821165>.

Wenger, E 2000, 'Communities of practice and social learning systems', *Organisation*, vol. 7, no. 2, pp. 225–246, http://dx.doi.org/10.1177/135050840072002.

Wheeldon, J & Faubert, J 2009, 'Framing experience: concept maps, mind maps, and data collection in qualitative research', *International Journal of Qualitative Methods*, vol. 8, no. 3, pp. 68–83, http://dx.doi.org/10.1177/160940690900800307.

White, DE, Oelke, ND & Friesen, S 2012, 'Management of a large qualitative data set: establishing trustworthiness of the data', *International Journal of Qualitative Methods*, vol. 11, no. 3, pp. 244–258, http://dx.doi.org/10.1177/160940691201100305.

Wicks, AC & Freeman, RE 1998, 'Organisation studies and the new pragmatism: positivism, anti-positivism, and the search for ethics', *Organisation Science*, vol. 9, no. 2, pp. 123–140, http://dx.doi.org/10.1287/orsc.9.2.123.

Van de Wiel, MWJ & Van den Bossche, P 2013, 'Deliberate practice in medicine: the motivation to engage in work-related learning and its contribution to expertise', *Vocations and Learning*, vol. 6, no. 1, pp. 135–158, http://dx.doi.org/10.1007/s12186-012-9085-x.

Wilcox, V, Trus, T, Salas, N, Martinez, J & Dunkin, BJ 2014, 'A proficiency-based skills training curriculum for the sages surgical training for endoscopic proficiency (step) program', *Journal of Surgical Education*, vol. 71, no. 3, pp. 282–288, http://dx.doi.org/10.1016/j.jsurg.2013.10.004.

Williams, AM, Ward, P, Knowles, JM & Smeeton, NJ 2002, 'Anticipation skill in a real-world task: measurement, training, and transfer in tennis', *Journal of Experimental Psychology: Applied*, vol. 8, no. 4, pp. 259–270, http://dx.doi.org/10.1037/1076-898X.8.4.259.

Williams, R, Faulkner, W & Fleck, J 1998, *Exploring expertise: issues and perspectives*, Palgrave Macmillan, Basingstoke, http://dx.doi.org/10.1007/978-1-349-13693-3_1.

Wolcott, HF 1994, *Transforming qualitative data: description, analysis, and interpretation*, Sage, Thousand Oaks.

Woodall, J 2000, 'Corporate support for work-based management development', *Human Resource Management Journal*, vol. 10, no. 1, pp. 18–32.

Wooderson, JR, Cuskelly, M & Meyer, KA 2017, 'Evaluating the performance improvement preferences of disability service managers: an exploratory study using Gilbert's behavior engineering model', *Journal of Applied Research in Intellectual Disabilities*, vol. 30, no. 4, pp. 661–671, http://dx.doi.org/10.1111/jar.12260.

Woolley, NN & Jarvis, Y 2007, 'Situated cognition and cognitive apprenticeship: a model for teaching and learning clinical skills in a technologically rich and authentic learning environment', *Nurse Education Today*, vol. 27, no. 1, pp. 73–9, http://dx.doi.org/10.1016/j.nedt.2006.02.010.

Worthen, BR & Sanders, JR 1987, *Educational evaluation: Alternative approaches and practical guidelines*, Longman, New York.

Wray, A & Wallace, M 2011, 'Accelerating the development of expertise: a step-change in social science research capacity building', *British Journal of Educational Studies*, vol. 59, no. 3, pp. 241–264, http://dx.doi.org/10.1080/00071005.2011.599790.

Wright, PM & McMahan, GC 2011, 'Exploring human capital: putting 'human' back into strategic human resource management', *Human Resource Management Journal*, vol. 21, no. 2, pp. 93–104, http://dx.doi.org/10.1111/j.1748-8583.2010.00165.x.

Yang, F, Li, FW & Lau, RW 2014, 'A fine-grained outcome-based learning path model', *IEEE Transactions on Systems, Man, and Cybernetics: Systems*, vol. 44, no. 2, pp. 235–245, http://dx.doi.org/10.1109/TSMCC.2013.2263133.

Yasin, S & Ali, Z 2016, 'Examining the competency mapping interventions impact on enhancing role efficacy', *International Journal of Academic Research in Accounting, Finance and Management Sciences*, vol. 6, no. 4, pp. 226–233, viewed 24 June 2017, <http://hrmars.com/hrmars_papers/Article_23_Examining_the_Competency_Mapping_Interventions_updated.pdf>.

Yates, K, Sullivan, M & Clark, R 2012, 'Integrated studies on the use of cognitive task analysis to capture surgical expertise for central venous catheter placement and open cricothyrotomy', *The American Journal of Surgery*, vol. 203, no. 1, pp. 76–80, http://dx.doi.org/10.1016/j.amjsurg.2011.07.011.

Yawson, RM 2013, 'Systems theory and thinking as a foundational theory in human resource development—a myth or reality?', *Human Resource Development Review*, vol. 12, no. 1, pp. 53–85, http://dx.doi.org/10.1177/1534484312461634.

Yen, M, Trede, F & Patterson, C 2016, 'Learning in the workplace: the role of nurse managers', *Australian Health Review*, vol. 40, no. 3, pp. 286–291, http://dx.doi.org/10.1071/AH15022.

Yin, RK 2014, *Case study research: design and methods*, 5th edn, Sage, Thousand Oaks.

Yousuf, MI 2007, 'Using experts' opinions through Delphi technique', *Practical Assessment, Research & Evaluation*, vol. 12, no. 4, pp. 1–8, viewed 24 June 2017, <https://www.researchgate.net/profile/M_Yousuf2/publication/253041760>.

Zachary, W, Hoffman, R, Crandall, B, Miller, T & Nemeth, C 2012, ''Rapidized' cognitive task analysis', *IEEE Intelligent Systems*, vol. 27, no. 2, pp. 61–66, viewed <https://pdfs.semanticscholar.org/00a0/3767acbc8c1c1290cfe56d876def3fda61d3.pdf>.

Zhamanov, A & Zhamapor, M 2013, 'Computer networks teaching by microlearning principles', *Journal of Physics: Conference Series*, vol. 423, no. 1, art. 012028, pp. 1-6, http://dx.doi.org/10.1088/1742-6596/423/1/012028.

Zhao, C & Wan, L 2006, 'A shortest learning path selection algorithm in e-learning', *Proceedings of the 6th International Conference on Advanced Learning Technologies (ICALT'06)*, Kerkrade, The Netherlands, 5-7 July, IEEE, http://dx.doi.org/10.1109/ICALT.2006.33.

Ziyani, I, Ehlers, V & King, L 2004, 'Using triangulation of research methods to investigate family planning practice in Swaziland', *Africa Journal of Nursing and Midwifery*, vol. 6, no. 1, viewed 24 June 2017, <http://uir.unisa.ac.za/bitstream/handle/10500/7008/sabinettriangulationhttp___content.ajarchive.org_cgi-bin_showfile.pdf?sequence=1>.

Zucker, DM 2009, How to do case study research, in M Garner, C Wagner & B Kawulich (eds.), *Teaching Research Methods in the Humanities and Social Sciences*, School of Nursing Faculty Publication Series, University of Massachusetts, Amherst, pp. 1–17, viewed 24 June 2017, <http://scholarworks.umass.edu/nursing_faculty_pubs/2>.

APPENDIX

Appendix 1 Participants' profiles

See section 3.3.6 and 3.4 for participant distribution
Total number of participants = 85
Number of practice leaders (Phase 1 interviews) = 25
Number of project leaders (Phase 2 interviews) = 62
Participated both as practice leader and project leader = 2

Type of participant	Pseudo name and code	Gender	Location	Experience range	Current industry (self-declared)	Title or position (grouped)	Education	Mode of participation	Document supplied	Expert Focus Group
Practice leader	Abbott, Practice Leader 1G	Female	USA	11 to 20	Information Technology & Services	CLO / CKO	Doctorate	Interview	4	
Practice leader	Andrew, Practice Leader 2G	Male	USA	21 to 30	Military	Researcher / Scientist / Academician / Author	Doctorate	Interview	-	
Practice leader	Bob, Practice Leader 22G	Male	USA	41 to 50	Management Consulting	Director / VP	Masters	Interview	1	
Practice leader	Christina, Practice Leader 13G	Female	UK	21 to 30	Education Management	President / CEO / MD / Founder	Bachelors	Interview	-	
Practice leader	Connan, Practice Leader 5G	Male	USA	31 to 40	Management Consulting	President / CEO / MD / Founder	Doctorate	Interview	1	
Practice leader	Dan, Practice Leader 6G	Male	UK	21 to 30	E-learning	Director / VP	-	Interview	-	
Practice leader	Ed, Practice Leader 7G	Male	USA	31 to 40	Higher Education	Researcher / Scientist / Academician / Author	Doctorate	Interview	-	
Practice leader	Em, Practice Leader 23G	Female	USA	11 to 20	Information Technology & Services	Trainer / Facilitator / Instructional Designer	Masters	Interview	4	
Practice leader	Emmy, Practice Leader 8G	Female	Australia	11 to 20	Professional Training & Coaching	President / CEO / MD / Founder	Bachelors	Interview	-	
Practice leader	Erik, Practice Leader 9G	Male	USA	31 to 40	Higher Education	Researcher / Scientist / Academician / Author	Doctorate	E-mail interview	-	
Practice leader	Fredrick, Practice Leader 10G	Male	Netherlands	Unknown	Higher Education	Researcher / Scientist / Academician / Author	Doctorate	Interview	-	
Practice leader	Kaufman, Practice Leader 11G	Male	USA	41 to 50	Management Consulting	Researcher / Scientist / Academician / Author	Doctorate	Interview	-	
Practice leader	Knox, Practice Leader 12G	Male	USA	21 to 30	Semiconductors	Trainer / Facilitator / Instructional Designer	Bachelors	Interview	-	
Practice leader	Lynn, Practice Leader 24G	Female	Australia	Unknown	-	Retired	-	Interview	-	
Practice leader	Mathews, Practice Leader 16G	Male	UK	31 to 40	Management Consulting	President / CEO / MD / Founder	Bachelors	Interview	1	
Practice leader	Merrill, Practice Leader 15G	Male	Netherlands	31 to 40	Education Technology	Researcher / Scientist / Academician / Author	Doctorate	Interview	-	
Practice leader	Rebecca, Practice Leader 3G	Female	USA	11 to 20	Professional Training & Coaching	President / CEO / MD / Founder	Masters	Interview	-	
Practice leader	Reese, Practice Leader 14G	Female	USA	21 to 30	Human Resources	Consultant	Doctorate	Interview	-	
Practice leader	Rickky, Practice Leader 18G	Male	USA	0 to 10	Professional Training & Coaching	Director / VP	Doctorate	Interview	-	

Role	Name	Gender	Country	Age	Industry	Title	Education	Method	Count	Other
Practice leader	Robert, Practice Leader 4G	Male	USA	41 to 50	Research	Researcher / Scientist / Academician / Author	Doctorate	Interview	-	
Practice leader	Robinson, Practice Leader 19G	Male	USA	31 to 40	Research	Researcher / Scientist / Academician / Author	Doctorate	Interview	-	
Practice leader	Ruthford, Practice Leader 21G	Female	USA	21 to 30	Professional Training & Coaching	President / CEO / MD / Founder	Masters	Interview	-	
Practice leader	Shane, Practice Leader 25G	Male	USA	11 to 20	Internet	President / CEO / MD / Founder	Masters	E-mail interview	1	
Project leader	Abigail, Project Leader 16	Female	USA	41 to 50	Management Consulting	President / CEO / MD / Founder	Bachelors	Interview	-	
Project leader	Aloha, Project Leader 19	Female	USA	21 to 30	Management Consulting	President / CEO / MD / Founder	Doctorate	Interview	1	
Project leader	Bella, Project Leader 28	Female	USA	21 to 30	Research	President / CEO / MD / Founder	Doctorate	Interview	-	
Project leader	Benny, Project Leader 1	Male	Singapore	11 to 20	Semiconductors	Trainer / Facilitator / Instructional Designer	Bachelors	Interview	-	
Project leader	Billy, Project Leader 2	Male	USA	11 to 20	Computer Software	Director / VP	Masters	Interview	-	
Project leader	Charlie, Project Leader 4	Male	UK	21 to 30	Management Consulting	Director / VP	Masters	Interview	4	Yes
Project leader	Christen, Project Leader 6	Male	USA	21 to 30	Banking	Program / Training Manager	Masters	Interview	2	
Project leader	Christian, Project Leader 5	Male	USA	11 to 20	Management Consulting	Consultant	Masters	Interview	-	
Project leader	Dany, Project Leader 8	Female	USA	11 to 20	Information Services	Consultant	Masters	Interview	1	
Project leader	Davidson, Project Leader 10	Male	USA	31 to 40	Oil & Energy	CLO / CKO	Bachelors	Interview	1	
Project leader	Diana, Project Leader 11	Female	USA	21 to 30	Professional Training & Coaching	President / CEO / MD / Founder	Masters	Interview	-	
Project leader	Dickenson, Project Leader 12	Male	USA	31 to 40	E-learning	President / CEO / MD / Founder	Masters	Interview	1	
Project leader	Elisa, Project Leader 30	Female	USA	11 to 20	Public Relations and Communications	Program / Training Manager	Bachelors	Interview	1	
Project leader	Ellis, Project Leader 14	Male	USA	31 to 40	Management Consulting	President / CEO / MD / Founder	Doctorate	Interview	1	
Project leader	Ferino, Project Leader 3	Male	Philippines	41 to 50	Professional Training & Coaching	Consultant	Masters	Questionnaire	-	
Project leader	Ford, Project Leader 7	Male	USA	31 to 40	Semiconductors	Program / Training Manager	Masters	Questionnaire	-	
Project leader	Frankstein, Project Leader 15	Male	USA	41 to 50	E-learning	President / CEO / MD / Founder	Masters	Interview	1	
Project leader	Hallmark, Project Leader 17	Male	USA	11 to 20	Professional Training & Coaching	President / CEO / MD / Founder	Masters	Interview	-	
Project leader	Harry, Project Leader 18	Male	USA	31 to 40	Professional Training & Coaching	Consultant	Doctorate	Interview	1	
Project leader	Hogdan, Project Leader 29	Female	USA	21 to 30	Professional Training & Coaching	Consultant	Masters	Interview	2	
Project leader	Huang, Project Leader 50	Male	Singapore	0 to 10	Oil & Energy	Program / Training Manager	-	Questionnaire	1	
Project leader	Jacky, Project Leader 20	Female	USA	31 to 40	Professional Training & Coaching	Director / VP	Masters	Interview	1	
Project leader	Jason, Project Leader 21	Male	USA	11 to 20	Computer Software	Consultant	Bachelors	Interview	-	
Project leader	Jessica, Project Leader 23	Female	USA	31 to 40	Management Consulting	President / CEO / MD / Founder	Doctorate	Interview	1	

Role	Name	Gender	Country	Age	Industry	Position	Education	Method	Count	Practice Leader
Project leader	Johnson, Project Leader 22	Male	USA	11 to 20	Semiconductors	Program / Training Manager	Masters	Interview	-	
Project leader	Kenny, Project Leader 27, 28 and 29	Male	USA	21 to 30	Management Consulting	President / CEO / MD / Founder	Masters	Interview	7	
Project leader	Kieve, Project Leader 24	Male	USA	11 to 20	Management Consulting	President / CEO / MD / Founder	-	Interview	1	
Project leader	Liza, Project Leader 13	Female	USA	11 to 20	Professional Training & Coaching	Consultant	Masters	Interview	1	
Project leader	Sunny, Project Leader 13A	Male	USA	11 to 20	Professional Training & Coaching	Consultant	Masters	Interview	1	
Project leader	Martin, Project Leader 31	Male	Netherlands	21 to 30	Research	Researcher / Scientist / Academician / Author	Doctorate	Interview	-	
Project leader	Matt, Project Leader 33	Male	USA	21 to 30	Education Management	Program / Training Manager	Masters	Interview	1	Yes
Project leader	Maximus, Project Leader 34	Male	Netherlands	21 to 30	Education Management	Program / Training Manager	Bachelors	Questionnaire	-	
Project leader	Mayer, Project Leader 9	Male	USA	31 to 40	Professional Training & Coaching	Director / VP	-	Interview	1	
Project leader	McDonalds, Project Leader 32	Male	USA	21 to 30	E-learning	CLO / CKO	Doctorate	Interview	4	Yes
Project leader	Meline, Project Leader 35	Female	USA	21 to 30	Professional Training & Coaching	President / CEO / MD / Founder	Masters	Interview	-	
Project leader	Mike, Project Leader 36	Male	USA	21 to 30	Professional Training & Coaching	President / CEO / MD / Founder	Masters	Interview	-	
Project leader	Mille, Project Leader 38	Male	USA	11 to 20	Electrical/Electronic Manufacturing	Program / Training Manager	Doctorate	Questionnaire	-	
Project leader	Mohammad, Project Leader 39	Male	Singapore	11 to 20	Semiconductors	Trainer / Facilitator / Instructional Designer	Bachelors	Interview	-	
Project leader	Murphy, Project Leader 37	Male	USA	21 to 30	Professional Training & Coaching	Consultant	Masters	Interview	-	Yes
Project leader	Patrick, Project Leader 40	Male	USA	31 to 40	Information Technology & Services	CLO / CKO	Bachelors	Interview	-	
Project leader* (practice leader)	Peterson, Project Leader 41	Male	USA	31 to 40	Higher Education	Researcher / Scientist / Academician / Author	Doctorate	Interview	-	
Project leader	Rahman, Project Leader 64	Male	UAE	11 to 20	Oil & Energy	Leadership / HRD Specialist	Doctorate	Questionnaire	-	
Project leader	Rayman, Project Leader 42 and 43	Male	USA	31 to 40	E-learning	President / CEO / MD / Founder	Doctorate	Interview	-	
Project leader	Reynold, Project Leader 49	Male	USA	31 to 40	Education Management	CLO / CKO	Doctorate	Interview	3	
Project leader	Richardson, Project Leader 45	Male	USA	21 to 30	Education Management	Program / Training Manager	Masters	Interview	-	
Project leader	Ricky, Project Leader 44	Male	USA	31 to 40	Management Consulting	Director / VP	Masters	Interview	-	Yes
Project leader	Rodridge, Project Leader 47	Male	USA	41 to 50	Management Consulting	President / CEO / MD / Founder	Doctorate	Interview	-	
Project leader* (practice leader)	Ron, Project Leader 48	Male	USA	Unknown	Higher Education	Researcher / Scientist / Academician / Author	Doctorate	Interview	2	
Project leader	Rustom, Project Leader 46	Male	USA	11 to 20	Semiconductors	Program / Training Manager	Bachelors	Interview	-	
Project leader	Sam, Project Leader 56	Male	USA	31 to 40	Financial Services	Director / VP	Masters	Interview	1	

Appendix

Project leader	Stacy, Project Leader 51	Female	USA	11 to 20	Broadcast Media	Leadership / HRD Specialist	Masters	Interview	1
Project leader	Stanley, Project Leader 52	Male	Australia	Unknown	Financial Services	Researcher / Scientist / Academician / Author	-	Interview	-
Project leader	Philly, Project Leader 67	Male	Australia	Unknown	Higher Education	Researcher / Scientist / Academician / Author	Masters	Interview	-
Project leader	Stephen, Project Leader 53, 54 and 55	Male	USA	31 to 40	Professional Training & Coaching	President / CEO / MD / Founder	Bachelors	Interview	4
Project leader	Stuart, Project Leader 65	Male	USA	31 to 40	Computer Software	President / CEO / MD / Founder	Bachelors	Interview	-
Project leader	Teresa, Project Leader 58	Female	Netherlands	31 to 40	Education Management	Trainer / Facilitator / Instructional Designer	Bachelors	Interview	-
Project leader	Thomson, Project Leader 59	Male	USA	11 to 20	Professional Training & Coaching	Consultant	Masters	Interview	-
Project leader	Todd, Project Leader 57	Male	Australia	11 to 20	Computer Software	President / CEO / MD / Founder	Masters	Interview	2
Project leader	Tony, Project Leader 60	Male	USA	31 to 40	Education Management	President / CEO / MD / Founder	Doctorate	Interview	-
Project leader	Tran, Project Leader 66	Male	USA	0 to 10	Computer Software	Consultant	Masters	E-mail interview	1
Project leader	Vasudevan, Project Leader 61	Male	USA	21 to 30	Computer Software	President / CEO / MD / Founder	Masters	Interview	1
Project leader	White, Project Leader 62 and 63	Male	USA	11 to 20	Research	Trainer / Facilitator / Instructional Designer	Doctorate	Interview	-

*Participated as practice leader in Stage 1

Appendix

Appendix 2 — Detailed project case profiles with contextual variables

See section 3.5.3 for classification of project cases per contextual variables
Total number of bounded project cases = 66
Total number of project leaders = 62
See section 3.6 for project case distribution of 60 selected cases

Project case ID	Project leader Pseudo name	Project case title	Location of project	Economic Sector (TRBC)	Business Sector (TRBC)	Industry Group (TRBC)	Nature of primary job role	Critical-to-success Skill	Complexity Rating	TTP results	Mode of collection
1	Benny, Project Leader 1	Customer service engineers troubleshooting and repairing complex semiconductor equipment	Singapore	TECHNOLOGY	Technology Equipment	Semiconductors & Semiconductor Equipment	Technical or Engineering	Complex troubleshooting	2. Medium-High	Direct	Interview
2	Billy, Project Leader 2	Customer service helpdesk taking inbound calls for sales of investment products	USA	FINANCIALS	Banking & Investment Services	Investment Banking & Investment Services	Sales - Non-Technical	Sales and negotiation	4. Medium-Low	Direct	Interview
3	Ferino, Project Leader 3	Technical trainers delivering food manufacturing process training	Philippines	CONSUMER NON-CYCLICALS	Food & Beverages	Food & Tobacco	Training or Education	Teaching and training	4. Medium-Low	None	Questionnaire
4	Charlie, Project Leader 4	Software engineers developing large scale information applications (books)	US/Thailand	TECHNOLOGY	Software & IT Services	Software & IT Services	Scientific or Development	Innovation and design	1. High	Direct	Interview
5	Christian, Project Leader 5	Cybersecurity analysts analysing and identifying cyber-threats on client enterprise networks	USA	TECHNOLOGY	Technology Equipment	Communications & Networking	Technical or Engineering	Technical Problem Solving	2. Medium-High	Direct	Interview
6	Christen, Project Leader 6	Insurance agents selling insurance products	USA	FINANCIALS	Insurance	Insurance	Sales - Non-Technical	Sales and negotiation	4. Medium-Low	Direct	Interview
7	Ford, Project Leader 7	Customer service engineers troubleshooting and repairing complex semiconductor equipment	USA	TECHNOLOGY	Technology Equipment	Semiconductors & Semiconductor Equipment	Technical or Engineering	Complex troubleshooting	2. Medium-High	Direct	Questionnaire
8	Dany, Project Leader 8	Console operators monitoring and controlling the processes at petrochemical plants	USA	ENERGY	Energy - Fossil Fuels	Oil & Gas	Technical or Engineering	Technical Problem Solving	2. Medium-High	Direct	Interview
9	Mayer, Project Leader 9	Service engineers troubleshooting and repairing telecommunication network equipment	USA	TELECOMMUNICATION SERVICES	Telecommunications Services	Telecommunications Services	Technical or Engineering	Complex troubleshooting	2. Medium-High	Direct	Interview
10	Davidson, Project Leader 10	Console operators monitoring and controlling the processes at petrochemical plants	USA	ENERGY	Energy - Fossil Fuels	Oil & Gas	Technical or Engineering	Technical Problem Solving	2. Medium-High	Direct	Interview
11	Diana, Project Leader 11	Pharmaceutical biochemists manufacturing sophisticated cancer drugs	USA	HEALTHCARE	Pharmaceuticals & Medical Research	Pharmaceuticals	Scientific or Development	Innovation and design	1. High	Direct	Interview
12	Dickenson, Project Leader 12	Managers managing retail doughnut baking stores	USA	CONSUMER NON-CYCLICALS	Food & Beverages	Food & Tobacco	Managerial, Supervisory	Supervisory	3. Medium	Direct	Interview
13	Liza, Project Leader 13	Claim processing executives examining and processing health insurance claims	USA	FINANCIALS	Insurance	Insurance	Financial services	Financial analysis	4. Medium-Low	Direct	Interview
14	Ellis, Project Leader 14	Sales representative selling pharmaceutical products	USA	HEALTHCARE	Pharmaceuticals & Medical Research	Pharmaceuticals	Sales - Technical	Sales and negotiation	4. Medium-Low	Direct	Interview
15	Frankstein, Project Leader 15	Insurance agents selling insurance products	USA	FINANCIALS	Insurance	Insurance	Sales - Non-Technical	Sales and negotiation	4. Medium-Low	Direct	Interview
16	Abigail, Project Leader 16	Console operators monitoring and controlling the processes at petrochemical plants	USA	ENERGY	Energy - Fossil Fuels	Oil & Gas	Technical or Engineering	Technical Problem Solving	2. Medium-High	Indirect	Interview
17	Hallmark, Project Leader 17	Customer service helpdesk taking inbound calls for hotel and travel related services	USA	CONSUMER NON-CYCLICALS	Cyclical Consumer Services	Hotels & Entertainment Services	Customer service helpdesk	Helpdesk support	5. Low	Direct	Interview
18	Harry, Project Leader 18	Managers managing supermarket chains	USA	CONSUMER NON-CYCLICALS	Retailers	Other Speciality Retailers	Managerial, Supervisory	Supervisory	3. Medium	Direct	Interview
19	Aloha, Project Leader 19	Energy Corporation top executives transferring knowledge to successors	USA	ENERGY	Energy - Fossil Fuels	Oil & Gas	Strategic Management, Leadership	Strategic thinking	1. High	Direct	Interview

#	Name	Description	Country	Sector	Industry	Sub-Industry	Category	Skill	Level	Contact	Method
20	Jacky, Project Leader 20	Hospital medical doctors and nursing staff providing paediatrics care services	USA	HEALTHCARE	Healthcare Services	Healthcare Providers & Services	Medical, Healthcare	Medical and psychological care	3. Medium	Direct	Interview
21	Jason, Project Leader 21	Customer helpdesk taking inbound calls to remotely troubleshoot client computer and software issues	USA	TECHNOLOGY	Software & IT Services	Software & IT Services	Technical or Engineering	Complex troubleshooting	2. Medium-High	Direct	Interview
22	Johnson, Project Leader 22	Customer service engineers troubleshooting and repairing complex semiconductor equipment	USA	TECHNOLOGY	Technology Equipment	Semiconductors & Semiconductor Equipment	Technical or Engineering	Complex troubleshooting	2. Medium-High	Direct	Interview
23	Jessica, Project Leader 23	School administrator and teachers instituting school improvement programs	USA	INDUSTRIALS	Industrial & Commercial Services	Professional & Commercial Services	Training or Education	Teaching and training	4. Medium-Low	Direct	Interview
24	Kieve, Project Leader 24	Warehouse professionals adopting SAP for supply chain and logistics transactions	USA	INDUSTRIALS	Transportation	Freight & Logistics Services	Warehouse	Data processing	5. Low	Direct	Interview
25	Kenny, Project Leader 25	Console operators monitoring and controlling the processes at petrochemical plants	USA	ENERGY	Energy - Fossil Fuels	Oil & Gas	Technical or Engineering	Technical Problem Solving	2. Medium-High	Indirect	Interview
26	Kenny, Project Leader 26	Young military officers on leadership pathway	USA	MILITARY/GOVERNMENT	Government / Military	Military	Strategic Management, Leadership	Strategic thinking	1. High	Indirect	Interview
27	Kenny, Project Leader 27	Military officers setting up a new command centre to prevent cyberterrorism	USA	MILITARY/GOVERNMENT	Government / Military	Military	Strategic Management, Leadership	Strategic thinking	1. High	Direct	Interview
28	Bella, Project Leader 28	Biotechnology scientists strategizing business of brain implant technology for curing neurological diseases	USA	HEALTHCARE	Pharmaceuticals & Medical Research	Biotechnology & Medical Research	Scientific or Development	Innovation and design	1. High	Direct	Interview
29	Hogdan, Project Leader 29	Machinists fabricating aircraft engine mechanical parts	USA	INDUSTRIALS	Industrial Goods	Aerospace & Defense	Production, Manufacturing	Precision machining	3. Medium	Direct	Interview
30	Elisa, Project Leader 30	Sales engineers selling hi-tech enterprise communication products	USA	TECHNOLOGY	Technology Equipment	Communications & Networking	Technical or Engineering	Project execution	2. Medium-High	Direct	Interview
31	Martin, Project Leader 31	Electronics technicians to troubleshoot and repair of complex Navy electronics equipment	Netherlands	TECHNOLOGY	Technology Equipment	Electronic Equipment & Parts	Technical or Engineering	Complex troubleshooting	2. Medium-High	Direct	Interview
32	McDonalds, Project Leader 32	Benefit Evaluators examining eligibility for Govt. run benefits	USA	MILITARY/GOVERNMENT	Government / Military	Public Services	Financial services	Financial analysis	4. Medium-Low	Direct	Interview
33	Matt, Project Leader 33	Sales engineers selling hi-tech enterprise computer and server systems	Netherlands	TECHNOLOGY	Technology Equipment	Communications & Networking	Technical or Engineering	Project execution	2. Medium-High	Direct	Questionnaire
34	Maximus, Project Leader 34	Customer service engineers troubleshooting and repairing complex semiconductor equipment	Netherlands	TECHNOLOGY	Technology Equipment	Semiconductors & Semiconductor Equipment	Technical or Engineering	Complex troubleshooting	2. Medium-High	Direct	Interview
35	Meline, Project Leader 35	Clinical staff and database administrators transitioning to new software for clinical trials data	USA	HEALTHCARE	Pharmaceuticals & Medical Research	Biotechnology & Medical Research	Technical or Engineering	Project execution	2. Medium-High	Indirect	Interview
36	Mike, Project Leader 36	Customer service helpdesk taking inbound calls for financial products	USA	FINANCIALS	Banking & Investment Services	Banking Services	Customer service helpdesk	Helpdesk support	5. Low	Direct	Interview
37	Murphy, Project Leader 37	Healthcare professionals providing assisted living services for elders	USA	HEALTHCARE	Healthcare Services	Healthcare Providers & Services	Medical, Healthcare	Medical and psychological care	3. Medium	Direct	Interview
38	Mille, Project Leader 38	Customer service engineers troubleshooting and repairing complex semiconductor equipment	USA	TECHNOLOGY	Technology Equipment	Semiconductors & Semiconductor Equipment	Technical or Engineering	Complex troubleshooting	2. Medium-High	Direct	Interview
39	Mohammad, Project Leader 39	Customer service engineers troubleshooting and repairing complex semiconductor equipment	Singapore	TECHNOLOGY	Technology Equipment	Semiconductors & Semiconductor Equipment	Technical or Engineering	Complex troubleshooting	2. Medium-High	Direct	Interview
40	Patrick, Project Leader 40	Insurance agents selling insurance products	USA	FINANCIALS	Banking & Investment Services	Investment Banking & Investment Services	Sales - Non-Technical	Sales and negotiation	4. Medium-Low	Direct	Interview
41	Peterson, Project Leader 41	Baseball players trying to recognise ball pitch	USA	SPORTS	Sports	Sports	Sports, Athletics	Perceptual and physical skills	2. Medium-High	Indirect	Interview
64	Rahman, Project Leader 64	Console operators monitoring and controlling the processes at petrochemical plants	UAE	ENERGY	Energy - Fossil Fuels	Oil & Gas	Technical or Engineering	Technical Problem Solving	2. Medium-High	Indirect	Questionnaire
42	Rayman, Project Leader 42	Managers managing retail store chains	USA	CONSUMER NON-CYCLICALS	Retailers	Other Speciality Retailers	Managerial, Supervisory	Supervisory	3. Medium	Direct	Interview
43	Rayman, Project Leader 43	Plant maintenance engineers to troubleshooting production machine issues	USA	INDUSTRIALS	Industrial Goods	Machinery, Equipment & Components	Technical or Engineering	Complex troubleshooting	2. Medium-High	Direct	Interview
44	Ricky, Project Leader 44	Sales representatives upselling strategic service products	USA	INDUSTRIALS	Industrial & Commercial Services	Professional & Commercial Services	Sales - Non-Technical	Sales and negotiation	4. Medium-Low	Direct	Interview
45	Richardson, Project Leader 45	Reactor operators manufacturing chemical paints	USA	BASIC MATERIALS	Chemicals	Chemicals -	Technical or Engineering	Technical Problem Solving	2. Medium-High	Direct	Interview
46	Rustom, Project Leader 46	Customer service engineers troubleshooting and repairing complex semiconductor equipment	USA	TECHNOLOGY	Technology Equipment	Semiconductors & Semiconductor Equipment	Technical or Engineering	Complex troubleshooting	2. Medium-High	Direct	Interview
47	Rodridge, Project Leader 47	Real estate agents booking mortgages and listings	USA	FINANCIALS	Real Estate	Real Estate Operations	Sales - Non-Technical	Sales and negotiation	4. Medium-Low	Indirect	Interview

Appendix

#	Name	Description	Country	Sector	Industry	Sub-Industry	Task	Complexity	Contact	Method
48	Ron, Project Leader 48	Truck assemblers assembling and fabricating automobiles	USA	CONSUMER NON-CYCLICALS	Automobiles & Auto Parts	Automobiles & Auto Parts	Assembly, Repair	Assembly	5. Low	Direct	Interview
49	Reynold, Project Leader 49	Maintenance engineers repairing and maintaining petroleum pipeline feeds	USA	ENERGY	Energy - Fossil Fuels	Oil & Gas Related Equipment and Services	Technical or Engineering	Complex troubleshooting	2. Medium-High	Direct	Interview
50	Huang, Project Leader 50	Machine operators fabricating mechanical parts for petroleum exploration equipment	Singapore	ENERGY	Energy - Fossil Fuels	Oil & Gas Related Equipment and Services	Production, Manufacturing	Precision machining	3. Medium	Direct	Questionnaire
51	Stacy, Project Leader 51	Managers adopting new conversation and coaching tool with their employees	USA	CONSUMER NON-CYCLICALS	Cyclical Consumer Services	Media & Publishing	Managerial, Supervisory	Supervisory	3. Medium	Indirect	Interview
52	Stanley, Project Leader 52	Financial analysts assessing corporate insolvency cases	Australia	INDUSTRIALS	Industrial & Commercial Services	Professional & Commercial Services	Management consulting	Business analysis	2. Medium-High	Indirect	Interview
65	Stuart, Project Leader 65	Service personnel handling automobile service experience	USA	CONSUMER NON-CYCLICALS	Automobiles & Auto Parts	Automobiles & Auto Parts	Sales - Non-Technical	Sales and negotiation	4. Medium-Low	None	Interview
53	Stephen, Project Leader 53	Healthcare professionals providing residential care for severely disabled	USA	HEALTHCARE	Healthcare Services	Healthcare Providers & Services	Medical, Healthcare	Medical and psychological care	3. Medium	Direct	Interview
54	Stephen, Project Leader 54	Sales engineers selling construction products and equipment	USA	INDUSTRIALS	Industrial Goods	Machinery, Equipment & Components	Sales - Technical	Sales and negotiation	4. Medium-Low	Direct	Interview
55	Stephen, Project Leader 55	Customer service helpdesk taking inbound calls for internet phone service	USA	TELECOMMUNICATION SERVICES	Telecommunications Services	Telecommunications Services	Customer service helpdesk	Helpdesk support	5. Low	Direct	Interview
56	Sam, Project Leader 56	Customer service helpdesk taking inbound calls for sales of financial products	USA	FINANCIALS	Banking & Investment Services	Banking Services	Sales - Non-Technical	Sales and negotiation	4. Medium-Low	Direct	Interview
57	Todd, Project Leader 57	Customer service helpdesk taking inbound calls for banking services	Australia	FINANCIALS	Banking & Investment Services	Investment Banking & Investment Services	Customer service helpdesk	Helpdesk support	5. Low	Direct	Interview
58	Teresa, Project Leader 58	Design engineers developing complex semiconductor equipment	Netherlands	TECHNOLOGY	Technology Equipment	Semiconductors & Semiconductor Equipment	Scientific or Development	Innovation and design	1. High	Direct	Interview
59	Thomson, Project Leader 59	Customer service helpdesk taking inbound calls for upselling of financial products	USA	FINANCIALS	Banking & Investment Services	Investment Banking & Investment Services	Sales - Non-Technical	Sales and negotiation	4. Medium-Low	Direct	Interview
60	Tony, Project Leader 60	Electrical engineers designing and repairing power plant equipment	USA	UTILITY	Utilities	Electrical Utilities & IPPs	Scientific or Development	Innovation and design	1. High	Direct	Interview
66	Tran, Project Leader 66	Computer programmers developing and testing general software	USA	TECHNOLOGY	Software & IT Services	Software & IT Services	Scientific or Development	Innovation and design	1. High	Indirect	E-mail inputs
61	Vasudevan, Project Leader 61	Sales engineers selling medical and surgical instruments	USA	HEALTHCARE	Healthcare Services	Healthcare Equipment & Supplies	Sales - Technical	Sales and negotiation	4. Medium-Low	Direct	Interview
62	White, Project Leader 62	Business managers developing strategies for unforeseen drop in gold prices	USA	BASIC MATERIALS	Mineral Resources	Metals & Mining	Strategic Management, Leadership	Strategic thinking	1. High	Direct	Interview
63	White, Project Leader 63	Underground miners preparing for unexpected underground fire during mining operations	USA	BASIC MATERIALS	Mineral Resources	Metals & Mining	Production, Manufacturing	Precision machining	3. Medium	Direct	Interview

Appendix

Appendix 3   Interview guide & questions

See section 3.4.5 for interview protocol

Raman K. Attri
Doctoral Research Student,
Southern Cross University, Australia

STRATEGIES TO ACCELERATE TIME-TO-PROFICIENCY OF EMPLOYEES IN ACQUIRING COMPLEX JOB SKILLS

TENTATIVE INTERVIEW QUESTIONS

RESEARCH QUESTION: *What (how and why) specific strategies (methods, techniques, mechanisms, systems, processes, instructional design, methodologies, interventions, etc.) have helped leading organisations to successfully "accelerate" acquisition of complex job skills of its employees?*

GOAL OF INTERVIEW: To deeply understand how you or your group selected and implemented various strategies (methods, methodologies, interventions, instructional design, processes, mechanisms, techniques or systems, etc.) in a project or bounded case and why these strategies worked in your context compressing time-to-proficiency?

This 60 minutes' interview is organised in 4 major sections:
A) Business challenge and context of the project
B) Old model and it's challenges to speed –to-proficiency
C) New model/strategies to speed up proficiency
D) Results of the new model in terms of accelerating time-to-proficiency

You can answer the questions either on your own behalf or your group/ team's behalf depending upon nature of the project.

Planned time: 60 minutes   **Recording mechanism:** Audio recording

Category of question	Topic	Tentative Question for the interview
Qualifying Question (to be confirmed before any interview)		Tell me about your background, work and experience
		Have you personally led, managed, designed, consulted, implemented or contributed to a project (or case) in which primary goal or the by-product of the project was to ACCELERATE OR SHORTEN the time taken by employees acquire desired expertise (proficiency or productivity) and come up to speed faster in their on-the-job skills?

		Do you have at least one success story, case study or a project (from your own organisation or from your client) that you plan to share with the researcher?
	Project role	Please briefly explain your or your group's role in the project (consultant, contributor, team leader, project manager, client, etc.).
Context of the project	company business / context	Tell me more about the background of the chosen project including industry sector and nature of business of the organisation.
	Nature of job role type	Please describe the type of work being performed and nature of job of the employee group targeted in above project. How was the composition of this employee group and their experience level in the job (new hires, experienced employees etc.)?
	Nature of primary skills	Please describe briefly the type of skills or knowledge involved in performing the said job/assignment. What level of competency or expertise was expected from the targeted employee group to perform their job?
	Skill or job role complexity	How would you rate the complexity level of skills of the targeted employee group? What made the skills complex in this job? Why?
Business challenge	Goal of project	What was the primary goal of the above-mentioned project?
	Focus on Accelerated Proficiency	In your own words, please explain how the goal of this project (directly or indirectly) involved shortening or accelerating time-to-proficiency of employees. Examples may include: bringing a new or an existing employee up to speed to certain pre-determined standards of expertise on a new job or driving employees to acquire new skills or new knowledge etc. to name a few.
	Business reason	What was the main business challenge that made the organisation or your group to focus on accelerating the acquisition of targeted skills of their employees to desired proficiency level? Why it was so important and critical for the organisation?
Old model and challenges (Solution before)	Previous solution, strategies	Please describe the old model (if any).
	Root cause/ challenges	Please highlight challenges associated with the previous model. Why was that model not working to accelerate time-to-proficiency?
New model and solution (Solution after)	New solution / strategies	Please describe solution your group proposed in terms of model, structure or plan. Highlight how selected strategies were implemented in the above project. Elaborate how various techniques were orchestrated to achieve the project goal.
	Training as solution	Why did your group choose "training" (as opposed to non-training solutions) as the primary solution for this project to shorten time-to-proficiency?
	Solutions and strategies	Please explain how solution proposed by your group focused mainly on methods & strategies to shorten time-to-proficiency (example: designing / orchestrating a training event, course or program or training solution).
	Influencing existing knowledge	Can you explain how your model of implementation was influenced by or drawn from any established or known training model?
	Guiding Philosophy	Please take some time to explain philosophy, premise, belief or guiding principle that guided you or your group the way strategies were implemented in the above project.
	Factors influencing choice	What factors made the selected strategies an ideal choice for the problem relative to other strategies available to you?
	Implementation	Tell me about how the nature of the job and nature of the business influenced the overall implementation of selected training strategies.
	Uniqueness	What did you do differently in this project as compared to traditional or pre-existing or known approaches?
Results & Effectiveness	Effectiveness	Can you elaborate how effective your chosen strategies were in shortening the time-to-proficiency of targeted group?

		Proficiency Indicators Measure of Proficiency	How did you measure the effectiveness of the chosen strategies? What KPIs were used as an indicator that targeted employee group has reached the 'desired proficiency' in the targeted skills?
		Proficiency Definition	In the settings of the project you mentioned, how did you define 'desired proficiency' of the target employee group?
		Determinants/Factors	In your opinion, what were the main reason or factors that led to the success of chosen strategies in achieving the goal?
		Bottlenecks in new solution	What was the major challenge or pitfall you faced while implementing these strategies?
		Contribution of training	Among other factors, what do you think how much accurate selection and deployment of strategies contributed in accelerating time-to-proficiency of the target employees? Less than 50% More than 50% More than 70% More than 90% Almost 100%
Transferability		Transferability	In your opinion, how could the strategy or model you applied in your context be applied successfully to other settings (jobs, industry sector, and business)? How would you recommend applying or implementing the same set of techniques in other practical corporate settings?
		Transferability	Have you tried the same model to any other context? If yes, which industry sector and job type

Appendix 4 Questionnaire interview template

See section 3.4.4 for details of questionnaire interviews

Category of question	Topic	Tentative Question for the interview
Qualifying Question (to be confirmed before any interview)		Tell me about your background, work and experience
		Have you personally led, managed, designed, consulted, implemented or contributed to a project (or case) in which primary goal or the by-product of the project was to ACCELERATE OR SHORTEN the time taken by employees acquire desired expertise (proficiency or productivity) and come up to speed faster in their on-the-job skills?
		Do you have at least one success story, case study or a project (from your own organisation or from your client) that you plan to share with the researcher?
	Project role	Please briefly explain your or your group's role in the project (consultant, contributor, team leader, project manager, client, etc.).
Context of the project	company business / context	Tell me more about the background of the chosen project including industry sector and nature of business of the organisation.
	Nature of job role type	Please describe the type of work being performed and nature of job of the employee group targeted in above project. How was the composition of this employee group and their experience level in the job (new hires, experienced employees etc.)?
	Nature of primary skills	Please describe briefly the type of skills or knowledge involved in performing the said job/assignment. What level of competency or expertise was expected from the targeted employee group to perform their job?
	Skill or job role complexity	How would you rate the complexity level of skills of the targeted employee group? What made the skills complex in this job? Why?
Business challenge	Goal of project	What was the primary goal of the above-mentioned project?
	Focus on Accelerated Proficiency	In your own words, please explain how the goal of this project (directly or indirectly) involved shortening or accelerating time-to-proficiency of employees. The examples may include: bringing a new or an existing employee up to speed to certain pre-determined standards of expertise on a new job or driving employees to acquiring new skills or new knowledge etc. to name a few.
	Business reason	What was the main business challenge that made the organisation or your group focus on accelerating the acquisition of targeted skills of their employees to desired proficiency level? Why it was so important and critical for the organisation?
Old model and challenges (Solution before)	Previous solution, strategies	Please describe the old model (if any).
	Root cause/ challenges	Please highlight challenges associated with the previous model. Why was that model not working to accelerate time-to-proficiency?
New model and solution (Solution after)	New solution / strategies	Please describe solution your group proposed in terms of model, structure or plan. Highlight how selected strategies were implemented in the above project. Elaborate how various techniques were orchestrated to achieve project goal.

	Training as solution	Why did your group choose "training" (as opposed to non-training solutions) as the primary solution for this project to shorten time-to-proficiency?
	Solutions and strategies	Please explain how solution proposed by your group focused mainly on methods & strategies to shorten time-to-proficiency (example: designing / orchestrating a training event, course or program or training solution).
	Influencing existing knowledge	Can you explain how your model of implementation was influenced by or drawn from any established or known training model?
	Guiding Philosophy	Please take some time to explain philosophy, premise, belief or guiding principle that guided you or your group the way strategies were implemented in the above project.
	Factors influencing choice	What factors made the selected strategies an ideal choice for the problem relative to other strategies available to you?
	Implementation	Tell me about how the nature of the job and nature of the business influenced the overall implementation of selected training strategies.
	Uniqueness	What did you do differently in this project as compared to traditional or pre-existing or known approaches?
Results & Effectiveness	Effectiveness	Can you elaborate how effective your chosen strategies were in shortening the time-to-proficiency of targeted group?
	Proficiency Indicators Measure of Proficiency	How did you measure the effectiveness of the chosen strategies? What KPIs were used as an indicator that targeted employee group has reached the 'desired proficiency' in the targeted skills?
	Proficiency Definition	In the settings of the project you mentioned, how did you define 'desired proficiency' of the target employee group?
	Determinants/Factors	In your opinion, what were the main reason or factors that led to the success of chosen strategies in achieving the goal?
	Bottlenecks in new solution	What was the major challenge or pitfall you faced while implementing these strategies?
	Contribution of training	Among other factors, what do you think how much accurate selection and deployment of strategies contributed in accelerating time-to-proficiency of the target employees? Less than 50% More than 50% More than 70% More than 90% Almost 100%
Transferability	Transferability	In your opinion, how could the strategy or model you applied in your context be applied successfully to other settings (jobs, industry sector, and business)? How would you recommend applying or implementing the same set of techniques in other practical corporate settings?
	Transferability	Have you tried the same model to any other context? If yes, which industry sector and job type

Appendix 5   Excerpt from questionnaire interview

See section 3.4.4 for details of questionnaire interviews

Q4.5 How would you rate the complexity level of skills of the targeted employee group? What made the skills complex in this job?

It depends on the product or service they will be supporting. Some of the pipelines are very difficult due to the complexity of the product or service provided. In the Auto Insurance New Hire program the new employee has to learn how to have the conversation, understand what advice they need to provide the member, and effectively use the correct system for fulfillment. Multi-tasking in this role is critical as speaking, typing and evaluating information proved by the member must all be done at the same time.

Q4.6 What was the primary goal of the above mentioned project?

To reduce the length of the learning solution, improve the quality of the graduate, and get the student to Time to Proficiency faster.

Q4.7 In your own words, please explain how the goal of this project (directly or indirectly) involved shortening or accelerating time-to-proficiency of technical professionals. Example may include: bringing a new or an existing employee up to speed to certain pre-determined standards of expertise on a new job or driving employees to acquiring new skills or new knowledge etc. to name a few. You may indicate if targeted employee group was non-technical.

The outcome of this project directly impacted our time to proficiency. First, we measured the graduates of the previous version of the course. Knowing that this course was poorly designed and bloated with a lot of content, we decided to measure how long it took graduates to achieve the time to proficiency. TTP was determined by the business using the same criteria they use in evaluating incumbent performers. It consisted of 11 key metrics and measures. A performer who meets certain thresholds was identified by the business as having achieved proficiency. We used these same standards to measure the graduates of the first program. After the build of the new course, we used the same criteria to measure the graduates of that course. Despite the course being 15 days shorter, participants in the new version were achieving TTP much faster. In fact, in the old version of the course, 33% of the graduates were proficient at week 10, but now with the new course we are experiencing 68% of graduates achieving proficiency by week 10.

Q4.8 What was the main business challenge that made organization or your group to focus on accelerating the acquisition of targeted skills of their employees to desired proficiency level? Why it was so important and critical for the organization?

The volatility of markets means when business surges, we need qualified people on the phones to meet member demand. Having a course which was long and slow in getting people to proficiency was not appealing to the business. Our desire was to shorten the learning cycle but simultaneously improving the quality of output..

Appendix 6 Sample invitation letter to participate in research

See section 3.4.5 for interview protocol

Raman K. Attri
Doctoral Research Student,
Southern Cross University, Australia

Subject: *Invitation to Participate in a Doctoral Research Study: Strategies to Accelerate Employee' Time-to-Proficiency*

Dear Industry Expert

My name is Raman K. Attri. I am a Senior Global Technical Training Manager at KLA-Tencor, a $10 billion semiconductor equipment giant. I found your contact from my LinkedIn connections and other industry/academic references. Based on your public profiles, I recognise your experience as training expert in semiconductor equipment sector. As a training thought leader, you may have significantly important opinions that can shape the findings of a unique research study I am conducting as part of my Doctorate in Business Administration (DBA) degree from Southern Cross University Australia on the topic of *"Strategies for Accelerating Employees' Time-to-Proficiency"*.

This research study is approved by the Human Research Ethics Committee at Southern Cross University wide approval number ECN-13-261 dated: 16-Oct-2013. For details on the research study scope and mode, please refer to attached information sheet.

As part of this research, I would like to hear your thoughts and experiences using different strategies to shorten (or accelerate) the time-to-proficiency of employees. With this letter, I am appealing for your kind and volunteer participation in this innovative research. The findings of this research may change the industry's perception about how to accelerate time-to-expertise of employees.

Should you volunteer to participate in this research; please click the link below to sign a consent form. https://www.surveymonkey.com/s/PTHWWFG

I really appreciate your interest and willingness to participate in this research. I will appreciate if you could take few moments to forward this letter to your colleague and experts in your network.

If you have further enquiries about the research, you can e-mail me at   . Alternatively, you may contact my research supervisor, Dr. Wing S. Wu at winswu@yahoo.com.

Yours sincerely

Raman K. Attri
LinkedIn Profile: www.linkedin.com/in/rkattri
Twitter: www.twitter.com/rkattri
Blog: http://managingtraining.wordpress.com

Appendix 7   Research information sheet

See section 3.4.5 for interview protocol

RESEARCH TITLE: STRATEGIES TO ACCELERATE EMPLOYEES' TIME-TO-PROFICIENCY

Research question	What specific strategies have helped leading organisations to successfully "accelerate" time-to-proficiency of its employees?
Researcher	**Raman K. Attri**
Research info:	Approval Number: ECN-13-261 dated: 16-Oct-2013 Degree: Doctorate of Business Administration Time frame for research: 2014-2015 Research Supervisor: Dr. Wing S. Wu
Aims of the research study	This research study is aimed at exploring and finding proven strategies (methods, mechanisms, structure, systems, methodologies, instructional design, processes and transformations, etc.) to train its employees to achieve the desired proficiency (also called productivity or expertise) in skills required to perform their job in lesser time.
Why this research?	As a hi-tech industry expert, you already may know noticed two drivers: 1) that organisations are striving to squeeze down the time-to-market of new technologies. 2) New technologies, equipment and processes are being invented at a fast speed to meet customer demands and needs. 3) Higher customer demands on efficiency and quality are making these technologies and systems highly complex. These three facts together are driving industry's need to develop top-notch capabilities of its employees in a shorter time. It is a general belief that industry is not able to accelerate time-to-proficiency of employees at the same speed as time-to-market. Through this doctoral research, I am hoping that we may be able to bring key semiconductor equipment industry thought leaders at same platform to solve this business challenge for a common cause.
Benefits of the research	- This research is expected to contribute a practical knowledge to the academic community by critically evaluating various strategies used by industry to meet this business challenge to speed up time-to-proficiency of employees. - The findings from this research are likely to be of great use by practitioners (like technical training managers, executives and instructional designers) to implement effective solutions in their organisations to meet their own specific challenges and save millions of dollars. - This research may be able to open gates for further research in exploring correct solutions to accelerate time-to-expertise of employees.
How will participants be selected?	Step-I: Online expression of interest Step-II: Online questionnaire to gather demographic details of participants Step-III: Select participants by applying a well-defined criterion to select the participants who possess directly or closely relevant expertise and experience which can benefit or impact the research findings.

	Criteria for selection include but not limited to several factors like relevancy of experience to the research area; exposure in Hi-Tech; specific job roles; authority/recognition in the industry, publication and authorship; leadership in technical training; projects pertaining to time-to-proficiency.
How long is participant engagement?	Interested participants will be expected to spare up to a maximum of 3 hours of time over the 1-2 years' time frame to participate in this research which includes: - Up to 15 minutes for data gathering questionnaire - Up to 90 minutes in-depth interview - Up to 30 minutes of follow-on interview (if needed) - Up to 60 minutes of focus group participation for select participants (optional)
How will participants be engaged in research?	Jan'14 – March'14 1. Participant fill expression of interest of participation in the research and consent form online (5 minutes) April'14 – June'14 2. All the interested participants will receive a link in e-mail to fill an online questionnaire and will be asked to provide specific details on demographic, experience, expertise, projects, cases and exposure in the subject-matter (15 minutes) Jul'14-Sept'14 3. Qualified participants, after applying the defined criteria, will receive an e-mail confirmation regarding proposed time / method of interview. Sample interview questions will also be sent to the participants (5 minutes) Oct'14 – March'15 4. Upon confirmation from participants to attend the interview, an in-depth interview will be conducted as per confirmed time and as per preferred method. (up to 90 minutes) 5. Some participants may be requested for a follow-on interview if any clarification is needed (up to 30 minutes) 6. All interviewed participants will receive a link in their e-mail for transcripts of their interview which they can review at their free will. (10 minutes optional) July'15 – Sept'15 7. Some key participants with demonstrated industry leadership will be invited for participation in a focus group (using Delphi method) to validate the research outcome. (60 minutes – optional) Jan'16- March'16 8. Participants will receive a thanks e-mail at the end of the research along with the link to download the copy of the final research report. (5 minutes)
How will participants be interviewed?	- The researcher will conduct the interview in a very semi-structured manner. The researcher will send you the intended questions beforehand. However, these may change based on dynamics of the conversation. - During the interviews, researcher will ask you to cite at least one success story (case, scenario, incident, project or example) in which your specific goal was to shorten time-to-proficiency of employees. - The researcher will ask you a series of semi-structured questions to explore your thoughts on the business challenge you encountered, type of training strategies deployed, implementation mechanism and level of success you noticed. - All efforts will be made not to ask any equipment, organisation or technology specific question or any other proprietary information. You will have the right not to respond to a particular question. - The researcher will set up interviews as per your convenient time zone, mode and technology (like WebEx, GoToMeeting online portal, Audio-video conference, Skype, Google HangOut etc.). The face-to-face interviews will be setup for local participants at your convenient time and place. - After the interview, you will be given a secure link to review or verify the accuracy of their interview transcripts at your own volition without any compulsion.
How confidentiality and privacy of participants will be protected?	- As per Ethics guidelines of Southern Cross University, the researcher will fully observe all the ethical measures. - All the participant information will be kept fully protected, private and confidential. - Privacy of the participants will be fully safeguarded. The real names, address, organisation, title, etc. will not be used anywhere. For interview transcripts storage and data reporting purposes, all

	participants and their organisations will be identified using pseudo-names to keep it non-identifiable. - The participant information will not be shared with any party under any circumstances. - Aggregated data will be correlated, and only group or category level results will be reported in the final research report without any mention of names of individuals or organisations. - The data gathered through research will be kept encrypted in a separate hard disk accessible to the researcher only and will be password protected to safeguard data and information pertaining to research participants' and the research itself. - All the data collected will be solely used for the aforementioned research only and will not be used for any commercial or business purposes. All the collected data will be kept confidential and with be retained by University for 7 years.
How findings will be published?	The result of the research will be reported in a thesis as per university guidelines. Interim results and findings are planned to be published in conferences and peer-reviewed scholarly international journals. All the confidentiality measures mentioned above will be strictly observed during any publication. Researcher's responsibility is to perform the trustworthy data analysis and report the result of the study which can benefit the larger community.
Complaints / concerns	During the research, if you have concerns about the ethical conduct of this research or the researchers, write to the following. University assured keeping all information confidential and handled as soon as possible. *The Ethics Complaints Officer, Southern Cross University, PO Box 157, Lismore NSW 2480 Australia* *Email: ethics.lismore@scu.edu.au*
Why should you be interested?	A copy of final research report will be provided to the interested participants. You as participants, among other practitioners, will be immensely benefitted from a final research report by gaining insight into various strategies that worked across the Hi-Tech industry in different settings and contexts.
Additional details	Click this link for a detailed presentation on the research: http://www.slideshare.net/rkattri/researchinvitation
Call for action	If you are interested to voluntarily participate in this research; please click this link to sign a consent form. https://www.surveymonkey.com/s/PTHWWFG

ABOUT THE RESEARCHER

Raman K. Attri is an organisational learning specialist and training management professional with specialisation on competitive training strategies, human performance improvement and expertise development in the complex corporate world. Raman is equipped with over 20 years of technical and training experience. Keenly interested in advanced research, he is currently pursuing is Doctorate in Business Administration (DBA) at Southern Cross University, Australia. He is conducting a ground-breaking research in training strategies to accelerate time-to-proficiency of employees performing complex jobs. As Senior Global Technical Training Manager for KLA-Tencor Corporation, a $10bn semiconductor equipment manufacturer and Training Magazine's one among Top 10 Hall of Fame companies for training excellence, he manages global field service training operations for semiconductor equipment service, maintenance and repair training. He has led several initiatives to restructure training programs to meet changing business needs with the complexity of equipment. He serves as a training and learning management consultant to leading professional bodies in several countries and participates in building the knowledge base of industry-wide best practices and transforming research into practical training strategies. Previously he has served as Sr. Scientist for 10 years in the area of research and development of sophisticated instrumentation and measurement technologies. Previously he earned a Professional Doctorate in Management, MBA in Operations Management, EMBA in Customer Relationships and a Master's Degree in Applied Electronics among several other international credentials and certifications.

ABOUT SOUTHERN CROSS UNIVERSITY

Southern Cross University (SCU) is a highly regarded Australian public university established under its own Act of Parliament. Southern Cross University is a research intensive university. The quality programs offered by the University have high academic standards combined with an industry and professional focus. In the Australian Research Council Excellence in Research for Australia 2012 Report, Southern Cross University achieved 10th position and acclaimed "well above world standard" in six fields of research. University profile can be seen at http://www.scu.edu.au .

Appendix 8   Web-based informed consent form at surveymonkey.com

See section 3.4.5 for details on interview protocols

---

1. I am volunteerily interested to participate in this research conducted by Raman K. Attri on accelerating time-to-expertise.

   ○ Yes   ○ No

2. I HAVE BEEN MADE FULLY AWARE BY THE RESEARCHER AND I UNDERSTAND THAT:
   - My participation in the research is voluntary
   - I can cease my participation at any time without any implications.
   - My participation in this research will be treated with confidentiality.
   - Any information identifying me will never be disclosed or published.
   - Any information that may identify me will be de-identified at the time of analysis of any data.
   - All information gathered during this research will be held by university confidentially for 7 years
   - I can contact the researchers at any time with any queries. Their contact details are provided to me.

   ○ Yes   ○ No

3. I understand the overall intent of the research and I fully understand the information provided by the researcher about my participation in the research project (time commitment, mode, steps and tentative plan).

   ○ Yes   ○ No

4. I agree that I will be able to commit about 3 hours of my time with the researcher for completing questionnaires, interviews or follow-ups over the next 1-2 years through a method and time convenient to me.

   ○ Yes   ○ No

5. I prefer to participate in research and respond to researcher's questions in following mode:

   ☐ Face-to-Face Interview only
   ☐ Online interview only (over the phone, audio/video or internet media)
   ☐ Online questionnaire only
   ☐ Any of the above

6. I prefer 'interview' as the primary mode to participate in this research. And I agree:
   - To be interviewed by the researcher as per mutually agreed mode and time.
   - To allow the interview to be "audio-taped and/or "video-taped" for the purposes of research.
   - To make myself available for further interview if required.

   ○ Yes   ○ No

7. I prefer 'questionnaire' as the primary mode to participate in the research. And I agree:
   - To complete any questionnaires that may be required to provide information about training strategies I used in accelerating employees' time-to-proficiency in my projects, or assignments
   - To fill the questionnaire with accurate information to the extent possible

   ○ Yes   ○ No

* 8. Please provide your full name

Name in full:

E-mail address:

LinkedIn Profile Link (if any):

Appendix 9 Web-based informed consent form at qualtrics.com

See section 3.4.5 for details on interview protocols

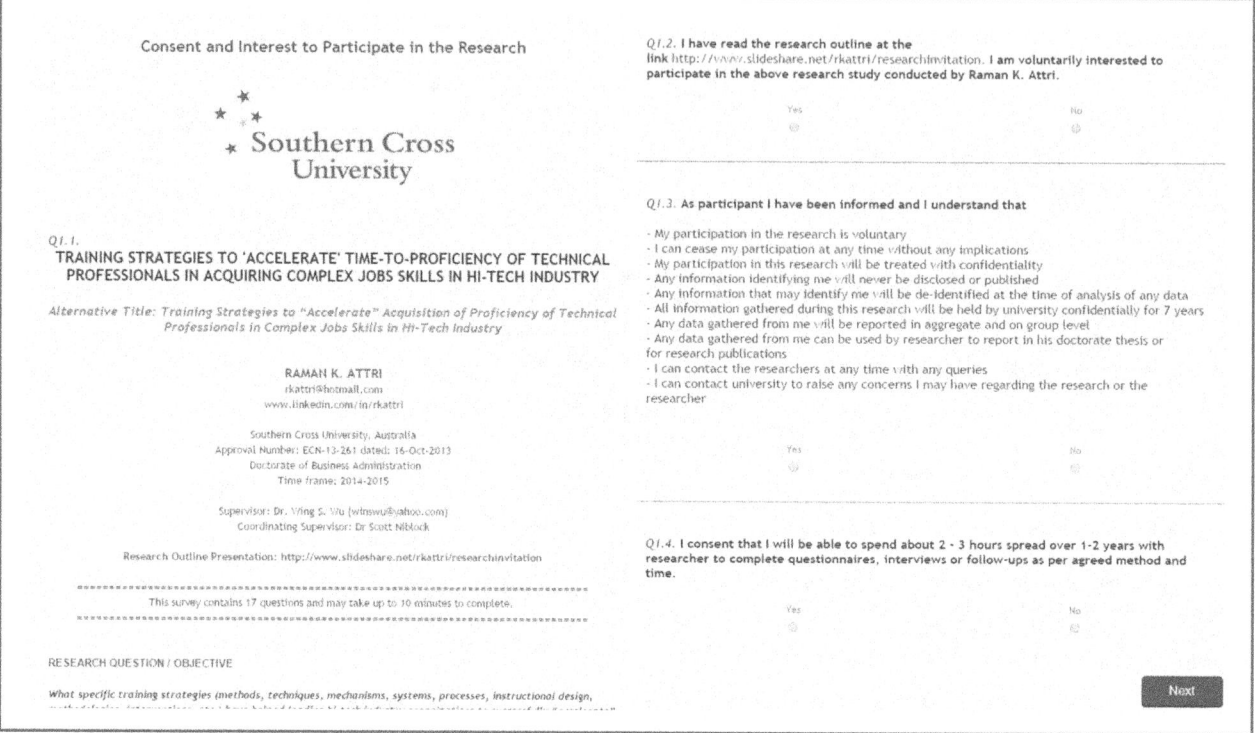

Appendix 10 Pre-interview expectation setting e-mail

See section 3.4.5 for details on interview protocols

Raman K. Attri
Doctoral Research Student,
Southern Cross University, Australia

Subject: Interview schedule and setting expectations

Dear XXXX

I appreciate your agreeing to participate in Doctorate research study I am conducting on **"Strategies to Accelerate Time-to-Proficiency of Employees".** This is an acknowledgement of the final interview date and time as per the date/time we discussed earlier. Based on your consent and agreement, I am setting up this 60-minutes in-depth interview as per details below:

Interview details
Date of interview: 23-April-2015 (Thursday)
Time: 9 AM Central (Minnesota)
Mode: Telephonic call Duration: 60 minutes

Please acknowledge this meeting invite. If you need to change the time or date for the interview, please feel free to send me an e-mail at

Though the interview is subject to go by the dynamics and flow of the conversation based on the experience shared by you, the tentative questions are attached for your review. Note that since the research is exploratory in nature, the interview questions are being updated continuously based on progressive interviews.

The objective of the interview is to explore your experience on **at least one case or project** to understand how you or your team selected the strategies and how your model of implementation looks like. It will be really great if you can think of one case or project you would want to discuss with the researcher. Once again, I would like to mention that all the data will be kept private and confidential and will be de-identified before storage. All the results will be reported in aggregate and on a group level. Your interview will entitle you to receive a copy of the research report which will be sent to you when ready.

I am truly thankful to your support for this unique research. Looking forward to talk to you soon.

Regards

Raman K. Attri

ATTACHED: Interview Questions and Research outline

Appendix 11 Concept map captured during interview (example)

See section 3.4.5 for details on interview protocols

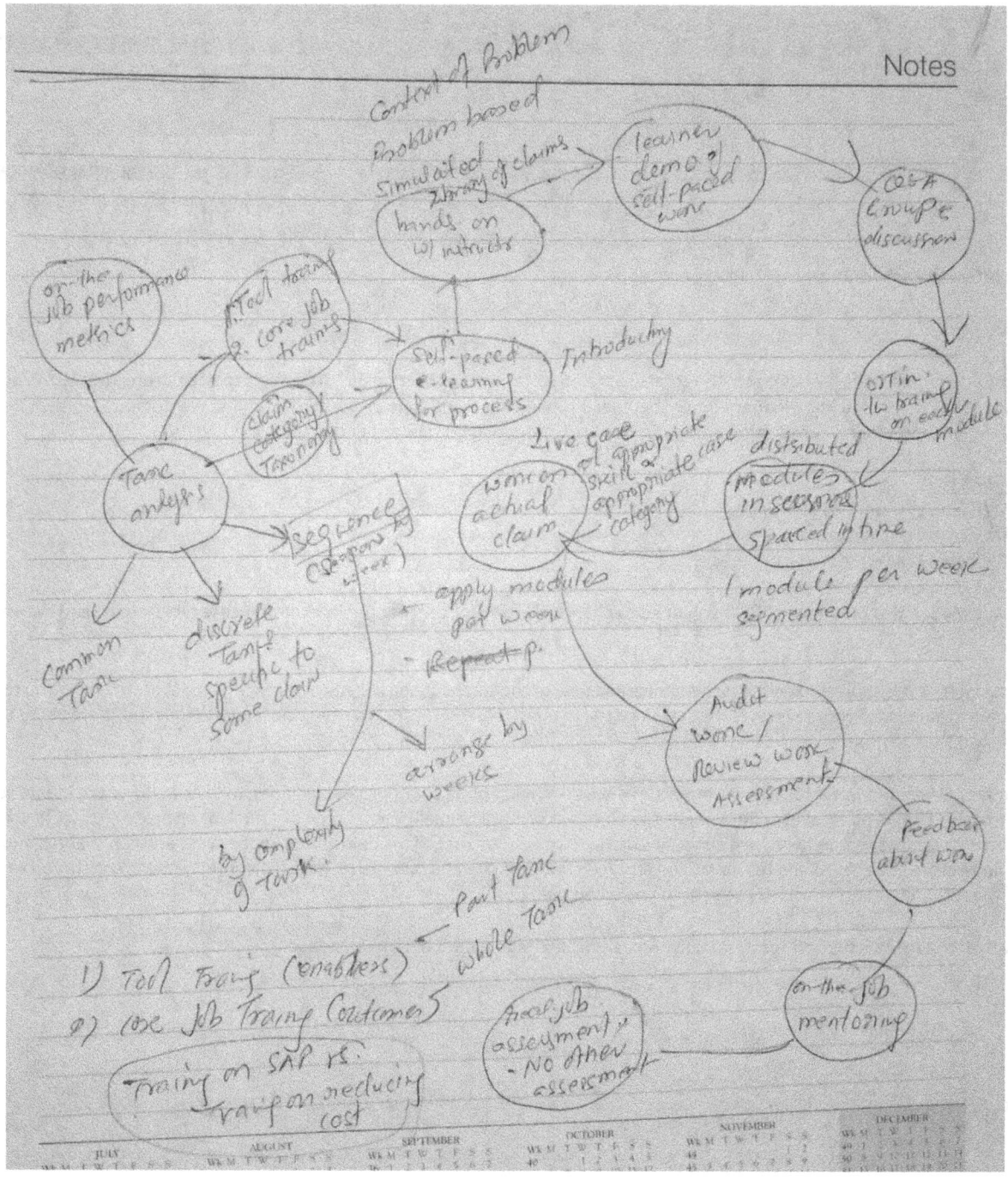

Appendix 12   Concept map updated and refined (example)

See section 3.4.5 for details on interview protocols

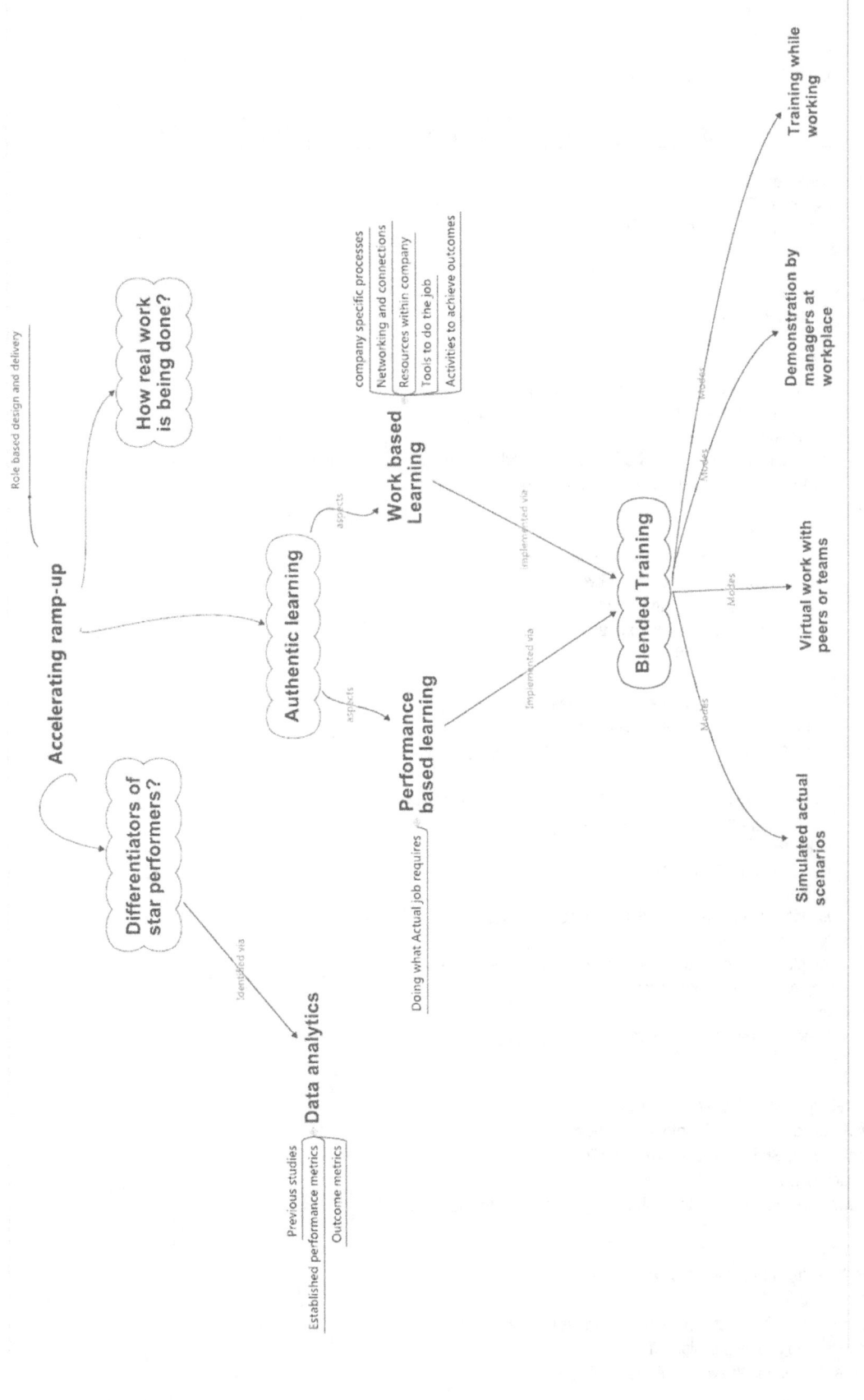

pg. 373

Appendix 13   Interview summary (example)

See section 3.5.1 for details on post-interview processing

Interview summary 23-Sep-2014: with Diana Project leader 11

Case Study Provided? **Yes**
Industry for the case study: Pharmaceutical
Specialisation of Participant: Instructional design
Usefulness: Good
Organisation: -
Position: Consultant
Nature of interview: Methodology

Key points
- Onboarding new hire challenge of longer proficiency
    - Precision skills and adhering to standards is crucial
- Information overload
    - Converting more procedural SOPs reading work into use-it--when-needed
    - Information not broken in a way it made sense
- Solution
    - 4 step approach
        - Read the SOP and answer questions
        - Go with mentor and observe it
        - Do it together with mentor
        - Do it while mentor observes
        - Mentor sign off
- SOP part
    - Organise the procedures around themes or practices
    - Chunks of short info courses or SOPs
    - Reading work on SOP followed by understanding type questions
- OJT
    - Coach's guide to help them coach the new hires on procedures
    - Coaches sign-off completing procedures
    - Structured OJT
    - No classroom type training
    - 100% on the job
    - Qualification criteria is standards posed by industry
- Complexity vs. frequency
    - Complexity is key to organising rather than frequency
    - Simple to complex progression
- Reading vs. doing
    - Method to change reading from using on the job

Reflections
- Accelerating cycle on learning by doing early
- Convert boring reading tasks into active doing tasks
- Use coaches or SMEs who are already skilled
- Use coaches to build sign-off process
- Take away non-value added time when they are not on their real job

Training Strategies
- Convert reading into a doing type of task
- Structured OJT
- Structure mentorship or coaching to perform task
- Use coaches to qualify and sign-off
- Organise information the way it will be used

Appendix

New Patterns
- **Structured OJT**
- **Re-organise the information**
- **Reading converted to doing**

Patterns Repeated
- **Mentorship / Coaching**
- **Learning by doing**

Takeaway
The key piece from interview today is that sometimes the work involves precision procedure but practice on those procedures in controlled environment is needed. This cannot be achieved with reading. Rather it should be converted into an active learning by doing task using mentors or coaches. Main use of structure OJT and structured coaching for sign-off. Bringing them to do fast under coach is the key to accelerating TTP.

Additional content

Appendix 14   Analytic memo of an interview (example)

See section 3.7.4 on using project case summary analytic memo to identify theme

---

Analytic Memo 26-Sep-2015: Matt's interview

Project core theme: Authentic learning at workplace

BIG IDEAS
star performers' differentiators
simulated scenarios
on-the-job learning
blended approach
authentic learning tasks
analytics on performance
training for outcomes
training for activities
analysis of real-work

MAJOR DETERMINANTS:

1. Authentic tasks accelerates proficiency
Matt's interview brought out an interesting point that 'learning should be authentic' on the authentic tasks what they are going to do to do their job. That requires using workplace and workplace activities as key methodologies to accelerate the ramp-up.

"We wanted sellers to actually be doing authentic things that they would have to do in their day jobs to be practicing those, getting better at those where they could make the transition to their day jobs as fast as possible."

2. Overall effectiveness to do the job is goal of accelerating proficiency
Another point to note is that when speeding up onboarding or ramping up, it is not about shortening the time in training or shortening the time overall. It is about quality and making sure the job they are going to do they can do effectively at experienced level.

3. Performance-based learning and work-based learning demarcation allows to address proficiency in both outcome-based tasks as well as ways to reach there

Another interesting task categorisation that came in Matt's interview was performance-based learning (which includes tasks related to outcome) and then work-based learning (tasks related to accompanied processes and activities to achieve the outcome). This makes great sense for task analysis. That means training strategies need to focus on outcomes and activities both.

The performance-based learning is similar to what Paul Mathew mentioned as 'outcome based training design'.
 If we're taking our sales example, performance-based learning basically means doing what you are going to have to do in your job in a safe environment where you get feedback, you get practice. If you're going to be a seller, it would be having a practice sales call where I'm playing the role of a client, you're trying to sell me something. When we're all done, I give you some feedback and some kind of assessment about how you did and then maybe you do it again and again. Now that's performance-based learning.

4. Understanding Differentiators of Star Performers helps set proficiency goals
Matt reiterated the strategy mentioned by Paul in regards to identifying, analysing star performers and understanding how they work and what makes them perform at that level. Mathew added 'data analytics' as a way to identify and analyse the star performers' outcomes.

STRATEGIES: Blended learning at workplace
As part of it, three training strategies that came into the picture: -
1. Simulated scenarios - designing authentic and realistic scenarios and adapting those to learning goals.
2. Workplace training - training in parallel to the normal work activities to ensure that learning is applied in workplace. The training assignments are done part of the job.
3. Doing the way they actually do the job. For example, the way they communicate with the customer in actual settings. It includes communicating and interacting with their peers virtually.

FURTHER EXPLORATION
How does data analytics act as a strategy to design-focused solutions?

Appendix 15 Master tracker and checklist for the research study (excerpt)

See section 3.5.2 for details on data management

Project code	ID for thesis	Mode	Mode	Interview date	Documents attached	Doc coding
1	Benny, Project Leader 1	Interview	Face-to-Face (in-person)	5/4/2015	-	-
2	Billy, Project Leader 2	Interview	Audio conference / Telephonic call	5/8/2015	-	-
3	Ferino, Project Leader 3	Questionnaire	Web-based Questionnaire	10/4/2014	-	-
4	Charlie, Project Leader 4	Interview	Skype / Video conference	10/6/2014	4	Yes
-	-	Interview	Skype / Video conference	10/6/2014	-	-
-	-	Interview	Skype / Video conference	10/6/2014	-	-
-	-	Interview	Skype / Video conference	10/6/2014	-	-
5	Christian, Project Leader 5	Interview	Audio conference / Telephonic call	4/28/2015	-	-
6	Christen, Project Leader 6	Interview	Webex internet meeting	4/23/2015	2	Yes
7	Ford, Project Leader 7	Questionnaire	Web-based Questionnaire	3/26/2015	-	-
8	Dany, Project Leader 8	Interview	Audio conference / Telephonic call	5/13/2015	1	Yes
9	Mayer, Project Leader 9	Interview	Audio conference / Telephonic call	9/19/2014	1	Yes
10	Davidson, Project Leader 10	Interview	Audio conference / Telephonic call	2/6/2015	1	Yes
11	Diana, Project Leader 11	Interview	Audio conference / Telephonic call	9/23/2014	-	-
12	Dickenson, Project Leader 12	Interview	Audio conference / Telephonic call	3/3/2015	-	-
13	Liza, Project Leader 13	Interview	Audio conference / Telephonic call	12/1/2014	1	Yes
14	Ellis, Project Leader 14	Interview	Audio conference / Telephonic call	10/16/2014	1	Yes
15	Frankstein, Project Leader 15	Interview	Webex internet meeting	4/27/2015	1	Yes
16	Abigail, Project Leader 16	Interview	Audio conference / Telephonic call	10/14/2014	-	-
17	Hallmark, Project Leader 17	Interview	Webex internet meeting	11/26/2014	1	No
18	Harry, Project Leader 18	Interview	Audio conference / Telephonic call	4/1/2015	1	No
19	Aloha, Project Leader 19	Interview	Audio conference / Telephonic call	11/26/2014	1	Yes
20	Jacky, Project Leader 20	Interview	Webex internet meeting	7/17/2015	-	-
21	Jason, Project Leader 21	Interview	Audio conference / Telephonic call	5/14/2015	-	-
22	Johnson, Project Leader 22	Interview	Audio conference / Telephonic call	11/5/2014	1	Yes
23	Jessica, Project Leader 23	Interview	Audio conference / Telephonic call	4/22/2015	1	Yes
24	Kieve, Project Leader 24	Interview	Webex internet meeting	5/1/2015	1	Yes
24	Kieve, Project Leader 24	Interview	Webex internet meeting	5/1/2015	-	-
25	Kenny, Project Leader 25	Interview	Audio conference / Telephonic call	3/16/2015	-	-
26	Kenny, Project Leader 26	Interview	Audio conference / Telephonic call	3/16/2015	-	-

Appendix 16 Job classification map

See section 3.5.3 for details on project case job classification system
Primary job nature derived by corroboration of participant account and classification under ISCO, SOC and DOT
Source: ISCO-08 http://www.ilo.org/public/english/bureau/stat/isco/isco08/index.htm
SOC-2010 https://www.bls.gov/soc/#classification
DOT https://www.oalj.dol.gov/LIBDOT.HTM

Primary Job Nature	Job type (per ISCO-08 3rd level)	Job type (per SOC 2010)	DOT Titles	Total No. of project cases
Technical or Engineering	Database and network professionals	Computer and Information Analysts	031.262-010 DATA COMMUNICATIONS ANALYST	1
		Computer Support Specialists	032.262-010 USER SUPPORT ANALYST	1
	Electrotechnology engineers	Precision Instrument and Equipment Repairers	003.187-018 CUSTOMER-EQUIPMENT ENGINEER	7
	Medical and pharmaceutical technicians	Clinical Laboratory Technologists and Technicians	079.362-014 - MEDICAL RECORD TECHNICIAN	1
	Physical and engineering science technicians	Electrical and Electronics Engineers	003.161-014 ELECTRONICS TECHNICIAN	1
		Industrial Machinery Installation, Repair, and Maintenance Workers	007.167-014 - PLANT ENGINEER	1
	Process control technicians	Geological and Petroleum Technicians	549.260-010 - REFINERY OPERATOR	5
		Industrial Machinery Installation, Repair, and Maintenance Workers	914.132-022 - SUPERVISOR, FIELD PIPELINES	1
		Miscellaneous Plant and System Operators	008.261-010 CHEMICAL-ENGINEERING TECHNICIAN	1
	Sales, marketing and public relations professionals	Sales Engineers	003.151-014 - SALES-ENGINEER, ELECTRONICS PRODUCTS	2
	Telecommunications and broadcasting technicians	Radio and Telecommunications Equipment Installers and Repairers	823.261-030 DATA COMMUNICATIONS TECHNICIAN	1
Sales - Non-Technical	Client information workers	Customer Service Representatives	205.362-026 CUSTOMER SERVICE REPRESENTATIVE (financial)	1
	Finance professionals	Securities, Commodities, and Financial Services Sales Agents	205.362-026 CUSTOMER SERVICE REPRESENTATIVE (financial)	2
			205.362-026 CUSTOMER SERVICE REPRESENTATIVE (financial)	1
	Sales and purchasing agents and brokers	Insurance Sales Agents	250.257-010 - SALES AGENT, INSURANCE	3
	Sales, marketing and public relations professionals	Sales Engineers	163.167-018 - MANAGER, SALES	1
		Sales Representatives, Wholesale and Manufacturing	185.167-058 - SERVICE MANAGER (automotive ser.)	1
Scientific or Development	Electrotechnology engineers	Electrical and Electronics Engineers	003.061-034 ELECTRONICS-DESIGN ENGINEER	1
	Life science professionals	Medical Scientists	019.061-010 BIOMEDICAL ENGINEER	1
	Physical and earth science professionals	Chemists and Materials Scientists	041.061-026 - BIOCHEMIST	1

Category	Occupation Group	DOT Code - Title	Count
	Physical and engineering science technicians	003.167-018 ELECTRICAL ENGINEER, POWER SYSTEM	1
	Miscellaneous Electrical and Electronic Equipment Mechanics, Installers, and Repairers		
	Software and applications developers and analysts	030.162-010 COMPUTER PROGRAMMER	2
	Software Developers and Programmers		
Strategic Management, Leadership	Business services and administration managers	166.117-018 MANAGER, PERSONNEL	1
	General and Operations Managers		
	Commissioned armed forces officers	166.117-018 MANAGER, PERSONNEL	1
	Military Officer Special and Tactical Operations Leaders		
		193.382-010 ELECTRONIC INTELLIGENCE OPERATIONS SPECIALIST	1
	Manufacturing, mining, construction, and distribution managers	183.117-010 - MANAGER, BRANCH	1
	General and Operations Managers		
Managerial, Supervisory	Hospitality, retail and other services managers	185.167-046 - MANAGER, RETAIL STORE	2
	First-Line Supervisors of Sales Workers		
		187.167-106 - MANAGER, FOOD SERVICE	1
	Information and communications technology service managers	166.117-018 MANAGER, PERSONNEL	1
	General and Operations Managers		
Customer service helpdesk	Client information workers	205.362-026 CUSTOMER SERVICE REPRESENTATIVE (financial)	2
	Customer Service Representatives		
		239.137-014 - CUSTOMER SERVICE REPRESENTATIVE	1
		239.362-014 - CUSTOMER SERVICE REPRESENTATIVE (phone)	1
Production, Manufacturing	Metal processing and finishing plant operators	609.362-010 - NUMERICAL CONTROL MACHINE OPERATOR	1
	Engine and Other Machine Assemblers		
	Mining and mineral processing plant operators	939.281-010 - MINER	1
	Mining Machine Operators		
	Process control technicians	609.362-010 - NUMERICAL CONTROL MACHINE OPERATOR	1
	Engine and Other Machine Assemblers		
Medical, Healthcare	Health professionals	187.117-010 - ADMINISTRATOR, HEALTH CARE FACILITY	1
	Medical and Health Services Managers		
	Other health associate professionals	355.674-014 - NURSE ASSISTANT	2
	Miscellaneous Healthcare Support Occupations		
Sales - Technical	Sales, marketing and public relations professionals	262.357-010 - SALES REPRESENTATIVE, CHEMICALS AND PHARMACEUTICAL	1
	Sales Representatives, Wholesale and Manufacturing		
		274.357-018 - SALES REPRESENTATIVE, BUILDING EQUIPMENT	1
		276.257-010 - SALES REPRESENTATIVE, DENTAL AND MEDICAL	1
Financial services	Financial and mathematical associate professionals	241.267-018 - CLAIM EXAMINER	2
	Claims Adjusters, Appraisers, Examiners, and Investigators		
Training or Education	Other teaching professionals	166.221-010 - INSTRUCTOR, TECHNICAL TRAINING	1
	Training and Development Specialists		
	Professional services managers	099.117-022 SUPERINTENDENT, SCHOOLS	1
	Education Administrators		
Warehouse	Business services agents	249.362-026 - ORDER CLERK (clerical)	1
	Logisticians		
Sports, Athletics	Sports and fitness workers	153.341-010 PROFESSIONAL ATHLETE	1
	Athletes, Coaches, Umpires, and Related Workers		
Management consulting	Finance professionals	161.167-010 - MANAGEMENT ANALYST	1
	Financial Analysts and Advisors		
Assembly, Repair	Assemblers	806.684-010 - ASSEMBLER, MOTOR VEHICLE	1
	Automotive Technicians and Repairers		
		Total	66

Appendix 17 Complexity levels (excerpt)

See section 3.5.3 for details on project case classification system
Complexity rating for job/skill was developed based on participant account corroborated with DOT complexity codes
See Appendix 18 for DOT job complexity codes

Project case #	Quote and associated complexity rating	Primary Critical-to-success (CTS) Skill involved	Complexity Rating	DOT complexity code
1	HIGH - "There was a lot at stake requiring quite a complex knowledge level and skill set level for these chemical reactor operator" "there is a very real, inherent danger in working with those chemicals in those quantities of a catastrophic runaway reaction"	Complex troubleshooting	2. High	261
2	HIGH - "how to identify and replace electronic products of the system, and optics with advanced lasers and optics and systems that they have to know how to measure and then align."	Complex troubleshooting	2. High	187
3	HIGH - "you can imagine it's quite a complicated system to be sure you get the right petroleum feedstock to the right client, and keep the pipelines full, because that's how you earn money, and it's really quite a complicated business."	Complex troubleshooting	2. High	132
4	MEDIUM - "The skills are complex due to the unique nature of our products, which are not found elsewhere in industry"	Precision technical skills	3. Medium-High	362
5	HIGH - "Very high .... there was a whole lot of qualitative as well as financial and quantitative **factors,** so it was a high level of decision making."	Higher order analysis / problem solving	2. High	167

Appendix

Appendix 18   The 3-digit DOT job complexity code

See section 3.5.3 for details on project case classification system
See Appendix 17 on how these codes were used to define the complexity levels

	Data		People		Things
0	Synthesizing	0	Mentoring	0	Setting up
1	Coordinating	1	Negotiating	1	Precision working
2	Analysing	2	Instructing	2	operating - controlling
3	Compiling	3	Supervising	3	Driving _ Operating
4	Computing	4	Diverting	4	Manipulating
5	Copying	5	Persuading	5	Tending
6	Comparing	6	Speaking - signalling	6	Feeding - off bearing
		7	Serving	7	Handling
		8	Taking instructions -helping		

Source: Dictionary of Occupational Titles (DOT)
US Department of Labor
https://www.oalj.dol.gov/LIBDOT.HTM
https://occupationalinfo.org/front_223.html

Appendix 19 Project cases excluded using criteria-based sampling

*See section 3.5.4 for definition of three criteria used to select the project cases
Total sample of project cases = 66
Total number of project excluded by applying criteria =6

Criteria*	ID for thesis	Ferino, Project Leader 3	Peterson, Project Leader 41	Rahman, Project Leader 64	Stacy, Project Leader 51	Stuart, Project Leader 65	Tran, Project Leader 66
1	Situated in business settings	Yes	No	Yes	Yes	Yes	No
	Goal is reducing time-t0-proficiency	No	Yes	No	No	No	Yes
	If no, actual goal of the project	Not clear	To acclerated sport performance in specific skill	Integrate young professionals (entry point) in a specific title within 30 months	Complete an e-learning course to 1400 managers in 30 days	To improve the customer satisfaction scores	Solid understanding of very fundamental programming concepts
	Time-to-proficiency reduction is a by-product	Yes	N/A	No	No	No	Yes
	Meets Criteria 1?	**No**	**Yes**	**No**	**No**	**No**	**Yes**
2	Direct results indicating reduction in time-to-proficiency	No	No	No	No	No	No
	If not, actual results reported	Almost immediately started teaching the course	Game performance improved	Post-class OJT was reduced substantially (no actual figures)	Trained 1400 managers in 30 days	No	Basic skills obtained in 5 days
	Meets Criteria 2?	**No**	**No**	**No**	**No**	**No**	**No**
3	Three essential structural elements described	Yes	Yes	Yes	Yes	Yes	No
	Business challenge	Yes	Yes	Yes	Yes	**Yes**	**No**
	Solutions implemented	Yes	Yes	Yes	Yes	Yes	Yes
	Results obtained	Yes	Yes	Yes	Yes	Yes	No
	Meets Criteria 3?	**Yes**	**Yes**	**Yes**	**Yes**	**Yes**	**No**
	Meet all criteria?	**No**	**No**	**No**	**No**	**No**	**No**

Appendix 20   Analytic memo for organising themes (example)

See section 3.7.6 on evolving first cycle codes and 3.7.8 on organising themes

Memo: Business Driver Theme (7-Nov-2016)

PROCESS

19 first cycle codes represented various reasons or triggers across all the bounded project cases that seem to drive the need for shorter time-to-proficiency.

Three different perspectives were tried to organise the codes into themes:

1. **by business impact**
2. **by transaction**
3. **by strategic intent**

By business impact

When codes were organised by the business impact, it appeared that first cycle codes could be grouped into two candidate themes – factors driving competition and factor driving costs. Since losing competition means the impact on cost. So a candidate theme could be COST which led to very little knowledge.

By transaction

The second perspective emerged organising the codes by type of transactions. This view led to the possibility of two candidate themes – factors impacting people's transactions and factors affecting financial transactions. However, this view did not match with data because participants described shortening time-to-proficiency as a strategic intent, and not the operational intent.

By strategic intent

Changing the perspective, the codes were re-arranged to see if there was some other relationship among them. Examining data and codes led to four groups of codes i.e., candidate themes – speed-related (SPEED), time-related (TIME), skills-related (SKILL) and cost or financial related (FINANCIAL). After the grouping of codes, the relationships within each group of codes were analysed. It appeared that time-related codes were communicating a sort of "pressure", while speed-related factors have a sense of "competition". The skill-related codes appeared to be indicating "deficiencies", and finance or cost-related codes just have an indication of lack of "cost efficiencies". Therefore, the description of themes was expanded as: TIME-RELATED PRESSURES, SPEED-RELATED COMPETITIVENESS, SKILL-RELATED DEFICIENCIES and COST OR FINANCIAL IMPLICATIONS. This view was much richer, explained the strategic intent of accelerated proficiency and reasonably explained what triggers organisations to institute the initiatives/projects to reduce time-to-proficiency.

Themes			First cycle code	Frequency	
By business impact	By transactions	By strategic intent		# of sources	# of references
COMPETITION	PEOPLE	SPEED	Rapid readiness	10	15
COMPETITION	MARKET	SPEED	Market urgency & pace of business	12	13
COMPETITION	MARKET	SPEED	New systems or processes or product	5	7
COMPETITION	PEOPLE	SPEED	Rapid hiring to support business	6	7
COMPETITION	MARKET	SPEED	New business and competition	4	6
COST	PEOPLE	TIME	Longer time-to-proficiency	23	29
COST	FINANCIAL	FINANCIAL	Other financial or cost-related impacts	17	18
COST	PEOPLE	SKILLS	Retiring expert workforce	13	17

COST	PEOPLE	SKILLS	Turnover and retention rate	11	14
COST	FINANCIAL	FINANCIAL	Cost of non-proficiency	6	12
COST	PEOPLE	SKILLS	Impact of critical errors	8	10
COST	PEOPLE	SKILLS	Performance issues with outdated skills	7	8
COST	FINANCIAL	TIME	Time value of proficiency	5	6
COST	PEOPLE	TIME	Length of training	4	4
COST	PEOPLE	SKILLS	Larger portfolio	4	4
COST	PEOPLE	SKILLS	Increasing complexity	2	3
COST	FINANCIAL	FINANCIAL	Cost of training	3	3
COST	FINANCIAL	FINANCIAL	Cost of lost opportunity	3	3
COST	PEOPLE	SKILLS	More knowledge less time	1	1

WRITE UP

The strategic intent varies from one organisation to another and that differentiation leads to competitive advantage. Cost saving is not always the strategy. While for one organisation a key strategy may be to focus on quality of skills to reduce errors, address complexity, performance issues or even impacting skills to new people coming in due to attrition, for another organisation, the priority that dictates strategy could mean supporting new business or pace of business at rapid rate by making people ready sooner, emphasising need for speed. For a different organisation, challenges may be simply too long a time taken by employees to reach desired performance standards as opposed to the quality of skills or speed of readiness. On similar grounds, errors in work or taking longer time to reach the desired standard or attending longer training sessions may amount to specific challenges of cost. Using this perspective, four clusters of pattern codes emerged – SPEED, TIME, SKILLS, FINANCIAL as business drivers for time-to-proficiency.

Themes

Major business drivers for time-to-proficiency is TIME-RELATED PRESSURES and SPEED-RELATED COMPETITIVENESS are related factors. Organisations are pressed to maintain their competitiveness in the market. However, market urgency and pace of business pushed them to set up new business, products, services in the market which in turn require them to rapidly hire the people to support the business or to rapidly prepare the existing workforce for new roles, challenges or standards. That's where longer training duration or longer time-to-proficiency becomes a detrimental factor to competitiveness.

SKILL- RELATED DEFICIENCIES are seen in another kind of organisations in form of skill gaps or workforce lifecycle. In some organisation the attrition of experienced workforce creates skill gaps, and they need to bring new workforce to desired proficiency in shorter time to sustain the business. In another kind of businesses, operating in precision and highly complex domains may need ways to develop proficiency employees equipped with new complex skills in shorter time to sustain their business.

COST OR FINANCIAL IMPLICATIONS, though important are not so prevailing. Mostly the direct financial and business success factors like need to implement regulatory compliance at faster speed are the drivers that may lead to a time-to-proficiency improvement project while indirect financial or cost drivers such as cost of long training are not that important, counter to the usual belief of organisations' focus to save money with every initiative/project.

Appendix 21 Thematic map of strategies (excerpt)

See section 3.7.7 on thematic networks to analyse themes for relationships

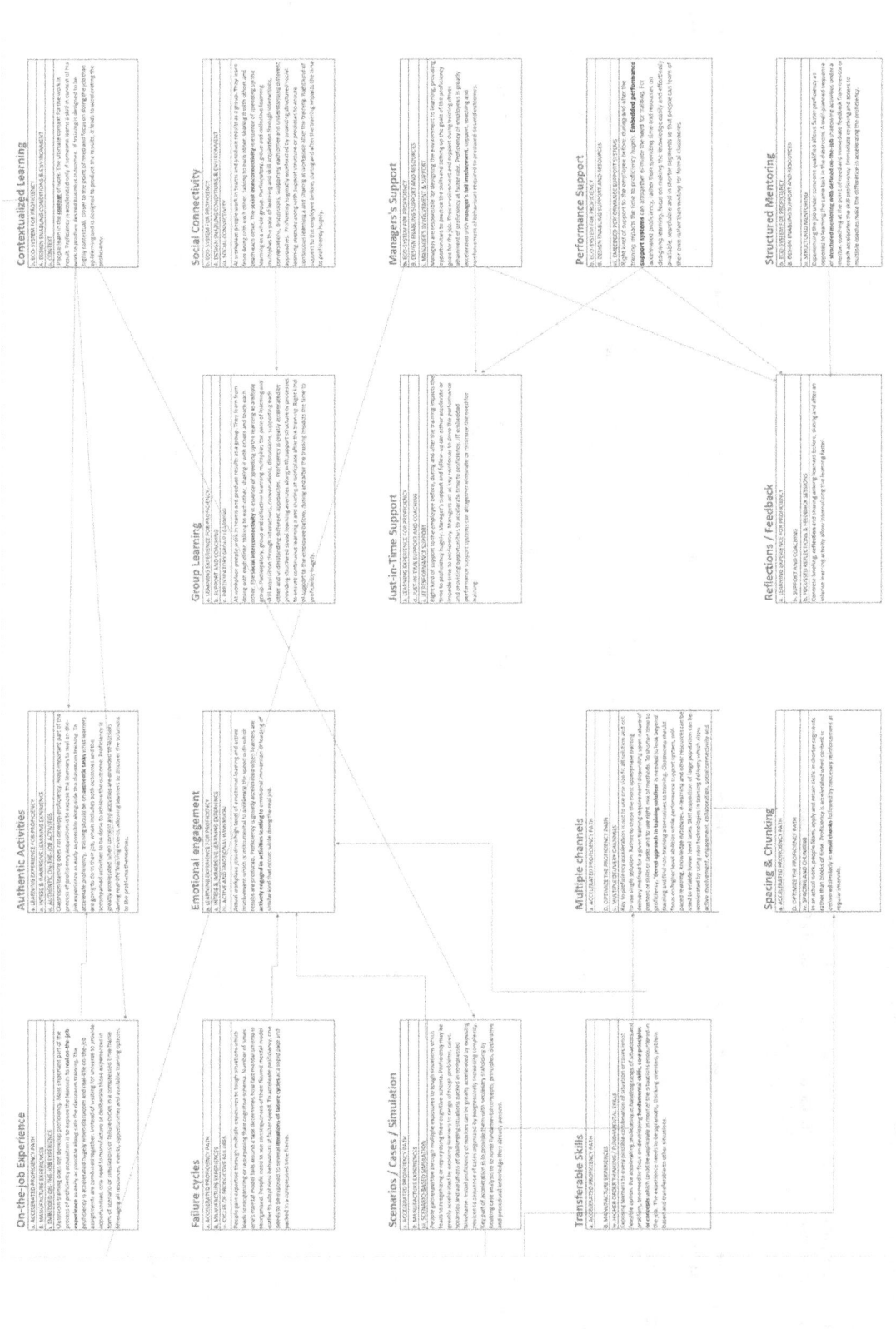

Appendix 22 Matrix of analytic memo for project case summary

See section 3.7.11 for cross-case analysis using matrix approach

Legend:
Yellow cells: codes/patterns related to scenarios, real-world cases or scenario-based training
Green cells: codes/patterns related to social connectivity, social and peer learning
Tan cells: codes/patterns related to performance support systems or its usage

ID for thesis	Big Idea #1	Big Idea #2	Big Idea #3	Big Idea #4	Big Idea #5	Determinant #1	Determinant #2	Determinant #3	Determinant #4	Strategy #1	Strategy #2	Strategy #3	Strategy #4	Strategy #5	Question to follow #1	Contradiction/outlier
Benny, Project Leader 1	Remove redundancy and wastage	Organise by Frequency and complexity	Pre-work and homework	Reinforcement OJT after formal class		Amount of overlapping content and skills	Spacing between consecutive formal classes	Post-training practice to gain required proficiency	Self-paced content for more hands-on in classroom	Remove redundancies, similarity, overlap and wastage from series of modules	Segregate skills by frequency and complexity	Keep optimal spacing between modules	Provide reinforcement practice OJT after formal class	Real-life scenario-based training in the classroom	Are other organisations practising structured OJT following formal training class (as opposed to the standard model of S-OJT) directly?	-
Charlie, Project Leader 4	Performance Support Systems	Manager support	Social interconnectivity	Take out informational content	Content, context and tasks	Manager	Environment	Informational content	Accountability	Social and peer learning	Social connectivity to star performers	Performance support systems				Opposes structure around informal, opposes traditional formal training

pg. 386

Name	Col 1	Col 2	Col 3	Col 4	Col 5	Col 6	Col 7	Col 8	Col 9	Col 10	Col 11	Col 12	Col 13	Col 14
Ford, Project Leader 7	Sequence of progression	compressed time-frame	Real-world scenarios		Stakeholder buy-in				Sequence of progressive difficulty	Embed or sequence group sharing, hands-on, scenarios and job shadowing	Real-world scenarios			-
Dany, Project Leader 8	DMX for rare 10% events	DMX instead of training	Critical Decision-making CTA with SMEs		Frequency				Critical incident method CTA with SMEs	Rare events training with DMXx	DMX Scenarios			Very similar to case study based on failures?
Mayer, Project Leader 9	Peer sharing	Social interconnectivity	Learning and workplace are one		Social connections				Interconnectivity	Learner guided learning	social interactions	group learning	participatory learning	
Davidson, Project Leader 10	DMX for rare 10% events	DMX instead of training	Critical Decision-making CTA with SMEs		facilitator				piece-meal scenarios	Facilitated discussions	DMX Scenarios			-
Diana, Project Leader 11	Sequencing	Pre-work	complexity based sequence	Structured OJT	Mentoring	Information overload		Manager	Pre-work	complexity based sequence	Structured OJT	Guided Mentoring		
Dickenson, Project Leader 12	Proficiency definition	Task analysis as major contributor	structured involvement of managers	Tap experts for task list sign-off	Performance consulting approach to gap analysis	Analysis	Attitude	Slowest learner in the class	Thorough performance analysis/gap analysis	Accurate Task list analysis	Pre-work to formal class	Performance support system instead of or support of training	Use experts to sign-off on task analysis	
Liza, Project Leader 13	E-learning	Mentorship	Combined ILT and OJT						self-paced	peer teaching	social connectivity	combined ILT and OJT	Feedback and review	

Appendix

Appendix 23 Example of case-ordered context matrix (excerpt)

See section 3.7.9 on constructing case-ordered, conceptually-ordered and descriptive matrices

Project case ID	Project Title	Context (company, business, environment, job type, challenge)	Context (Quotes)
1	Customer service engineers troubleshooting and repairing complex semiconductor equipment	A high-tech semiconductor equipment company in high-paced technology business pressed hard to keep customers' production running and keeping equipment uptime commitments. Required to develop proficient skills of its engineers in repair and service of equipment in shorter time.	as per customer requirement, all engineers need to undergo formal training and gets to be certified before they are allowed to maintain the tools on the customer site.... They need to perform the maintenance of the tool, preventive maintenance, troubleshooting the tool if there are some issues on the tool, maintaining the tool as per customer requirement.... business needs is typically around three to six months, the engineers should be proficient enough in time to readiness for him to be proficient enough to be deployed in the field. That's the main target for now.
4	Software engineers developing large scale information applications (books)	An information technology company with 65 software development centres spread worldwide with 5000 software developers, offshored 1800 software developers to low-cost countries replacing existing expert workforce. Formal training was too long and coaching with leaving experts was not feasible. Required to develop skills of offshored developers to the desired proficiency in the shorter timeframe before existing experts are gone.	"And the company had 65 software development centers spread around the world.... We had about – say about 5,000 software developers and database center managers. And the company took a decision to restructure its development, to reduce those numbers of centres and to move some of them to lower cost areas. So we established a big development centre in Thailand, called Company R Software Thailand in Bangkok, and a big development centre in Beijing. And we recruited people rapidly into those development centres. Now in Bangkok, we recruited 1,500 software – no, 1,800 software developers and database experts, technical experts, 1,800 in 15 months.... One was that the formal structured training programs just took too long, just were taking too much time over too long."
5	Cybersecurity analysts analysing and identifying cyber-threats on client enterprise networks	A hi-tech internet infrastructure and cyber security company required new engineers to come up to speed in highly technical skills in shorter time.	a very high-tech company focused on internet infrastructure and cyber security....and then that continued to evolve into, "Well, we really think to really understand everything, if we would do everything in a system, right now it takes about a year." And I went, "Whoa, that's a long time to wait for people to be ready to go to work".
7	Customer service engineers troubleshooting and repairing complex semiconductor equipment	A high-tech semiconductor equipment company in high-paced technology business pressed hard to keep customers' production running and keeping equipment uptime commitments. Required to develop proficient skills of its engineers in repair and service of equipment in shorter time.	The technicians hired would mostly be incoming zero experience semiconductor technicians working in all areas of the semiconductor manufacturing structure.... we bring a new employee (or existing promoted employee) up to speed to a pre-determined standard of technical expertise. We introduce them to the demands of life in the Fab by slowly integrating them into the highly volatile environment.

8	Console operators monitoring and controlling the processes at petrochemical plants	An oil and gas company in exploratory operations faced with the rapid retirement of their aged and experienced board operators. Required to develop technical and decision-making skills of younger new hired operators to proficiency before the current experts are gone.	they were dealing with or continued to deal with a pretty rapid rate of attrition among the operators, and losing their less experienced operators, needing to bring newer people up to speed really quickly because this is also an industry that's really heavily regulated, and so needing to make sure that people can maintain safe and efficient conditions.... That's part of the performance case of people who are able to monitor the data and information and make decisions on the job and also as a business case of making sure they're maintaining operations within those regulatory requirements.
9	Service engineers troubleshooting and repairing telecommunication network equipment	A large telecommunication company providing high-speed Internet services to end users and pressed hard to keep the downtime of services to a minimum. Required to develop proficiency of their engineers' skills in troubleshooting issues in the installation of a completely new technology telecommunication equipment.	A large telecommunication company in US [referred as Company A]... They had a program in [DSL]... Yes, well DSL is a communications protocol that the engineers have to master, you know for communicating data in terms of new equipment that they are building and so on ... Well, there were several goals. It was to reduce downtime, you know, to get outages corrected more quickly, so you don't lose the customer connections, and to demonstrate everyone's ability to do that.
10	Console operators monitoring and controlling the processes at petrochemical plants	An oil and gas company in exploratory operations faced with the rapid retirement of their aged and experienced board operators. Required to develop technical and decision-making skills of younger new hired operators to proficiency before the current experts are gone.	at least in the United States, we're experiencing a significant workforce turnover due to- there was a period of time where plants weren't hiring people and so now you've got a case where you're seeing significant losses due to retirements and workforce is getting younger very fast.

Appendix

Appendix 24 Example of case-ordered themes (excerpt)

See section 3.7.9 on constructing case-ordered, conceptually-ordered and descriptive matrices
See section 4.4.2 for description of overarching theme of business drivers,
See section 4.7.2 for description of emergent themes of four business drivers
See section 5.4.2 for discussion on business drivers

Project case ID	Project case title	Time-related pressures	Speed-related competitiveness	Cost or financial implications	Skill-related deficiencies	Analytic Comments
50	Machine operators fabricating mechanical parts for petroleum exploration equipment			Financial/Business Drivers: "In order to meet production requirements and targets, it is important to get the new employees up to speed quickly"	Skill drivers: "No room for error" "without incurring any safety related incidents."	Skill drivers due to pressure of impact of non-proficiency and critical errors on production. Financial drivers due to impact on production and loss of revenue due to non-proficient employees.
29	Machinists fabricating aircraft engine mechanical parts	Time drivers: "longer that it takes somebody to learn, the more difficult it is to complete our process and ship to the customer on time"	Speed drivers: "Massive recruitment efforts yielded few potential employees."	Cost drivers: "In addition, the company wanted to reduce costs (including recruitment costs)"	Skill drivers: "a severe skills shortage" "The sooner people are fully competent to perform job, new employee becomes more safe and productive"	Time/ Speed drivers due to rapid hiring to support business and pressures due to time to market. Skills drivers due to precision work involved and need to prepare employees to a proficiency level of error-free work. Financial drivers due to impact of non-proficiency on production and opportunity cost lost in the wait time.
49	Maintenance engineers repairing and maintaining petroleum pipeline feeds	Time drivers: "shortening the time-to-proficiency came to the top of the list"		Financial/regulatory drivers: "So if you could shave a week, even two weeks off that, or a month or more ... when they began to be productive, produced very extraordinary savings"	Skill drivers: "doing so safely and in accordance with federal and state regulations requires well-trained and highly knowledgeable employees"	Time/speed drivers due to urgency to resolve the issue quickly to avoid impact on production and impact on customers. Skill drivers due to impact of critical errors on production, which leads to revenue loss. Financial drivers due to cost of longer training.
27	Military officers setting up a new command centre to prevent cyberterrorism	Time drivers: "it would take one year to take these core business processes."	Speed drivers: "getting them quickly to what they refer to as "initial operating capability."			Time/speed drivers due to need for rapid readiness for new operations or processes in place. Skill drivers are implicit because team lacked the skills required to erect new infrastructure fast.

Appendix pg. 390

Appendix 25 Example of variable-ordered themes (excerpt)

See section 3.7.9 on constructing case-ordered, conceptually-ordered and descriptive matrices

Complexity Rating	Time-related pressures	Speed-related competitiveness	Cost or financial implications	Skill-related deficiencies	Analytic Comments
HIGH	Time drivers: "it would take one year to take these core business processes."	Speed drivers: "getting them quickly to what they refer to as 'initial operating capability.'"			Time/speed drivers due to need for rapid readiness for new operations or processes in place. Skill drivers are implicit because team lacked the skills required to erect new infrastructure fast.
MEDIUM HIGH	Time drivers: "shortening the time-to-proficiency came to the top of the list."		Financial/regulatory drivers: "So if you could shave a week, even two weeks off that, or a month or more ... when they began to be productive, produced very extraordinary savings."	Skill drivers: "doing so safely and in accordance with federal and state regulations requires well-trained and highly knowledgeable employees."	Time/speed drivers due to urgency to resolve the issue quickly to avoid impact on production and impact on customers. Skill drivers due to impact of critical errors on production, which leads to revenue loss. Financial drivers due to cost of longer training.
			Financial/Business Drivers: "In order to meet production requirements and targets, it is important to get the new employees up to speed quickly."	Skill drivers: "No room for error" without incurring any safety related incidents."	Skill drivers due to pressure of impact of non-proficiency and critical errors on production. Financial drivers due to impact on production and loss of revenue due to non-proficient employees.
MEDIUM	Time drivers: "longer that it takes somebody to learn, the more difficult it is to complete our process and ship to the customer on time"	Speed drivers: "Massive recruitment efforts yielded few potential employees."	Cost drivers: "In addition, the company wanted to reduce costs (including recruitment costs)"	Skill drivers: "a severe skills shortage" "The sooner people are fully competent to perform job, new employee becomes more safe and productive"	Time/ Speed drivers due to rapid hiring to support business and pressures due to time to market. Skills drivers due to precision work involved and need to prepare employees to a proficiency level of error-free work. Financial drivers due to impact of non-proficiency on production and opportunity cost lost in the wait time.

Appendix 26 Checklist matrix for time-to-proficiency results reported in project cases

Includes results of only 60 selected projects
See section 4.9.1 for classification of direct/indirect indicators of proficiency
See section 3.7.9 on constructing checklist matrix

Project case ID	Case Title	Direct or Indirect results?	Indicators					
			Time-to-Proficiency	Time-to-Readiness	Training Duration	Comparative performance	Proficient population	Rate of learning
1	Customer service engineers troubleshooting and repairing complex semiconductor equipment	Direct	YES	-	YES	-	-	-
2	Customer service helpdesk taking inbound calls for sales of investment products	Direct	YES	-	YES	YES	-	-
4	Software engineers developing large scale information applications	Direct	-	YES	-	-	-	-
5	Cybersecurity analysts analysing and identifying cyber-threats on client enterprise networks	Direct	YES	-	-	YES	-	-
6	Insurance agents selling insurance products	Direct	YES	-	-	YES	-	-
7	Customer service engineers troubleshooting and repairing complex semiconductor equipment	Direct	YES	-	-	-	-	-
8	Console operators monitoring and controlling the processes at petrochemical plants	Direct	-	YES	-	-	-	-
9	Service engineers troubleshooting and repairing telecommunication network equipment	Direct	-	-	YES	-	-	YES
10	Console operators monitoring and controlling the processes at petrochemical plants	Direct	-	YES	-	-	-	-
11	Pharmaceutical biochemists manufacturing sophisticated cancer drugs	Direct	YES	-	-	-	-	-
12	Managers managing retail doughnut baking stores	Direct	YES	-	YES	-	-	YES
13	Claim processing executives examining and processing health insurance claims	Direct	YES	-	YES	-	-	-
14	Sales representative selling pharmaceutical products	Direct	YES	-	-	-	-	-
15	Insurance agents selling insurance products	Direct	-	YES	-	-	-	-
16	Console operators monitoring and controlling the processes at petrochemical plants	Indirect	-	-	-	YES	-	-
17	Customer service helpdesk taking inbound calls for hotel and travel related services	Direct	-	-	YES	YES	-	YES
18	Managers managing supermarket chains	Direct	YES	-	YES	-	-	-
19	Energy Corporation top executives transferring knowledge to successors	Direct	YES	-	-	-	-	YES
20	Hospital medical doctors and nursing staff providing paediatrics care services	Direct	-	YES	-	-	-	-
21	Customer helpdesk taking inbound calls to remotely troubleshoot client computer and software issues	Direct	YES	-	YES	YES	-	YES
22	Customer service engineers troubleshooting and repairing complex semiconductor equipment	Direct	YES	-	-	-	-	-
23	School administrator and teachers instituting school improvement programs	Direct	-	YES	-	-	-	-
24	Warehouse professionals adopting SAP for supply chain and logistics transactions	Direct	-	YES	-	-	-	-
25	Console operators monitoring and controlling the processes at petrochemical plants	Indirect	-	-	-	-	-	YES
26	Young military officers on leadership pathway	Indirect	-	-	-	YES	-	YES
27	Military officers setting up a new command centre to prevent cyber terrorism	Direct	-	YES	YES	-	-	-

#	Description							
28	Biotechnology scientists strategizing business of brain implant technology for curing neurological diseases	Direct	-	YES	-	-	-	-
29	Machinists fabricating aircraft engine mechanical parts	Direct	YES	-	-	-	-	YES
30	Sales engineers selling hi-tech enterprise communication products	Direct	YES	-	-	YES	-	YES
31	Electronics technicians to troubleshoot and repair of complex Navy electronics equipment	Direct	-	-	YES	-	-	-
32	Benefit evaluators examining eligibility for Govt. run benefits	Direct	YES	-	-	-	-	YES
33	Sales engineers selling hi-tech enterprise computer and server systems	Direct	YES	-	-	YES	-	YES
34	Customer service engineers troubleshooting and repairing complex semiconductor equipment	Direct	YES	-	-	-	-	YES
35	Clinical staff and database administrators transitioning to new software for clinical trials data	Indirect	-	-	-	-	-	YES
36	Customer service helpdesk taking inbound calls for financial products	Direct	YES	-	YES	-	-	-
37	Healthcare professionals providing assisted living services for elders	Direct	YES	-	-	-	-	-
38	Customer service engineers troubleshooting and repairing complex semiconductor equipment	Direct	-	YES	-	-	-	YES
39	Customer service engineers troubleshooting and repairing complex semiconductor equipment	Direct	YES	-	-	-	-	YES
40	Insurance agents selling insurance products	Direct	-	-	YES	-	-	YES
42	Managers managing retail store chains	Direct	-	-	YES	-	-	YES
43	Plant maintenance engineers to troubleshooting production machine issues	Direct	-	-	YES	-	-	YES
44	Sales representatives upselling strategic service products	Direct	-	YES	-	-	-	-
45	Reactor operators manufacturing chemical paints	Direct	YES	-	-	-	-	-
46	Customer service engineers troubleshooting and repairing complex semiconductor equipment	Direct	-	YES	YES	-	-	-
47	Real estate agents booking mortgages and listings	Indirect	-	-	-	-	-	YES
48	Truck assemblers assembling and fabricating automobiles	Direct	YES	-	-	-	-	YES
49	Maintenance engineers repairing and maintaining petroleum pipeline feeds	Direct	YES	-	-	-	-	-
50	Machine operators fabricating mechanical parts for petroleum exploration equipment	Direct	YES	-	-	-	-	-
52	Financial analysts assessing corporate insolvency cases	Indirect	-	-	-	-	-	YES
53	Healthcare professionals providing residential care for severely disabled	Direct	YES	-	-	-	-	-
54	Sales engineers selling construction products and equipment	Direct	YES	-	-	-	-	-
55	Customer service helpdesk taking inbound calls for internet phone service	Direct	YES	-	-	-	-	-
56	Customer service helpdesk taking inbound calls for sales of financial products	Direct	-	-	YES	-	YES	-
57	Customer service helpdesk taking inbound calls for banking services	Direct	YES	-	YES	-	-	-
58	Design engineers developing complex semiconductor equipment	Direct	YES	-	-	-	-	YES
59	Customer service helpdesk taking inbound calls for upselling of financial products	Direct	YES	-	-	-	-	YES
60	Electrical engineers designing and repairing power plant equipment	Direct	YES	-	-	-	-	-
61	Sales engineers selling medical and surgical instruments	Direct	-	YES	-	-	-	-
62	Business managers developing strategies for unforeseen drop in gold prices	Direct	-	YES	-	-	-	-
63	Underground miners preparing for unexpected underground fire during mining operations	Direct	-	YES	-	-	-	-

Appendix

Appendix 27   Matrix of time-to-proficiency results reported in project cases

Includes results of only 60 selected projects
See section 4.9.1 for classification of direct/indirect indicators of proficiency
See section 0 for analysis of results of project cases in terms of time-to-proficiency
See section 4.7.1 for magnitude and scale of time-to-proficiency metrics before starting a project case

Project case ID	Project case title	Direct indicators		Training Duration Reduction	Indirect indicators
		Time-to-Proficiency reduction	Time-to-Readiness reduction		
1	Customer service engineers troubleshooting and repairing complex semiconductor equipment	67% (53 weeks to 18 weeks)	-	45% (from 13 weeks to 7 weeks)	-
2	Customer service helpdesk taking inbound calls for sales of investment products	33% (from 12 weeks to 8 weeks)	-	INCREASED (from 4 weeks to 12 weeks)	Productivity- 34% faster (achieved same productivity and quality scores in 8 weeks as the 12 weeks old graduates)
4	Software engineers developing large scale information applications (books)	-	Readiness of offshore centres Reduced by several months	-	-
5	Cybersecurity analysts analysing and identifying cyber-threats on client enterprise networks	50% (180 days to 90 days)	-	-	Producing in 30 days equivalent to previously trained people's productivity in 6 months
6	Insurance agents selling insurance products	83% (18 months to 3 months)	-	-	Strong performance equivalent to tenure staff
7	Customer service engineers troubleshooting and repairing complex semiconductor equipment	over 50% (from several months to 5 weeks)	-	-	-
8	Console operators monitoring and controlling the processes at petrochemical plants	-	(Simulated) - from several years to few days for 10% rare events	-	-
9	Service engineers troubleshooting and repairing telecommunication network equipment	-	-	13 hours per week (5 hours a week)	Reduce training development from 240 hours to 166 hours
10	Console operators monitoring and controlling the processes at petrochemical plants	-	(Simulated) - from several years to few days for 10% rare events	-	-
11	Pharmaceutical biochemists manufacturing sophisticated cancer drugs	50% (from 6 months to 15 weeks)	-	-	-
12	Managers managing retail doughnut baking stores	50% (4 weeks to 2 weeks)	-	50% (4 weeks to 2 weeks)	Consistent and better skill ratings than before
13	Claim processing executives examining and processing health insurance claims	80% (5 months to 1 month)	-	33% (from 15 weeks to 10 weeks -check)??	-
14	Sales representative selling pharmaceutical products	25% (From 24 weeks to 18 weeks)	-	-	-
15	Insurance agents selling insurance products	-	Certification: Over 50% (from X days to 90 days)	-	-
16	Console operators monitoring and controlling the processes at petrochemical plants	-	-	-	Most successful transition compared to peers (as cited by client)
17	Customer service helpdesk taking inbound calls for hotel and travel related services	-	-	25% (from 4 weeks to 3 weeks)	Strong performance equivalent to tenure staff, much shorter time to readiness (able to handle live calls out of training)
18	Managers managing supermarket chains	80% (14 months to 14 weeks)	-	50% (13 weeks to 5 -7 weeks)	-
19	Energy Corporation top executives transferring knowledge to successors	50% (as compared to time taken by veterans)	-	-	Improvement in Proficiency scores

Appendix   pg. 394

#	Role	Col3	Col4	Col5
20	Hospital medical doctors and nursing staff providing paediatrics care services	-	Ramp-up: 66% (Expected 12 months to 4 months)	-	-
21	Customer helpdesk taking inbound calls to remotely troubleshoot client computer and software issues	22% (9 weeks to 7 weeks)	-	60% (5 weeks to 2 weeks)	Higher level performance in 4 weeks compared to previous graduates, 10 points higher for graduate of 3 weeks training than graduates of 5 weeks training
22	Customer service engineers troubleshooting and repairing complex semiconductor equipment	Target 75% (from 2-3 years to 6 months) - work-in-progress	-	-	-
23	School administrator and teachers instituting school improvement programs	-	Certification: over 50% (from X years to 4 months)	-	-
24	Warehouse professionals adopting SAP for supply chain and logistics transactions	-	Accelerated ramp up of 12 sites by several months	-	-
25	Console operators monitoring and controlling the processes at petrochemical plants	-	-	-	Accelerated knowledge acquisition for new hires
26	Young military officers on leadership pathway	-	-	-	time with improved effectiveness (Young leader ready to lead sooner than before)
27	Military officers setting up a new command centre to prevent cyberterrorism	-	Ramp-up 50% (from 1 year to 6 months)	-	-
28	Biotechnology scientists strategizing business of brain implant technology for curing neurological diseases	-	(simulated) - 2 years' worth of change in 2 days for anticipated rare events	-	-
29	Machinists fabricating aircraft engine mechanical parts	40% (151 days to 92 days)	-	-	At better rate than average time to competence
30	Sales engineers selling hi-tech enterprise communication products	50% (1 years to 6 months)	-	-	Productivity- 10% increase in efficiency than past graduates, much shorter time to readiness (becoming productive sales representatives at faster speed) Time-to-proficiency - Shortened compared to veterans Performance Indicators - immediately start generating revenue (earning during 120 days of hiring)
31	Electronics technicians to troubleshoot and repair of complex Navy electronics equipment	-	-	42% (7 weeks to 4 weeks)	-
32	Benefit evaluators examining eligibility for Govt. run benefits	over 50% (from 1-3 years to few months)	-	-	Employee up to speed in shorter time with improved effectiveness (able to handle cases right away)
33	Sales engineers selling hi-tech enterprise computer and server systems	50% (26 weeks to 12 weeks for new hires and 6 weeks for experienced sellers)	-	-	Productivity - 70% higher sales by new hires over 3 quarters Productivity - 2X likely to achieve average quota than experienced sellers
34	Customer service engineers troubleshooting and repairing complex semiconductor equipment	Target 50% (1-2 years to 6 -12 months) - work-in-progress	-	-	Employee up to speed in shorter time with improved effectiveness (troubleshooting skills of engineers)
35	Clinical staff and database administrators transitioning to new software for clinical trials data	66% (1 year to 4 months)	-	-	Much shorter time to readiness (on new system)
36	Customer service helpdesk taking inbound calls for financial products	77% (90 days to 20 days)	-	50% (from X to Y)	-
37	Healthcare professionals providing assisted living services for elders	-	-	-	-
38	Customer service engineers troubleshooting and repairing complex semiconductor equipment	-	Certification: Target 50% (1-2 years to less than 1 year) - work-in-progress	-	Much shorter time to readiness
39	Customer service engineers troubleshooting and repairing complex semiconductor equipment	Over 50% (from 1-2 years to 6 months)	-	-	Much shorter time to readiness
40	Insurance agents selling insurance products	-	-	80% (5 days to 1 day)	Employee up to speed in shorter time with improved effectiveness
42	Managers managing retail store chains	-	-	87% (8 weeks to 1-week instructor-led)	Much shorter time to readiness (doing most essential tasks in XX weeks)

Appendix

#	Role			
43	Plant maintenance engineers to troubleshooting production machine issues	-	-	66% (18 weeks of instructor-led to 6 weeks on-the-job training)	Reduced time of learning
44	Sales representatives upselling strategic service products	-	Significant shorter time to sales quota	-	-
45	Reactor operators manufacturing chemical paints	50% (18-24 months to 9-12 months)	-	-	-
46	Customer service engineers troubleshooting and repairing complex semiconductor equipment	-	Certification: 80% (6 months to 6 weeks) for 80% population	66% (6 weeks to 2 weeks)	-
47	Real estate agents booking mortgages and listings	-	-	-	Reduced time of sales performance (results interrupted due to acquisition)
48	Truck assemblers assembling and fabricating automobiles	90% (from 5 days to 0.5 days)	-	-	Productivity - Improved by 66% (3 defects to 1 defect per week)
49	Maintenance engineers repairing and maintaining petroleum pipeline feeds	Target 75% (1 year to 3 months)	-	-	-
50	Machine operators fabricating mechanical parts for petroleum exploration equipment	50% (4 weeks to 2 weeks) for 95% cases	-	-	-
52	Financial analysts assessing corporate insolvency cases	-	-	-	Excelled in simulated performance, New hires up to speed on basic decision making
53	Healthcare professionals providing residential care for severely disabled	77% (9 months to 2 months)	-	-	-
54	Sales engineers selling construction products and equipment	33% (from 18 months to 12 months)	-	-	-
55	Customer service helpdesk taking inbound calls for internet phone service	over 30% (from 12 weeks to 8 weeks)	-	-	-
56	Customer service helpdesk taking inbound calls for sales of financial products	-	-	30% (from 51 days to 36 days)	Population to Proficiency - Increased from 33% to 55% (or 68%) in 10 weeks
57	Customer service helpdesk taking inbound calls for banking services	66% (6 weeks to 2 weeks) -post training	-	50% (12 weeks to 6 weeks)	-
58	Design engineers developing complex semiconductor equipment	Target 66% (from 3 years to 1 year) - work-in-progress	-	-	Much shorter time to readiness
59	Customer service helpdesk taking inbound calls for upselling of financial products	50% (3 months to 1.5 months)	-	-	Much shorter time to readiness (faster on the floor)
60	Electrical engineers designing and repairing power plant equipment	(Expected) 33% to 50% reduction (from 2 years to 1 year)	-	-	-
61	Sales engineers selling medical and surgical instruments	-	Significant shorter time to quota	-	-
62	Business managers developing strategies for unforeseen drop in gold prices	-	(Simulated) - From 10-20 years to 3 days for anticipated rare events	-	-
63	Underground miners preparing for unexpected underground fire during mining operations	-	(Simulated) - From 8-10 years to 2 days for anticipated rare events	-	-

Appendix

Appendix 28 Matrix of business benefits reported in project cases

Includes results of only 60 selected projects
See section 3.7.9 on constructing case-ordered, conceptually-ordered and descriptive matrices
See section 4.7.3 on grouping of business benefits and analysis

Project case ID	Case Title	Business gains (Business, productivity, operational metrics)
1	Customer service engineers troubleshooting and repairing complex semiconductor equipment	Cost saving - Saved travel expenses by 40%
2	Customer service helpdesk taking inbound calls for sales of investment products	-
4	Software engineers developing large scale information applications (books)	Productivity- Saved 45500 hours of 1250 people per year Productivity - saved 4.9 hours per month on an average for 62% workforce Productivity - Reduced need to take people away from job
5	Cybersecurity analysts analysing and identifying cyber-threats on client enterprise networks	-
6	Insurance agents selling insurance products	Operation Metrics - Retention improved from 10% to 25.5% (4 years) Operation Metrics - Retention rates increased by more than 50% (1st year)
7	Customer service engineers troubleshooting and repairing complex semiconductor equipment	-
8	Console operators monitoring and controlling the processes at petrochemical plants	-
9	Service engineers troubleshooting and repairing telecommunication network equipment	Business gains - Client cited phenomenal results
10	Console operators monitoring and controlling the processes at petrochemical plants	-
11	Pharmaceutical biochemists manufacturing sophisticated cancer drugs	Productivity-- Supervisor more productive
12	Managers managing retail donut baking stores	-
13	Claim processing executives examining and processing health insurance claims	Productivity - 25% increase in claim processing and 60% reduction in errors. Productivity - Reduction in errors and spills (payment errors are expected to drop by 60%)
14	Sales representative selling pharmaceutical products	Cost saving - Millions of dollars for 600 people
15	Insurance agents selling insurance products	-
16	Console operators monitoring and controlling the processes at petrochemical plants	Business gains - Client cited phenomenal results
17	Customer service helpdesk taking inbound calls for hotel and travel related services	-
18	Managers managing supermarket chains	Cost saving - Tremendous savings with OJT
19	Energy Corporation top executives transferring knowledge to successors	-
20	Hospital medical doctors and nursing staff providing paediatrics care services	Business gains - Onboarding of 400 new staff in shorter time
21	Customer helpdesk taking inbound calls to remotely troubleshoot client computer and software issues	Business gains - High customer satisfaction
22	Customer service engineers troubleshooting and repairing complex semiconductor equipment	-
23	School administrator and teachers instituting school improvement programs	-
24	Warehouse professionals adopting SAP for supply chain and logistics transactions	Business gains -12 site ready with software deployments
25	Console operators monitoring and controlling the processes at petrochemical plants	-
26	Young military officers on leadership pathway	-
27	Military officers setting up a new command centre to prevent cyberterrorism	-
28	Biotechnology scientists strategizing business of brain implant technology for curing neurological diseases	Business gains - stock 5X, market cap 3X and 0 debt
29	Machinists fabricating aircraft engine mechanical parts	Cost saving - cost avoidance of $145K in 1 year
30	Sales engineers selling hi-tech enterprise communication products	Business gains - Needed 40% fewer staff to execute the program Cost saving - Reduced cost by 24%
31	Electronics technicians to troubleshoot and repair of complex Navy electronics equipment	Productivity - Troubleshooting performance increased from 45% to 100%
32	Benefit evaluators examining eligibility for Govt. run benefits	-

#	Description	Results
33	Sales engineers selling hi-tech enterprise computer and server systems	Business gains - $1.8M additional net profit per seller Productivity - 26% higher quota attainment over 6 quarters
34	Customer service engineers troubleshooting and repairing complex semiconductor equipment	-
35	Clinical staff and database administrators transitioning to new software for clinical trials data	-
36	Customer service helpdesk taking inbound calls for financial products	-
37	Healthcare professionals providing assisted living services for elders	Business gains - improved sales and internal efficiencies
38	Customer service engineers troubleshooting and repairing complex semiconductor equipment	-
39	Customer service engineers troubleshooting and repairing complex semiconductor equipment	-
40	Insurance agents selling insurance products	-
42	Managers managing retail store chains	-
43	Plant maintenance engineers to troubleshooting production machine issues	Operation Metrics - Increased engineer's availability on-the-job
44	Sales representatives upselling strategic service products	Business gains - Shortened sales cycle substantially and increased market share
45	Reactor operators manufacturing chemical paints	Productivity - Reduction in errors and spills
46	Customer service engineers troubleshooting and repairing complex semiconductor equipment	Cost Saving - 8-10 Million dollars Operation Metrics - Reduced training load by 75% Business gains - High customer satisfaction
47	Real estate agents booking mortgages and listings	-
48	Truck assemblers assembling and fabricating automobiles	-
49	Maintenance engineers repairing and maintaining petroleum pipeline feeds	-
50	Machine operators fabricating mechanical parts for petroleum exploration equipment	-
52	Financial analysts assessing corporate insolvency cases	-
53	Healthcare professionals providing residential care for severely disabled	Operation Metrics - Retention improved from 55% to 95%
54	Sales engineers selling construction products and equipment	Operation Metrics - Retention improved in 1st year
55	Customer service helpdesk taking inbound calls for internet phone service	Operation Metrics - Retention improved in 1st year
56	Customer service helpdesk taking inbound calls for sales of financial products	Productivity - 53% drop in misdirected calls Cost saving - $682K in 1 year and 5.68M in 2 years with shorter course
57	Customer service helpdesk taking inbound calls for banking services	Operation Metrics - Cut Manager to employee ratio by 50% (1:20 to1:40) 20% reduction in new hire induction training cycle (this is not the job training) Productivity - improved 25% from 120 to 150 per day
58	Design engineers developing complex semiconductor equipment	-
59	Customer service helpdesk taking inbound calls for upselling of financial products	Operation Metrics - Retention improved to 90%
60	Electrical engineers designing and repairing power plant equipment	-
61	Sales engineers selling medical and surgical instruments	-
62	Business managers developing strategies for unforeseen drop in gold prices	-
63	Underground miners preparing for unexpected underground fire during mining operations	-

Appendix

Appendix 29 Proficiency measures matrix (excerpt)

See section 3.7.9 on constructing case-ordered, conceptually-ordered and descriptive matrices
Also see section 4.6.13) for analysis of proficiency measures

Project case ID	Project case title	Measures	Proficiency Measure and definition
1	Customer service engineers troubleshooting and repairing complex semiconductor equipment	Measure by performance specs	Measure by performance specs ("proper skills proficient enough to repair, perform trouble shootings, execute preventive maintenance, and maintain the tool to its utmost performance following with respect to customer requirements.")
4	Software engineers developing large scale information applications	Measure by behaviour change Measure by outcomes	Measure by outcomes ("you know this person is working in a contact center for example, are they achieving first time resolution of their clients' or their customers' problems, or if they are sales person, are they achieving greatest sales figures that the organisation wants, which may be more sales or maybe be greater retention of clients or whatever it maybe." Measure by behaviour change ("you are looking at measuring real learning which is behavior change. Are they doing – are they behaving and performing better?") () ()
5	Cybersecurity analysts analysing and identifying cyber-threats on client enterprise networks	Measure by observable actions Measure by activities and outcomes	Measure by observable actions ("they are evaluating you to say, "They've now been through all this. I've shown them how to do it, they've asked questions", and that way, that person can really see the improvement in that person that they've been working with, and they can evaluate it based on that." Measure by activities and outcomes ("we just knew that the customer had to be helped. That was the ultimate outcome.... So there was when an attack was actually happening, that was one thing that they had to know how to react to that, you had to know all the different items we need to do.")
7	Customer service engineers troubleshooting and repairing complex semiconductor equipment	Measure by performance specs	Measure by performance specs ("we bring a new employee (or existing promoted employee) up to speed to a pre-determined standard of technical expertise." "technicians are certified to perform vacuum technology repairs, including leak checking.")
8	Console operators monitoring and controlling the processes at petrochemical plants	Measure by observable actions	Measure by observable actions ("to maintain safe and efficient operations")
9	Service engineers troubleshooting and repairing telecommunication network equipment	Measure by KPI improvements	Measure by KPI improvements ("And their results are to speed-to-installation of new equipment, to reduce turnaround time for troubleshooting, for problem-solving, etc., etc… It was to reduce downtime, you know, to get outages corrected more quickly, so you don't lose the customer connections")
10	Console operators monitoring and controlling the processes at petrochemical plants	Measure by observable actions	Measure by observable actions ("to maintain safe and efficient operations")

Appendix 30 Code matrix (excerpt)

See section 3.7.9 on constructing case-ordered, conceptually-ordered and descriptive matrices

Mode		Interview	Interview	Interview	Interview
Case ID		40	56	57	59
Industry Group (TR)		Investment Banking & Investment Services	Investment Banking & Investment Services	Investment Banking & Investment Services	Investment Banking & Investment Services
Business Sector (TR)		Banking & Investment Services	Banking & Investment Services	Banking & Investment Services	Banking & Investment Services
Primary job Nature		Sales - Non-Technical	Customer service helpdesk	Sales - Non-Technical	Sales - Non-Technical
Critical to success Skill		Sales and negotiation	Helpdesk support	Sales and negotiation	Sales and negotiation
Complexity Rating		4. Medium-Low	5. Low	4. Medium-Low	4. Medium-Low
Case Title		Insurance agents selling insurance product	Customer service helpdesk taking inbound calls for s	Customer service helpdesk taking inbound calls for t	Customer service helpdesk taking inbound
2. REFERENCE MODEL OF PROFICIENCY	1st Level	1	1	1	0
a. TASK ANALYSIS FOR OUTCOMES	2nd Level	0	1	0	0
i. Skills, Tasks and Knowledge	3rd Level	0	0	0	0
ii. Work Analysis	3rd Level	0	0	0	0
b. PROFILE CAPABILITIES OF PERFOMERS	2nd Level	0	0	0	0
i. Performers' capability and capacity	3rd Level	0	0	0	0
c. MODEL STAR PERFORMERS' SUCCESS BEHAVIOUR	2nd Level	1	1	0	0
i. Star Performers	3rd Level	0	0	0	0
ii. Success behaviours	3rd Level	1	1	0	0
d. OPERATING CONDITIONS AND LIMITING FACTORS	2nd Level	0	1	0	0
i. Limiting factors and hurdles to accelerate proficiency	3rd Level	0	0	0	0
ii. Operational & job environment	3rd Level	0	1	0	0
3. EFFICIENT PROFICIENCY PATH	1st Level	1	1	1	1
a. SEGMENTATION WITH TASK & ACTIVITIES ANALYTICS	2nd Level	1	1	1	1
i. Segment by Complexity	3rd Level	0	1	0	0
ii. Segment by Frequency and usage	3rd Level	0	1	0	0
iii. Segment by Impact and importance	3rd Level	0	1	0	0
iv. Segment by Nature of skills	3rd Level	0	0	0	0
v. Tradeoffs	3rd Level	0	1	0	1
b. LOGICAL SEQUENCE EXPERIENCES	2nd Level	1	1	1	1
i. Sequence by Task characteristics	3rd Level	0	0	0	0
ii. Sequence by organizing principles	3rd Level	1	0	0	0
iii. Sequence for proficiency	3rd Level	1	0	1	1
c. OPTIMIZE THE PATH FOR EFFICIENCY & TIME	2nd Level	0	1	1	1
i. Optimize with Lean process improvement	3rd Level	1	1	0	0
ii. Optimize with multiple delivery channels	3rd Level	0	1	1	1
iii. Optimize for time-spaced activities	3rd Level	1	0	0	0

Appendix 31 Descriptive meta-matrix for themes and sub-themes arranged by complexity (example)

See section 3.7.9 on constructing case-ordered, conceptually-ordered and descriptive matrices

Analysis strategies	Very High complexity	High complexity	Medium-High complexity	Medium complexity	Summary / Analytics notes
ANALYSIS >> ENVIRONMENT	Analysis of available training resources (2) Analysis of headcount resources (1) Analysis of limiting factors, beliefs and mindsets (1) Analysis of operational and job environment (6) Analysis of personal capacity and capabilities (0) Barriers to achieve proficiency (0) Example of thorough need assessment (0) Thorough need assessment (0)	Analysis of available training resources (2) Analysis of headcount resources (2) Analysis of limiting factors, beliefs and mindsets (7) Analysis of operational and job environment (7) Analysis of personal capacity and capabilities (3) Barriers to achieve proficiency (0) Example of thorough need assessment (1) Thorough need assessment (3)	Analysis of available training resources (4) Analysis of headcount resources (2) Analysis of limiting factors, beliefs and mindsets (1) Analysis of operational and job environment (9) Analysis of personal capacity and capabilities (0) Barriers to achieve proficiency (0) Example of thorough need assessment (0) Thorough need assessment (0)	Analysis of available training resources (1) Analysis of headcount resources (1) Analysis of limiting factors, beliefs and mindsets (4) Analysis of operational and job environment (4) Analysis of personal capacity and capabilities (0) Barriers to achieve proficiency (0) Example of thorough need assessment (0) Thorough need assessment (0)	At higher side of the complexity, analysis of operational and job environment is critical because environment is dynamic and changing. Also there is trend of analyzing beliefs and mindset that can potentially hamper the proficiency. However, on the lower side, more analysis of available training resources as the environment becomes more predictable.
ANALYSIS >> JOB ANALYSIS >> PERFORMERS	Analysis of capabilities of performers (0) Analysis of Job roles & levels (1) Analysis of self-assessment & prior skills (1)	Analysis of capabilities of performers (0) Analysis of Job roles & levels (5) Analysis of self-assessment & prior skills (2)	Analysis of capabilities of performers (1) Analysis of Job roles & levels (0) Analysis of self-assessment & prior skills (2)	Analysis of capabilities of performers (1) Analysis of Job roles & levels (0) Analysis of self-assessment & prior skills (0)	At higher side of the complexity, understanding job roles and levels and associated expectations with a given job role is important while at lower side it becomes importance to understand the pre-existing capabilities of the performers.
ANALYSIS >> JOB ANALYSIS >> MEASURES	Analysis of business goals & outcomes (3) Analysis of Job goals (3) Analysis of Proficiency statements (0) Baseline time to proficiency numbers (0)	Analysis of business goals & outcomes (2) Analysis of Job goals (5) Analysis of Proficiency statements (2) Baseline time to proficiency numbers (1)	Analysis of business goals & outcomes (0) Analysis of Job goals (0) Analysis of Proficiency statements (0) Baseline time to proficiency numbers (2)	Analysis of business goals & outcomes (7) Analysis of Job goals (1) Analysis of Proficiency statements (0) Baseline time to proficiency numbers (1)	Analysis of outcomes and job goals is critical across all complexity levels
ANALYSIS >> JOB ANALYSIS >> OUTCOMES	Analysis of Job performance (1) Analysis of outcomes of star performers (0) Analysis of payback or value of learning (0)	Analysis of Job performance (5) Analysis of outcomes of star performers (2) Analysis of payback or value of learning (0)	Analysis of Job performance (2) Analysis of outcomes of star performers (0) Analysis of payback or value of learning (1)	Analysis of Job performance (10) Analysis of outcomes of star performers (5) Analysis of payback or value of learning (1)	Analysis of job performance and outcomes of the star performers is critical on lower side of the complexity probably because of more defined nature of measurements and outcomes. At higher side of the complexity, such analysis becomes difficult.
ANALYSIS >> JOB ANALYSIS >> TASKS & SKILLS	Analysis of skills required in cases (0) Analysis of tasks, skills and knowledge (8) Analyze task relationships and dependencies (0) Cognitive work analysis (0) Decompose a complex skill into part-tasks (0)	Analysis of skills required in cases (0) Analysis of tasks, skills and knowledge (10) Analyze task relationships and dependencies (1) Cognitive work analysis (1) Decompose a complex skill into part-tasks (1)	Analysis of skills required in cases (0) Analysis of tasks, skills and knowledge (3) Analyze task relationships and dependencies (0) Cognitive work analysis (0) Decompose a complex skill into part-tasks (2)	Analysis of skills required in cases (0) Analysis of tasks, skills and knowledge (2) Analyze task relationships and dependencies (0) Cognitive work analysis (0) Decompose a complex skill into part-tasks (0)	Tasks, skills and knowledge is important at all levels while at higher side of the complexity it is key given the fuzzy nature of the skills.

ANALYSIS >> TASK ANALYTICS	Analysis of activities analytics (0) Analysis of common or base skills (0) Analysis of complexity (2) Analysis of critical volume (80-20 rule) (0) Analysis of data to define scope (0) Analysis of difficulty (1) Analysis of error-proneness (0) Analysis of frequency and usage (1) Analysis of importance & criticality (4)	Analysis of activities analytics (2) Analysis of common or base skills (0) Analysis of complexity (5) Analysis of critical volume (80-20 rule) (0) Analysis of data to define scope (1) Analysis of difficulty (0) Analysis of error-proneness (1) Analysis of frequency and usage (6) Analysis of importance & criticality (3)	Analysis of activities analytics (1) Analysis of common or base skills (0) Analysis of complexity (2) Analysis of critical volume (80-20 rule) (0) Analysis of data to define scope (0) Analysis of difficulty (0) Analysis of error-proneness (1) Analysis of frequency and usage (0) Analysis of importance & criticality (0)	Analysis of activities analytics (0) Analysis of common or base skills (0) Analysis of complexity (1) Analysis of critical volume (80-20 rule) (0) Analysis of data to define scope (2) Analysis of difficulty (1) Analysis of error-proneness (1) Analysis of frequency and usage (1) Analysis of importance & criticality (1)	Importance and criticality of a skill or task becomes important on higher side of the complexity and drives the design. In addition, analysis of complexity and frequency becomes key to reducing the scope. There do not appear to be many references on any major analysis on the lower side of the complexity
ANALYSIS >> CURRENT MODEL	Alignment to corporate statement (0) Analysis of current curriculum (1) Analysis of delivery modes (2) ANALYSIS OF INEFFICIENCIES OF CURRENT MODE (9)	Alignment to corporate statement (0) Analysis of current curriculum (0) Analysis of delivery modes (0) ANALYSIS OF INEFFICIENCIES OF CURRENT MODE (86)	Alignment to corporate statement (0) Analysis of current curriculum (0) Analysis of delivery modes (0) ANALYSIS OF INEFFICIENCIES OF CURRENT MODE (8)	Alignment to corporate statement (0) Analysis of current curriculum (2) Analysis of delivery modes (0) ANALYSIS OF INEFFICIENCIES OF CURRENT MODE (33)	At higher side of the complexity, analyzing current model of curriculum is critical while at lower side, the curriculum is more or less deemed acceptable.
ANALYSIS >> MODEL EXPERTS	Analyze and map out how experts operate (CTA) (17) Analyze components of expertise (2) Analyze how experts learned a task (0) Analyze success behavior of star performers (reference model) (2) Analyze variance between good, solid and star performers (0) Identify top or star performers (0) Observe off-normal activities or exceptions (0)	Analyze and map out how experts operate (CTA) (24) Analyze components of expertise (2) Analyze how experts learned a task (1) Analyze success behavior of star performers (reference model) (3) Analyze variance between good, solid and star performers (1) Identify top or star performers (0) Observe off-normal activities or exceptions (0)	Analyze and map out how experts operate (CTA) (0) Analyze components of expertise (0) Analyze how experts learned a task (2) Analyze success behavior of star performers (reference model) (1) Analyze variance between good, solid and star performers (0) Identify top or star performers (0) Observe off-normal activities or exceptions (0)	Analyze and map out how experts operate (CTA) (6) Analyze components of expertise (0) Analyze how experts learned a task (1) Analyze success behavior of star performers (reference model) (12) Analyze variance between good, solid and star performers (0) Identify top or star performers (0) Observe off-normal activities or exceptions (1)	Analysis of how expert operates is key analysis at higher side of the complexity due to several unknowns at higher side.

Appendix 32 Example of case-ordered conceptually clustered matrix (except only)

See section 3.7.9 on constructing case-ordered, conceptually-ordered and descriptive matrices

Case title	Business sector	Drivers (combined)	Drivers (Analytics)	Context (company, business, environment, job type, challenge)	Context (Quotes)	Traditional training challenges	Measures	Proficiency Definition
Customer service engineers troubleshooting and repairing complex semiconductor equipment	Technology Equipment	Speed drivers: "business needs is typically around three to six months; the engineers should be proficient enough in time to readiness for him to be deployed in the field. That's the main target for now." ..."as per customer requirement, all engineers need to undergo formal training and gets to be certified before they are allowed to maintain the tools on the customer site."	NOT MENTIONED: Time/speed drivers due to customer expectations or pressures and need to get engineers ready with skills in shorter time to be able to support customers. Also longer time in training and long TTP is a contributor. Skill drivers due to engineers not being able to perform the expected tasks proficiently.	A high-tech semiconductor equipment company in high paced technology business pressed hard to keep customers' production running and keeping equipment uptime commitments. Required to develop proficient skills of its engineers in repair and service of equipment in shorter time.	as per customer requirement, all engineers need to undergo formal training and gets to be certified before they are allowed to maintain the tools on the customer site.... They need to perform the maintenance of the tool, preventive maintenance, troubleshooting the tool if there are some issues on the tool, maintaining the tool as per customer requirement.... business needs is typically around three to six months, the engineers should be proficient enough in time to readiness for him to be proficient enough to be deployed in the field. That's the main target for now.	ineffective OJT and coaching, long cycle, instructor-centered, inefficient design	Measure by performance specs	"proper skills proficient enough to repair, perform trouble shootings, execute preventive maintenance, and maintain the tool to its utmost performance following with respect to customer requirements."
Offshoring - Software engineers developing large scale information applications	Software & IT Services	Speed drivers: "And we recruited people rapidly into those development centres.... 1,800 in 15 months" Time drivers: "One was that the formal structured training programs just took too long, just were taking too much time over too long." Cost drivers: "we're going to have to reduce these training programs from five days to three days. And if	Time/speed drivers and skill drivers because business required to develop skills of newly hired 1800 software engineers to proficiency in shorter time frame due to rapid hiring and replacement of existing workforce.	An information technology company with 65 software development centres spread worldwide with 5000 software developers offshored 1800 software developers to low-cost countries replacing existing expert workforce. Formal	"And the company had 65 software development centres spread around the world.... We had about – say about 5,000 software developers and database centre managers. And the company took a decision to restructure its development, to reduce those numbers of centres and to move some of them to lower cost areas. So we established a big development centre in Thailand, called Company R Software	content heavy, costly, long cycle	Measure by behavior change Measure by outcomes	"you are looking at measuring real learning which is behavior change. Are they doing – are they behaving and performing better?" "you know this person is working in a contact center for example, are they achieving first time resolution of their clients' or their customers' problems, or if they are sales person, are they achieving greatest sales figures that the organisation wants, which may be

Appendix pg. 403

		we do that, there will be huge cost savings." "Increasing number of jobs that require dealing with ambiguity and decision-making and higher cognitive skills" Skill drivers: "We were replacing vastly experienced people across Europe and North America"	training was too long and coaching with leaving experts was not feasible. Required to develop skills of offshored developers to the desired proficiency in the shorter timeframe before existing experts are gone.	Thailand in Bangkok, and a big development centre in Beijing. And we recruited people rapidly into those development centres. Now in Bangkok, we recruited 1,500 software – no, 1,800 software developers and database experts, technical experts, 1,800 in 15 months.... One was that the formal structured training programs just took too long, just were taking too much time over too long.		more sales or maybe be greater retention of clients or whatever it maybe."
Cybersecurity analysts analysing and identifying cyber-threats on client enterprise networks	Technology Equipment	Time drivers: "right now it takes about a year"	Time/speed mainly because it was taking long for employees to reach desired proficiency. Skill drivers are implicit.	A hi-tech internet infrastructure and cyber security company required new engineers to come up to speed in highly technical skills in shorter time.	a very high-tech company focused on internet infrastructure and cyber security….and then that continued to evolve into, "Well, we really think if we would do everything in a system, right now it takes about a year." And I went, "Whoa, that's a long time to wait for people to be ready to go to work".	long cycle	Measure by observable actions Measure by activities and outcomes	"they are evaluating you to say, "They've now been through all this. I've shown them how to do it, they've asked questions", and that way, that person can really see the improvement in that person that they've been working with, and they can evaluate it based on that." "we just knew that the customer had to be helped. That was the ultimate outcome.… So there was when an attack was actually happening, that was one thing that they had to know how to react to that, you had to know all the different items we need to do."

Appendix

Appendix 33   Member (participant) checking questionnaire

See section 3.8.7 for member (participation) checking method

Question #	Question
1.	During Aug 2014 to June 2015, during an interview with the researcher, you described a project case in which you and your team implemented certain specific training / learning strategies to shorten time-to-proficiency of employees. On the scale of 1 to 10, 10 being highest, how well do you think that the aggregate model represents the project case you explained to the researcher?
2.	Based on the response to the question #1, please highlight the concepts, strategies or elements of the model, which you think has represented your project case accurately.
3.	Based on the response to the question #1, please highlights the concepts, strategies of elements of the model, which you think did <u>not</u> represent your project case accurately.
4.	Does the proposed model miss out anything of importance to you when it comes to accelerating time-to-proficiency? Is there anything you strongly applied in your project but do not see it in the aggregated model? Please explain.
5.	On the scale of 1 to 10, 10 being highest how well you see your general viewpoint and concept of accelerating speed to proficiency in the aggregated model explained in previous pages. Please explain.
6.	If there is a chance to lead another project in your settings with a goal to accelerate proficiency of specific group of employees, do you think that you could use the previous model with reasonable success. If yes, indicate which sections of the model, in particular, you think you could be applied to other settings.
7.	Did you face any issue understanding any of the following? If yes, please highlight the issue face and how you suggest it could be improved. a. The high level visual, conceptual model of the 6 concepts b. Written summary of the 6 concepts c. Detailed conceptual model (both tabular view and transfer function view)
8.	Do you have any concerns, inputs, or feedback regarding the findings described in the preceding pages? It may be related to any aspect of explanation, language, or visual representations or otherwise. Is there any specific aspects you do not see reported in this document but would like the researcher to investigate and report?

Appendix 34 Example of data triangulation of interview codes with document codes

See section 3.8.3 for methodology on data triangulation using project case documents

Overarching themes	DEVELOP REAL-WORLD LEARNING EXPERIENCES		DELIVER INTEGRATED INTERVENTIONS	
	First cycle codes (with quotes)	Code hierarchy	Codes (with Quotes)	Code hierarchy
From Interview	**Real-world cases and scenarios** ("there were actual insolvency cases that we had held") **Library of scenarios** ("then we tried to build a very rich description of a number of cases, real cases that we heard about") **Library of scenarios** ("we just had to collect cases") **Piece-meal scenarios** ("I think the case describes the circumstances and then once you've understood the circumstances at this particular point in time you have to make a decision about the future of the company") **Case-based learning** ("within the firms themselves, their training of junior practitioners was also around recent cases") **Variations and variety** ("Within that case they have a lot of problems that arise") **Spaced scenarios** (over three days or they had something like four cases a day.") **Distributed and time spaced learning experience** ("When we were using IN System in training experiments, that's how we deployed IN System over three days or they had something like four cases a day.")	DEVELOPMENT >> FAILURE CYCLES DEVELOPMENT >> SCENARIO-BASED SIMULATION DEVELOPMENT >> SPACING AND CHUNKING	**Immediate feedback during training** ("we try to provide feedback at the end of each stage. Yeah, we sometimes had a short commentary from an expert, which said what they would have done in the circumstances.")	DELIVERY >> REFLECTIONS AND FEEDBACK
From Document	**Real-world cases and scenarios** (@validate that the cases descriptions were authentic and that the information was sufficient for forming opinions and appropriate conclusions for each stage.) **Piece-meal scenarios** ("Cases that are able to be broken into stages are appropriate for the IN system.")	DEVELOPMENT >> SCENARIO-BASED SIMULATION	**Targeted and focused reflection** ("IN System also requires learners to reflect on their proposed solutions.") **Attention and deeper focus** ("The first element is attention. Activities that are interesting and engaging that promote focus will lead to stronger encoding in the learners' memory.") **Immediate feedback during learning** ("Following the 'make a recommendation task' at each stage of a case, learners are presented with the advice of an expert on the current state of the case.") **Conversation and discussions** (The chat feature allows learners to discuss their recommendation with others)	DELIVERY >> PARTICIPATORY GROUP LEARNING DELIVERY >> REFLECTIONS AND FEEDBACK DELIVERY >> ACTIVE AND IMMERSIVE LEARNING

Appendix 35 Thematic prevalence of six practices arranged by contextual variables

See section 3.7.9 on constructing prevalence matrix
See section 3.8.5 on method of using prevalence analysis to assess generalizability and transferability of themes

	Contextual Variable	Number of projects	1. BUSINESS-DRIVEN PROFICIENCY	2. PROFICIENCY REFERENCE MAP	3. EFFICIENT PROFICIENCY PATH	4. ACCELERATED CONTEXTUAL EXPERIENCES	5. ACTIVE EMOTIONAL IMMERSION	6. PROFICIENCY ECO-SYSTEM
Across Complexity	1. High	9	100%	100%	56%	100%	100%	78%
	2. Medium-High	22	91%	95%	91%	100%	95%	100%
	3. Medium	9	89%	100%	89%	100%	100%	89%
	4. Medium-Low	14	100%	93%	100%	86%	100%	100%
	5. Low	6	83%	67%	100%	100%	100%	100%
	COMPLEXITY LEVELS AVERAGE		**93%**	**91%**	**87%**	**97%**	**99%**	**93%**
Across primary job roles	Scientific or Development	5	100%	100%	80%	100%	100%	80%
	Strategic Management, Leadership	4	100%	100%	25%	100%	100%	75%
	Management consulting	1	100%	100%	100%	100%	100%	100%
	Technical or Engineering	21	90%	95%	90%	100%	95%	100%
	Managerial	3	100%	100%	100%	100%	100%	100%
	Medical, Healthcare	3	67%	100%	100%	100%	100%	100%
	Production, Manufacturing	3	100%	100%	67%	100%	100%	67%
	Financial services	2	100%	100%	100%	100%	100%	100%
	Sales - Non-Technical	8	100%	88%	100%	75%	100%	100%
	Sales - Technical	3	100%	100%	100%	100%	100%	100%
	Training or Education	1	100%	100%	100%	100%	100%	100%
	Assembly	1	100%	100%	100%	100%	100%	100%
	Customer service helpdesk	4	75%	75%	100%	100%	100%	100%
	Warehouse	1	100%	0%	100%	100%	100%	100%
	JOB ROLES AVERAGE		**95%**	**90%**	**90%**	**98%**	**100%**	**94%**
Across critical to success skills	Innovation and design	5	100%	100%	80%	100%	100%	80%
	Strategic thinking	4	100%	100%	25%	100%	100%	75%
	Business analysis	1	100%	100%	100%	100%	100%	100%
	Complex troubleshooting	12	100%	92%	100%	100%	92%	100%
	Project execution	3	100%	100%	100%	100%	100%	100%
	Technical Problem solving	6	67%	100%	67%	100%	100%	100%
	Supervisory	3	100%	100%	100%	100%	100%	100%
	Medical and psychological care	3	67%	100%	100%	100%	100%	100%
	Precision machining	3	100%	100%	67%	100%	100%	67%
	Financial analysis	2	100%	100%	100%	100%	100%	100%

	Sales and negotiation	11	100%	91%	100%	82%	100%	100%
	Teaching and training	1	100%	100%	100%	100%	100%	100%
	Assembly	1	100%	100%	100%	100%	100%	100%
	Helpdesk support	4	75%	75%	100%	100%	100%	100%
	Data processing	1	100%	0%	100%	100%	100%	100%
	CTS SKILLS AVERAGE		**94%**	**91%**	**89%**	**99%**	**99%**	**95%**
Across economic sectors	BASIC MATERIALS	3	100%	100%	67%	100%	100%	33%
	CONSUMER NON-CYCLICALS	5	100%	80%	100%	100%	100%	100%
	ENERGY	7	71%	100%	71%	100%	100%	100%
	FINANCIALS	10	90%	90%	100%	90%	100%	100%
	HEALTHCARE	8	88%	100%	88%	100%	100%	88%
	INDUSTRIALS	7	100%	100%	86%	86%	100%	100%
	MILITARY/ GOVERNMENT	3	100%	100%	33%	100%	100%	100%
	TECHNOLOGY	14	100%	93%	100%	100%	93%	100%
	TELECOMMUNICATION SERVICES	2	100%	100%	100%	100%	100%	100%
	UTILITY	1	100%	100%	100%	100%	100%	100%
	ECONOMIC SECTORS AVERAGE		**94%**	**96%**	**83%**	**97%**	**99%**	**91%**
Across business sectors	Chemicals	1	100%	100%	100%	100%	100%	100%
	Mineral Resources	2	100%	100%	50%	100%	100%	0%
	Automobiles & Auto Parts	1	100%	100%	100%	100%	100%	100%
	Cyclical Consumer Services	1	100%	0%	100%	100%	100%	100%
	Food & Beverages	1	100%	100%	100%	100%	100%	100%
	Retailers	2	100%	100%	100%	100%	100%	100%
	Energy - Fossil Fuels	7	71%	100%	71%	100%	100%	100%
	Banking & Investment Services	6	83%	83%	100%	100%	100%	100%
	Insurance	3	100%	100%	100%	100%	100%	100%
	Real Estate	1	100%	100%	100%	0%	100%	100%
	Healthcare Services	4	75%	100%	100%	100%	100%	100%
	Pharmaceuticals & Medical Research	4	100%	100%	75%	100%	100%	75%
	Industrial & Commercial Services	3	100%	100%	100%	67%	100%	100%
	Industrial Goods	3	100%	100%	67%	100%	100%	100%
	Transportation	1	100%	100%	100%	100%	100%	100%
	Government / Military	3	100%	100%	33%	100%	100%	100%
	Software & IT Services	2	100%	100%	100%	100%	100%	100%
	Technology Equipment	12	100%	92%	100%	100%	92%	100%
	Telecommunications Services	2	100%	100%	100%	100%	100%	100%
	Utilities	1	100%	100%	100%	100%	100%	100%
	BUSINESS SECTORS AVERAGE		**96%**	**94%**	**90%**	**93%**	**100%**	**94%**

Appendix 36   Feedback from expert focus group

See section 3.4.3 on phase 3 data collection using expert focus group
See section 3.8.9 on method of using expert focus group to validate research findings

Feedback Elements	Expert Focus Group Feedback Quotes
General impression of the model	Thorough model (Expert 1) ... The model strikes me as solid (Expert 1). The six core concepts as representative of concepts I discussed in my case examples (Expert 2). Transfer function view on page 11 has elements that seem a little more familiar (Expert 2). Recognise inputs and outputs as a familiar model characteristic (Expert 2). 'proficiency eco-system concept most accurately represents my case examples in this model' [Expert 2] Model is very good (Expert 3). Eco system [concept] is very good (Expert 3). Very effective and saves time for the project manager/trainer (Expert 3).
Elements of model that represented the strategies in practice	Reflective of my input (Expert 1). I recognise my view points, philosophy, and strategies scattered throughout the findings and models, but not in any unified way (Expert 2). Strongly recognise - measures of proficiency; baseline time to proficiency; learning in the context of the job; focused reflection and feedback; task analytics and segmentation; optimise the proficiency path; structured monitoring (Expert 2). Up front explain the path, show the metrics and drive for results (Expert 3) Goes way beyond a 'check list' to a competency of job (Expert 3). Represented almost all of the strategies that we have employed (Expert 5).
Elements of the model that did not represent the strategies in practice	The accelerators and blockers of high performance (Expert 1). Learning approaches that mirror the actual work environment (Expert 1). Do not strongly recognise - JIT Performance Support Systems; active and emotional immersion; operating conditions; understanding the cause of a long time to proficiency (Expert 2). Drive for results is a team effort (Expert 3). Longer time to proficiency is not the function of several training and non-training factors (Expert 4). Proficiency is defined and measured for a job as a whole (Expert 4). Focus on work analysis as opposed to task analysis for a given job (Expert 4). Learner profiling and preparation (Expert 4). Multiple level assessment (Expert 4). While the lean optimization of the path is a great way to go, we rarely get to do that in practice – once the learning path is done, the client is usually not wanting to spend time and money on further optimization. It should be done (and in the model) – we just get to do it (Expert 5).
Potential areas which could be extended in the model	Role of coaching / expert feedback within the simulations (Expert 1). Not strongly enough emphasise the importance of linking time-to-proficiency to the business or strategic goals of the organisation (Expert 2). Strategies for getting the business to really understand what proficiency means (Expert 3). Everything is covered to an extent. The concept that training or learning a priori as preparation to working is not always applied in my work with clients (Expert 4). Just more detail – but related to the Reference Model (Expert 5).
Extent to which model reflects viewpoint and approaches in practice	This work reflects how I think about accelerating time to proficiency as a learning design leader (Expert 1). I do find some accuracy in the 26 "strategies" (Expert 2). Twenty-six is a rather large number (Expert 2). I can't say that all 26 strategies were present in each of the time-to-proficiency projects I worked on (Expert 2). Enjoyed his [meta] questions in each section. This is excellent (Expert 3). Generally the thesis represents my experiences/cases very closely (Expert 4). 9.5 of 10 - very similar to my approach (Expert 5).
Extent to which model is useful and applicable in other contexts to reduce time-to-proficiency with reasonable success	The model lends itself to a checklist which could increase the odds of such an effort succeeding (Expert 1). Elements of the model would find use in a future proficiency project (Expert 1). Overarching model would not guide me in such a project (Expert 2). Model enriches best practices that I have seen (Expert 3). It aligns closely with the model I have worked on and developed (advocated in other places) (Expert 4). For the most part, yes. I'd say the biggest organisational stumbling block relates to the eco-system – the manager/coach is critical to success; however, many managers don't coach well or at all. So a key to the success of this approach is support for manager coaching through change management, expectation setting, manager

		training on how to implement this, and technology tools to make it easier for them and for tracking and accountability. If this piece is not in place – the rest of the model is unlikely to succeed (Expert 5).
	Extent to which model can be understood easily in practice	*Clear model that is easily understandable (Expert 3).* *Written descriptions of the six core concepts muddled and confusing (Expert 2). Advise striving for clearer use of language to define these concepts (Expert 2)* *Differentiate between drivers and metrics (Expert 2).* *Very clear model (Expert 5).*
	Areas of improvement / extension	*Helpful to have the components of the model validated by direct research / experimentation (Expert 1).* *Refining the grammatical presentation of the models and strategies (Expert 2).* *Illustrating the validity of a hypothetical model by showing how it is applied to a case example (Expert 2).* *At times it is a bit too general (Expert 3). He can be stronger in 'what does success look like.' (Expert 3).* *A lessons learned session would be helpful (Expert 3).* *Some research and evidence that this approach really works and leads to ROI (Expert 5). Good have more detail on HOW to implement this model (Expert 5).*

Appendix 37 Explaining a project case using 6/24 framework of strategies

See section 3.8.10 for method of rick and thick description as a validation method
See section 5.6.1 for conceptual model and 5.6.2 framework used to describe following project case

Note: Sam, Project Leader 56, made all quotes used in this section. Attributions to project leader are omitted from the narrative for the purposes of describing the case and to avoid repetition of same name. Quotes are integrated into the narrative by the researcher.

Case title: Customer service representatives in a Fortune 500 financial company providing advisory and sales service for insurance and financial products

Project case ID: 56

Contextual variables

Economic sector: financials
Business sector: banking and investment services
Industry group: banking services
Job type: sales non-technical
Skill critical-to-success: sales and negotiation
Complexity of job or skill: medium-low

Organisation: The organisation was a US-based Fortune 500 financial services company employing 28000 employees. They were offering banking, investing and insurance products to 10 million members. The company employed direct marketing employing its own employees rather than agents and most of the business was conducted over internet and phone. The target group of employees was customer services representatives taking inbound from and making outbound calls to their customers for products and services.

Target employees: The target audience was new customer service representatives who took inbound calls from members regarding new products and services or serviced existing accounts. They were responsible for sales and service. '*This target audience were new hires with less than 2-4 weeks on the job (having just completed new employee orientation, licensing, and basic training)*'.

Target skills: The new hires needed to develop advisory skills, conversational skills, channel skills and product technical skills. 'In the auto insurance new hire program, the new employee has to learn how to have the conversation, understand what advice they need to provide the member, and effectively use the correct system for fulfillment'. Multi-tasking in this role is critical, as speaking, typing and evaluating information provided by the customer must all be done at the same time. Complexity varied among pipelines. '*Some of the pipelines are very difficult due to the complexity of the product or service provided.*'

Magnitude and scale of the problem: This project targeted one insurance product pipeline in which new hires were required to attend ten weeks of training program just to be able to start doing the job. Time-to-proficiency of new hires spanned several weeks. In a year the organisation was training 1200 employees in this program translating to a large sum of money being invested in the program. Project leader mentioned: '*Time to proficiency is a key metric for this population*'.

Business drivers: The project was driven mainly by long length-of-training pipeline which was a time-related driver and the need for rapid readiness following raid hiring sprints, which was a speed-related driver. 'New hire pipelines, which are multi-week learning courses built around the products or services the [executive] will support…. The volatility of markets means when business surges, we need qualified people on the phones to meet member demand. Having a course which was long and slow in getting people to proficiency was not appealing to the business.'

Project goal: The goal of the project was to get faster time- to- proficiency of new hires. A secondary goal was to streamline multi-week courses, making them more effective and efficient, reduce the length of the learning solution and improve the quality of the graduate.

Challenges of the previous solution: Previous training program design was ineffective because it covered everything whether an event was happening or not. The subsequent analysis indicated that '20 percent of calls were responsible for 80 percent of the volume' while the previous program was targeting to train people on everything. Therefore, it led to retention issues. 'We were teaching people how to do something, how to handle a call that they may get one or two of those calls a year, and they'll never remember it when that call finally comes.' The previous training program was too content-heavy. 'There's no way that this learner is going to remember all of this content. It's just way too much.' The previous model was instructor-focused relying heavily on lecture formats. 'In the old version of the program, it was a lot of lecture. You had somebody standing in front of the room talking and sometimes demonstrating how to fulfill something, and then we would turn them loose to work on it.' The program was topic-based. 'topic-based learning sessions were too much'. Due to massive content the most important things for the jobs were getting out of focus. 'We had so much content in there that the real critical things got lost in the content. It became very difficult for the learner to really focus on what is it that's really important, what is it I really need to know to hit the ground running when I go out on a production floor.' Further, the program 'didn't validate trainees' proficiency'. Finally, the pipelines for new hires ended up as multi-week learning courses which resulted in long time-to-proficiency of new hires.

New solution and strategies described with 6/24 framework: To explain the interplay of strategies used in the project case, the 6/24 framework of six practices and twenty-four strategies is used as a structural framework to assess how well original case is explained by the framework.

Practices		Strategies	Practices employed in the project case
P1	Defining business-driven proficiency measures	P1.1 Starting with end in mind- Upfront definition and measures of proficiency in terms of business outcomes and link it to business needs	The organisation defined the proficiency measures in terms of business outcomes and results. Performance specs were used as indicators for the proficiency. The criteria used to evaluate the new people were same as used for seasoned performers. 'TTP [time-to-proficiency] was determined by the business using the same criteria they used in evaluating incumbent performers. It consisted of eleven key metrics and measures. A performer who met certain thresholds was identified by the business as having achieved proficiency.' Business pre-defined the proficiency upfront in terms of the business outcomes. 'For example in auto insurance new hire, there are seven key metrics that they use'. Consistently was expressed as the key piece of proficiency. 'There are three times that they're evaluated against those metrics and if they consistently hit those thresholds, then we would say that they're proficient'.
		P1.2 Baseline current time-to-proficiency and establish new time-to-proficiency goals based on business drivers	The time-to-proficiency of the previous program was baselined. Project leader and his team 'immediately put process in place to measure the graduates of the old program and how long it took them to achieve time-to-proficiency'. The time-to-proficiency of new program was measured using same metrics and was compared with previous program. 'We then took those same metrics and we started to apply those to the graduates of the new program to see if we were able to get them to achieve time-to-proficiency at a faster pace'.
P2	Developing a proficiency reference map	P2.1 Conduct upfront comprehensive work analysis drawn from the outcomes	The program was already in place but was leading to longer time-to-proficiency. Therefore, elements of work analysis, performer's capabilities and capacities, success behaviours of exemplary performers were available or fine-tuned from previous program.
		P2.2 Profile capabilities and capacities of the job performers	

Appendix

	P2.3	Model success behaviours of exemplary performers	
	P2.4	Understand job operating conditions and environment influences	Overall job conditions were analysed from previous solutions that was existing before starting this new initiative. Market conditions and job environment such as regulatory protocols were particularly analysed in which job was operating. 'But the big one we ran into because of increased compliance means more documentation, more things from regulations surrounding this.' The job was operating within complex socio-psychological interactions with the client. 'they're trying to go from an emotional end point. We're not just doing the balance sheet; we're also trying to find out where they have passion around their life.'
	P2.5	Analyse roadblocks and hindrances that lead to longer time-to-proficiency	The complexity of interactions made lack of abilities like right emotional quotient and empathy with the client as key roadblock. 'On the adviser side is extremely complex, systems, behavioral economics. It's also that psychological aspect of really finding out who this person loves and who they love and how they feel about it …' Project leader also assessed 'do they have enough infrastructure?' Old training model and curriculum was analysed and found to very inefficient. 'it was "training" in a sense I'm going to tell you everything you need to know about our business, about people, and then we're going to unleash you and you have to figure out how to work with people.'
P3		Sequencing an efficient proficiency path	
	P3.1	Segment tasks and activities based on characteristics with analytics	Data analytics from historical records as well as qualitative feedback from managers was gathered to understand trends on activities and tasks. 'We pulled information and data from our quality control group and we also talked to managers out on the floor of those things that are activities that they found themselves having coach and correct people so continually.' The analysis led to the segmentation of tasks by criticality or error-prone tasks. 'Through that, we created the list of critical mistakes'. These error-prone tasks were categorised for impact. 'It really is looking at those things that have the greatest impact when that mistake is made'. Focusing on the segment of most important tasks was the key to the shortening time-to-proficiency. Focus on the more important things and not have to worry about everything else that was in the old version of the program. That I think is probably our greatest asset in getting toward time-to-proficiency.' Further, they used 80%-20% rule for segmenting tasks by frequency. 'In the new course we focused on making them experts on the 20% of call-types that represented 80% of the call volumes we received. Segmentation was also done by nature of skills and trade-offs like what must be trained on and what can be done through performance support systems. 'then taught them how to look up the answers for the other 80% of call volumes which only represented 20% of the call volumes.
	P3.2	Create logical sequence of experiences in form of complete path	Once tasks segmentation was done, a logical sequence of experience is created based on frequency of events. They focused on most occurring calls. 'We want to teach them to be an expert in the calls that they get a lot.' By doing so the overall inventory of calls or events one needed to master was much smaller.
	P3.3	Optimise the proficiency path for efficiency and time saving	The sequence thus created was optimised by removing waste and non-value-added content. Project leader considered two factors as the biggest ones that led to shorter time-to-proficiency. One is removing waste and non-value added content and second is training people only on most frequent calls. 'being able to say let's eliminate a lot of this content and make them an expert on that call-types that they get the most of and focus on that only and just teach them how to find and research the answers of others, that was probably the biggest thing for helping us toward time-to-proficiency.'

Appendix

P4	**Manufacturing accelerated contextual experiences**		Further, the proficiency path was optimised by using multiple modalities and delivery channels. Project leader attributed project success to this factor as: 'more that you can offer modalities for people to get information or have questions answered quickly, the greater the chance are that you can shorten that time-to-proficiency cycle'.
		P4.1	Assign performers on authentic job activities that allow practice on generating job-specific outcomes	A key focus was to have learners work on authentic work assignments or at least get them involved in the ongoing experience. 'we want them to get the experience of talking to live members with a lot of coaches helping them through that before we actually put them out on the production floor.' The organisation made a point to provide intense practical experience on actual work rather than mock-ups within a high coaching environment. A new hire will take 'over 300 calls in that last half of that last part of their pipeline experience'.
		P4.2	Embed learning into the work and focus on doing the job rather than topic-wise learning	The training and work assignments were interleaved to embed learning and work together. The focus was on doing the job rather than just learning. 'And we have classroom facility and we have the actual stations that they would take calls in. They learn in the classroom, they come out to the lab for application of skills to take their self-paced learning.' The learning is embedded into work or work is embedded into learning in such a way that it is relevant to the real-world. 'What we try to do is replicate that environment so they know what it feels like to be sitting in front of the dual screen monitors with the same applications.'
		P4.3	Expose performers to multiple cycles of deliberate and purposeful failures at a rapid rate or in a compressed time-frame	They designed the entire programs based on critical mistakes and teaching through multiple cycles of failures. 'We used Critical Mistake Methodology... We wanted the student o not be lectured to like the old version of the program, but to be given scenarios and allow them to learn by making mistakes and learning the right way.' Historical data were used to identify the past failures or incidents not handled well and those purposeful failures were inserted into training program. Branching simulations were used to expose learners to multiple mistakes and failures. 'And through that branching simulation, they'll either end up with a member who is very satisfied at the conclusion of the call or in some cases; you have a member that hangs up because they're not happy with the service. And that again is an example of a critical mistake, a critical instant mistake that they have to learn from.' Learners were exposed continuously to the series of such failures till learner demonstrated desired proficiency.
		P4.4	Compress hard-to-obtain experiences on known situations in highly contextualised realistic cases, gamified scenarios, and representative simulations	The organisation used case studies, simulations, role plays and scenarios heavily. Primary method was to use the real-world events and cases into the training program. 'we actually take actual calls and we use those for training and simulation purposes.' Most of the learning was being delivered through self-paced online simulations. 'Through the simulations and the case studies and the role plays, they basically go through the content on their own, self-paced.' Project leader commented: '[self-pace] allowed students to advance faster'. Gamified scenarios were other method used by them. 'we actually do put games into the actual design of the program where they have the opportunity to respond to various scenarios that are on online learning solutions...all designed into really building competition and fun into that learning process.' The program also incorporated role plays among learners as well with experts. 'we actually bring these subject matter experts in who pose as members and we'll do role plays with actual business leaders come in and work with the classes.'
		P4.5	Strengthen generic, transferable, principle-based, fundamental skills to handle unfamiliar or unknown situations	Providing the most fundamental judgment skills to discern elements of a good call was another important aspect.' giving them the ability to identify what right sounds like and looks like.'

Appendix   pg. 414

P5	Promoting an active emotional immersion	P5.1	Active engagement and emotional immersion with the tasks and situations similar to the workplace	Organisation inserted some sort competition and pressure through gamification. 'it's actually putting that competition in that way to track and monitor people's progression…. it becomes more of an internal competition in the class to see who could progress to and hit the thresholds that they need to be performing to.'

They used learning by doing as the main approach 'Leveraging learning by doing techniques was a change in our approach to learning'. The learners were made to work on the actual calls while they were also being monitored and assessed. 'rather than having somebody sit right next to the individual and tell them every single step, we give them the basics and then let them go into the system and actually attempt to perform something and learn from the mistakes that they made.'

Also, the learner's accountability is a key factor used in this program that allowed learners to go at their pace while getting actively engaged with the task. 'the learner learns better when they're able to go at their own pace, put hands-on training, and learn from the mistakes that they make as they go through the process.'

Assessment has the consequence component as well to drive required emotional loading. 'Failure to eventually perform will lead to being washed out of the program.' |
| | | P5.2 | Provide immediate feedback and allow moments of focused reflection | Feedback was a critical instrument used in this program. The feedback was immediate, and it happened from several different levels and in several different ways. Like by the instructor 'the instructor actually facilitates' as well as by the learners 'students analyze the call and say what went well and what didn't go well in that call'. Another way was instant feedback from online simulations. 'They get instantaneous feedback through simulators…if they're correct, they'll get confirmation, the correct decision. If they're incorrect, it takes them back.' Assessment forms a good feedback mechanism too. 'They have full visibility in their progression [report]'.

Further reflection during skill acquisition was incorporated. 'asked them to rethink their response and give them the opportunity to respond again.' |
| | | P5.3 | Assess performers through job-specific, continuous, multi-level assessment beyond a training intervention | In this project, distributed and continuous assessment technique was used to assess proficiency. Trainees were tested three times. 'They have to pass three different assessments to ensure that they are performing at the level we need them to before we graduate them out to the production floor.' The assessment uses same standards as demanded by the actual job. 'same criteria that we have in our call quality team is the same instrument tool that we use in assessing our new hires as they're coming through that program.'
This is done continuous 'three times over a two-week period'.
The assessment uses non-negotiable criteria and person is continuously assessed until he reaches desired proficiency. 'if they fail one of those assessments then instead of getting three of those, they'll get four of them or however many they need to have until they demonstrate three in a row successfully and that indicates to us that they're ready to out to the production floor.'
The of proficiency evaluation was consistency. 'if they consistently hit those thresholds, then we would say that they're proficient'. |
| P6 | Setting up a proficiency eco-system | P6.1 | Create enabling and supportive environment | Organisation ensured that a supporting and enabling environment is created in which trainees could gain experience and could make mistakes safely but get coached for corrections 'When they see somebody who's not going as well, they can actually go over the station and start coaching and providing some additional insights to that student'. |
| | | P6.2 | Structured involvement, accountability, support and reinforcement from manager | Manager's involvement is not very evident in this project. However, managers were available to support if people run into an issue at work 'the manager then walks over to the station and is able to provide the answer'. |

Appendix

P6.3	Institute a structured mentoring and coaching process at workplace	The organisation deployed highly structured mentoring and coaching process in form of nesting for few weeks before they go independent. 'The production floor has an area that they call nesting which is where all the new employees will come into a unit that's overseen by an experienced manager.' During this period, they get high level of support, coaching, help and guidance while performing the actual job. 'We call that nesting because they get very high coaching and follow-up by the leaders while they're in that nesting period'.
P6.4	Design opportunities for social connectivity and structured informal learning	Social connectivity was seen as an important component in changing times particularly for its value in connecting new people to master performers and building their learning networks. 'future of learning is less and less now about building formal solutions and more and more about building social networks that allow learners to connect with master performers and learn from the master performer rather than focusing strictly on formal learning events.' Therefore, they focused on implementing purpose-driven social interconnectivity to impact learning. 'how do we get employees to help train and teach other employees through this process of building up these social networks.' They built several opportunities for participatory group learning and peer sharing that encouraged social interactions. 'in that SharePoint site, they can actually share tips and ideas back and forth or the instructor will actually throw out exercises or activities for them to do through that social site.' The social interconnectivity continues to the workplace. 'they continue to use that site when they're out on the production floor to communicate with one another and share ideas and concepts with one another.' Incorporating and putting a structure around informal learning proved quite valuable to the organisation. 'come up with shortcuts or ideas to how to do things more effectively and efficiently'.
P6.5	Deploy on-demand performance support systems embedded in workflow and learning	Organisation set up an on-demand performance system with searchable information to give them ability to look for answers about 80% infrequent calls. 'It's got a Google-like search so that they can go into that knowledge management system with a question on a call type they may not receive very frequently and can't remember the answer to'. Just-in-time information systems were employed through instant messengers. 'they will use instant messaging and blast that question out to the members of their team. Invariably, you can get back within 30 seconds a correct response from somebody who is quite familiar with the procedure or process.'
P6.6	Leverage subject matter experts strategically	Not used

Success indicators of success of strategies: After implementing new strategies, this project case reported three results. Training duration was shortened by 30% from 10 weeks to 7 weeks. Despite that '*participants in the new version were achieving TTP much faster…we're certainly getting people hitting that time-to-proficiency a lot faster in the new programs than we are in the older programs*'.

Time-to-proficiency was measured using comparative performance indicators. At ten weeks mark, while earlier program led to 33% of the population being proficient per standards, in the new program at the same ten weeks mark, 68% of the population was deemed proficient using same metrics. That indirectly indicated that the population in a given job role were becoming proficient faster. This also means that in the new program, the time-to-proficiency of the majority of employees (68%) was ten weeks on an average.

Business gains reported in the project case: In addition to the reduction in time-to-proficiency, this project case also showed two business results as reported by the project leader:

- Improvement in productivity: 53% drop in misdirected calls
- Cost-saving: Organisation saved $682K in 1 year and 5.68M in 2 years with the shorter course for 1600 new hires.

Appendix

Appendix 38   Reflexivity journals (examples)

See section 3.8.11 for method of using reflexivity journals as one of the techniques for validation and reliability of research study by keeping audit and decision trails (section 3.8.6)

Reflexivity journal: 9-March-2015

It is not about learning, it is about organisational competencies

This research is not how to make employee learn fast to learn what he needs to do the job. This research is about discretionary mechanisms and strategies put in place by organisations to drive their employees to attain organisational and task related competencies faster.

Organisational competencies include

- Job role specific competencies
- Task specific competencies
- Business specific competences

At this point my stand is that it is not about how people learn, though learning organisational competencies have a lot to do with how people learn, but the point is to put certain intentional systems in place to have people learn the competencies the way usually people learn fast.

Further proficiency is not about just learning. It is about demonstration of the attainment of the competencies to the desired level of performance. Learning processes are all pervasive and all over, but key thing is achieving level of performance recognised by organisations indicating desired proficiency level in terms of business outcomes.

Performance vs. competencies
The thesis would need to defend that I am looking at organisational performance and then looking at when an employee or group of employee delivers that kind of organisational performance, then he is deemed proficient.

Reflexivity journal: 16-May-2015

What is my unit of analysis?

I am rethinking my definition of unit of analysis. Is my unit of analysis **a Case** (how it was done in a project?) or a **participant** (how he did it) or **organisation** (how an organisation did it)? This needs to be connected to research questions.

Rethinking the scope

Is my question pertaining to training strategies?

a) used by "different experts" (then it needs unit of analysis as expert or individual,
b) or is it "different organisation" (then unit of analysis should be organisations)
c) or if it is "different contexts" (then unit of analysis should be contexts for same kind of job).
d) or if it is different complex jobs (then unit of analysis should be different complex jobs
e) or if it is different complex skills (then unit of analysis should be different skills)

Rethinking context

Looking back at interviews and data collected so far, what is the pattern? I have interviewed people in different "contexts". They had different business challenges and they eventually applied the training strategies to address the challenge to drive TTP down. Context could be represented as type of job, type of organisation or type of business. In my research most feasible context is "type of sector or type of organisation". Definition of sectors are more easily understood using some established industry classification system. It may be much easier and defensible to use it as context rather than skills, jobs, organisation type etc.

Does the definition of context change the research question to "training strategies to accelerate time-to-proficiency of employees in different contexts"?

Rethinking unit of analysis

My unit of analysis should be a case. How training strategies were applied in a case?
I am looking for different case in different contexts - I may have several cases in one context and many other in other contexts.

Settings:
- Organisations (Government or educational)
- Corporations or companies

Participants:
- External Training Consultants
- Senior officials in training positons
- Recognised Thought leaders
- Researchers in training and learning domain
- Project managers and project leaders with different characteristics (background, area of expertise, industry sector)

Boundary conditions
Mainly one common characteristic is that "project leader" was interviewed whether in the role of designer, implementer, manager or consultant. The interview and data collection has been from his angle how he viewed the business challenge, how he made the changes and how he viewed the results.

Events:
- On boarding
- Ramp-up
- Time-to-proficiency

Processes
- What training strategies are applied by training experts in various settings or contexts?
- How do they apply those in different settings or contexts?

Rethinking scope

Gathering bounded cases in various settings, contexts and organisations in different industry sectors to understand commonality and generalization what kind of training strategies have been applied with direct or indirect results of shortening time-to-proficiency of employees?

Appendix 39 Thematic structure of overarching themes and emergent themes in three research questions

See section 4.2 for description of thematic structure of themes identified in this study
See sections 4.3, 4.4, and 4.5 for description of overarching themes
See sections 4.6, 4.7 and 4.8 for description of emergent themes
See sections 5.3, 5.4 and 5.5 for discussion on overarching themes and emergent themes

	Overarching themes		Emergent themes
Research question #1: What does the concept of accelerating proficiency or accelerating time-to-proficiency mean to organisations?			
C1	Proficiency	C1.1	Proficiency refers to meeting established performance thresholds for a job role.
		C1.2	Consistency is the hallmark of the state of proficiency of a job role.
		C1.3	Proficiency is measured by business outcomes of the job role or observable actions linked to outcomes.
		C1.4	Proficiency is not just about learning an isolated skill, task or activity in a job
C2	Accelerated proficiency	C2.1	Accelerated proficiency is measured in terms of reduction in time-to-proficiency.
		C2.2	A clear definition of proficiency for a job role is the most critical requirement to baseline, monitor and shorten time-to-proficiency.
		C2.3	Accelerated proficiency is not accelerated learning or accelerated training.
		C2.4	Training alone rarely leads to accelerating proficiency, it requires solutions beyond training.
Research question #2: What business factors do drive the need for reducing time-to-proficiency of the workforce and how do organisations benefit from achieving it?			
D1	Magnitude and scale (of time-to-proficiency business problem)	D1.1	Magnitude of time-to-proficiency problem
		D1.2	Scale of time-to-proficiency problem
D2	Business drivers (for accelerating proficiency)	D2.1	Time-related pressures
		D2.2	Speed-related competitiveness
		D2.3	Skill-related deficiency
		D2.4	Cost or financial implications
D3	Business benefits (of reduced time-to-proficiency)	D3.1	Business gains
		D3.2	Improvement in operational metrics
		D3.3	Improvement in productivity
		D3.4	Cost savings

Research question #3: What core practices and strategies do business leaders and practitioners adopt to achieve shorter time-to-proficiency of the workforce in a given job?

P1	Defining business-driven proficiency measures	P1.1	Starting with end in mind: upfront definition and measures of proficiency in terms of business outcomes and link it to business needs.
		P1.2	Baseline and establish time-to-proficiency targets based on business drivers.
P2	Developing a proficiency reference map	P2.1	Conduct upfront comprehensive work analysis drawn from the outcomes.
		P2.2	Profile capabilities and capacities of the job performers.
		P2.3	Model success behaviours of exemplary performers.
		P2.4	Understand job operating conditions and environmental influences.
		P2.5	Analyse roadblocks and hindrances that lead to longer time-to-proficiency.
P3	Sequencing an efficient proficiency path	P3.1	Segment tasks and activities based on characteristics from analytics.
		P3.2	Create logical sequence of experiences as a complete path.
		P3.3	Optimise the proficiency path for efficiency and time saving.
P4	Manufacturing accelerated contextual experiences	P4.1	Assign performers on authentic job activities that allow practice on generating job-specific outcomes.
		P4.2	Embed learning into the work and focus on doing the job rather than topic-wise learning.
		P4.3	Expose performers to multiple cycles of deliberate and purposeful failures at a rapid rate or in a compressed time-frame.
		P4.4	Compress hard-to-obtain experiences on known situations in highly contextualised realistic cases, gamified scenarios and representative simulations.
		P4.5	Strengthen generic, transferable, principle-based, fundamental skills to handle unfamiliar or unknown situations.
P5	Promoting an active emotional immersion	P5.1	Active engagement and emotional immersion with the tasks and situations similar to the workplace.
		P5.2	Provide immediate feedback and allow moments of focused reflection.
		P5.3	Assess performers through job-specific, continuous, multi-level assessment beyond a training intervention.
P6	Setting up a proficiency eco-system	P6.1	Create enabling and supportive environment.
		P6.2	Structured involvement, accountability, support and reinforcement from manager.
		P6.3	Institute a structured mentoring and coaching process at workplace.
		P6.4	Design opportunities for purpose-driven social connectivity and structured informal learning in the workplace.
		P6.5	Deploy on-demand performance support systems embedded in workflow and learning.
		P6.6	Leverage subject matter experts strategically.

Appendix 40   Summary of research propositions

See sections 5.3, 5.4 and 5.5 detailing how each of the research propositions was evolved

Research question #1— What does the concept of accelerating proficiency or accelerating time-to-proficiency mean to organisations?

Job-role proficiency denotes a state of performance at which performers produce business outcomes or deliverables consistently to the set performance thresholds expected from a given job role. It refers to achieving and maintaining one pre-established performance level and does not imply progression through different stages or levels of performance. It refers to the business performance of the job role and does not convey an individual's performance demonstrated on a task or skill.

Accelerating proficiency means shortening the time someone takes in a given job role to reach to a state of consistent performance that meets the set thresholds. This is measured in time-to-proficiency. A clearer definition of job-role proficiency and its measures are the foremost critical requirement to the acceleration of proficiency. Accelerated proficiency is not about learning a body of content faster or shortening the training duration because the solution to a shorter time-to-proficiency lies beyond training interventions.

Research question #2 — Why is reducing time-to-proficiency of the workforce important to organisations and how do they benefit from achieving it?

The magnitude of time-to-proficiency in any job role is typically significantly large. This magnitude, when multiplied across all the individuals serving same job role becomes a business problem of such a large scale that organisations are not able to ignore its impacts. The impacts manifest in the form of time-related pressures, speed-related competitiveness, skill-related deficiencies or cost or financial implications. These business needs trigger organisations to institute initiatives/projects with a goal to shorten time-to-proficiency. Such initiatives/projects lead to substantial business gains and improvement in operational metrics. Saving cost and financial implications are not usually the primary drivers to institute such initiatives/projects. However, financial gains are invariably attained in every such initiative/project.

Research Question #3: What core practices and strategies do business leaders and practitioners adopt to achieve shorter time-to-proficiency of the workforce in a given job?

Proficiency of individuals in a given job role in the workplace is accelerated through six business-level practices/processes which all interact with each other in an input-output-feedback system. Job-role proficiency is positively accelerated when the six business practices are orchestrated together in the workplace as a closely-loop system.

Defining business-driven proficiency measures: Any initiative/project setup with a goal to accelerate proficiency and shorten time-to-proficiency at workplace starts with defining proficiency measures based on business needs and then defining current and target time-to-proficiency. This practice specifies starting with the end in mind, defining proficiency and its measures upfront in terms of business outcomes and linking it to business needs. Managers baseline and establish time-to-proficiency targets based on business drivers.

Developing a proficiency reference map: The second practice involves developing an overall proficiency reference map mapping out all the inputs required to produce the outcomes in a given job role and mapping out all the conditions and limitations that may influence attaining such outcomes in shorter time. This practice specifies conducting upfront comprehensive work analysis drawn from the outcomes; profiling capabilities and capacities of the job performers; modelling success behaviours of exemplary performers; understanding job operating conditions and environmental influences; and analysing roadblocks and hindrances that lead to longer time-to-proficiency.

Sequencing an efficient proficiency path: The third practice involves sequencing the needed experiences effectively and optimising the sequence to build proficiency in a shorter time and most efficient manner. This practice specifies segmenting tasks and activities based on characteristics from analytics; creating a logical sequence of experiences as a complete path; and optimising the proficiency path for efficiency and time-saving.

Manufacturing accelerated contextual experiences: The fourth practice involves assembling contextual experience for the inputs defined in the proficiency reference map either by leveraging job or by designing interventions. This practice specifies assigning performers on authentic job activities that allow practice on generating job-specific outcomes; embedding learning into work and focus on doing rather than learning; exposing performers to multiple cycles of deliberate and purposeful failures at a rapid rate or in a compressed time-frame; compressing hard-to-obtain experiences on known situations in highly contextualised realistic cases, gamified scenarios and representative simulations; and strengthening generic, transferable, principle-based, fundamental skills to handle unfamiliar or unknown situations.

Promoting an active emotional immersion: The fifth practice involves delivering contextual experiences in such a way that drive active engagement and high emotional loading for the performers. This practice specifies ensuring active engagement and emotional immersion with the tasks and situations similar to the workplace; providing immediate feedback and allow moments of focused reflection; and assessing performers through job-specific, continuous, multi-level assessment beyond a training intervention.

Setting up a proficiency eco-system: The sixth practice involves setting an eco-system around the performers on the job with timely support with resources. This practice specifies creating a enabling and supportive environment; structuring involvement, accountability, support and reinforcement from the manager; instituting a structured mentoring and coaching process in the workplace; designing opportunities for social connectivity and structured informal learning; deploying on-demand performance support systems embedded in workflow and learning; and leveraging subject matter experts strategically.

The six practices are implemented through 24 strategies. Each strategy has a definite purpose and addresses an important element of a given practice. Though a particular strategy may serve its intended purpose on its own, the real results of shorter time-to-proficiency are achieved when all the strategies within a practice are implemented as a process and when all the practices are implemented together as a system to attain meaningful improvement in time-to-proficiency.

Appendix 41 6/24 framework of strategies to reduce time-to-proficiency (research output #1)

See section 5.6.2 describing emergence of 6/24 framework of strategies

	Business practices		**Strategies**
P1	Defining business-driven proficiency measures	P1.1	Starting with end in mind: upfront definition and measures of proficiency in terms of business outcomes and link it to business needs.
		P1.2	Baseline and establish time-to-proficiency targets based on business drivers.
P2	Developing a proficiency reference map	P2.1	Conduct upfront comprehensive work analysis drawn from the outcomes.
		P2.2	Profile capabilities and capacities of the job performers.
		P2.3	Model success behaviours of exemplary performers.
		P2.4	Understand job operating conditions and environmental influences.
		P2.5	Analyse roadblocks and hindrances that lead to longer time-to-proficiency.
P3	Sequencing an efficient proficiency path	P3.1	Segment tasks and activities based on characteristics from analytics.
		P3.2	Create logical sequence of experiences as a complete path.
		P3.3	Optimise the proficiency path for efficiency and time saving.
P4	Manufacturing accelerated contextual experiences	P4.1	Assign performers on authentic job activities that allow practice on generating job-specific outcomes.
		P4.2	Embed learning into the work and focus on doing the job rather than topic-wise learning.
		P4.3	Expose performers to multiple cycles of deliberate and purposeful failures at a rapid rate or in a compressed time-frame.
		P4.4	Compress hard-to-obtain experiences on known situations in highly contextualised realistic cases, gamified scenarios and representative simulations.
		P4.5	Strengthen generic, transferable, principle-based, fundamental skills to handle unfamiliar or unknown situations.
P5	Promoting an active emotional immersion	P5.1	Active engagement and emotional immersion with the tasks and situations similar to the workplace.
		P5.2	Provide immediate feedback and allow moments of focused reflection.
		P5.3	Assess performers through job-specific, continuous, multi-level assessment beyond a training intervention.
P6	Setting up a proficiency eco-system	P6.1	Create enabling and supportive environment.
		P6.2	Structured involvement, accountability, support and reinforcement from manager.
		P6.3	Institute a structured mentoring and coaching process at workplace.
		P6.4	Design opportunities for purpose-driven social connectivity and structured informal learning in the workplace.
		P6.5	Deploy on-demand performance support systems embedded in workflow and learning.
		P6.6	Leverage subject matter experts strategically.

Appendix 42 Accelerated Proficiency Model (APM) (research output #2)

See section 5.6.1 describing development and emergence of conceptual model

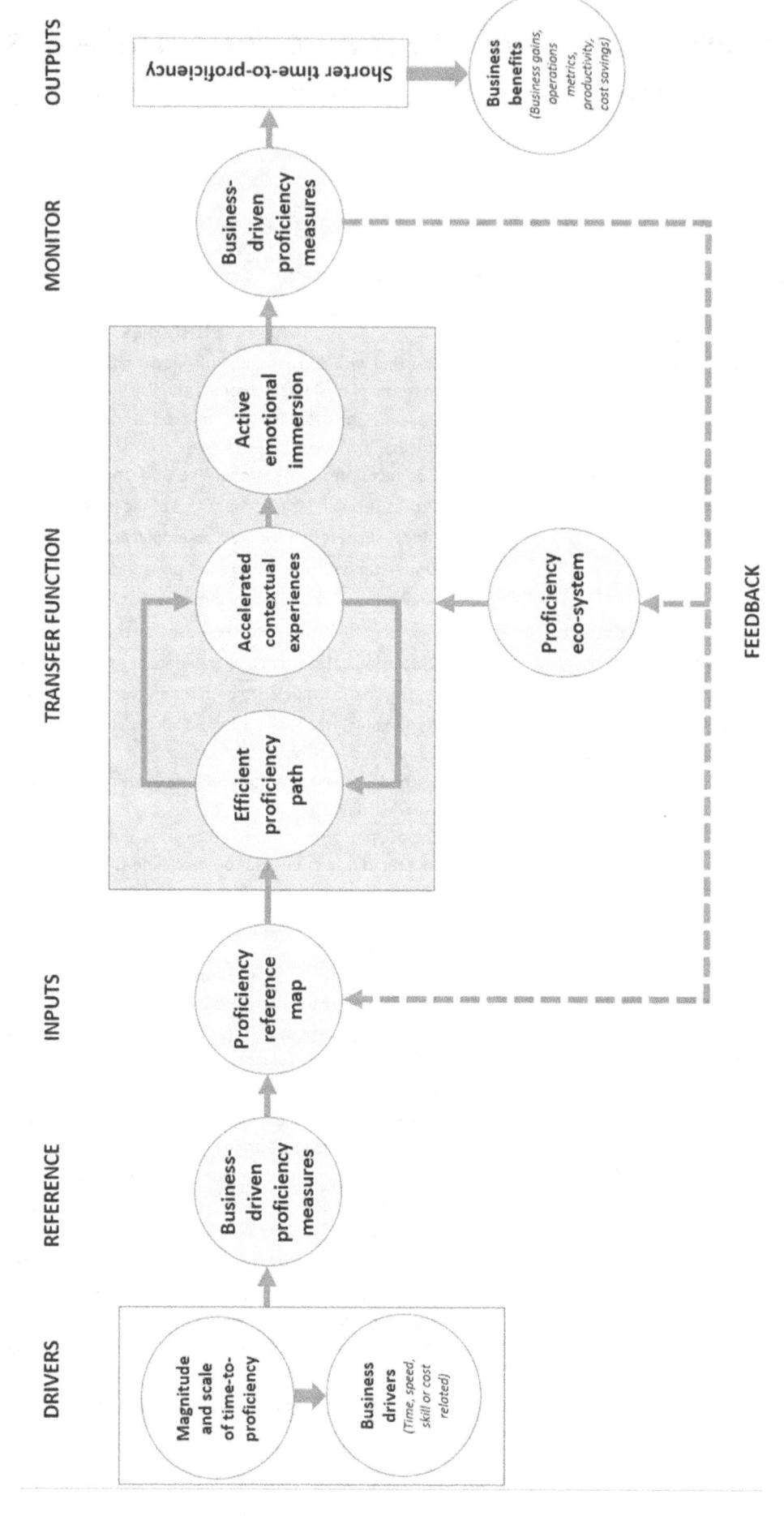

Appendix 43 Research questions mapped to interview questions

RQ No.	Question	Focus Area	Tentative Question for the interview
1	What does the concept of accelerating proficiency or accelerating time-to-proficiency mean to organisations?	Context	Tell me more about the background of the chosen project including industry sector and nature of business of the organisation.
			Please describe the type of work being performed and nature of job of the employee group targeted in above project. How was the composition of this employee group and their experience level in the job (new hires, experienced employees etc.)?
			How would you rate the complexity level of skills of the targeted employee group? What made the skills complex in this job? Why?
			Please describe briefly the type of skills or knowledge involved in performing the said job/assignment. What level of competency or expertise was expected from the targeted employee group to perform their job?
		Meaning of proficiency	What KPIs were used as an indicator that targeted employee group has reached the 'desired proficiency' in the targeted skills?
			In the settings of the project you mentioned, how did you define 'desired proficiency' of the target employee group?
		Meaning of accelerated proficiency	What was the primary goal of the above-mentioned project?
			In your own words, please explain how the goal of this project (directly or indirectly) involved shortening or accelerating time-to-proficiency of employees. Examples may include: bringing a new or an existing employee up to speed to certain pre-determined standards of expertise on a new job or driving employees to acquire new skills or new knowledge etc. to name a few.
2	What business factors drive the need for reducing time-to-proficiency of the workforce and how do organisations benefit from achieving it?	Magnitude and scale	What was the primary goal of the above-mentioned project?
			In your own words, please explain how the goal of this project (directly or indirectly) involved shortening or accelerating time-to-proficiency of employees. Examples may include: bringing a new or an existing employee up to speed to certain pre-determined standards of expertise on a new job or driving employees to acquire new skills or new knowledge etc. to name a few.
		Business drivers	What was the main business challenge that made the organisation or your group to focus on accelerating the acquisition of targeted skills of their employees to desired proficiency level? Why it was so important and critical for the organisation?
		Business benefits	Can you elaborate how effective your chosen strategies were in shortening the time-to-proficiency of targeted group?
			How did you measure the effectiveness of the chosen strategies?
3	What core practices and strategies do business leaders and practitioners adopt to achieve shorter time-to-proficiency of	Previous solution, strategies	Please describe the old model (if any).
			Please highlight challenges associated with the previous model. Why was that model not working to accelerate time-to-proficiency?
		New solution / strategies	Please describe solution your group proposed in terms of model, structure or plan. Highlight how selected strategies were implemented

	the workforce in a given job?		in the above project. Elaborate how various techniques were orchestrated to achieve the project goal.
			Why did your group choose "training" (as opposed to non-training solutions) as the primary solution for this project to shorten time-to-proficiency?
			Please explain how solution proposed by your group focused mainly on methods & strategies to shorten time-to-proficiency (example: designing / orchestrating a training event, course or program or training solution).
			Can you explain how your model of implementation was influenced by or drawn from any established or known training model?
			Please take some time to explain philosophy, premise, belief or guiding principle that guided you or your group the way strategies were implemented in the above project.
			What factors made the selected strategies an ideal choice for the problem relative to other strategies available to you?
			Tell me about how the nature of the job and nature of the business influenced the overall implementation of selected training strategies.
			What did you do differently in this project as compared to traditional or pre-existing or known approaches?
			In your opinion, what were the main reason or factors that led to the success of chosen strategies in achieving the goal?
			What was the major challenge or pitfall you faced while implementing these strategies?
			Among other factors, what do you think how much accurate selection and deployment of strategies contributed in accelerating time-to-proficiency of the target employees? Less than 50% More than 50% More than 70% More than 90% Almost 100%
		Success evidence	Can you elaborate how effective your chosen strategies were in shortening the time-to-proficiency of targeted group?
			How did you measure the effectiveness of the chosen strategies?
			What KPIs were used as an indicator that targeted employee group has reached the 'desired proficiency' in the targeted skills?
		Transferability	In your opinion, how could the strategy or model you applied in your context be applied successfully to other settings (jobs, industry sector, and business)? How would you recommend applying or implementing the same set of techniques in other practical corporate settings?
			Have you tried the same model to any other context? If yes, which industry sector and job type

THE AUTHOR

Dr Raman K Attri is a global authority on speed in personal and professional space. He is a performance and learning leader with over 25 years of international experience. His specializes in equipping professional and organizations with proven competitive strategies to speed up human learning, expertise, and performance by 2X. An accomplished business researcher, he is one among few experts in the world who have cracked the code to reduce time to proficiency of employees by 50%. An organizational learning leader, he manages a Hall of the Fame training organization, named one among the top 5 globally, at a $40bn technology corporation. Passionate about learning, he holds two doctorates in human performance apart from earning over 100 international educational credentials and being nominated for some of the world's highest certifications. An inspiring personality, he speaks internationally to guide leaders and professionals on research-based best practices, models, and frameworks to solve tough workplace performance problems. A prolific author of 20 multi-genre books, he writes about the deeper aspects of human excellence and capabilities. A powerhouse of positivity, despite his disability since childhood, he made his mission to teach others how to accelerate the path to excellence and walk faster in all walks of life.

LinkedIn https://www.linkedin.com/in/DrRamanKAttri
Facebook https://www.facebook.com/DrRamanKAttri
Website http://ramankattri.com
Website: https://get-there-faster.com

FROM THE SAME AUTHOR

DESIGNING TRAINING TO SHORTEN TIME TO PROFICIENCY: Online, Classroom and On-the-Job Learning Strategies from Research

ISBN: 978-981-14-0633-1 (e-book)
ISBN: 978-981-14-0632-4 (paperback)
ISBN: 978-981-14-0645-4 (hardcover)

Available with major retailers, distributors and market places

ACCELERATE YOUR LEADERSHIP DEVELOPMENT IN TRAINING DOMAIN: Proven Success Strategies for New Training & Learning Managers

ISBN: 978-981-11-8991-3 (e-book)
ISBN: 978-981-14-0066-7 (paperback)

Available with major retailers, distributors and market places

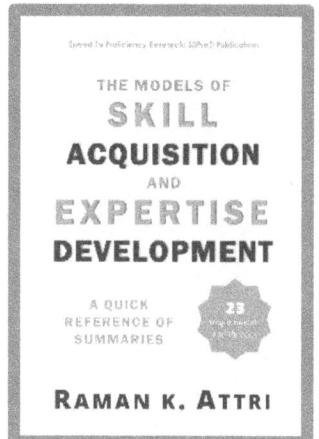

THE MODELS OF SKILL ACQUISITION AND EXPERTISE DEVELOPMENT: A Quick Reference of Summaries

SBN: 978-981-11-8988-3 (e-book)
ISBN: 978-981-14-1122-9 (paperback)
ISBN: 978-981-14-1130-4 (hardcover)

Available with major retailers, distributors and market places

TRAINING EFFECTIVENESS MEASUREMENT FOR LARGE SCALE PROGRAMS: DEMYSTIFIED! A 4-Tier Practical Model for Technical Training Managers

ISBN: 978-981-11-8990-6 (e-book)
ISBN: 978-981-11-417672 (paperback)

Available with major retailers, distributors and market places

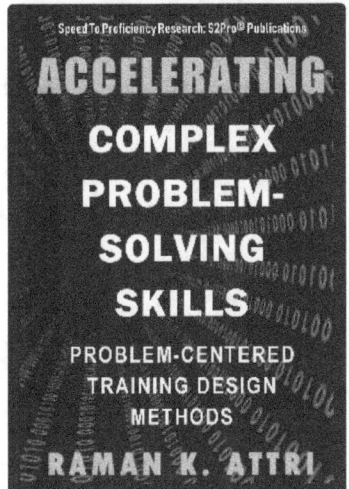

ACCELERATING COMPLEX PROBLEM-SOLVING SKILLS: Problem-Centered Training Design Methods

ISBN: 978-981-11-8991-2 (e-book)
ISBN: 978-981-14-1766-5 (paperback)

Available with major retailers, distributors and market places

SPEED TO PROFICIENCY IN ORGANIZATIONS: Model, Practices and Strategies to Shorten Time To Proficiency

ISBN 978-981-14-0753-6 (e-book)

Available with major retailers, distributors and market places

ACCELERATED PROFICIENCY FOR ACCELERATED TIMES: A Review of Key Concepts and Methods to Speed Up Performance

ISBN: 978-981-14-6276-4 (e-book)
ISBN: 978-981-14-6275-7 (paperback)
ISBN: 978-981-14-6274-0 (hardcover)

Available with major retailers, distributors and market places

SPEED MATTERS: Why best in class business leaders priotize workforce time to proficiency metrics

ISBN: 978-981-18-0536-3 (e-book)
ISBN: 978-981-18-0535-6 (paperback)
ISBN: 978-981-18-0534-9 (hardcover)

Available with major retailers, distributors and market places

www.ingramcontent.com/pod-product-compliance
Lightning Source LLC
LaVergne TN
LVHW081533070526
838199LV00005B/349